W9-AYD-441

COMPLETE FIX-IT-YOURSELF MANUAL

PRENTICE HALL PRESS
NEW YORK • LONDON • TORONTO • SYDNEY • TOKYO

Time-Life Books Complete Fix-It-Yourself Manual
was produced by
ST. REMY PRESS

MANAGING EDITOR	Kenneth Winchester
MANAGING ART DIRECTOR	Pierre Léveillé
Editor	Katherine Zmetana
Art Director	Solange Pelland
Senior Art Director	Diane Denoncourt
Contributing Editors	Fiona Gilsenan, Kathleen M. Kiely
Illustrators	Robert Paquet
Electronic Designers	Daniel Bazinet, Maryse Doray
Index	Christine M. Jacobs
Administrator	Denise Rainville
Coordinator	Michelle Turbide
Systems Manager	Shirley Grynspan
Systems Analyst	Simon Lapierre
Proofreaders	Billy Wisse, Jeffrey Yagod

Time-Life Books Complete Fix-It-Yourself Manual was adapted from
the Fix It Yourself series, produced by **ST. REMY PRESS** for
TIME-LIFE BOOKS INC.

EDITOR	George Constable
Executive Editor	Ellen Phillips
Director of Design	Louis Klein
Director of Editorial Resources	Phyllis K. Wise
Editorial Board	Russell B. Adams Jr., Dale M. Brown, Roberta Conlan, Thomas H. Flaherty, Lee Hassig, Donia Ann Steele, Rosalind Stubenberg, Henry Woodhead
Director of Photography and Research	John Conrad Weiser
Asst. Director of Editorial Resources	Elise Ritter Gibson
PRESIDENT	Christopher T. Linen
Chief Operating Officer	John M. Fahey Jr.
Senior Vice Presidents	Robert M. DeSena, James L. Mercer
Vice Presidents	Stephen L. Bair, Ralph J. Cuomo, Neal Goff, Stephen L. Goldstein, Juanita T. James, Hallett Johnson III, Carol Kaplan, Susan J. Maruyama, Robert H. Smith, Joseph J. Ward
Director of Production Services	Robert J. Passantino

BOMC offers recordings and compact discs, cassettes
and records. For information and catalog write to
BOMR, Camp Hill, PA 17012.

CONSULTING EDITOR

Richard Day, a do-it-yourself writer for nearly a
quarter century, is a founder of the National
Association of Home and Workshop Writers and the
author of several home repair books. He has built
two houses from the ground up, and now lives in
southern California.

THE CONSULTANTS

John Banks, Bruce Barcomb, Klaus Bremer,
John Dinolfo, Steven J. Forbis, Ira Gladstone,
David L. Harrison, William J. Hawkins,
Oleh Z. Kowalchuk, John Lefever, Jeff Lefever,
Elliot Levine, Michael R. MacDonald, Evan Powell,
Mark M. Steele, Joseph A. Tedesco, Steve Toth,
Eldon Wilson

 Prentice Hall Press
Gulf+Western Building
One Gulf+Western Plaza
New York, New York 10023

Copyright © 1989 by Time-Life Books Inc.

Library of Congress Cataloging-in-Publication Data
Time-Life Books Complete fix-it-yourself manual.
    p.   cm.
   Includes index.
   ISBN 0-13-921651-0
   1. Dwellings—Maintenance and repair—Amateurs'
manuals. 2. Household appliances—Maintenance and
repair—Amateurs' manuals. I. Time-Life Books.
TH4817.3.C63 1989
643'.7—dc 19   88-39712
                          CIP

Manufactured in the United States of America

HOW TO USE THIS BOOK

The *Time-Life Books Complete Fix-It-Yourself Manual* is a comprehensive guide to maintaining, troubleshooting and repairing almost everything in your home. Whether you have a refrigerator that won't cool, a washerless faucet that drips, or a microwave oven that is slow to cook your meals, you'll find the solution to the problem in this book. Compiled from the best-selling *Time-Life Books Fix-It-Yourself* series, this manual shows you how to repair a range of household items—from appliances and electronic units to plumbing, electricity, and home heating and cooling systems.

The *Complete Fix-It-Yourself Manual* is divided into eight chapters that are color-coded for easy reference:

The **Emergency Guide** shows you what to do when you need to take immediate action; its troubleshooting guide on pages 14–15 directs you to the quickest, most effective way to deal with an emergency situation. A list of safety tips warns you of potential hazards involved in various repairs and tells you when you need to take precautions; such as discharging the capacitor in a heat pump or microwave oven before working inside the unit.

Repair chapters—the heart of the book— cover the six subject areas shown at right. These chapters lead you through dozens of repair jobs, including; removing a jammed audiocassette, testing a multi-control switch, replacing a faulty oven element, and servicing a leaking toilet. Time and difficulty ratings let you know what to expect in advance, so you can plan ahead for a major job.

Tools & Techniques presents both the basic and specialized tools that you will need for the repairs covered in this book, and provides tips on how to use them. If you are unfamiliar with special techniques, such as silver soldering or stripping electrical wires, you'll find the procedures described in detail in this section.

The Complete Fix-It-Yourself Manual provides a simple and straightforward system to home repair. Sample pages, and an explanation of how to go about diagnosis and repair, are shown an page 8. Whether you are an experienced do-it-yourselfer or a novice to home repair, you can use this book to save yourself time, money, and aggravation.

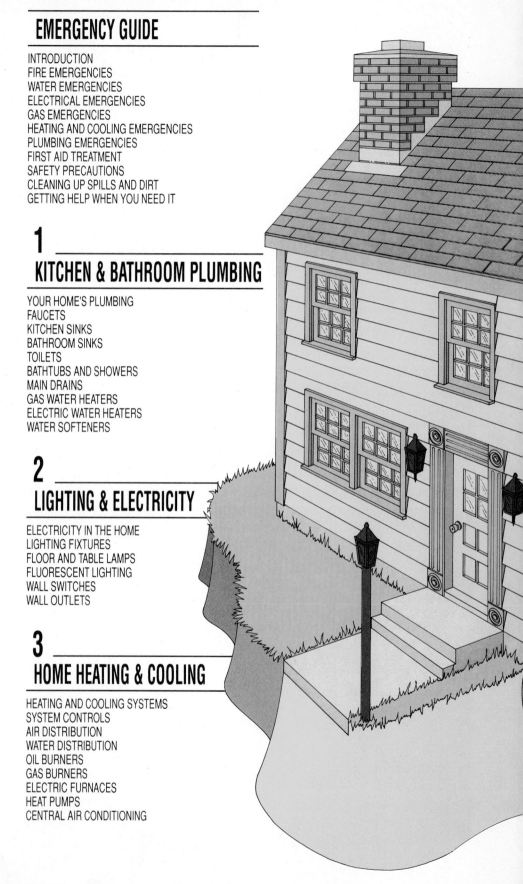

EMERGENCY GUIDE

INTRODUCTION
FIRE EMERGENCIES
WATER EMERGENCIES
ELECTRICAL EMERGENCIES
GAS EMERGENCIES
HEATING AND COOLING EMERGENCIES
PLUMBING EMERGENCIES
FIRST AID TREATMENT
SAFETY PRECAUTIONS
CLEANING UP SPILLS AND DIRT
GETTING HELP WHEN YOU NEED IT

1
KITCHEN & BATHROOM PLUMBING

YOUR HOME'S PLUMBING
FAUCETS
KITCHEN SINKS
BATHROOM SINKS
TOILETS
BATHTUBS AND SHOWERS
MAIN DRAINS
GAS WATER HEATERS
ELECTRIC WATER HEATERS
WATER SOFTENERS

2
LIGHTING & ELECTRICITY

ELECTRICITY IN THE HOME
LIGHTING FIXTURES
FLOOR AND TABLE LAMPS
FLUORESCENT LIGHTING
WALL SWITCHES
WALL OUTLETS

3
HOME HEATING & COOLING

HEATING AND COOLING SYSTEMS
SYSTEM CONTROLS
AIR DISTRIBUTION
WATER DISTRIBUTION
OIL BURNERS
GAS BURNERS
ELECTRIC FURNACES
HEAT PUMPS
CENTRAL AIR CONDITIONING

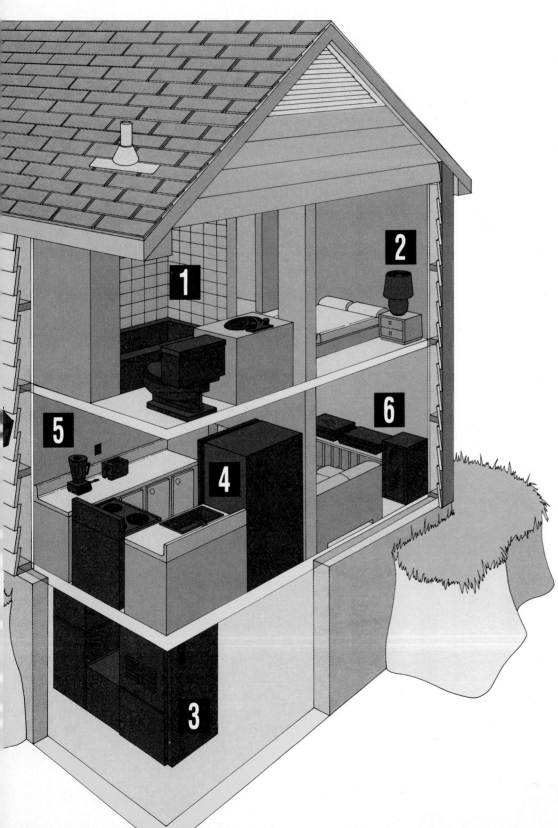

Pictured below are four sample pages from the section on Dishwashers—of the Major Appliances chapter—with captions describing the various features of the book and how they work. If your dishes are dirty and spotted after washing, for example, consult the troubleshooting guide on pages 253–254 for a number of possible causes, ranging from incorrect loading of dishes to a faulty timer. If you identify a clogged spray arm, you will be directed to page 262 for detailed, step-by-step instructions on servicing the spray arm and tower. Refer to the exploded diagram to discover the inner workings of a typical dishwasher and to locate the source of trouble; it will help you identify each of the machine's parts—to know where the part goes, and how to ask for a replacement by name. Read the introductory text to learn how the dishwasher functions and the typical problems you can expect. You will also find tips on keeping your appliance performing at its best.

Each repair has been rated by degree of difficulty and the average time it will take for a do-it-yourselfer to complete. Keep in mind that this rating is only a suggestion. Before deciding whether you should attempt a job, first read all the instructions carefully. Then be guided by your own confidence, and the tools and time available to you. For complex

Introductory text
Describes proper use and care of the appliance or unit, most common breakdowns and basic safety precautions.

"Exploded" and cutaway diagrams
Locate and describe the various mechanical, electrical and plumbing parts of the appliance or unit.

Troubleshooting Guide
To use this chart, locate the symptom in column 1 that most closely resembles your problem, review the possible causes in column 2, then follow the recommended procedures in column 3. Simple fixes may be explained on the chart; in most cases you will be directed to an illustrated, step-by-step repair sequence.

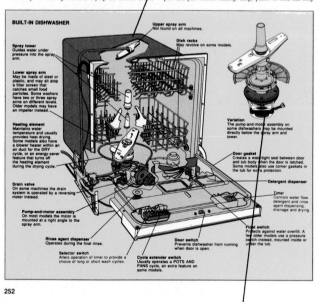

Variations
Differences in popular models are described throughout the book, particularly if a repair procedure varies from one instance to another.

Degree of difficulty and time
Rate the complexity of each repair, and how much time the job should take for a homeowner with average do-it-yourself skills.

Special tool required
Some repairs, such as those requiring electrical tests, require a multitester or other special tool (page 417).

repairs, such as servicing a clogged pump, you may be directed to call for professional service. You will still have saved time and money by diagnosing the problem yourself.

Most repairs in *The Complete Fix-It-Yourself Manual* can be made with basic tools, including screwdrivers, wrenches, and utility pliers. When procedures require a specialized tool, such as a multitester for testing electrical components, a symbol on the Troubleshooting Guide lets you know in advance. The tools you need—and how to use them—are presented in Tools & Techniques *(page 417)*. If you are a novice at home repair, read this section in preparation for a job.

Home repair is easy and safe if you work logically and follow all precautions. Turn off power or disconnect the unit or appliance as directed. Close the appropriate shutoff valve before working on a fixture connected to supply lines, and have a bucket and rags at hand. For small appliances and electronic units, set up on a clean work table, write down the sequence of disassembly steps, and store fasteners and other small parts in labeled containers. The Emergency Guide *(pages 11-31)* provides information that can be indispensable, even lifesaving, in the event of a household emergency. Study this section *before* you need the important advice it contains.

Name of repair
You will be referred by the Troubleshooting Guide to the first page of a specific repair.

Step-by-step procedures
Follow the numbered repair sequence carefully. Depending on the result of each step, you may be directed to a later step, or to another part of the book, to complete the repair.

Tools and techniques
When a tool or method is required for a job, it is described within the step-by-step repair. General information on working with tools, including the use of continuity testers and multitesters, is covered in the Tools & Techniques chapter *(page 417)*.

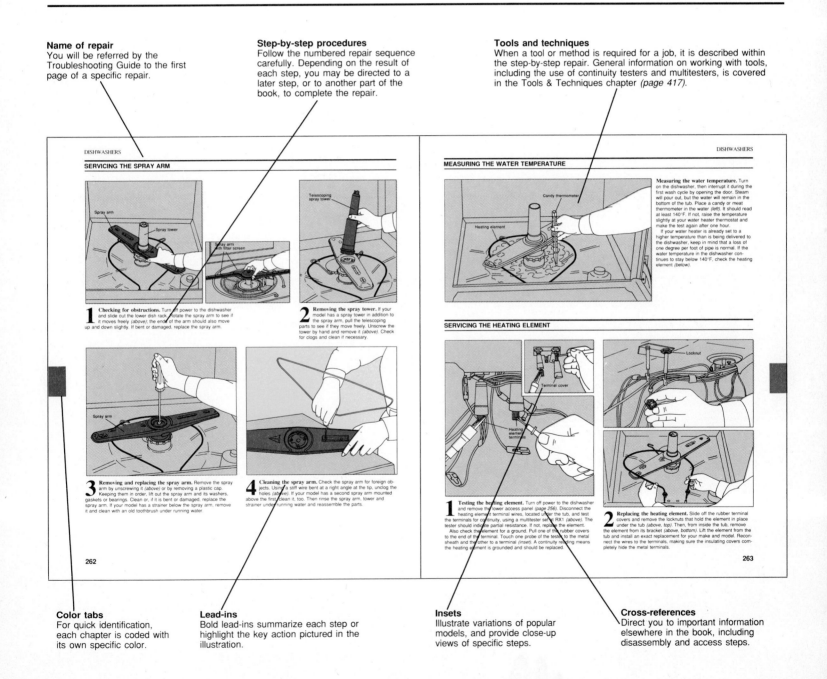

Color tabs
For quick identification, each chapter is coded with its own specific color.

Lead-ins
Bold lead-ins summarize each step or highlight the key action pictured in the illustration.

Insets
Illustrate variations of popular models, and provide close-up views of specific steps.

Cross-references
Direct you to important information elsewhere in the book, including disassembly and access steps.

EMERGENCY GUIDE

EMERGENCY GUIDE

Preventing home emergencies. Plumbing, electricity and heating and cooling systems today are so reliable that homeowners take safe, uninterrupted service for granted—until an emergency occurs. Installed according to strict codes and safety standards, these systems rarely pose a hazard, as long as they are properly maintained. Appliances and electronic units, too, have been expertly designed to give years of safe, worry-free use. With proper care and maintenance, most of them can last a lifetime. Familiarize yourself with the owner's manual for the recommended use and care of your appliance, electronic unit or heating and cooling system.

The repair of household systems, appliances and electronic units need not be any more dangerous than their routine use. Indeed, a repair procedure that is properly performed can prevent hazardous conditions. The safety tips at right cover basic guidelines to performing the repairs in this book; consult the individual chapters for more specific advice.

Fire and electrical shock are life-threatening emergencies that can happen in even the most safety-conscious of homes. Deprive fire of its sneak attack by installing smoke alarms judiciously throughout the house *(page 17)*. Have the correct fire extinguisher on hand to snuff out a blaze before it gets the upper hand, and learn how to use it before you need it *(page 16)*. Always turn off the power before working on electrical boxes, fixtures or appliances wired to a circuit *(page 102)* and confirm that it is off by using a voltage tester *(page 424)*. Alert family members by affixing a tag labeled "DO NOT TURN ON" to the main service panel and unit disconnect switch. If you must rescue someone frozen by live current, do not touch him; use a wooden broom handle or wooden chair to push him free of the electrical circuit *(page 23)*.

Prepare yourself to handle emergencies before they occur. Read the troubleshooting guide on page 14, which places emergency procedures at your fingertips. It lists quick-action steps to take and refers you to pages 16–31 for detailed instructions. Also review Tools & Techniques *(page 417)* for information on repairs and on the safe use of tools.

Get technical assistance when you need it. If you are in doubt about your ability to handle a repair, call a professional for help *(page 31)*. Even in non-emergency situations, an inspector from your utility company or fire department can answer questions concerning the condition and proper use of your home's plumbing, gas and electrical systems.

Post the telephone numbers for the fire department, medical emergency services, electricity and plumbing utilities, as well as gas and oil suppliers near the telephone—and do not hesitate to use them. In most areas, you can dial 911 in case of a life-threatening emergency.

SAFETY TIPS

1. Before attempting any repair in this book, read the entire procedure. Familiarize yourself with the safety information presented below and in the chapters for each appliance.

2. Refer to Tools & Techniques *(page 417)* for correct tool use and instructions on getting help when you need it.

3. Use the right tools for the job, with insulated handles when available, and do not substitute tools or materials.

4. Light the work area well, and do not reach into any area of an appliance or electronic unit you cannot see clearly.

5. Keep children and pets away from all work areas, controls and toxic substances. Store tools and supplies out of reach.

6. Keep protective equipment handy: wear safety goggles and work gloves when recommended, and rubber-soled shoes in damp conditions.

7. Remove watches and jewelry before starting a repair. Avoid loose-fitting clothes and tie back long hair.

8. Use only replacement parts and wiring of the same specifications as the original. Look for the UL (Underwriters Laboratories) or CSA (Canadian Standards Association) label on new parts. If in doubt, consult the manufacturer or take the original part to the dealer.

9. Except for temporary repairs in an emergency, use only materials permitted by local plumbing, building and electrical codes. If in doubt, check with local authorities before working on your system.

10. Familiarize yourself with the correct procedure for shutting off your home's power, water and fuel supplies. For quick identification, label the main gas and water shutoff valves.

11. Whenever instructed, turn off electrical power to any unit or appliance under repair. Let appliances, fixtures and electronic units cool before working on them.

12. Label your main service panel with the locations of the appliance and outlet circuit breakers or fuses. Map and label your home's electrical circuits *(page 106)*.

13. When resetting a circuit breaker or replacing a fuse at the main service panel, work with one hand, holding the other hand behind you or using it to grasp a plastic flashlight.

14. Complete the repair before reconnecting the electricity, water or gas. Open water supply lines slowly at first to allow air to escape, then fully to flush debris from the pipes and faucets.

15. Never work with electricity in wet conditions and do not use wet electrical cords, tools or appliances. Use grounded or GFCI-protected outlets in bathrooms and kitchens.

16. Never bypass or alter any component when repairing appliances or units. Ensure that all wiring connections are tight and that no wires or fuel lines are pinched. Do not remove the ground prong of a three-prong cord.

17. Do not run power cords under carpets or through heavily trafficked areas. Do not use extension cords as permanent wiring for an appliance or electronic unit.

18. Perform a cold check for leaking voltage before plugging in and using any appliance or unit after a repair *(page 427)*.

19. Catch draining fuel or water in a sturdy basin and wipe up spills immediately. Discard used oil and other flammable substances according to local environmental regulations.

20. Never smoke or light a flame when there is a smell of gas or when working with gas.

SAFETY TIPS

PLUMBING

1. Identify and label the shutoff valves for all plumbing fixtures as well as the house main shutoff valve.
2. Avoid using caustic chemical drain openers—particularly those containing lye—in a drain that is completely blocked. If the chemical doesn't clear the drain, you will be exposed to it as you plunge, auger or open the trap.
3. Do not use a power auger for clearing drains unless you are confident in working with power tools.
4. If hair and soap frequently clog bathroom drains, install a strainer in the bathroom sink. Do not rinse fats and coffee grounds down a kitchen sink, and avoid using the toilet as a wastebasket.
5. When hot water is not used for two weeks or more, hydrogen gases can build up in the water heater and pipes. Before turning on appliances that use water, run all hot-water faucets in the house for two minutes to clear out the gas.

LIGHTING AND ELECTRICITY

1. Read the introductory chapter *Electricity in the Home (page 98)* to better understand how to live and work safely with electricity.
2. Never work on service panel wiring. Entrance wires remain live even when the main breaker or fuse is off.
3. Do not touch a metal faucet, pipe or appliance, or any other ground, when working with electricity.
4. Before working on a circuit, switch off the power at the service panel *(page 102)*. Leave a note on the panel so that no one switches it back on while you are working.
5. Never wipe a hot bulb with a damp cloth.

HEATING AND COOLING

1. The diagnosis and repair of some heating and cooling problems are beyond the scope of the homeowner. Never attempt a repair that you are unqualified to do; call for professional service where recommended.
2. Avoid damage to refrigerant coils and lines; have them serviced by a professional.
3. Discharge capacitors safely before working in the electrical service box of an air conditioning or heat pump unit.
4. Keep furniture and curtains away from baseboard heaters and make sure that air distribution registers are unblocked.
5. If there is an odor of gas that does not dissipate, do not attempt to relight a gas-burner pilot light; do not light matches or touch electrical outlets or switches. Ventilate the area, leave the house, and call the gas company.
6. Ask the fuel company for an annual system checkup, including a measurement of the carbon monoxide level in your home. If the safety of your heating or cooling system or of any repair is in doubt, call for professional advice.

APPLIANCES

1. Familiarize yourself with the owner's manual for each appliance. If you have mis-placed it, purchase a new one from an authorized service center.
2. Never allow small children to play with or operate appliances. If children are nearby, do not leave working appliances unattended. Store small appliances out of the reach of children when not in use.
3. Do not submerge a small appliance in water or any other liquid to clean it.
4. Never use or clean small appliances near the bath or shower. If an appliance has fallen into water, do not unplug it. Turn off the power at the main service panel, then unplug the appliance and retrieve it.
5. Do not poke anything inside a small appliance when the power is connected.
6. Discharge the capacitor safely before working inside a microwave oven.

HOME ELECTRONICS

1. Read *Entertainment Systems (page 354)* to understand the interrelationship of electronic units that are hooked up together.
2. Never look directly at the laser in a compact disc player that is plugged in and turned on; it can cause eye damage.
3. Wear eye protection when making repairs inside a television. Prevent injury from picture-tube implosion by asking a service technician to dispose safely of an old set.
4. Keep food and beverages away from electronic units and make sure air vents remain unobstructed and dust-free.
5. Unplug electronic units and external antenna connections from the television before going away on vacation.

TROUBLESHOOTING GUIDE

SYMPTOM	PROCEDURE
FIRE EMERGENCIES	
Cooking fire	Turn off burners and exhaust hood fan. Slide fitted lid onto pan *(p. 16)*
	Pour baking soda or salt on fire to smother it *(p. 16)*. Do not apply water, baking powder or flour to fire
	Close oven door to smother flames and turn off oven to allow it to cool. If flames spread, use fire extinguisher *(p. 16)*
Grease fire in range hood	Turn off range hood fan; if flames do not subside, use fire extinguisher *(p. 16)*
Fire inside toaster or microwave oven	Do not open door of appliance. Shut off power at main service panel *(p. 22)*; then unplug appliance from wall outlet *(p. 24)*
Burning smell or smoke from appliance	Do not open appliance door. Unplug power cord *(p. 24)* and allow appliance to cool. If flames develop, use fire extinguisher *(p. 17)*
Clothes burning or melting in dryer	Close dryer door to smother fire. Shut off power at main service panel *(p. 22)*; allow dryer to cool before removing clothes. If flames develop, use fire extinguisher *(p. 17)*
Fire in electrical outlet, switch, fixture, appliance, unit or power cord	Call fire department. Use fire extinguisher rated for electrical fires *(p. 17)*. Shut off power at main service panel *(p. 22)*; then, unplug unit power cord from wall outlet *(p. 24)*
	If flames or smoldering continue, leave house and wait for fire department
Heating or cooling unit on fire	Use fire extinguisher *(p. 17)*; call fire department
Burning or other peculiar odor coming from electronic unit	Turn off unit and unplug unit power cord from wall outlet *(p. 24)*; wait until odor dissipates before servicing unit
	Locate and repair cause of odor or take unit for professional service
WATER EMERGENCIES	
Clothes washer overflowing	Turn off washer. Set timer on final spin cycle and turn on washer to pump out water. If water doesn't drain: Unplug power cord *(p. 24)* and bail or siphon out water *(p. 19)*
Dishwasher overflowing	Turn off dishwasher at timer. Turn off dishwasher valve under sink *(p. 19)*. Turn on dishwasher and let run to empty water
	If water doesn't drain: Shut off power *(p. 102)* and bail or siphon out water *(p. 19)*
Water heater, washing machine, dishwasher or garbage disposer leaking	Turn off machine. Unplug power cord without touching the machine *(p. 24)*, or shut off power *(p. 102)*. Turn off water supply at machine *(p. 19)* or close main shutoff valve *(p. 18)*. Bail out or siphon out machine if full of water
Water on floor from appliance leak or overflowing appliance	If you must stand in water to mop it, first unplug power cord *(p. 24)* or shut off power *(p. 102)*. Dam area around water with washable, absorbent rags; clean up with mop or towels *(p. 19)*
Basement flooded	Close main shutoff valve *(p. 18)*. Mop up, bail out or shovel water *(p. 19)*. For 1/2 inch or less, use a wet-and-dry shop vacuum; for more than 1/2 inch, use a sump pump *(p. 21)*
Ceiling sagging from weight of flooded water	Poke a small hole in ceiling with a large nail and catch water in a bucket *(p. 21)*
Electronic unit is flooded	Do not touch unit or any plumbing fixture; dry yourself if you are wet. Shut off power at service panel *(p. 102)*; then unplug unit power cord from wall outlet *(p. 24)*
	Dry unit with absorbent cloth and hair dryer
ELECTRICAL EMERGENCIES	
Child or adult victim of electrical shock	Push victim away with wooden spoon, broom handle or chair. Treat victim for injuries and call for help *(p. 23)*
Switch sparking or hot to the touch	Turn off switch using a wooden spoon or broom handle *(p. 24)*.
Arcs and sparks at service panel	Do not touch service panel; call power company to have power turned off or call an electrician
Cord or plug discolored, hot or melting	Shut off power at service panel *(p. 102)*. Unplug cord using a towel *(p. 24)*. Call an electrician
Appliance, lamp or electronic unit gives off sparks or shocks user	Unplug cord *(p. 24)* without touching appliance or unit, or shut off power at service panel *(p. 102)* and unplug unit
	Take appliance or unit for service
Appliance excessively hot	Shut off power at service panel *(p. 102)*, then unplug appliance from wall outlet *(p. 24)*. Clean the appliance as instructed in service manual, or take it for service
Beverage or other foreign material spilled into electronic unit	Unplug unit power cord from wall outlet *(p. 24)*. Dry unit with absorbent cloth and hair dryer if wet; or clean the components *(p. 31)*
Small appliance falls in sink or bathtub	Do not touch appliance or any plumbing fixture. If you are dry, pull out cord *(p. 24)* or shut off power to appliance at service panel *(p. 102)* and unplug appliance
	Take appliance for service

TROUBLESHOOTING GUIDE

SYMPTOM	PROCEDURE
ELECTRICAL EMERGENCIES	
Large appliance or outlet wet or submerged	Do not enter room. If conditions around service panel are dry, turn off power at service panel *(p. 22)*; otherwise, leave house and call power company
Power failure	Turn off all appliances with motors or heating elements; including furnace, air conditioner, heater, washer and dryer, to prevent overloading system when power is restored
	Check service panel. If main circuit breaker has tripped or main fuses have blown, call an electrician or power company to inspect system
	Have emergency supplies on hand, including a small space heater and lantern, flashlight or candles. A portable generator can provide a limited amount of emergency power *(p. 25)*
	Leave several lights on so that you will know when power has been restored
Lightning storm	Unplug electronic devices or use a surge suppressor to protect them. Be careful near windows, doors, fireplaces, radiators, stoves, sinks and pipes
GAS EMERGENCIES	
Pilot light out in gas appliance	Relight pilot *(p. 26)*
Odor of escaping gas	Ventilate room *(p. 26)*. Do not touch electrical outlets or switches and extinguish all flames
	Check pilots of all gas appliances and relight if necessary *(p. 26)*
	Leave house and call gas company if odor persists
HEATING AND COOLING EMERGENCIES	
No heat due to clogged air filter in air distribution system	Clean or replace air filter *(p. 27)*
No heat due to faulty thermostat	Jumper thermostat *(p. 27)*; have thermostat replaced as soon as possible
No heat due to faulty aquastat in water distribution system	Jumper aquastat *(p. 27)*; Caution: If burner aquastat is jumpered, allow system to run for only one 30-minute cycle every hour. Have aquastat replaced as soon as possible
	Call for service
PLUMBING EMERGENCIES	
Small object dropped down sink	Do not run water in sink. Carefully remove trap under sink *(p. 28)*; have a bucket handy
Faucet burst or fixture leaking or overflowing	Turn off faucets if possible. Close shutoff valves at fixture or close main shutoff valve *(p. 18)*
Supply pipe leaks	Close main shutoff valve *(p. 18)*
	Patch hole temporarily with electrical tape or hose clamps and bicycle inner tube *(p. 20)*
Supply pipe bursts	Close main shutoff valve *(p. 18)*. Call municipality or utility company
Supply pipe freezes	Turn up heat in house. Close main shutoff valve *(p. 18)* and open nearest faucet. Thaw with a hair dryer or heating tape *(p. 18)*
Toilet blocked or overflowing	Do not flush; bail out half the water, then dislodge clog and flush *(p. 65)*
Sewage fumes	Check fixture traps to be sure they have not run dry; run water to refill traps. Pour a bucket of water in basement floor drain to replenish house trap, if any
Sewage backs up into house	Call municipality
Possibility of water contamination from back-siphonage or pollution	Do not attempt to flush out the supply lines yourself. Call local health department
FIRST AID TREATMENT	
Burn or scald	Soak injury in cold water. Do not apply any ointment or butter. If severe, cover with sterile gauze *(p. 29)* and seek medical help
Refrigerant burn	Apply non-adhesive sterile gauze *(p. 29)*; seek medical help immediately
Electrical burn	Soak injury in cold water and cover with sterile gauze if severe
	Seek medical attention immediately, since electrical burns can cause internal injury
Chemical splashed in eye.	Flush eye with clean water for 10 minutes *(p. 29)*. Seek medical help
Skin cut	Wrap cut with a clean, dry cloth; elevate cut and apply pressure until bleeding stops, then wash wound with soap and water and bandage with a sterile dressing *(p. 29)*
	Seek medical help if bleeding persists or wound is deep or gaping

FIRE EMERGENCIES: COOKING FIRES

Smothering a cooking fire in a pan. Do not move the pan. Turn off the burner controls and the range hood fan. Protecting your hand with an oven mitt or a pot holder, slide a fitted lid onto the pan *(above)*. If no lid is available, use a plate or platter a bit larger than the pan. Do not clap the cover straight down; the rush of air can spread the flames. Let the pan cool before removing the cover. If the fire spreads, apply baking soda *(above, right)*.

Controlling a cooking fire on the range top. Do not move the pan. Turn off the burner controls and the range hood fan. Pour baking soda liberally over the flames until they are out *(above)*. If baking soda is not available, use salt. **Caution:** Do not put water, baking powder or flour on a cooking fire; they will spread the flames. Allow the range to cool before removing the pan and cleaning the range top. If the fire spreads, use a fire extinguisher *(below)*.

Using a fire extinguisher. To snuff an oven fire, first turn off the oven control and close the door; lack of oxygen should kill the flames. If the fire spreads, use a fire extinguisher rated ABC or BC. Stand near an exit, 6 to 10 feet from the fire. Pull the lock pin out of the extinguisher handle and, holding the extinguisher upright, aim the nozzle at the base of the flames. Squeeze the two levers of the handle together, spraying in a quick side-to-side motion *(left)*. The fire may flare and appear to grow at first before subsiding. If the discharge stream scatters the flames, move back. Keep spraying until the fire is completely extinguished. Watch carefully for "flashback," or rekindling, and be prepared to spray again. Allow the appliance to cool completely before cleaning it.

FIRE EMERGENCIES: ELECTRICAL FIRES

ABC or BC
fire extinguisher

Extinguishing an electrical fire. Have someone call the fire department immediately. If flames or smoke are coming from the walls or ceiling, leave the house to call for help. To snuff a small electrical fire, use a dry-chemical fire extinguisher rated ABC or BC. Stand near an exit, 6 to 10 feet from the fire. Holding the extinguisher upright, pull the lock pin out of the handle and aim the nozzle at the base of the flames. Squeeze the handle and spray in a quick side-to-side motion *(left)* until the fire is completely out. Watch for "flashback," or rekindling, and be prepared to spray again. You may also have to turn off power at the service panel *(page 22)* to remove the source of heat at the fire. If the fire spreads, leave the house.

FIRE EMERGENCIES: SAFETY ACCESSORIES

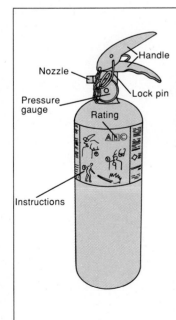

Handle
Nozzle
Pressure gauge
Lock pin
Rating
ABC
Instructions

A household fire extinguisher. Best for use in the home is a multi-purpose dry-chemical extinguisher rated ABC *(left)*. A and B ratings indicate effectiveness against fires in wood or upholstery and flammable liquids such as grease or paint, while an extinguisher rated C can be used for electrical fires. A numerical rating indicates what size fire the extinguisher can combat. An extinguisher of convenient size holds a pressurized load of 2 1/2 to 7 pounds. Check the pressure gauge monthly. After any discharge or loss of pressure, recharge or replace the tank according to the manufacturer's instructions. Mount extinguishers, using the wall brackets provided, near doors to the kitchen, utility room, garage and basement.

Ionization alarm

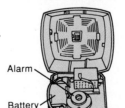

Alarm

Battery

Photoelectric alarm

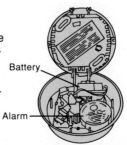

Battery

Alarm

Two kinds of smoke alarms. Ionization alarms *(left, top)* which sense atomic particles, respond quickly to hot fires with little smoke, but may set off annoying false alarms in the presence of normal cooking fumes.

Photoelectric alarms *(left, bottom)* "see" smoke particles; they respond best to the smoldering typical of cooking, appliance and upholstery fires.

Install at least one smoke alarm in a central hallway, near the kitchen, bedrooms and head of the stairs, as well as in the garage and basement. Mount a battery-powered smoke alarm on the ceiling. Replace the battery once a year—the detector emits a chirping sound when the battery runs low.

WATER EMERGENCIES

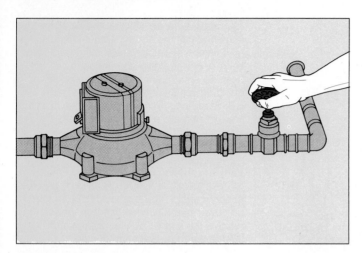

Locating shutoff valves. If water is spraying from a broken faucet, or pouring from a burst pipe, the first step before attempting any repair is to turn off the water supply. Look for shutoff valves directly beneath the broken appliance or fixture where the water supply connects to it. If you don't see any handles there, or if the problem is a leaking pipe, look for the main shutoff valve supplying water to the entire house. This is usually a gate valve located near the water meter in the basement *(above, left)*, utility room, crawlspace or even outside in mild climates. Turn the valve clockwise to shut off the water supply. To stop an overflowing toilet, close its single shutoff valve *(above, right)* or support the float ball and arm with a bent coat hanger *(inset)*.

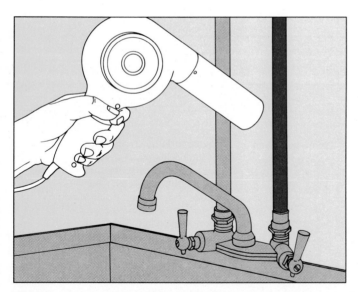
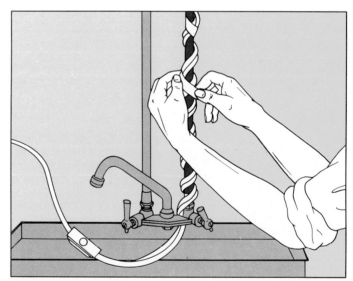

Thawing frozen pipes. When thawing frozen pipes, always open the nearest faucet to allow melting ice to drain, and close the main shutoff valve about 3/4 off. If you still have electricity, one of the safest remedies is to aim a hair dryer 3 to 4 inches from the affected area. Apply heat to the open faucet first, then work back along the pipe *(above, left)*. When water begins to trickle from the spout, open the main shutoff; the flow of water will speed thawing.

Electric heating tape draws only a small amount of current to keep tap water safely above the freezing point. Some models are equipped with a thermostat that turns the tape on and off as needed; these may be permanently plugged in. Starting at a faucet or fixture, wrap the tape tightly around the exposed pipe, taking 6 to 8 turns per foot. Secure the spirals with plastic tape every 6 inches *(above, right)*.

WATER EMERGENCIES: LEAKING APPLIANCES

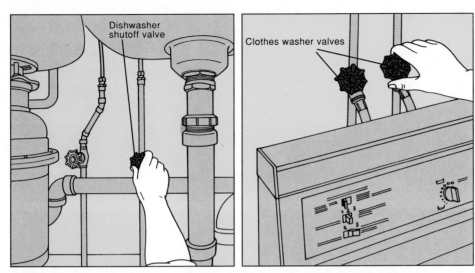

1 **Turning off the water supply to appliances. Caution:** If an electrical appliance is submerged, do not enter the room; disconnect power at the service panel *(page 22)*. If an appliance is leaking or overflowing, unplug the power cord *(page 24)*, then turn off the water at the shutoff valve to the appliance. For a dishwasher, the valve is usually under the sink *(above, left)*. Clothes washer valves are on the wall behind the machine *(above, right)* or at the utility sink faucet; shut off both the hot and cold water supply. If the valve is leaking, or there is no valve, turn off the house water supply at the main shutoff valve *(page 18)*, located near the water meter or where the main water supply pipe enters the house. To service a leaking valve, see Tools & Techniques *(page 417)*.

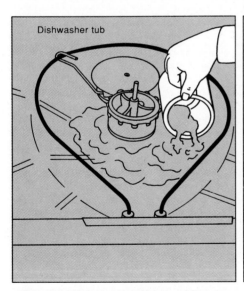

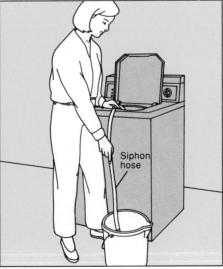

2 **Emptying an appliance of water.** If a clothes washer stops working in the wash or rinse cycle, try setting it on the spin cycle to drain the water. To empty an overflowing dishwasher, turn off the water valve under the sink *(step 1)* and turn on the dishwasher. If a water-filled appliance does not work at all, unplug it and let the water cool. Bail out the water *(above, left)*, or use a hose to siphon it out into a bucket on the floor *(above, right)*. To start the water flow, suck on the end of the hose; the flow will continue as long as the end of the hose is lower than the level of the water. Consult the appliance chapter to troubleshoot the problem.

3 **Damming a leak.** Disconnect power to the appliance without stepping in the water. To keep water on the floor from spreading, surround it with a dam of washable, rolled-up rugs or towels. Clean up water within the dammed area with a mop or heavy cotton towels *(above)*, not paper towels.

WATER EMERGENCIES: LEAKING PIPES

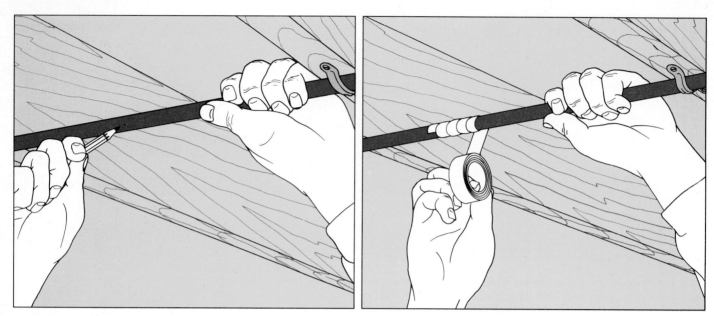

Quick fix for a pinhole leak. If you suspect a leak in the supply line, first check the water meter. If its needle or dial is moving and no one in the house is using a faucet or appliance, there is a leak somewhere. To locate it, look for stains on ceilings and walls, and listen carefully along supply pipes. As a temporary repair, turn off the water supply at the main shutoff valve *(page 18)*, jam a pencil point into the hole and break it off *(above, left)*. A toothpick may also work, but for steel pipes, the graphite in the pencil lead will better seal the leak. To secure the plug, dry the surface of the pipe and wrap two or three layers of plastic electrical tape around the pipe for three inches on each side of the leak, overlapping each turn by half *(above, right)*. For a lasting solution, have the damaged section of pipe replaced.

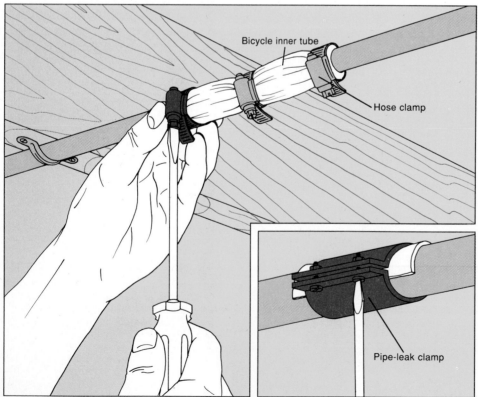

Bicycle inner tube

Hose clamp

Pipe-leak clamp

Sealing cracks or punctures. For a larger crack or puncture, close the main shutoff valve *(page 18)* and drain the supply line by opening a nearby faucet. Wrap the pipe with an old bicycle inner tube and secure it with hose clamps *(left)*. Turn the water back on, slowly at first, to test for leaks. Have the damaged section replaced as soon as possible.

To install a commercial pipe-leak clamp, remove the screws that hold the two halves of the clamp together, then fit them over the damaged pipe so that the rubber cushion seals the leak. Insert and tighten the screws *(inset)*.

Small leaks can also be patched using pipe cement or epoxy. The pipe must be drained of water and dried thoroughly for the cement to set properly. Roughen the damaged area with emery cloth, apply a thick coat of cement and allow it to dry overnight. Point a heat lamp or 100-watt bulb at the pipe to speed curing.

WATER EMERGENCIES: FLOODS

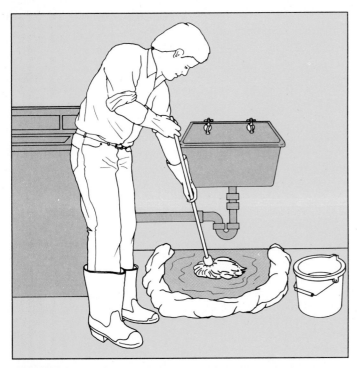

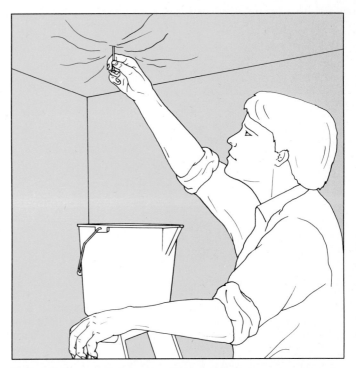

Damming the flood. Caution: If an appliance or outlet is submerged, do not enter the room; disconnect power at the service panel if it is safe to do so *(page 22)*. Unplug the appliance. Turn off water to the leaking or overflowing fixture at its shutoff valves, or close the main shutoff valve *(page 18)*. To keep water on the floor from spreading, surround it with a dam of washable, rolled-up rugs or towels. Then mop up the water within the dammed area *(above)*.

Puncturing a waterlogged ceiling. If flood water has collected above the ceiling and caused it to sag, stand on a stepladder and puncture it with a heavy nail *(above)*. Place a bucket directly under the hole to catch the water as it pours out. When the water has drained, place a dehumidifier or space heater close to the damaged area to speed drying and prevent mildew. Have the hole patched only when the ceiling is completely dry.

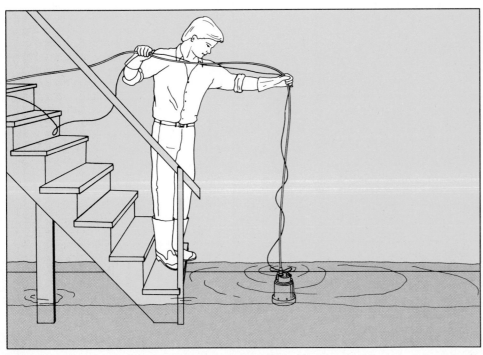

Using a sump pump. To get rid of water following a major flood, rent an electric or gas-powered sump pump from a tool-rental dealer. Flood water should be more than 1/2-inch deep to reach the pump impeller. Connect a long garden hose, or 1 1/4-inch flexible pipe to the discharge fitting, then run the hose outside or to a working drain in the house. Next, lower the sump pump into the water to be drained *(left)*. To avoid electrical shock, never stand in the water while the sump pump is operating. While you are high and dry, plug the pump into a grounded outlet. Drain as much water as you can, but do not run the pump without water or you may damage its water-lubricated bearing. Stop the pump when it no longer sucks up water and remove any remaining water on the floor by bailing and mopping. Run clean water through the pump to flush its mesh filter and hose.

ELECTRICAL EMERGENCIES

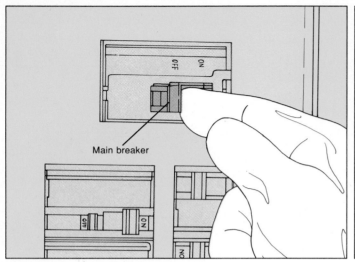

Main breaker

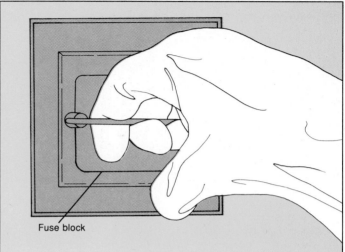

Fuse block

Shutting down the entire electrical system. If the floor is wet around the service panel, stand on a dry board or rubber mat, or wear rubber boots. Wear heavy rubber gloves or use a wooden broom handle. Work with one hand only, to protect your body from becoming a path for electrical current, and keep the other hand in your pocket or behind your back. At a circuit breaker panel *(above, left)*, flip off the main breaker. As an added precaution, use your knuckle; any shock will jerk your hand away from the panel. At a fuse panel *(above, right)*, remove the main fuse block by gripping its metal handle and pulling it from the box. Remove all main fuse blocks if there is more than one. Some fuse panels have a shutoff lever instead of a fuse block. To shut off power to only one circuit at the main service panel, go to page 102.

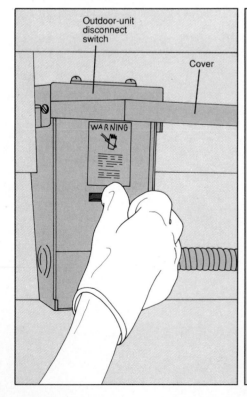

Outdoor-unit
disconnect
switch

Cover

WARNING

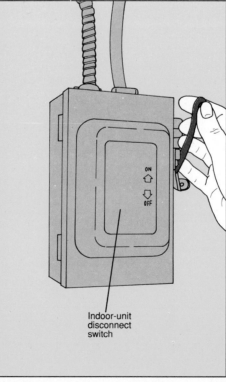

ON

OFF

Indoor-unit
disconnect
switch

Turning off power at the unit disconnect switch. A unit disconnect switch accompanies most electrically controlled systems—electric furnaces, air conditioners and heat pumps. Locate the unit disconnect switch indoors, near the furnace or boiler, or outdoors, mounted on or near the heat pump or central air conditioning unit. If the floor or ground in that vicinity is wet, stand on a dry board or rubber mat, or wear rubber boots; also wear heavy rubber gloves. Using one hand, shift an indoor-unit disconnect switch to the OFF position *(near left)*. On an outdoor-unit disconnect switch, lift up the weatherproof cover *(far left)* to access the ON/OFF switch. As an extra safety precaution, also shut off power to the heating or cooling unit at the main service panel *(page 102)*. After completing a repair, restore the power at the service panel, then at the unit disconnect switch.

ELECTRICAL EMERGENCIES: ELECTRICAL SHOCK

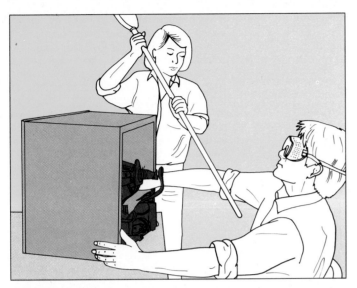 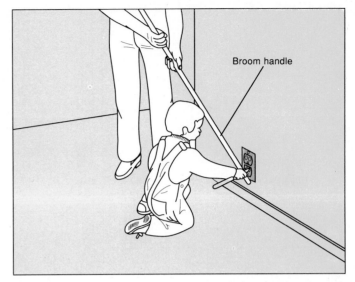

Broom handle

Freeing someone from a live current. Usually a person who contacts live current will be thrown back from the source. But sometimes muscles contract involuntarily around a wire or component. Do not touch the victim or the unit. Pull the power cord plug from the wall outlet *(page 24)* or shut off power at the main service panel *(page 22)*. If the power cannot be cut immediately, use a wooden broom handle or wooden chair to knock the person free *(above, left and right)*. Cover unused outlets with plastic safety caps *(page 101)* to prevent such accidents where young children can reach.

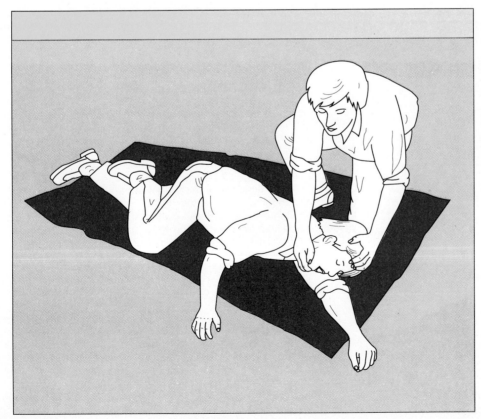

Handling a victim of electrical shock. Call for help immediately. Check the victim's breathing and heartbeat. If there is no breathing or heartbeat, give mouth-to-mouth resuscitation or cardiopulmonary resuscitation (CPR) only if you are qualified to do so. If the victim is breathing and has not sustained back or neck injuries, place him in the recovery position *(left)*. Tilt the head back with the face to one side and the tongue forward to maintain an open airway. Keep the victim calm and comfortable until help arrives.

ELECTRICAL EMERGENCIES: SPARKING SWITCHES

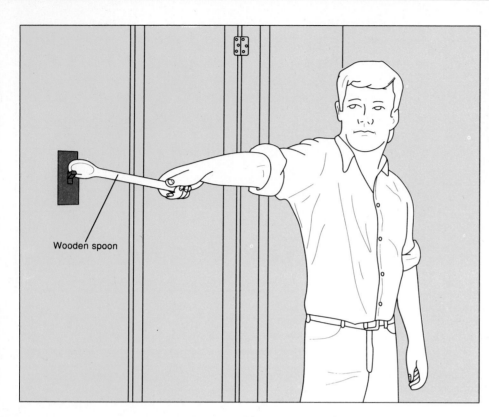

Wooden spoon

Switching off electrical hazards. If a switch, outlet or fixture makes snapping or crackling sounds, or if visible sparks, smoke or flames appear, immediately shut off power to that circuit at the service panel *(page 102)*. If in doubt about which fuse or breaker controls the circuit, shut off all electricity *(page 22)*. Inspect the electrical boxes along the affected circuit for loose or broken wires *(page 431)* and have repairs made before restoring power to the circuit.

Never touch a burning or sparking switch to turn it off. Stand away from it and use a wooden spoon *(left)* to flip off the toggle.

ELECTRICAL EMERGENCIES: HOT CORD, PLUG OR APPLIANCE

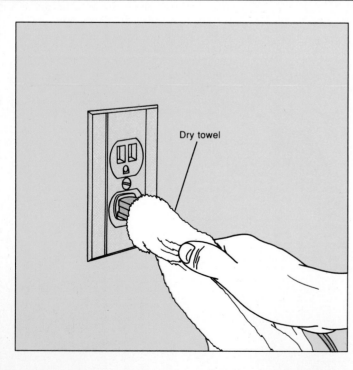

Dry towel

Pulling the power cord from the wall outlet. If the floor or counter is wet, or the outlet itself is sparking or burning, do not touch the cord, lamp or appliance. Instead, shut off power to the circuit at the service panel *(page 102)*. If the lamp or appliance sparks, shocks you, feels hot or is burning, disconnect the plug. Protect your hand with a thick, dry towel or a heavy work glove. Without touching the wall outlet, grasp the cord with one hand several inches from the plug, as shown, and pull it out *(left)*. Locate and repair the problem before using the device again.

ELECTRICAL EMERGENCIES: POWER FAILURE

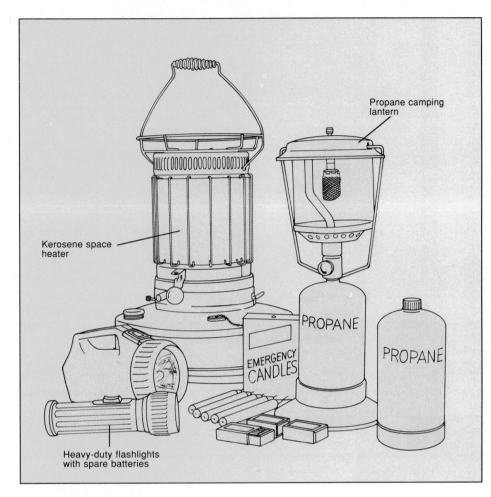

Propane camping lantern

Kerosene space heater

Heavy-duty flashlights with spare batteries

Emergency supplies. Plan in advance for power failure or heating malfunction. Candles, a reliable source of light, provide a surprising amount of warmth. Keep candles, matches and a flashlight in a familiar, accessible location. A propane lantern will provide bright, long-lasting light but should be used with caution; when fuel-fired heaters are used indoors, always open a door or window slightly for proper ventilation. A kerosene heater rated for indoor use is a safe temporary source of heat, provided the manufacturer's instructions regarding fuel, ventilation and operation are strictly followed.

To prepare for power restoration, reduce the load on your electrical system by turning off or unplugging all heating and motorized equipment. Open your refrigerator or freezer as little as possible; spoilage will not likely occur within 24 hours.

A portable electrical generator. A gasoline generator can be rented to deal with long-term power failure. A generator must be operated in a dry, sheltered, ventilated area; a garage or porch is ideal. Only appliances that can use extension cords should be attached to a generator. Permanent hookup to the house wiring must be left to a professional. A 2200-watt unit *(left)* is large enough to operate a refrigerator or electric space heater and several lamps. To run appliances that have a compressor, a generator with surge capacity is needed. Calculate the load you need to run *(page 443)* in order to choose the right size.

GAS EMERGENCIES

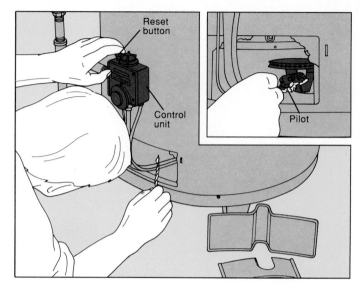

Relighting the pilot in a gas heater. Remove the burner access panels to gain access to the pilot. Turn the temperature control to its lowest setting and the gas control knob to OFF. **Caution:** Wait at least five minutes for the gas to clear. Depress the reset button *(above)* while placing a lighted match near the tip of the pilot *(inset)*. If the pilot is hard to reach, make a taper from a tightly rolled piece of paper. When there is no reset button, hold down the gas control knob while lighting the pilot. Should the pilot fail to light immediately, close the gas shutoff valve and call the gas company. If it lights, continue to depress the reset button or gas control knob for one minute, then release it and set the temperature control. If the pilot goes out, turn the gas control knob to OFF and call for service.

Ventilating a gas-filled room. First open all windows and doors in the room *(above)*. **Caution:** Extinguish all flames, except for pilot lights. Do not use electrical switches or outlets—a spark could ignite the gas. Turn off controls to all gas appliances in the room. When the gas has dissipated, relight any pilots that are out *(next step)*. If the gas odor persists, leave the house and call the gas company for service. If you return home and smell a strong odor of gas, DO NOT enter the building; call the gas company from a neighbor's house. Gas inhalation symptoms include nausea and choking; take victims outdoors immediately, and call for medical help.

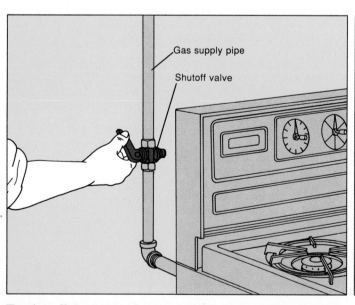

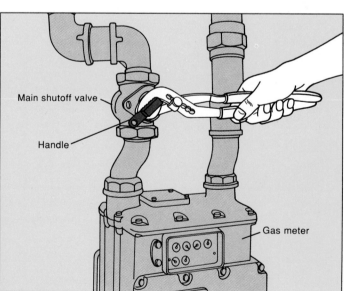

Turning off the gas supply. If the appliance has a valve on its gas supply pipe, turn the handle perpendicular to the pipe to shut off the gas *(above, left)*. The gas supply to the whole house may be turned off at the meter; using a wrench, turn the main valve so that its handle is perpendicular to the pipe *(above, right)*. If the gas in the room does not dissipate, leave the house and call the gas company.

HEATING AND COOLING EMERGENCIES

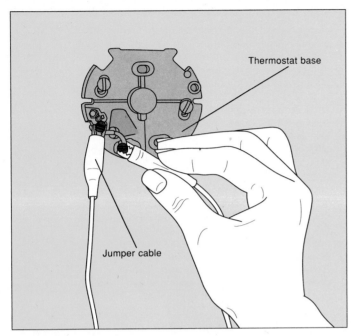

Thermostat base

Jumper cable

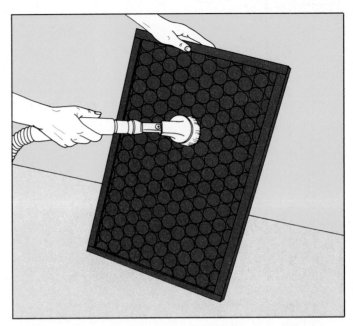

Jumpering a low-voltage thermostat. If the cause of a heating system failure is a faulty thermostat, you can jumper the thermostat, bypassing it to get the system going temporarily. Shut off power to the heating system at the main service panel *(page 102)* and unit disconnect switch *(page 22)*. Access the low-voltage connections on the thermostat base *(page 166)*. Locate the terminals marked "R" and "W" connected to the red and white wires from the wall. Attach one clip of a jumper cable to each terminal *(above)*. Turn on power to the system. When the house temperature has reached a comfortable point, shut off power. Repeat as necessary. Have the thermostat replaced as soon as possible.

Cleaning a disposable air filter. If an air distribution system malfunctions due to a clogged filter, and you do not have a spare filter on hand, take out the filter *(page 171)* and use a vacuum cleaner with a brush attachment to remove debris embedded in the filter's fibers *(above)*. Reinstall the filter; replace it with a new one as soon as possible.

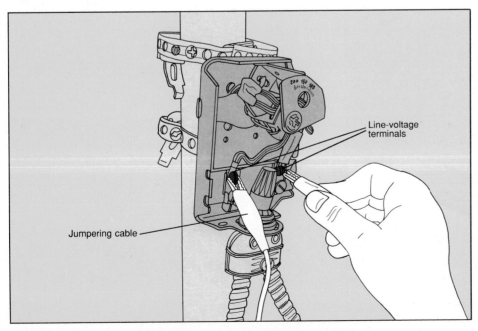

Line-voltage terminals

Jumpering cable

Jumpering an aquastat. If you have diagnosed a faulty burner aquastat or pump aquastat *(page 177)*, you can get the system operating temporarily—just until a replacement part is available. Shut off power to the boiler at the main service panel *(page 102)* and unit disconnect switch *(page 22)*. Remove the cover on the aquastat to access the line-voltage terminal screws *(page 184)*. Use a voltage tester to confirm that power is off *(page 424)*. Attach one clip of a jumper cable of the proper gauge to each line-voltage terminal on the aquastat *(left)*. Turn on power to the system. Do not touch the terminals or jumper cable while power is on. **Caution:** When the burner aquastat is jumpered, the safety shutoff system is bypassed; allow the system to run for only 30 minutes every hour. Shut off power to the system immediately if the pressure gauge on the boiler exceeds 30 psi (pounds per square inch).

PLUMBING EMERGENCIES

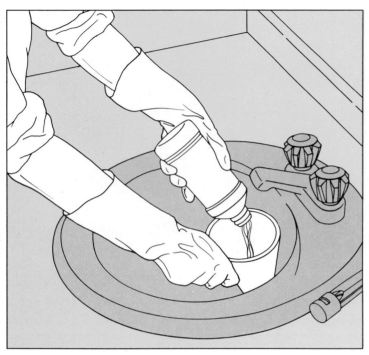

Clearing clogs with chemicals. To unblock a sluggish drain with a chemical drain opener, use a liquid, alkali-based brand (with the ingredient sodium hydroxide—lye—listed on the label). Bail out any standing water in the sink or bathtub and place a funnel in the drain. Wearing rubber gloves (and safety goggles for extra protection), pour a small amount of drain cleaner into the funnel, being careful not to splash any of the chemical on your skin or in your eyes *(left)*. Use it only once on the drain. After 15 minutes, test the drain by flushing with cold water. If the sluggishness remains, work directly on the trap.

Because it reacts with water to produce toxic fumes, caustic soda is not recommended for household drains. It may also crystallize, inhibiting the use of a plunger or auger. Acid-based drain openers can corrode pipes and should never be used after an alkali-based variety has failed. Remember that all chemical drain openers are dangerous. They can burn eyes and skin, and must be kept out of reach of children.

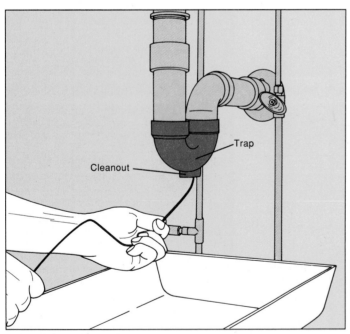

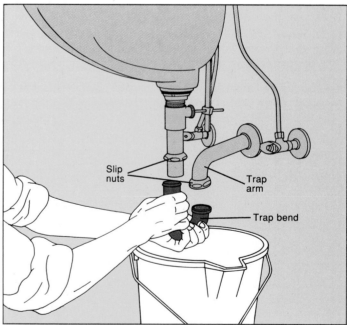

Cleaning a trap bend. Place a pan or pail under the bend of the trap and have some rags at hand. If there is a cleanout plug, loosen it with an adjustable wrench, then remove it by hand, catching water and debris in the pail. With a bent coat hanger *(above, left)*, probe into the opening and try to snag and remove any debris. Replace the cleanout plug and test the drain. If the clog remains, or if there is no cleanout plug, you must remove the trap bend.

Supporting the trap bend with one hand, loosen the two slip nuts with a monkey wrench or tape-covered pliers. (Loosen the slip nut on the trap arm first.) Unscrew the slip nuts by hand and slide them away from the connections. To loosen corroded nuts, apply penetrating oil and wait 15 minutes before trying again. Pull the trap bend down and off *(above, right)* and empty the water into the pail. Clean out the trap with the coat hanger or use a bottle brush.

FIRST AID TREATMENT

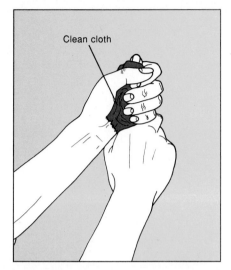

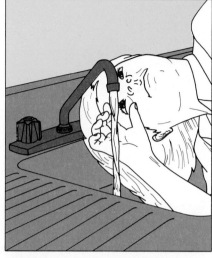

Cuts and scratches. To stop bleeding, wrap a clean cloth around the cut and apply direct pressure with your hand, elevating the limb *(above)*. If the cloth becomes blood-soaked, add another cloth at the wound without removing the first one. Continue applying pressure, keeping the limb elevated, until the bleeding subsides. If the wound is minor, wash it with soap and water and bandage it. Seek medical attention if bleeding persists or if the wound is deep or gaping.

Toxic vapors.. Exposure to toxic vapors can cause headache, dizziness, faintness, fatigue or nausea. At the first sign of any of these symptoms, leave the work area immediately and get fresh air. Remove all clothing that has been splashed by chemicals. Loosen your clothing at the waist, chest and neck. If you feel faint, sit with your head lowered between your knees *(above)*. Have someone ventilate the work area, close all containers, read instructions on the container labels and call the poison control center in your area for medical advice.

Flushing chemicals from the eye. A liquid chemical accidentally splashed in the eye must be washed out quickly. Holding the eyelids apart with your fingers, position the injured eye under a gentle flow of cool water, tilting the head to prevent the chemical from being washed into the uninjured eye *(above)*. Flush the eye for 10 minutes, then cover it with a sterile gauze bandage and seek medical attention immediately.

Treating a liquid refrigerant burn. A liquid refrigerant "burn" is actually a form of severe frostbite, caused when the skin comes in contact with an extremely cold fluorocarbon chemical escaping under high pressure. If the affected area is red—indicating a first-degree burn—but shows no sign of blistering, apply a layer of nonadherent, sterile gauze moistened with lukewarm water *(left)*. **Caution:** Do not apply antiseptic sprays, ointments or chemical neutralizers of any kind. A minor wound will heal itself. If blisters appear—indicating a second-degree burn—keep the area dry. Protect the burn with a layer of nonadherent sterile gauze and seek medical help immediately.

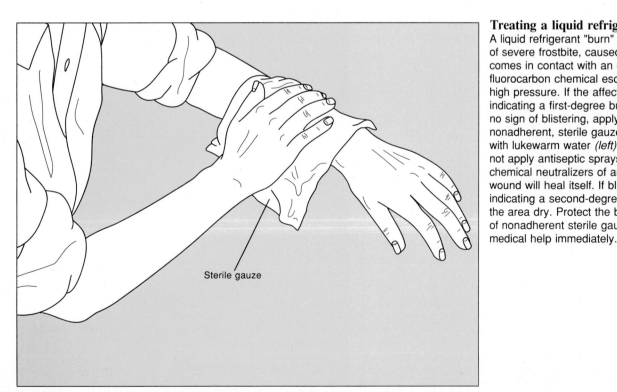

SAFETY PRECAUTIONS

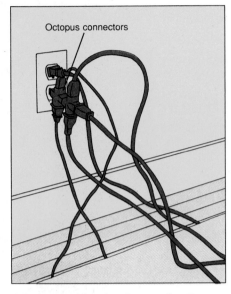

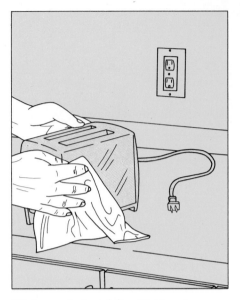

Adapters and extension cords. Do not use "octopus connectors" *(above)*. Plugging too many cords into one outlet could overload the circuit. If a plug is loose or its prongs exposed, the poor connection could produce heat and sparking. Use an extension cord only temporarily. Do not tack it down or run it under a rug.

Pulling the plug. When unplugging an appliance or electronic unit, grasp the plug, not the power cord, firmly *(above)* and work the plug out of the socket. If you suspect that a plug is hot, wrap your hand in a thick towel and then pull the power cord *(page 24)*. If you see sparks, shut off power at the main service panel first *(page 102)*. Replace a frayed power cord immediately *(pages 429–430)*

Water and electricity. Wet hands can create an alternate path for electrical current. Unplug a small appliance before cleaning it with a wet cloth *(above)*. Dry your hands and the appliance before plugging it back in. Never immerse an appliance in water. If it falls into water accidentally, shut off power at the service panel *(page 102)*, then unplug and retrieve it.

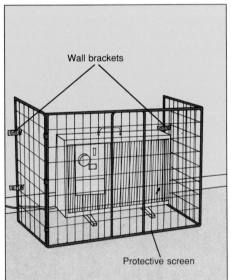

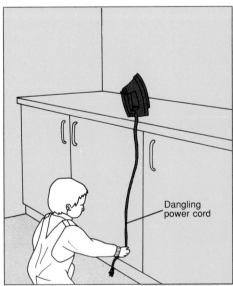

Using appliances around children. Avoid leaving heating appliances such as toasters or irons unattended, especially with young children around. Place fans and heaters out of reach, or install a permanently mounted protective screen around them *(above, left)*. Don't let power cords dangle; a small child may grab the cord and pull the appliance down *(above, center)*. Kettles and irons are particular hazards, because the water inside remains hot enough to scald long after the appliance is turned off. Unplug an appliance after use and coil the power cord out of reach. Chopping and cutting appliances such as blenders and food processors, and their blades, are best stored on a high shelf *(above, right)* or in a locked cupboard when not in use.

CLEANING UP SPILLS AND DIRT

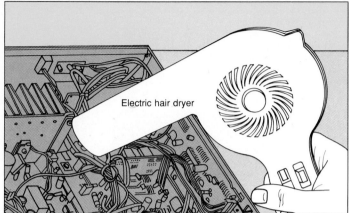

Electric hair dryer

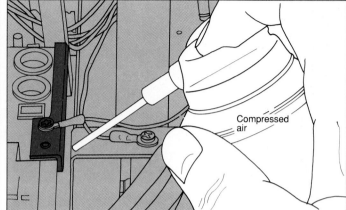

Compressed air

Drying and cleaning internal components of an electronic unit. Turn off the unit and unplug it from the wall outlet. Disconnect its cables and any ground wire hooked up to it *(page 359)*. Set the unit on a clean work table. Refer to the chapter on the electronic unit for instructions on reaching the internal components. Using a lint-free, absorbent cloth, carefully soak up pools of liquid. Dry the internal components thoroughly using a hair dryer set on the no-heat or low-heat position *(above, left)*; aim with slow,

sweeping motions to avoid heating up a component. To remove sticky dust or dirt particles from components, spray them with short bursts of compressed air *(above, right)*. Use foam swabs to clean components; apply denatured alcohol to metal or plastic, rubber-cleaning compound to rubber, and electronic contact cleaner to circuit boards and switches. Finally, lubricate moving parts by applying light machine oil to metal and white grease to plastic. Perform a cold check for leaking voltage *(page 427)* after reassemby.

GETTING HELP WHEN YOU NEED IT

To replace a broken part, first determine the appliance's model and serial number, stamped on a plate attached to the cabinet:

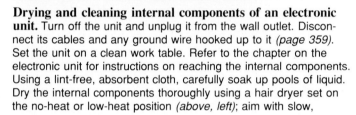

BRAND NAME		
MODEL NO:		SERIAL NO:
MBD64000DYAR		MA 98678A
120/240V 3 WIRE	60hz 5600W	24A
CLOTHES DRYER MADE IN U.S.A		259995827

If you can't locate the plate, consult the owner's manual. Some components carry their serial numbers stamped on the part or listed in the manual. Armed with this information, you can call the dealer to make sure the part is in stock. If possible, take the defective part with you for comparison.

Most dealers do not permit returns or exchanges, so make sure the replacement is identical—especially since an incorrect part could damage your appliance or, in the case of an electrical component, cause a fire. So-called "universal" parts are standard for most brands of appliances. Before buying such parts, however, make sure they are approved for your machine. The parts dealer or distributor should be able to

advise you. If you need more information, many manufacturers maintain toll-free "hot lines to answer customers' questions. Look in your owner's manual for the number, or call 1-800-555-1212 to find out if the manufacturer is listed. Complex mechanical parts such as transmissions or motors can sometimes be rebuilt rather than replaced, saving you money. Ask your dealer or distributor whether this is an option. You have several sources of replacement parts from which to choose:

Independent appliance dealers. If a store does not carry the parts you need, the dealer may be able to order them for you or tell you where to find them.

Major retail chains. Hardware or department stores stock parts of the brands they carry, as well as universal parts.

Appliance parts distributors. These outlets usually sell parts to dealers and repairmen, but often welcome do-it-yourselfers as customers. If necessary, you may be able to order hard-to-find parts through the mail. Distributors usually carry service and repair manuals for appliances.

Manufacturers. Many do not sell parts directly to the public, but they may direct you to a retail source.

When it's time to call in a professional for repairs, choose carefully. Ask friends or neighbors for advice, or consult the retailer who sold you the appliance. Make sure whoever you find is authorized to service your brand of appliance; if not, the repair may not be covered under the warranty. When you phone to arrange a service call, be prepared to supply as much information as possible. Know the model of your appliance, its age and condition. Take careful note of the problem: When did it occur (in which cycle or function), what sounds did the machine make, were there telltale odors, and is this a recurring problem? With these details, a repairman is more likely to bring the proper replacement parts. If your problem involves a flooded dishwasher or washing machine, you can save the repairman time—and yourself money—by bailing out the appliance before he arrives *(page 19)*.

You and your warranty. Before attempting any repair, check the appliance's warranty; take note that some parts may be warranted for a longer period than that of the entire appliance. If the warranty is still in effect, you may void coverage if you undertake the repair yourself. Only an authorized technician should make the needed repairs.

KITCHEN & BATHROOM PLUMBING 33

YOUR HOME'S PLUMBING

Domestic plumbing consists of three basic systems: supply lines, fixtures and drainpipes. Although it may appear a random puzzle of pipes and fittings, the system and its various components work in a logical way.

The supply system is made up of pipes, fittings and valves that carry potable water throughout the house. Water enters your property under pressure from a reservoir, municipal water system or, in rural areas, from the pump-and-tank system of a private well. Typically, the water passes through a curb valve near the street (owned by the water utility), a water meter and the main shutoff valve. The meter is usually on the street side of the house, and the pipe enters a basement, crawlspace or, if your house is built on a slab, a utility center. Water pressure in the supply lines ranges from 35 to 100 pounds per square inch; the ideal pressure is 40-50 psi. Lower pressure may cause insufficient flow at fixtures; higher pressure may encourage water hammer or burst pipes.

From the cold water main, one supply pipe branches off to the water heater to begin a second, parallel run called the hot water main. From there, secondary branches of hot and cold water spaced about 6 inches apart snake through walls and ceilings to the various fixtures. In a well-designed system, each branch contains a shutoff valve near the point where it leaves the main line. Thus you can turn off an individual run without cutting off water to the entire house.

Plumbing fixtures include sinks, bathtubs, showers, toilets, sprinkler systems and appliances that use water and connect either permanently or temporarily to the supply and drainage systems. Not all fixtures need both of the supply lines; a toilet tank has only a cold water line, a dishwasher only a hot one. Once again, in a good system, shutoff valves control each fixture. Behind the wall at most fixtures are air chambers—capped vertical pipes that trap a column of air to cushion onrushing water when the faucet is turned off. Without an air chamber, an abrupt turn-off might create several hundred pounds of pressure within the supply system and result in water hammer.

The DWV (drain-waste-vent) system is the least visible part of the plumbing system, but the most strictly regulated by plumbing codes. The system is not under pressure, but depends on gravity to carry waste water out of the house. Each fixture is connected to a drainpipe by a P- or S-shaped trap filled with water that prevents harmful sewer gas from entering the home. When a toilet is flushed or a sink emptied, the water in the trap is replaced.

Branch drains lead to a larger vertical pipe called a stack, which drops to the level of the outgoing sewer line, and projects up through the roof to vent sewer gas and maintain atmospheric pressure in the system. (Larger dwellings may have two or more stacks.) At ground level (or below if there is a basement), the stack makes a near-45-degree turn to become the main drain, then slopes away from the house to enter a public sewer line or private septic system.

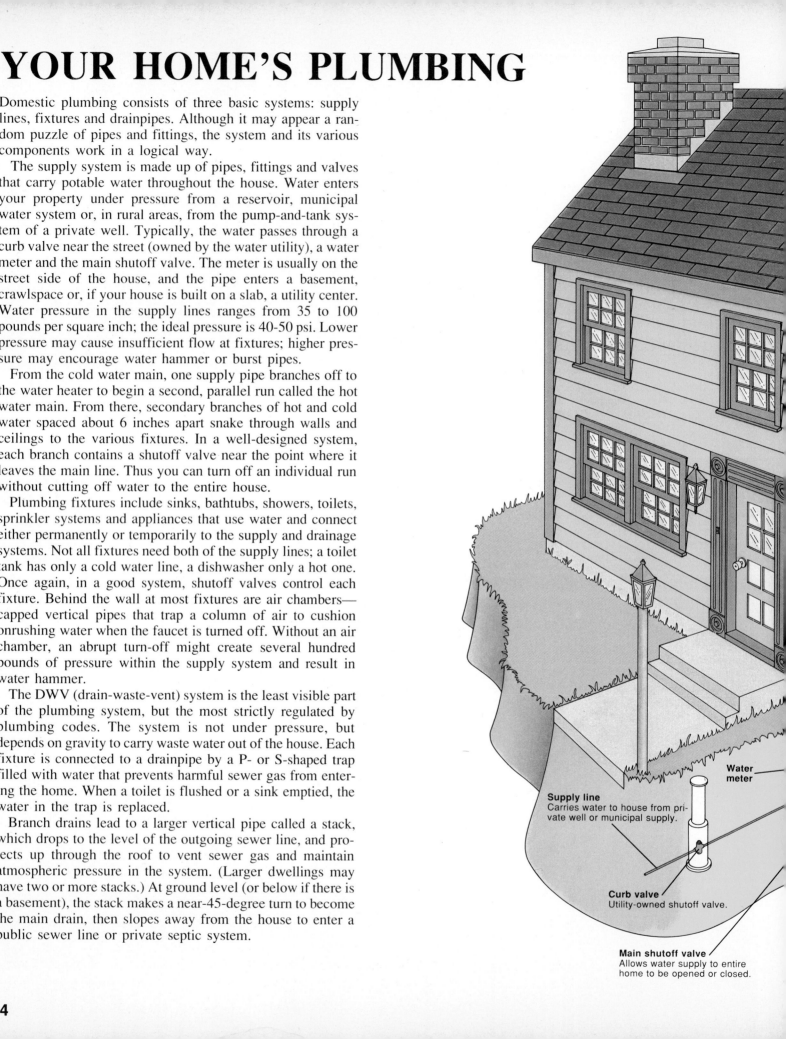

Water meter

Supply line
Carries water to house from private well or municipal supply.

Curb valve
Utility-owned shutoff valve.

Main shutoff valve
Allows water supply to entire home to be opened or closed.

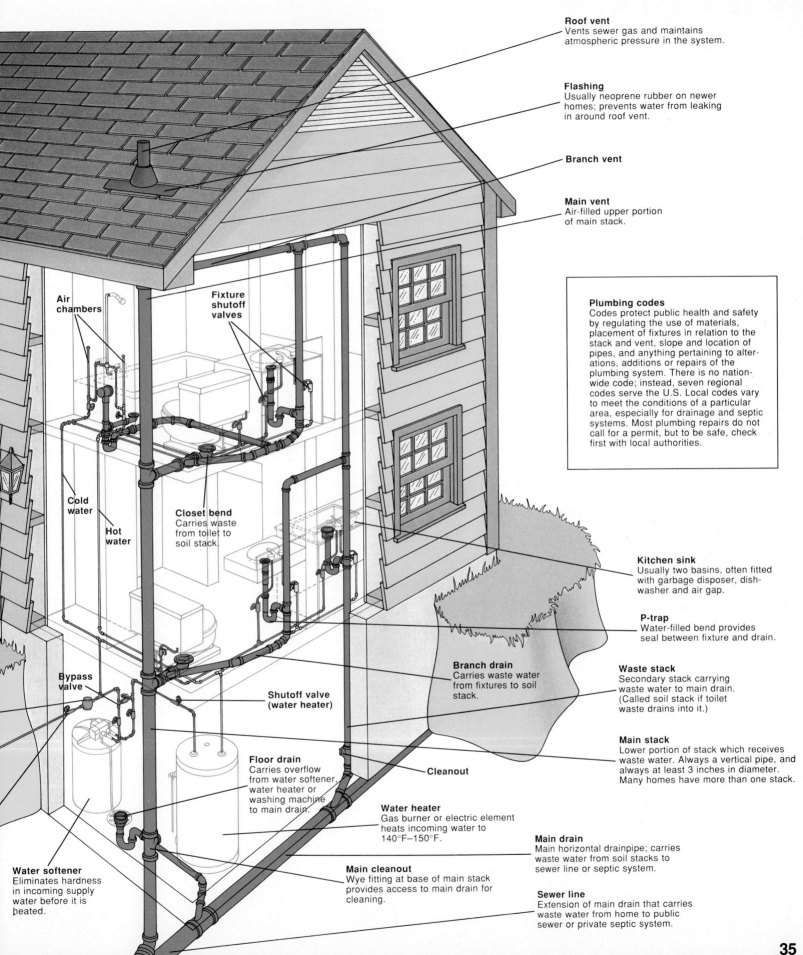

Roof vent
Vents sewer gas and maintains atmospheric pressure in the system.

Flashing
Usually neoprene rubber on newer homes; prevents water from leaking in around roof vent.

Branch vent

Main vent
Air-filled upper portion of main stack.

Plumbing codes
Codes protect public health and safety by regulating the use of materials, placement of fixtures in relation to the stack and vent, slope and location of pipes, and anything pertaining to alterations, additions or repairs of the plumbing system. There is no nationwide code; instead, seven regional codes serve the U.S. Local codes vary to meet the conditions of a particular area, especially for drainage and septic systems. Most plumbing repairs do not call for a permit, but to be safe, check first with local authorities.

Air chambers

Fixture shutoff valves

Cold water

Hot water

Closet bend
Carries waste from toilet to soil stack.

Bypass valve

Shutoff valve (water heater)

Floor drain
Carries overflow from water softener, water heater or washing machine to main drain.

Water softener
Eliminates hardness in incoming supply water before it is heated.

Cleanout

Water heater
Gas burner or electric element heats incoming water to 140°F–150°F.

Main cleanout
Wye fitting at base of main stack provides access to main drain for cleaning.

Kitchen sink
Usually two basins, often fitted with garbage disposer, dishwasher and air gap.

P-trap
Water-filled bend provides seal between fixture and drain.

Waste stack
Secondary stack carrying waste water to main drain. (Called soil stack if toilet waste drains into it.)

Branch drain
Carries waste water from fixtures to soil stack.

Main stack
Lower portion of stack which receives waste water. Always a vertical pipe, and always at least 3 inches in diameter. Many homes have more than one stack.

Main drain
Main horizontal drainpipe; carries waste water from soil stacks to sewer line or septic system.

Sewer line
Extension of main drain that carries waste water from home to public sewer or private septic system.

FAUCETS

Sink faucets are simple valves that control the flow of thousands of gallons of water each year in the kitchen and bathroom. Faucet trouble usually announces itself as a steady drip, drip, drip from the spout, or as a slow leak from around the handle or collar. To solve the problem, you must first identify what kind of faucet you have so that you can buy the exact replacement parts. In most cases, this means disassembling the faucet, then comparing it to those illustrated in this chapter.

Compression faucets, always double-handle, have a washer that rests on a seat at the bottom of the stem. When a compression faucet is turned on, the washer rises to allow water to flow to the spout. A variation is the reverse-compression faucet; when it is turned on, the stem lowers to create a space between the washer and seat, allowing water up. Refer to the section on compression faucets for repairing both types. Simply changing the stem washer will often stop the spout from dripping. Replacing the O-ring or packing in the stem will usually stop leaks from the handle.

A *diaphragm* faucet, another type of double-handle faucet, is easily repaired. A change of O-ring stops most leaks from the handle. Replacing the diaphragm, which controls water flow, stops leaks from both the spout and the handle.

A *disc* faucet, double-handle or single-lever, has a pair of plastic or ceramic discs that move up and down to regulate the volume of water, and rotate to control temperature. The disc assembly rarely needs changing, but the inlet ports can become clogged, and the seals can wear out.

A *rotating-ball* faucet, another single-lever faucet, employs a slotted plastic or brass ball set atop a pair of spring-loaded rubber seats. The handle rotates the ball to adjust water temperature and flow. When this faucet leaks from the spout, its springs and seats probably need replacing. Seepage around the handle points to worn O-rings or a loose adjusting ring.

A *cartridge* faucet regulates water flow by means of a cartridge controlled by a single lever. Repairs involve changing the O-rings or replacing the entire cartridge.

Leaks under the sink may be a result of loose connections between the faucet body and the supply plumbing. Refer to the illustrations below and check all locknuts and coupling nuts for snugness, tightening one-half turn where necessary. Leaks around the aerator or a reduced flow from the spout may be caused by an accumulation of sediment on the screen inside. Every few months, unthread the aerator from the spout and brush it clean with a toothbrush and vinegar.

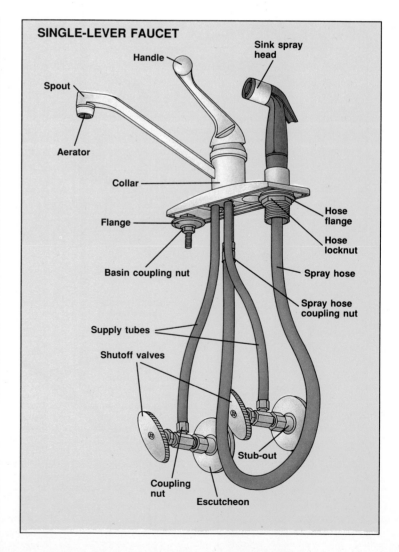

DOUBLE-HANDLE FAUCET
Handles
Spout
Faucet body
Flange
Locknut
Faucet tailpiece
Basin coupling nut
Supply tubes
Coupling nut
Stub-out
Escutcheon
Shutoff valves

SINGLE-LEVER FAUCET
Handle
Sink spray head
Spout
Aerator
Collar
Flange
Hose flange
Hose locknut
Basin coupling nut
Spray hose
Spray hose coupling nut
Supply tubes
Shutoff valves
Stub-out
Coupling nut
Escutcheon

TROUBLESHOOTING GUIDE

SYMPTOM	POSSIBLE CAUSE	PROCEDURE
Double-handle compression faucet drips from spout	Washer worn or damaged	Replace washer (p. 38) □○
	Seat pitted or corroded	Newer models: replace or dress seat (p. 38) ◨◕▲ ; older models: dress seat (p. 38) ◨◕▲, or have faucet replaced
Double-handle compression faucet leaks from handle	O-rings worn or damaged (newer models)	Replace O-rings (p. 39) □○
	Packing nut loose (older models)	Tighten packing nut (p. 40) □○
	Stem packing worn (older models)	Replace packing (p. 40) □○
	Stem bent (older models)	Straighten or replace stem (p. 40) □○ Have faucet replaced
Double-handle disc faucet leaks from handle	O-ring on disc assembly worn	Replace O-ring (p. 41) □○
Double-handle disc faucet drips from spout	Disc cracked or pitted	Replace disc assembly (p. 41) □○
	Seat assembly worn	Replace seat assembly (p. 41) □○
Double-handle diaphragm faucet leaks from handle	O-ring on sleeve worn	Replace O-ring (p. 42) □○
Double-handle diaphragm faucet drips from spout	Diaphragm worn	Replace diaphragm (p. 42) □○
Ceramic disc faucet leaks around base or flow from spout reduced	Aerator blocked	Unscrew aerator from spout and clean it
	Inlet ports blocked	Clean inlet ports (p. 43) □○
	Disc cracked or pitted	Replace disc assembly (p. 43) □○
	Inlet seals worn	Replace inlet seals (p. 43) □○
Single-lever rotating-ball faucet leaks from handle or drips from spout	Adjusting ring loose	Tighten adjusting ring (p. 44) □○
	Cam assembly worn	Replace cam assembly (p. 44) □○
	Seat assembly worn	Replace seat assembly (p. 44) □○
	Ball cracked or pitted	Replace ball (p. 44) □○
Single-lever rotating-ball faucet leaks from collar	Collar O-rings worn	Replace O-rings (p. 44) □○
Single-lever cartridge faucet leaks from handle or drips from spout	Cartridge worn, cracked or pitted	Replace cartridge (p. 46) □○
Single-lever cartridge faucet leaks around spout collar	Collar O-rings worn	Replace O-rings (p. 46) □○
Water under sink	Faucet set loose	Tighten locknuts under faucet set
	Supply tube or shutoff valve leaks	Tighten coupling nut at shutoff valve □○ Service or replace shutoff valves (p. 417) □○
	Faucet body worn	Have faucet replaced
Flow from spout reduced	Aerator blocked	Unscrew aerator from spout and clean it

DEGREE OF DIFFICULTY: □ Easy ◨ Moderate ■ Complex
ESTIMATED TIME: ○ Less than 1 hour ◕ 1 to 3 hours ● Over 3 hours ▲ Special tool required

DOUBLE-HANDLE COMPRESSION FAUCET (Newer models)

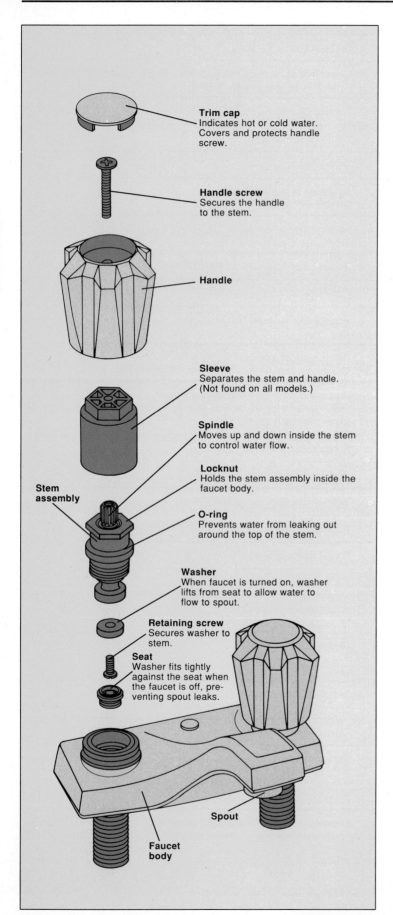

Trim cap
Indicates hot or cold water. Covers and protects handle screw.

Handle screw
Secures the handle to the stem.

Handle

Sleeve
Separates the stem and handle. (Not found on all models.)

Spindle
Moves up and down inside the stem to control water flow.

Locknut
Holds the stem assembly inside the faucet body.

Stem assembly

O-ring
Prevents water from leaking out around the top of the stem.

Washer
When faucet is turned on, washer lifts from seat to allow water to flow to spout.

Retaining screw
Secures washer to stem.

Seat
Washer fits tightly against the seat when the faucet is off, preventing spout leaks.

Spout

Faucet body

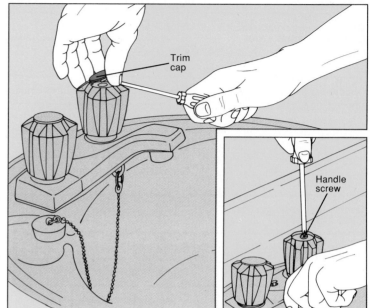

Trim cap

Handle screw

1 **Opening up the faucet.** To find out which handle needs servicing when the spout drips, turn off one of the shutoff valves underneath the sink. If the leak stops, the problem is with that handle; if it persists, the other handle is at fault. (When there are no individual shutoff valves for the sink, service both handles.) Turn off the water supply, open the faucet and close the drain to prevent loss of parts. Carefully pry off the trim cap with a knife or small screwdriver *(above)*. Remove the screw that secures the handle to the stem *(inset)*.

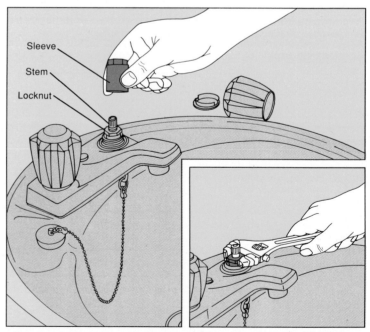

Sleeve

Stem

Locknut

2 **Gaining access to the stem.** Lift off the faucet handle and sleeve *(above)*. If it will not budge, apply penetrating oil and wait an hour before trying again. Never strike the handle or sleeve with a hammer; you might damage the soft brass stem. Open the faucet one-half turn, then unscrew the locknut that secures the stem to the faucet body *(inset)*.

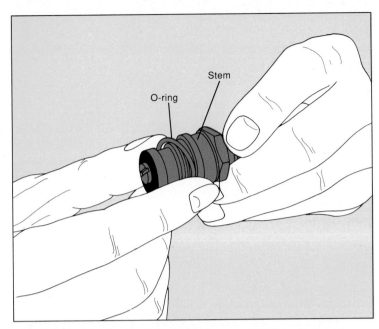

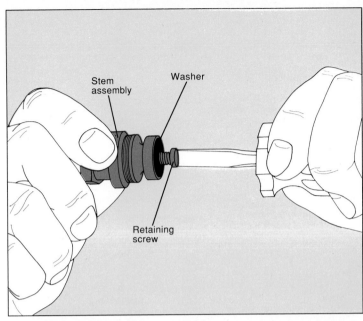

3 **Replacing the O-ring.** Grasp the stem spindle with taped pliers and lift it out of the faucet body. To stop leaks around the handle, pinch off the O-ring *(above)*, lubricate a new O-ring with petroleum jelly, then roll it onto the stem until it is firmly seated. Reassemble and test the faucet.

4 **Replacing the washer.** A dripping spout points to a worn stem washer. Carefully remove the retaining screw *(above)* and pry the washer from the stem with the tip of a screwdriver or knife. (If the screw is tight, install the faucet handle on the stem for better leverage.) Replace with an identical washer, its flat side facing the stem. With the washer in place, tighten the retaining screw until it presses the washer squarely into the stem. Reassemble and test the faucet. If the spout still leaks, replace or dress the seat *(step 5).*

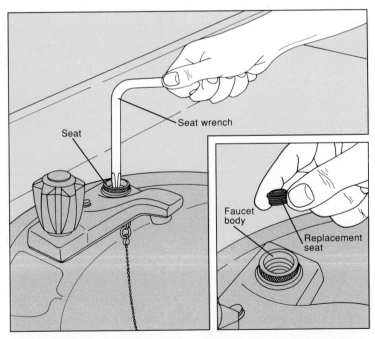

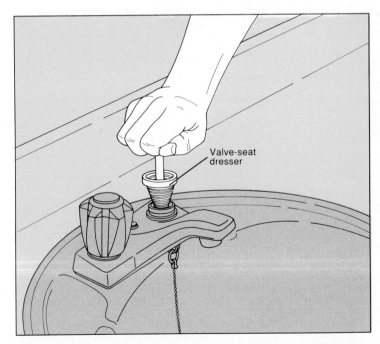

5 **Removing the seat.** Use a hex wrench or special faucet seat wrench *(above)* to unscrew a leaking seat by turning it counter-clockwise. If the seat will not budge, apply penetrating oil, wait overnight and try again. Once the old seat is free, fit an identical replacement seat into the faucet body by hand *(inset)* or with a pair of long-nose pliers. Screw it in tightly with the hex wrench or seat wrench. If the seat cannot be removed—it may be built into the faucet—it must be ground smooth with a valve-seat dresser *(next step).*

6 **Dressing the seat.** Buy or rent a valve-seat dresser with the largest cutter that fits the faucet body, and screw on a guide disc that fits the valve-seat hole. Slide the cone down snugly into the faucet body. Turn the handle clockwise several times to grind the seat smooth *(above)*. Wipe out the filings with a damp cloth, and reassemble the faucet. If the leak persists, try again; if a second attempt fails, the entire faucet set should be replaced.

DOUBLE-HANDLE COMPRESSION FAUCETS (Older models)

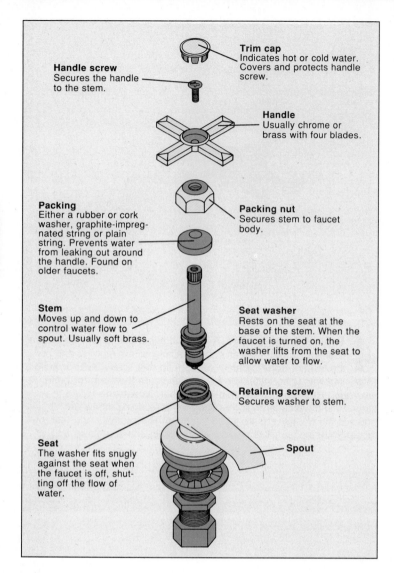

Trim cap
Indicates hot or cold water. Covers and protects handle screw.

Handle screw
Secures the handle to the stem.

Handle
Usually chrome or brass with four blades.

Packing
Either a rubber or cork washer, graphite-impregnated string or plain string. Prevents water from leaking out around the handle. Found on older faucets.

Packing nut
Secures stem to faucet body.

Stem
Moves up and down to control water flow to spout. Usually soft brass.

Seat washer
Rests on the seat at the base of the stem. When the faucet is turned on, the washer lifts from the seat to allow water to flow.

Retaining screw
Secures washer to stem.

Seat
The washer fits snugly against the seat when the faucet is off, shutting off the flow of water.

Spout

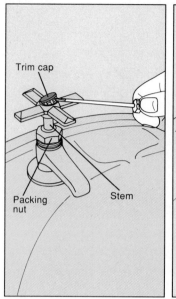
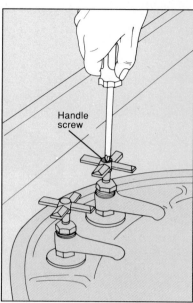

Trim cap

Packing nut

Stem

Handle screw

1 Opening up the faucet. To stop leaks around the handle, try tightening the packing nut by turning it clockwise with an adjustable wrench, its jaws taped to protect the chrome finish. If this has no effect, service the packing washer or string *(step 2)* or the stem and washer *(page 38)*. Turn off the water. Carefully pry off the trim cap with a small screwdriver *(above, left)* or knife. Then unscrew the handle screw *(above, right)* and pull off the handle. If a bent stem appears to be causing the leak, you can try to straighten it with a pair of tape-covered pliers. If the stem is badly damaged, the entire faucet should be replaced.

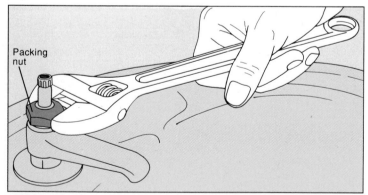

Packing nut

2 Removing the old packing. Use an adjustable wrench to unscrew the packing nut from the faucet body *(above)*. Pry off the old packing washer or unwind old packing string. Scour the base of the stem thoroughly with steel wool to remove mineral deposits, and replace the packing *(step 3)*. If the spout drips, also change the washer at the base of the stem or dress the valve seat *(page 39)*. Kitchen faucets may have additional packing at the base of the spout. Unscrew the spout nut with tape-covered pliers, lift off the spout, remove the packing and replace it as in step 3.

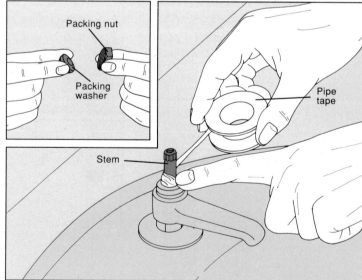

Packing nut

Packing washer

Pipe tape

Stem

3 Changing the packing. Insert a replacement packing washer into the packing nut *(inset)*; replace packing string with pipe tape *(above)* or new packing string. Wrap the tape or string several times around the base of the stem, stretching and pressing it down as you go. Thread the packing nut back on, but do not overtighten. The nut will compress the packing when you screw it down. Reassemble the handle and test the repair.

DOUBLE-HANDLE FAUCETS (Disc type)

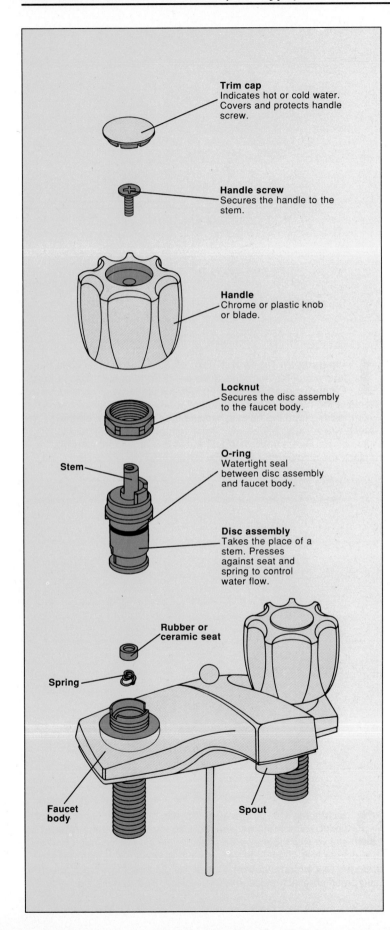

Trim cap
Indicates hot or cold water. Covers and protects handle screw.

Handle screw
Secures the handle to the stem.

Handle
Chrome or plastic knob or blade.

Locknut
Secures the disc assembly to the faucet body.

O-ring
Watertight seal between disc assembly and faucet body.

Stem

Disc assembly
Takes the place of a stem. Presses against seat and spring to control water flow.

Rubber or ceramic seat

Spring

Faucet body

Spout

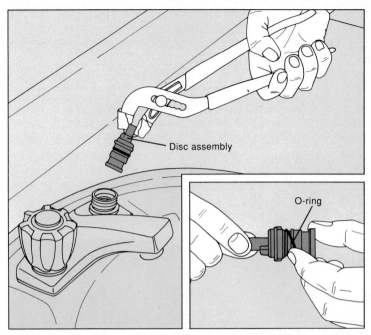

Disc assembly

O-ring

1 **Replacing the O-ring.** Turn off the water, open the faucet one-half turn and close the drain to prevent loss of parts. Carefully pry off the trim cap with a knife or small screwdriver. Remove the handle screw and pull off the handle. Unscrew the locknut with a taped adjustable wrench. Lift the cartridge from the faucet body *(above)*. Water leaking around the handle may be caused by a cracked or pitted disc assembly. If so, buy a new assembly and O-ring. Insert the assembly, lining up its slots with those on the faucet body. If only the O-ring is worn, pinch it off the assembly *(inset)*, lubricate an exact replacement with petroleum jelly and slip it on. Reassemble the faucet.

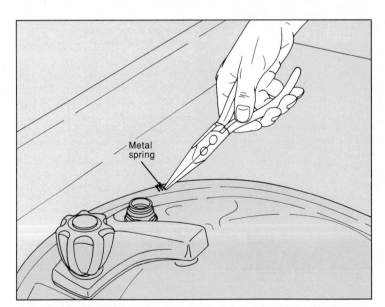

Metal spring

2 **Replacing the seat and spring.** To stop water dripping from the spout, use long-nose pliers to pick the rubber seat and spring out of the faucet body *(above)*. (Instead of a seat and spring there may be a ceramic seal and O-ring.) Replace these with parts from a repair kit for the same make and model of faucet. Then insert the disc assembly, lining up its slots with the faucet body, and reassemble the faucet.

DOUBLE-HANDLE FAUCETS (Diaphragm type)

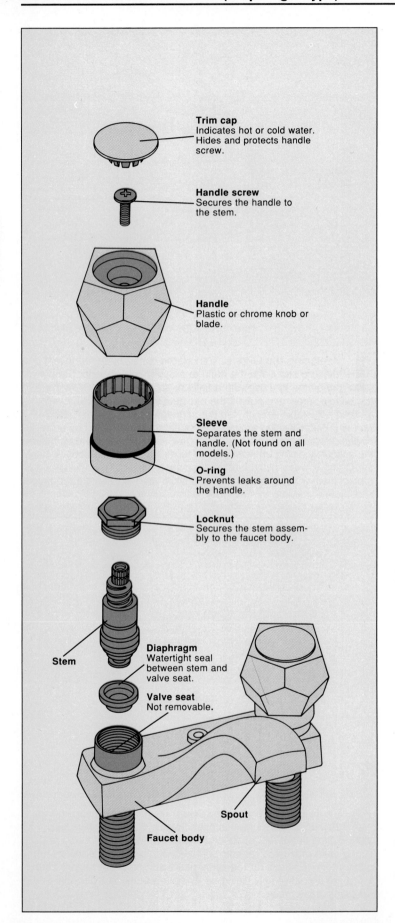

Trim cap
Indicates hot or cold water. Hides and protects handle screw.

Handle screw
Secures the handle to the stem.

Handle
Plastic or chrome knob or blade.

Sleeve
Separates the stem and handle. (Not found on all models.)

O-ring
Prevents leaks around the handle.

Locknut
Secures the stem assembly to the faucet body.

Stem

Diaphragm
Watertight seal between stem and valve seat.

Valve seat
Not removable.

Spout

Faucet body

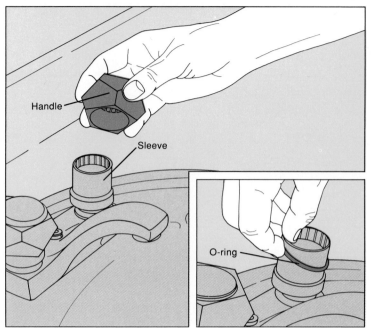

Handle

Sleeve

O-ring

1 Opening up the faucet. Turn off the water supply, open the faucet one-half turn and close the drain to prevent loss of parts. Carefully pry off the trim cap with a knife or small screwdriver. Remove the handle screw and pull off the handle *(above)*. To stop water leaking from the handle, replace the O-ring. Roll it off the sleeve *(inset)*, lubricate a new O-ring with petroleum jelly and roll it into place. Reassemble and test the faucet. If the leak persists, replace the diaphragm *(next step)*.

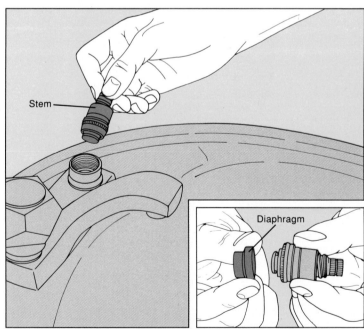

Stem

Diaphragm

2 Replacing the diaphragm. To stop leaks from the handle or spout, replace the hat-shaped diaphragm. Lift off the chrome sleeve with tape-covered pliers, exposing the locknut. Unscrew the locknut with a tape-covered adjustable wrench and lift the stem from the faucet body *(above)*. Pry off the diaphragm by hand *(inset)*, and press an exact replacement into place. Reassemble the faucet.

SINGLE-LEVER FAUCETS (Ceramic-disc type)

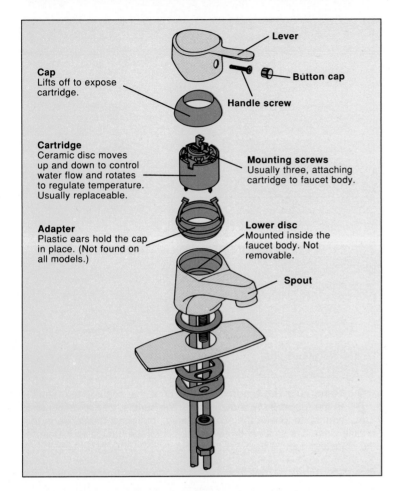

Cap
Lifts off to expose cartridge.

Lever

Button cap

Handle screw

Cartridge
Ceramic disc moves up and down to control water flow and rotates to regulate temperature. Usually replaceable.

Mounting screws
Usually three, attaching cartridge to faucet body.

Adapter
Plastic ears hold the cap in place. (Not found on all models.)

Lower disc
Mounted inside the faucet body. Not removable.

Spout

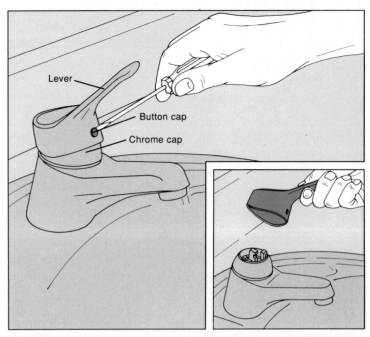

Lever

Button cap

Chrome cap

1 **Removing the lever.** Turn off the water supply and drain the faucet by lifting the lever to its highest position. Close the drain to prevent loss of parts. Pry off the button cap at the base of the lever with a knife or small screwdriver *(above)*, and remove the handle screw. (On some models the screw is underneath the lever body and there is no cap.) Lift off the handle *(inset)*.

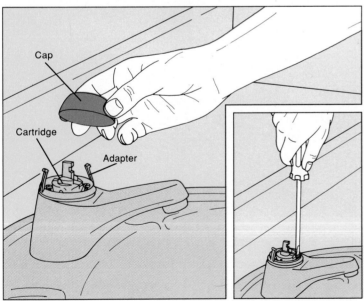

Cap

Cartridge

Adapter

2 **Freeing the cartridge.** Pry the cap off its plastic adapter *(above)* or, on some faucets, unscrew it from the faucet body. Loosen the two or three brass screws holding the cartridge to the faucet body *(inset)*, and lift out the cartridge.

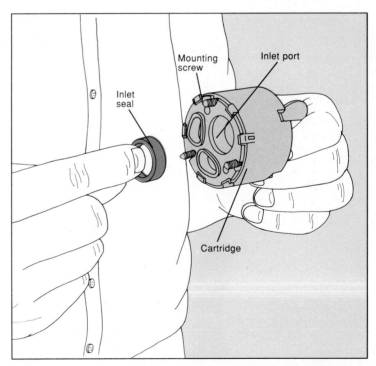

Mounting screw

Inlet port

Inlet seal

Cartridge

3 **Servicing the cartridge.** First check to be sure that the leak is not caused by a piece of dirt caught between the ceramic discs. Clean the inlet ports and the surface of the bottom disc. If the upper disc is cracked or pitted, buy a replacement cartridge for the same make and model. Insert the new seals in the disc, position the cartridge in the faucet body and screw it in place. Check that the three ports on the bottom of the cartridge align with those of the faucet body.

SINGLE-LEVER FAUCETS (Rotating-ball type)

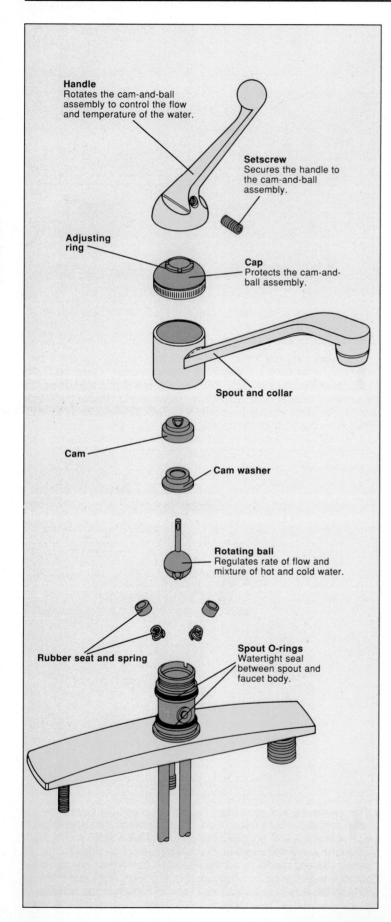

Handle
Rotates the cam-and-ball assembly to control the flow and temperature of the water.

Setscrew
Secures the handle to the cam-and-ball assembly.

Adjusting ring

Cap
Protects the cam-and-ball assembly.

Spout and collar

Cam

Cam washer

Rotating ball
Regulates rate of flow and mixture of hot and cold water.

Rubber seat and spring

Spout O-rings
Watertight seal between spout and faucet body.

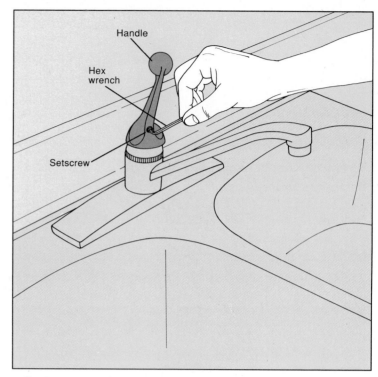

Handle

Hex wrench

Setscrew

1 Removing the handle. The setscrew that secures the handle to the faucet body is underneath the handle. Use a small hex wrench to loosen the screw *(above)*, but leave the screw in the handle since it is small and easily lost. Lift off the handle to expose the adjusting ring.

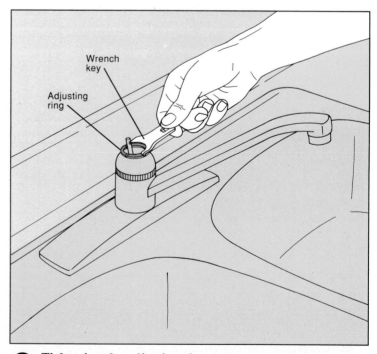

Wrench key

Adjusting ring

2 Tightening the adjusting ring. To stop water leaking from the faucet handle, use the edge of an old dinner knife or a special wrench included in the repair kit to tighten the adjusting ring clockwise, as shown. (The ball should move easily without the handle attached.) Reassemble the handle and test for leaks. Tighten the adjusting ring again, if necessary. If the leak persists, go to step 3.

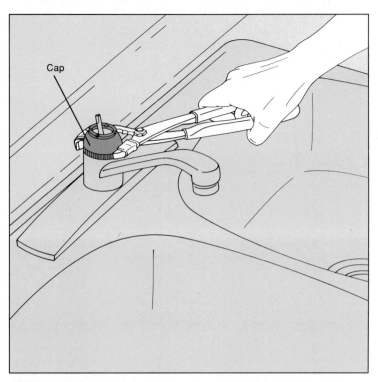

3 **Removing the cap.** Service the cam-and-ball assembly if the handle continues to leak after you have tightened the adjusting ring, or if the spout drips. First turn off the water supply, open the faucet and close the drain to prevent loss of parts. Unscrew the cap by hand or with a pair of channel-joint pliers taped to protect chrome parts *(above)*.

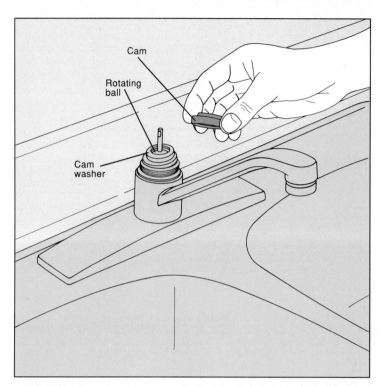

4 **Replacing the cam assembly.** Lift off the plastic cam *(above)*, exposing the cam washer and rotating ball. Buy a repair kit that includes replacement parts for your make and model of faucet. Service worn or damaged parts individually *(step 5)* or replace all of them while the faucet is disassembled.

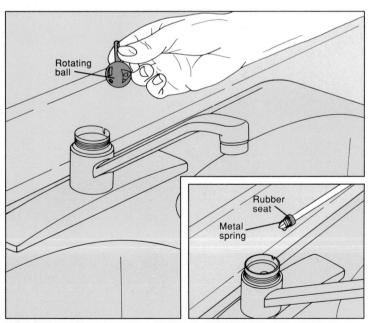

5 **Replacing the seats, springs and ball.** Lift the rotating ball from the faucet body *(above)*, then reach into the faucet body with long-nose pliers or the end of a screwdriver and remove the two sets of rubber seats and metal springs *(inset)*, or two sets of ceramic seals and O-rings. Replace these parts from the kit, making sure they are properly seated in the faucet body before reassembling the faucet. If the cam-and-ball assembly appears damaged, replace it at the same time.

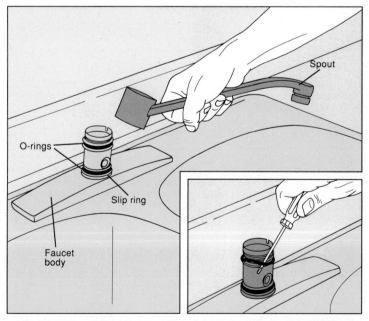

6 **Replacing the spout O-rings.** If water leaks from the spout collar, twist the spout off *(above)* to expose its O-rings. Slip the end of a small screwdriver under the O-rings to pry them off the faucet body *(inset)*. Lubricate the new O-rings with petroleum jelly, and roll them into place. Lower the spout straight down over the body and rotate it until it rests on the plastic slip ring at the base. Reassemble the faucet.

SINGLE-LEVER FAUCETS (Cartridge type)

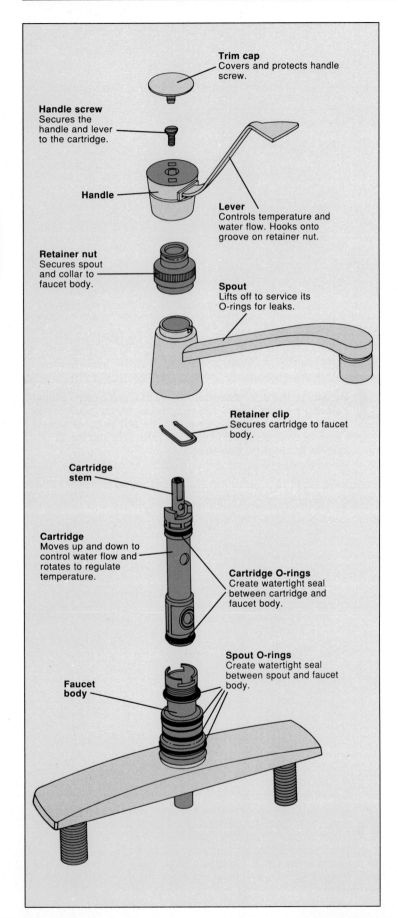

Trim cap
Covers and protects handle screw.

Handle screw
Secures the handle and lever to the cartridge.

Handle

Lever
Controls temperature and water flow. Hooks onto groove on retainer nut.

Retainer nut
Secures spout and collar to faucet body.

Spout
Lifts off to service its O-rings for leaks.

Retainer clip
Secures cartridge to faucet body.

Cartridge stem

Cartridge
Moves up and down to control water flow and rotates to regulate temperature.

Cartridge O-rings
Create watertight seal between cartridge and faucet body.

Spout O-rings
Create watertight seal between spout and faucet body.

Faucet body

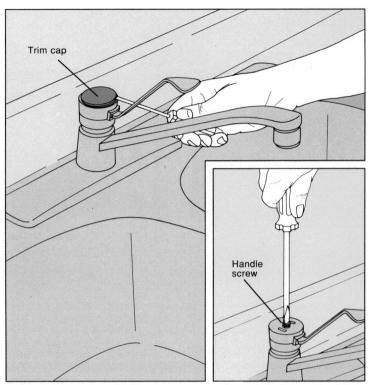

Trim cap

Handle screw

1 **Opening up the faucet.** Turn off the water supply, lift the handle several times to drain the faucet, and close the drain to prevent loss of parts. Carefully pry off the trim cap with a small screwdriver *(above)* or knife. Remove the handle screw that secures the handle assembly to the cartridge *(inset)*.

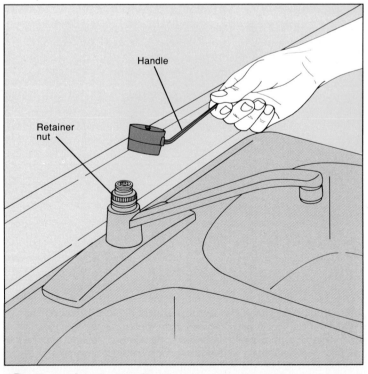

Handle

Retainer nut

2 **Removing the handle.** The faucet handle attaches to the lip of the retainer nut much like a bottle opener to a cap. Tilt the handle lever up sharply to unhook it from the nut, then lift it free.

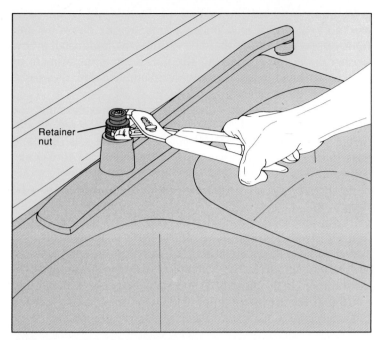

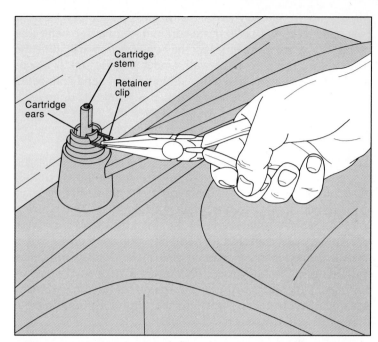

3 **Removing the retainer nut.** Unscrew the retainer nut with taped channel-joint pliers *(above)* and lift it off the faucet body. To stop a leaking handle or a dripping spout, replace the O-rings or the entire cartridge *(step 4)*. To stop leaks from the spout collar, replace the spout O-rings *(step 6)*.

4 **Freeing the cartridge.** Locate the U-shaped retainer clip that holds the cartridge in place in the faucet body. Using long-nose pliers or tweezers, pull the clip from its slot *(above)*, being careful not to drop it down the drain.

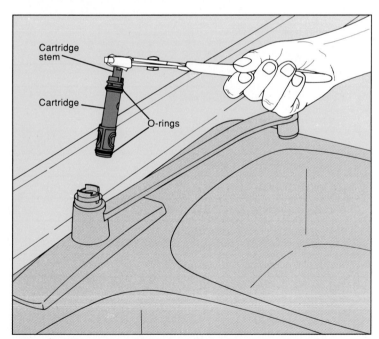

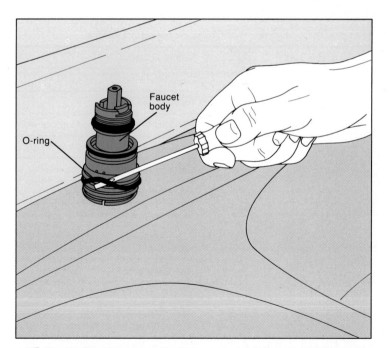

5 **Servicing the cartridge.** Grasping the cartridge stem with taped pliers, lift the cartridge out of the faucet body *(above)*. Examine the O-rings and replace them if they are worn or cracked. Pry the old rings off the cartridge with the tip of an awl or other pointed tool. Lubricate the new O-rings with a dab of petroleum jelly and roll them down over the cartridge until they rest in the appropriate grooves. If the cartridge itself is worn or damaged, replace it with a new one. Reinsert the cartridge, align it properly in its seat, and replace the retainer clip and retainer nut. Attach the handle by hooking its inside lever on the lip of the retainer nut. If the hot and cold water are reversed, remove the handle and rotate the cartridge stem one-half turn.

6 **Replacing the spout O-rings.** If water leaks around the spout collar, replace the spout O-rings. Lift off the spout and pry off the cracked or worn rings *(above)*. Lubricate new O-rings with petroleum jelly and roll them into the grooves on the faucet body. Replace the spout and reassemble the faucet, hooking the inside edge of the handle lever onto the lip of the retainer nut.

KITCHEN SINKS

Most modern kitchen sinks are made of stainless steel or enameled steel, with two basins draining into a trap bend that blocks sewer gas from entering the house. A trap arm joins the bend to the drainpipe at the wall. Under a single sink is a one-piece fixed or swivel trap, consisting of a trap bend connected to a trap arm. A dishwasher fits under any sink; its drain hose attaches to an air gap—a simple device that prevents back-siphonage—and another hose leads to the garbage disposer or sink tailpiece.

The two problems that most frequently plague kitchen sinks, clogged drains and leaky supply pipes, can be handled with basic plumbing tools. You can avoid clogs altogether by placing strainer baskets in the drain openings and not pouring grease or coffee grounds down the drain. If a sink does back up, a plunger or manual auger will break up most clogs. Use a chemical opener in a porcelain sink if the drain is only partially clogged, but never use chemicals in an enamel or stainless-steel sink; they will mar the finish. More serious blockages can be cleared by opening the trap or by probing the drainpipe behind the wall.

You may only need to tighten a loose slip nut on the drain assembly to stop a leak under a sink. If this doesn't work, remove that part of the trap nearest the leak and install a new washer under the connecting slip nut. Keep an assortment of washers on hand; whenever you disassemble a trap it's wise to replace all the washers.

When you remove part of a trap, you may decide that the piece is too corroded to reinstall. You can replace it with metal, polypropylene or PVC plastic. Because it is light and easy to work with, plastic is especially suited for do-it-yourself plumbing. (If you leave for the plumbing supply store, close the shutoff valves to ensure that the faucet will not be turned on.)

Check that the water under the sink is not leaking from a faulty dishwasher drain hose. If the hose is at fault, turn off power to both the dishwasher and the disposer and close the dishwasher shutoff valve. Then tighten the hose clamps at the disposer and at the air gap. Trim a damaged hose with a utility knife and replace the clamps with new ones, taking care to push the ends onto the connections before tightening.

TROUBLESHOOTING GUIDE

SYMPTOM	POSSIBLE CAUSE	PROCEDURE
Water seeps from sink	Sink basket displaced	Twist basket into place
	Sink basket not sealing	Clean or replace basket
Water under sink	Faucet set loose	Tighten locknuts under faucet set
	Faucet set worn	Have faucet replaced
	Trap fittings loose	Tighten slip nuts on trap assembly (p. 52) □○
	Dishwasher hose clamp loose or worn	Tighten or replace clamp
	Dishwasher drain hose worn	Trim or replace hose
	Garbage disposer drainpipe washer worn	Replace washer (p. 52) ◩●
	Trap or drain washers worn	Replace worn parts (p. 52) ◩●
	Tailpiece or washers worn	Replace worn parts (p. 52) ◩●
	Leaky joint at sink strainer	Tighten locknut or retainer screws (p. 53) □○ Replace plumber's putty or worn parts (p. 53) ◩●
	Trap assembly worn or damaged	Replace trap assembly (p. 52) ◩●
	Supply tubes or fittings leak	Tighten coupling nut at shutoff valve (p. 417) □○ Replace supply tubes or shutoff valves (p. 417) ◩●
	Sink damaged or corroded	Have sink replaced
Drain blocked or sluggish	Clog in trap bend or arm	Use boiling water, plunger or hose (p. 50) □○ Work through cleanout plug (p. 50) □○ or trap (p. 51) ◩●
	Clog in branch drain	Auger behind the wall (p. 51) ◩●
More than one sink clogged	Main drain or vent blocked	Unblock main drain or vent (p. 76) ◩●

DEGREE OF DIFFICULTY: □ Easy ◩ Moderate ■ Complex
ESTIMATED TIME: ○ Less than 1 hour ◖ 1 to 3 hours ● Over 3 hours

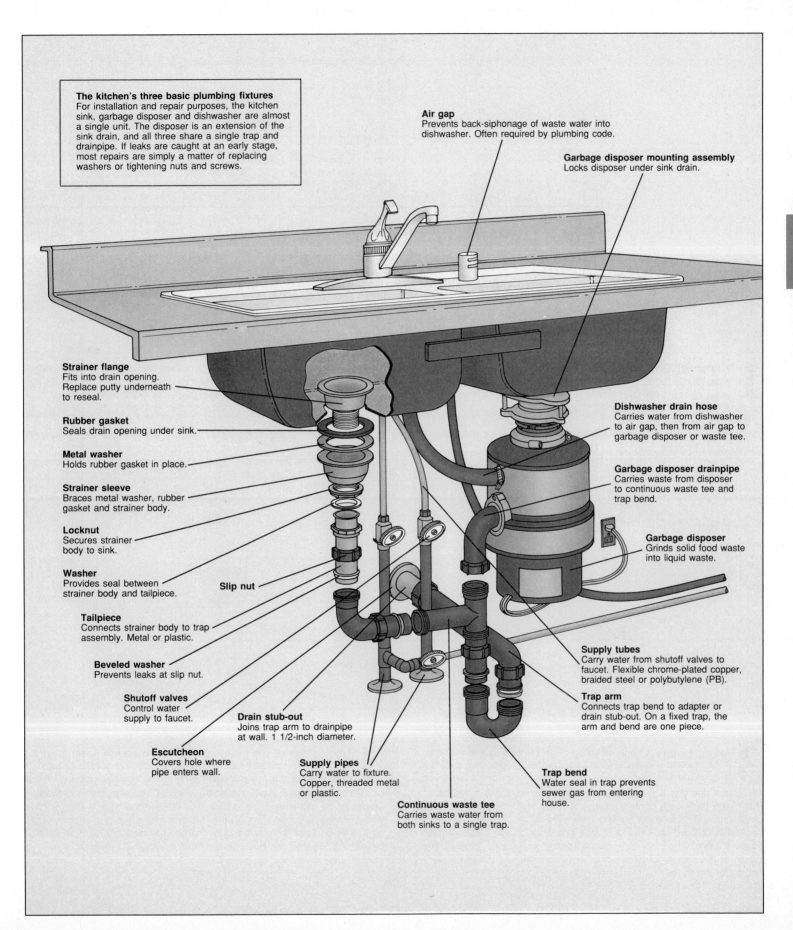

The kitchen's three basic plumbing fixtures
For installation and repair purposes, the kitchen sink, garbage disposer and dishwasher are almost a single unit. The disposer is an extension of the sink drain, and all three share a single trap and drainpipe. If leaks are caught at an early stage, most repairs are simply a matter of replacing washers or tightening nuts and screws.

Air gap
Prevents back-siphonage of waste water into dishwasher. Often required by plumbing code.

Garbage disposer mounting assembly
Locks disposer under sink drain.

Strainer flange
Fits into drain opening. Replace putty underneath to reseal.

Rubber gasket
Seals drain opening under sink.

Metal washer
Holds rubber gasket in place.

Strainer sleeve
Braces metal washer, rubber gasket and strainer body.

Locknut
Secures strainer body to sink.

Washer
Provides seal between strainer body and tailpiece.

Slip nut

Tailpiece
Connects strainer body to trap assembly. Metal or plastic.

Beveled washer
Prevents leaks at slip nut.

Shutoff valves
Control water supply to faucet.

Drain stub-out
Joins trap arm to drainpipe at wall. 1 1/2-inch diameter.

Escutcheon
Covers hole where pipe enters wall.

Supply pipes
Carry water to fixture. Copper, threaded metal or plastic.

Continuous waste tee
Carries waste water from both sinks to a single trap.

Dishwasher drain hose
Carries water from dishwasher to air gap, then from air gap to garbage disposer or waste tee.

Garbage disposer drainpipe
Carries waste from disposer to continuous waste tee and trap bend.

Garbage disposer
Grinds solid food waste into liquid waste.

Supply tubes
Carry water from shutoff valves to faucet. Flexible chrome-plated copper, braided steel or polybutylene (PB).

Trap arm
Connects trap bend to adapter or drain stub-out. On a fixed trap, the arm and bend are one piece.

Trap bend
Water seal in trap prevents sewer gas from entering house.

CLEARING A CLOGGED DRAIN

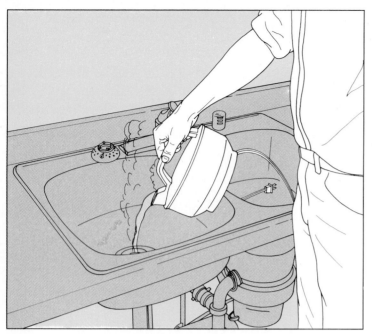

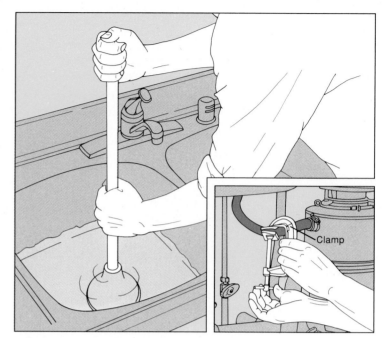

1 **Removing grease clogs.** Bail out any standing water in the sink, lift out the sink basket and clear any debris caught in the drain opening. Pour in boiling water to break up a grease clog *(above)*, but only if your drain has metal or polypropylene drainpipes, and there is no garbage disposer beneath that particular basin. If the blockage remains, or the sink is fitted with a disposer or PVC drain-pipes, use a plunger *(step 2)*.

2 **Using a plunger.** If there is a dishwasher attached to the sink, seal off the drain hose between the air gap and the disposer by tightening a C-clamp over two pieces of wood placed on each side of the hose *(inset)*. Then, for a double sink, pack several rags wrapped in plastic into one drain opening. Run enough water in the other sink to cover the plunger cup, and set the plunger squarely over the drain. Pump up and down about a dozen times without lifting the cup *(above)*, then pull away sharply. Repeat several times. If this is ineffective, use a hose *(step 3)*.

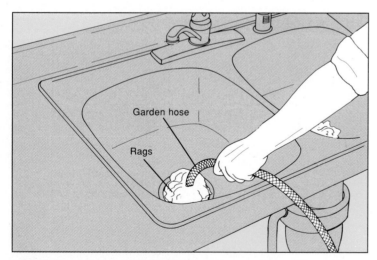

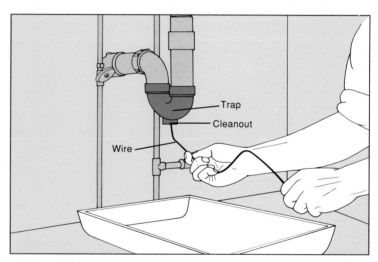

3 **Using a hose.** A hose attached to an outdoor faucet—or the drain valve of a water heater—may reach the sink through a window. If not, you will need to adapt the hose to fit the kitchen faucet. Block one drain of a double sink, feed the hose down the other drain, and pack rags tightly around the hose. Hold the hose firmly in place and turn the faucet on and off several times *(above)*. If water backs up, remove the hose and rags and work on the cleanout *(next step)*. If there is no cleanout, you must remove the trap *(step 5)*. Because of the danger of back-siphonage, do not leave the hose attached to the faucet.

4 **Unblocking at the cleanout.** A plastic drainpipe under a single sink will often be fitted with a cleanout. Place a bucket or pan beneath the trap. Loosen and remove the cleanout plug by hand or with channel-joint pliers. Water pouring out indicates that the blockage must be elsewhere; go to step 5 to remove the trap. If little or no water emerges, probe through the opening with an auger or bent coat hanger to snag or loosen the clog. Tighten the cleanout plug. Turn the water back on and run hot water to flush the trap. If the drain is still sluggish, remove the trap *(step 5)*.

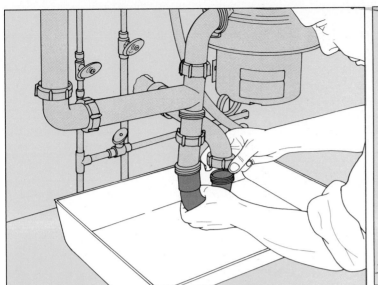

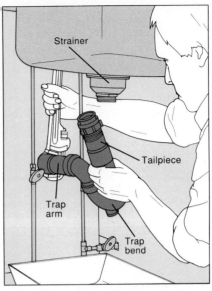

5 **Removing the trap.** With the pan still under the trap, support the bend with one hand and loosen the slip nuts on each end, using channel-joint pliers if metal. Push the loosened slip nuts and beveled washers onto the pipes above, and pull the trap free *(above, left)*. Empty the bend into a container, scrub it with a flexible brush—or use an auger—then rinse with water. If you removed the obstruction, reinstall the trap using new washers and test the drain. Otherwise, remove the trap arm *(step 6)*. If the trap is under a single sink, use channel-joint pliers to remove the slip nuts connecting one end of the tailpiece to the strainer body, and the other end to the trap bend. For a fixed trap, push the tailpiece down into the trap and loosen the slip nut at the stub-out with a pipe wrench *(above, right)*. Then remove the trap assembly from the drainpipe by hand. For a swivel trap, loosen the slip nuts, pull the trap bend free and empty it into a container. Scrub the bend with a brush, then rinse. Replace the cleaned trap and test the drain. If you found no clog, clear the drainpipe behind the wall *(step 7)*.

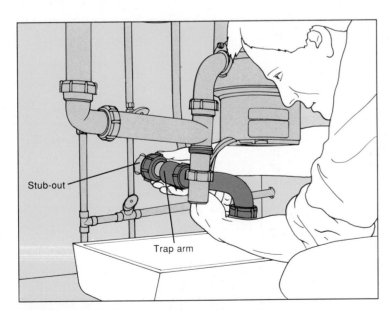

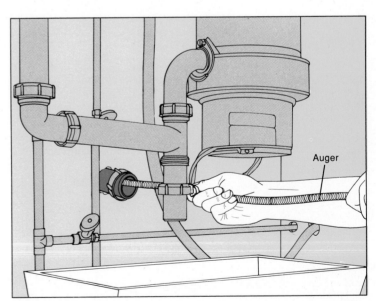

6 **Removing the trap arm.** Loosen the slip nut that joins the trap arm to the drain stub-out with channel-joint pliers—it may be covered by an escutcheon—then unthread the trap assembly by hand *(above)*. Pull out the trap arm and clean it as in step 5. If you removed the clog, reconnect the trap arm and bend, and run water to test the drain. If it remains blocked, work behind the wall to clear the branch drain *(step 7)*.

7 **Augering into the branch drain.** Probe into the branch drain behind the wall with a manual auger *(above)*. Work carefully with the auger. Ramming it too vigorously can loosen fittings behind the wall and could pierce an old, deteriorated pipe. Reconnect the trap assembly using new washers, and tighten all slip nuts. Test the drain. If it is still clogged, work on the main drain *(page 76)*.

SERVICING THE TRAP AND DRAIN

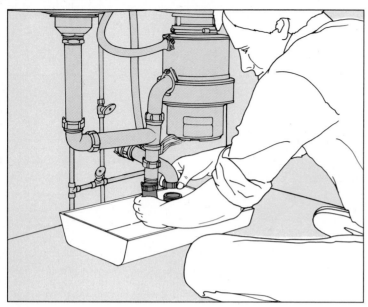

1 **Servicing the trap bend.** To stop leaks at the trap bend, first try tightening the slip nuts a quarter-turn. If this fails, remove the bend *(page 51, step 5)*. Replace if corroded or cracked, and change the washer where the bend meets the trap arm. If you are replacing a metal trap with a plastic one, install a new plastic slip nut on the pipe above. Push the trap bend back onto the pipe above, as shown. If there are leaks from other fittings, go to steps 2, 3 or 4 before reassembling the trap. To reconnect the bend, turn it so that it is directly under the trap arm or stub-out opening and thread the slip nut onto the bend by hand. Tighten metal slip nuts a quarter-turn with channel-joint pliers. Hand-tighten plastic connections.

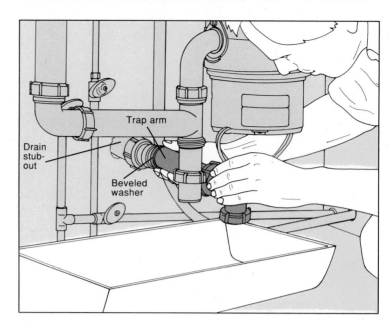

2 **Servicing the trap arm.** Move the pan under the drain stub-out or place rags below it. Remove the trap bend, if you have not already done so, then the trap arm *(page 51, step 6)*. Replace corroded parts, and install new washers. For additional protection against leaks, spread a coat of plumber's putty or silicone sealant inside the slip nuts. Hold the trap arm up to the stub-out and thread the slip nut back on *(above)*. Reconnect the trap bend to the trap arm *(step 1)* and turn on the faucet. If leaks persist, tighten the slip nuts a quarter-turn.

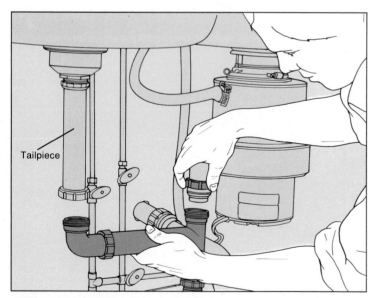

3 **Servicing other drain fittings.** Place a container under the drain fittings to catch water runoff and debris. One by one, tighten the slip nuts to stop a leak. If this doesn't work, remove the trap bend, then disassemble the fittings and inspect them for damage *(above)*. Replace any part that is cracked or corroded. If there are leaks at the sink strainer and tailpiece, go to step 4. Reassemble the drain and trap using new washers, and coat the inside of the slip nuts with putty or silicone sealant before tightening the connections.

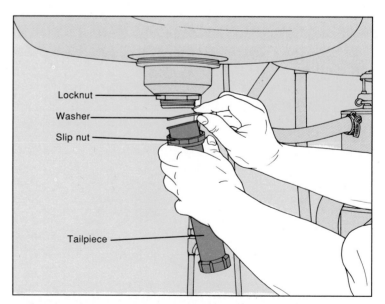

4 **Servicing the tailpiece.** With channel-joint pliers, loosen the slip nut that connects the tailpiece to the sink. If you have not already removed the drain fittings, loosen one or more other slip nuts as needed to lower the tailpiece an inch or so from the sink. Slip the flat tailpiece washer out *(above)*, insert a new washer, and reconnect the tailpiece. Reconnect the drain fittings as in step 3, or if water leaks from the sink strainer, reseal or replace it.

SERVICING THE STRAINER

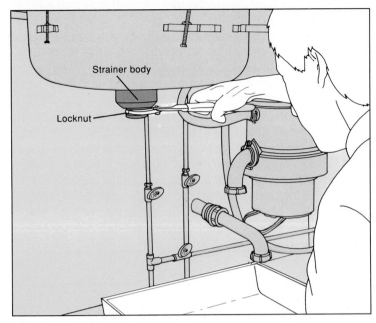

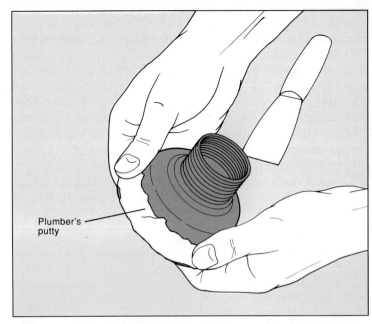

1 **Freeing the strainer.** Leaks arise here when the strainer body wears through or the putty that seals it to the sink dries out or erodes. To gain access to the strainer, first loosen and remove the faucet tailpiece *(page 52, step 4)*. Next, unscrew the locknut that secures the strainer body to the sink *(above)*. If the strainer body starts to turn in the sink while you loosen the locknut, wedge a screwdriver into the drain and hold it steady with your free hand. Another type of strainer is held in place by a plastic retainer and three screws; remove them and twist the retainer a quarter-turn to unlock the strainer body.

2 **Stopping leaks around the strainer.** If water leaks from around the sink opening, replace the putty and, if necessary, the strainer. Push the strainer body out of the sink from underneath. Scrape the putty off the drain hole, and off the old strainer if you plan to reuse it. Apply a 1/2-inch strip of plumber's putty under the lip of the strainer, as shown. Note that some strainers come with adhesive-coated rubber gaskets, and need no putty.

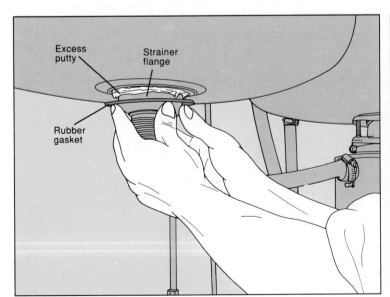

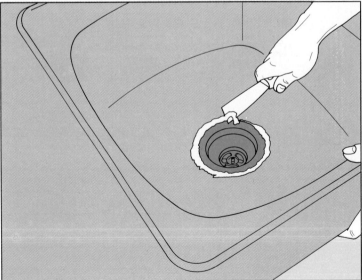

3 **Installing the strainer.** Lower the strainer body into the sink opening from above. From underneath the sink, slip the rubber and metal washers over the neck of the strainer *(above, left)*, then secure the locknut or retainer and screws. Raise the tailpiece into place and tighten the coupling nuts. Scrape away any excess putty around the sink opening with a putty knife *(above, right)*, being careful not to scratch the surface.

BATHROOM SINKS

With only a single trap and drain, a bathroom sink is far simpler to repair than a kitchen sink with two drains, garbage disposer, dishwasher and maze of drainpipes. Because they are often exposed, supply lines and drains may be more accessible in the bathroom than kitchen. Bathroom drainpipes are also narrower—1 1/4 inches in diameter—since they do not carry grease or food waste. Bathroom sinks are always fitted with a trap to prevent sewer gases from entering the house: P-shaped if it joins a branch drain in the wall, or S-shaped if it drains through the floor.

While a simple rubber plug is still the most reliable way to keep water from seeping down the drain, most sinks today are equipped with the more convenient pop-up stopper. Pulling one end of a lift rod between the faucet handles causes the stopper to drop into the drain, sealing it. If water seeps away while the basin is full, or drains too slowly when the lift rod is lowered, the stopper or its lift mechanism may be at fault.

The two most common sink problems are leaks and clogs. Water under the sink usually points to worn faucet parts (page 36) or faulty supply fittings or shutoff valves (page 417). If drain fittings are loose, replacing dried putty, tightening a slip nut or changing a washer may fix the trouble.

Because the bathroom sink trap is narrow, it tends to clog as soap and hair accumulate in the tailpiece, bend or arm. Start by removing the stopper and clearing the drain opening with a bent coat hanger. Then look beneath the sink for a cleanout

TROUBLESHOOTING GUIDE

SYMPTOM	POSSIBLE CAUSE	PROCEDURE
Water seeps from sink	Accumulation of soap or hair on stopper	Clean stopper (p. 56) □○
	Stopper O-ring worn	Replace O-ring (p. 56) □○
	Stopper worn	Replace stopper (p. 56) □○
	Lift mechanism too long	Adjust or replace lift mechanism (p. 56) ◨⬤
Pop-up stopper does not open or close properly	Lift mechanism disconnected	Reconnect below sink (p. 56) □○
	Lift mechanism broken or out of adjustment	Service lift mechanism (p. 56) □○ Replace drain body and pop-up assembly (p. 56) ◨⬤
Water under sink	Faucet set loose	Tighten locknuts under faucet set (p. 36) □○
	Putty under sink flange cracked or gasket worn	Loosen locknut on drain body and pry up sink flange. Replace putty or gasket (p. 53) ◨⬤
	Faucet set worn	Have faucet set replaced
	Joint at pivot rod loose	Tighten retaining nut (p. 55) □○
	Sink tailpiece or fittings worn	Tighten connections (p. 55) □○
	Trap fittings worn	Tighten connections; replace worn washers (p. 52) ◨⬤
	Trap bend or trap arm damaged	Repair temporarily with tape (page 20). □○ Replace trap bend or arm (p. 51) ◨⬤
	Supply tube leaks	Tighten coupling nut at shutoff valve or service valve (p. 417) □○ Replace supply tubes or shutoff valves (p. 417) ◨⬤
Drain slow or blocked	Accumulation of soap or hair on stopper	Clean stopper (p. 56) □○
	Pop-up lift mechanism too short	Adjust or replace lift mechanism (p. 56) □○
	Clog in trap bend or arm	Use plunger or auger (p. 72) □○ Clean trap (p. 50) ◨⬤
	Object dropped down drain	Retrieve object from trap (p. 51) ◨⬤
	Clog in drainpipe beyond trap	Auger behind wall (p. 51) ◨⬤
Sink needs replacement	Basin chipped, cracked or discolored	Have sink replaced

DEGREE OF DIFFICULTY: □ Easy ◨ Moderate ■ Complex
ESTIMATED TIME: ○ Less than 1 hour ◖ 1 to 3 hours ● Over 3 hours

plug on the trap; place a pan under the trap to catch waste water, then remove the plug and probe through the opening to snag or loosen the clog. Otherwise, fill the sink halfway, plug the overflow opening with tape or a rag wrapped in plastic, and use a plunger—this is far safer for both you and your pipes than a caustic chemical drain opener.

If the clog remains, use a manual auger to reach down into the drain from the sink. Refer to Bathtubs *(page 72)* for unblocking the drain with an auger, but work it directly into the drain opening as far as the bend of the trap. If this fails, you will need to disassemble the trap and clean its various sections one by one *(page 52)*. Repairs to the exposed trap of the bathroom sink are virtually the same as for the kitchen sink; the

Troubleshooting Guide refers you directly to that section. Have a container and rags at hand to catch water runoff when working on drainpipes. While plastic fittings can often be taken apart by hand, use channel-joint pliers or a monkey wrench to take apart chrome pipes. Prevent damage to the chrome finish by wrapping it first with a soft cloth or by taping the jaws and teeth of the pliers with a piece of tape.

Before working on faucets or supply lines, close the shutoff valves beneath the sink (or the main shutoff valve if the fixture has none) and cover the drain to prevent loss of parts. If the sink is set in a narrow vanity, half of the repair may involve getting at the plumbing. A basin wrench, with its long shaft and spring-loaded jaws, is useful in such cramped quarters.

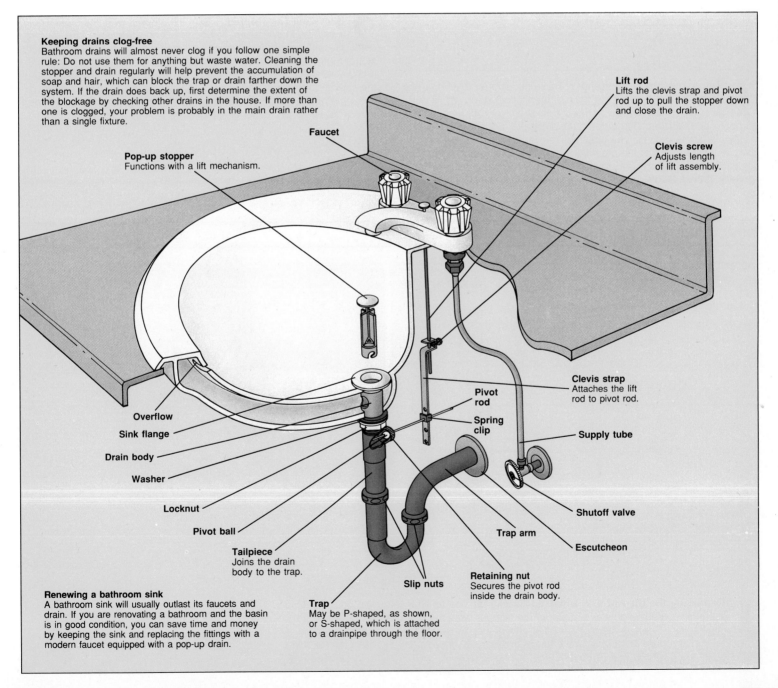

Keeping drains clog-free
Bathroom drains will almost never clog if you follow one simple rule: Do not use them for anything but waste water. Cleaning the stopper and drain regularly will help prevent the accumulation of soap and hair, which can block the trap or drain farther down the system. If the drain does back up, first determine the extent of the blockage by checking other drains in the house. If more than one is clogged, your problem is probably in the main drain rather than a single fixture.

Lift rod
Lifts the clevis strap and pivot rod up to pull the stopper down and close the drain.

Faucet

Clevis screw
Adjusts length of lift assembly.

Pop-up stopper
Functions with a lift mechanism.

Clevis strap
Attaches the lift rod to pivot rod.

Pivot rod

Spring clip

Supply tube

Overflow

Sink flange

Drain body

Washer

Shutoff valve

Trap arm

Locknut

Escutcheon

Pivot ball

Retaining nut
Secures the pivot rod inside the drain body.

Tailpiece
Joins the drain body to the trap.

Slip nuts

Renewing a bathroom sink
A bathroom sink will usually outlast its faucets and drain. If you are renovating a bathroom and the basin is in good condition, you can save time and money by keeping the sink and replacing the fittings with a modern faucet equipped with a pop-up drain.

Trap
May be P-shaped, as shown, or S-shaped, which is attached to a drainpipe through the floor.

REMOVING AND CLEANING THE STOPPER

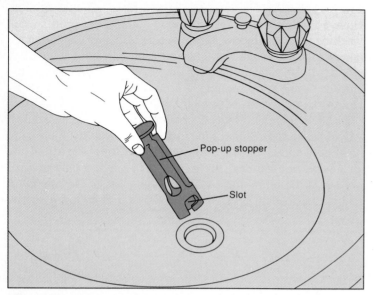

Pop-up stopper

Slot

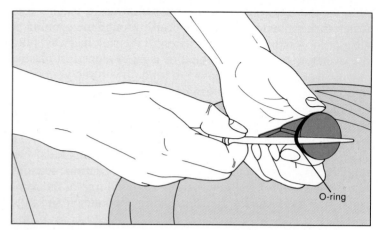

O-ring

1 **Removing a pop-up stopper.** Raise the stopper to its open position and pull it out of the drain. If the stopper does not lift out, turn it counterclockwise to free it from the pivot rod, then pull the stopper out as shown. Do not force the stopper if it does not lift out easily. On some models, you must unscrew a retaining nut below the sink. Pull the rod out of the drain body and lift out the stopper from above the sink. Service the stopper *(step 2)* or replace a badly worn stopper. If unavailable, install a new pop-up mechanism *(below)*.

2 **Servicing the stopper.** Clean the stopper with fine steel wool or a stiff brush and soap. Pry off the O-ring *(above)*, if any, and replace it. Lower the stopper back into the drain. Rotate a slotted stopper into place. If the stopper has an eye, position the eye so that it faces the pivot hole. Thread the pivot rod into the eye from beneath the sink and tighten the retaining nut. Run water through the drain. If any water leaks from the retaining nut, or if the stopper does not open fully or close tightly, adjust or replace the lift mechanism.

REPLACING THE POP-UP LIFT MECHANISM

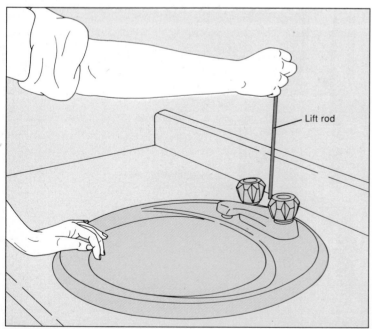

Lift rod

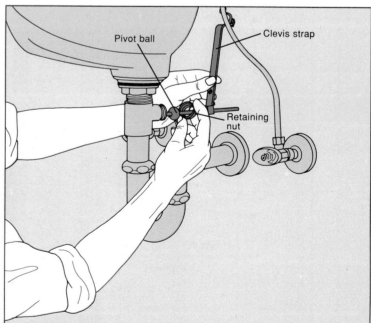

Pivot ball

Clevis strap

Retaining nut

1 **Removing the lift rod and pivot.** If adjusting the pop-up lift mechanism does not stop water from seeping down the drain, or the stopper does not open properly, replace the mechanism. Remove the stopper *(step above)* then loosen the clevis screw under the sink. Pull the lift rod up and out from the faucet body or sink *(above, left)*. Loosen the retaining nut and pull the pivot rod and ball out of the drain body *(above, right)*. Replace a damaged lift mechanism if parts are available for your make and model *(step 2)*.

REPLACING THE POP-UP LIFT MECHANISM (continued)

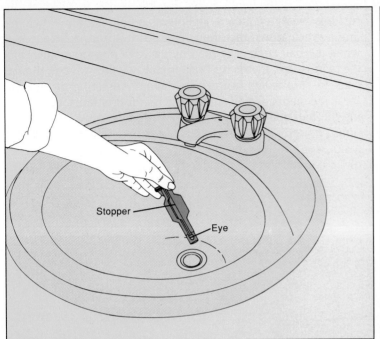

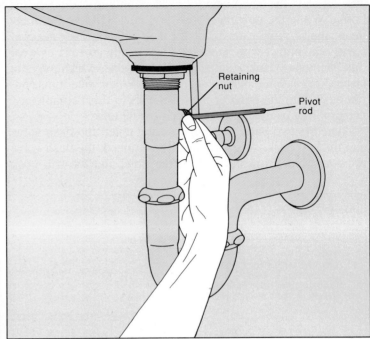

2 **Installing the stopper and pivot rod.** In this example, the pivot rod fits into an eye in the bottom of the stopper. With one hand, position the stopper in the drain opening with the eye facing the pivot rod *(above, left)*. With the other hand, place the rod into the drain body, then screw on the retaining nut *(above, right)* with pliers or an adjustable wrench. If you are installing a slotted stopper, rotate it until the slot catches the pivot rod. Some stoppers simply rest on the pivot rod.

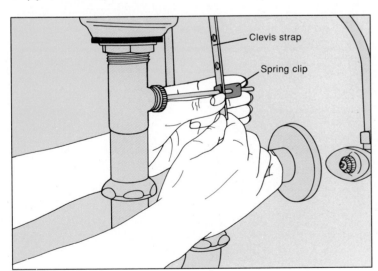

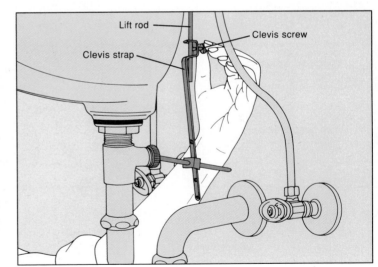

3 **Connecting the lift rod.** Pinch the spring clip to slide the free end of the pivot rod into a hole in the clevis strap *(above)*, then release the clip to hold it in place. From above, slip the lift rod into the hole between the faucet handles. From below, feed the lift rod into the clevis strap and tighten the clevis screw. Test the lift assembly and adjust if the stopper is not properly seated *(next step)*.

4 **Adjusting the assembly.** Loosen the clevis screw with pliers, then unscrew it by hand *(above)*. To keep water from seeping out of the sink when the stopper is in place, push the clevis strap up the lift rod to shorten the assembly. Pulling the strap down will lengthen the assembly, and allow faster draining. Tighten the clevis screw and test, readjusting its length if necessary. If the stopper assembly is difficult to operate, pinch the spring clip to slide the pivot rod out of the clevis strap and move it to a higher or lower hole.

TOILETS

The toilet is the most heavily used plumbing fixture in the home. While the porcelain bowl and tank will last for many years, the working parts inside the tank will not. They are constantly in contact with water, and eventually corrode or wear out. Many new tanks contain all-plastic parts, which may not last as long as brass, but do not corrode. When water runs continuously into the bowl or the toilet fails to flush completely, the problem can usually be traced to the tank.

There are two basic mechanisms in a toilet: the flush valve and the ball cock. When the handle is tripped, the flush valve releases water from the tank to the bowl and the ball cock opens to fill the tank. Each time the toilet is flushed, the rushing water creates a siphoning action in the bowl that draws waste down the drain. Water flows in to refill the tank when the ball cock is opened by the lowering float ball. Once the tank is full, the rising float arm closes the valve in the ball cock to stop water from overflowing. Adjusting or cleaning these mechanisms will solve most minor problems, but replacing the ball cock or flush valve is often the only lasting solution. Though most flush toilets use conventional tank components, certain new designs work more efficiently than their older counterparts. Consider replacing the ball cock with a

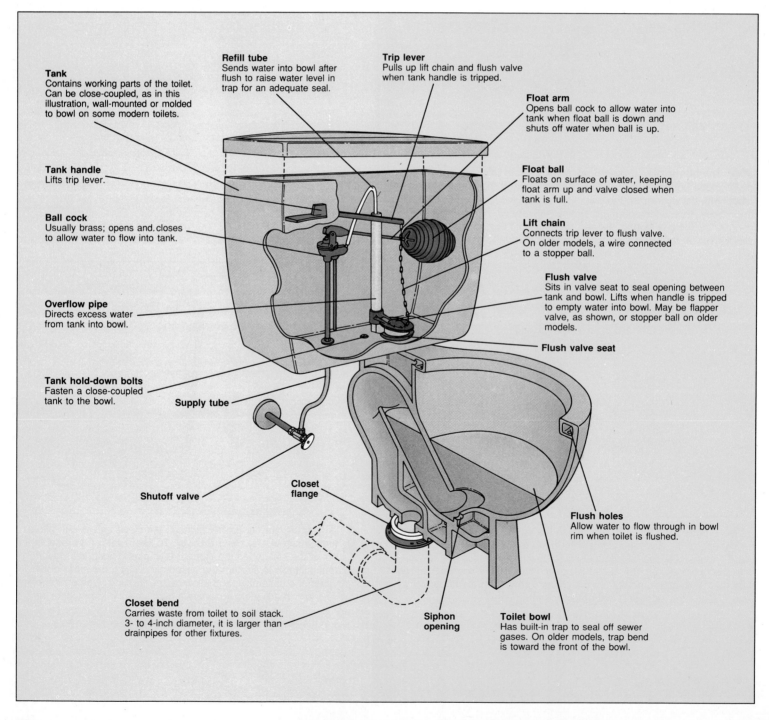

Tank
Contains working parts of the toilet. Can be close-coupled, as in this illustration, wall-mounted or molded to bowl on some modern toilets.

Refill tube
Sends water into bowl after flush to raise water level in trap for an adequate seal.

Trip lever
Pulls up lift chain and flush valve when tank handle is tripped.

Float arm
Opens ball cock to allow water into tank when float ball is down and shuts off water when ball is up.

Tank handle
Lifts trip lever.

Float ball
Floats on surface of water, keeping float arm up and valve closed when tank is full.

Ball cock
Usually brass; opens and closes to allow water to flow into tank.

Lift chain
Connects trip lever to flush valve. On older models, a wire connected to a stopper ball.

Flush valve
Sits in valve seat to seal opening between tank and bowl. Lifts when handle is tripped to empty water into bowl. May be flapper valve, as shown, or stopper ball on older models.

Overflow pipe
Directs excess water from tank into bowl.

Flush valve seat

Tank hold-down bolts
Fasten a close-coupled tank to the bowl.

Supply tube

Shutoff valve

Closet flange

Flush holes
Allow water to flow through in bowl rim when toilet is flushed.

Closet bend
Carries waste from toilet to soil stack. 3- to 4-inch diameter, it is larger than drainpipes for other fixtures.

Siphon opening

Toilet bowl
Has built-in trap to seal off sewer gases. On older models, trap bend is toward the front of the bowl.

plastic water-intake assembly that eliminates the need for a float ball and float arm. An old-fashioned flush valve, such as a stopper ball, can be replaced with a flapper valve.

When a small clog causes a toilet to drain slowly, use a plunger or closet auger to clear the blockage before an emergency develops. (Never use a power auger in a toilet drain or closet bend.) For a serious blockage it may be necessary to remove and reseat the toilet to get at it from underneath—perhaps a full afternoon's job for a plumber. Never use chemical drain openers to clear a clogged toilet. Chemicals are usually ineffective in a toilet and can be dangerous since the

heat they produce can crack the bowl. To prevent clogs, put only toilet paper down the toilet and keep dental floss, cotton swabs and paper towels out.

Most toilets manufactured today are insulated to prevent drips on the floor from condensation. You can stop an older tank from sweating by lining it with flexible foam (page 66). Instead of placing a brick in the tank to conserve water, bend the float arm down an inch or so. When working on a toilet, take care to place the tank cover in a safe place, and do not overtighten bolts. Porcelain cracks very easily, which usually means replacing the entire toilet.

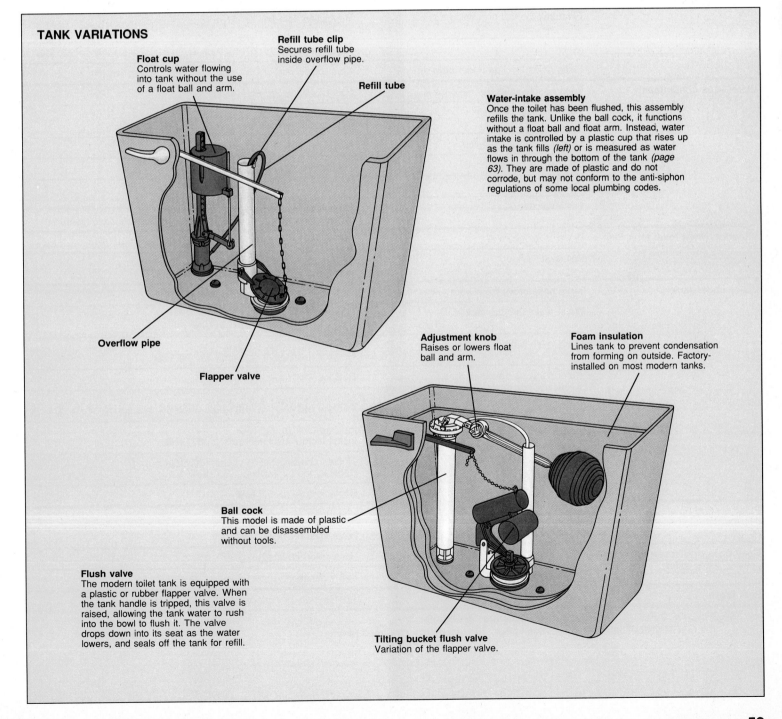

TANK VARIATIONS

Float cup
Controls water flowing into tank without the use of a float ball and arm.

Refill tube clip
Secures refill tube inside overflow pipe.

Refill tube

Water-intake assembly
Once the toilet has been flushed, this assembly refills the tank. Unlike the ball cock, it functions without a float ball and float arm. Instead, water intake is controlled by a plastic cup that rises up as the tank fills (left) or is measured as water flows in through the bottom of the tank (page 63). They are made of plastic and do not corrode, but may not conform to the anti-siphon regulations of some local plumbing codes.

Overflow pipe

Flapper valve

Adjustment knob
Raises or lowers float ball and arm.

Foam insulation
Lines tank to prevent condensation from forming on outside. Factory-installed on most modern tanks.

Ball cock
This model is made of plastic and can be disassembled without tools.

Flush valve
The modern toilet tank is equipped with a plastic or rubber flapper valve. When the tank handle is tripped, this valve is raised, allowing the tank water to rush into the bowl to flush it. The valve drops down into its seat as the water lowers, and seals off the tank for refill.

Tilting bucket flush valve
Variation of the flapper valve.

TROUBLESHOOTING GUIDE

SYMPTOM	POSSIBLE CAUSE	PROCEDURE
Toilet bowl overflows	Blockage in bowl or drain	Use plunger or auger (p. 65) □○ Have toilet removed to unblock it
Toilet does not flush	Water supply turned off	Turn on water supply
	Handle loose, broken or disconnected	Tighten or replace handle (p. 64) □○
	Lift chain broken or disengaged	Service lift chain (p. 64) □○
	Lift chain too loose	Shorten lift chain (p. 64) □○
	Ball cock faulty	Service ball cock (p. 61) ◨◕ Replace ball cock (p. 63) ◨◕
Toilet bowl drains sluggishly	Blockage in bowl or drain	Use plunger or auger (p. 65) □○ Have toilet removed to unblock it
	Float ball too low or rubbing against tank wall	Reposition float ball (p. 61) □○
	Water level too low	Adjust float arm (p. 61) □○ or water-intake assembly (p. 63) ◨◕
	Flush holes blocked under bowl rim	Clear holes with unbent coat hanger and clean bowl
Water runs continuously	Tank handle stuck	Service handle (p. 64) □○
	Water level in tank high	Reposition or replace float ball (p. 61) □○ Adjust water-intake assembly (p. 63) □○
	Lift chain short or tangled	Adjust or replace lift chain (p. 64) □○
	Lift wire bent or corroded	Service lift wire (p. 64) □○
	Ball cock faulty	Service ball cock (p. 61) ◨◕
	Flush valve leaking	Service or replace valve (p. 64) ◨◕ Clean valve seat or replace flush-valve assembly (p. 64) ◨◕
Vibration when toilet tank fills	Water level incorrect	Adjust float arm (p. 61) □○ or water-intake assembly (p. 63) □○
	Ball cock faulty	Service ball cock (p. 61) ◨◕ Replace ball cock (p. 63) ◨◕
Water under tank	Tank loose or washers worn	Tighten nuts or replace washers (p. 66) □○
	Water leaks through handle	Lower float ball (p. 61) □○ Shorten overflow pipe (p. 64) ◨◕
	Flush valve leaks	Replace gasket (p. 66) ◨◕ Replace flush-valve assembly (p. 64) ◨◕
	Water spraying from refill tube	Replace refill tube
	Water spraying from ball cock	Service ball cock (p. 61) ◨◕ Replace ball cock (p. 63) ◨◕
	Condensation on tank	Insulate tank (p. 66) □◕ Install factory-insulated tank (p. 67) ◨●
	Shutoff valve leaks	Tighten coupling nut at shutoff valve □○ Replace shutoff valve (p. 417) ◨◕
	Hairline crack in tank	Replace tank (p. 67) ◨●
Floor around bowl wet	Wax gasket faulty	Have toilet reseated
	Crack in bowl	Have toilet replaced
Dampness or discoloration on ceiling below toilet	Wax gasket faulty	Have toilet reseated
	Drainpipe cracked	Call a plumber
Seat loose	Seat bolts corroded or seat cracked	Tighten bolts or replace seat (p. 67) □○

DEGREE OF DIFFICULTY: □ **Easy** ◨ **Moderate** ■ **Complex**
ESTIMATED TIME: ○ **Less than 1 hour** ◕ **1 to 3 hours** ● **Over 3 hours**

SERVICING THE FLOAT ASSEMBLY

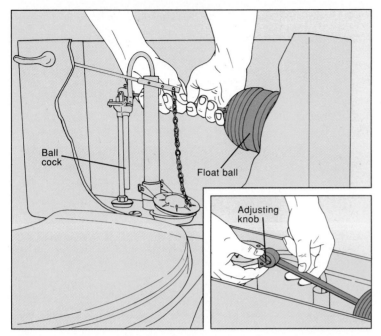

Ball cock

Float ball

Adjusting knob

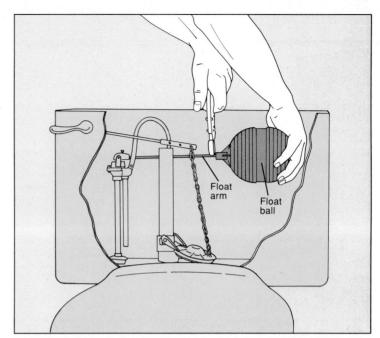

Float arm

Float ball

1 **Adjusting the float arm.** Water running over the top of the overflow pipe, or leaking through the handle, means that the water level is too high. Gently lift the float arm and bend it down slightly, as shown, to keep the water level 1/2 to 1 inch below the top of the overflow pipe. If water continues to run, go to step 2. An incomplete flush means that the water level is too low. Bend the float arm to raise the float ball, making sure the ball does not rub the tank. To raise or lower a plastic float arm, turn the knob at the ball cock *(inset)*.

2 **Replacing the float ball.** A cracked float ball contains water that prevents it from rising high enough to close the ball cock. To remove the ball, grasp the float arm with locking pliers *(above)* and twist the float ball counterclockwise. If it will not come off, use the pliers to unthread the float arm from the ball cock. Replace the ball, coating the threads of the float arm with petroleum jelly, and screw the arm back onto the ball cock. Adjust the float level as in step 1. If water still runs, repair or replace the ball cock *(below)*.

SERVICING THE BALL COCK

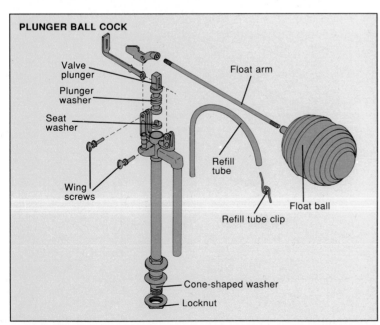

PLUNGER BALL COCK

Valve plunger

Plunger washer

Seat washer

Wing screws

Float arm

Refill tube

Refill tube clip

Float ball

Cone-shaped washer

Locknut

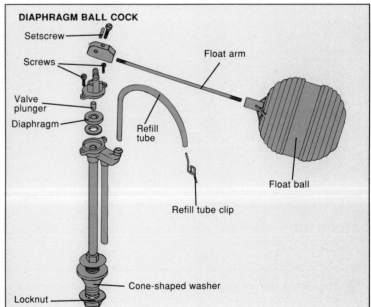

DIAPHRAGM BALL COCK

Setscrew

Screws

Valve plunger

Diaphragm

Float arm

Refill tube

Float ball

Refill tube clip

Cone-shaped washer

Locknut

Ball-cock assemblies. Ball cocks allow water to flow into the tank when the toilet is flushed and the float ball and arm lower, and close when the float ball and arm rise. In the plunger-type ball cock *(above, left)*, the float arm applies pressure on a valve plunger and washer to seal off incoming water. In a diaphragm type *(above, right)* the plunger presses on a rubber diaphragm. In water-intake assemblies *(page 63)* a plastic cup or fill valve controls water flow.

SERVICING THE BALL COCK (continued)

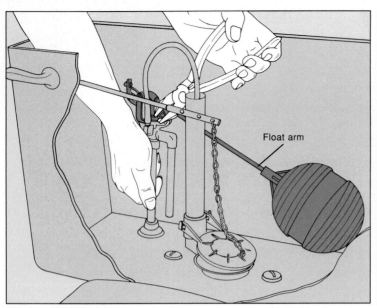

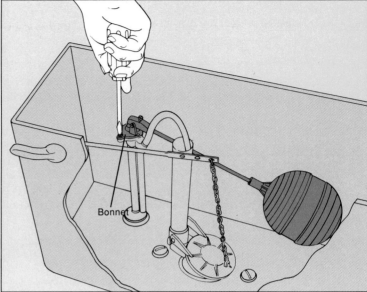

Float arm

Bonnet

1 **Access to the ball-cock assembly.** When possible, buy replacement parts for your make and model of toilet before disassembling it. Turn off the water supply and flush the toilet to empty the tank. Remove the tank cover and carefully lay it aside. To disassemble a plunger ball cock *(above, left)*, remove the wing screws by hand, or with pliers if stubborn. Slide out the float arm, then pull up on the valve plunger to remove it. To access a diaphragm ball cock, remove the screws on the bonnet *(above, right)*, then lift up the float arm with the bonnet attached. This will expose the diaphragm and valve plunger. If the assembly is too corroded to service, replace it *(page 63)*.

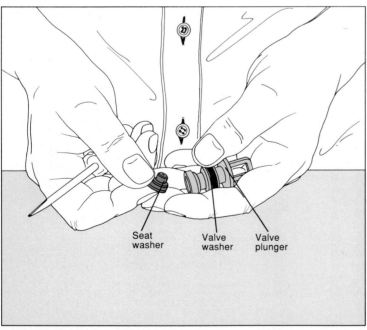

Seat washer

Valve washer

Valve plunger

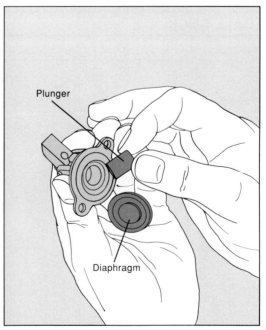

Plunger

Diaphragm

2 **Replacing the washers and diaphragm.** Use a small screwdriver to pry the washers off the valve plunger *(above, left)* or diaphragm *(above, right)* from the ball-cock assembly. Scrape away sediment inside the ball cock with a small knife or toothbrush and vinegar. Then replace the washers and plunger, or diaphragm. Reassemble the ball cock, turn on the water and flush to test the repair. If leaks persist, replace the ball cock *(page 63)*.

REPLACING THE BALL COCK

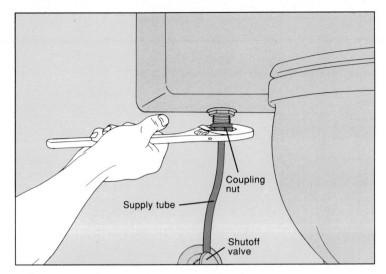

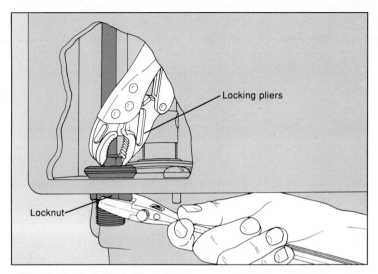

1 **Preparing the tank.** You can replace a worn or broken ball cock with an identical assembly *(next step)* or with a plastic water-intake assembly *(step 3)*. Remove the tank cover and carefully lay it aside. Place a container on the floor beneath the tank to catch water runoff. Shut off the water supply and flush the toilet, holding the handle down to drain as much water from the tank as possible. Remove the float arm from the ball cock *(page 62)* and pull the refill tube from the overflow pipe. Sponge up any remaining water in the bottom of the tank. With an adjustable wrench, disconnect one end of the supply tube from the tank *(above)* and the other end from the shutoff valve. Gently push the supply tube aside or remove it to avoid kinking.

2 **Replacing the ball cock.** To prevent the ball cock from turning inside the tank, attach locking pliers at its base, then wedge them against the tank wall, as shown. Loosen the locknut under the ball cock with an adjustable wrench. If necessary, apply penetrating oil, wait 15 minutes, then try again. If all else fails, cut through the shaft of the ball cock between the locknut and the tank, protecting the tank with plastic tape. Pull the ball cock up and out. Place a strip of plumber's putty around the cone-shaped washer of the new ball cock, then set the assembly firmly into the tank opening. Hold the ball cock with one hand while you tighten the locknut, first by hand, then one-half turn with an adjustable wrench. Place the refill tube into the overflow pipe and reinstall the float arm and ball. Reconnect the supply tube and slowly turn on the water. Flush and check the water level, adjusting the float arm if necessary *(page 61)*.

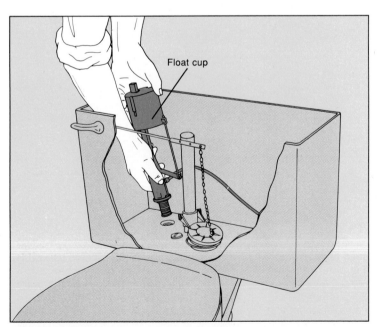

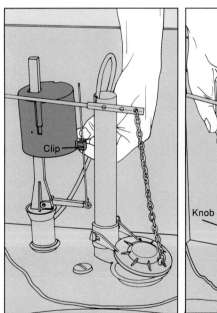

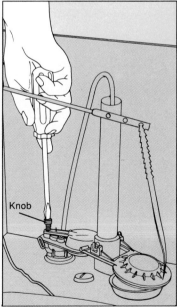

3 **Installing a water-intake assembly.** If you prefer to replace a conventional ball cock with a water-intake assembly, install it in the same way. Use caution when tightening the retaining nut on the underside of the tank; the plastic threads on the assembly shaft may strip and crack under excessive force. Reconnect the supply tube using the washers provided with the new assembly and turn on the water supply, slowly at first, to check for leaks.

4 **Adjusting the water level.** Flush the toilet and check the water level in the tank. It should be 1/2 to 1 inch below the top of the overflow pipe, and just below the handle. To adjust the water level for a float cup *(above, left)*, pinch the clip and slide the cup 1/2 inch at a time: up to raise the water level, or down to lower it. Adjust the water level for a metered fill valve *(above, right)* by turning the adjustment knob by hand or with a screwdriver, one-half turn at a time: clockwise to raise the water level, counterclockwise to lower it.

SERVICING THE FLUSH ASSEMBLY

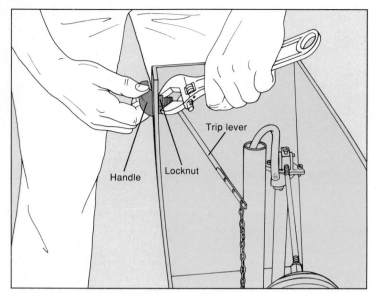

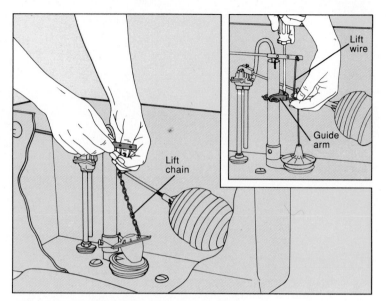

1 **Adjusting the handle.** Remove the tank cover and carefully lay it aside. For a loose tank handle, tighten the locknut inside the tank counterclockwise with an adjustable wrench *(above)*. If sediment and corrosion are blocking the handle, apply penetrating oil to the threads, wait 15 minutes, then unscrew the locknut. If the nut is impossible to remove, cut through the handle shaft with a hacksaw and replace the handle and trip lever. Unhook the chain from the trip lever and slide the trip lever, with the handle attached, through the hole in the tank. Scrub the handle threads with a toothbrush and vinegar. Reinstall the entire assembly, tightening the locknut counterclockwise.

2 **Adjusting the lift chain.** If the handle must be held down to flush the toilet, the chain may be too long. To shorten it, try hooking the chain through a different hole in the trip lever *(above)*, or use long-nose pliers to open and remove chain links. A slow flush may indicate a short or broken chain. To lengthen it, you must replace the chain. Do not try to repair or lengthen the chain by adding a safety pin or piece of wire; a second metal will promote corrosion. To adjust the length of an older flush assembly, loosen the screw on the guide arm *(inset)*, then slide the guide arm up to shorten, or down to lengthen it.

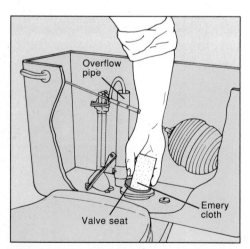

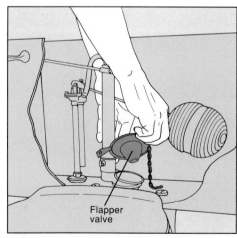

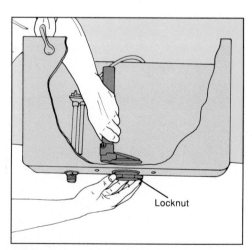

3 **Cleaning the valve seat.** Mineral deposits and sediment on the valve seat can prevent the flapper valve from sealing tightly and permit water to run continuously into the bowl. Turn off the water supply, or use a coat hanger to hold up the float ball *(page 18)*. Flush the toilet to drain the tank, then remove the flapper valve by unhooking it, or by sliding it up the overflow pipe. Gently scour inside the seat and its rim with emery cloth *(above)*, and coat the rim with petroleum jelly. Turn on the water supply and flush to check for leaks.

4 **Replacing the flapper valve.** A flapper valve that is soft or distorted allows water to leak into the bowl between flushes. Unhook the lift chain and remove the flapper valve *(above)*. Buy a replacement that fits the valve seat in your tank and install it. If you cannot find a valve that fits your seat, or if leaks persist after replacing the flapper valve, replace the entire assembly *(step 5)*.

5 **Replacing the flush-valve assembly.** For this repair you must first remove the tank *(page 67)*. Cut the new overflow pipe with a hacksaw to 1/2 inch below the tank handle. Apply a thin strip of plumber's putty to the cone-shaped washer on the flush-valve assembly. Then fit the assembly snugly into the tank opening and scrape away excess putty. Thread on the retaining nut, as shown, tightening it with a spud wrench or monkey wrench. Then push a new conical gasket up over the locknut. Ease the tank onto the bowl and reconnect them.

UNCLOGGING THE TOILET

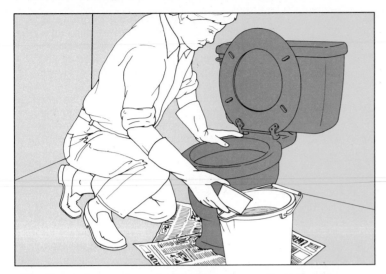

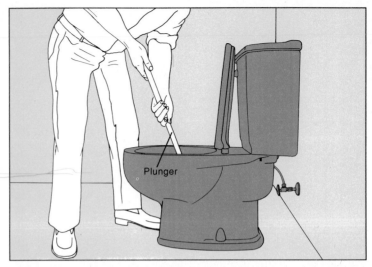

1 **Preparing to clear the blockage.** Do not flush the toilet. Spread newspaper around the base of the bowl. If the bowl is overflowing, put on rubber gloves and use a plastic container to bail out half the water *(above)*. If the bowl is empty, add water to half-full, then go to step 2 to clear the blockage with a plunger.

2 **Using a plunger.** A flanged plunger fits into the toilet drain and exerts more pressure than the regular type. Place the rubber cup squarely over the drain opening—the larger one if there are two. Keep the cup below the water level, pump up and down rapidly 8 to 10 times, then pull the plunger up sharply. If the water rushes away, you may have released the blockage. Use the plunger once again, to be sure the water is draining freely. Pour in a pail of water to test and repeat if necessary.

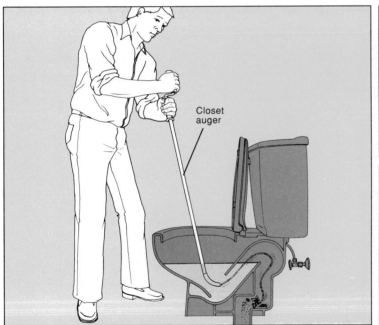

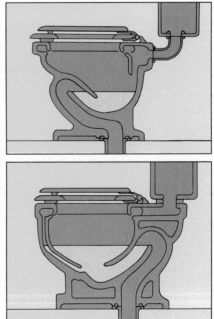

3 **Using an auger.** If possible, use a closet auger to clear a clogged toilet. Its long sleeve is curved to help start the coil into the toilet bend without scratching the porcelain. With the help of the illustrations above, determine the direction in which to guide the auger in your toilet. Feed the curved tip into the drain opening *(above)*. Crank clockwise until the auger tightens up, then continue cranking in the other direction. When the auger tightens again, reverse the direction until the auger is as far in the drain as it will go. Then pull the handle up and out to remove the auger. If it jams, push gently, then pull again. You may have to turn the handle as you pull up. Then use a plunger to ensure that the drain runs freely. Repeat with the auger if necessary. As a last resort, it may be necessary to remove the toilet to reach the blockage from underneath.

INSULATING THE TANK

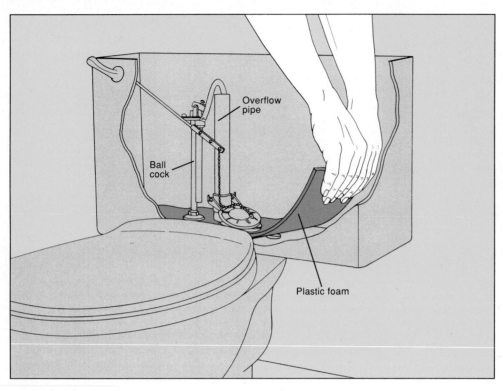

Overflow pipe

Ball cock

Plastic foam

1 Lining the tank with foam. Lining a sweating tank will often stop drips caused by condensation, especially in hot weather. Remove the tank cover and carefully lay it aside. Mark the water level inside the tank; the foam should cover the tank to 1/2 inch above this line. Shut off the water supply and flush, holding the handle to drain as much water as possible. For easier access, remove the float ball and float arm *(page 61)*. Sponge up any remaining water and use a hair dryer to dry the tank walls completely. Cut and install the foam *(left)* according to instructions in the kit, applying a bead of adhesive over all edges and seams. Replace the float ball and arm. Leave the tank cover off and allow the adhesive to set overnight before turning on the water supply and filling the tank.

STOPPING LEAKS FROM THE TANK

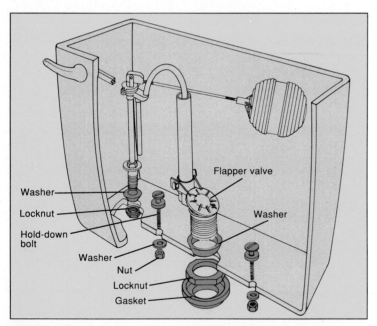

Flapper valve

Washer

Washer

Locknut

Hold-down bolt

Washer

Nut

Locknut

Gasket

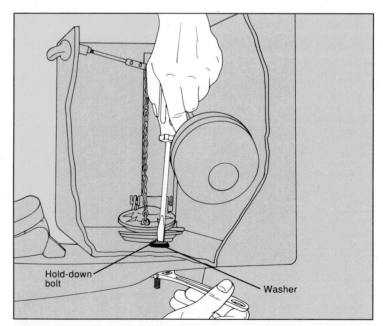

Hold-down bolt

Washer

1 Finding the source of a leak. The diagram above shows where leaks occur if seals are not watertight. First look through the Troubleshooting Guide on page 60 to check for obvious causes of leaks and ensure that no tank parts are at fault. If you are unable to find the leak, pour a few drops of food coloring into the tank, and wait—up to a day—to see where the coloring shows up.

2 Stopping leaks under the tank. To tighten a tank hold-down bolt, secure it inside the tank with a screwdriver *(above)*, and tighten the nut with an adjustable wrench. If leaks persist, loosen and remove the hold-down bolts and replace the washers. For a hairline crack in the tank, replace the tank. Tighten a loose locknut at the ball cock a quarter-turn with an adjustable or open-end wrench, holding the ball cock inside the tank steady with the other hand.

REPLACING THE TANK

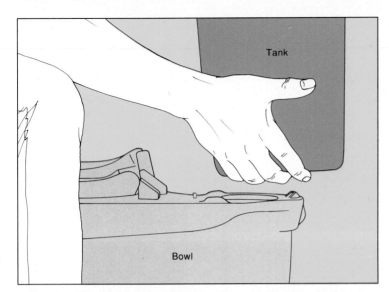

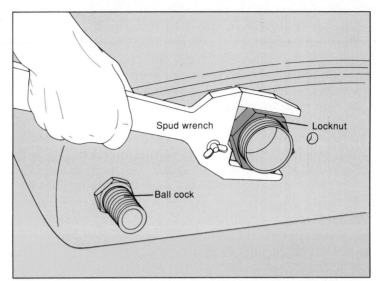

1 **Disconnecting the tank.** Shut off the water supply. Remove the tank cover and carefully lay it aside. Flush, drain and sponge out any remaining water in the tank. With an adjustable wrench or channel-joint pliers, loosen the coupling nuts at the supply tube. Gently push the tube aside or remove it to avoid kinking. To remove the hold-down bolts, hold the bolt on the inside of the tank with a flat-tipped screwdriver and loosen the nut with an adjustable wrench *(page 66)*. Lift the tank up and off the bowl *(above)*, twisting carefully if there is resistance from the tank gasket. Gently lay the tank on a rug or pad of newspapers. Pry or scrape the old gasket off the tank and bowl.

2 **Replacing the tank.** If you are reusing the old tank, first remove the exposed locknut with a spud wrench, turning it counterclockwise *(above)*. If the threads are badly corroded, apply penetrating oil and wait at least 15 minutes before trying again. Hold on to the overflow pipe and valve seat, and pull the flush-valve assembly free. Install the new assembly as described on page 64. Place the tank back on the bowl and, keeping it parallel to the wall, install new hold-down bolts and washers. Reconnect the supply tube and turn the water on slowly. Flush to test for leaks, and tighten the connections one-quarter turn if necessary.

REPLACING THE TOILET SEAT

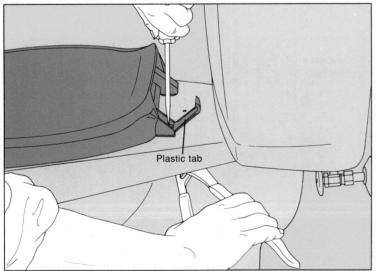

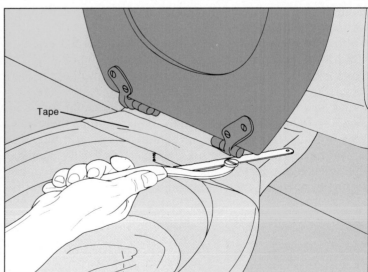

Removing the seat bolts. Measure both the width and length of the seat before buying a replacement. To remove the seat bolts, which may be hidden under plastic tabs, hold one bolt steady with a screwdriver, then unscrew the nut with a socket wrench or pliers *(above, left)*. To loosen corroded bolts, apply penetrating oil, wait overnight, then try again. If necessary, protect the bowl with tape or a thin piece of cardboard and cut through the bolts with a hacksaw *(above, right)*. Replace the seat and bolts, and hand-tighten the nuts. Check that the seat aligns with the bowl, and tighten the nuts one-quarter turn with a wrench.

BATHTUBS AND SHOWERS

Since one-third of a typical household's water pours through the shower head and tub spout—and down the bathtub drain—it's not surprising that these fixtures can call for a variety of repairs. On the supply side, tub spouts may drip, faucet handles leak and diverters refuse to send water to the shower head. On the drainage side, the tub may empty too slowly or water may seep away annoyingly during a bath.

Leaks around the faucet handles, diverter or shower head call for a while-you're-at-it approach to repair. While the fixture is removed and disassembled, clean it thoroughly with vinegar and a wire brush, and replace any parts that appear worn, pitted or heavily corroded with exact duplicates. The Troubleshooting Guide on page 69 will refer you to Faucets for specific repairs. Bathtub faucets differ from sink faucets in that you may need to pry off the escutcheon after removing the handle in order to gain access to working parts. For a double-handle faucet, using a reversible ratchet with a deep socket will make it easier to remove the stem. In the case of older or less expensive fixtures, it may be less trouble to have the entire faucet, spout or shower head replaced rather than hunt for replacement parts.

Clogged drains are usually caused by an accumulation of soap and hair, or by foreign objects such as stray hairpins or plastic toys. But don't reach for the chemical drain opener as soon as the drain backs up. A plunger or auger is much safer for the trap and drain than caustic chemicals.

Simple maintenance can prevent most drain problems. Use a drop-in basket strainer to catch hair and stray objects. Clean the strainer or stopper regularly (and put the debris in the garbage, not down the drain). And don't cure a slow drain by removing the strainer or stopper to let the water out. Unblock the drain immediately, to prevent more serious problems farther down the system.

When tackling repairs to the supply pipes and fixtures, be sure to first turn off the water. To locate the shutoff valves, look for an access panel on the other side of the wall where the faucets are located. It is usually fastened by screws in each corner, and lifts off to expose the pipes. The shutoff valves should be behind this panel or in the basement directly below the tub. If not, turn off the main shutoff valve. Most tub and shower repairs require only a screwdriver, adjustable wrench, pipe wrench and locking pliers. Protect chromed parts from the bite of a wrench by wrapping them with friction or plastic tape. And be sure to have a pail and rags close at hand to sop up any water that spills from the system.

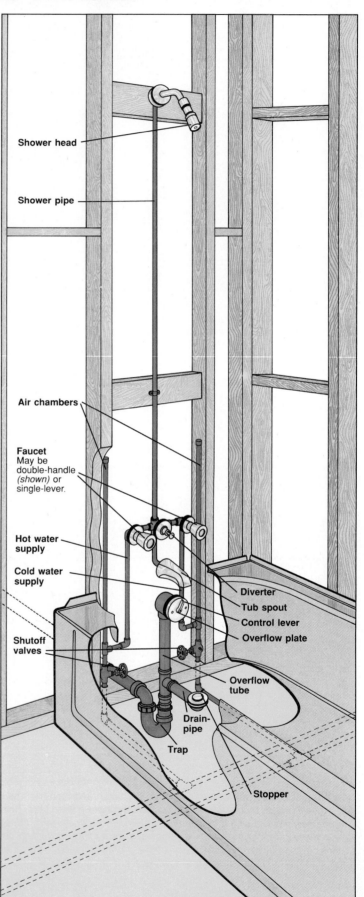

TROUBLESHOOTING GUIDE

SYMPTOM	POSSIBLE CAUSE	PROCEDURE
Water seeps from bathtub (pop-up drains)	Accumulation of hair or soap around stopper	Remove and clean stopper (p. 70) □○
	Accumulation on lift assembly	Remove and clean lift assembly (p. 70) □○
	Lift assembly too long	Adjust lift assembly (p. 70) □○
	Lift assembly worn or damaged	Replace lift assembly (p. 70) □○
Water seeps from bathtub (trip-lever drains)	Accumulation on plunger	Remove and clean lift assembly (p. 70) □○
	Lift assembly too short or plunger worn	Adjust or replace lift assembly (p. 70) □○
Control lever won't stay in position	Lever mechanism corroded	Adjust or replace lift assembly (p. 70) □○
Water drains too slowly from bathtub (pop-up drains)	Accumulation around stopper	Clean stopper (p. 70) □○
	Lift assembly clogged, corroded or too short	Clean and adjust lift assembly (p. 70) □○
Water drains too slowly from bathtub (trip-lever drains)	Lift assembly clogged, corroded or too long	Clean and adjust lift assembly (p. 70) □○
	Lift assembly worn or damaged	Replace lift assembly (p. 70) □○
Drain slow or blocked	Drainpipes clogged	Open drainpipe with a plunger, auger or hose (p. 72) □○
	Trap blocked	If trap is accessible, unblock through cleanout plug or remove trap (p. 50) ◻●. If not accessible, call for service
Faucet handle leaks (double-handle faucets)	Compression type (newer): O-rings worn or damaged	Replace O-rings (p. 38) □○
	Compression-type (older): packing nut loose, packing or washer worn	Tighten nut or replace worn parts (p. 40) □○
	Disc type: O-ring worn	Replace O-ring (p. 41) □○
	Diaphragm type: O-ring worn	Replace O-ring (p. 42) □○
Faucet handle leaks (single-lever faucets)	Disc type: inlet seals worn or disc cracked	Replace seals or disc assembly (p. 43) □○
	Ball type: adjusting ring loose or O-rings worn	Tighten adjusting ring or replace O-rings (p. 44) □○
	Cartridge type: O-rings or cartridge worn	Replace O-rings or cartridge (p. 46) □○
Water leaks from tub spout or shower head (double-handle faucets)	Compression type (newer): washer worn or seat damaged	Replace washer (p. 38) □○ or replace or redress seat (p. 38) ◻●▲
	Compression type (older): washer worn or seat damaged	Replace washer (p. 40) □○ or redress seat (p. 38) ◻●▲ or have faucet replaced
	Disc type: seat assembly worn	Replace seat assembly (p. 41) □○
	Diaphragm type: diaphragm worn	Replace diaphragm (p. 42) □○
Water dripping from tub spout or shower head (single-lever faucets)	Disc type: disc cracked or worn	Replace disc assembly (p. 43) □○
	Ball type: ball assembly worn	Replace worn parts (p. 44) □○
	Cartridge type: cartridge worn	Replace cartridge (p. 46) □○
	Faucet body worn	Have faucet replaced
Water incompletely diverted from spout to shower (tub-spout diverters)	Diverter worn	Replace tub spout (p. 73) □○
Water leaks around diverter handle (push-pull diverters)	O-rings worn	Replace O-rings or diverter (p. 74) ◻●
	Diverter worn	Replace diverter (p. 74) ◻●
Water incompletely diverted from spout to shower (push-pull diverters)	O-rings worn	Replace O-rings or diverter (p. 74) ◻●
	Diverter coated with sediment	Clean diverter (p. 74) ◻●
	Diverter worn	Replace diverter (p. 74) ◻●
Weak or uneven pressure from shower head	Mineral buildup on shower head	Clean or replace shower head (p. 75) ◻●
Shower head leaks	Connections at shower head and arm loose	Tighten shower head to arm or seal joint with pipe tape (p. 75) □○

DEGREE OF DIFFICULTY: □ Easy ◻ Moderate ◼ Complex
ESTIMATED TIME: ○ Less than 1 hour ● 1 to 3 hours ● Over 3 hours   ▲ Special tool required

BATHTUB DRAINS

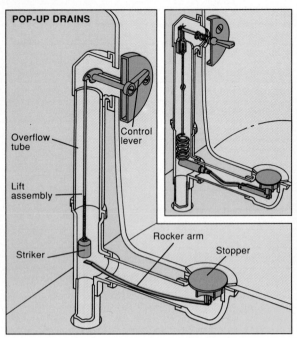

POP-UP DRAINS

Overflow tube

Control lever

Lift assembly

Striker

Rocker arm

Stopper

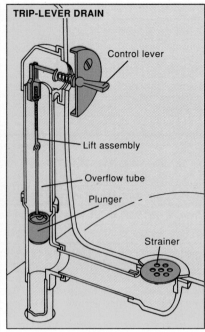

TRIP-LEVER DRAIN

Control lever

Lift assembly

Overflow tube

Plunger

Strainer

Pop-up drains. The distinguishing feature of a pop-up drain *(far left)* is a curved rocker arm attached to the stopper. The arm extends to the intersection of the drain, where a lift assembly in the overflow tube rests. The control lever raises the assembly so the striker at the bottom lifts off the rocker. As that end of the rocker springs up, the stopper falls to close the drain. When the lift assembly is lowered, the striker presses down on the rocker, pushing up the stopper to open the drain.

Trip-lever drain. Tubs with trip-lever drains *(near left)* usually have a strainer in the drain, but no stopper. Inside the overflow tube a hollow brass plunger is suspended from the lift assembly. The control lever lowers the plunger down the tube, blocking the intersection of the drain. When the plunger is raised, the water runs freely down the drain.

SERVICING THE DRAIN ASSEMBLY

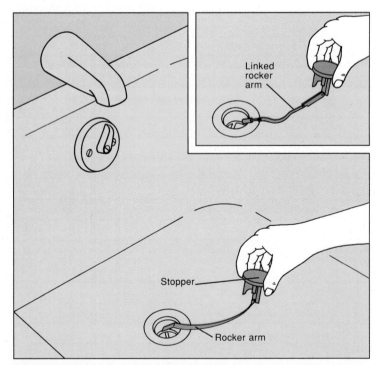

Linked rocker arm

Stopper

Rocker arm

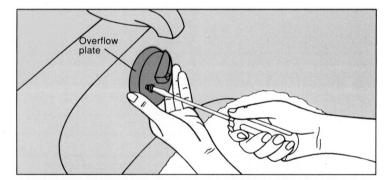

Overflow plate

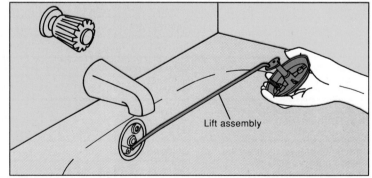

Lift assembly

1 **Cleaning the pop-up stopper.** If water seeps down the bathtub drain when it is closed, or the tub drains too slowly, the pop-up stopper may be clogged. To remove the stopper, turn the control lever to open the drain, pull up the stopper, and work the rocker arm clear of the drain opening *(above)*. Scour the stopper assembly with fine steel wool. Feed it back into the drain with the rocker arm curving downward in the drainpipe. Wiggle a linked rocker arm *(inset)* back and forth until it sits back in place. If either problem persists, go to step 2.

2 **Removing the pop-up or trip-lever assembly.** Cover the drain with a bathmat to protect the tub and prevent loss of parts. Remove the screws on the overflow plate and pull it away from the tub, as shown. To remove a stubborn lift assembly, spray penetrating oil down the overflow tube and wait 15 minutes before trying again. Pull the lift assembly up through the overflow opening. Clean the assembly *(step 3)*, adjust it *(step 4)*, or replace a badly worn assembly *(step 5)*.

SERVICING THE DRAIN ASSEMBLY (continued)

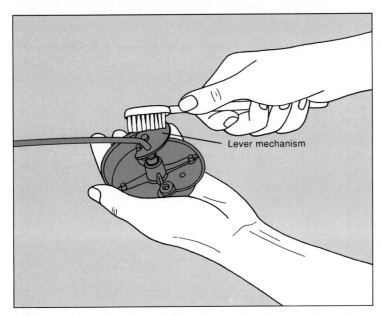

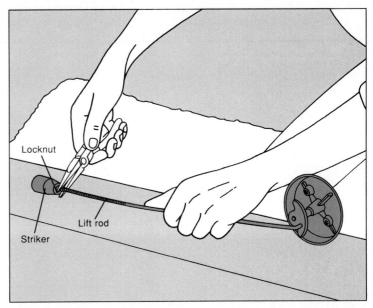

3 **Cleaning the lift assembly.** Wash off debris around the striker, spring or plunger. Remove corrosion from the assembly using vinegar and steel wool or an old toothbrush. Clean the lever mechanism on the back of the overflow plate *(above)* to ensure that the control lever stays in position. Lubricate the entire mechanism lightly with petroleum jelly or silicone lubricant.

4 **Adjusting the lift assembly.** If the stopper does not fit snugly into the drain, or does not rise far enough to drain properly, the lift assembly may need adjustment. Loosen the locknut that holds the striker in place. Rotate the nut down the threaded rod to lengthen the lift assembly, or up to shorten it, then retighten *(above)*. Reassemble and test. If problems persist, replace the drain assembly *(next step)*.

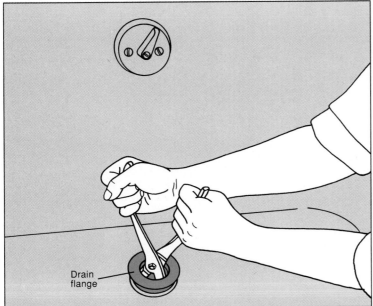

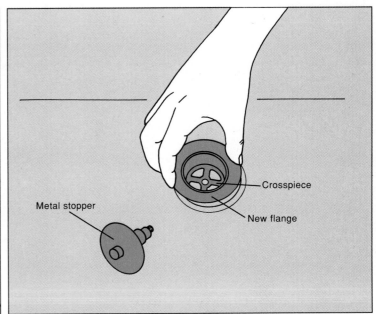

5 **Replacing the assembly.** When a drain assembly of the same make and model as the old one is not available, simply replace the assembly with a rubber plug and drop-in basket strainer. Pull out the pop-up stopper or pry up the trip-lever strainer and remove the overflow plate with the lift assembly attached. Remove the cotter pin to release the lift assembly or cut the linkage. Screw the overflow plate back in place. If the lift assembly cannot be disconnected from the back of the overflow plate, buy a replacement overflow plate with screws that line up with the holes in the overflow tube.

You can also use a metal stopper that opens and closes the drain at a touch. With the stopper or strainer removed, unscrew the drain flange counterclockwise, using pliers *(above, left)*. To increase leverage, insert the handle of a wrench between the handles of the pliers. Take the flange to a plumbing supply store; its threads must match those of the stopper's flange. Apply a strip of plumber's putty under the lip of the new flange. Screw the flange into the drain opening *(above, right)* and thread the metal stopper into the crosspiece.

CLEARING A CLOGGED DRAIN

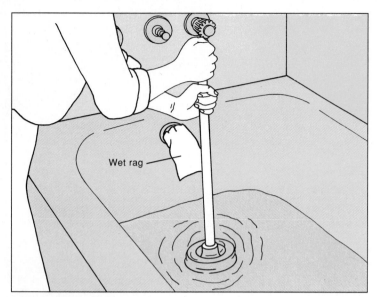

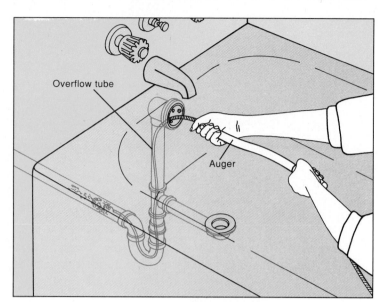

1 **Using a plunger.** If there is a tub stopper, remove it and the overflow plate *(page 70)*. Plug the overflow opening with tape, a large, wet rag or a rag wrapped in plastic. Coat the plunger rim with petroleum jelly and run enough water into the tub to cover the plunger cup. Insert the plunger at an angle so that no air remains trapped under it. Push down and pull up forcefully, keeping the plunger upright and the cup sealed over the drain opening *(above)*. Repeat the process many times; patience is the key to plunging. If the clog remains, use an auger *(step 2)*, or if local codes permit, a hose *(steps 3-4)*.

2 **Using an auger.** Have a pail ready to catch any debris snagged by the end of the auger. In a shower stall, pry up or unscrew the strainer and work through the drain opening. In a bathtub, remove the stopper and the lift assembly *(page 70),* and feed the auger down the overflow tube *(above)*. Maneuver the auger around the corners in the drain, rotating it clockwise to break up the clog. Remove the auger slowly and run water to test the drain. If the clog remains, use a hose *(steps 3-4)*. If the trap is accessible, work directly on the trap *(page 50)*.

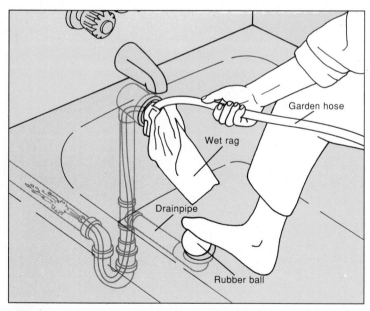

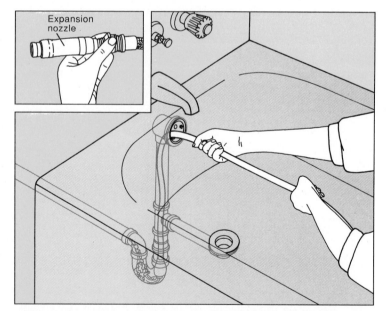

3 **Using a hose.** A hose attached to an outdoor faucet may reach the tub through a window. If not, attach the hose to an indoor faucet using a threaded adapter. Close all nearby drains, feed the hose down the overflow tube and pack rags tightly around the hose. (When the overflow tube is too narrow for the hose, feed the hose down the drain opening as far as possible.) Press down firmly on the plug or a rubber ball *(above)* to seal the tub drain. Hold the hose firmly while someone turns the water on full force and then off again several times to flush the blockage.

4 **Using an expansion nozzle.** This attachment, available at plumbing supply stores, expands to seal the overflow tube and force water through the drain in jets, increasing the effectiveness of the hose. Measure the opening to determine which nozzle will fit that diameter of pipe. Attach the nozzle to the hose *(inset)* and the hose to a faucet. Seal off all nearby drains. Insert the hose as in step 3, and turn the water slowly to full force *(above)*. Turn the water off, detach the hose from the faucet, and wait for the nozzle to deflate before removing it.

REPLACING A SCREW-ON TUB SPOUT

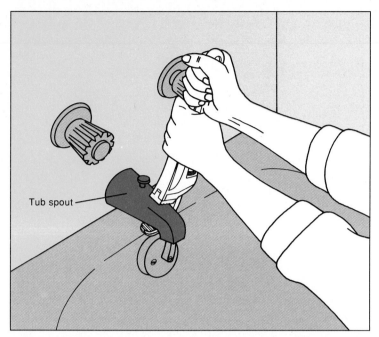

Tub spout

Nipple

1 Loosening the spout. If the tub spout contains a diverter valve that is not completely diverting water from the spout to the shower head, replace the tub spout. Check under the spout for a setscrew; if there is one, it is a slip-fit spout *(page 74)*. Otherwise, grip the spout with a pipe wrench and turn counterclockwise to loosen it *(above)*. If the spout will not move and there is access from behind, apply penetrating oil, wait 15 minutes and try again. Do not use too much force, or you might damage the plumbing behind the wall.

2 Removing the spout. Twist the loosened spout off the nipple by hand *(above)* or off the adapter at the end of a copper pipe. If you can find a replacement spout, go to step 4. If a compatible spout is unavailable, go to step 3.

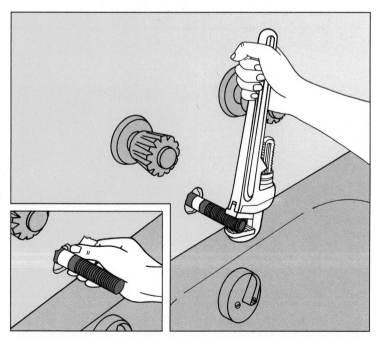

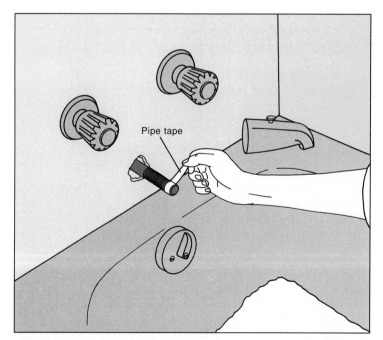

Pipe tape

3 Removing the nipple. Wrap masking tape around the nipple to mark the point where it protrudes from the wall *(inset)*, then unscrew it with a pipe wrench *(above)*. Take the nipple and tub spout to a plumbing supply store. Fit the nipple into a new spout and measure the difference between the tape and the edge of the spout. Buy a threaded brass nipple that is the length of the old one minus this difference, or have one cut to that length. Apply pipe tape to the threads, then screw the nipple into the wall by hand.

4 Mounting the tub spout. Clean the threads of the nipple with steel wool or a wire brush. Apply pipe tape to the threads (unless the directions on the new spout advise otherwise) and silicone sealant to the base of the spout. Thread the spout onto the nipple and tighten it by hand, then wrap the tub spout with masking tape and tighten with a pipe wrench.

REPLACING A SLIP-FIT TUB SPOUT

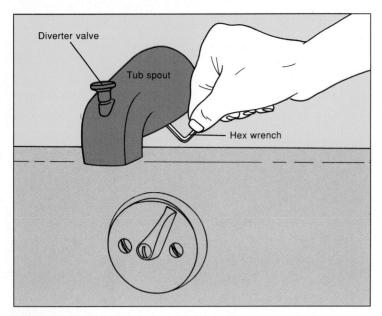

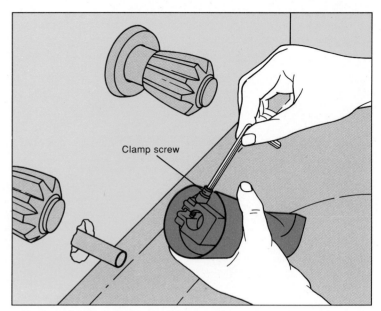

1 **Removing the old spout.** Loosen the clamp screw on the underside of the spout with a hex wrench *(above)*. Grasp the spout firmly and twist it off the copper pipe.

2 **Mounting the new spout.** Loosen the clamp screw on the new spout with a hex wrench *(above)*, and twist the spout onto the copper pipe. Turn the spout so that the clamp screw faces up, and partially tighten the screw. Twist the spout into position and finish tightening the screw with the hex wrench. Do not overtighten.

REPAIRING PUSH-PULL DIVERTERS

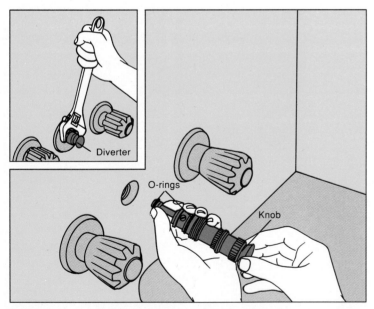

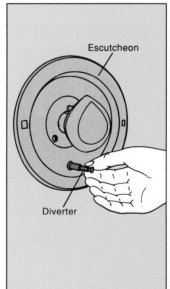

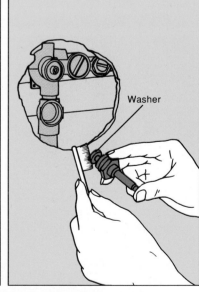

Repairing a push-pull diverter (double-handle faucets). Turn off the water supply and open the faucets. Close the drain and set a bath-mat down to prevent loss of parts and protect the tub. To remove a diverter located between two faucet handles, wrap it in tape and un-screw it with an adjustable wrench *(inset)*, exposing two O-rings. Un-screw the diverter knob by hand *(above)* to reveal another O-ring and a spring. Clean the spring and lubricate it lightly with petroleum jelly or silicone lubricant. Replace any O-rings that appear cracked or worn. If problems persist, replace the entire diverter with an identical part.

Repairing a diverter (single-lever faucets). Remove the faucet handle according to your faucet type *(page 36)*. Remove any screws securing the escutcheon and pry it off, then unscrew the diverter *(above, left)*. If water is not being properly diverted from the tub spout to the shower head, clean any sediment off the washer with vinegar and an old toothbrush *(above, right)*. If water leaks from around the diverter, or if its parts are worn, replace the entire mechanism with one of the same make.

REPAIRING A SHOWER HEAD

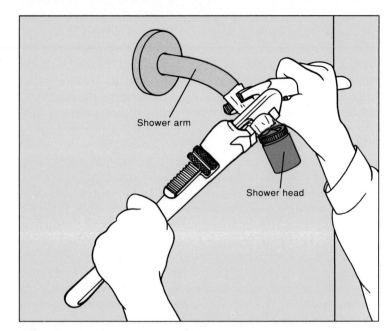

1 **Removing the shower head.** If the flow of water from a shower head is uneven or insufficient, first disassemble and clean it. Close the drain and cover it with a bathmat to prevent loss of parts and to protect the tub. Wrap the shower head collar in masking tape and turn it counterclockwise with a pipe wrench. Or use a strap wrench, which requires no tape. For greater leverage, grip the shower arm with one wrench and turn the collar counterclockwise with a second wrench *(above)*. Twist off the loosened shower head by hand.

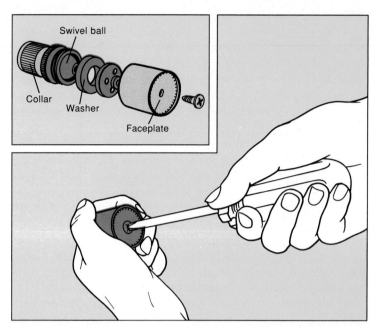

2 **Disassembling the shower head.** Remove the screw *(above)* or the knob that secures the faceplate to the shower head. Unscrew the collar from the shower head to reveal the swivel ball, and pry out the washer. To clean the disassembled parts *(inset)*, go to step 3. If the parts appear badly worn or corroded replace the shower head *(step 4)*.

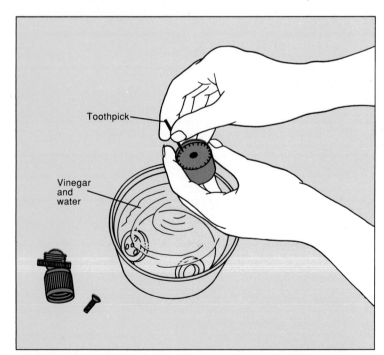

3 **Cleaning the shower head.** Soak the entire shower head or its disassembled parts overnight in vinegar. Scrub with steel wool or an old toothbrush, and clear the spray holes with a needle or toothpick *(above)*. If possible, buy replacements for the worn parts of an expensive shower head rather than buying a new one. Lubricate the swivel ball with petroleum jelly or silicone lubricant and reassemble the parts in reverse order.

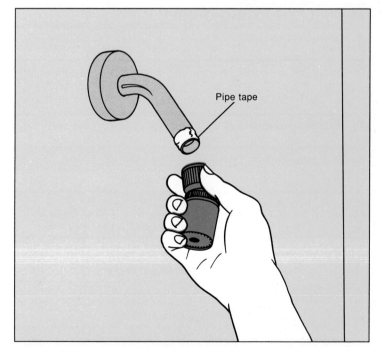

4 **Installing the shower head.** When replacing an old shower head with a new one, consider water-saving heads, heads with adjustable spray, and heads with plastic parts that collect less sediment. Clean the pipe threads of the shower arm with steel wool or a wire brush. Apply pipe tape to the threads to seal the joints. Hand-tighten the head on the shower arm *(above)*. Turn on the water to test the shower; if it leaks, tighten it an additional half-turn.

MAIN DRAINS

The home drainage system is called the drain-waste-vent (DWV) system because of its three major functions: drainage, waste removal and venting of sewer gas, all of which are interconnected. The DWV system is completely separate from the supply system and, because it must maintain modern sanitation standards, it is closely regulated by plumbing codes. Consult local authorities regarding these codes before working on your home drainage system.

Under each sink, bathtub and toilet is a P- or S-shaped trap containing water, which acts as a seal to prevent waste and gases from rising out of the drainage system and into the home. Beyond the traps, gravity carries the waste along horizontal branch drains to the main stack. A waste stack is always a vertical drainpipe. If the stack carries toilet waste as well, it is referred to as a soil stack. Most fixtures and appliances are clustered around this main drainpipe *(page 34)*. Local plumbing codes regulate how many fixtures can empty into a stack, so a house may have more than one stack.

The portion of the soil stack above the branch drains is called the vent, a single pipe rising through the roof. Atmospheric pressure in the vent prevents fixture traps from being siphoned dry each time they are used. A common problem is ice or leaves blocking the vent, creating a vacuum that can siphon all the water from traps in the system. In the harsh winters of some parts of the United States and Canada, snow and ice would soon block the standard vent; codes there call for oversize pipes, sometimes fitted with cages or screens.

At the bottom of the soil stack, the pipe makes a gentle 90-degree turn to become the main drain, which slopes to a public sewer or private septic system. The main cleanout, which provides access to the main drain, is located near this turn. In warmer climates, or in houses without basements, the cleanout may be outside, above the point where the main drain leaves the foundation. Another access point in some older homes is the house trap, identifiable by its two cleanout plugs close to the foundation wall.

Two or more clogged or sluggish drains point to blockage somewhere in the branch drains, soil stack, main drain or sewer line. Often the hardest step in dealing with such a problem is opening a rusted cleanout plug or house trap. It may be easier to gain access by working down from the vent stack on the roof. (However, because a roof is high and often steeply pitched, it is best to hire a plumber for this job.) When you can open the cleanout, a garden hose, especially with a rubber expansion nozzle, or a manual auger will usually clear the drain. Power augers are available from plumbing supply or rental companies, but you should consider this as a last resort, and only if you have experience with heavy power tools. Have the rental company teach you how to start and operate the machine. Wear safety goggles to protect your eyes. Sometimes a blockage affecting the entire drainage system is caused by a crack in the sewer pipe. Repairing the pipe is a formidable job, requiring an experienced plumber and often permission from local authorities before digging.

TROUBLESHOOTING GUIDE

SYMPTOM	POSSIBLE CAUSE	PROCEDURE
Drain sluggish or backed up	Trap or branch drain clogged at fixture	Clear trap or drain at fixtures: Sinks *(p. 50)* Toilets *(p. 65)* Bathtubs and showers *(p. 72)*
Two or more drains backed up	Drainage system blocked below fixtures	Unblock main drain from main cleanout *(p. 77)* ◪◓ Have soil stack unblocked from roof vent
Odors or gurgling from drains	Vent blocked	Have soil stack unblocked from roof vent
	Septic tank full	Have septic system serviced professionally
Basement floor drain backed up	Main drain blocked	Unblock main drain from main cleanout *(p. 77)* ◪◓
	House trap or sewer line blocked	Call for service
All drains sluggish or backed up	Main drain blocked	Unblock main drain from main cleanout *(p. 77)* ◪◓
	Sewer line blocked	Call for service
	Leak in sewer line	Call for service
	Septic tank full	Have septic system serviced professionally
	Main drain or sewer line has insufficient slope	Call for service

DEGREE OF DIFFICULTY: ☐ Easy ◪ Moderate ■ Complex
ESTIMATED TIME: ○ Less than 1 hour ◓ 1 to 3 hours ● Over 3 hours

ACCESS TO THE MAIN CLEANOUT

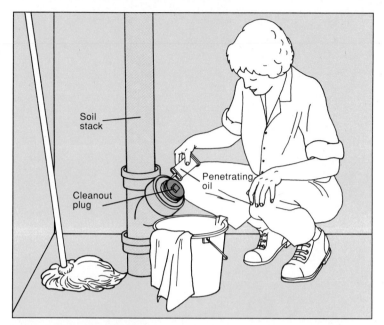

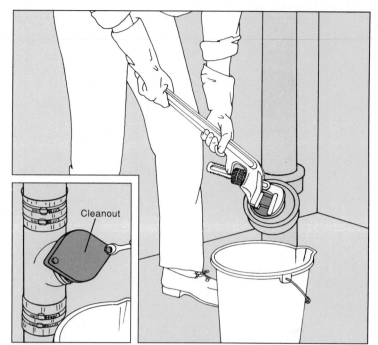

1 **Loosening the cleanout plug.** The main cleanout is usually near the bottom of the soil stack, in the basement or crawlspace, close to where the stack makes a 90-degree turn to leave the house. If the main cleanout is hard to find, locate the vent on the roof and follow it down to the corresponding spot in the basement, crawlspace or lawn. Before opening the cleanout, either shut off the main water supply or do not use any water in the house. Allow waste to drain out of the system, preferably overnight, so that water does not pour out after the cleanout plug is off. Have a mop, rags and a bucket ready. If the cleanout plug is metal, it may be stubborn. Apply penetrating oil to the threads, as shown, waiting overnight if possible before trying to remove it.

2 **Removing the cleanout plug.** Loosen, but do not remove, the cleanout plug with a large pipe wrench *(above)*. If the nut has been rounded off from previous repairs, first file it square with a metal file. If it still does not loosen, go to step 3. Let some of the trapped water ooze out into the bucket, tighten the nut and mop up, repeating the process until no water remains. Clear the blockage with an auger or hose *(page 78)*. Some cleanouts have a metal cover secured by two brass bolts. Apply penetrating oil, wait a few minutes and use an open-end wrench *(inset)* or adjustable wrench to loosen the bolts.

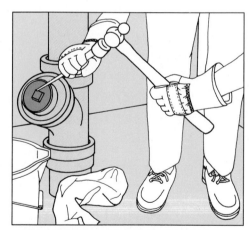

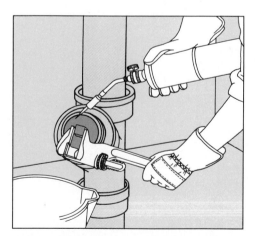

3 **Loosening the plug with a hammer and chisel.** If the plug remains stubborn, place a cold chisel on one edge of the nut and tap it firmly counterclockwise with a ball-peen hammer, as shown, then move to the next face. Continue hammering until the plug is loose enough to turn with a wrench. If the nut remains stubborn, apply heat with a propane torch *(next step)*.

4 **Applying heat to the plug.** If the plug will not move because it has rusted in place, try burning off the rust with a propane torch. The heat needed to loosen the plug dissipates very quickly, so hold the wrench with one hand while you play the torch over the rusted fitting with the other hand *(above)*.

5 **Breaking the plug.** As a last resort, you may have to destroy a rusted cleanout plug and replace it with a new one. Using a power drill with a 3/8-inch metal bit, drill a ring of holes within 1/4 inch of the edge of the plug *(above)*. With a hammer and chisel, knock out the center of the plug, then the pieces between the holes. Do not let the pieces fall down the drain. Replace the plug after you have serviced the drain.

UNBLOCKING THE MAIN DRAIN

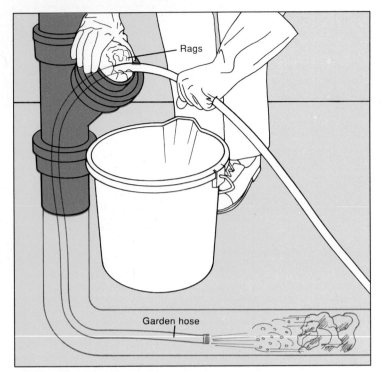

1 **Using a hose to break up small blockages.** Insert a garden hose as far as possible into the cleanout, or until you hit the blockage. Pack large, wet rags around the hose to create a seal. Hold the rags and hose firmly with both hands *(above)*, while a helper turns on the water full pressure. (Do not use water elsewhere in the house while doing this.) If the blockage seems to have been cleared, test the drain *(step 4)*. If not, add an expansion nozzle to the hose *(step 2)* or use an auger *(step 3)*.

2 **Using an expansion nozzle.** Choose a nozzle made to fit a 3- to 6-inch drainpipe, available at a plumbing supply or hardware store, and screw it to the end of the hose *(inset)*. Push the hose as far as possible into the drain and turn on the water. The nozzle will expand to seal the pipe *(above)*, forcing the water to blast the line clear if the blockage is not too large. If the blockage seems to have been cleared, turn off the water, detach the hose from the faucet, and wait a few minutes for the nozzle to deflate before removing it.

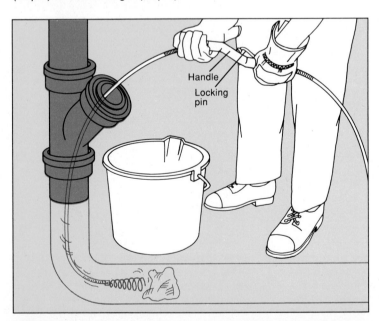

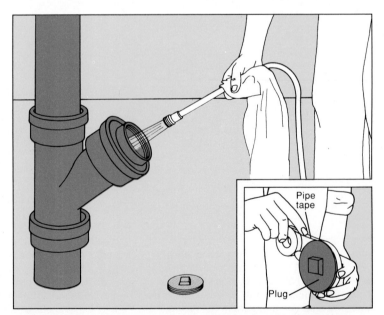

3 **Using a manual auger.** Use a drain auger 1/4 inch in diameter and 25 to 100 feet long. Uncoil it on the floor, allowing enough room to push and pull. Feed the auger as far as possible into the drain, lock the handle in place, then wind it clockwise to break up the blockage *(above)*. When the auger moves freely, test the drain *(step 4)*. If the blockage remains intact or out of reach, rent a power auger *(page 79)*.

4 **Testing the drain.** Test a cleanout located near the floor by sending water through it with a hose *(above)*. If the cleanout is near the ceiling, replace the plug, then turn on a faucet upstairs. When the water runs freely through the drain, rub petroleum jelly or wind pipe tape on the threads of the plug *(inset)* and reinstall it.

UNBLOCKING THE MAIN DRAIN WITH A POWER AUGER

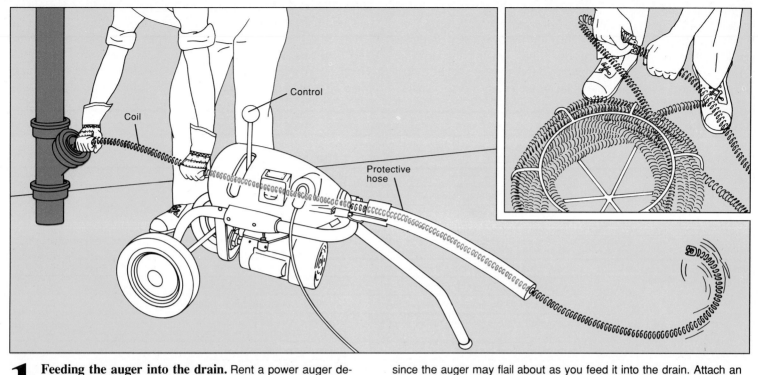

1 **Feeding the auger into the drain.** Rent a power auger designed for a 3- or 4-inch drain, with a single length of coil rolled on a drum and several cutting heads. Power augers are heavy-duty tools that must be used with great care to protect pipes; follow the manufacturer's directions carefully. (Some augers have automatic feed, for example.) Wear work gloves, heavy boots and eye protection,

since the auger may flail about as you feed it into the drain. Attach an all-purpose head, which breaks up loose blockages such as grease, fabric, hair and sand, to a length of coil. With the motor off, feed the coil into the drain by hand *(above)*. If the first length of coil does not reach the blockage, clip a second length of coil to the end of the first *(inset)* and continue feeding it down the drain.

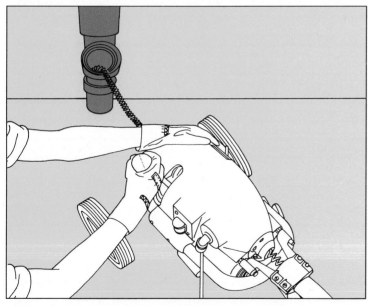

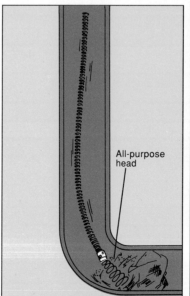

2 **Activating the auger.** Depending on the model, turn the control to the drive position *(above)* or press the foot pedal to activate the auger. Keep hands and feet clear of all moving parts. As its cutting head turns, the auger will begin to break up the blockage. If it jams, pull the auger out a few inches, then advance it again. When the auger spins freely, turn the control to the idle position, feed a few more inches of coil into the drain, then activate the auger again. Repeat this procedure until the blockage is cleared, then turn off the auger and pull out the coils by hand. If the blockage remains, switch to a heavier-duty head *(next step)*.

3 **Changing the cutting head.** When the all-purpose cutting head *(above, left)* fails to break up the blockage, or you suspect that tree roots are the cause, replace the head with a root-cutting head *(above, right)*. The spinning blades will scrape the sides of the pipe to remove tree roots, rust and mineral deposits. **Caution**: Do not turn on the auger until it reaches the blockage. When the drain is clear, turn off the auger before removing it. Do not use sharp or saw-tooth heads for plastic drainpipe.

GAS WATER HEATERS

A gas-fired water heater typically heats about 60 gallons of water to 140°F each day. When a hot water faucet is turned on, hot water flows from the tank through the hot water outlet as cold water enters through the dip tube. Sensing the drop in temperature, the thermostat opens a valve that sends gas to the burner, where it is ignited by the pilot or an electric spark.

Heated air is vented from the burner chamber through the flue and its heat-retaining baffle and out the draft hood and vent.

The number of gallons that can be heated from 50°F to 150°F in one hour is known as a heater's recovery capacity. This figure, and the capacity of the tank, is stamped on a metal plate affixed to most heaters. The common complaint of insuf-

TROUBLESHOOTING GUIDE

SYMPTOM	POSSIBLE CAUSE	PROCEDURE
No hot water	Pilot light out	Relight pilot (p. 82) □○
	Pilot light does not stay lit	Replace thermocouple (p. 83) ▭○
	Repeated pilot outages	Check for floor drafts, check and clean flue and vent (p. 84) ▭●
	Temperature control turned off	Reset temperature control (p. 82) □○
	Temperature control faulty	Call for service
Not enough hot water or water not hot enough	Heavy household demand for hot water	Stagger use of hot water or have a larger water heater installed
	Temperature control set too low	Raise temperature control setting (p. 82) □○
	Poor burner flame slows recovery time	Check and clean flue and vent (p. 84) ▭●
	Sediment in tank slows heater recovery time	Drain and refill tank (p. 85) □◑ If rate of sedimentation is high, have a water softener installed
	Hot water faucet leaks	Repair faucet (p. 36)
	Loss of heat	Insulate tank and hot water pipes (p. 85) □○
	Incoming water too cold	Raise temperature control setting (p. 82) □○
	Dip tube broken	Call for service
Water too hot	Temperature control set too high or frequent short draws of hot water cause buildup of very hot water in top of tank	Lower temperature control setting (p. 82) □○
	Temperature control faulty	Call for service
Relief valve leaks continuously	Relief valve faulty	Test and replace valve (p. 86) ▭◑. If pressure reducing valve in system, call for service
Relief valve leaks and hot water has not been used	Excessive pressure in supply water	Lower temperature control dial setting (p. 82) □○ Have pressure reducing valve installed
Relief valve drips after heavy use of hot water	Water at top of tank too hot	Stagger hot water use or lower temperature (p. 82) □○ Test and replace valve (p. 86) ▭◑
Drain valve leaks	Valve loose or faulty	Tighten valve handle; replace washer or valve (p. 87) ▭◑
Cold water supply valve leaks	Valve faulty	Replace valve (p. 417) ▭◑
Water pipes leak	Pipes broken or corroded	Have pipes replaced
Hot water rusty	Water heater tank corroded	Drain and refill tank (p. 85) ▭◑ Check and replace anode rod (p. 83) ▭◑ Lower temperature control dial setting (p. 82) □○ Have water heater replaced
	Galvanized steel water pipes corroded	Have pipes replaced
Hot water smells bad	Magnesium anode rod reacting with sulfurous hot water	Replace with aluminum anode rod (p. 83) ▭◑ Have water heater replaced
Water heater rumbling	Sediment in tank traps pockets of very hot water	Drain and refill tank regularly (p. 85) □◑ Have water softener installed if sedimentation rate is high
Water heater sizzles	Water leaks into burner chamber	Have water heater replaced
Water heater noisy	Burner pops when heater turned on or off	Have gas company check burner and gas pressure
	Noisy combustion from burner flame	Eliminate any strong floor drafts. If problem persists, have gas company check burner and gas pressure
Hot water or tank sooty	Improper ventilation	Check and clean flue and vent (p. 84) ▭◑ If problem persists, have burner and gas pressure checked

DEGREE OF DIFFICULTY: □ Easy ▭ Moderate ■ Complex
ESTIMATED TIME: ○ Less than 1 hour ◑ 1 to 3 hours ● Over 3 hours

ficient hot water is often caused by heavy demand on a too-small heater, rather than mechanical failure.

A few routine maintenance chores will increase the heater's efficiency. Vacuum under and around the heater to keep dust from clogging the pilot and the burner. (Be careful not to snuff the pilot, however.) Drain the tank periodically to check for sediment. Once a year, disassemble and clean the vent and draft hood, and test the heater's relief valve.

Before working on a gas water heater, be sure to close the gas shutoff valve: turn the handle perpendicular to the pipe *(page 26)*. For repairs to the control unit, pilot, burner and gas supply lines, call for professional service.

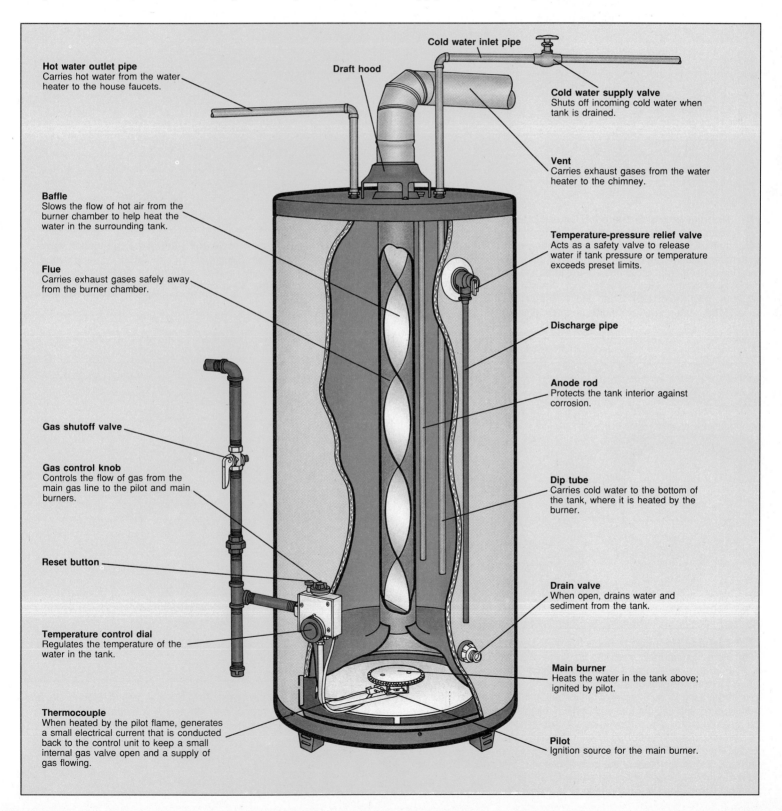

Cold water inlet pipe

Hot water outlet pipe
Carries hot water from the water heater to the house faucets.

Draft hood

Cold water supply valve
Shuts off incoming cold water when tank is drained.

Vent
Carries exhaust gases from the water heater to the chimney.

Baffle
Slows the flow of hot air from the burner chamber to help heat the water in the surrounding tank.

Temperature-pressure relief valve
Acts as a safety valve to release water if tank pressure or temperature exceeds preset limits.

Flue
Carries exhaust gases safely away from the burner chamber.

Discharge pipe

Anode rod
Protects the tank interior against corrosion.

Gas shutoff valve

Gas control knob
Controls the flow of gas from the main gas line to the pilot and main burners.

Dip tube
Carries cold water to the bottom of the tank, where it is heated by the burner.

Reset button

Drain valve
When open, drains water and sediment from the tank.

Temperature control dial
Regulates the temperature of the water in the tank.

Main burner
Heats the water in the tank above; ignited by pilot.

Thermocouple
When heated by the pilot flame, generates a small electrical current that is conducted back to the control unit to keep a small internal gas valve open and a supply of gas flowing.

Pilot
Ignition source for the main burner.

LIGHTING A GAS WATER HEATER

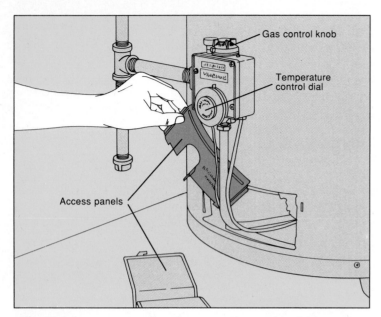

1 **Gaining access to the pilot.** Carefully remove the burner access panels by lifting them off the heater *(above)* or sliding them sideways. To light a pilot that has blown out (there will be no flame visible in front of the burner), turn the temperature control dial to its lowest setting and the gas control knob to OFF. **Caution:** Wait at least five minutes for the gas to clear. Then, if there is no gas odor, relight the pilot *(next step)*. If gas odor lingers, close the gas shutoff valve to the heater, ventilate the room and call the gas company.

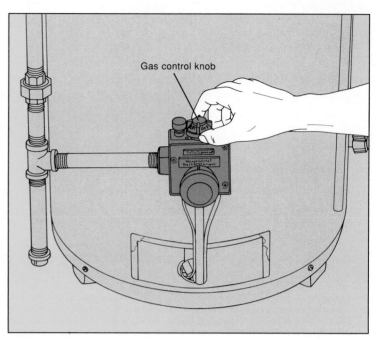

2 **Checking the gas flow to the pilot.** If the gas shutoff valve is already open, turn the gas control knob to PILOT *(above)*. But if the gas shutoff valve was closed, open it and wait about five minutes for the gas to reach the control unit before turning the control knob to PILOT.

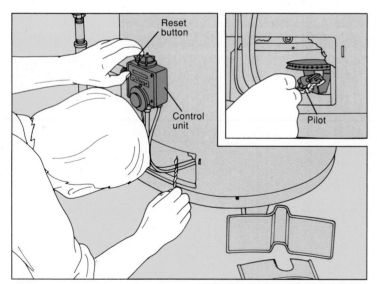

3 **Lighting the pilot.** Depress the reset button *(above)* while placing a lighted match near the tip of the pilot *(inset)*. If the pilot is hard to reach, make a taper from a tightly rolled piece of paper. When there is no reset button, hold down the gas control knob while lighting the pilot. Should the pilot fail to light immediately, close the gas shutoff valve and call the gas company. If it lights, continue to depress the reset button or gas control knob for one minute, then release it and set the temperature control *(step 4)*. If the pilot goes out, turn the gas control knob to OFF. Try tightening the hexagonal nut connecting the thermocouple to the base of the control unit, first by hand, then by giving it a quarter-turn with an open-end wrench. Relight the pilot. If it goes out again, service the thermocouple *(page 83)*.

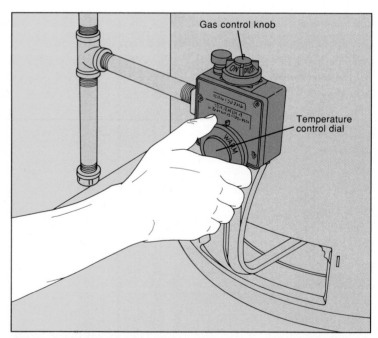

4 **Setting the temperature.** Turn the gas control knob to ON and the temperature control dial between 120°F and 130°F (or just above WARM), as shown. A moderate setting lowers heating costs, prolongs tank life, and reduces the risk of scalding. Replace the access panels.

REPLACING THE THERMOCOUPLE

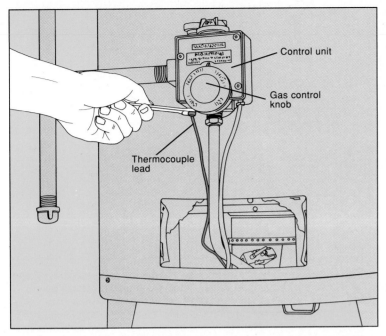

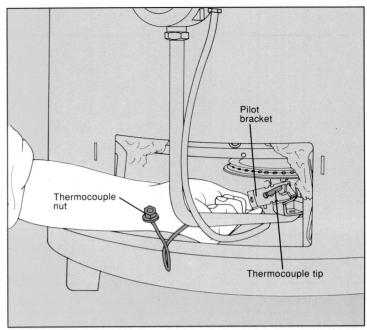

Disconnecting the thermocouple. Turn the gas control knob to OFF and close the gas shutoff valve. With an open-end wrench, loosen the nut that secures the thermocouple to the control unit *(above, left)*, then unscrew it by hand. Pull down on the copper lead to detach the end of the thermocouple from the control unit. There may be a second nut attaching the thermocouple tip to the pilot bracket; unscrew it and slide it back along the copper lead. Grip the base of the thermocouple *(above, right)* and pull firmly, sliding it out of the pilot bracket.

Buy an exact replacement for the old thermocouple at a plumbing or heating supplier. Push the tip of the new thermocouple into the pilot bracket clip as far as it will go. If there is a hexagonal nut at its tip, screw it to the bracket. Run the lead out and bend it up into a gentle curve. Screw the nut on the end of the thermocouple to the control unit by hand, then give it a quarter-turn with an open-end wrench. Relight the pilot *(page 82)*. If it does not stay lit, close the gas shutoff valve and call for service.

REPLACING THE ANODE ROD

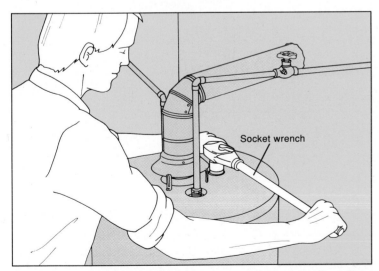

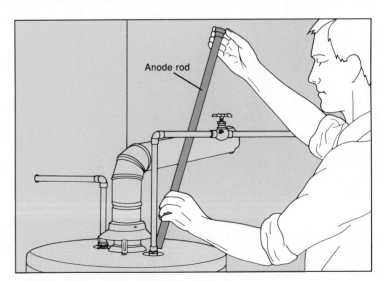

1 **Removing the anode plug.** Before removing the old anode rod, buy an exact replacement from the manufacturer or a heating supply company. Close the cold water supply valve and turn the gas control knob to OFF. Since the hexagonal plug that secures the anode may be rusted tight to the tank, borrow or rent a socket wrench with a 24-inch handle for better leverage. Drain two to three gallons of water from the tank *(page 85)*. Fit the socket over the anode plug and apply strong, even pressure to turn the ratchet counterclockwise *(above)*, while someone else braces the tank if necessary.

2 **Replacing the anode rod.** Raise the anode rod as far as possible with the socket wrench, then unscrew the last few inches by hand. Lift the rod straight up and out of the tank *(above)*. Apply only a single width of pipe tape to the threaded upper end of the new rod. Insert the rod into the tank, screw it in as far as possible by hand, then tighten it clockwise with the socket wrench. Open the cold water supply valve and relight the pilot *(page 82)*.

SERVICING THE FLUE AND VENT

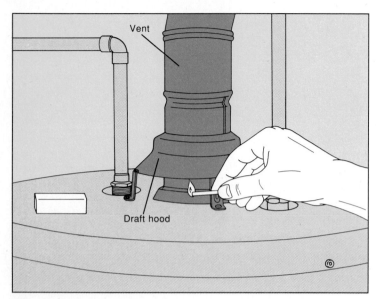

1 Testing the vent. Wait until the burner has been on for 5 to 10 minutes, then hold a lighted match under the draft hood *(above)*. If the vent is working properly, the match flame will be drawn in under the edge of the hood. If the flame is blown away from the draft hood or snuffed out, there may be a blockage within the vent. Clean the vent once a year *(step 2)* to ensure proper ventilation and prevent the backup of dangerous carbon monoxide fumes.

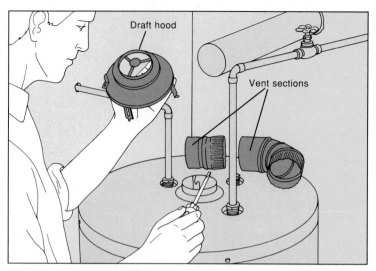

2 Disassembling the vent. Turn the gas control knob to OFF and close the gas shutoff valve. Remove the burner access panels *(page 82)* and cover the burner and floor with newspapers to catch soot and debris. Remove any sheet metal screws at joints, mark the vent sections for reassembly and tie up any overhead runs of ductwork with a cord or wire to prevent them from falling while you remove the vertical sections below. Finally, unscrew and remove the draft hood from the top of the tank *(above)*. Shake the hood and vent sections over the newspapers to release dirt, then scrub the insides with a wire brush. Replace any ductwork that is rusted or perforated.

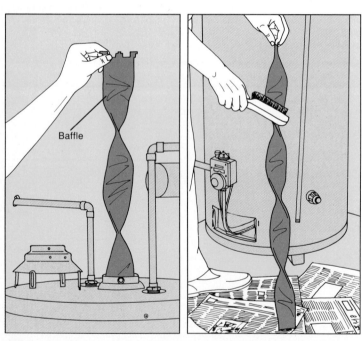

3 Cleaning the baffle. With the vent removed, you now have access to the heater flue and its removable baffle. Lift the baffle from the flue *(above, left)* and scrub it with a wire brush *(above, right)* to remove dust and soot. If there is not enough room to pull the baffle all the way out, lift it as high as possible, clean it, then rattle it to dislodge debris.

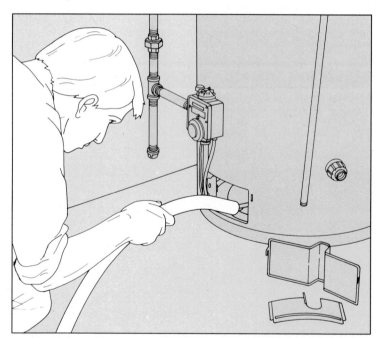

4 Cleaning the combustion chamber. Vacuum the inside of the combustion chamber *(above)*, then clean the burner and its ports with a soft brush. Use an old toothbrush to clean around the pilot. Replace the baffle, draft hood and vent, then vacuum the combustion chamber again. Relight the pilot *(page 82)*, and test the vent with a lighted match as in step 1. If the flame is not drawn up the vent, turn the gas control knob to OFF, close the gas shutoff valve, then recheck the pilot, burner and vent. Turn on the gas, relight the pilot and test again. If the test fails, there may be a blockage in the main chimney—call for service.

INSULATING THE WATER HEATER

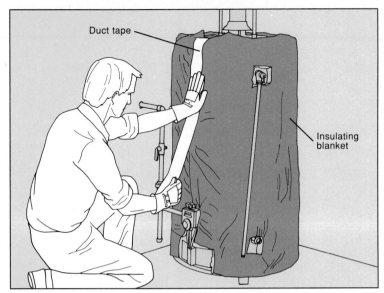

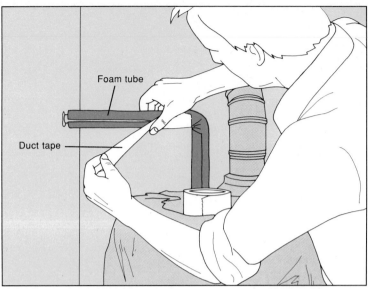

Insulating the tank and pipes. Energy-saving foam or fiberglass blankets are available for various sizes of water heaters. For a gas heater, first turn the gas control knob to OFF and close the gas shutoff valve. On an electric heater, shut off power at the main service panel *(page 102)*. With waterproof duct tape, fasten the insulating blanket to the top of the tank—but not over the top—then tape the edges of the blanket together to form a neat, vertical seam *(above, left)*.

Use a utility knife to cut away all insulation from around the access panels, relief valve, drain valve, control panel and the space between the tank and the floor. Turn the gas or electricity back on and restart the heater. To prevent heat loss, you can also insulate runs of hot water pipe that pass through unheated areas with adhesive-backed foam, fiberglass tape or pre-slit foam tubes secured with duct tape *(above, right)*. For this, it is not necessary to turn off the gas or electricity first.

DRAINING AND FILLING THE TANK

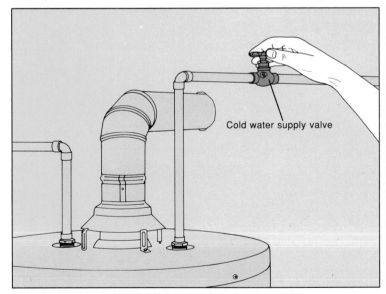

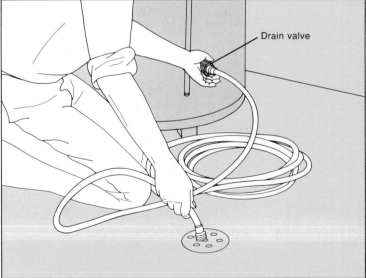

Draining the water heater. Turn the gas control knob to OFF and close the gas shutoff valve. For an electric water heater, shut off power at the main service panel. Close the cold water supply valve *(above, left)* and open a hot water faucet in the house to speed draining. Attach a hose to the drain valve and run it to a nearby floor drain *(above, right)* or into a bucket beneath the drain valve. Turn the drain valve clockwise to open it. As the tank empties, the valve may clog with sediment; open the cold water supply valve for a few minutes to allow the water pressure to clear the blockage. If you are using a

bucket, watch carefully and turn the drain valve off before the bucket overflows; the process may take up to an hour. To refill the tank, close the drain valve tightly, open the cold water supply valve and open the hot water faucet farthest from the tank. When water flows from that faucet, the tank is full; close the faucet. Be sure the heater is full before turning on the gas or electricity, then relight the pilot *(page 82)* or turn the power back on. Two or three gallons can be drawn off in this manner every few months to check for sediment.

SERVICING THE TEMPERATURE-PRESSURE RELIEF VALVE

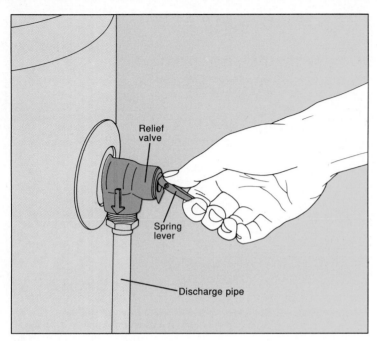

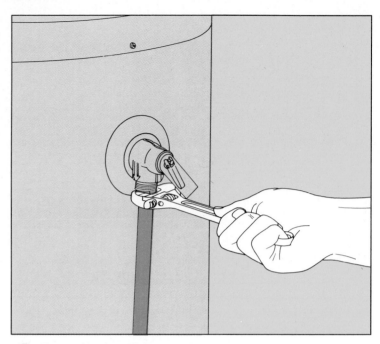

1 **Testing the relief valve.** In the unlikely event that the temperature or water pressure rises too high inside the water heater, the relief valve opens to prevent the tank from exploding. To test the valve, simply lift the spring lever *(above)*, keeping clear of the outlet or discharge pipe as hot water escapes. One-half to one cup of water should spurt out. Lift the lever several times to clear the valve of sediment. If no water spurts out, or if water continues to drip after the valve is released, it should be replaced. If there is a discharge pipe, remove it first *(step 2)*; if not, go to step 3.

2 **Removing the discharge pipe.** Turn the gas control knob to OFF and close the gas shutoff valve. For an electric water heater, shut off power at the main service panel *(page 102)*. Close the cold water supply valve. If the relief valve is located on top of the water heater, drain one gallon of water from the tank *(page 85)*; drain four to five gallons if the valve is on the side of the tank. Loosen and remove the discharge pipe, which may be threaded directly to the relief valve or to an adapter *(above)*.

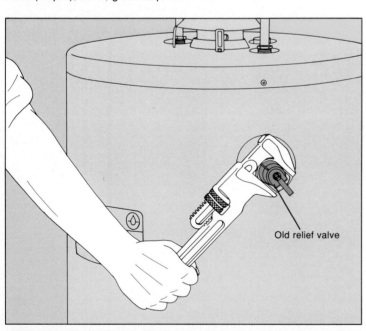

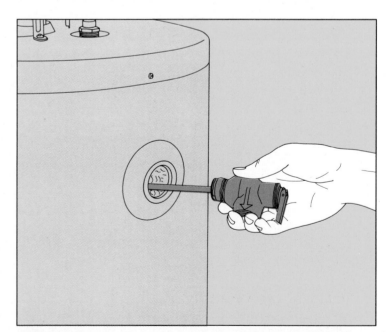

3 **Removing the old relief valve.** Fit a pipe wrench over the old relief valve and turn counterclockwise to unscrew the valve from the tank *(above)*. If the tank is old, the valve may be difficult to remove. Use firm, steady pressure (have a helper brace the tank if necessary), but do not jerk the valve—you might damage the tank. When the valve is loose, unscrew it by hand and pull it out.

4 **Installing a new relief valve.** Take the old valve with you to buy an exact replacement. (The model type and size often appear on a metal tag hanging from the old valve.) Apply pipe tape to the threads of the new relief valve and screw it into the tank by hand, then tighten with a pipe wrench. Screw the discharge pipe (if any) back into the valve outlet. Refill the water heater and relight the pilot *(page 82)* or turn the electricity back on. If the valve continues to leak, have a plumber check the house water pressure.

SERVICING THE DRAIN VALVE

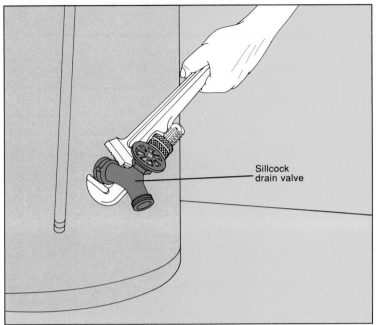

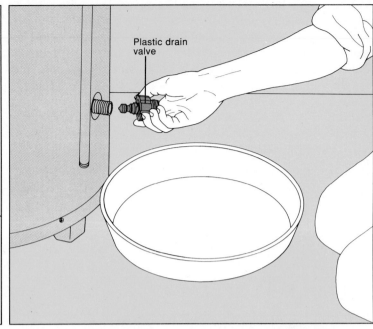

Plastic drain valve

Sillcock drain valve

1 **Repairing a leaking drain valve.** Turn the gas control knob to OFF and close the gas shutoff valve. For an electric water heater, shut off power at the main service panel. Close the cold water supply valve and drain the heater completely *(page 85)*. If the drain valve has a removable handle, unscrew it and replace the washer behind it. Reassemble the handle, refill the tank and check the valve for leaks. If the handle cannot be removed, or the drain valve is made of plastic, replace the entire valve. Fit a pipe wrench over the

base of the drain valve and turn it counterclockwise to unscrew the valve from the tank *(above, left)*, then go to step 2. If the valve is plastic, first turn the handle counterclockwise by hand, four complete revolutions. Then, while pulling firmly on the handle, turn the valve handle clockwise six complete turns to free it from the tank *(above, right)*. Replace it with an identical valve by pushing down on the handle and turning counterclockwise six times, then clockwise four times. You can also replace a plastic valve with a sillcock valve *(step 2)*.

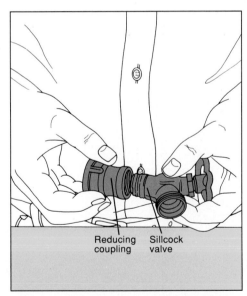

Reducing coupling Sillcock valve

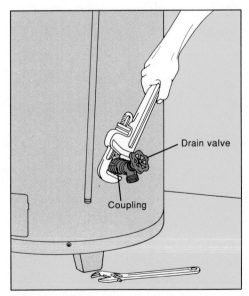

Drain valve

Coupling

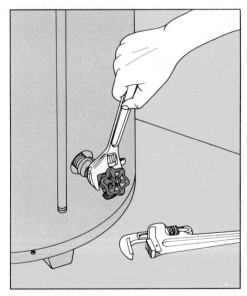

2 **Assembling the new drain valve.** Because it is both durable and contains a washer (and can therefore be serviced), a sillcock valve is the recommended replacement. When selecting the valve, also buy a 3/4-to-1/2-inch reducing coupling to match the valve to the tank. Wrap pipe tape around the threaded end of the sillcock valve and screw it into the 1/2-inch end of the reducing coupling *(above)*.

3 **Installing the new valve.** Apply pipe tape to the threaded end of the nipple on the water heater tank. Screw the coupling and valve onto the nipple and tighten as far as possible by hand. Finish tightening the coupling with a pipe wrench *(above)*.

4 **Aligning the valve.** Fit an adjustable wrench over the body of the sillcock valve (but not over its outlet), and turn it clockwise to tighten the valve so that it faces down toward the floor *(above)*. Refill the tank and relight the pilot *(page 82)* or turn the electricity back on.

ELECTRIC WATER HEATERS

Electric water heaters usually have an upper and a lower heating element, each controlled by its own thermostat. The upper element has, in addition, a high-limit temperature cutoff to keep hot water from reaching the boiling point. Basic maintenance and repair—testing the relief valve, replacing the anode—are the same as for a gas water heater. The Trouble-shooting Guide on page 89 will refer you to that section *(page 80)*. To test the electrical components, use a multitester as directed in Tools & Techniques *(page 417)*.

First, adjust the multitester to zero. Set the selector switch to RX1, then touch the probes together. Using the ohms-adjust dial, align the needle exactly over 0. A reading of 0 ohms

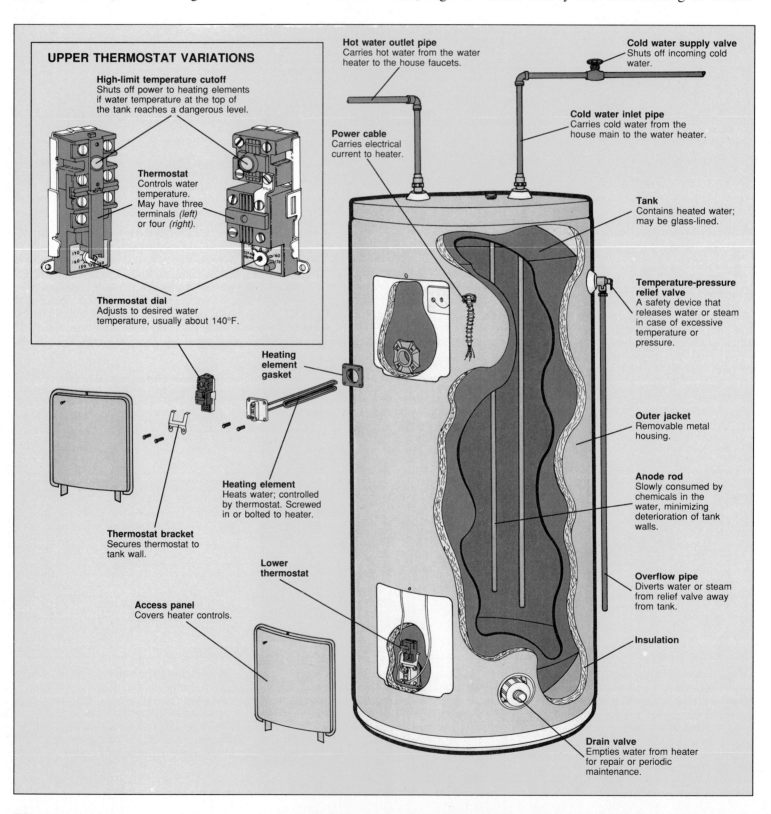

UPPER THERMOSTAT VARIATIONS

High-limit temperature cutoff
Shuts off power to heating elements if water temperature at the top of the tank reaches a dangerous level.

Thermostat
Controls water temperature. May have three terminals *(left)* or four *(right)*.

Thermostat dial
Adjusts to desired water temperature, usually about 140°F.

Hot water outlet pipe
Carries hot water from the water heater to the house faucets.

Cold water supply valve
Shuts off incoming cold water.

Power cable
Carries electrical current to heater.

Cold water inlet pipe
Carries cold water from the house main to the water heater.

Tank
Contains heated water; may be glass-lined.

Temperature-pressure relief valve
A safety device that releases water or steam in case of excessive temperature or pressure.

Heating element gasket

Outer jacket
Removable metal housing.

Heating element
Heats water; controlled by thermostat. Screwed in or bolted to heater.

Anode rod
Slowly consumed by chemicals in the water, minimizing deterioration of tank walls.

Thermostat bracket
Secures thermostat to tank wall.

Lower thermostat

Overflow pipe
Diverts water or steam from relief valve away from tank.

Access panel
Covers heater controls.

Insulation

Drain valve
Empties water from heater for repair or periodic maintenance.

indicates continuity, or a completed circuit, while a reading of infinity indicates resistance, a total lack of current flow. The heating elements must have partial resistance; the needle should move to the middle range of the scale. To test for voltage, set the multitester at 250 volts AC, and read the results on the AC scale.

Observe strict safety precautions when working on an electric heater. Wear rubber-soled shoes, and make sure the floor around the heater is dry. Do not skip steps in doublechecking that power to the heater is indeed turned off. Post a sign on the disconnect switch box or service panel to stop someone from turning on the power while you work.

TROUBLESHOOTING GUIDE

SYMPTOM	POSSIBLE CAUSE	PROCEDURE
No hot water	Heater disconnect switch off	Turn switch on
	Fuse blown or circuit breaker tripped	Replace fuse or reset breaker (p. 102) □○
	High-limit temperature cutoff faulty	Test temperature cutoff (p. 91) ◪●▲
	Thermostat faulty	Test thermostats (p. 92) ◪●▲
	Element faulty	Test element (p. 93) ◪●▲
Not enough hot water or water not hot enough	Heavy household demand for hot water or cold incoming water slows recovery time	Stagger use of hot water or install a larger water heater
	Washing machine mixing valve or shower combination valve faulty	Check for hot water in the toilet tank refill tube; call for service
	Thermostat control set too low	Raise thermostat control setting to 140°F (p. 92) □○
	High-limit temperature cutoff faulty	Test temperature cutoff (p. 91) ◪●▲
	Thermostat faulty	Test lower thermostat (p. 92) ◪●▲
	Sediment in tank slows heater recovery time	Drain and refill tank (p. 85) □●
	Heating element faulty	Test heating element (p. 93) ◪●▲
	Loss of heat	Insulate tank and hot water pipes (p. 85) □○
Water too hot	Thermostat control set too high	Lower thermostat control setting to 140°F (p. 92) □○
	Thermostat improperly mounted	Reposition lower thermostat (p. 92) ◪●▲
	High-limit temperature cutoff faulty	Test cutoff (p. 91) ◪●▲
	Thermostat faulty	Test thermostat (p. 92) ◪●▲
	Heating element faulty	Test heating element (p. 93) ◪●▲
Fuse blows or breaker trips repeatedly	Wire in heater loose or broken	Check heater wiring (p. 92) □○
	House wiring faulty	Call an electrician
Temperature-pressure relief valve leaks continuously	Relief valve unseated	Pop spring lever to reseat valve (p. 86) □○
	Relief valve faulty	Replace valve (p. 86) ◪●
	Thermostat faulty	Test thermostat (p. 92) ◪●▲
Drain valve leaks	Valve loose or faulty	Tighten valve handle; replace washer or valve (p. 87) ◪●
Heater wet or dripping	Tank leaks	Have water heater replaced
Insulation wet	Leak around element	Tighten loose element; change gasket (p. 93) ◪●▲
Hot water discolored	Sediment in tank	Drain and refill tank (p. 85) □●
	Anode rod deteriorated	Replace anode rod (p. 83) ◪●
	Tank interior corroded	Have water heater replaced
Hot water smells bad	Magnesium anode rod reacting with sulfurous hot water	Replace with aluminum anode rod (p. 83) ◪● Have water heater replaced
Water heater noisy	Sediment in tank	Drain and refill tank (p. 85) □●
	Temperature-pressure relief valve faulty	Test valve (p. 86) ◪●
	Mineral scale on element	Clean or replace element (p. 93) ◪●▲

DEGREE OF DIFFICULTY: □ Easy ◪ Moderate ■ Complex
ESTIMATED TIME: ○ Less than 1 hour ● 1 to 3 hours ● Over 3 hours   ▲ Multitester required

CHECKING THE VOLTAGE

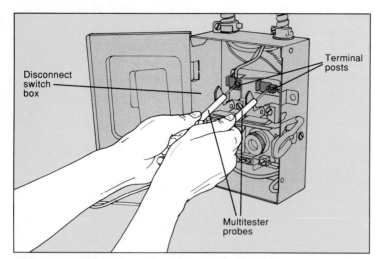

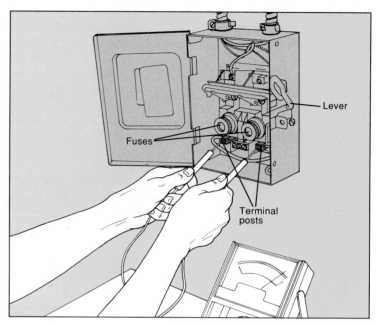

1 **Checking the voltage at the disconnect switch box.** If your water heater does not have its own switch box, check the main service panel for a blown fuse or tripped circuit breaker. (A 240-volt heater may have two fuses or breakers.) Replace or reset them, if necessary. If the heater still does not work, shut off the house's main power switch at the service panel, and label it so that no one will turn it on. Then access the controls *(step 1, below)*. If the water heater has a disconnect switch box, turn it off and replace any blown fuses. Then use a multitester set at 250 volts AC to verify incoming power to the switch box. **Caution:** Do not touch the switch box. Hold the tester probes by the insulated handles only and touch one probe to each of the upper terminals, as shown. The tester should read between 200 and 250 volts. Next touch one probe to the left terminal and the other to the grounding screw on the back of the box. The tester should read about 120 volts. Test the right terminal the same way. If all results are what they should be, go to step 2. If not, call an electrician.

2 **Testing the lower terminals.** With the power on, test the two lower terminals as you tested the upper terminals in step 1; the results should be the same. If all the readings in both steps are what they should be, enough power is getting to the heater. If not, call an electrician. Before working on any part of the heater, test that the power is off: Shift the lever arm of the disconnect switch box to the OFF position and test the lower terminals as you tested the upper terminals in step 1. This time the tester should show zero volts in all cases. If the tester shows that the disconnect switch box conducts any power at all while in the OFF position, do not work on the switch box or the water heater; call an electrician.

ACCESS TO THE CONTROLS

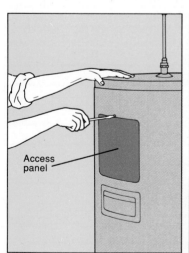

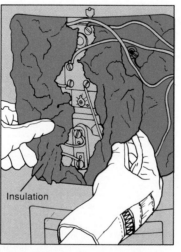

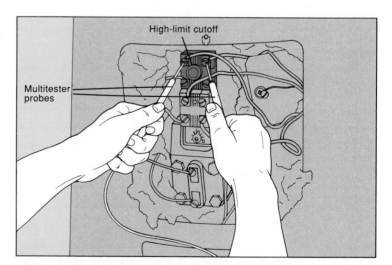

1 **Accessing the controls.** Shut off power to the heater at the main service panel or at the disconnect switch box, and test that it is off *(step 2, above)*. To reach the heater controls, unscrew and remove the upper and lower access panels *(above, left)*. Wearing gloves, turn aside insulation that is pre-slit *(above, right)*, or cut the insulation away with a serrated knife, being careful not to damage the controls behind it. Save any insulation you remove. You now have access to the high-limit cutoff, thermostats and heating elements.

2 **Verifying power shutoff at the heater.** With the power off, set a multitester at 250 volts AC and touch a probe to each of the upper terminals of the high-limit cutoff, as shown. Then touch one probe to the exposed interior tank wall and the other to each terminal, in turn. The tester should show zero volts each time. If the power is off and the readings are not zero, do not work on the heater; call an electrician. Tighten any loose mounting bracket bolts and any loose electrical connections at the upper and lower controls.

TESTING THE HIGH-LIMIT TEMPERATURE CUTOFF

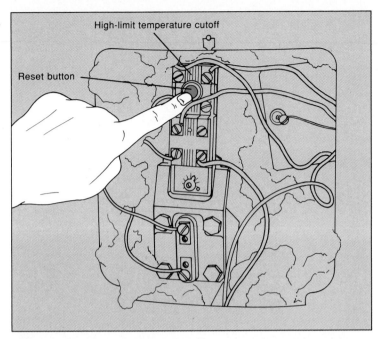

1 Checking the reset button. Disconnect power to the heater at the main service panel or switch box and verify that it is off, then remove the upper access panel and use a multitester to verify that power is off *(page 90)*. If the high-limit cutoff's reset button has popped out, push it in, as shown, and listen for a click. Turn on the power and wait three hours. If the interior tank wall feels warm near the bottom, turn off the power, replace the insulation and access panels and turn the power back on. If not, test the high-limit cutoff.

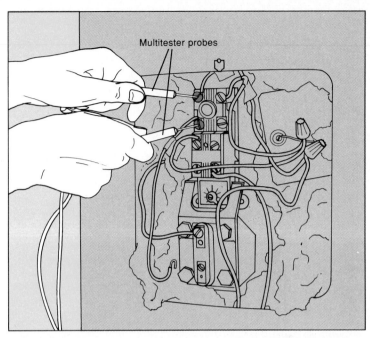

2 Testing the cutoff for continuity. With the power off, label the position of one of the element wires with masking tape, and disconnect it by removing its terminal screw. With a multitester set at RX1, touch a probe to each of the cutoff's two left terminals, as shown, and then to the two right terminals. The tester needle should sweep to zero each time, indicating continuity. If the cutoff shows continuity, test the thermostat *(page 92)*; if not, replace the cutoff *(step 3)*.

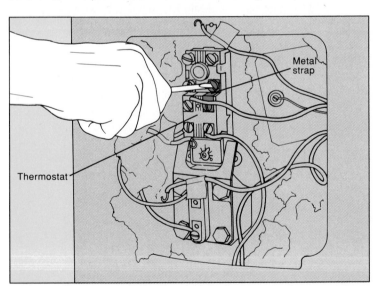

3 Removing the cutoff. With the power still off, tag the wires to each of the cutoff terminals with masking tape to identify their positions for reassembly. To disconnect the cutoff's wires, loosen the terminal screws and gently unhook the wires. Remove the screws that hold the metal strap connecting the cutoff to the thermostat; the strap may be at the front *(above)* or the side. Take off the strap. Pull the cutoff up to release it from the spring clips that hold it to the heater, or pry it free with a screwdriver.

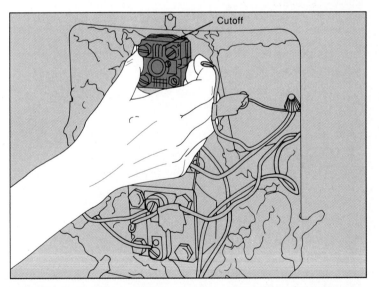

4 Replacing the cutoff. Buy a new cutoff of the same make and model from a heating or plumbing supplier. Before installing it, depress the reset button and test it for continuity *(step 2)*. Snap the new cutoff into place *(above)*. Reconnect the wires and metal strap in their proper positions, then turn on the power and wait three hours. If the interior tank feels warm near the lower element, the heater is working properly. Turn off the power, repack the insulation, install the access panels and turn the power on. If the tank does not become warm, test the thermostats *(page 92)* and elements *(page 93)*.

TESTING THE THERMOSTATS

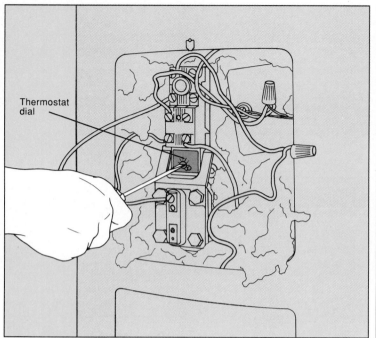

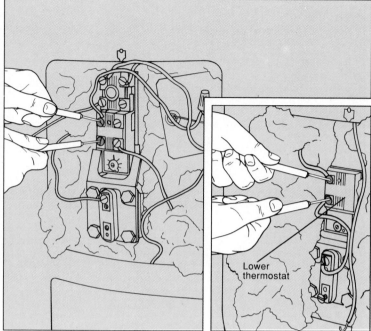

1 **Testing the thermostats.** Turn off power to the water heater at the disconnect switch box or the main service panel and test that it is off, then access the upper and lower controls *(page 90)*. Turn the thermostat dial counterclockwise to its lowest temperature setting *(above, left)* and listen for a click. If you hear no click, turn the dial clockwise to its highest point, run a hot water tap until the water runs lukewarm, and move the dial to its lowest setting; you should now hear a click. Label and disconnect the wire to the upper element. With a multitester set at RX1, touch a probe to each of the left terminals *(above, right)*. The tester needle should remain at infinity. Then touch a probe to each of the two right terminals on a four-screw thermostat, or to the upper left and upper right terminals on a three-screw model. The tester needle should swing to zero. Adjust the thermostat to its highest setting; you should hear a click. Repeat the two tests; this time the results should be reversed. To test the lower thermostat *(inset)*, first adjust the upper thermostat to its lowest setting. Then turn the lower dial to its lowest setting; the tester needle should remain at infinity. Finally, turn the dial to the highest setting; the needle should swing to zero. If any of your results differ, replace the thermostat *(step 2)*. If the thermostats test OK, test the elements *(page 93)*.

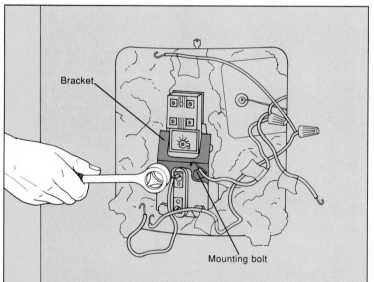

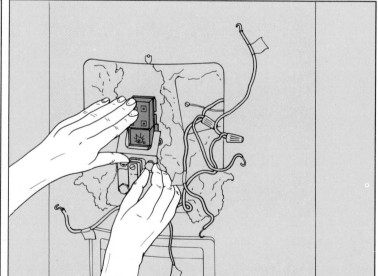

2 **Replacing the thermostat.** With the power still off, remove the cutoff *(page 91)*, and label and disconnect the wires to the thermostat. Using a socket wrench, loosen the two bolts on the thermostat mounting bracket *(above, left)*. Slip the thermostat up and out of the bracket. Buy a new thermostat of the same make and model at a heating or plumbing supplier, and test it for continuity *(step 1)*. Insert the new thermostat behind the bracket *(above, right)* and tighten the bolts, making sure the back of the thermostat fits flush with the heater wall. Adjust the thermostat to the medium setting, or 140°F. If the heater has two thermostats, adjust both to the same setting. Reinstall the cutoff *(page 91)*, reconnect all the wires and turn on the power. Wait three hours and if the exposed tank wall feels warm near the lower element, the heater is working properly. Turn off the power, repack the insulation uniformly, replace the access panels and turn the power back on. If the tank is not warm, test the heating elements *(page 93)*.

TESTING THE HEATING ELEMENTS

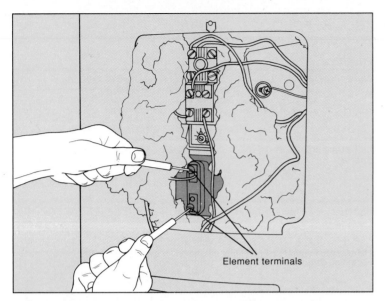

Element terminals

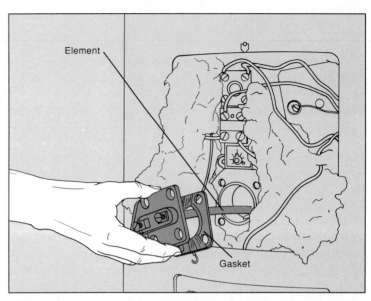

Element

Gasket

1 Testing the element. Turn off power to the water heater, and test that it is off *(page 90)*. To test the upper or lower element, disconnect one of its wires. Using a multitester set at RX1000, touch one probe to an element mounting bolt or the thermostat bracket, and the other to each element terminal screw in turn. If the tester needle moves at all, the element is grounded and should be replaced *(step 2)*. To test whether the element works, set the multi-tester at RX1 and touch a probe to each of the two terminal screws *(above)*. The tester should indicate resistance in the medium range of the ohms scale; if not, replace it *(step 2)*.

2 Removing the element. Drain the heater *(page 85)*. Disconnect the remaining element wire and label the position of each wire with masking tape. If the element is held by mounting bolts, use a socket wrench to remove them. Carefully lift off the thermostat brack-et—the thermostat will hang by its wires. If you do not see mounting bolts, the element itself is screwed in; use a socket wrench to unscrew it. To remove either type of element, pull it straight out *(above)*, gently working it loose if the shape has become distorted. Clean mineral scale from a working element by soaking it in vinegar for several hours, then use an old knife to chip off the scale.

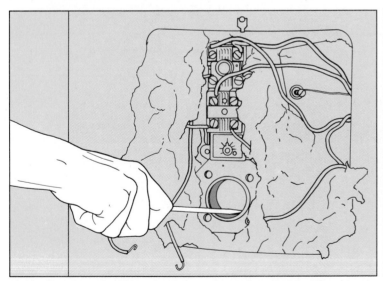

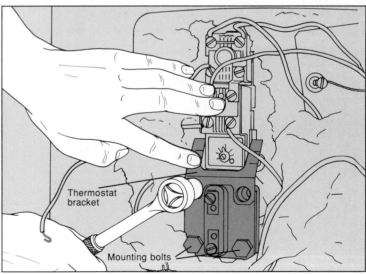

Thermostat bracket

Mounting bolts

3 Replacing the element. Test a new element *(step 1, above)* before you install it. Whether replacing an element or reinstalling a cleaned one, buy a new gasket. Using an old screwdriver, scrape scale and rust from the inside surface of the element fitting *(above, left)* so the gasket can form a tight seal. Remove the old gasket and thread the new gasket onto the element, then ease the element into the heater. If the element was bolted in place, install the two lower mounting bolts, then reposition the thermostat and thermostat bracket *(above, right)* and tighten the two upper bolts. If the element is a screw-in type, install it using a socket wrench. Install a lower element the same way, and reconnect all the wires. Refill the heater *(page 85)*, turn it on and wait three hours; if the exposed tank wall feels warm near the lower element, the heater is working properly. Turn off the power, repack the insulation uni-formly, replace the access panels and turn the power back on.

WATER SOFTENERS

Hard water combines with soap to leave a dull film on fixtures, tubs and sinks. Mineral buildup can also block pipes and corrode water heaters, washing machines and faucets. A water softener effectively reduces hardness by exchanging magnesium and calcium ions, which react with soap, for sodium ions, which do not react.

Although its various cycles may seem complex, the water softener is a simple plumbing fixture to maintain. On an automatic softener, check the brine line and injector for blockages every six months, and clean or replace the injector screen. If a softener is installed in a warm place, such as near a furnace, condensation may form in the brine tank. This results in compacted salt—known as salt bridging—which blocks the flow of salt water from the brine tank to the resin tank. Break up or remove a salt bridge when this occurs. Iron, if heavily concentrated in supply water, breaks down the resin beads, which may then block hoses or valves. If your water contains up to 3 parts per million (ppm) of iron, add a bag of resin cleaner to the resin tank; install an iron filter on the supply pipe if the water contains more than 3 ppm of iron.

TROUBLESHOOTING GUIDE

PROBLEM	PROCEDURE
Water remains hard	Check and refill salt in brine tank
	Set timer to regenerate more often
	Have water checked for iron content and install iron filter if necessary
Salt compacts to form a bridge	Poke salt bridge with broom handle to loosen salt pellets. If salt is hard, disconnect softener, empty tank, and lift out the salt bridge. Replenish with fresh salt
Softener not drawing brine	Flush brine line (p. 95) □○
	Clean or replace injector and filter screen (p. 95) □○
Softener doesn't work at all	Remove control unit and take to dealer to service motor and timer (p. 95) ■●

DEGREE OF DIFFICULTY: □Easy ▬Moderate ■Complex
ESTIMATED TIME: ○Less than 1 hour ●1 to 3 hours

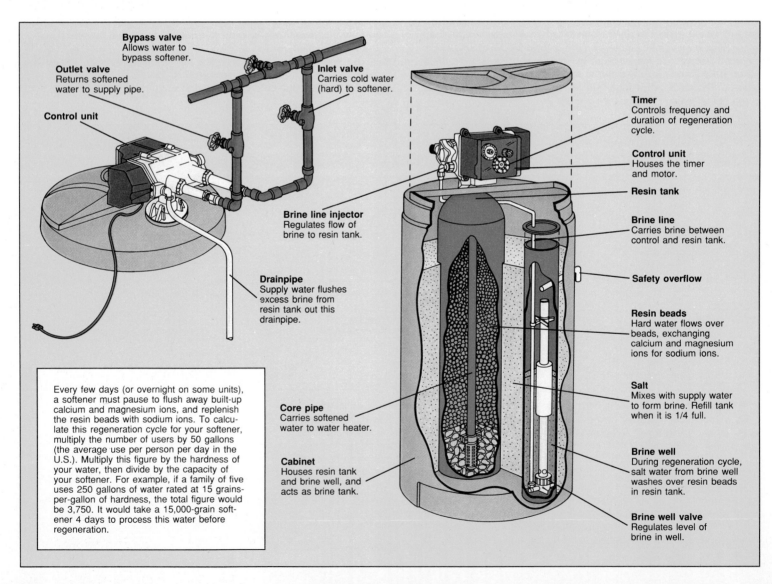

Bypass valve
Allows water to bypass softener.

Outlet valve
Returns softened water to supply pipe.

Inlet valve
Carries cold water (hard) to softener.

Control unit

Timer
Controls frequency and duration of regeneration cycle.

Control unit
Houses the timer and motor.

Resin tank

Brine line injector
Regulates flow of brine to resin tank.

Brine line
Carries brine between control and resin tank.

Safety overflow

Drainpipe
Supply water flushes excess brine from resin tank out this drainpipe.

Resin beads
Hard water flows over beads, exchanging calcium and magnesium ions for sodium ions.

Salt
Mixes with supply water to form brine. Refill tank when it is 1/4 full.

Every few days (or overnight on some units), a softener must pause to flush away built-up calcium and magnesium ions, and replenish the resin beads with sodium ions. To calculate this regeneration cycle for your softener, multiply the number of users by 50 gallons (the average use per person per day in the U.S.). Multiply this figure by the hardness of your water, then divide by the capacity of your softener. For example, if a family of five uses 250 gallons of water rated at 15 grains-per-gallon of hardness, the total figure would be 3,750. It would take a 15,000-grain softener 4 days to process this water before regeneration.

Core pipe
Carries softened water to water heater.

Cabinet
Houses resin tank and brine well, and acts as brine tank.

Brine well
During regeneration cycle, salt water from brine well washes over resin beads in resin tank.

Brine well valve
Regulates level of brine in well.

SERVICING THE BRINE LINE AND INJECTOR

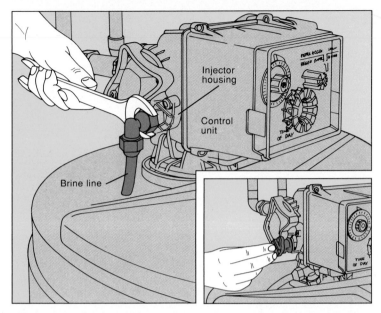

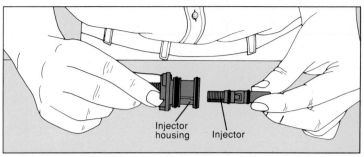

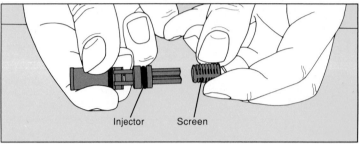

1 **Inspecting the brine line.** Unplug the softener. Close the main shutoff valve and open the nearest hot water faucet to lower the water level in the softener below the inlet valve. With a wrench, loosen the nut connecting the brine line to the injector housing *(above)* and gently pull the brine line free. If there is an obstruction in the line, use an oven baster to flush it out with warm water. Next, unscrew the injector housing from the control unit by hand *(inset)*.

2 **Cleaning the injector.** Gently pull the injector from its housing *(above, top)*, then remove the small filter screen from the injector *(above, bottom)*. Clean a clogged screen in warm, soapy water; replace a broken one. Next, remove any obstruction in the injector by blowing gently. (Do not use a sharp object to remove a blockage.) Replace the screen, then fit the injector back in its housing. Screw the injector housing to the control unit and reattach the brine line. Turn the water back on and plug in the softener.

SERVICING THE CONTROL UNIT

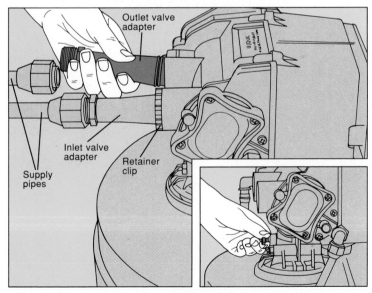

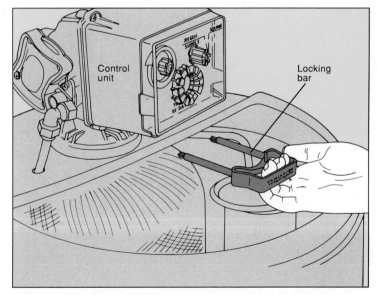

1 **Disconnecting the control unit.** Unplug the softener. Close the main shutoff valve and open the nearest hot water faucet to lower the water level in the softener below the inlet valve. Unscrew the fittings joining the supply pipes to the inlet and outlet valve adapters, then pry off the retainer clips that secure the adapters to the control unit *(above)*. Push the pipes back to provide enough space to remove the control unit. Next, unscrew the nuts securing the locking bar rods beneath the inlet and outlet valves *(inset)*, then remove the brine line from the injector housing *(step 1, above)*.

2 **Replacing the control unit.** Lift off the cabinet lid and pull out the locking bar from beneath the control unit *(above)*. Grasp the control unit firmly and pull it up and off the cabinet. Take the unit to the dealer to repair a faulty timer or motor. To reinstall the unit, reposition it on top of the cabinet, insert the locking bar rod and replace the nuts. Push the inlet and outlet valve adapters back into the control unit and reattach their retainer clips. Push the pipes back in place and screw the fittings onto the adapters. Reconnect the brine line, turn on the water and plug in the softener.

LIGHTING & ELECTRICITY

ELECTRICITY IN THE HOME

The first time you lift off a switch cover plate or disassemble a table lamp, you may be overwhelmed by the tangle of wires ("This looks much too complicated!"). Or you may be daunted by the notion that electrical repair is dangerous ("Electricity can kill, can't it?"). But one of the best things about electricity is that it follows a relentless logic. If you have a basic understanding of your home's wiring, work methodically and take reasonable precautions, you can tackle any repair in this book with confidence.

Electrical current flows in a continuous path, or circuit, from a power source through various switches, fixtures and appliances, and then back to the source. In a household electrical system, the source is the main service panel and the path is your home's wiring. Electricity always takes the path of least resistance. Copper and aluminum are good conductors of electricity and are therefore used to carry current; plastic, rubber, glass and porcelain are non-conductive and are used as insulators for electrical equipment.

The power company delivers electricity to your home via three, or in some cases four, large overhead or underground wires that arrive at the service entrance. From there, electricity passes through a meter into the main service panel, where it is divided into branch circuits and distributed throughout the house. Two of the service wires are hot and carry 120 volts each, providing power to operate 120-volt and 240-volt appliances.

To prevent damage to the wiring and guard against fire and shock, each circuit is protected by a fuse or circuit breaker. If there is an overload in the circuit, this device will instantly stop the flow of current. The main service panel is also equipped with a fuse or circuit breaker that will turn off all incoming current at the panel.

Normally, branch-circuit cables that carry 120-volt current contain a black wire, a white wire and a bare copper grounding wire. From the service panel, the black (hot) wire delivers 120 volts of current "under pressure" to light a bulb or run an appliance. The white wire carries the electrons back to the service panel at close to zero volts. In an analogy to home plumbing, the black wire is equivalent to the supply pipe and the white wire serves as the drainpipe.

The bare copper grounding wire (or insulated green wire) in each circuit safeguards the system by providing a second path for electricity to return to the service panel. A main grounding wire, or service-grounding wire, runs from the service panel to a metal grounding rod that is buried in the earth.

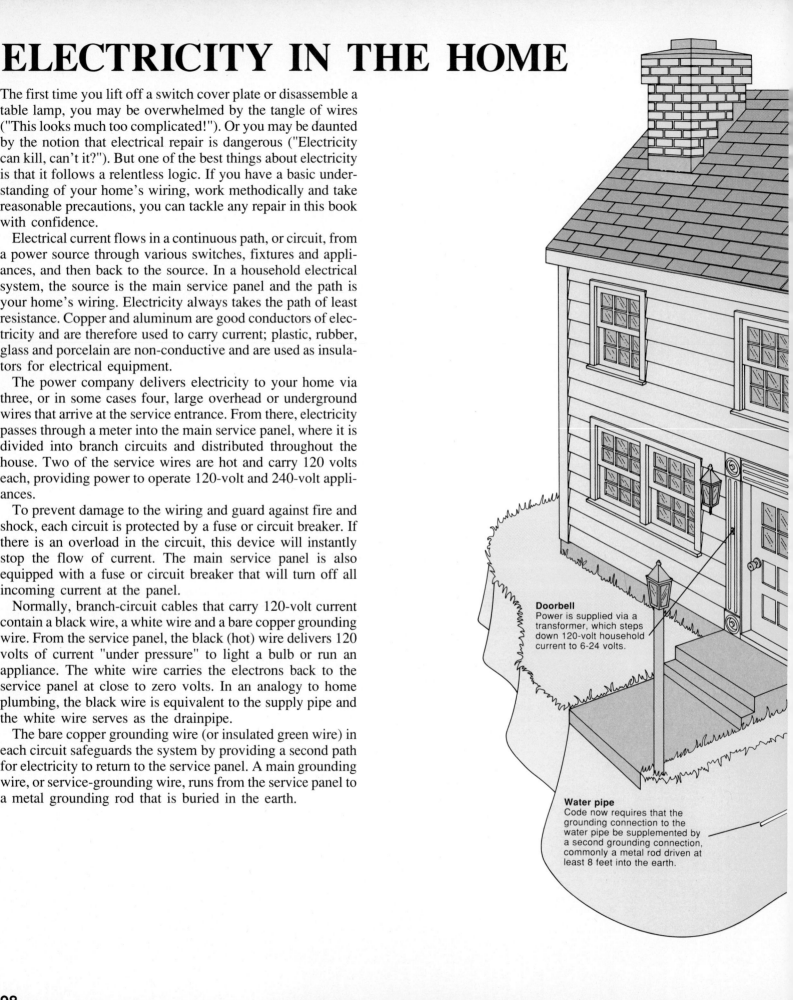

Doorbell
Power is supplied via a transformer, which steps down 120-volt household current to 6-24 volts.

Water pipe
Code now requires that the grounding connection to the water pipe be supplemented by a second grounding connection, commonly a metal rod driven at least 8 feet into the earth.

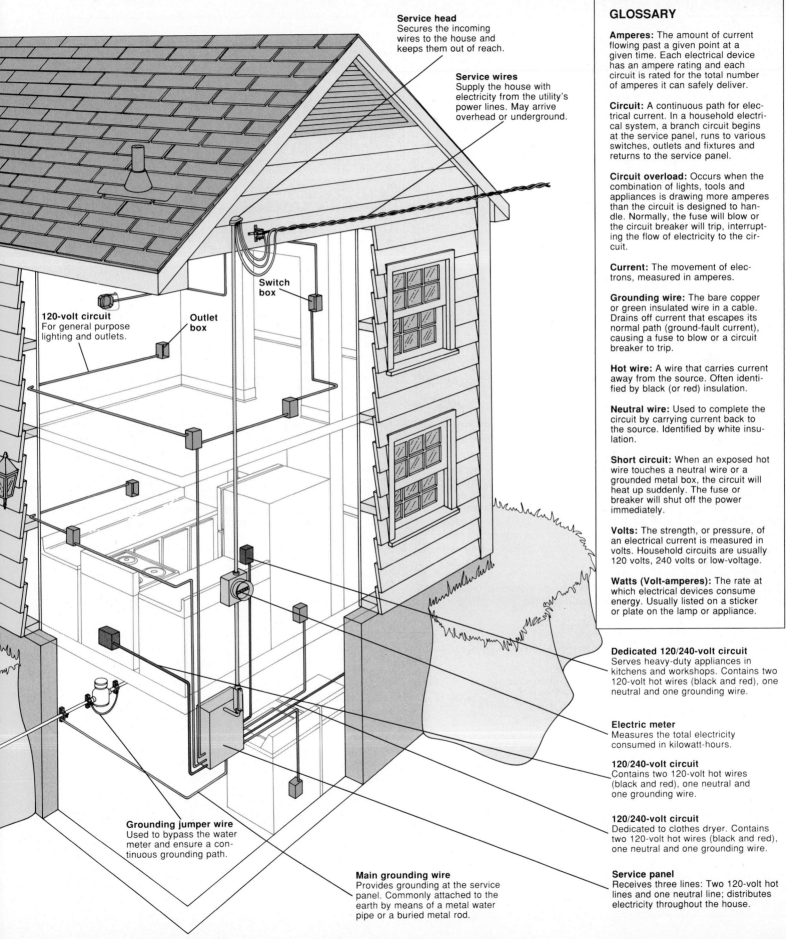

Service head
Secures the incoming wires to the house and keeps them out of reach.

Service wires
Supply the house with electricity from the utility's power lines. May arrive overhead or underground.

Switch box

120-volt circuit
For general purpose lighting and outlets.

Outlet box

Grounding jumper wire
Used to bypass the water meter and ensure a continuous grounding path.

Main grounding wire
Provides grounding at the service panel. Commonly attached to the earth by means of a metal water pipe or a buried metal rod.

GLOSSARY

Amperes: The amount of current flowing past a given point at a given time. Each electrical device has an ampere rating and each circuit is rated for the total number of amperes it can safely deliver.

Circuit: A continuous path for electrical current. In a household electrical system, a branch circuit begins at the service panel, runs to various switches, outlets and fixtures and returns to the service panel.

Circuit overload: Occurs when the combination of lights, tools and appliances is drawing more amperes than the circuit is designed to handle. Normally, the fuse will blow or the circuit breaker will trip, interrupting the flow of electricity to the circuit.

Current: The movement of electrons, measured in amperes.

Grounding wire: The bare copper or green insulated wire in a cable. Drains off current that escapes its normal path (ground-fault current), causing a fuse to blow or a circuit breaker to trip.

Hot wire: A wire that carries current away from the source. Often identified by black (or red) insulation.

Neutral wire: Used to complete the circuit by carrying current back to the source. Identified by white insulation.

Short circuit: When an exposed hot wire touches a neutral wire or a grounded metal box, the circuit will heat up suddenly. The fuse or breaker will shut off the power immediately.

Volts: The strength, or pressure, of an electrical current is measured in volts. Household circuits are usually 120 volts, 240 volts or low-voltage.

Watts (Volt-amperes): The rate at which electrical devices consume energy. Usually listed on a sticker or plate on the lamp or appliance.

Dedicated 120/240-volt circuit
Serves heavy-duty appliances in kitchens and workshops. Contains two 120-volt hot wires (black and red), one neutral and one grounding wire.

Electric meter
Measures the total electricity consumed in kilowatt-hours.

120/240-volt circuit
Contains two 120-volt hot wires (black and red), one neutral and one grounding wire.

120/240-volt circuit
Dedicated to clothes dryer. Contains two 120-volt hot wires (black and red), one neutral and one grounding wire.

Service panel
Receives three lines: Two 120-volt hot lines and one neutral line; distributes electricity throughout the house.

WORKING SAFELY WITH ELECTRICITY

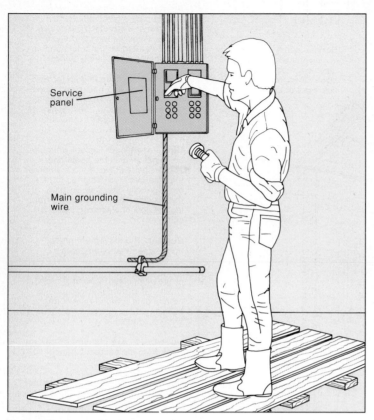

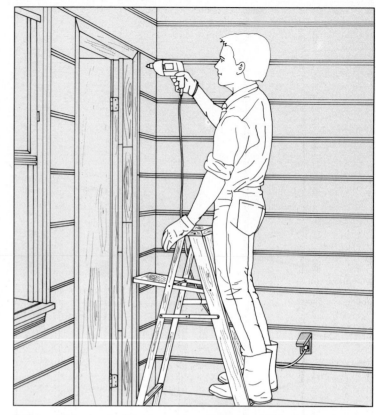

Safety at the service panel. When working at the service panel, even to change a fuse or reset a circuit breaker *(page 102)*, be sure to take basic safety precautions. Dry any water on the floor. To protect your body from making a circuit to the ground, stand on boards or wear dry rubber boots and heavy rubber gloves *(above)*. Work with one hand only, keeping the other in your pocket or behind your back to avoid touching anything metal. Have a flashlight at a convenient spot near the service panel so that you do not have to change a fuse in the dark. Do not touch a service panel that is sparking, blackened or rusted; call an electrician. Do not remove the panel cover to expose the service cables; even if you have turned off the main breaker or pulled the main fuse block, parts of the box remain charged with current.

Safety outdoors. Code now requires that new outdoor outlets be protected by a GFCI (ground-fault circuit interrupter). This safety device is especially important in damp locations, where electrical shocks can be severe. When working outdoors with a power tool, be sure that it is properly grounded. As an added safety precaution, stand on a wooden plank or rubber mat and use a wooden ladder and heavy rubber gloves *(above)*. Be careful not to touch overhead power lines when working on your roof or siding. Call the power company to locate any underground power lines before digging in the yard.

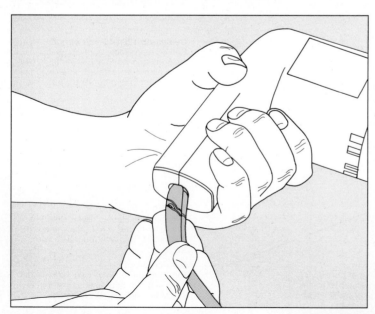

Safety and power tools. Inspect power tools regularly for signs of wear. Look for corroded, loose or bent plug prongs and examine the cord for cracked or frayed insulation *(left)*; some tools have a strain-relief sleeve to protect the cord from wear at the point where it is joined to the tool. To prevent electrical shock, power tools should have a three-prong plug or double insulation—a plastic housing that isolates metal parts from contact with the hand. Do not touch a faucet, water pipe or another grounded appliance while using a power tool. If a tool sparks, shocks or becomes hot to the touch, it must be repaired or replaced. Never carry a power tool by its cord. All pliers, screwdrivers and stripping tools used for electrical work should have insulated handles, or handles wrapped in electrical tape.

LIVING SAFELY WITH ELECTRICITY

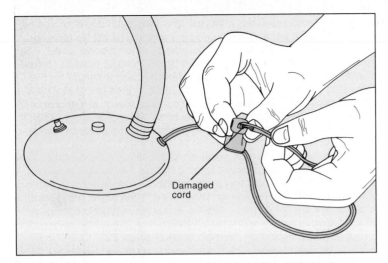

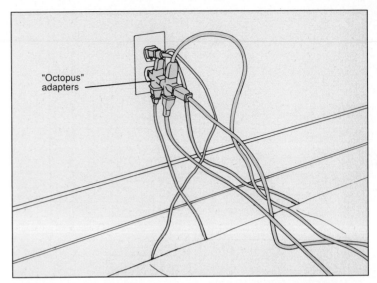

Cords and plugs. Inspect cords and plugs regularly and replace them if they appear damaged *(above)* or heat up when the appliance is in use. Cords tend to crack or fray at the plug and at the appliance. Any cracking or rubbing of the insulation will eventually expose bare wire and create a fire or shock hazard. Keep cords away from heat and water, which can damage the insulation, and do not run them under rugs, where they are subject to abrasion. Plugs with removable insulating discs are unsafe, especially if the disc is missing and the wire ends are exposed. When removing a plug from an outlet, pull on the plug, not the cord. Never break off the third prong on a grounded plug to adapt it to a two-slot outlet. Instead, replace the two-slot outlet with a three-slot, grounded outlet *(page 158)* or a GFCI outlet *(page 156)*.

Adapters and extension cords. Do not use "octopus" connections; plugging too many cords into one outlet could overload the circuit *(above)*. If a plug is loose or its prongs exposed, the poor connection could produce heat and sparking. Extension cords are not designed to take the place of permanent wiring; use them to bring power into an area only temporarily. Never attach extension cords with tacks or pins. Permanent use of extension cords and octopus adapters is an indication that your home's wiring is inadequate and should be updated.

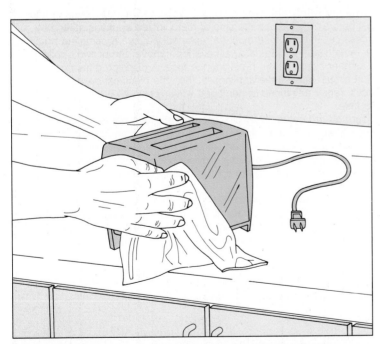

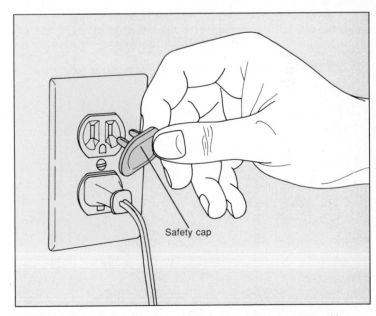

Water and electricity. Wet hands can create an alternate path for electrical current. Unplug a small appliance before cleaning it with a wet cloth *(above)*, then dry your hands—and the appliance—thoroughly before plugging it back in. Radios and hair dryers are particular hazards in bathrooms. Areas of the home where there is plumbing or dampness should be protected by a ground-fault circuit interrupter *(page 105)*, which will shut down the circuit if leakage is detected.

Children and electricity. Teach children to treat electricity with respect. Instruct them not to play with cords and wires and never to poke things into appliances or outlets. To protect curious fingers from a nasty shock, cover all unused outlets with plastic safety caps *(above)* that fit tightly in the slots.

THE MAIN SERVICE PANEL

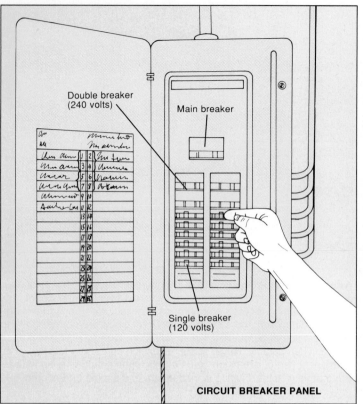

CIRCUIT BREAKER PANEL

Double breaker (240 volts)

Main breaker

Single breaker (120 volts)

Turning off and resetting a circuit breaker. Each circuit served by the circuit breaker panel is controlled by a switch that will flip off automatically if there is a short circuit or overload. When tripped, some breakers flip to the OFF position; others flip to a middle position *(below)*. To reset a breaker that is in the tripped position, wait a minute for the heater strip to cool, then push the toggle to OFF, then to ON *(left)*. If the breaker snaps off again immediately, disconnect one or two appliances, or inspect the electrical boxes along the circuit for a short *(page 417)*. If the problem is not a short circuit or an overload, have an electrician inspect the panel.

Before working on a switch, outlet, fixed appliance or light fixture, turn off the circuit that supplies power to it by flipping the breaker toggle to the full OFF position. Work only in dry conditions, use one hand, and do not touch any metal parts with the other hand. If the circuit breakers in the panel box are not correctly labeled, follow the instructions on page 106 to map your home's wiring. In an emergency, the entire system can be shut down by flipping off the main breaker *(page 22)*.

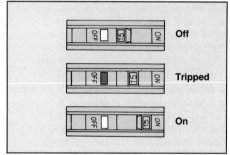

Off

Tripped

On

Removing and replacing a fuse. Fuse panels can be found in houses built before 1960. When the strip of metal inside a fuse is melted by excess current, the fuse must be replaced *(below)*. A complete break in the metal strip indicates a circuit overload; move one or two appliances to another circuit before replacing the fuse. A discolored fuse points to a short circuit. Inspect the appliances, then the electrical boxes along the circuit; repair any loose or damaged wires *(page 417)* before replacing the fuse.

Turn off or unplug the appliances on the circuit before removing a plug fuse. Grasp the fuse by its insulated rim only and unscrew it *(left)*; use one hand and do not touch any metal parts. Replace a blown fuse with one of the same ampere rating. Inspect the fuse panel every six months and check that the fuses are tight. A loose fuse can overheat and cause arcing at the panel.

Before working on a switch, outlet or fixture, remove the fuse that supplies power to that circuit *(left)*. The 240-volt outlets are controlled by cartridge fuses housed in fuse blocks or in a separate panel. Work only in dry conditions, use one hand, and do not touch any metal parts with the other hand. If the fuses in the panel box are not correctly labeled, follow the instructions on page 106 to identify the circuits. In an emergency, turn off power to all circuits by pulling the main fuse blocks *(page 22)*.

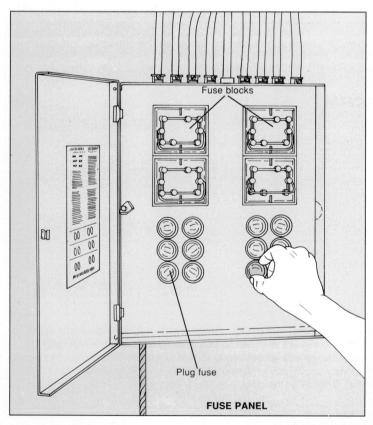

Fuse blocks

Plug fuse

FUSE PANEL

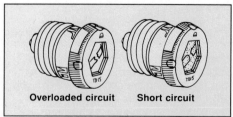

Overloaded circuit   Short circuit

PLUG AND CARTRIDGE FUSES

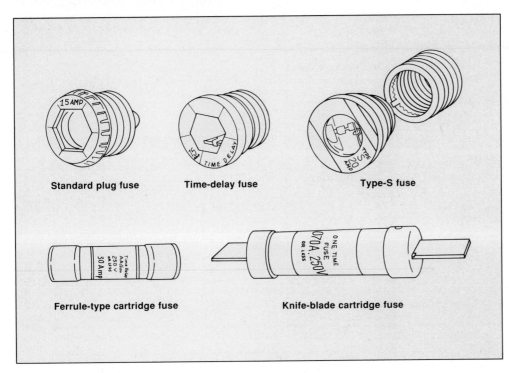

Standard plug fuse

Time-delay fuse

Type-S fuse

Ferrule-type cartridge fuse

Knife-blade cartridge fuse

Standard plug fuse. Plug fuses come in 15-, 20- and 30-ampere versions; their ampere rating must match the gauge of the wire in the circuit. Never replace a blown fuse with one of a higher ampere rating.

Time-delay fuse. The metal strip of a time-delay fuse will withstand the momentary power surge created when an appliance motor starts up, but will blow if there is a sustained overload or a short circuit.

Type-S fuse. This fuse is designed to fit into an adapter that screws into the panel. The adapter accepts only a Type-S fuse of matching ampere rating, guarding against accidental installation of a higher ampere fuse.

Ferrule-type cartridge fuse. Found in fuse blocks in the main, or in a separate panel, this fuse protects a separate circuit for a large appliance; available for 10 to 60 amperes.

Knife-blade cartridge fuse. This cartridge fuse—rated over 60 amperes—is used to protect the house electrical system.

TESTING AND REPLACING CARTRIDGE FUSES

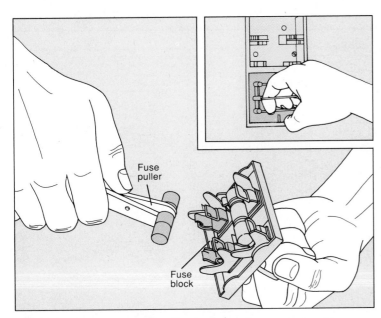

Fuse puller

Fuse block

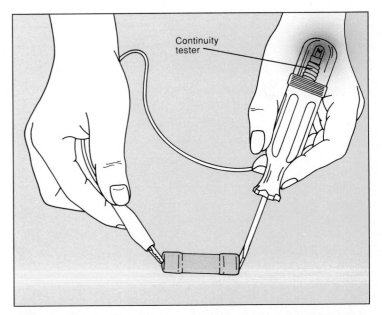

Continuity tester

1 **Removing a cartridge fuse.** If an appliance protected by a cartridge fuse fails to work, turn off or unplug the appliance and check the fuse. If the fuse is housed in a block in the main service panel, grasp the handle of the fuse block firmly with one hand and pull it out *(inset)*. Release the fuse from the spring clips with a fuse puller *(above)* or by hand. Do not touch the metal ends, which may be hot. If the cartridge fuse is housed in a separate panel box, use the plastic fuse puller to remove it. Work only in dry conditions, use one hand, and do not touch any metal parts.

2 **Testing the fuse.** Since a cartridge fuse shows no visible sign of damage, you will need a continuity tester to determine if it is blown. Touch the alligator clip to the metal cap at one end of the fuse and touch the tester probe to other end *(above)*. The tester will light if the fuse is good. If the tester doesn't light, replace the fuse with one of the same ampere rating. Push the new cartridge fuse against the spring clips until it snaps into place. If the new fuse blows when the appliance is turned on, there is probably a short circuit in the appliance.

GROUNDING FOR SAFETY

Grounding at the service panel. Grounding is a safety precaution built into every modern electrical system. At the service panel, the main grounding wire is connected to a metal water pipe or grounding rod that is buried in the earth, providing excess current with a direct path to the ground.

In the house wiring, a bare copper or green insulated grounding wire provides an alternate path for leaking current, protecting the circuit from damage and the user from shock. In the example at right, the hot wire supplying current to a lighting fixture has become disconnected from its socket terminal. This is called ground fault. Since the circuit cannot be completed via the neutral wire, the metal box would become electrified and dangerous. But the grounding wire picks up this leaking current and returns it to the service panel, where it trips the breaker or blows the fuse cutting off the fault current.

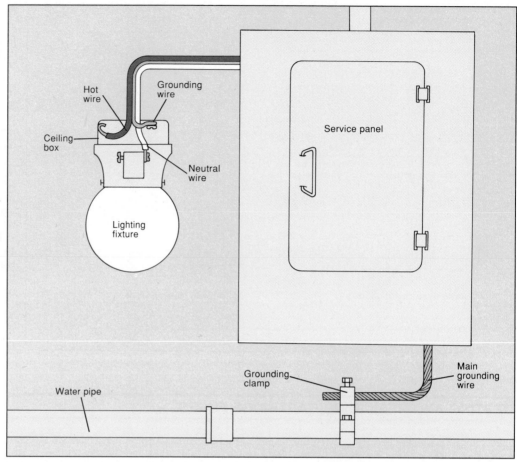

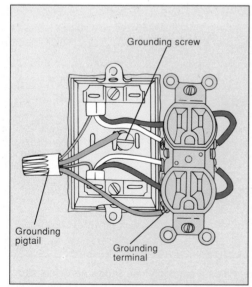
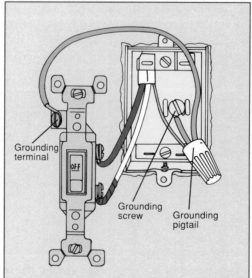
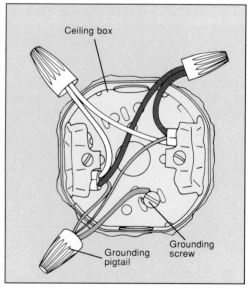

Grounding in outlet, switch and ceiling boxes. The bare copper grounding wire in the cable provides protection against ground-fault leakage at an electrical box. It is attached to the grounding screw at the back of a metal box and to the grounding terminal *(above)* on a switch or outlet, and grounds the box, the mounting strap, the device or fixture and all three-prong appliances that are plugged into a grounded outlet. When there is more than one cable in the electrical box, grounding is accomplished using jumper wires in a pigtail connection *(page 417)*. In Canada, more than one grounding wire may be attached to the grounding screw at the back of the box.

GROUND-FAULT CIRCUIT INTERRUPTERS

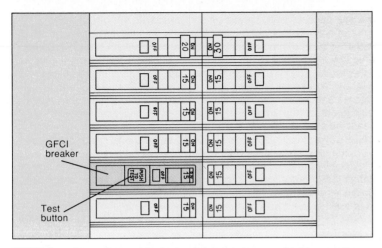

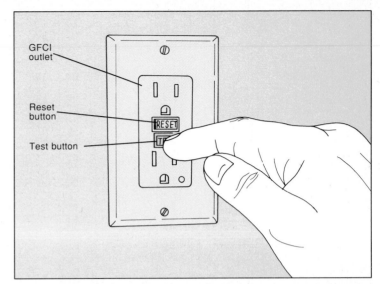

GFCI breakers. Ground-fault circuit interrupters are highly sensitive breakers that measure the current entering and leaving a device along the circuit. If the difference is greater than .007 amperes, the breaker instantly interrupts the flow of current, shutting down the circuit before anyone can be seriously hurt. A GFCI breaker *(above)* replaces a regular breaker in a service panel. It comes in 15- to 30-ampere versions and is available for both 120- and 240-volt circuits. The GFCI should be checked regularly by pressing the TEST button. If the breaker is good, it will trip; to reset it, flip the toggle back to the ON position.

GFCI outlets. If it is installed at the first outlet box in the circuit, most GFCI outlets *(above)* will protect all outlets along the circuit. The National Electrical Code now requires that new outlets within 6 feet of the kitchen sink and in bathrooms, garages, basements and outdoors must be GFCI-protected. Also available is a portable, plug-in GFCI that fits into any three-slot outlet *(page 159)*. To test a GFCI outlet, push the TEST button; the RESET button will pop out. Reactivate the GFCI by pressing the RESET button. To service a GFCI outlet, see page 156.

POLARIZATION IN LAMPS AND FIXTURES

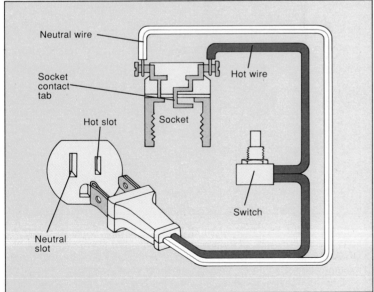

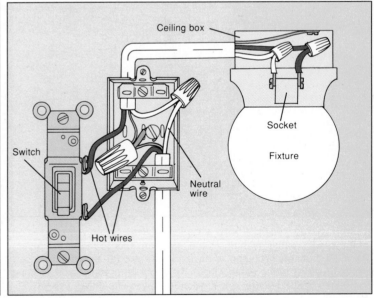

Stopping current at the switch. In a properly wired lamp or lighting fixture, the switch interrupts the hot wire that carries current forward, ensuring that no electricity flows to the lamp or fixture when the switch is turned off. If polarity is reversed, an exposed socket can give a shock even though the switch is off. Polarization in a lamp *(above, left)* begins at the wall outlet. The narrow slot of the outlet is hot; when a polarized lamp cord is plugged into the outlet, power enters the plug through the narrow prong and is transmitted through the hot, unmarked wire, through the switch, to the brass socket terminal. In a lighting fixture *(above, right)*, current flows from the hot wire at the wall switch to the brass terminal of the fixture socket.

MAPPING YOUR HOME'S WIRING

Tracing each circuit. Labels on service panels are often incorrect or out-of-date. Before performing any work on your home's electrical system, it is important to locate and correctly label the branch circuits served by the service panel. Begin by sketching a map of each floor of the house. Then walk around each floor, sketching in the outlets, switches, fixtures and major appliances in each room. Next, turn off all switches and appliances. At the service panel, post a new label, which you can obtain from the power company or an electrical supplier. Clearly number each fuse or circuit breaker in the service panel, then turn off power to circuit Number 1, using one hand to remove the fuse or trip the circuit breaker *(page 102)*.

To identify the devices on the circuit, find the switches, outlets and fixtures that are no longer receiving power. Flip on switches and small appliances and plug a reliable lamp into the upper and lower receptacle of each outlet; those that do not work are controlled by circuit Number 1. (Note that a circuit can serve more than one room or floor.) On your map, write the circuit number beside each switch, outlet or fixture served by the first circuit, then return to the service panel and turn on the power to that circuit. Turn off power to the second circuit and repeat the procedure until you have mapped all the circuits *(inset)*. Include 240-volt circuits that serve major appliances and are controlled by double breakers or fuse blocks. Use the information recorded on the floor plans to label the various breakers or fuses *(left)*. Leave unused breakers turned off and unused fuse sockets empty, and label them.

INSPECTING THE CIRCUITS

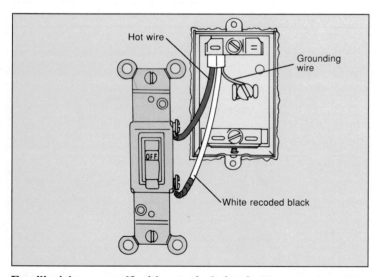

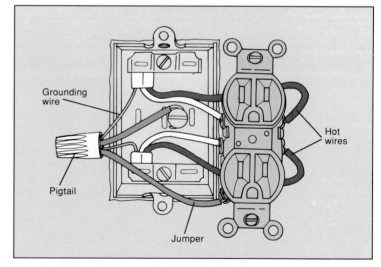

Familiarizing yourself with a typical circuit. Begin your inspection at the service panel. With one hand, open the door to reveal the fuses or circuit breakers. You should have 15-, 20- and 30-ampere fuses or circuit breakers in the panel. Check the condition of the cables entering the panel. If you discover any cracked or frayed sheathing, call for a professional inspection of your house wiring. Note that the wiring behind the panel cover is live and dangerous, to be serviced only by an electrician.

Turn off power to one circuit by removing the fuse or tripping the circuit breaker *(page 102)*. Examine each switch and outlet cover on the circuit. Check for warm or discolored cover plates, indicating poor connections at the device. Next, look inside two typical boxes, following the instructions for Switches *(page 140)* and Outlets *(page 148)* to free each device from its box and confirm that the power is off. Examine the

condition of the switch or outlet and look for dirty or loose wire connections at the terminals. (If the switch and outlet are stamped AL/CU or CO/ALR and the bare wire ends appear white, you probably have aluminum wiring. Call an electrician to inspect your system.)

Note the number of cables entering the box. One cable *(above, left)* means that the switch or outlet is located at the end of the circuit; two or more cables *(above, right)* indicate that the device is installed mid-circuit. Locate the black (hot) wire, the white (neutral) wire and the bare grounding wire leading from each cable. When the white wire is used as a hot wire, it is recoded black with electrical tape or black paint *(above, left)*. Sometimes a short piece of insulated wire, called a jumper, is used to link two or more wires to a screw terminal. It is attached to the other wires in a pigtail connection *(above, right)*.

LIGHTING FIXTURES

Lighting fixtures illuminate halls and stairways and brighten dim rooms. Incandescent fixtures are still the most common type for home use, although fluorescent fixtures offer a practical alternative for kitchens and workrooms.

When a fixture doesn't light, first check the bulb. If it must be replaced, choose one according to the maximum recommended wattage, as indicated on the sticker found near the socket of most lamps and fixtures. Never use a bulb that exceeds this wattage; the heat produced could melt the shade or damage the wire insulation. Take care to also match the bulb's socket size and depth. To repair the fixture, you will have to take it down from the wall or ceiling. Disconnecting and reconnecting the wiring is relatively simple; taking down and remounting the fixture, especially if it is heavy or has older mounting hardware, can be hard work.

Simple ceiling and wall fixtures are mounted directly to an electrical box. Heavier fixtures, such as chandeliers, must be secured with a mounting strap; a threaded nipple secures the strap to the stem of the fixture. Older fixtures may be supported by a threaded stud mounted to the back of the box. The versatile track fixture clips onto its channel; to disengage it, simply turn the lever on the stem.

Carefully follow safety procedures when working on a fixture. Always flip off the wall switch and turn off power to the circuit by removing the fuse or tripping the circuit breaker *(page 102)*. Use a sturdy ladder to reach an overhead fixture and have a helper ready when taking down a heavy chandelier. Once you have exposed the wire connections, test as indicated to confirm that power is off.

When reconnecting a fixture, pay special attention to the color coding of the wires. Fixture leads are black or unmarked (hot) and white or marked with a ridge, stripe or threaded tracer in the strands (neutral). Protect against shock with correct polarity *(page 105)*; connect the hot wire to the brass terminal on the socket and to the black house wire, and connect the neutral wire to the silver terminal on the socket and to the white house wire. If there is a bare or green grounding wire, connect it to the metal ceiling box. Replacement wire should be the same gauge as the old wire, and its insulation rated to withstand high temperatures.

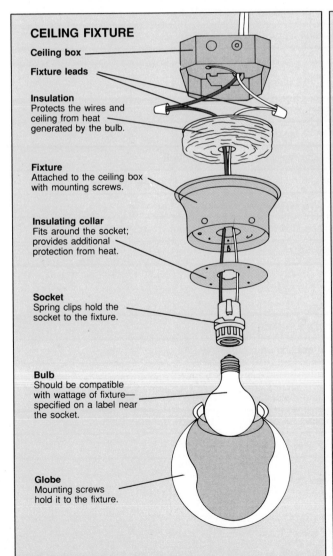

CEILING FIXTURE

Ceiling box

Fixture leads

Insulation
Protects the wires and ceiling from heat generated by the bulb.

Fixture
Attached to the ceiling box with mounting screws.

Insulating collar
Fits around the socket; provides additional protection from heat.

Socket
Spring clips hold the socket to the fixture.

Bulb
Should be compatible with wattage of fixture—specified on a label near the socket.

Globe
Mounting screws hold it to the fixture.

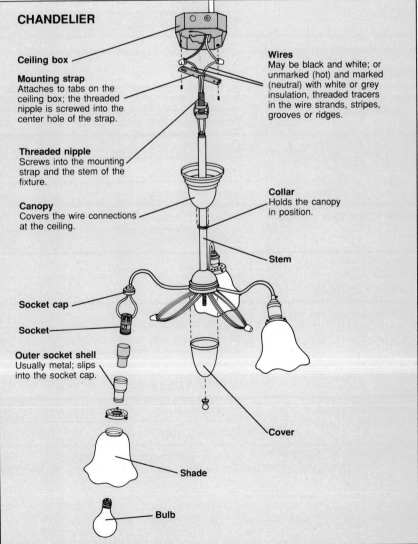

CHANDELIER

Ceiling box

Mounting strap
Attaches to tabs on the ceiling box; the threaded nipple is screwed into the center hole of the strap.

Threaded nipple
Screws into the mounting strap and the stem of the fixture.

Canopy
Covers the wire connections at the ceiling.

Socket cap

Socket

Outer socket shell
Usually metal; slips into the socket cap.

Wires
May be black and white; or unmarked (hot) and marked (neutral) with white or grey insulation, threaded tracers in the wire strands, stripes, grooves or ridges.

Collar
Holds the canopy in position.

Stem

Cover

Shade

Bulb

TROUBLESHOOTING GUIDE

SYMPTOM	POSSIBLE CAUSE	PROCEDURE
CEILING FIXTURE		
Bulb flickers or does not light	Bulb loose or burned out	Tighten or replace bulb
	No power to fixture	Replace fuse or reset circuit breaker *(p. 102)* □○
	Wall switch faulty	Check wall switch *(p. 140)*
	Socket contact dirty or bent too far down	Clean or bend up tab *(p. 109)* □○
	Socket and wires faulty	Test and replace socket and wires *(p. 109)* ⬓○
	Socket or switch faulty (pull-chain socket)	Test socket and switch and replace socket *(p. 111)* ⬓○
WALL FIXTURE		
Bulb flickers or does not light	Bulb loose or burned out	Tighten or replace bulb
	No power to fixture	Replace fuse or reset circuit breaker *(p. 102)* □○
	Wall switch faulty	Check wall switch *(p. 140)*
	Socket contact dirty or bent too far down	Clean or bend up tab *(p. 112)* □○
	Socket and wires faulty	Test and replace socket and wires *(p. 112)* ⬓○
CHANDELIER		
One bulb (or more) flickers or does not light	Bulb loose or burned out	Tighten or replace bulb
	Socket contact dirty or bent too far down	Clean or bend up tab *(p. 113)* □○
	Socket faulty	Test and replace socket *(p. 113)* ⬓◒
	Socket wires faulty	Test and replace socket wires *(p. 113)* ⬓◒
	Wires in stem faulty	Test and replace wires in stem *(p. 113)* ⬓◒
Entire fixture does not light	No power to fixture	Replace fuse or reset circuit breaker *(p. 102)* □○
	Wall switch faulty	Check wall switch *(p. 140)*
TRACK LIGHTING		
Bulb flickers or does not light	Bulb loose or burned out	Tighten or replace bulb
	Socket contact dirty or bent too far down	Clean or bend up tab *(p. 116)* □○
	Track contacts dirty	Clean track contacts *(p. 116)* □○
	Socket and wires faulty	Test and replace socket and wires *(p. 116)* ⬓◒
All fixtures on track do not light	No power to track	Replace fuse or reset circuit breaker *(p. 102)* □○
	Wall switch faulty	Check wall switch *(p. 140)*

DEGREE OF DIFFICULTY: □ **Easy** ⬓ **Moderate** ■ **Complex**
ESTIMATED TIME: ○ **Less than 1 hour** ◒ **1 to 3 hours** ● **Over 3 hours**

SERVICING CEILING FIXTURES

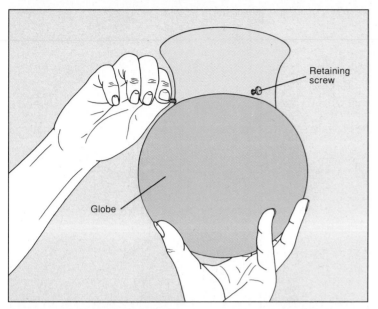

Globe

Retaining screw

1 **Dismounting the fixture.** Flip off the wall switch. Loosen any retaining screws holding the globe to the fixture *(above)*, then remove the globe. Tighten a loose bulb or replace a burned-out bulb with one of the same wattage. Flip on the switch. If the fixture lights, reinstall the globe. If it doesn't, turn off power to the fixture by removing the fuse or tripping the circuit breaker *(page 102)*. Use a screwdriver to remove the mounting screws holding the fixture to the ceiling box.

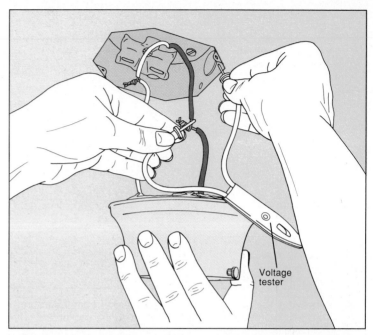

Voltage tester

2 **Testing for voltage.** Have someone hold the fixture, then twist off the wire caps to expose the connections, taking care not to touch any bare wire ends. Use a voltage tester to confirm that the power is off by touching one probe to the black wire connection and the other first to the grounded metal box *(above)*, then to the white wire connection. Then test between the white wire connection and the box. The tester should not glow in any test. If it does, return to the service panel and turn off power to the correct circuit. When the power is confirmed off, untwist the connections and take down the fixture.

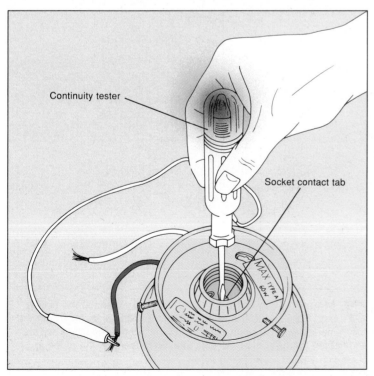

Continuity tester

Socket contact tab

3 **Testing the socket.** Pull away the insulation, if any, to expose the base of the socket. Scrape off any corrosion from the socket contact tab and pry it up slightly to improve contact with the bulb. Place the alligator clip of a continuity tester on the bare end of the black wire from the fixture and touch the tester probe to the socket contact tab *(left)*. Then place the alligator clip on the white wire end and touch the probe to the threaded metal tube of the socket. The tester should light in both tests. If it doesn't, the socket and wires must be replaced *(step 4)*.

SERVICING CEILING FIXTURES (continued)

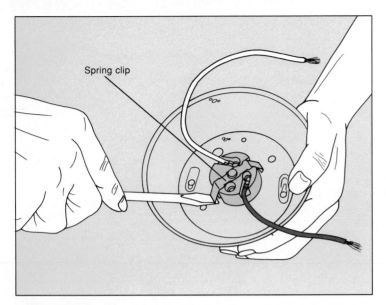

Spring clip

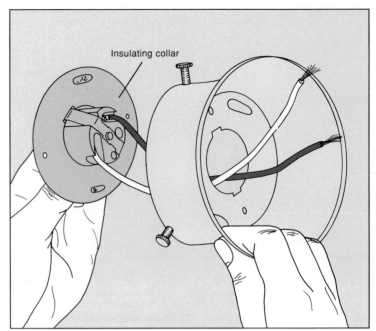

Insulating collar

4 **Removing the old socket.** To free the socket from the fixture, insert a screwdriver under the spring clip on the socket and press on the clip *(above)*. On other models, you may have to unscrew the two parts of the socket to remove it. Pull the socket and wires out of the fixture. Take the old socket with you to buy a compatible replacement with wires attached.

5 **Installing the new socket.** Thread the socket wires through the insulating collar, if any, then through the fixture *(above)*. If the new socket has spring clips, as on the model shown, push the socket into the fixture until the clips snap into place. If the replacement is a two-part, screw-type socket, fit the bottom half through the back of the fixture and screw the top half onto it from the front.

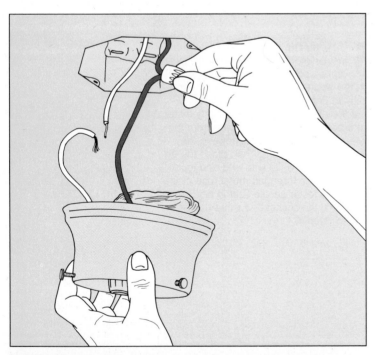

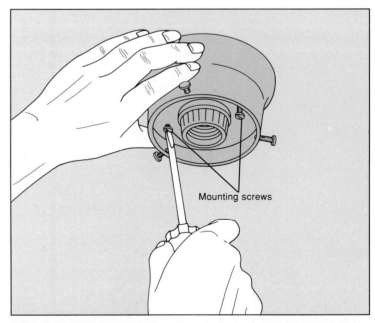

Mounting screws

6 **Connecting the wiring.** To improve the connections, strip back the wires inside the box *(page 417)*. Twist together the black fixture lead with the black wire from the ceiling box, and the white fixture lead with the white wire from the box, then screw a wire cap onto each connection *(above)*.

7 **Mounting the fixture.** Gently fold the wires into the ceiling box. Position the fixture so that its mounting slots align with the mounting holes on the ceiling box. Insert the mounting screws and tighten them *(above)*. Screw in the bulb, then set the globe in place and tighten its retaining screws.

REPLACING A PULL-CHAIN SOCKET

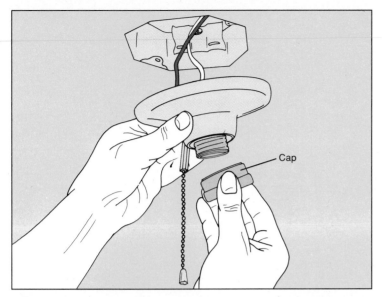

Cap

1 Access to the socket. The ceiling fixture shown above is usually made of porcelain and often found in garages, basements and closets. It has no wire leads; it is simply a housing for a socket that connects directly to the house wires. If the switch breaks or the socket fails, simply replace the socket. Turn off power to the fixture by removing the fuse or tripping the circuit breaker *(page 102)*. Take out the bulb, then loosen the screws that hold the fixture to the ceiling. Unscrew the cap from the socket *(above)*, then lower the fixture. Do not touch the socket or any metal parts until you have confirmed that the power is off *(step 2)*.

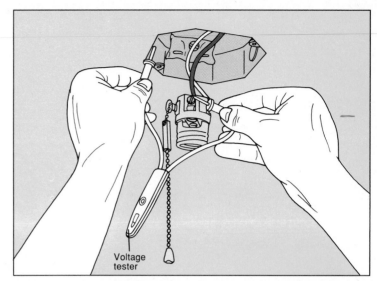

Voltage
tester

2 Testing for voltage. Use a voltage tester to confirm that the power is off by touching one probe to the brass socket terminal and the other first to the grounded metal box *(above)*, then to the silver terminal screw. Then test from the silver terminal screw to the grounded box. The tester should not glow in any test. If it does, return to the service panel and turn off power to the correct circuit.

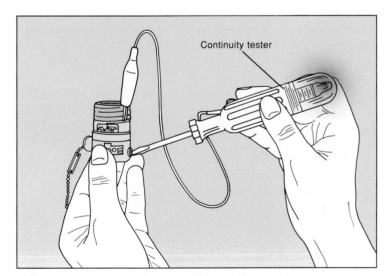

Continuity tester

3 Testing the socket and switch. With the power confirmed off, disconnect the wires from the terminal screws and take down the socket. Use a continuity tester to check the socket and switch. Place the alligator clip on the threaded metal tube and touch the tester probe to the silver terminal screw *(above)*. The tester should light. Then place the alligator clip on the brass terminal screw and touch the tester probe to the socket contact tab. Pull the switch. The tester should light when the switch is in one position and not when it is in the other. If the socket fails either test, it should be replaced.

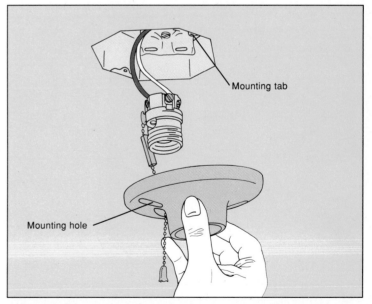

Mounting tab

Mounting hole

4 Replacing the socket. Take the old socket with you to buy a compatible replacement. To improve the connections, strip back the wires inside the box *(page 417)*. Connect the black wire to the brass terminal screw, then connect the white wire to the silver terminal screw. Gently fold the wires into the ceiling box. Thread the pull chain through its hole in the fixture *(above)*, then position the fixture so that its mounting holes align with the mounting tabs in the ceiling box. Insert the mounting screws and fasten them tightly with a screwdriver, reattach the cap and screw in the bulb. Turn on the power.

SERVICING WALL FIXTURES

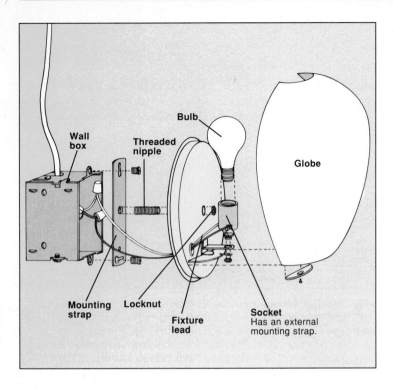

Wall box

Threaded nipple

Bulb

Globe

Mounting strap

Locknut

Fixture lead

Socket
Has an external mounting strap.

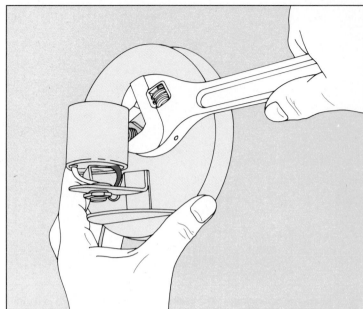

1 **Removing the fixture.** Flip off the wall switch and remove the globe. Tighten a loose bulb or replace a burned-out bulb with one of the same wattage. Flip on the switch. If the fixture lights, reinstall the globe. If it doesn't, turn off power to the fixture by removing the fuse or tripping the circuit breaker *(page 102)*. Unscrew the bulb. Use an adjustable wrench to loosen the locknut holding the fixture to the threaded nipple *(above)*, then pull the fixture away from the wall.

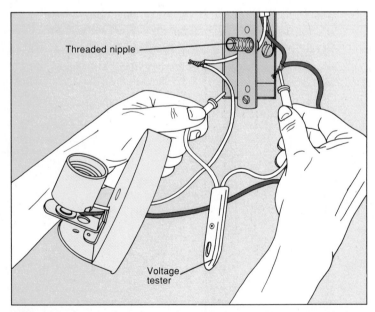

Threaded nipple

Voltage tester

2 **Testing for voltage.** Unscrew the wire caps from the black and white wire connections, taking care not to touch any exposed wire ends. Have someone support the fixture if it is heavy. Use a voltage tester to confirm that the power is off by touching one probe to the black wire connection and the other first to the grounded metal box *(above)*, then to the white wire connection. Then test between the white wire connection and the grounded box. The tester should not glow in any test. If it does, return to the service panel and turn off power to the correct circuit. When the power is confirmed off, untwist the connections and take down the fixture.

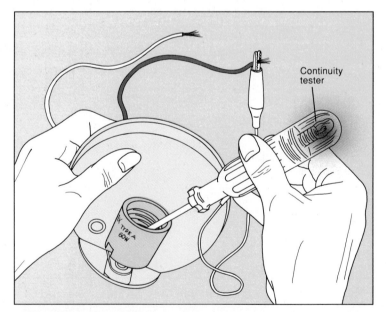

Continuity tester

3 **Testing the socket and wires.** Scrape off any corrosion from the socket contact tab and pry it up slightly to improve contact with the bulb. Place the alligator clip of a continuity tester on the black wire end and touch the tester probe to the socket contact tab *(above)*. Then place the alligator clip on the white wire end and touch the probe to the threaded metal tube of the socket. The tester should light in both tests. If not, replace the socket and wires *(step 4)*.

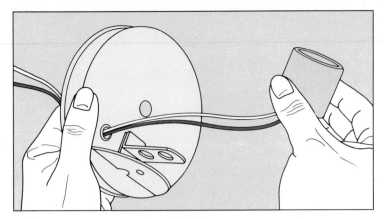

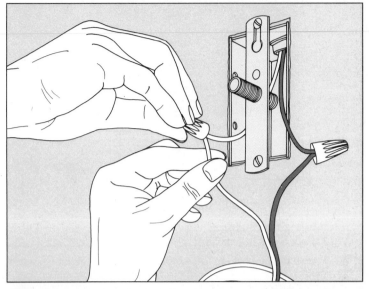

4 **Replacing the socket and wires.** Loosen the mounting screw holding the socket to the fixture, then pull the socket and the wires free of the fixture *(above)*. Buy a compatible socket with preattached wires or a socket with terminal screws and two pieces of wire the same gauge, length and color as the old ones. To connect the wires to the socket terminals, strip back the insulation *(page 417)*, twist the strands together and curl them into a hook, then loop the black wire end around the brass terminal screw and the white wire end around the silver terminal screw and tighten the connections. Thread the wires back through the hole in the fixture and tighten the mounting screw to secure the socket to the fixture.

5 **Reinstalling the fixture.** To improve the connections, strip back the wires inside the box *(page 417)*. Twist together the black lead from the fixture with the black wire in the box and screw on a wire cap. Join the white wires in the same way *(above)*. Gently fold the wires back into the box. Fit the fixture over the threaded nipple and position it against the wall, then slip on the locknut that holds the fixture to the nipple and tighten it. Screw in the bulb and replace the globe. Turn on the power.

SERVICING CHANDELIERS

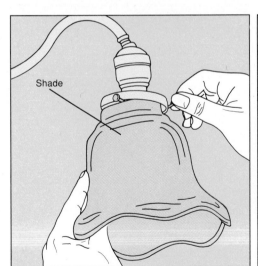

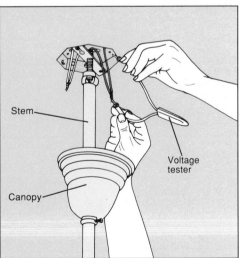

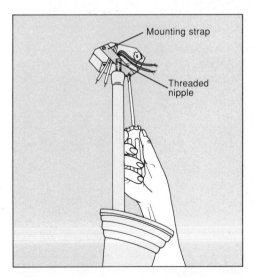

1 **Testing for voltage.** After confirming that the problem is not a loose or burned-out bulb, flip off the wall switch and unscrew the light bulbs, then take off the shades *(above, left)* and carefully set them aside. Turn off power to the chandelier by removing the fuse or tripping the circuit breaker *(page 102)*. Loosen any screws holding the canopy in place against the ceiling and slide it down the stem to expose the ceiling box. Unscrew the wire caps from the connections, taking care not to touch any exposed wire ends. Use a voltage tester to confirm that the power is off by touching one of the tester probes to the black wire connection and the other probe first to the grounded metal box *(above, right)*, then to the white wire connection. Then test between the white wire connection and the grounded metal box. The tester should not glow in any test. If it does, return to the service panel and turn off power to the correct circuit.

2 **Dismounting the chandelier.** When the power is confirmed off, untwist the wire connections. Before dismounting the chandelier, use masking tape to tag the faulty part. Have a helper support the chandelier while you unscrew the mounting strap *(above)*, and gently lower the fixture from the ceiling.

SERVICING CHANDELIERS (continued)

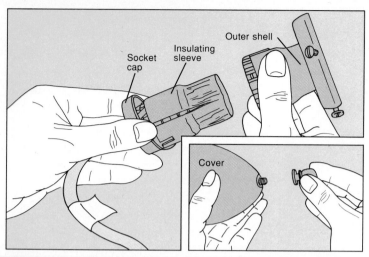

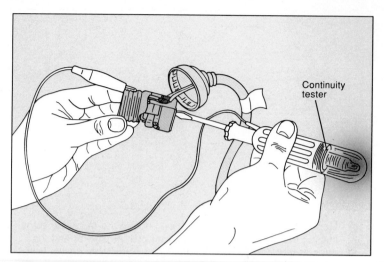

3 **Access to the socket.** To provide enough slack at the tagged sockets, remove the cover at the base of the fixture *(inset)*, pull out the wires and disconnect them. At the socket, press in with your thumb where the word "PRESS" is stamped and lift away the outer shell *(above)*. Then pull off the socket insulating sleeve. Pull the socket away from the socket cap so that at least 1 inch of wire is drawn out with it.

4 **Testing the socket.** Scrape any corrosion from the socket contact tab and pry it up slightly to improve contact with the bulb. To test the socket, place the alligator clip of a continuity tester on the threaded metal tube of the socket and touch the tester probe to the silver terminal screw *(above)*. Then place the alligator clip on the brass terminal screw and touch the tester probe to the socket contact tab. The tester should light in both tests. If not, loosen the socket terminal screws, detach the wires, remove the socket and install a replacement *(next step)*. If the socket tests OK, test the socket wires *(step 6)*.

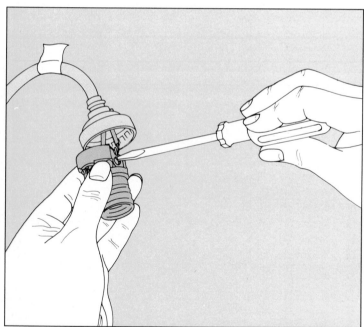

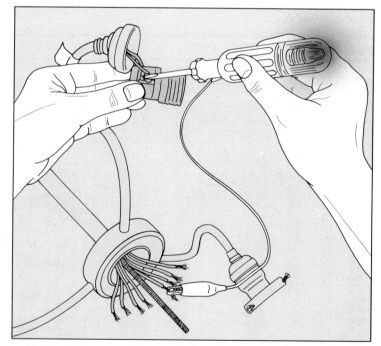

5 **Replacing the socket.** Buy a compatible socket with an insulating sleeve, an outer shell, and a socket cap. Replace only the faulty parts—in this case, the socket and insulating sleeve. Begin by removing the outer shell and insulating sleeve. Hook the marked wire around the silver socket terminal and tighten the connection, making sure there are no stray strands. Next, hook the unmarked wire around the brass socket terminal *(above)*. Slip the new insulating sleeve over the new socket, then push the outer shell into the cap until it snaps into place. At the base of the fixture, twist together the unmarked wires, then twist together the marked wires. Screw a wire cap onto each connection. Remount the chandelier *(step 10)*.

6 **Testing the socket wires.** Place the alligator clip of the continuity tester on the marked socket wire at the base of the fixture and touch the tester probe to the silver socket terminal *(above)*. Then place the alligator clip on the unmarked socket wire and touch the tester probe to the brass socket terminal. The tester should light in both tests. If not, loosen the socket terminal screws, detach the wires, remove the socket and replace the socket wires *(step 7)*. If the socket wires are good, go to step 8 to test the wires in the stem.

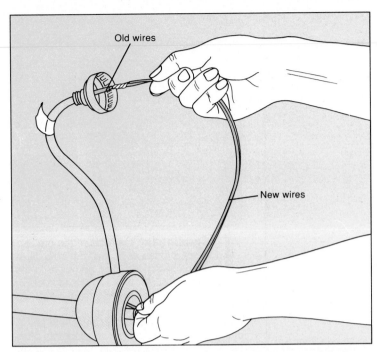

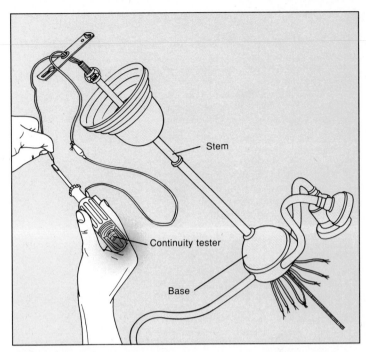

7 **Replacing the socket wires.** Buy insulated wire of the same gauge and length as the old wire. Strip 3/4 inch of insulation from both ends of each wire *(page 417)*. Use the old wire to pull the new wire through the fixture arm. At the socket, hook the wires together and secure the connection with electrical tape, keeping the connection as thin as possible. Then, at the base of the fixture, pull out the old wires, bringing the new wires into the arm *(above)*. Connect the socket as in step 5. Remount the chandelier *(step 10)*.

8 **Testing the wires in the stem.** At the base of the fixture, twist together the two wires leading up the stem. At the top of the fixture, place the alligator clip of the continuity tester on one wire end and touch the tester probe to the other wire end *(above)*. The tester should light. If it doesn't, replace the wires in the stem of the fixture *(step 9)*.

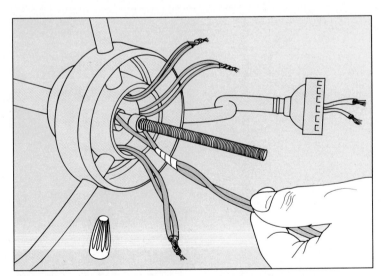

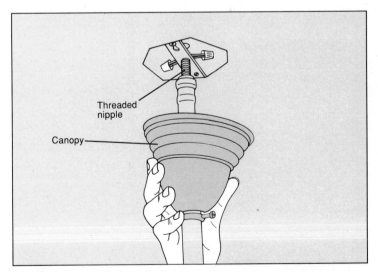

9 **Rewiring the chandelier.** Buy wire of the same gauge and length as the old wire. Strip 3/4 inch of insulation from both ends of each wire *(page 417)*. Use the old wire to pull the new wire through the fixture stem. At the top of the stem, hook the wires together and secure the connection with electrical tape, keeping the connection as thin as possible. Then, at the base of the fixture, pull out the old wires, bringing the new wires through the stem *(above)*. Twist the marked socket wires together with the marked stem wire and screw on a wire cap. Repeat the procedure for the unmarked wires.

10 **Remounting the chandelier.** Fold the wire connections into the wiring compartment and screw on the cover. Strip back the wires inside the box to improve the connections *(page 417)*. While a helper supports the chandelier, tighten the mounting strap to the ceiling box. Twist together the marked fixture wire with the white wire in the box, and the unmarked fixture wire with the black wire in the box, then secure the connections with wire caps. Gently fold the wires into the box. Slide the canopy up the stem until it is flat against the ceiling *(above)* and tighten any screws to secure it. Screw in the bulbs and reattach the shades.

SERVICING TRACK FIXTURES

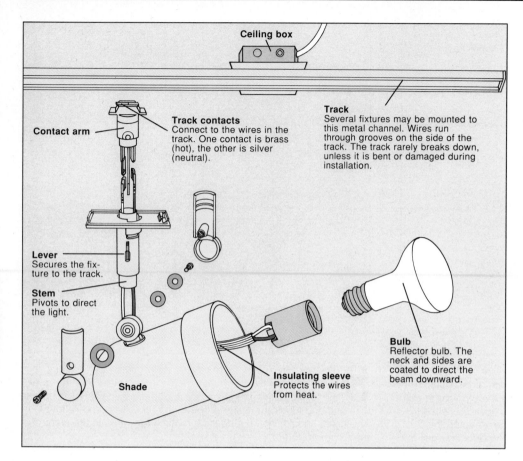

Ceiling box

Contact arm

Track contacts
Connect to the wires in the track. One contact is brass (hot), the other is silver (neutral).

Track
Several fixtures may be mounted to this metal channel. Wires run through grooves on the side of the track. The track rarely breaks down, unless it is bent or damaged during installation.

Lever
Secures the fixture to the track.

Stem
Pivots to direct the light.

Bulb
Reflector bulb. The neck and sides are coated to direct the beam downward.

Insulating sleeve
Protects the wires from heat.

Shade

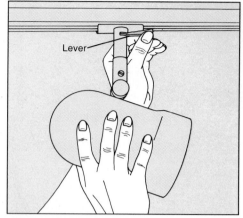

Lever

1 **Cleaning the contacts.** If the problem is not a loose or burned-out bulb, flip off the switch and turn off power to the track *(page 102)*. Allow the fixture to cool, then turn the lever to release the fixture from the track *(above)*. Do not touch any wires in the track. Use fine sandpaper to clean any dirt or corrosion from the track contacts on the fixture. Remove the bulb, then scrape any corrosion from the socket contact tab and pry it up slightly to improve contact with the bulb. Screw in the bulb, position the fixture in the track and flip on the switch. If the bulb still doesn't light, go to step 2.

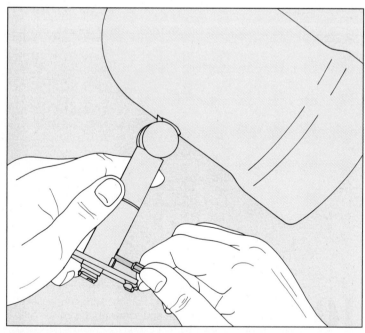

2 **Access to the socket.** Turn off power to the track and take down the fixture. To provide enough slack at the socket, unscrew the lever by hand *(above)*, then use a screwdriver to loosen the screw in the stem. Disassemble the stem. Remove the screws holding the socket to the shade and pull the socket free of its mounting.

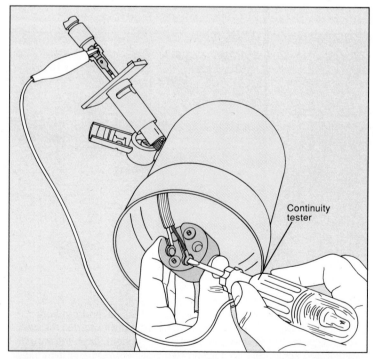

Continuity tester

3 **Testing the socket.** Place the alligator clip of a continuity tester on the brass track contact and touch the tester probe to the black wire connection at the socket terminal *(above)*. Then place the alligator clip on the silver track contact and touch the tester probe to the white wire connection. The tester should light in both tests. If it doesn't, replace the socket and its wires *(step 4)*.

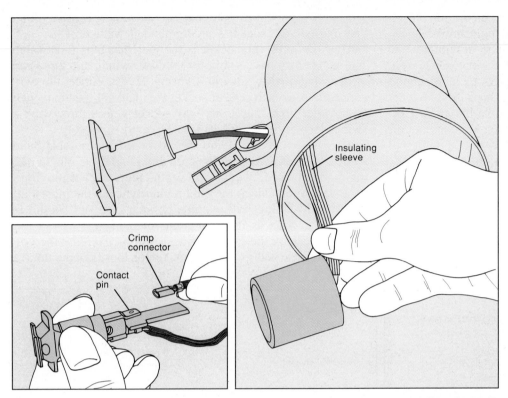

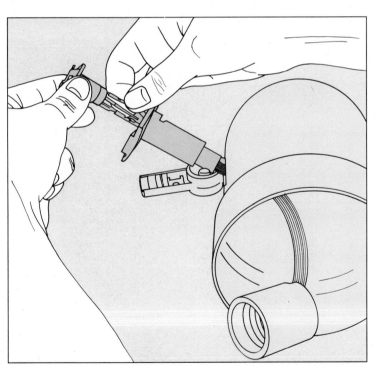

4 **Removing the old socket.** To release the wire connections at the base of the stem, pull the connectors free of the contact pin terminals *(inset)*. Then pull the socket out of the shade *(left)*, bringing with it the wires and insulating sleeve. Slip the wires out of the insulating sleeve and set the sleeve aside; do not discard it. Take the socket and wires with you to buy a compatible socket with wires attached. Also buy two crimp-style connectors the same size and shape as the old ones.

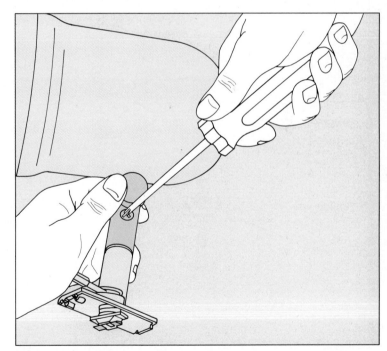

5 **Installing the new socket.** Slip the insulating sleeve over the new wires, then thread the wires through the hole in the shade and through both parts of the stem. Strip 1/4 inch of insulation from the wire ends *(page 417)*, then twist the strands tightly and push each wire end into a wire connector. Use a multi-purpose tool to crimp the connectors. Next, push the connector attached to the black wire onto the brass contact pin and the connector attached to the white wire onto the silver contact pin *(above)*.

6 **Reassembling the fixture.** Set the socket in the shade and tighten the screws to secure it. Screw the lever into the stem by hand, then reassemble the stem and screw it together *(above)*. To mount the fixture, fit the stem in the track and turn the lever a quarter-turn. Do not touch any wires in the track. Screw in the bulb, turn on the power and flip on the switch.

FLOOR AND TABLE LAMPS

Lamps, unlike fixtures, are portable; they can be moved at whim to brighten a dark corner or to shed light on the latest mystery novel. Whether floor or table, modern or antique, the parts and wiring of lamps are basically the same. Once you know how to fix one, you need never throw out a lamp again.

When a lamp is not working properly, check first for the simplest cause—a loose or burned-out bulb, a blown fuse or tripped circuit breaker, or a plug that has been knocked out of the wall outlet. Confirm that the outlet is not at fault by plugging another lamp into it. Finally, check the lamp socket, switch, plug and wiring.

When choosing a replacement bulb, consider your lighting requirements. Bulbs come in different wattages; the higher the wattage, the more light it will provide—but the more electricity it will consume. Lightbulbs in frosted and coated versions create special atmospheres. Globe bulbs are ideal for makeup mirrors. To prevent a potential fire hazard, never use a bulb that exceeds the socket's recommended wattage.

After the bulb, the socket is the part that fails most often. The socket may have a simple ON/OFF switch, or a three-way switch that offers several lighting levels. Since the wire connections to each type of socket are identical, you may want to consider replacing a one-way socket with a three-way. A switch located in a cord can be repaired separately.

Always unplug the lamp before beginning a repair and, while you're at it, inspect the cord and plug. To avoid damaging the lamp cord, always pull on the plug when removing it from the outlet. Check the plug regularly; even the most carefully handled plug will eventually wear out, and should be replaced as soon as it shows signs of damage.

If you suspect the lamp wiring is faulty, examine the cord for frayed, cracked or bare wires, or for loose connections at

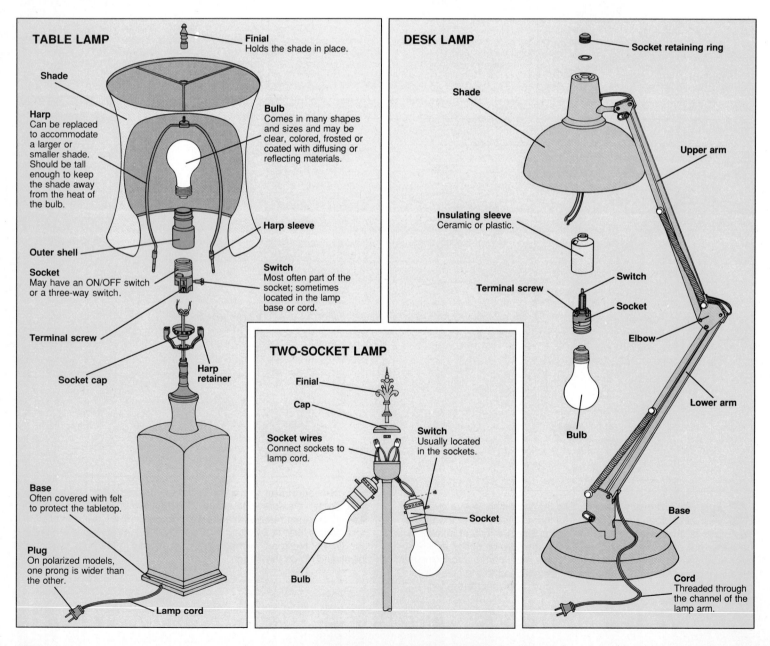

TABLE LAMP

Finial
Holds the shade in place.

Shade

Harp
Can be replaced to accommodate a larger or smaller shade. Should be tall enough to keep the shade away from the heat of the bulb.

Bulb
Comes in many shapes and sizes and may be clear, colored, frosted or coated with diffusing or reflecting materials.

Harp sleeve

Outer shell

Socket
May have an ON/OFF switch or a three-way switch.

Switch
Most often part of the socket; sometimes located in the lamp base or cord.

Terminal screw

Socket cap

Harp retainer

Base
Often covered with felt to protect the tabletop.

Plug
On polarized models, one prong is wider than the other.

Lamp cord

TWO-SOCKET LAMP

Finial

Cap

Socket wires
Connect sockets to lamp cord.

Switch
Usually located in the sockets.

Socket

Bulb

DESK LAMP

Socket retaining ring

Shade

Upper arm

Insulating sleeve
Ceramic or plastic.

Switch

Terminal screw

Socket

Elbow

Bulb

Lower arm

Base

Cord
Threaded through the channel of the lamp arm.

the plug. It is common to find a broken or damaged wire at the plug or at the lamp base. Never splice a worn lamp cord; replace it with a new one.

If you have never wired anything before, lamps are a good place to start. When you replace the cord, select one the same gauge as the old cord; most lamps use No.18/2 lamp cord (also called zip cord). To determine how much cord to buy, measure the old cord and add the height of the lamp; then add at least another foot. Replace the entire cord and, for maximum safety, replace the plug at the same time. (Sometimes you can buy the cord and plug as one piece.)

Lamp cord has many fine wire strands beneath its plastic insulation. When making connections with this type of cord, you must twist the strands together to be sure there are no stray wire ends. First strip the insulation from the wire end with wire strippers or a multi-purpose tool, then twist the bare strands together tightly in a clockwise direction between your thumb and forefinger. If there are any stray or broken strands, snip the wire end and start again. To join stranded wire to solid wire, wrap the twisted strands in a spiral over the solid wire and screw on a wire cap to secure the connection. To fit the wire over a terminal connection, bend the twisted wire into a hook as for solid wire *(page 417)*.

When rewiring a lamp, be sure to polarize it *(page 105)* so that the lamp switch interrupts the current-carrying hot wire. That way, when the lamp is turned off, there will be no power flowing through it. You will need a polarized plug, which has one prong wider than the other, and polarized cord, which is ribbed or color-coded on one side or has a thread evident in the strands of one wire. This is the neutral side, and should be connected to the silver terminal of the socket and the wide prong of the polarized plug.

TROUBLESHOOTING GUIDE

SYMPTOM	POSSIBLE CAUSE	PROCEDURE
Bulb flickers or does not light	Plug or bulb loose	Check plug in wall outlet; tighten bulb in socket
	Bulb burned out	Replace bulb
	Wall outlet faulty	Test lamp in another outlet. If it lights, service outlet *(p. 148)*
	Socket contact tab bent	Pry up contact tab *(p. 120)* □○
	Socket faulty	Replace socket *(p. 120)* □○
	Lamp switch faulty	Test and replace switch *(socket with switch, p. 120* □○*; switch in lamp base, p. 123* □○*; flat-cord switch, p. 124* ▣○*; round-cord switch, p. 124* ▣○*)*
	Plug faulty	Replace plug *(flat-cord plug, p. 126* □○*; quick-connect plug, p. 126* □○*; round-cord plug, p. 127* □○*)*
	Lamp cord faulty	Test and rewire lamp *(one-socket lamp, p. 128* ▣◕*; two-socket lamp, p. 129* ▣◕*; desk lamp, p. 131* ▣◕*)*
Lamp blows fuse or trips circuit breaker	Overload circuit	Move a high-wattage appliance to another circuit. Have an electrician run a new circuit from the circuit panel
	Short circuit in lamp cord	Test and rewire lamp *(one-socket lamp, p. 128* ▣◕*; two-socket lamp, p. 129* ▣◕*; desk lamp, p. 131* ▣◕*)*
	Plug faulty	Replace plug *(flat-cord plug, p. 126* □○*; quick-connect plug, p. 126* □○*; round-cord plug, p. 127* □○*)*
	Socket faulty	Test and replace socket *(p. 120)* □○
Bulb broken or seized	Socket corroded or damaged	Remove bulb base *(p. 125)* □○; replace socket *(p. 120)* □○
Bulb burns out too quickly	Heavy use of lamp	Install long-life bulb or bulb-life extender
Shock when changing bulb	Socket faulty	Replace socket *(p. 120)* □○
	Polarity reversed	Check polarity in cord and plug *(p. 128)* □○
Shock when plugging or un-plugging lamp	Plug faulty	Replace plug *(flat-cord plug, p. 126* □○*; quick-connect plug, p. 126* □○*; round-cord plug, p. 127* □○*)*
	Lamp cord faulty	Rewire lamp *(one-socket lamp, p. 128* ▣◕*; two-socket lamp, p. 129* ▣◕*; desk lamp, p. 131* ▣◕*)*

DEGREE OF DIFFICULTY: □ **Easy** ▣ **Moderate** ■ **Complex**
ESTIMATED TIME: ○ **Less than 1 hour** ◕ **1 to 3 hours** ● **Over 3 hours**

TESTING AND REPLACING THE SOCKET

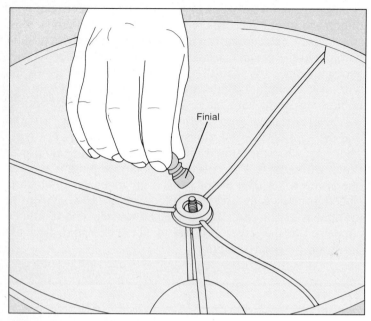

1 **Removing the shade.** Unplug the lamp. If there is a finial securing the shade to the harp, unscrew it *(above)*, then lift off the shade and unscrew the light bulb. Screw the finial back onto the harp to avoid losing it.

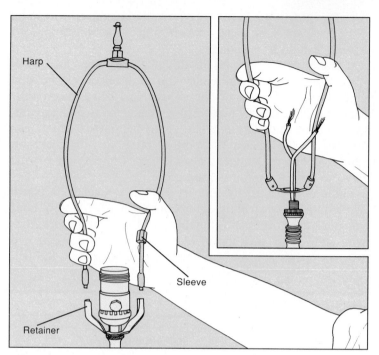

2 **Removing the harp.** Most one-socket lamps have a harp that is held to a retainer by metal sleeves. To remove it, push up the sleeves, then squeeze the harp and lift it out of the retainer, as shown. On some lamps, the harp cannot be lifted off the lamp until the socket is removed *(inset)*.

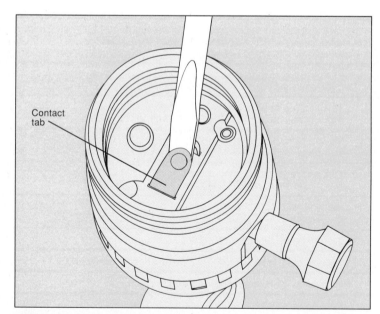

3 **Cleaning and adjusting the contact tab.** With a flat-tipped screwdriver, scratch any dirt off the surface of the contact tab. If the tab is corroded or broken, remove and replace the socket *(step 4)*. If you suspect the tab does not protrude enough to make contact with the bottom of the bulb, use a screwdriver to pry the end up slightly *(above)*, and try the bulb again. The contact tab is delicate; prying it up more than a few times may break it. If the bulb still does not light, or if the contact tab snaps, unplug the lamp again, unscrew the bulb and go to step 4.

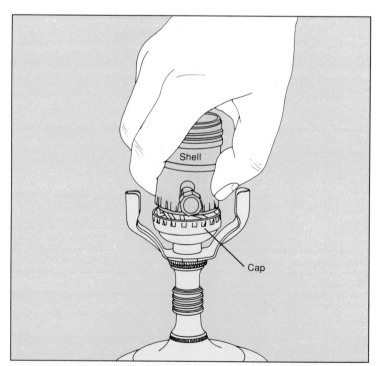

4 **Removing the outer shell and insulating sleeve.** Look for the word "PRESS" on the outer shell of the socket near the switch, then press hard with your thumb *(above)*. You may also have to wiggle the cap slightly to release its grip; do not twist it. Lift the shell free. Slip off the cardboard insulating sleeve if it does not lift off with the shell. If the sleeve is damaged, the socket must be replaced.

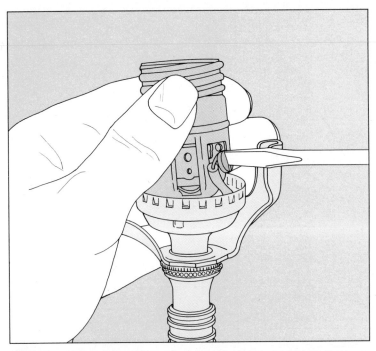

5 **Detaching the socket.** On lamps that have no terminal screws, clip the wires near the socket, lift the socket off and go to the next step. If there are screw terminals, check for a loose wire connection; if a wire is loose, rehook it around the terminal screw and tighten the screw. Then screw in the light bulb, plug in the lamp and turn it on to test. If the lamp still does not light, unplug it and remove the bulb. Detach the socket wires *(above)*, and lift the socket up and off the lamp.

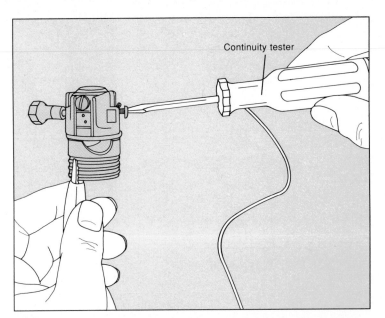

6 **Testing the socket.** If the socket has screw terminals, place the alligator clip of a continuity tester on the threaded metal base and touch the tester probe to the silver (neutral) terminal, as shown. Then place the alligator clip on the brass terminal screw and touch the tester probe to the socket contact tab. The tester should light in both tests. If the socket tests OK, check the switch in the socket *(page 122)*, or reinstall the socket and check the switch in the lamp base *(page 123)* or cord *(page 124)*. If the tester does not light, go to the next step.

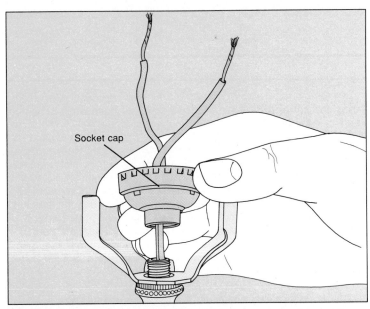

7 **Removing the socket cap.** To remove the socket cap from the lamp, first untie the cord if it is knotted. Loosen the setscrew at the base of the cap, if there is one, then unscrew the cap. Pull it off the center pipe *(above)*. If the socket cap holds the lamp body to the center pipe, support the lamp so that the lamp does not come apart. While the lamp is disassembled, inspect its cord. If the cord is in poor condition, rewire the lamp *(pages 128, 129 and 131)*.

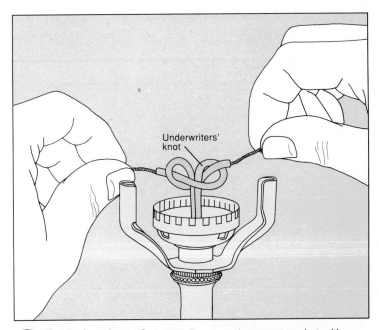

8 **Replacing the socket cap.** Buy a replacement socket with screw terminals. New sockets fit most lamps and come with a socket cap. Thread the lamp cord through the cap, then screw the cap onto the center pipe. If the cord is new, part it about 2 inches back and strip the insulation from the separated ends *(page 417)*. To protect the terminals from strain, tie an Underwriters' knot with the two wire ends, as shown.

TESTING AND REPLACING THE SOCKET (continued)

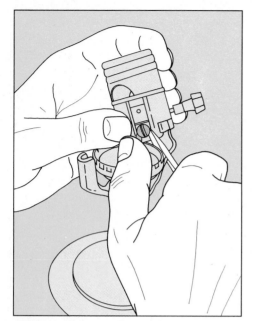

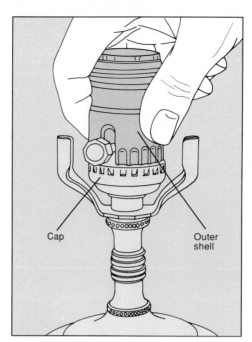

Cap

Outer shell

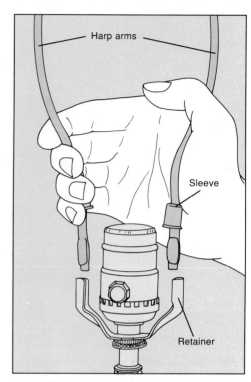

Harp arms

Sleeve

Retainer

9 **Wiring the new socket.** Twist the strands of each exposed wire end clockwise so that there are no frayed ends. Then, using a screwdriver, hook each wire end clockwise around a terminal screw *(above)*. Make sure the neutral wire of the cord (the ridged or marked wire) connects to the silver socket terminal and the wide plug prong. The hot or unmarked wire of the cord connects to the brass socket terminal and the narrow plug prong. Tighten the screws, making sure there are no stray wire strands.

10 **Installing the socket.** Slip the insulating sleeve and outer shell onto the socket, fitting the notched opening over the socket switch, as shown. Push the shell into the rim of the cap until it snaps into place. Screw in the bulb, then plug in the lamp and turn it on. If it works, reinstall the harp and lamp shade *(next step)*. If it doesn't, remove the bulb and test the switch *(below, pages 123 and 124)*.

11 **Reassembling the lamp.** Squeeze the arms of the harp to-gether and fit them back into the retainer *(above)*, then lower the sleeves in place. Screw in the light bulb and reattach the shade and finial.

TESTING A SOCKET SWITCH

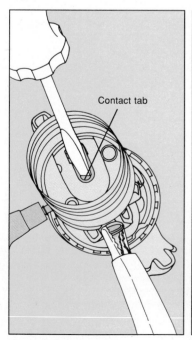

Contact tab

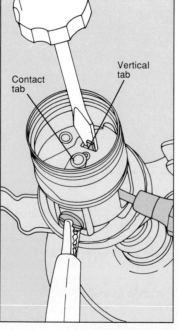

Contact tab

Vertical tab

Testing for continuity. If a socket switch seems loose when turned on and off, or if the bulb flickers as the lamp is jiggled, the switch should be checked. Unplug the lamp, remove the shade, unscrew the bulb and lift off the harp, if any. Lift out the socket shell and insulating sleeve *(page 120)* to expose the terminals on the side of the socket. To test a regular ON/OFF switch *(far left)*, place the alligator clip of a continuity tester on the brass terminal and touch the tester probe to the socket contact tab. The tester should light when the switch is on, but not when the switch is off. To test the switch on a three-way socket, place the alligator clip of the continuity tester on the brass screw terminal and touch the tester probe to the small vertical tab in the base of the socket *(near left)*, then to the contact tab. Turn the switch to the three ON positions, then to the OFF position. The tester should light as follows:

POSITION:	The tester should light when the probe touches:
FIRST	Vertical tab
SECOND	Contact tab
THIRD	Each tab
OFF	The tester should not light

If the switch is faulty, detach and replace the socket *(page 120)*. If the switch tests OK and the socket is good, test the cord and plug *(pages 128, 129 and 131)*.

REPAIRING A SWITCH IN THE LAMP BASE

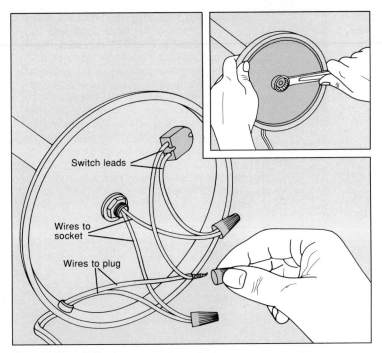

Switch leads

Wires to socket

Wires to plug

1 Access to the switch leads. Flip the switch while the lamp is plugged in. If the switch feels loose when it is turned on and off, or the bulb flickers as the switch is jiggled, the switch is probably faulty. Unplug the lamp and set it on its side. Carefully peel back the protective cover, which is usually felt. If there is a bottom plate, use a wrench to remove the locknut holding it in place *(inset)*, then pull off the plate. If the switch is connected to the lamp cord with wire caps, unscrew the caps *(above)*, then untwist the wires.

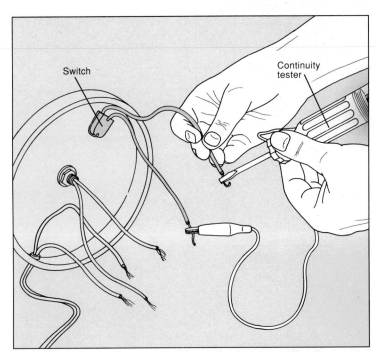

Switch

Continuity tester

2 Testing the switch. Locate the two switch leads. Place the alligator clip of a continuity tester on the bare end of one lead and touch the tester probe to the end of the other lead *(above)*. The tester should light when the switch is in one position, but not the other. If the switch fails the test, replace it.

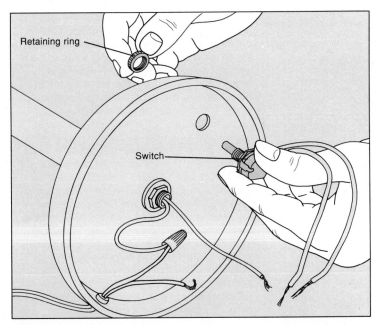

Retaining ring

Switch

3 Removing the switch. Unscrew the retaining ring on the lamp base, then pull the switch out through the bottom of the base *(above)*. Take the switch to a hardware store or electrical supplier and buy a compatible replacement.

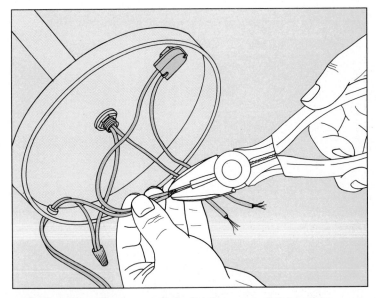

4 Installing the new switch. Set the new switch into the lamp base from the bottom and tighten the retaining ring to hold it in place. Connect the unmarked wire from the plug to the unmarked switch lead *(above)*. Next, connect the marked wire from the plug to the marked socket wire. Then connect the marked switch lead to the unmarked socket wire. Screw a wire cap onto each connection. Fit the bottom plate back on and tighten the locknut. Secure the protective cover to the lamp base with cloth glue.

REPAIRING A FLAT-CORD SWITCH

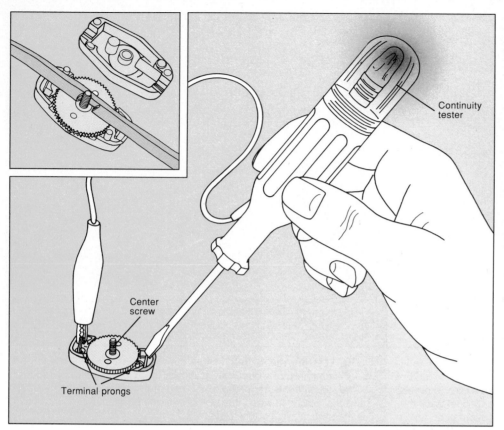

Testing and replacing the switch. Unplug the lamp. Unscrew the switch cover and remove the switch from the lamp cord. Place the alligator clip of a continuity tester on one terminal prong and touch the tester probe to the other prong *(left)*. The tester should light only when the switch is in the ON position. If the switch is defective, buy a new flat cord and flat-cord switch. Rewire the lamp *(pages 128, 129 and 131)*. Then choose the most convenient place along the cord to install the new switch. Unscrew the switch cover and separate the switch in two pieces. Using a utility knife, cut a notch large enough to accommodate the center screw of the switch. Set the cord into the switch *(inset)*, then place the switch cover on the cord, making sure that both prongs of the switch pierce the same wire of the cord. If the lamp is polarized, the prongs must pierce the hot (unmarked) wire of the lamp cord. Screw on the switch cover securely.

REPAIRING A ROUND-CORD SWITCH

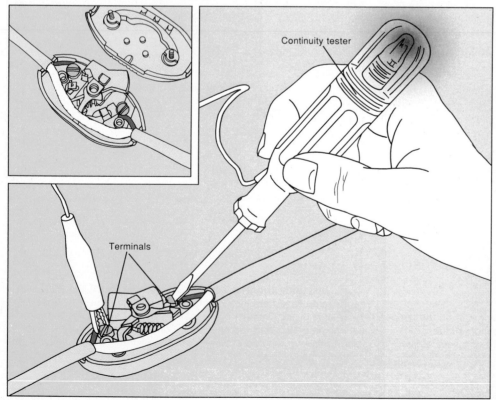

Testing and replacing the switch. Unplug the lamp. Unscrew the switch cover to reveal the terminal connections *(inset)*. Loosen the terminal screws to release the wires and remove the switch from the lamp cord. Place the alligator clip of a continuity tester on one of the switch terminals and touch the tester probe to the other terminal *(left)*. The tester should light when the switch is in one position but not in the other position. If the switch fails this test, buy a new round cord and switch. Rewire the lamp *(pages 128, 129 and 131)*, then choose the most convenient place along the cord to install the new switch. Unscrew the switch cover. Using a utility knife, part the cord, then strip a section of outer insulation from the cord, long enough to accommodate the new switch. Do not strip the neutral (marked) wire. Clip the hot (unmarked) wire and strip back the insulation on both ends. Attach each hot wire to a terminal screw. Screw on the switch cover securely.

PLUGS

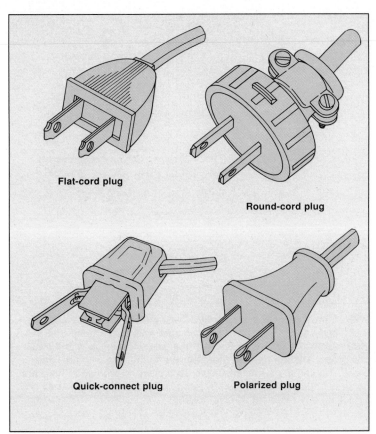

Flat-cord plug

Round-cord plug

Quick-connect plug

Polarized plug

Servicing 120-volt plugs. A glance will tell you whether a plug's casing is cracked or the prongs are loose, bent or corroded. In any of these cases, the plug should be replaced. If a test of the plug and cord *(pages 128, 129 and 131)* shows no continuity, tighten connections between the two and test again. If there is still no continuity, rewire the lamp and replace the plug *(page 126)*.

As a rule of thumb, replace a defective plug with one of the same type *(left);* also select the same type of cord (most lamps use No. 18/2 lamp wire, called zip cord). The most common type of plug is the flat-cord plug, connected to the lamp cord with terminal screws. An Underwriters' knot is often made in the cord to guard the terminals from strain.

Some lighting devices (such as swag lamps that hang by their cords) need the extra strength of a round cord, which must be fitted with a special plug. If the insulating disc is missing from an old round-cord plug, the plug is unsafe and should be replaced with a modern plug.

By far the easiest plug to install is the quick-connect plug. However, its connections are not as sturdy as the other types, and it should be used only for lamps that are seldom unplugged.

When buying a replacement, look for a polarized plug, with one narrow prong and one wide prong. The wider (neutral) prong will not fit into the narrow (hot) slot of modern outlets. By connecting the marked wire of the cord to the wide prong at the plug and the silver terminal at the socket, you can ensure that the lamp switch interrupts the hot wire, and no current flows to the light when the switch is off *(page 105)*.

REPLACING A BROKEN BULB

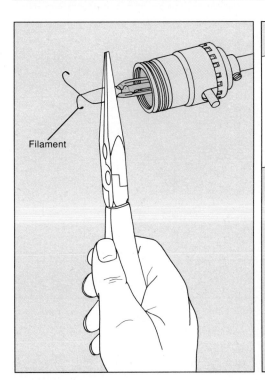

Filament

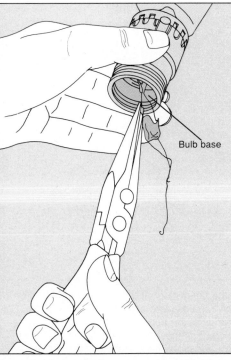

Bulb base

Safely removing a broken light bulb.
When a bulb seizes in its socket, do not force it. Unplug the lamp or turn off power to the fixture. Squirt lubricating oil into the socket and gently ease out the bulb. Occasionally, the bulb breaks, leaving its base in the socket. To remove it, use long-nose pliers to grasp the filament *(far left)* and turn counterclockwise until the base can be removed by hand. (Wear eye protection when working on overhead fixtures.) If the filament is also broken *(near left)*, grasp the bulb base with long-nose pliers and turn it counterclockwise until the base can be removed by hand. Once the bulb is completely removed, examine the socket. Replace it if corroded or damaged.

REPLACING A FLAT-CORD PLUG

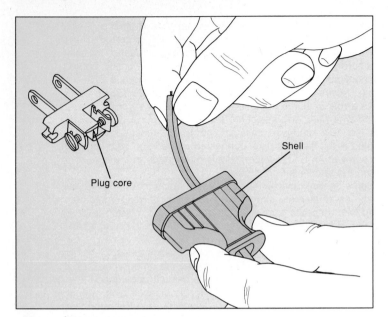

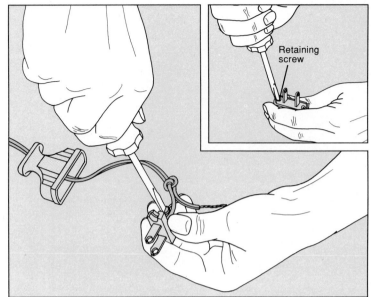

1 Setting the new plug in place. Unplug the lamp. Snip the faulty plug off the old wire with a utility knife or diagonal-cutting pliers. For best results, remove the lamp cord and rewire the lamp *(pages 128, 129 and 131)*. If the new plug has a core and shell, separate them and slip the cord through the shell *(above)*. Peel apart the two wires at the end of the cord and strip about 3/4 inch of insulation from each wire end *(page 417)*. To protect the terminals, tie an Underwriters' knot *(page 121, step 8)* with the two wire ends.

2 Connecting the terminals. Twist the wire strands clockwise and use a screwdriver to hook each wire end around a terminal screw. Attach the unmarked (hot) wire to the side with the narrow prong, and the marked (neutral) wire to the side with the wide prong. Tighten the terminal screws, as shown, making sure there are no stray ends. Close the plug by snapping the core into the shell and tightening any retaining screws *(inset)*.

INSTALLING A QUICK-CONNECT PLUG

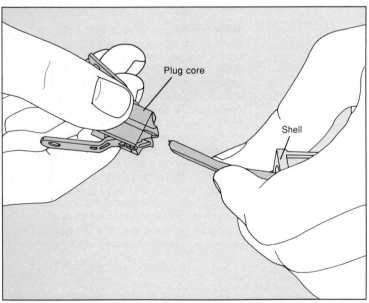

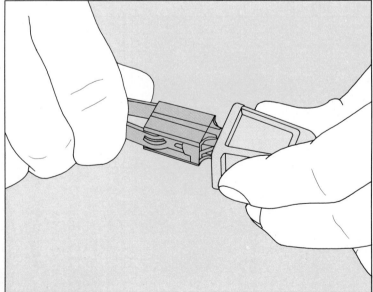

Taking a wiring shortcut. Unplug the lamp. Snip the faulty plug off the old wire with a utility knife or diagonal-cutting pliers. For best results, remove the old wire and plug and rewire the lamp *(pages 128, 129 and 131)*. Spread open the prongs of the new plug by hand or, on some quick-connect plugs, by lifting a lever on top of the plug, then insert the cord into the plug core *(above, left)*. Insert the unmarked wire of the cord on the side of the narrow prong. Then squeeze the prongs together by hand or with the lever, piercing the cord. Slide the shell, if any, over the plug *(above, right)*.

SERVICING A ROUND-CORD PLUG

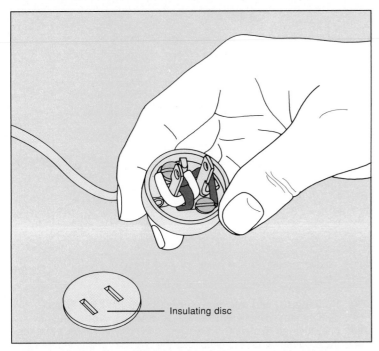

Insulating disc

1 **Removing the old plug.** Unplug the lamp and inspect the plug *(above)*. If the insulating disc is missing, or the prongs are bent or broken, snip the faulty plug off the old wire with a utility knife or diagonal-cutting pliers. For best results, remove the old wire and rewire the lamp *(pages 128, 129 and 131)*. Then replace the plug *(step 2)*.

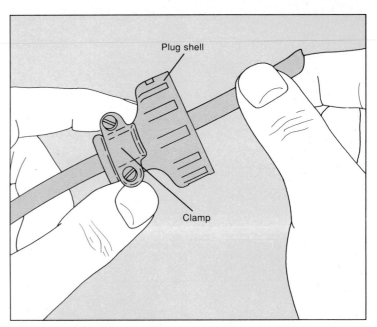

Plug shell

Clamp

2 **Preparing the new plug.** Buy a replacement round-cord plug and pry off the shell with a flat-tipped screwdriver. (Modern plugs do not have insulating discs—they are no longer approved for use.) Slide the shell onto the cord, as shown, and strip 1 1/2 inches of insulation from each wire end *(page 417)*. Tie an Underwriters' knot *(page 121, step 8)* with the two wire ends.

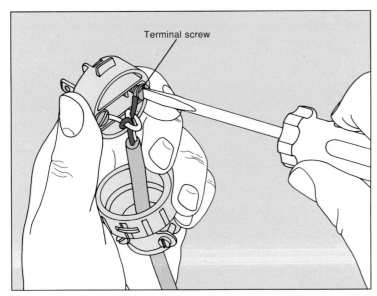

Terminal screw

3 **Making the connections.** Connect the wire ends clockwise to the terminal screws of the new plug *(above)*, hooking the white wire around the silver screw and the black wire around the brass screw. Tighten the connections, making sure there are no stray ends.

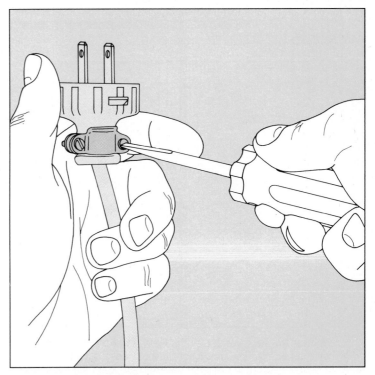

4 **Tightening the clamp.** Fit the plug shell over the core and snap them together. (In some plugs, the core is fastened to the shell with screws.) Secure the plug by tightening the two screws on the plug clamp *(above)*.

REWIRING A ONE-SOCKET LAMP

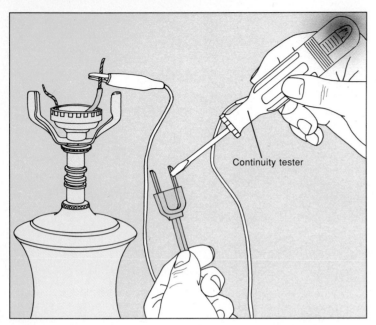

Continuity tester

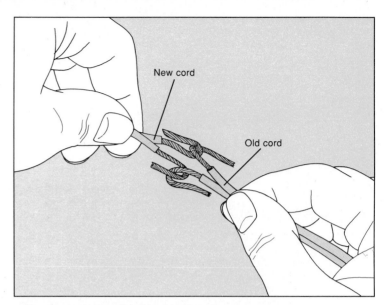

New cord

Old cord

1 **Testing the cord and plug.** Unplug the lamp. Remove the shade, unscrew the bulb and lift off the harp, then remove the socket *(page 120)*. If the plug is not polarized, place the alligator clip of a continuity tester on one wire end and touch the tester probe first to one plug prong *(above)*, then to the other. The tester should light for only one prong. Repeat the test for the other wire end. If the plug is polarized (one prong is wider than the other), place the alligator clip of the continuity tester on the end of the unmarked wire and touch the tester probe to the narrow plug prong. Repeat the test for the wide prong and marked wire. On a good cord and plug, the tester should light for both tests. If the tester does not light, tighten the plug connections and test again. If the cord and plug fail the second test, replace them *(next step)*.

2 **Splicing the old and new cords.** If your lamp has a short, straight pipe, simply remove the old cord and feed in the new one, then go to step 4. If the lamp is tall or you suspect that the center pipe bends inside the lamp, use the old cord to pull the new cord through the lamp. Part the new cord 2 inches back, then strip 3/4 inch of insulation from each wire end *(page 417)*. Twist the strands clockwise, then hook the ends of the old and new cords together *(above)*. Secure the splice by wrapping it tightly with electrical tape so that it will fit through the lamp. If the splice is too thick, unwrap it and use a single wire from each cord *(page 131, step 2)*.

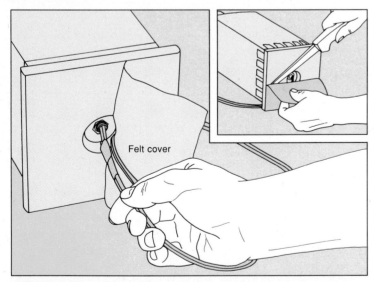

Felt cover

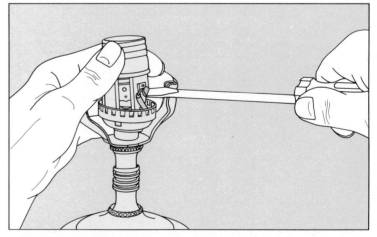

3 **Fishing the new cord.** Using a knife, carefully pry the felt cover away from the lamp base *(inset)*. Peel it back far enough to reveal the cord in the lamp base. (Try to keep the felt in one piece for later regluing.) Feed the splice into the center pipe at the top of the lamp. Then, from the base, pull on the old cord until the splice appears *(above)*. Remove the tape, undo the splice and discard the old cord. Continue pulling the new cord through, leaving enough at the top to attach the socket.

4 **Reassembling the lamp.** Thread the new lamp cord through the socket cap, then screw the cap to the lamp. Part the cord about 2 inches back and strip 3/4 inch of insulation from the separated ends *(page 417)*. Tie an Underwriters' knot with the two wire ends. Hook the unmarked wire around the brass socket terminal and the marked wire around the silver socket terminal, then tighten the connections *(above)*. Slip the insulating sleeve and outer shell onto the socket, and push the shell into the cap. Install a new plug *(page 126)*. Reattach the bulb, harp and shade. Plug in the lamp and test it.

REWIRING A TWO-SOCKET LAMP

Finial

Cover

1 **Access to the wiring.** Unplug the lamp. Remove the light bulbs, then unscrew the finial and lift off the lamp shade. Unscrew the cover at the junction of the sockets *(above)*. Then press on the outer shell of one socket and pull it off with its insulating sleeve. Loosen the terminals on the socket, disconnect the wires and set the socket aside.

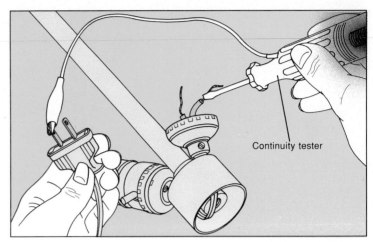

Continuity tester

2 **Testing the cord and plug.** If the plug is not polarized, place the alligator clip of the continuity tester on one plug prong and touch the tester probe first to one wire end *(above)*, then to the other. The tester should light when only one wire end is touched. Repeat the test for the other prong. If the plug is polarized (one prong is wider than the other), place the alligator clip of the continuity tester on the narrow plug prong and touch the tester probe to the unmarked wire at the socket end of the cord. Repeat the test for the wide prong and marked wire. The tester should light in both cases. If it doesn't, tighten the connections and retest. If the cord and plug fail the second test, rewire the lamp *(step 3)*. Otherwise, disassemble and test the second socket.

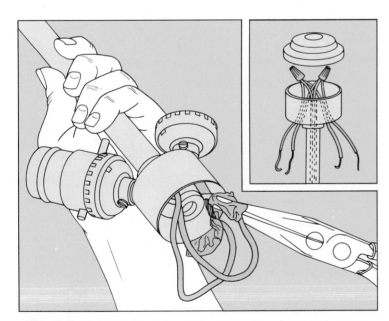

3 **Disconnecting the wires.** Using long-nose pliers, pull out the wires that connect the sockets to the lamp cord *(above)*. Note how the lamp is wired. In most cases, the main lamp cord is parted and each wire is joined with a wire cap to a wire from each socket *(inset)*. The marked wires are joined with one wire cap and the unmarked wires with another. Remove any electrical tape, twist off the wire caps and disconnect the wires.

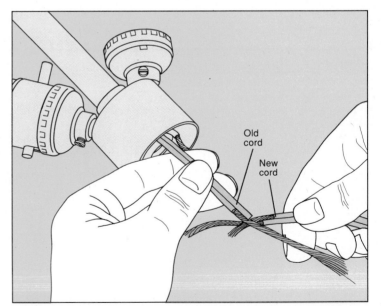

Old cord

New cord

4 **Splicing the old and new cords.** Pull the socket wires out of the lamp and keep them aside to measure new wires in step 6. If your lamp has a short, straight center pipe, simply remove the old cord and feed in the new cord, then go to step 6. If the lamp has a long center pipe, or you suspect that the center pipe bends inside the lamp, use the old cord to pull the new cord through the lamp. Part the new cord about 2 inches back and strip 3/4 inch of insulation from each wire end *(page 417)*. Twist the strands clockwise, then hook the ends of the old and new cords together *(above)*. Secure the splice by wrapping it with electrical tape, keeping the splice as thin as possible so that it will fit through the lamp. If the splice is too thick, undo it and use a single wire from each cord *(page 131, step 2)*.

129

REWIRING A TWO-SOCKET LAMP (continued)

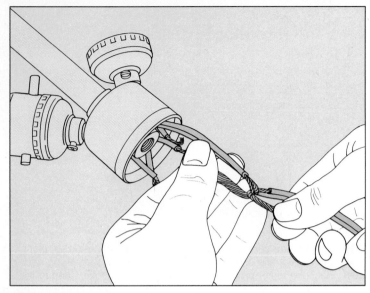

5 **Fishing the new cord.** Feed the splice into the top of the lamp, pushing it into the center pipe. Then pull gently on the old cord at the lamp base until the new cord appears. Disconnect the splice *(above)* and discard the old cord. Install a new plug *(page 126)*.

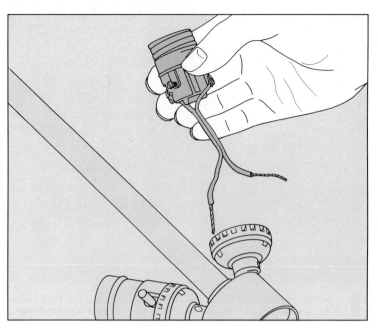

6 **Replacing the socket.** Cut a piece of lamp cord the same length as the old socket wires, part the cord 1 1/2 inches back and strip both ends *(page 417)*. Wrap the unmarked wire around the brass socket terminal and the marked wire around the silver socket terminal, then tighten the connections. Return the socket to the lamp *(above)*, feeding the wires through the socket cap and the top of the lamp. Slip the insulating sleeve and socket shell onto the socket and push the shell into the rim of the cap until it snaps into place.

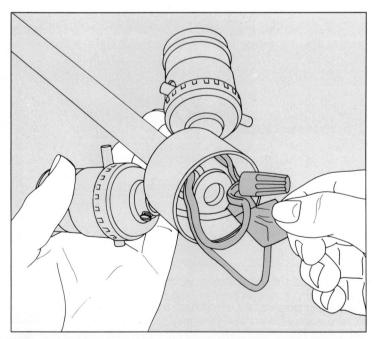

7 **Connecting the socket wires and lamp cord.** Twist the marked wire of the new lamp cord together with the two marked socket wires. Screw on a wire cap. Repeat the procedure for the unmarked wire of the new lamp cord and the two unmarked socket wires. As an extra precaution, secure the connections by wrapping the wire caps with electrical tape *(above)*.

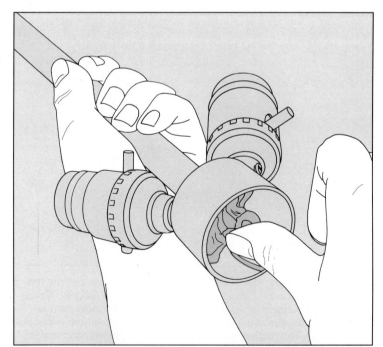

8 **Reassembling the lamp.** Fold the wires back into the top of the lamp, as shown. Replace the cover, shade and finial. Screw in the light bulbs and plug in the lamp to test it.

REWIRING A DESK LAMP

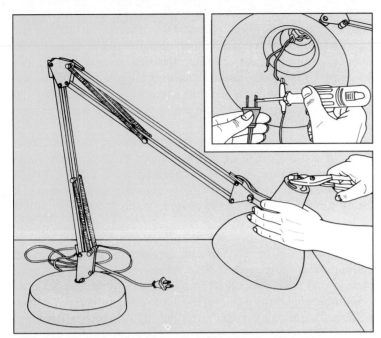

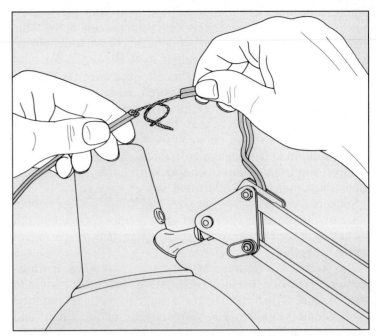

1 **Testing the cord and plug.** Unplug the lamp and remove the light bulb. Use pliers to unscrew the socket retaining ring *(above)*. Then push the cord in at the bottom of the lamp to gain some slack and pull the socket out of its ceramic or plastic insulating sleeve. Loosen the terminals with a screwdriver and disconnect the wires. Remove the socket and set it aside. If the plug is not polarized, place the alligator clip of the continuity tester on one wire end and touch the tester probe first to one plug prong *(inset)*, then the other. The tester should light for only one prong. Repeat the test for the other wire end. If the plug is polarized (one prong is wider than the other), place the alligator clip on the unmarked wire end and touch the tester probe to the narrow prong. Repeat the test for the marked wire end and wide prong. The tester should light for both tests. If not, tighten the connections and test again. If the cord and plug fail the second test, replace them *(next step)*.

2 **Splicing the old and new cords.** Untie the Underwriters' knot, if any, in the old cord, then pull the cord through the hole in the lamp shade so that its wire ends are exposed at the top of the upper arm. To create a splice that is thin enough to feed through the channel of the lamp arm, hook together only one wire of the old and new cords *(above)*. Secure the splice with electrical tape.

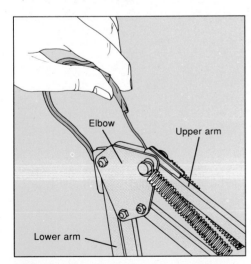

Elbow
Upper arm
Lower arm

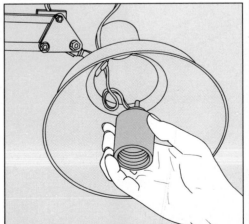

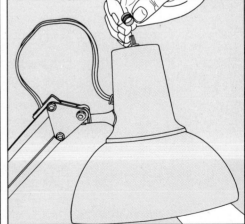

3 **Fishing the new cord.** Use the old cord to pull the new cord through the upper arm until the splice appears at the elbow *(above)*, then continue pulling the new cord through the lower arm to the base. Undo the splice and remove the old wire.

4 **Reassembling the lamp.** Feed the end of the new cord into the lamp shade, then part it and strip back 3/4 inch of insulation from each wire. Attach the ends to the socket terminals *(page 122, step 9)* and insert the socket into the insulating sleeve. Then pull the cord at the lamp elbow to create 3 or 4 inches of slack. Set the socket assembly inside the shade *(above, left)*, screw on the socket retaining ring *(above, right)* and tighten with pliers. Remove all but 2 inches of slack at the elbow by pulling the cord through from the base. Install a new plug *(page 126)*, then screw in a light bulb, plug in the lamp and test the repair.

FLUORESCENT LIGHTING

Fluorescent tubes can give six times more light per watt of power and last five times longer than incandescent bulbs. This makes fluorescent lighting an economical choice for kitchens, workshops and areas where bright light is needed for long periods of time. The color of light cast, once only a cold blue-white, can now be almost any desired shade.

The working parts common to all fluorescent fixtures and lamps are tubes, sockets and ballasts; starters or trigger switches are also found on some models. Tubes *(page 134)* can be straight to fit rectangular fixtures, circular to fit circline fixtures, and U-shaped to fit one-socket fixtures. Replacement tubes must match the ballast and socket wattage.

Sockets come in a variety of sizes and shapes and are held in place by the fixture frame, cover plate or a socket bracket. If a socket is broken or its metal contacts are bent or corroded, replace it *(page 136)*.

The heart of a fluorescent fixture is the ballast, a transformer-like device that initially boosts the incoming current to start the tubes, then reduces the voltage to the level required for continuous lighting. The ballast can last up to 12 years and is generally the most expensive part to replace; when it does fail, you might want to consider replacing the fixture altogether. One sign of a faulty ballast is a black resin that drips out of the ballast casing, caused by overheating. Take care not to touch the leaking fluid when handling an old ballast; it contains harmful chemicals.

There are two basic types of fluorescent fixtures for household use: the starter type (sometimes called pre-heat) and the rapid-start. Starter-type fixtures, usually older units of 30 watts or less, have two circuits: the first provides the initial surge of voltage; the second supplies current for continuous lighting. Rapid-start models do not require a starter for the initial power surge. They are quicker to light but consume slightly more power.

When a fluorescent fixture is not working properly, first look for a blown fuse or tripped circuit breaker at the main service panel *(page 102)*. Next check for a burned-out tube, a faulty wall switch *(page 140)* or, on starter-type fixtures, a faulty starter. You may have to replace the socket, the ballast or the entire fixture.

A fluorescent fixture may be surface-mounted on a wall or ceiling in a kitchen or bathroom, or recessed in a suspended ceiling of a recreation room. When replacing the fixture, choose one that is mounted in the same way as the old one.

Fluorescent lamps work on the same basic principle as fluorescent fixtures. One popular model, the trigger-switch lamp *(page 138)*, resembles a starter-type fixture. The switch performs the same function as the starter; pressing it for several seconds provides the necessary surge of voltage to start the lamp. A more recent generation of fluorescent lamps includes a compact, one-socket model *(page 139)*, identified by its small, U-shaped tube.

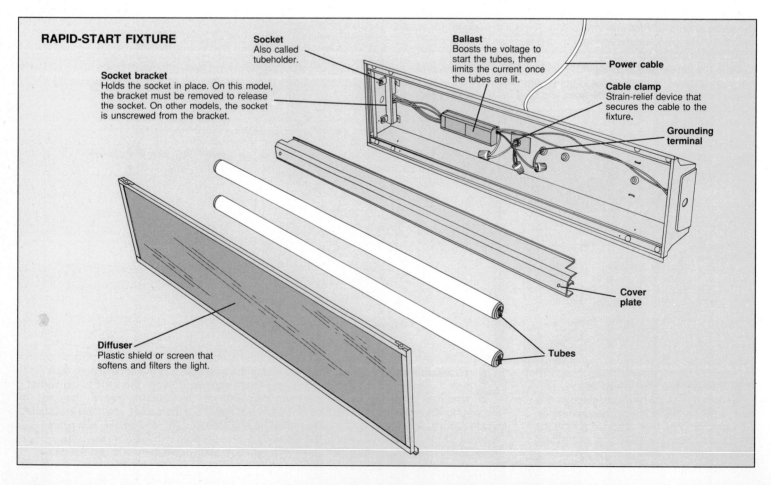

RAPID-START FIXTURE

Socket
Also called tubeholder.

Socket bracket
Holds the socket in place. On this model, the bracket must be removed to release the socket. On other models, the socket is unscrewed from the bracket.

Ballast
Boosts the voltage to start the tubes, then limits the current once the tubes are lit.

Power cable

Cable clamp
Strain-relief device that secures the cable to the fixture.

Grounding terminal

Cover plate

Tubes

Diffuser
Plastic shield or screen that softens and filters the light.

TROUBLESHOOTING GUIDE

SYMPTOM	POSSIBLE CAUSE	PROCEDURE
Fixture doesn't light or ends of tube glow but center doesn't	No power to fixture	Replace fuse or reset circuit breaker (p. 102) □○
	Tube burned out	Replace tube (p. 135) □○
	Wall switch faulty	Check wall switch (p. 140)
	Tube pins making poor contact in sockets	Reseat tube (p. 135) □○; replace sockets (p. 136) ▣○
	Starter faulty	Replace starter (p. 135) □○
	Ballast faulty	Replace ballast (p. 137) ▣◕; replace fixture (recessed or surface-mounted, p. 137; mounted in suspended ceiling, p. 138) ▣◕
	Grounding connections faulty (rapid-start)	Tighten grounding connections (p. 136) □○
Tube blinks, flickers or is slow to light	Tube damp or dirty	Wipe tube with window cleaner and dry thoroughly
	Short, frequent use; tube requires time to stabilize	Leave light on for longer periods
	Starter faulty	Replace starter (p. 135) □○
	Tube pins making poor contact in sockets	Reseat tube (p. 135) □○; replace sockets (p. 136) ▣◕
	Ballast faulty	Replace ballast (p. 137) ▣◕; replace fixture (recessed or surface-mounted, p. 137; mounted in suspended ceiling, p. 138) ▣◕
	Location too cold	Install ballast rated for cold temperatures
Fixture hums	Ballast vibrating	Remount ballast (p. 137) □○
	Ballast faulty	Replace ballast (p. 137) ▣◕; replace fixture (recessed or surface-mounted, p. 137; mounted in suspended ceiling, p. 138) ▣◕
Black resin seeps from fixture	Ballast faulty	Replace ballast (p. 137) ▣◕; replace fixture (recessed or surface-mounted, p. 137; mounted in suspended ceiling, p. 138) ▣◕
Desk lamp doesn't light or lights incompletely	Tube burned out	Replace tube (trigger-switch, p. 138; one-socket, p. 139) □○
	No power to lamp	Plug lamp into another outlet to test
	Switch faulty	Replace switch (trigger-switch, p. 138; one-socket, p. 139) ▣◕
	Tube pins making poor contact in sockets	Reseat tube (p. 135) □○; replace sockets (trigger-switch, p. 138; one-socket, p. 139) ▣○
	Ballast faulty	Replace ballast (trigger-switch, p. 138; one-socket, p. 139) ▣◕

DEGREE OF DIFFICULTY: □Easy ▣Moderate ■Complex
ESTIMATED TIME: ○Less than 1 hour ◕1 to 3 hours ●Over 3 hours

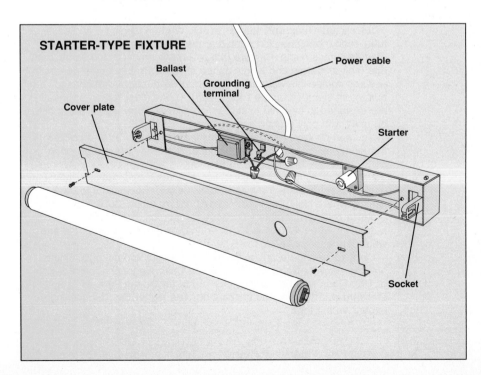

STARTER-TYPE FIXTURE
Ballast
Grounding terminal
Power cable
Cover plate
Starter
Socket

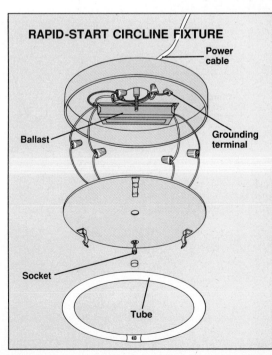

RAPID-START CIRCLINE FIXTURE
Power cable
Ballast
Grounding terminal
Socket
Tube

FLUORESCENT TUBES

Care of fluorescent tubes. Unlike incandescent bulbs, which light when current flows through the filament, a fluorescent tube lights when electricity charges a gas inside the tube, causing the phosphorus-coated inner surface to glow. Age, rapid switching, humjdity, dirt and cold can create an electrochemical imbalance inside the tube and result in swirling, fluttering or blinking. Follow these steps to enhance the performance of the fluorescent tubes:

• Remove a dirty or damp tube, wipe it with a clean cloth dampened with window cleaner and dry it thoroughly.

• Leave a fluorescent light on for several hours rather than switching it on and off for occasional use. Life expectancy drops with increased switching.

• Allow a flickering tube, new or old, to stabilize by leaving it on for several hours.

• Do not expect a fluorescent fixture to perform well at temperatures below 50°F. Install a cold-rated ballast for unheated basements or garages. Shielded tubes are available if wind is a problem.

• Take care when handling a broken fluorescent tube; the mercury inside is poisonous and the glass can cause cuts and slivers.

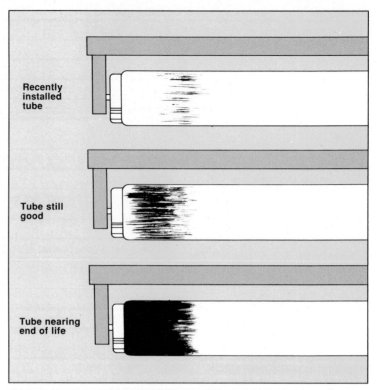

How to spot a burned-out tube. As the cathode filaments of a fluorescent tube wear away, they form black deposits at each end. Light discoloration at the ends indicates a nearly new tube, a wider band of gray is a normal mid-life condition and a blackened end means that the tube is almost finished. If only one end is blackened, reverse the tube to extend its life.

CHOOSING A TUBE

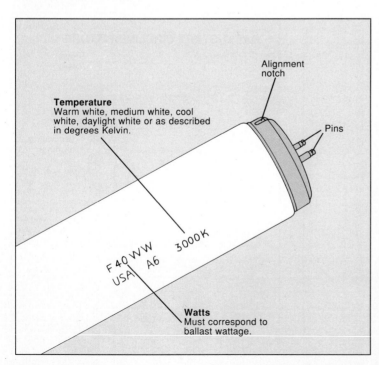

Fluorescent color and temperature. When changing a fluorescent tube, read the information printed at the end of the tube near the manufacturer's name. Be sure to buy a replacement of the same wattage (volt-amperes) and length as the old one. Proper length generally assures compatible wattage; if you are unsure, check the wattage requirement stamped on the ballast *(left)*. Tubes identified as pre-heat are designed to be used in starter-type fixtures, but regular tubes can be used with only slightly less efficiency.

You can choose from a wide variety of temperatures and colors. Temperature ratings range from cool to warm and are measured in degrees Kelvin (or °K). Cool tubes (4000°K and up) produce the harsh factory light that has given fluorescents a bad name for home use. These tubes are the least expensive and most useful for task lighting where high visibility is needed. Warm tubes (3000°K or less) produce light comparable to incandescent bulbs. If in doubt, choose a medium tube (3000 to 4000°K) or, in double-tube fixtures, use one warm and one cool tube.

Color rendering describes the ability of a light source to illuminate objects. Sunlight is the standard, with a Color Rendering Index (CRI) of 100. Fluorescent grow tubes for plants rate in the 90's, while a standard warm white tube is about 50. The higher the CRI, the more expensive the tube.

REPLACING THE TUBE AND STARTER

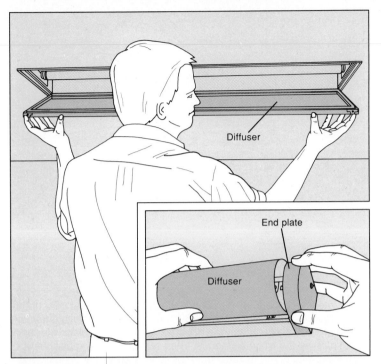

1 **Access to the tube.** Fluorescent fixtures often have a translu-
cent cover, or diffuser, which must be removed to gain access to
the tube. If the diffuser rests in a metal frame with pins on one
side and clips on the other, slide in the clips to release one side and let
the diffuser hang by the pins *(above)*. To release a diffuser held by end
plates *(inset)*, pull one end plate out with one hand and pull the diffuser
free with the other.

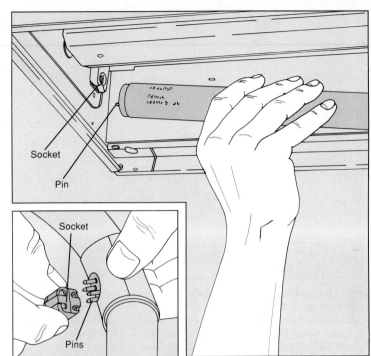

2 **Removing the tube.** Rotate the tube a quarter-turn in either
direction and lower the pins from the sockets, as shown. To
detach a circline tube, unplug the tube pins from the socket, then
pull the tube free of its clips *(inset)*. To replace a starter, go to step 3.
To replace a burned-out fluorescent tube, go to step 4.

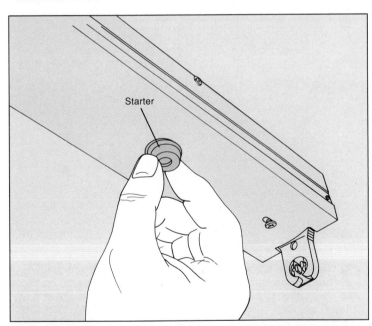

3 **Replacing the starter.** A defective starter is a likely cause of
flickering or blinking and is much cheaper to replace than a tube.
Push in the starter and twist it counterclockwise a quarter-turn
(above), then pull it out. Take it to a lighting store for a correct match;
the wattage of the starter should correspond to that of the tube and
ballast. Push in the new starter until its pins enter the slots, then turn
clockwise until it clicks into place.

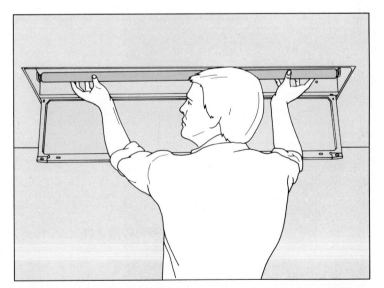

4 **Installing the tube.** Position the pins in the sockets *(above)*,
then twist the tube a quarter-turn to seat it. The tube should fit
snugly; if not, the socket may need replacement *(page 136)*. Install a circline tube by lining up the pins with the holes in the socket
and connecting them, then pushing the tube past the clips. Replace
the diffuser.

SERVICING THE GROUNDING CONNECTIONS

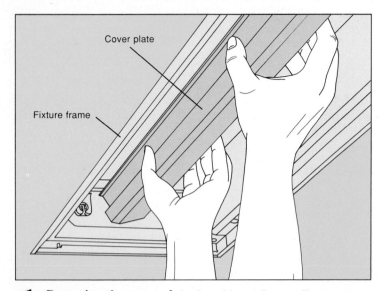

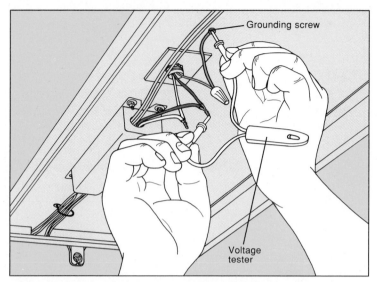

1 **Removing the cover plate.** A rapid-start fixture will not operate correctly if it is improperly grounded. To expose the wire connections, turn off power to the fixture by removing the fuse or tripping the circuit breaker *(page 102)*, then remove the diffuser and tubes *(page 135)*. Squeeze the cover plate to release it from the frame *(above)*, exposing the fixture's wiring.

2 **Testing for voltage and checking the grounding.** Unscrew the wire caps from the black and white leads, taking care not to touch any bare wire ends. Touch one probe of a voltage tester to the grounding screw and the other probe first to the black wire ends *(above)*, then the white wire ends. Then test between the black and white wire ends. The tester should not glow. Inspect the connections at the grounding screw and pigtail and tighten them if necessary. Remount the cover plate and install the tubes *(page 135)*. Turn on the power and flip on the switch. If the fixture lights, put back the diffuser.

REPLACING THE SOCKET

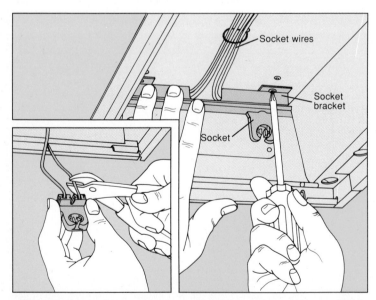

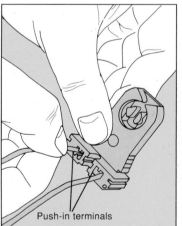 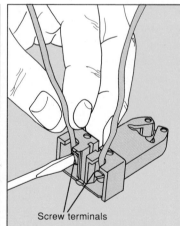

1 **Removing the socket.** Turn off the power *(page 102)*, remove the diffuser and tube *(page 135)*, take off the cover plate and test for voltage *(steps 1 and 2, above)*. Access the socket connections by unscrewing the socket bracket, as shown. To disconnect a socket with push-in terminals, insert a paper clip into each terminal slot and pull out the wire. To disconnect a socket with screw terminals, loosen the screws and unhook the wires. Sockets with preattached wires cannot be disconnected; cut the wires close to the socket *(inset)*, leaving long leads on the ballast.

2 **Replacing the socket.** Take the socket (and its removable bracket, if any) to a lighting store for the best possible match. Push each ballast wire end into a terminal *(above, left)* and tug gently to test for a secure connection. For screw terminals, curl each wire end clockwise around a terminal *(above, right)* and tighten. Screw the socket and bracket, if any, back in place. Then reassemble the fixture, turn on the power and flip on the wall switch. If the fixture lights, replace the diffuser. If it doesn't, check the ballast *(page 137)*.

REPLACING THE BALLAST

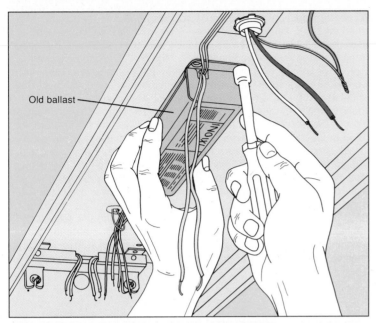

Old ballast

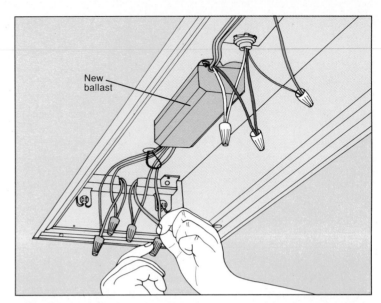

New ballast

1 **Removing the old ballast.** To test the ballast, flip off the wall switch and turn off power to the fixture at the service panel *(page 102)*. Expose the ballast by removing the diffuser and tubes *(page 135)*, then the cover plate *(page 136)*. Do not touch any leaking fluid. Twist the wire caps off the black and white leads and grounding pigtail, taking care not to touch any exposed wire ends. Use a voltage tester to confirm that the power is off *(page 136)*. Release the sockets from their brackets, if any, then disconnect the ballast from both sockets. For sockets with preattached wires, cut the wires near the ballast, leaving a long lead on each socket. Since the ballast is the heaviest part of the fixture, it should be supported firmly with one hand while removing its mounting nuts or screws *(above)*. Take the old ballast with you for a correct match, then dispose of it safely.

2 **Mounting the new ballast.** Set the new ballast in position with its black and white leads facing the incoming house wiring and hold it firmly while tightening the mounting nuts or screws. Connect the ballast to the sockets, twisting together the leads and screwing a wire cap on each connection *(above)*. Set the sockets back in place, then screw or snap on the cover plate, making sure that the wires are not pinched. Install the tubes *(page 135)*, turn on the power and flip on the wall switch. If the ballast hums excessively, turn off the power and tighten the mounting nuts. Replace the diffuser and turn on the power.

REPLACING RECESSED OR SURFACE-MOUNTED FIXTURES

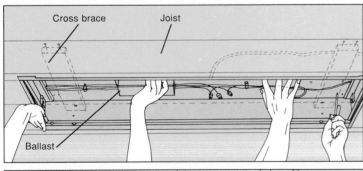

Cross brace   Joist

Ballast

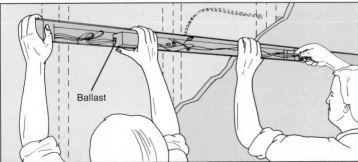

Ballast

Flip off the wall switch and turn off power to the fixture at the service panel *(page 102)*. Remove the diffuser and tubes *(page 135)*, then the cover plate *(page 136)*. Twist the wire caps off the black and white leads and grounding pigtail, taking care not to touch any exposed wire ends, then use a voltage tester to confirm that the power is off *(page 136)*. If the power cable is attached to the fixture with a cable clamp, unscrew the locknut on the clamp. Recessed fixtures are held to cross braces between the joists with mounting screws *(left, top)*. Surface-mounted fixtures are usually attached directly to the ceiling or wall *(left, bottom)*. Have someone support the fixture and ballast while you remove the screws, then lower the fixture. Do not touch any leaking fluid—it contains harmful chemicals—and dispose of the old ballast in a sealed bag.

To install a new fixture, have someone hold it while you push the power cable into the unit through the knockout on the back plate. Drill new holes in the cross brace, if necessary, then secure the fixture by tightening the mounting screws at both ends of the fixture. Connect the fixture's black lead to the black house wire and the white lead to the white house wire. Then make a new grounding pigtail by connecting a jump-er wire to the grounding terminal in the back of the fixture, and twisting it together with the bare grounding wire from the cable. Secure the connections with wire caps. Replace the cover plate, then install the tubes and diffuser.

REPLACING A FIXTURE IN A SUSPENDED CEILING

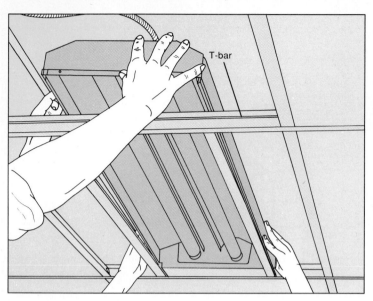

Accessing and replacing the fixture. With power to the fixture turned off at the service panel *(page 102)*, remove the diffuser and tubes *(page 135)*, then the cover plate *(page 136)*. Twist the wire caps off the black and white leads and grounding pigtail, taking care not to touch any exposed wire ends, then use a voltage tester to confirm that power is off *(page 136)*. Unscrew the locknut on the cable clamp so that the cable can be pulled free from the fixture. Remove the ceiling tiles around the fixture, then reach in and detach any safety chains or straps securing the fixture. With a helper, lift, tilt and lower the fixture from the ceiling *(left)*. Buy a replacement fixture of the same dimensions.

Have someone hold the new fixture while you push the power cable through the knockout on the back plate and secure it by tightening the cable clamp. Set the fixture into the T-bar frame, then reattach any safety chains or straps. Connect the black fixture lead to the black house wire and the white lead to the white house wire. Then make a new grounding pigtail by hooking a jumper wire around the grounding terminal in the back of the fixture and twisting it together with the bare grounding wire from the cable. Secure the connections with wire caps, screw or snap on the cover plate, then install the tubes and diffuser.

SERVICING TRIGGER-SWITCH LAMPS

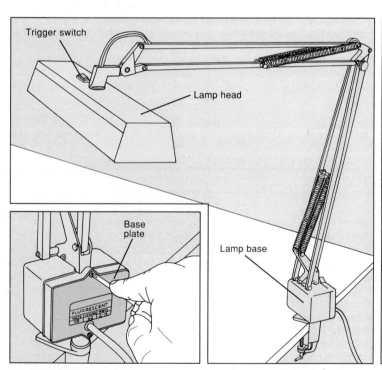

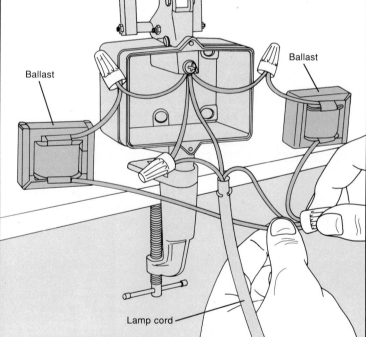

Servicing the tube, the ballast and the trigger switch. Turn off and unplug the lamp. Then check the tube *(page 134)*; if it is burned out, install a compatible replacement. If the tube is good, look for visible damage in the plug and cord; replace them in the same way as for an incandescent lamp *(page 118)*. Also replace a broken or damaged socket *(page 136)*.

More often than not, the problem is with the ballast. Lamp ballasts are small and, because they are quite heavy, are usually located in the lamp base. When the lamp has two tubes, it often has a separate ballast for each. You can save time by replacing both ballasts while the lamp is disassembled. With the lamp unplugged, unscrew the base plate *(inset)* and slide it out of the way. Gently pull the wires out

of the base but do not detach them. Remove any mounting screws and place the ballasts beside the base. Twist off the wire caps *(above, right)*, and detach the two wires from one ballast at a time. If the wires are not color-coded, twist them together to identify them as a pair. Take the ballasts to the store for a correct match. To reassemble the lamp, twist each of the new ballast wires together with a lamp wire and screw on a wire cap. Set the ballasts and wiring back into the base, making sure that no wires are pinched.

If the problem is not the ballast, the trigger switch may be at fault. To access it, remove any snap-in or screw-on cover in the lamp head. Disconnect the wires from the three terminals and install a compatible replacement. Screw on the cover, plug in the lamp and test.

SERVICING ONE-SOCKET LAMPS

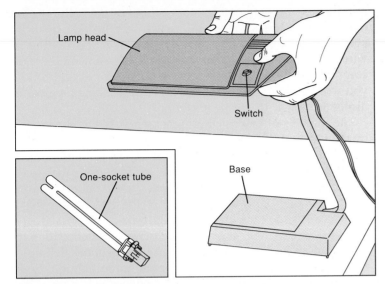

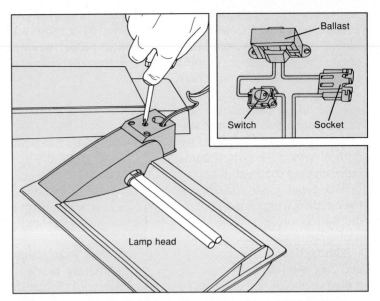

1 **Replacing the tube and removing the lamp head.** Most servicing of the compact, one-socket lamp takes place at the lamp head. To remove a burned-out tube, turn off the lamp and unplug it. Then grasp the tube as close to the base as possible, wiggle it back and forth and gently pull it free. Since the shape of the tube base changes with wattage, take the old tube with you to purchase a replacement. Holding the new tube at the base, push it firmly into the socket.

If there is visible damage to the plug and cord, replace them as for an incandescent lamp *(page 118)*. If not, loosen any screws or clamps holding the lamp head on the stem, then slide it up and off *(above)*.

2 **Disassembling the lamp head.** Remove any screws from the component case in the lamp head *(above)* and pry off the cover with a screwdriver. Take note, as the lamp head is opened, of how the ballast, switch and socket are connected *(inset)*, as well as their positions in the lamp head. To replace the socket, go to the next step; to replace the switch or ballast, go to step 4.

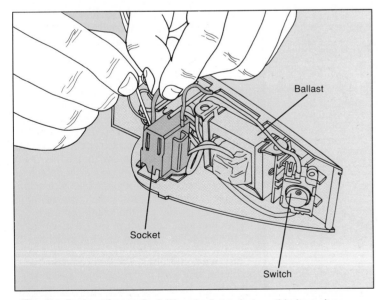

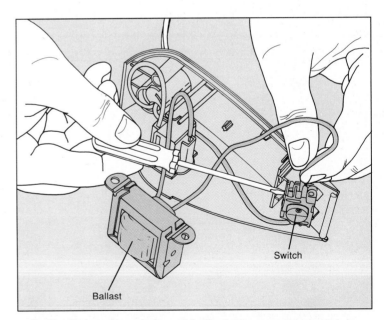

3 **Replacing the socket.** The single socket on this lamp has two push-in terminals. To disconnect the socket, push a pin or paper clip into the slot beside the wire and pull the wire free *(above)*. Then squeeze the two plastic prongs together and pull the socket out of the lamp. Buy a replacement socket of the same wattage and push it into place until the prongs catch, then test it with a light tug. Set the components back into the case, tuck in the wires, and reattach the cover plate. Return the assembled head to the lamp arm.

4 **Replacing the switch and ballast.** Disconnect the switch by detaching the wires at its two screw terminals. Disconnect the ballast by detaching one wire at the switch terminal and the other wire at the socket terminal. Take the old ballast or switch for a correct match. Reconnect the wires to the switch at the two screw terminals; reconnect one ballast wire to a switch terminal and the other to the socket terminal. Set the parts back into the lamp head, tuck in the wires, and reattach the cover plate. If the lamp still doesn't work, test the cord and plug as for an incandescent desk lamp *(page 118)*.

WALL SWITCHES

With a few inexpensive tools such as an insulated screwdriver, voltage tester and continuity tester *(page 417)*, any wall switch can be safely replaced or restored to proper working order. The job can be as simple as cleaning corroded wire ends or tightening loose connections.

Switches found in most homes fall into three general categories, based on the number used to operate a single fixture: single-pole, three-way, and least common, four-way *(below)*.

When a fixture controlled by a wall switch does not work, do not service the switch immediately. First replace the light bulb, change the fuse or reset the circuit breaker at the main service panel *(page 102)*. If you suspect that the problem is in the circuit wiring, flip on the other switches and test a lamp in the outlets on that circuit. After eliminating these potential problems, look to the switch.

Although wall switches may last up to twenty years, heavy use can wear out the mechanism. Most moving parts are sealed inside the housing and cannot be accessed. When the mechanism fails, simply replace the switch.

When removing a wall switch from its box, do not be surprised by wiring variations. Hookups in switch boxes differ according to the number of terminals on the switch *(below)*, grounding variations *(page 142)*, the number of cables enter-ing the box and the number of switches housed within it. The main trick to replacing a wall switch is simply to hook the correct wire around the correct terminal. Color coding on wires and terminals will help you do this. In some of the more complicated installations described on the pages that follow, you will be instructed to tag a wire with masking tape before disconnecting it to aid in reassembly.

The number of cables entering a switch box is determined by the location of the switch in the electrical circuit. A switch installed mid-circuit is called middle-of-the-run and has two (or more) cables in the box—one leading from the power source, the other going out to the next switch, outlet or fixture on the circuit. A switch installed at the end of the run is connected to the single cable in the box.

Manufacturers offer a wide range of wall switches for various locations and special needs. There are switches that turn a fixture on and off automatically, or set mood lighting. Some switches are fitted with a pilot light or oversize handle; others can be locked to protect dangerous power tools. Most can be installed using the procedures shown for single-pole switches. Be sure to read the markings on the switch *(page 141)*. Choose a replacement that is compatible and follow the manufactur-er's instructions carefully.

SINGLE-POLE SWITCH

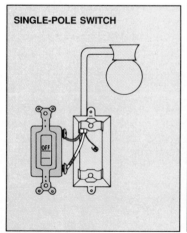

THREE-WAY SERIES

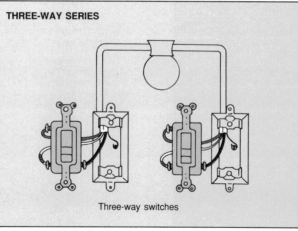

Three-way switches

FOUR-WAY SERIES

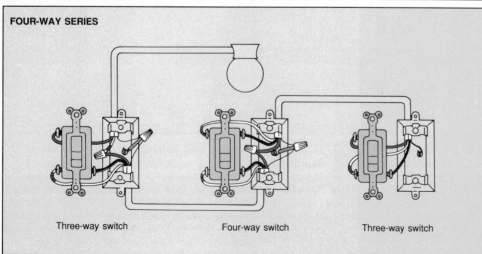

Three-way switch   Four-way switch   Three-way switch

Single-pole switch. The most common switch found in the home, it controls one or more fixtures (or an outlet) from a single location. The switch has two brass screw terminals, each connected to a hot wire. If one wire is black and the other is white, the white wire should be recoded black with electrical tape or black paint to indicate that it is a hot wire.

Three-way switches. A light that can be turned on from two separate locations is controlled by three-way switches, which are always installed in pairs. The term three-way refers to the number of terminals per switch and not the number of switches controlling the fixture. The three-way switch has no ON or OFF markings on the toggle. The darker (black or copper) common terminal connects to a black wire that feeds in from the power source or leads out to the fixture. The two lighter terminals connect to the black, white or red wires that run between the switches.

Four-way switches. Far less common than the three-way switch, the four-way switch is likely to be found near stairs or along hallways. It is always installed in the circuit between a pair of three-way switches. The combination of three-way and four-way switches allows someone to operate a fixture from three or more locations. A four-way switch has four brass screw terminals and no ON or OFF markings on the toggle.

TROUBLESHOOTING GUIDE

SYMPTOM	POSSIBLE CAUSE	PROCEDURE
Fixture does not light or lights intermittently	Light bulb burned out	Replace light bulb
	Fuse blown or circuit breaker tripped	Replace fuse or reset circuit breaker *(p. 102)* □○
	Wires in box damaged	Repair wires in box *(p. 417)* ◪○
	Switch connections loose	Tighten connections *(single-pole, p. 143; three-way, p. 145; four-way, p. 147)* □○
	Switch faulty	Test and replace switch *(single-pole, p. 143; three-way, p. 145; four-way, p. 147)* ◪○
	Fixture faulty	Service fixture *(p. 107)*
Fuse blows or circuit breaker trips when switch flipped on	Too many fixtures or appliances on circuit	Move an appliance to another circuit
	Short circuit in wiring system	Check wiring and boxes along the circuit *(p. 417)* ◪○
Sparks or crackling noise or light flickers when switch on	Switch connections loose	Tighten connections *(single-pole, p. 143; three-way, p. 145; four-way, p. 147)* □○
	Switch faulty	Test and replace switch *(single-pole, p. 143; three-way, p. 145; four-way, p. 147)* ◪○
Toggle does not stay in ON position	Switch faulty	Replace switch *(single-pole, p. 143; three-way, p. 145; four-way, p. 147)* ◪○
Both switches must be flipped to turn on fixture (three-way series)	Loose connection at one of the switches	Tighten connections of one switch at a time *(p. 145)* □○
	One of the switches faulty	Test switches one at a time and replace if faulty *(p. 145)* ◪○
Fixture does not light (four-way series)	Three-way switch connection loose	Tighten connections of one switch at a time *(p. 145)* □○
	One of the three-way switches faulty	Test switches one at a time and replace if faulty *(p. 145)* ◪○
	Four-way switch connection loose	Tighten connections *(p. 147)* □○
	Four-way switch faulty	Test and replace switch *(p. 147)* ◪○

DEGREE OF DIFFICULTY: □ **Easy** ◪ **Moderate** ◼ **Complex**
ESTIMATED TIME: ○ **Less than 1 hour** ◖ **1 to 3 hours** ● **Over 3 hours**

READING A SWITCH

Examining a single-pole switch. Look at the mounting strap for switch ratings and tester listing marks *(right)*. The symbols UL and UND.LAB.INC.LIST confirm that the switch meets the Underwriters Laboratories safety standards. (A CSA monogram is the Canadian Standards Association stamp.) Check maximum ampere and voltage ratings. For example, 15A-120V indicates that the switch can be used for up to 15 amperes of current at 120 volts. 15A-120VAC, or AC ONLY stamped elsewhere on the switch, indicates that it can only be used in alternating current systems, now almost universal in homes.

The two brass terminals of the single-pole switch are normally found on the side of the housing. The most common configuration of side-wired switches has an upper and lower terminal on the same side.

Some switches have a grounding terminal on the mounting strap at the top or bottom. The terminal is hexagonal, often colored green or marked GR. These switches are especially recommended for use in plastic boxes that do not contain a grounding bar *(page 142)*.

Wire specifications appear on the mounting strap and on the back of the switch. Switches rated at 30 amperes and above and with CU/AL markings accept copper, copper-clad aluminum, or aluminum wiring. A 15-or 20-ampere switch with a CO/ALR stamp can also be used with copper, copper-clad aluminum or aluminum wire. Switches without these markings are for use with copper wire only. Prescribed wire size, ranging from No. 10 to No. 14, normally appears on the back; most circuits with light fixtures use No. 12 or No. 14 wire. On the back of some switches are push-in terminals and an accompanying wire strip gauge. When the switch has both push-in and screw terminals, use the screw terminals to provide a more secure connection.

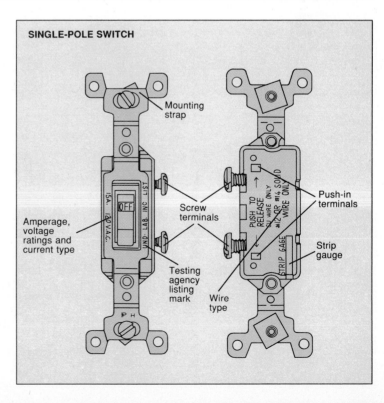

SINGLE-POLE SWITCH

Mounting strap

Amperage, voltage ratings and current type

Testing agency listing mark

Screw terminals

Push-in terminals

Strip gauge

Wire type

GROUNDING SWITCHES AND SWITCH BOXES

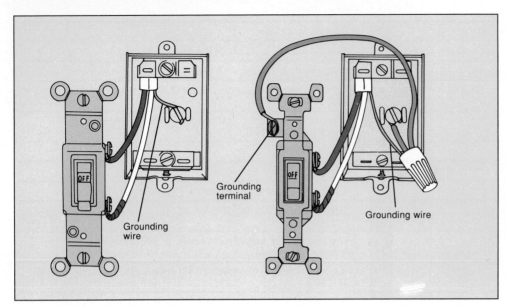

Grounding terminal

Grounding wire

Grounding wire

Grounding in metal boxes (one cable).
Grounding is an important safety precaution *(page 104)*. Replace a defective switch with one that has its own grounding terminal so that the switch can be grounded directly. If the switch does not have a grounding terminal, a grounded metal box normally provides a ground to the switch through its mounting screws.

When the switch does not have a grounding terminal, secure the bare copper grounding wire from the cable to the back of the metal box *(far left)*.

If the switch has a grounding terminal, fashion a pigtail *(page 417)* to ground the switch *(near left)*. Attach a jumper wire to the grounding terminal, and another to a screw at the back of the box. Twist the ends of these jumpers together with the bare wire from the cable and screw on a wire cap.

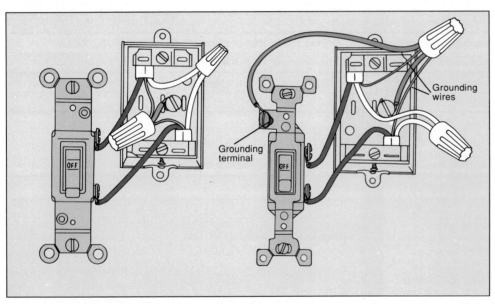

Grounding wires

Grounding terminal

Grounding in metal boxes (two cables).
If the switch does not have a grounding terminal, fashion a pigtail connection from the two grounding wires and jumper *(far left)*. Attach the jumper wire to the screw terminal on the back of the box, twist the other end of the jumper together with the bare grounding wires from each cable and screw on a wire cap. In Canada, code allows both of the grounding wires entering the box to be hooked around a screw on the back of the metal box.

When there is a grounding terminal on the switch, attach the jumper wire to the terminal and connect the jumper to the other grounding wires with a wire cap *(near left)*.

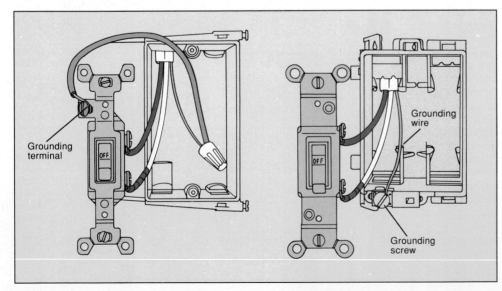

Grounding terminal

Grounding wire

Grounding screw

Grounding in plastic boxes. Some plastic boxes have a grounding screw on a metal bar. When there is no grounding terminal on the switch, ground the box by attaching the grounding wire to the metal bar *(near left)*.

Where the switch has a grounding terminal and the box does not, attach a jumper wire to the switch grounding terminal and connect it to the bare grounding wire from the cable with a wire cap *(far left)*. If the switch and the box have a grounding terminal, make a pigtail as shown in the previous step to connect both the switch and box to the grounding wire from the cable. Where two cables enter the box, include the grounding wire from both cables in the pigtail.

SERVICING SINGLE-POLE SWITCHES

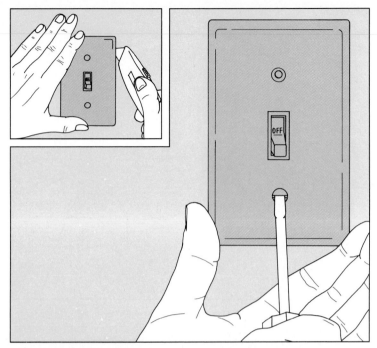

1 **Removing the cover plate.** Turn off power to the switch by removing the fuse or tripping the circuit breaker *(page 102)*. Remove the two screws on the cover plate *(above)* and lift it away from the wall. If the cover plate is stuck to the wall with paint or plaster, use a sharp knife to cut neatly around its edge *(inset)*. Tape the screws to the cover plate to avoid losing them.

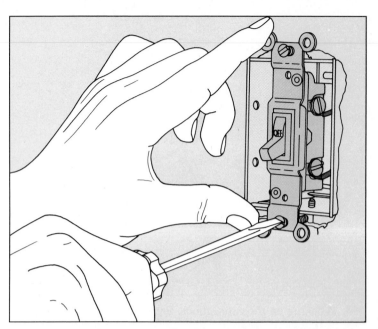

2 **Freeing the switch from the box.** Release the switch from the box by loosening the mounting screws located at the top and bottom of the mounting strap *(above)*. Grasp the mounting strap and pull the switch out of the box to expose the wires. Do not touch any wires or terminals until you have checked for voltage *(step 4)*.

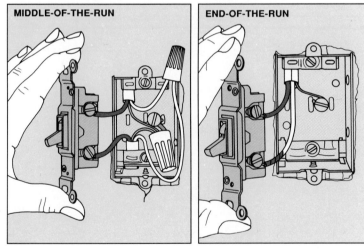

MIDDLE-OF-THE-RUN   END-OF-THE-RUN

3 **Identifying the wiring.** Check the number of cables entering the box. When the switch is middle-of-the-run, at least two cables enter the box *(above, left)*. Each cable has one black wire, one white wire, and a copper grounding wire. The black wires are hot and are connected to the switch terminals. The white wires are neutral and are joined inside the box with a wire cap. When the switch is end-of-the-run *(above, right)*, only one cable enters the box. Both the black and white wires connected to the switch terminals are hot. The white wire should be recoded black (hot) with electrical tape or black paint.

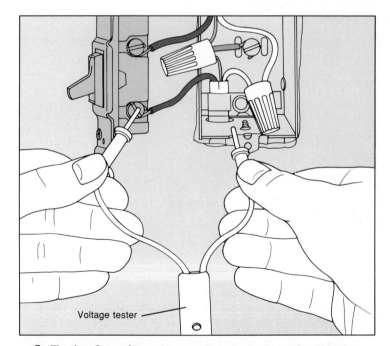

Voltage tester

4 **Testing for voltage.** Use a voltage tester to confirm that the power is off by touching one of the tester probes to the grounded metal box and the other probe to the terminal where a black wire is connected *(above)*. For plastic boxes, touch one probe to the switch terminal with the black wire and the other probe to the green grounding terminal on the switch (or to the metal grounding bar on the box or bare grounding wire). Repeat the procedure for the other switch terminal. The tester should not glow. If it does, return to the service panel and turn off power to the correct circuit.

SERVICING SINGLE-POLE SWITCHES (continued)

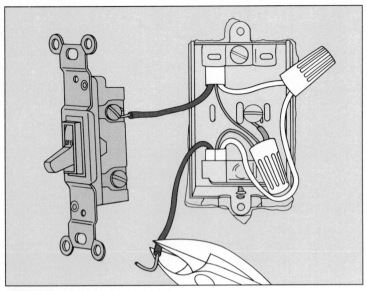

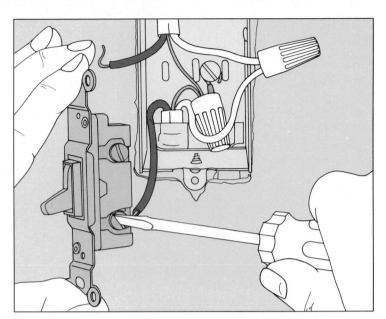

5 **Working on the connections.** Begin by checking the connections at the terminals. If a wire is loose, rehook it around the terminal and tighten the screw. If the connections appear dirty, detach the wires and clean the terminals and wire ends with fine sandpaper. Or clip the wires *(above)* and restrip the insulation to expose clean wire *(page 417)*. With long-nose pliers, form the wire ends into a hook and secure each wire clockwise under its terminal screw. Then screw the switch back into the box, turn on the power and flip on the switch to see if there is power to the fixture. If the switch works, put on the cover plate. If it doesn't work, turn off the power, take the switch out of the box and test it *(step 6)*.

6 **Removing the switch.** Loosen the terminal screws and detach the wires *(above)*. When there is a single cable in the box, mark the white wire with electrical tape or black paint, if it is not already marked. If there is a green grounding terminal on the switch, loosen the terminal screw and remove the grounding wire. If the wires are attached to push-in terminals on the back of the switch *(page 141)*, insert a small screwdriver blade into the release slot of each terminal and pull the wires free.

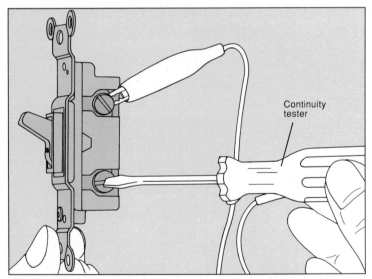

Continuity tester

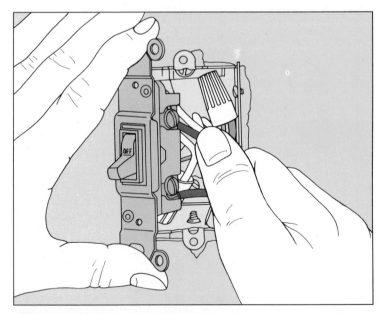

7 **Testing the switch.** Set the switch in the ON position. (Some switches have ON and OFF marked on the toggle; others have only a small, round bump to indicate the ON position.) Place the alligator clip of a continuity tester on one of the terminals and touch the tester probe to the opposite terminal *(above)*. Then set the switch in the OFF position and repeat the procedure. On a good switch, the continuity tester will light when the switch is on, but not when the switch is off. If the switch passes the test, reconnect it, screw it back into the box, put on the cover plate and turn on the power. If the switch is defective, replace it *(step 8)*.

8 **Installing the new switch.** Loosen the terminal screws of the new switch. Hold the switch so that the toggle points down when it is off. Hook the wires clockwise around the correct terminals: Connect one black wire to each terminal; or if one cable enters the box, the black wire to one terminal and the recoded white wire to the other. Tighten the connections firmly. If there is a green grounding terminal on the switch, ground it *(page 142)*. Set the switch into the box *(above)*, carefully folding the wires to make them fit. Screw the mounting strap back onto the box, making sure that the switch is straight. Put on the cover plate and turn on the power.

SERVICING THREE-WAY SWITCHES

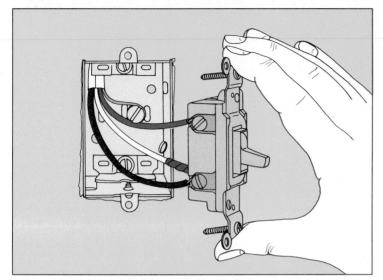

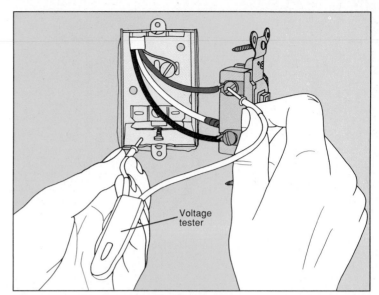

1 Freeing the switch from the box. Three-way switches are always installed in pairs *(page 140)*. To correct a problem in a three-way series, follow the procedure shown here for one of the switches; if it is not faulty, repeat the procedure for the other. Start by turning off power to the switch at the service panel *(page 102)*. Remove the screws on the cover plate and lift it away from the wall. Loosen the screws on the mounting strap and pull the switch out of the box to expose the wires *(above)*. Whether one or two cables enter the box, there are always three wires connected to the switch. The wire that feeds in from the power source or leads to the fixture is attached to the darker screw terminal. The two wires that run between the switches are connected to the silver or brass teminals.

2 Testing for voltage. Use a voltage tester to confirm that the power is off by touching one of the tester probes to the grounded metal box and the other probe to one of the three switch terminals *(above)*. For plastic boxes, touch one probe to a switch terminal and the other probe to the green grounding terminal on the switch (or the metal grounding bar on the box or bare grounding wire). Repeat the procedure for the other two switch terminals. The tester should not glow. If it does, return to the service panel and find the correct fuse or circuit breaker and turn off the power to the switch.

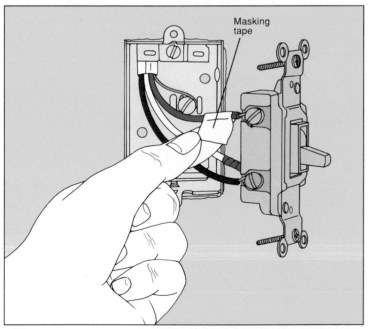

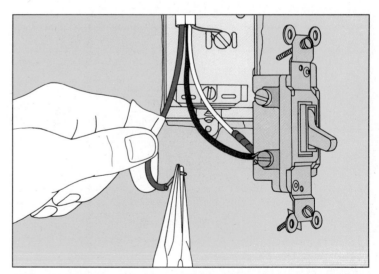

3 Marking the wires. All three wires connected to the switch are hot. A black wire is attached to the darker (copper or black) terminal. To help you when reconnecting the switch, mark this wire with a piece of masking tape *(above)*. The other two wires are connected to the silver or brass terminals. One is red, the other is black (or white recoded black.) If the white is not recoded to indicate that it is hot, mark the end with tape or black paint .

4 Working on the connections. Check the connections at the terminals. If a wire is loose, rehook it around the terminal and tighten the screw. If the connections appear dirty, clean the terminals and wire ends with fine sandpaper. It may be necessary to snip back the wire ends and strip the insulation *(page 417)*. Then recurl the wire ends *(above)* and hook each wire clockwise around its terminal. If there are two cables in the box, check the connections under the wire caps. Screw the switch back into the box, turn on the power and flip on the switch to see if there is power to the fixture. If the switch works, put on the cover plate. If it doesn't, turn off the power again and take the switch out of the box *(step 5)*.

SERVICING THREE-WAY SWITCHES (continued)

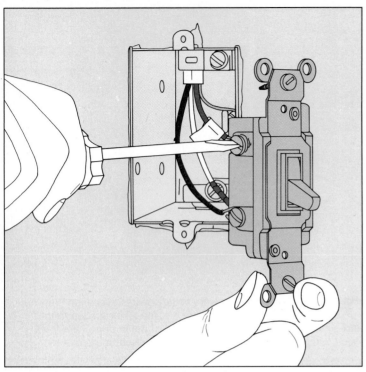

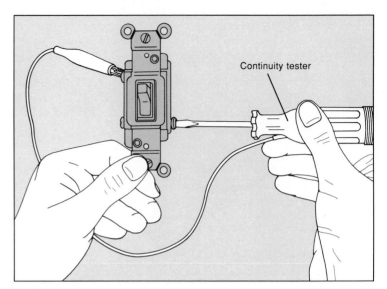

Continuity tester

5 **Removing the old switch.** Loosen the screw terminals *(above)*. Disconnect the tagged wire from the darker terminal. Disconnect the other two wires from their terminals and remove the switch.

6 **Testing the switch.** Place the alligator clip of a continuity tester on the darker (black or copper) terminal. Touch the tester probe to one of the other terminals *(above)*. Flip the switch on, then off. The tester should glow in one position and not in the other. Set the toggle to the position in which the tester glows and touch the tester probe to the opposite terminal. The tester should not glow with the toggle in this position but should glow when the toggle is moved to the other position. If the switch fails any of these tests, replace it *(next step)*. If the switch passes the tests, reconnect it, put it back in the box and put on the cover plate. Then check the other three-way switch.

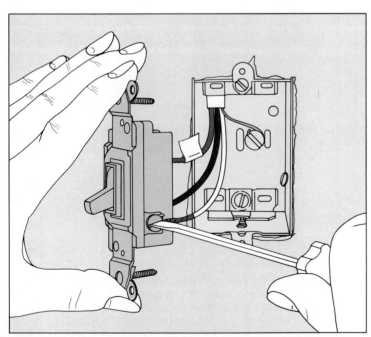

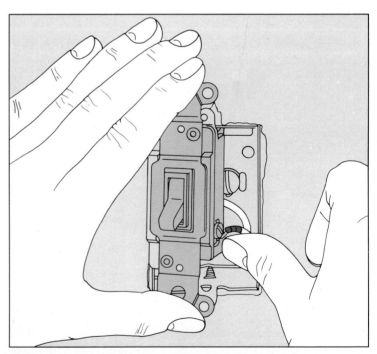

7 **Connecting the new switch.** Hook the tagged wire around the black or copper terminal of the new switch and tighten the screw. Connect the other two wires to their terminals in the same way *(above)*. Either wire can be connected to either terminal. If there is a grounding terminal on the switch, ground it *(page 142)*.

8 **Setting the switch into the box.** Grasp the switch by the mounting strap and push it into the box, as shown, carefully folding the wires to make them fit. Screw the mounting strap back onto the box, making sure the switch is straight. Put on the cover plate and turn on the power.

SERVICING FOUR-WAY SWITCHES

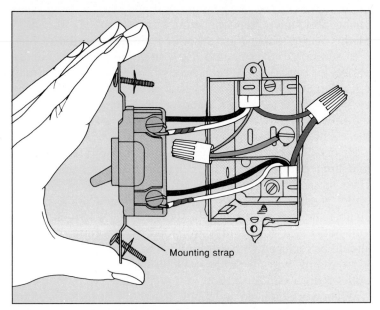

Mounting strap

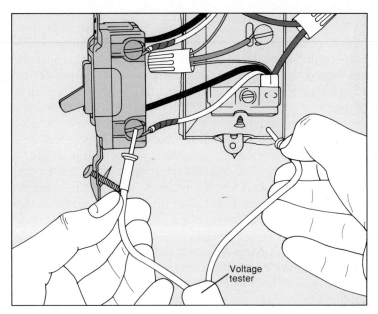

Voltage tester

1 **Freeing the switch from the box.** Turn off power to the switch at the service panel *(page 102)*. Remove the cover plates of all switches that operate the fixture. Identify the three-way and four-way switches: Three-ways have three terminals, four-ways have four terminals. Begin by servicing the three-way switches *(page 145)*; if none of these is faulty, test the four-way switch in the series. Loosen the screws on the mounting strap and pull the switch from the box to expose the wires. There are two cables entering the box; all four wires connected to the switch are hot. Two wires connected to one side of the switch are red; two attached to the other side are either black or white recoded black *(above)*.

2 **Testing for voltage and checking the connections.** Use a voltage tester to confirm that the power is off by touching one of the tester probes to the grounded metal box and the other probe to one of the four screw terminals *(above)*. For plastic boxes, touch one probe to the switch terminal and the other probe to the green grounding terminal on the switch (or to the metal grounding bar on the box or bare grounding wire). Repeat the procedure for all four terminals. The tester should not glow. If it does, return to the service panel and turn off power to the correct circuit. Next check for loose or dirty connections. Clean the wires and screw terminals, stripping the wires if necessary *(page 417)*. Tighten the terminal screws and wire caps. Screw the switch back into the box and turn on the power. If the switch works, put on the cover plate. If it doesn't, turn off the power, take the switch out of the box and go to step 3.

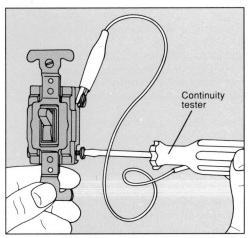

Continuity tester

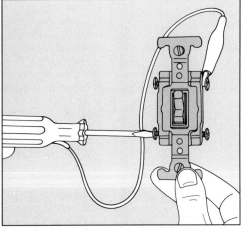

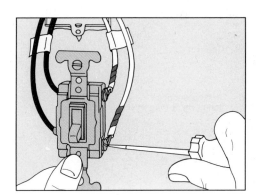

4 **Installing the new switch.** Hook the tagged red wire around an upper terminal. Attach the tagged white wire to the upper terminal on the opposite side. Then connect the other red and white wires *(above)*. Screw the switch back into the box, making sure that it is straight. Put on the cover plate and turn on the power.

3 **Testing the switch.** To help you when reconnecting the switch, use masking tape to tag the wires connected to the two upper terminals. Then disconnect the switch. Place the alligator clip of a continuity tester on one of the upper terminals. Touch the tester probe to the lower terminal on the same side *(above, left)*. If the tester fails to light, set the switch toggle to the other position. The tester should light. Next, touch the tester probe to the lower terminal on the opposite side *(above, right)*, and move the toggle to the other position. The tester should light. Remove the alligator clip from the terminal, place it on the upper terminal on the opposite side, and repeat the procedure. The tester should not light. If the switch fails any of these tests, install a replacement *(step 4)*. If the switch is good, reconnect it, put it back in the box and put on the cover plate. Then check any other four-way switches in the series.

WALL OUTLETS

The common wall outlet is essentially inert. Current arrives at its hot side and is kept on hold until an appliance is plugged into it, completing the circuit. A standard 15-ampere, 120-volt, grounded duplex outlet has an upper and lower receptacle, each with three slots. It is a sturdy and long-lasting device; any problems can usually be traced to the lamp or appliance plugged into the outlet rather than the outlet itself. When it does wear out, or it no longer makes contact with the plug prongs, an outlet can be quickly and inexpensively replaced.

Once the cover plate is removed, you will find one of a number of wiring variations inside an outlet box. The number of cables is determined by the location of the outlet along the circuit. An outlet that is installed mid-circuit (middle-of-the-run) will have two or more cables in the box: One cable coming in from the power source and the other going out to the next box on the circuit. An outlet box located at the end of the circuit (end-of-the-run) has a single incoming cable. An outlet is also wired differently if it is controlled by a switch, or if it is supplied by a 240-volt split circuit *(page 155).*

The trick to attaching an outlet is simply to connect the correct wire to the correct terminal. Black (sometimes red) wires connect to brass terminals and white wires connect to silver terminals. Upper and lower terminals on the same side of the outlet operate as a single unit and may be used interchangeably unless the connecting tab is removed. Variations of this wiring pattern are described within each repair.

In addition to the standard 120-volt duplex outlet, there is a variety of outlets for special needs. The GFCI (ground-fault circuit interrupter) is an important safety feature required by code in bathrooms, garages and outdoor circuits. It monitors the flow of electricity at an outlet and shuts off all current in the event of a leak.

Heavy-duty, 240-volt outlets—which will accept only matching plugs—are found behind most major appliances. Have these outlets serviced by a qualified electrician. Both the outlet and its box must be grounded *(page 159)* to protect against shock in the event of a short circuit. A two-slot, 120-volt outlet will not admit a grounded (three-prong) plug and should be replaced with a grounded three-slot outlet if there is a grounding wire in the box. Otherwise, replace a two-slot outlet with a GFCI outlet.

When working in an outlet box, use a voltage tester rated for 240 volts *(page 417)* and proceed carefully. Work only in dry conditions. Do not touch any terminals or wire ends until you have turned off power to the outlet and used a voltage tester to confirm that the power is off.

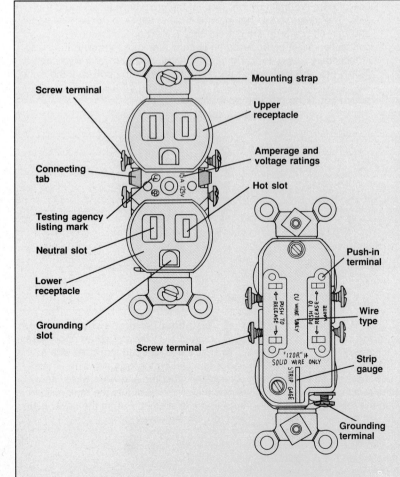

Screw terminal
Mounting strap
Upper receptacle
Amperage and voltage ratings
Connecting tab
Hot slot
Testing agency listing mark
Neutral slot
Push-in terminal
Lower receptacle
Wire type
Grounding slot
Screw terminal
Strip gauge
Grounding terminal

Reading an outlet. The standard grounded duplex outlet has an upper and lower receptacle. Each receptacle has a long (neutral) slot for the wide prong of a plug, a shorter (hot) slot for the narrow prong, and a D-shaped grounding slot.

Look on the front and back of the outlet to find ratings and tester stamps. The symbol UL, or UND.LAB.INC.LIST, confirms that the outlet meets the Underwriters Laboratories standardized tests. (CSA is the Canadian Standards Association monogram.) Voltage and ampere ratings, stamped on the front of the outlet, stipulate the maximum levels at which the outlet can be safely used. For example, 15A-125V indicates that the outlet is designed for up to 15 amperes of current at 125 volts.

Two brass terminals are found on one side of the outlet and two silver terminals on the other side. Sometimes WHITE is stamped on the back of the outlet to identify the side with the silver terminals. A connecting tab links the terminals on each side; when the tab between the brass terminals is snapped off, the upper and lower receptacles function independently. The grounding terminal of the outlet is hexagonal and colored green.

Wire specifications appear on the mounting strap or the back of the outlet. Outlets rated at 30 amperes and above and with a CU/AL marking take copper, copper-clad aluminum or aluminum wiring. A 15- or 20-ampere outlet with a CO/ALR stamp can be used with copper, copper-clad aluminum or aluminum wiring. Unmarked 15- or 20-ampere outlets take only copper or copper-clad wire. Prescribed wire size, usually ranging from No. 10 to No. 14 gauges, normally appears on the back. On the back of some outlets there are also push-in terminals and an accompanying wire-strip gauge. When the outlet has both push-in and screw terminals, hook the wires clockwise around the screw terminals to provide a more secure connection.

TROUBLESHOOTING GUIDE

Most outlet problems can be solved by servicing the connections or replacing the outlet. At right is a quick-reference guide to various outlets in this chapter.

TYPE OF OUTLET	TIGHTEN CONNECTIONS	REPLACE OUTLET
Standard duplex outlet *(p. 150)*	□○	▣○
Switch-controlled outlet (switch controls upper and lower receptacles) *(p. 152)*	□○	▣○
Switch-controlled outlet (switch controls one receptacle) *(p. 153)*	□○	▣○
Split-circuit outlet *(p. 155)*	□○	▣○
GFCI outlet *(p. 156)*	□○	▣○

SYMPTOM	POSSIBLE CAUSE	PROCEDURE
ALL OUTLET TYPES		
Appliance in outlet does not work	Appliance faulty	Check appliance *(Major Appliances, p. 225; Small Appliances, p. 289)*
	No power to outlet	Replace fuse or reset circuit breaker *(p. 102)* □○
	Outlet connections loose	Service connections *(above)*
	Outlet faulty	Replace outlet *(above)*
Fuse blows or breaker trips when plugging in or turning on appliance	Circuit overloaded	Move appliance to another circuit
	Appliance faulty	Check appliance *(Major Appliances, p. 225; Small Appliances, p. 289)*
	Short circuit in wiring system	Check boxes along circuit *(p. 417)* ▣○
Appliance plug falls out easily	Appliance plug faulty	Service appliance plug *(p. 417)* ▣◐
	Outlet worn	Test outlet with reliable plug; if plug falls out, replace outlet *(above)*
Appliance runs intermittently or lamp flickers	Appliance or lamp faulty	Check appliance *(Major Appliances, p. 225; Small Appliances, p. 289)* or lamp *(p. 118)*
	Outlet connections loose	Service connections *(above)*
Sparks or mild shock when plugging in appliance	Appliance is turned on	Turn off appliance before plugging it in
	Fingers contacting plug prongs	Hold plug by insulation
	Appliance faulty	Check appliance *(Major Appliances, p. 225; Small Appliances, p. 289)*
	Outlet connections loose	Service connections *(above)*
SWITCH-CONTROLLED OUTLET		
Outlet does not deliver power	Wall switch faulty	Check wall switch *(p. 140)*
SPLIT-CIRCUIT DUPLEX OUTLET		
Only one receptacle in duplex works	Outlet connections loose	Service connections *(p. 155)* □○
GFCI OUTLET		
GFCI trips constantly	Appliance faulty	Check appliance *(Major Appliances, p. 225; Small Appliances, p. 289)*
	Outlet connections loose	Service connections *(p. 156)* □○
	GFCI faulty	Replace outlet *(p. 156)* ▣◐
	Faulty appliance or wiring in box elsewhere on same circuit	Check appliances on circuit *(Major Appliances, p. 225; Small Appliances, p. 289)*; check wiring in boxes along the circuit *(p. 417)* ▣○
TWO-SLOT OUTLET		
Outlet will not accept grounded (three-prong) plugs	Older, two-slot outlet	Install grounding-adapter plug temporarily *(p. 159)*; replace two-slot outlet with three-slot outlet *(p. 158)* ▣◐ or GFCI outlet *(p. 156)* ▣◐

DEGREE OF DIFFICULTY: □ Easy   ▣ Moderate   ■ Complex
ESTIMATED TIME: ○ Less than 1 hour   ◐ 1 to 3 hours   ● Over 3 hours

149

SERVICING DUPLEX OUTLETS

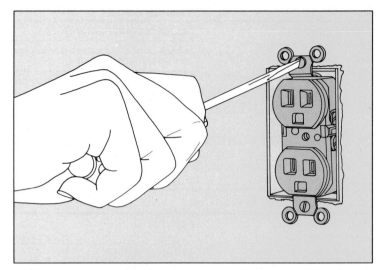

1 **Removing the cover plate.** Turn off power to the outlet by removing the fuse or tripping the circuit breaker *(page 102)*. Remove the screw on the cover plate *(above)* and lift it away from the wall. If the cover plate is stuck to the wall with paint or plaster, use a utility knife or single-edge razor blade to cut neatly around its edge *(inset)*. Tape the screw to the cover plate to avoid losing it.

2 **Freeing the outlet from the box.** Release the outlet from the box by loosening the mounting screws located at the top and bottom of the mounting strap *(above)*. Grasp the mounting strap and pull the outlet out of the box to expose the wires. Do not touch any wires or terminals until you have tested for voltage *(step 4)*.

MIDDLE-OF-THE-RUN

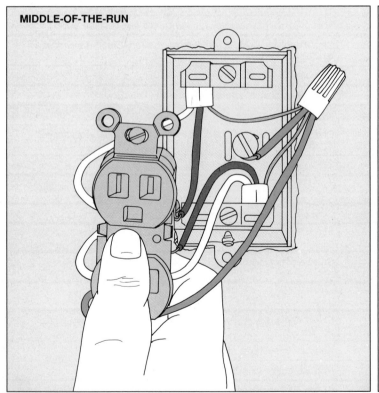

END-OF-THE-RUN

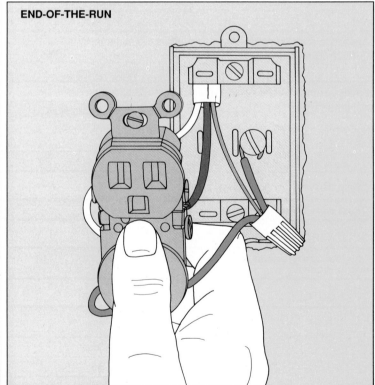

3 **Identifying the wiring.** Check the number of cables entering the box. When the outlet is middle-of-the-run, two cables enter the box *(above, left)*, each with one black wire, one white wire, and a bare copper grounding wire. The black wires are hot and are connected to the brass terminals on the outlet. The white wires are neutral and are connected to the silver terminals. When the outlet is end-of-the-run, only one cable enters the box *(above, right)*. The cable contains one black wire, one white wire and a bare grounding wire. The black wire is attached to a brass terminal and the white wire is attached to a silver terminal. In both cases, a grounding jumper is attached to the grounding terminal on the outlet.

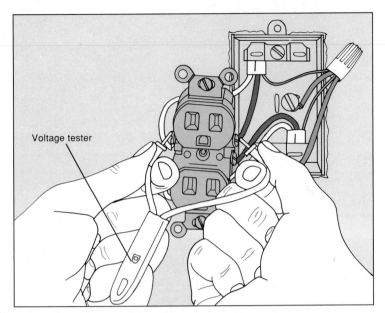

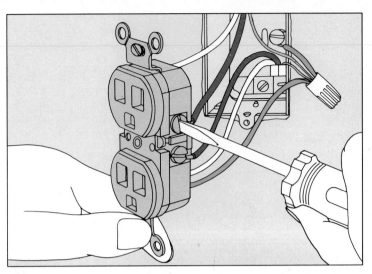

4 **Testing for voltage.** Use a voltage tester to confirm that the power is off by touching one of the tester probes to a brass terminal where a wire is connected and the other probe to a silver terminal where a wire is connected (above). If there are wires connected to the other set of terminals, repeat the procedure for these too. Then test between the grounding terminal and the brass and silver terminals in succession. The tester should not glow in any test. If it does, return to the service panel and turn off power to the correct circuit.

5 **Servicing the connections.** Check the connections at each terminal. If a wire is loose, rehook it around the terminal and tighten the screw. If the connections appear dirty, detach the wires and clean the terminals and wire ends with fine sandpaper. Or clip the wires and strip the insulation to expose clean wire (page 417), then form each wire end into a hook and secure it to the terminal screw (above). Screw the outlet back into the box, turn on the power, and plug a lamp into each receptacle in turn. If the lamp doesn't work in either receptacle, turn off the power and replace the outlet (next step).

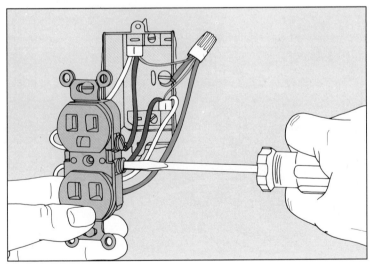

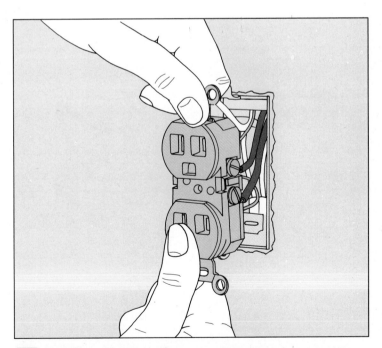

6 **Removing the old outlet.** Loosen the terminal screws and disconnect the black and white wires, as shown. Detach the grounding jumper from the green grounding terminal on the outlet.

7 **Installing the new outlet.** Loosen the terminal screws of the new outlet. Hook each black wire around a brass terminal and tighten the connections, then hook each white wire around a silver terminal and tighten the connections. Connect the grounding jumper to the green grounding terminal on the outlet. Gently fold the wires into the box and set the outlet in place (above). Screw the mounting strap to the box, making sure that the outlet is straight. Put on the cover plate and turn on the power.

SERVICING SWITCH-CONTROLLED DUPLEX OUTLETS (Switch controls both receptacles)

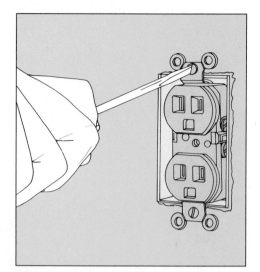

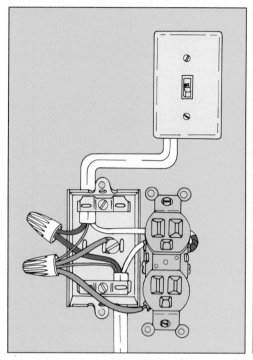

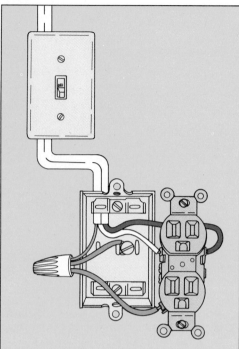

1 Removing the outlet. When an outlet controlled by a wall switch is not operating, first check the switch *(page 140)*. If the problem persists, service the outlet. Begin by flipping off the switch that controls the outlet, then turn off the power by removing the fuse or tripping the circuit breaker *(page 102)*. Unscrew the cover plate, loosen the mounting strap *(above)* and pull the outlet from the box, taking care not to touch any exposed wire ends or terminals.

2 Identifying the wiring. If two cables enter the box *(above, left)*, one of the white wires may be attached to a brass terminal; this white wire should be recoded black with electrical tape or black paint to indicate that it is hot (it carries current to the switch). The other white wire is attached to a silver terminal. The black wires are connected under a wire cap. If one cable enters the box *(above, right)*, the black wire is attached to a brass terminal and the white wire is attached to a silver terminal.

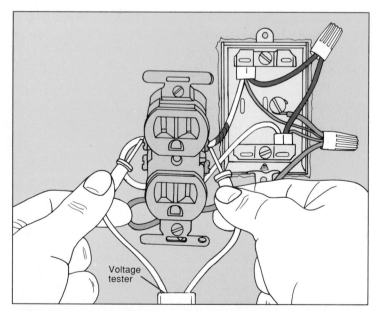

Voltage tester

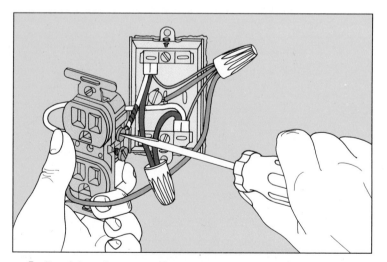

3 Testing for voltage. Use a voltage tester to confirm that the power is off by touching one of the tester probes to the brass terminal where a wire is connected and the other probe to the silver terminal where a wire is connected *(above)*. Then test between the grounding terminal and the brass and silver terminals in succession. The tester should not glow in any test. If it does, return to the service panel and turn off power to the correct circuit *(page 102)*.

4 Servicing the connections. Check the connections at each terminal. If a wire is loose, rehook it around the terminal and tighten the screw. If the connections appear dirty, detach the wires and clean the terminals and wire ends with fine sandpaper. Or clip the wires and strip the insulation to expose clean wire *(page 417)*, then form each wire end into a hook and secure it to the terminal *(above)*. Screw the outlet back into the box, turn on the power, flip on the wall switch and plug a lamp into each receptacle. If the lamp doesn't work in either receptacle, turn off the power, disconnect the outlet and install a replacement *(step 5)*.

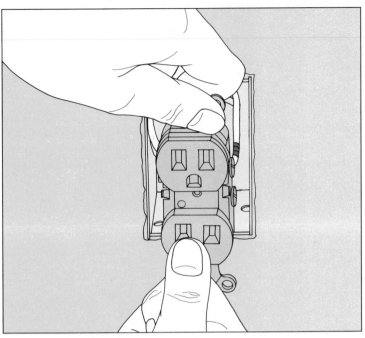

5 **Replacing the outlet.** With the power off, remove the old outlet and loosen the terminal screws on the new outlet. If there are two cables in the box, hook the white wire with the black marking clockwise around a brass terminal and tighten the connection, then hook the other white wire clockwise around a silver terminal and tighten it. If there is one cable in the box, attach the black wire to a brass terminal and the white wire to a silver terminal. Reconnect the grounding jumper to the green grounding terminal on the outlet. Gently fold the wires into the box and set the outlet in place *(left)*. Screw the mounting strap onto the box, making sure that the outlet is straight. Put on the cover plate and turn on the power.

SERVICING SWITCH-CONTROLLED OUTLETS (Switch controls one receptacle)

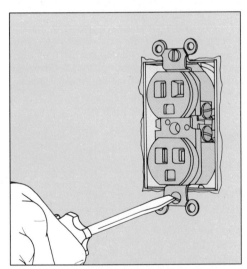

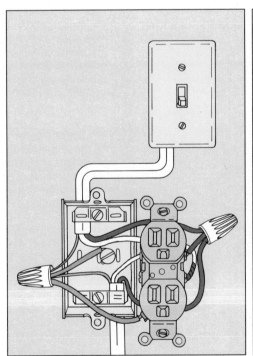

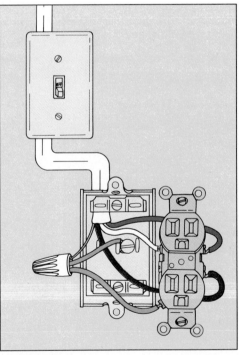

1 **Removing the outlet.** This duplex outlet is wired so that one receptacle (upper or lower) is controlled by a wall switch; the other receptacle is independent of the switch. When the outlet does not operate correctly, first check the switch *(page 140)*. If the problem persists, service the outlet. Turn off the power by removing the fuse or tripping the circuit breaker *(page 102)*. Unscrew the cover plate, loosen the mounting strap and pull the outlet from the box, taking care not to touch any exposed wire ends or terminals.

2 **Identifying the wiring.** If two cables enter the box *(above, left)*, the black wires are connected to a jumper that hooks around a brass terminal. One of the white wires is attached to a silver terminal. The other white wire is attached to a brass terminal; this white wire should be recoded black with electrical tape or black paint, indicating that it is hot (it carries current to the switch). If one cable enters the box *(above, right)*, it has two hot wires (one black and one red) to deliver power to the receptacles individually. The black and red wires are attached to brass terminals. The white wire is attached to a silver terminal. In both cases, the connecting tab between the brass terminals has been removed, interrupting the flow of power between the upper and lower receptacles.

SERVICING SWITCH-CONTROLLED OUTLETS (Switch controls one receptacle, continued)

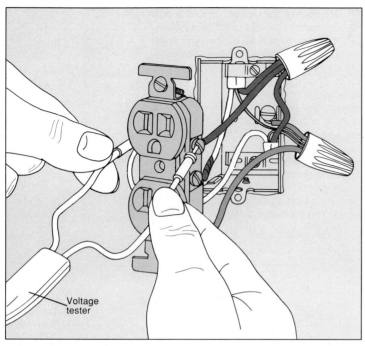

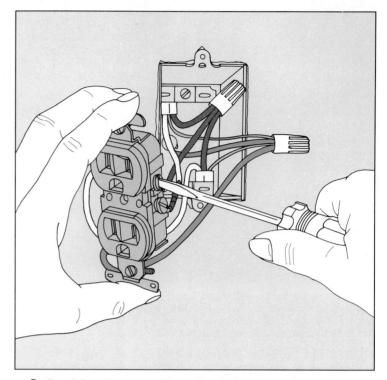

3 **Testing for voltage.** Use a voltage tester to confirm that the power is off by touching one of the tester probes to one brass terminal and the other probe to the silver terminal where the wire is connected *(above)*. Repeat the procedure for the same silver terminal and the other brass terminal. Then test between the grounding terminal and the brass and silver terminals in succession. The tester should not glow in any test. If it does, return to the service panel and turn off power to the correct circuit.

4 **Servicing the connections.** Check the connections at the terminals. If a wire is loose, rehook it around the terminal and tighten the screw. If the connections appear dirty, detach the wires and clean the terminals and wire ends with fine sandpaper. Or clip the wires and strip the insulation to expose clean wire *(page 417)*, then form each wire end into a hook and secure the wires clockwise under the terminals *(above)*. Screw the outlet back into the box, turn on the power, flip on the wall switch and plug a lamp into each receptacle. If the lamp doesn't work in either receptacle, turn off the power, disconnect the outlet and install a replacement *(step 5)*.

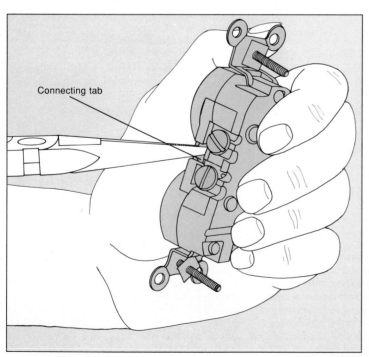

Connecting tab

5 **Installing the new outlet.** Confirm that power is off *(step 3, above)*. To ensure that the two receptacles of the new outlet will operate independently, use long-nose pliers or a screwdriver to snap off the connecting tab between the brass terminals *(left)*; do not snap off the tab between the silver terminals. If there are two cables in the box, hook the white wire with the black marking around one brass terminal and the jumper from the pigtail of black wires around the other brass terminal and tighten the connections. Connect the white wire to a silver terminal. If there is one cable in the box, attach the black wire to one brass terminal, the red wire to the other brass terminal, and the white wire to a silver terminal. Reconnect the grounding jumper to the green grounding terminal on the outlet. Screw the outlet into the box, making sure that it is straight, then put on the cover plate and turn on the power.

SERVICING SPLIT-CIRCUIT DUPLEX OUTLETS

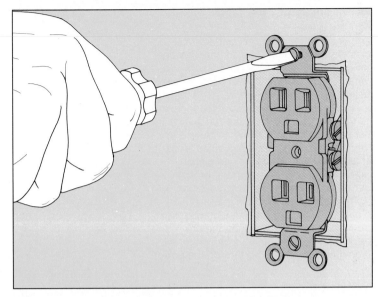

1 **Removing the outlet.** On a split-circuit duplex outlet, the upper and lower receptacles of the outlet operate independently, each connected to half of a dedicated 120/240-volt circuit. Commonly found in kitchens, the split-circuit duplex provides power for appliances, such as toasters, electric kettles and coffeemakers, which consume a great deal of electricity. When the outlet is not operating correctly, turn off power to the 120/240-volt circuit at the main service panel *(page 102)*, or at a switch beside the panel. Unscrew the cover plate, loosen the mounting strap *(above)* and pull the outlet from the box. Take care not to touch any exposed wire ends or terminals.

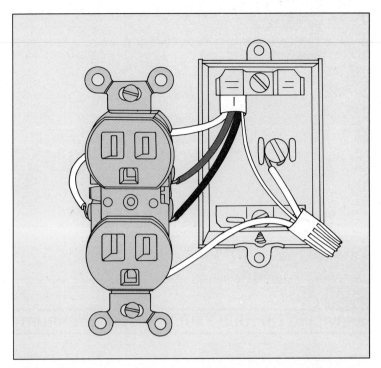

2 **Identifying the wiring.** One cable enters the box *(above)*; it has two hot wires (one black and one red), each attached to a brass terminal. The white wire is attached to a silver terminal. The connecting tab between the brass terminals has been removed, interrupting the power between the upper and lower receptacles.

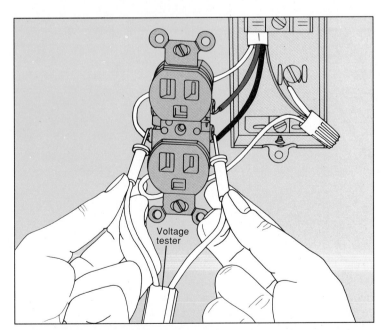

Voltage tester

3 **Testing for voltage.** Use a voltage tester to confirm that the power is off by touching one of the tester probes to a brass terminal and the other probe to the silver terminal where a wire is connected *(above)*. Repeat the procedure for the same silver terminal and the other brass terminal, then between the two brass terminals. Test between the grounding terminal and the brass and silver terminals in succession. The tester should not glow in any test. If it does, return to the service panel and turn off power to the correct circuit.

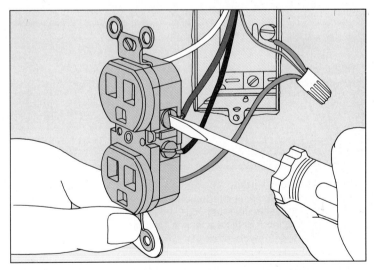

4 **Servicing the connections.** Check the connections at the terminals. If a wire is loose, rehook it around the terminal and tighten the screw. If the connections appear dirty, detach the wires and clean the terminals and wire ends with fine sandpaper. Or clip the wires and strip the insulation to expose clean wire *(page 417)*, then form the wire ends into hooks and secure each wire clockwise under its terminal *(above)*. Screw the outlet back into the box, turn on the power, and test the outlet. If the outlet still doesn't work, turn off the power, disconnect the outlet and install a replacement *(next step)*.

SERVICING SPLIT-CIRCUIT DUPLEX OUTLETS (continued)

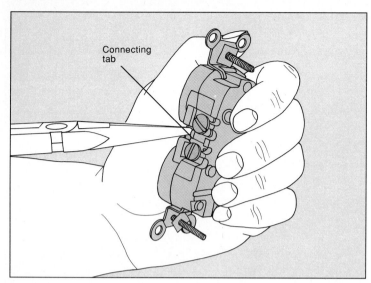

Connecting tab

5 **Installing the new outlet.** Confirm that power is off *(page 155, step 3)*. To ensure that the upper and lower receptacles of the new outlet will operate independently, use long-nose pliers or a screwdriver to snap off the connecting tab between the brass terminals *(left)*; do not snap off the tab between the silver terminals. Attach the black wire to one brass terminal, the red wire to the other brass terminal, and the white wire to a silver terminal. If there are two white wires, join them first with a jumper and pigtail *(page 417)* and connect the jumper to the silver terminal. Reconnect the grounding jumper to the green grounding terminal on the outlet. Gently fold the wires into the box. Screw the mounting strap onto the box, making sure that the outlet is straight, then put on the cover plate and turn on the power.

SERVICING GROUND-FAULT CIRCUIT INTERRUPTERS

1 **Testing the outlet.** The GFCI (ground-fault circuit interrupter) outlet protects the circuit—and you—by tripping instantly when it detects a leak in current *(page 105)*. Code now requires that GFCI outlets be installed in new and remodeled bathrooms, kitchens and garages; they are also recommended in workshops, laundry rooms and other damp locations. To ensure continued protection, check the GFCI outlet every month by pressing the TEST button; if the RESET button does not pop out, service the outlet. When a GFCI outlet is not delivering power to an appliance, the fault could be with the appliance or the outlet. Unplug the appliance and press the RESET button. If the GFCI still doesn't work, go to step 2.

MIDDLE-OF-THE-RUN

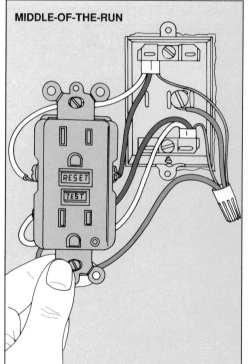

END-OF-THE-RUN

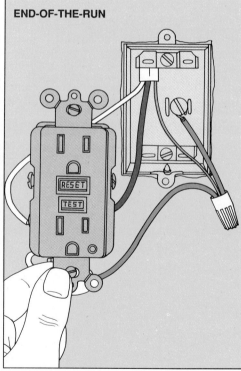

2 **Identifying the wiring.** Turn off power to the outlet by removing the fuse or tripping the circuit breaker *(page 102)*. Unscrew the cover plate, loosen the mounting strap and pull the outlet from the box, taking care not to touch any exposed wire ends or terminals. If two cables enter the box *(above, left)*, each of the black wires is connected to a brass terminal and each of the white wires is connected to a silver terminal. If one cable enters the box *(above, right)*, the black wire is attached to the brass terminal marked LINE and the white wire is attached to the opposite silver terminal. Some GFCI outlets have leads in the place of terminals: two white, two black and one green grounding lead.

SERVICING GROUND-FAULT CIRCUIT INTERRUPTERS (continued)

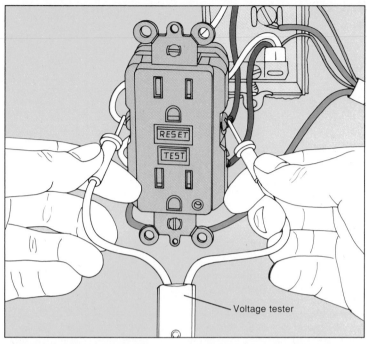

Voltage tester

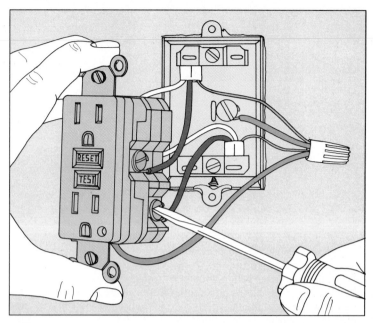

3 Testing for voltage. Use a voltage tester to confirm that the power is off by touching one of the tester probes to the brass terminal where a wire is connected and the other probe to the silver terminal where a wire is connected *(above)*. If there are wires connected to the other set of terminals, repeat the procedure for these. Then test between the grounding terminal and the brass and silver terminals in succession. The tester should not glow in any test. If it does, return to the service panel and turn off power to the correct circuit.

4 Servicing the connections. Check the connections at the terminals. If a wire is loose, rehook it around the terminal and tighten the screw. If the connections appear dirty, detach the wires and clean the terminals and wire ends with fine sandpaper. Or clip the wires and strip the insulation to expose clean wire *(page 417)*, then form the wire ends into hooks and secure each wire clockwise under its terminal, as shown. Screw the outlet back into the box, turn on the power and press the RESET button. If the outlet still doesn't work, turn off the power, free the outlet from the box and go to step 5.

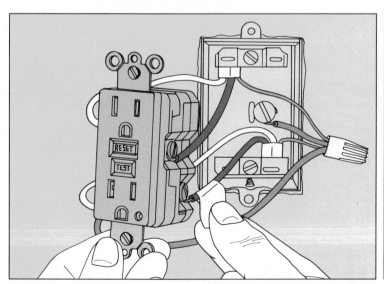

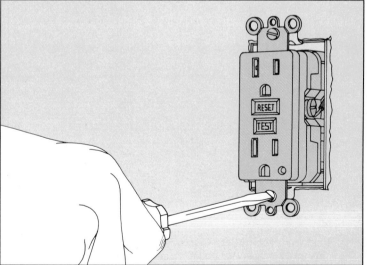

5 Replacing the outlet. If there are two cables in the box, tag the wires to help you when reconnecting the new outlet. Wrap masking tape around the black and white wires connected to the terminals marked LINE *(above, left)*. Disconnect the outlet and buy a replacement. If there are two cables in the box, hook the tagged black wire around the brass terminal marked LINE, and connect the tagged white wire to the opposite silver terminal. Then connect the second black wire to the second brass terminal and the second white wire to the second silver terminal. If there is one cable in the box,

attach the black wire to the brass terminal marked LINE and the white wire to the opposite silver terminal. Reconnect the grounding jumper to the green grounding terminal on the GFCI outlet. Gently fold the wires back into the box and screw the mounting strap to the box *(above, right)*, making sure that the outlet is straight. Put on the cover plate, turn on the power and press the RESET button. If the outlet still doesn't work and there are two cables in the box, a faulty appliance or connection at another point along the circuit may be causing the GFCI to trip. Check the other boxes along the same circuit *(page 417)*.

REPLACING A TWO-SLOT DUPLEX OUTLET

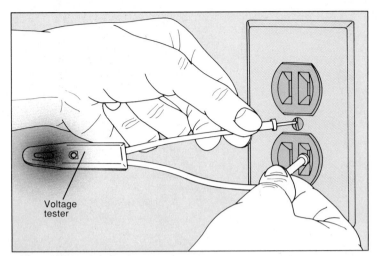

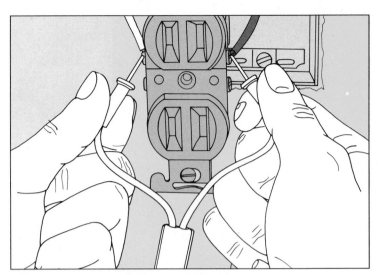

1 **Testing for grounding.** To determine whether you can replace a two-slot outlet with a three-slot grounded outlet, first confirm that the outlet box is grounded. **Caution:** This is a live voltage test. Be sure to hold the voltage tester by its insulated handles, or use the one-hand technique shown in Tools & Techniques *(page 417)*. With the power on, place one probe of the voltage tester on the cover plate screw and insert the other probe into one slot in the outlet *(above)*, then into the other slot. The tester should glow when the probe is in one slot (the hot slot) and not in the other. If it doesn't glow, the cover plate is not grounded; replace it with a GFCI outlet or a two-slot outlet, or have an electrician extend a grounded circuit to the box.

2 **Testing for voltage.** Turn off power to the outlet by removing the fuse or tripping the circuit breaker *(page 102)*. Free the outlet from the box, taking care not to touch any exposed wire ends or terminals. Use a voltage tester to confirm that the power is off by touching one probe to a brass terminal where a wire is connected and the other probe to the silver terminal on the opposite side. Repeat the test for the other brass and silver terminals if wires are connected to them. Then test between the grounded metal box and the brass and silver terminals in succession. The tester should not glow in any test. If it does, return to the service panel and turn off power to the correct circuit.

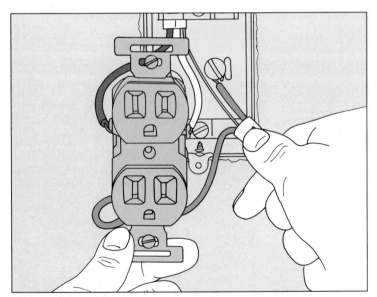

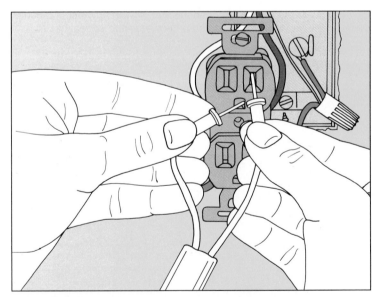

3 **Replacing the outlet.** Disconnect the old outlet and buy a three-slot replacement outlet. To attach the new outlet, hook the black wire around a brass terminal and the white wire around a silver terminal, then tighten the connections. Next, disconnect the grounding wire from the grounding screw at the back of the box. Cut two jumper wires *(page 417)*. Hook one jumper around the grounding screw at the back of the box, and the other around the grounding terminal on the new outlet, then twist together the bare grounding wire with the jumpers and screw on a wire cap *(above)*. Some armored cable has no grounding wire; to ground the outlet, attach a jumper to the screw at the back of the box and hook the other end around the grounding terminal on the outlet. Screw the outlet into the box, put on the cover plate and turn on the power.

4 **Checking the grounding.** Use the voltage tester to confirm that the outlet is properly grounded by inserting one tester probe into the D-shaped grounding slot and the other into the long (neutral) slot, then into the shorter (hot) slot, as shown. **Caution:** This is a live voltage test. Be sure to hold the tester by its insulated handles, or use the one-hand technique shown in Tools & Techniques *(page 417)*. The tester should glow when the probe is in the hot slot and not when it is in the neutral slot. If the outlet fails the test, turn off the power and check the grounding connections; polarity may be reversed.

ADAPTERS AND EXTENSIONS

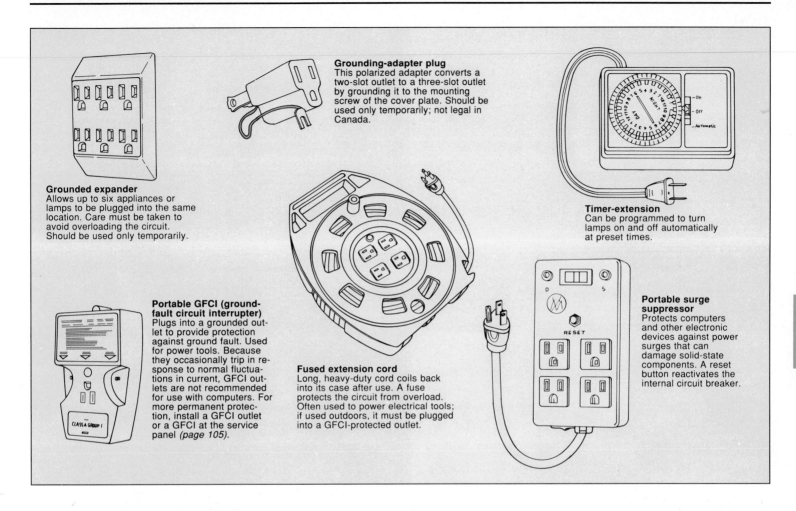

Grounded expander
Allows up to six appliances or lamps to be plugged into the same location. Care must be taken to avoid overloading the circuit. Should be used only temporarily.

Grounding-adapter plug
This polarized adapter converts a two-slot outlet to a three-slot outlet by grounding it to the mounting screw of the cover plate. Should be used only temporarily; not legal in Canada.

Timer-extension
Can be programmed to turn lamps on and off automatically at preset times.

Portable GFCI (ground-fault circuit interrupter)
Plugs into a grounded outlet to provide protection against ground fault. Used for power tools. Because they occasionally trip in response to normal fluctuations in current, GFCI outlets are not recommended for use with computers. For more permanent protection, install a GFCI outlet or a GFCI at the service panel *(page 105)*.

Fused extension cord
Long, heavy-duty cord coils back into its case after use. A fuse protects the circuit from overload. Often used to power electrical tools; if used outdoors, it must be plugged into a GFCI-protected outlet.

Portable surge suppressor
Protects computers and other electronic devices against power surges that can damage solid-state components. A reset button reactivates the internal circuit breaker.

GROUNDING IN OUTLET BOXES

METAL BOX

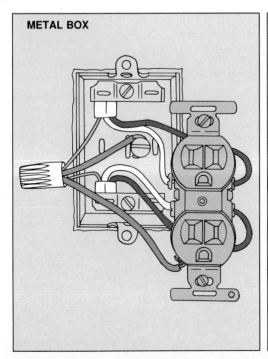

PLASTIC BOX

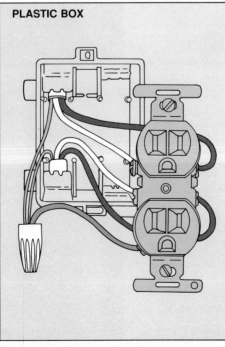

Grounding in metal boxes. All three-slot outlets must be grounded *(page 104)*. To ground an outlet in a metal box *(far left)*, attach a jumper wire to the grounding screw at the back of the box and another to the grounding terminal on the outlet. Then twist the ends of these jumpers together with the bare wires entering the box and screw on a wire cap. (In Canada, code allows the bare grounding wire entering the box and the jumper on the outlet to be connected directly to the grounding screw at the back of the box.) Some armored cable has no grounding wire; to ground the outlet, attach a jumper to the grounding screw at the back of the box and the grounding terminal on the outlet.

Grounding in plastic boxes. To ground an outlet in a plastic box *(near left)*, attach a jumper wire to the grounding terminal on the outlet, then twist the end of the jumper together with the bare wires entering the box and screw on a wire cap. If there is only one bare wire entering the box, connect it directly to the grounding terminal on the outlet.

159

HOME HEATING & COOLING

HEATING AND COOLING SYSTEMS

No matter what heating or cooling system you have, your home's climate is unique. Your comfort depends on the house's insulation, location and exposure, as well as how your heating and cooling system is maintained.

The system's design may be as simple as a single baseboard heater in each room, or more complicated, such as an air distribution system using a heat pump plus an oil-fired furnace and central humidifier. All systems, however, have four things in common. Each system has a *heat producer*—an oil or gas burner or an electric heating element, and a *heat exchanger*—a furnace where air is heated or a boiler where water is heated. A system's *heat distributor* may be the ducts and registers that circulate air throughout the home, or the pipes and radiators that circulate water. Finally, each system has a *control*—a thermostat or humidistat. When troubleshooting a heating or cooling problem, make sure to refer to all chapters pertaining to your system.

Listen to how your system sounds when it operates properly. This will give you important clues when something goes wrong: Does the blower start and stop too frequently? Do you

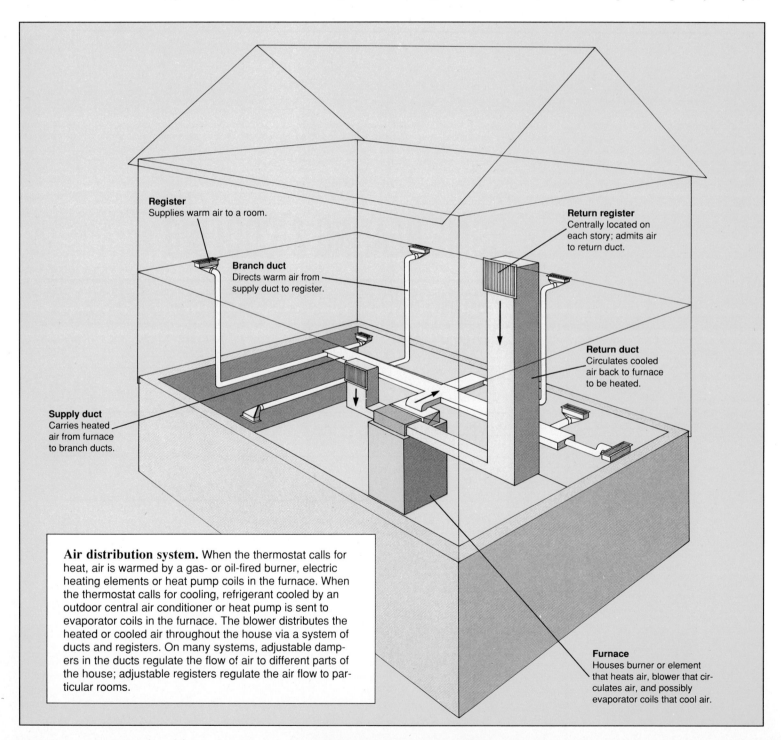

Register
Supplies warm air to a room.

Branch duct
Directs warm air from supply duct to register.

Return register
Centrally located on each story; admits air to return duct.

Return duct
Circulates cooled air back to furnace to be heated.

Supply duct
Carries heated air from furnace to branch ducts.

Furnace
Houses burner or element that heats air, blower that circulates air, and possibly evaporator coils that cool air.

Air distribution system. When the thermostat calls for heat, air is warmed by a gas- or oil-fired burner, electric heating elements or heat pump coils in the furnace. When the thermostat calls for cooling, refrigerant cooled by an outdoor central air conditioner or heat pump is sent to evaporator coils in the furnace. The blower distributes the heated or cooled air throughout the house via a system of ducts and registers. On many systems, adjustable dampers in the ducts regulate the flow of air to different parts of the house; adjustable registers regulate the air flow to particular rooms.

hear any unusual noises? The answers to questions like these can help you locate a problem more easily.

Pictured below are two representative home heating and cooling systems. Remember that these systems can be assembled and wired in a variety of ways, depending on the model, its age, and the space it occupies. If necessary, ask a service technician to help you identify your system's components.

For many families, heating and cooling is a major monthly expense. By keeping your system well maintained, you can minimize the energy it uses. To use that energy most efficient-

ly, make sure your home is well insulated, and weather-strip, caulk, or add storm windows and doors if necessary. Lined draperies help insulate windows and stop drafts; keep draperies open during the day in winter to let the sunshine in, and close them at night. Shut off most of the heat to unused rooms by closing registers, dampers or radiators. Set your thermostat back at night and when you're not at home, or install an electronically timed thermostat. Do not allow furniture or draperies to block registers, radiators, convectors or baseboard heaters. Keep the fireplace damper closed when not in use.

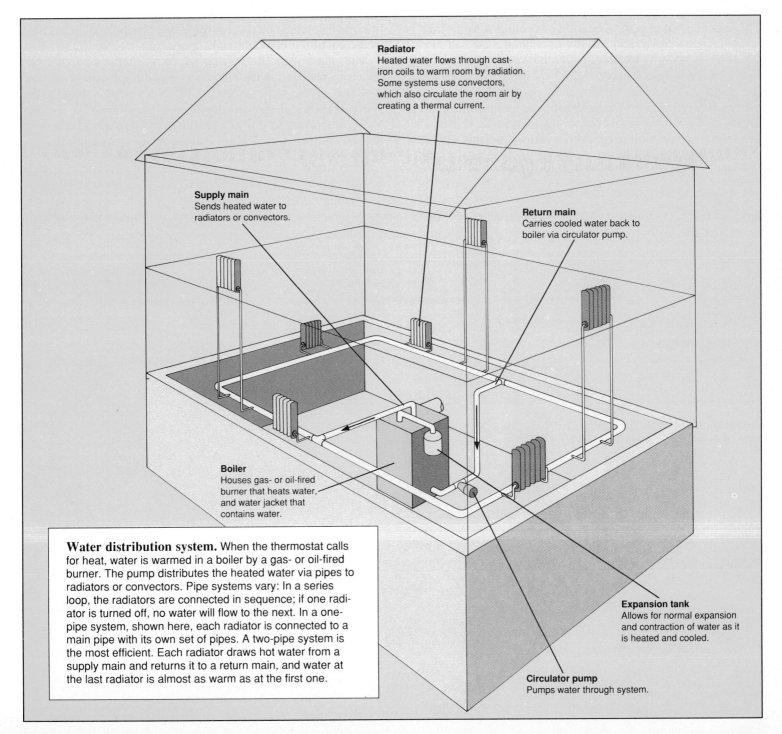

Radiator
Heated water flows through cast-iron coils to warm room by radiation. Some systems use convectors, which also circulate the room air by creating a thermal current.

Supply main
Sends heated water to radiators or convectors.

Return main
Carries cooled water back to boiler via circulator pump.

Boiler
Houses gas- or oil-fired burner that heats water, and water jacket that contains water.

Expansion tank
Allows for normal expansion and contraction of water as it is heated and cooled.

Circulator pump
Pumps water through system.

Water distribution system. When the thermostat calls for heat, water is warmed in a boiler by a gas- or oil-fired burner. The pump distributes the heated water via pipes to radiators or convectors. Pipe systems vary: In a series loop, the radiators are connected in sequence; if one radiator is turned off, no water will flow to the next. In a one-pipe system, shown here, each radiator is connected to a main pipe with its own set of pipes. A two-pipe system is the most efficient. Each radiator draws hot water from a supply main and returns it to a return main, and water at the last radiator is almost as warm as at the first one.

SYSTEM CONTROLS

The thermostat and humidistat provide fingertip control of complicated systems. The thermostat turns on the heating or air conditioning system when the room temperature strays outside the level you set, and turns it off when the temperature is correct. An electronic thermostat can be programmed to turn the system on and off at certain times of day, or to change the preset temperature levels automatically. Small batteries run its display functions. The humidistat senses moisture in the air to activate a humidifier or, in some cases, a dehumidifier, built into the heating system. It may be located on the wall, the air duct or the plenum.

Three typical thermostats are pictured below and at right. Those connected to central heating or cooling systems may be round or rectangular, and usually operate in a 24-volt circuit; the voltage rating is marked inside the cover or on the body. The household line voltage—120 or 240 volts—that powers the heating or cooling system is stepped down by a transformer before it passes to the thermostat circuit. Based on its setting and the room temperature, the thermostat signals various relays in its circuit to turn on or turn off heating elements,

gas valves, blowers and other components in the system. The anticipator indicator maintains even room temperature by turning the heating unit off and on ahead of the room's needs. This chapter covers maintenance and repair of the thermostat wall unit; to troubleshoot other parts in the thermostat circuit or controlled by it, see the chapter on the particular system.

Most low-voltage thermostats use a temperature-sensitive bimetal coil that opens and closes a switch to turn the system on and off. The switch is commonly a mercury bulb type, in which a ball of mercury rolls toward or away from electrical contacts. Such a thermostat must be installed perfectly level. Heat pump systems with an auxiliary heating unit use a staged thermostat, which has two or three mercury bulb switches. It is serviced like a conventional thermostat.

The line-voltage thermostat *(right, bottom)* is wired to an electric baseboard heater that runs on 240-volt household line voltage. (Some heaters run on 120 volts.) Since voltage to the thermostat is not stepped down by a transformer, it is especially important to turn off power to the heater at the service panel, and test that it is off before touching the wires.

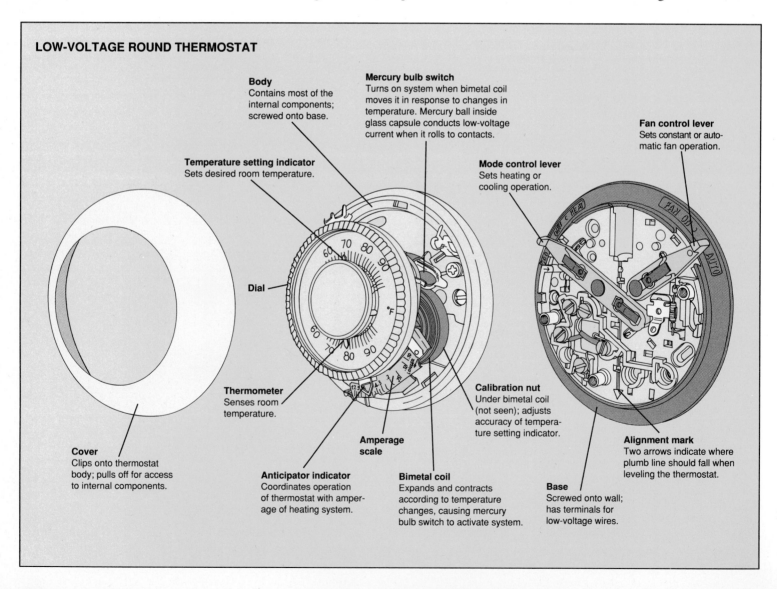

LOW-VOLTAGE ROUND THERMOSTAT

Body
Contains most of the internal components; screwed onto base.

Mercury bulb switch
Turns on system when bimetal coil moves it in response to changes in temperature. Mercury ball inside glass capsule conducts low-voltage current when it rolls to contacts.

Fan control lever
Sets constant or automatic fan operation.

Temperature setting indicator
Sets desired room temperature.

Mode control lever
Sets heating or cooling operation.

Dial

Thermometer
Senses room temperature.

Calibration nut
Under bimetal coil (not seen); adjusts accuracy of temperature setting indicator.

Amperage scale

Cover
Clips onto thermostat body; pulls off for access to internal components.

Anticipator indicator
Coordinates operation of thermostat with amperage of heating system.

Bimetal coil
Expands and contracts according to temperature changes, causing mercury bulb switch to activate system.

Base
Screwed onto wall; has terminals for low-voltage wires.

Alignment mark
Two arrows indicate where plumb line should fall when leveling the thermostat.

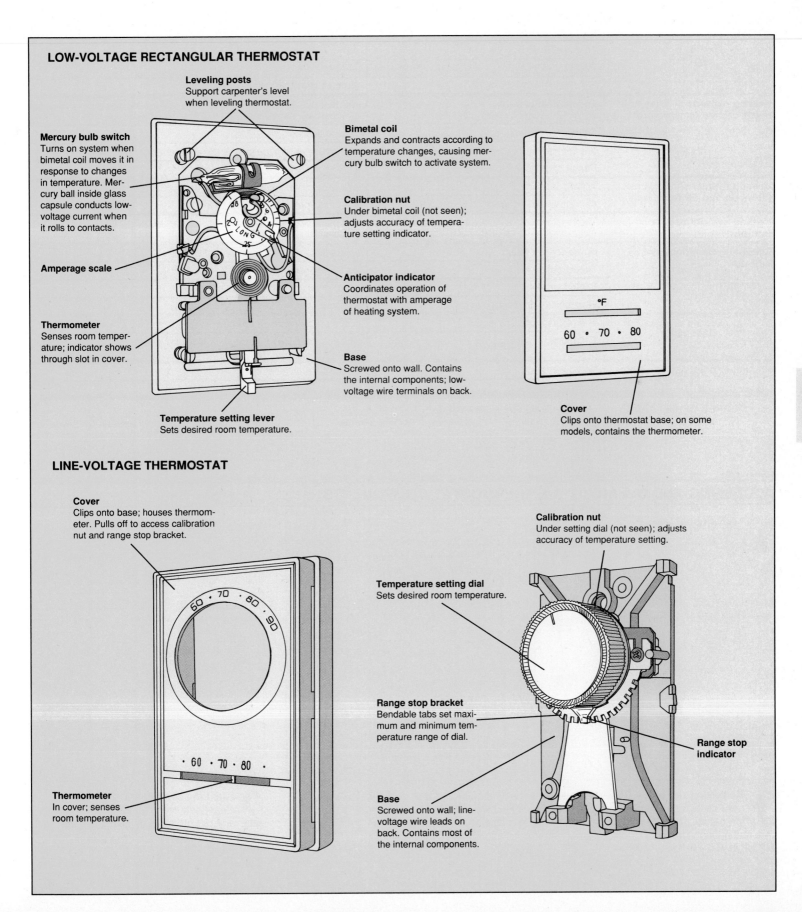

LOW-VOLTAGE RECTANGULAR THERMOSTAT

Leveling posts
Support carpenter's level when leveling thermostat.

Mercury bulb switch
Turns on system when bimetal coil moves it in response to changes in temperature. Mercury ball inside glass capsule conducts low-voltage current when it rolls to contacts.

Amperage scale

Thermometer
Senses room temperature; indicator shows through slot in cover.

Temperature setting lever
Sets desired room temperature.

Bimetal coil
Expands and contracts according to temperature changes, causing mercury bulb switch to activate system.

Calibration nut
Under bimetal coil (not seen); adjusts accuracy of temperature setting indicator.

Anticipator indicator
Coordinates operation of thermostat with amperage of heating system.

Base
Screwed onto wall. Contains the internal components; low-voltage wire terminals on back.

°F

60 · 70 · 80

Cover
Clips onto thermostat base; on some models, contains the thermometer.

LINE-VOLTAGE THERMOSTAT

Cover
Clips onto base; houses thermometer. Pulls off to access calibration nut and range stop bracket.

60 · 70 · 80 · 90

· 60 · 70 · 80 ·

Thermometer
In cover; senses room temperature.

Calibration nut
Under setting dial (not seen); adjusts accuracy of temperature setting.

Temperature setting dial
Sets desired room temperature.

Range stop bracket
Bendable tabs set maximum and minimum temperature range of dial.

Range stop indicator

Base
Screwed onto wall; line-voltage wire leads on back. Contains most of the internal components.

TROUBLESHOOTING GUIDE

SYMPTOM	POSSIBLE CAUSE	PROCEDURE
No heat	No power to system	Replace fuse or reset circuit breaker *(p. 102)* □○
	Thermostat dirty	Clean thermostat *(p. 166)* □○
	Thermostat faulty	Call for service
	Electronic thermostat batteries weak or dead	Replace batteries
Heating exceeds or does not reach desired temperature	Thermostat not level	Level thermostat with carpenter's level on leveling posts or with plumb line along alignment mark
	Anticipator set incorrectly	Adjust anticipator *(p. 167)* □○
	Thermostat out of calibration	Recalibrate low-voltage or line-voltage thermostat *(p. 168)* ◓◑▲
	Range stop incorrect	Call for service
Heating system short cycles (turns on and off repeatedly)	Thermostat dirty	Clean thermostat *(p. 166)* □○
	Anticipator set incorrectly	Adjust anticipator *(p. 167)* □○
Heating system does not turn off	Thermostat not level	Level thermostat with carpenter's level on leveling posts or with plumb line along alignment mark
Cooling system does not turn on	No power to system	Replace fuse or reset circuit breaker *(p. 102)* □○
	Thermostat dirty	Clean thermostat *(p. 166)* □○
	Thermostat faulty	Call for service
	Electronic thermostat batteries weak or dead	Replace batteries
Cooling exceeds or does not reach set temperature	Thermostat out of calibration	Recalibrate low-voltage or line-voltage thermostat *(p. 168)* ◓◑▲
	Thermostat not level	Level thermostat with carpenter's level on leveling posts or with plumb line along alignment mark
Humidifier does not turn on	No power to system	Replace fuse or reset circuit breaker *(p. 102)* □○
	Humidistat faulty	Call for service

DEGREE OF DIFFICULTY: □ Easy ◓ Moderate ■ Complex
ESTIMATED TIME: ○ Less than 1 hour ◑ 1 to 3 hours ● Over 3 hours

▲ Special tool required

ACCESSING AND CLEANING THE THERMOSTAT COMPONENTS

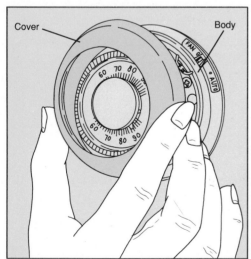

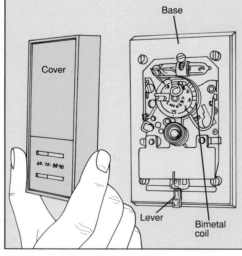

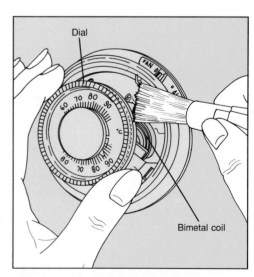

1 **Removing the cover.** Turn off power to the heating system at the main service panel *(page 102)*. Access the bimetal coil, anticipator, mercury bulb switch and lever contacts by snapping the cover of a round thermostat off its body *(above, left)* or a rectangular thermostat off its base *(above, right)*.

2 **Cleaning the bimetal coil.** Use a clean, soft brush to wipe built-up dust and dirt off the bimetal coil. Turn a round thermostat's dial *(above)* or a rectangular thermostat's lever from the lowest to the highest setting to help dislodge stubborn particles. If your thermostat is round, go to step 3; if it is rectangular, go to step 4.

ACCESSING AND CLEANING THE THERMOSTAT COMPONENTS (continued)

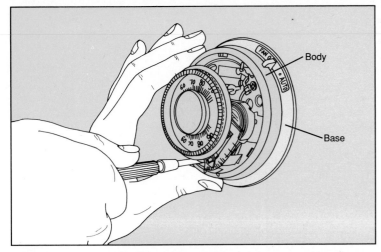

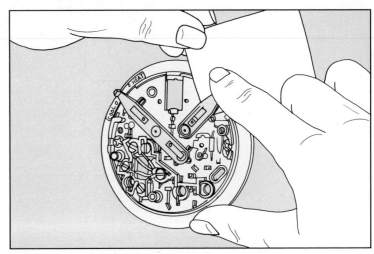

3 **Removing the body.** Use a screwdriver to loosen the screws securing a round thermostat's body to its base *(above)*; on many models, the screws will remain attached to the body. Take care not to remove recessed screws that secure electrical components. Remove the body and set it aside.

4 **Cleaning the switch contacts.** With a round thermostat's cover and body removed, or with a rectangular thermostat's cover removed, lift the lever and slip a strip of white bond paper between it and the contacts *(above)*. Shift the lever across the contacts and slide the paper to clean them. Tighten any loose wire connections. Remount a round thermostat body, replace the thermostat cover and turn on the heating system.

ADJUSTING THE ANTICIPATOR

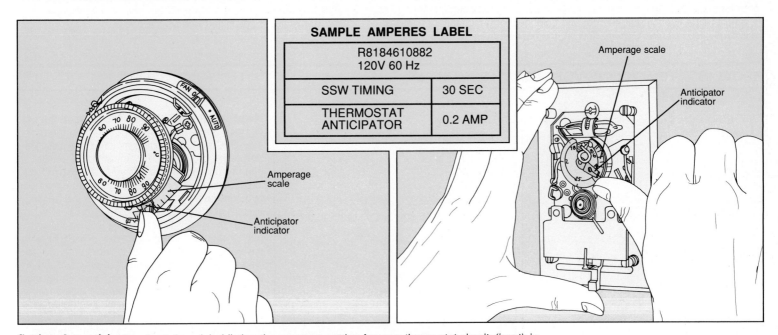

SAMPLE AMPERES LABEL	
R8184610882 120V 60 Hz	
SSW TIMING	30 SEC
THERMOSTAT ANTICIPATOR	0.2 AMP

Setting the anticipator. Look for a label listing the amperes setting for your thermostat circuit *(inset)*: in your system's instruction manual, on an electric furnace's service panel, or on an oil- or gas-fired furnace or boiler's transformer or relay box. Turn off power to the heating system at the main service panel *(page 102)*, and remove the thermostat cover *(page 166)*. Check the position of the anticipator indicator on its scale. On an air distribution system, the indicator should point to the recommended amperes setting; on a water distribution system, the indicator should point to a number 1.4 times the amperes setting. If the anticipator is not correctly set, use your fingernail or a pen point to adjust the indicator; along a round thermostat's linear scale *(above, left)* or a rectangular thermostat's circular scale *(above, right)*. A two-stage thermostat has two adjustable anticipators; adjust each according to the recommended amperes setting for its heating unit.

RECALIBRATING A LOW-VOLTAGE THERMOSTAT

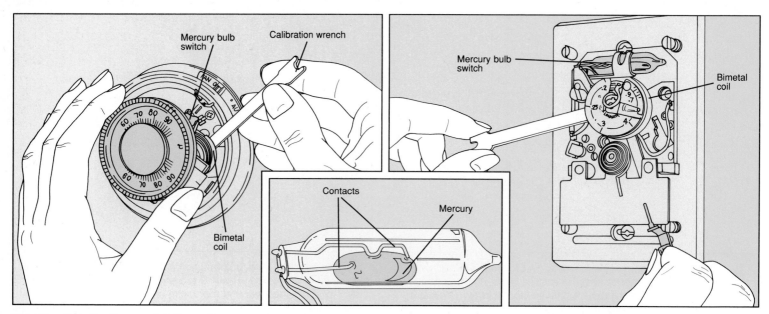

Recalibrating the thermostat. Turn off power to the heating system at the main service panel *(page 102)*. Pull off the thermostat cover *(page 166)* and check the calibration: Set the dial or lever at the actual room temperature; use a room thermometer to check the accuracy of the thermostat's thermometer. If this is the exact setting at which the mercury *(inset)* shifts from one end of the bulb to the other, the thermostat is properly calibrated. To recalibrate, set the thermostat 5°F above room temperature. Look for the calibration nut under the bimetal coil. Fit a calibration wrench onto the nut and hold the thermostat dial or lever firmly. Do not touch, or breathe on, the heat-sensitive bimetal coils. Slowly rotate the nut, clockwise on most thermostats *(above, left and right)*, just until the mercury rolls to the right of the contacts. Turn the temperature setting down 10°F and wait five minutes, then set the thermostat dial or lever to match the room temperature reading. Holding the thermostat dial or lever firmly, turn the calibration nut in the opposite direction just until the mercury rolls back to the contacts. Allow the recalibrated thermostat to stabilize for 30 minutes. Check whether the room temperature matches the set temperature, and recalibrate again, if necessary. Reinstall the cover and turn on the power.

RECALIBRATING A LINE-VOLTAGE THERMOSTAT

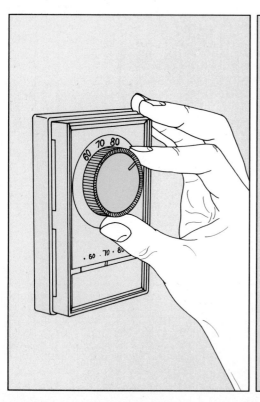

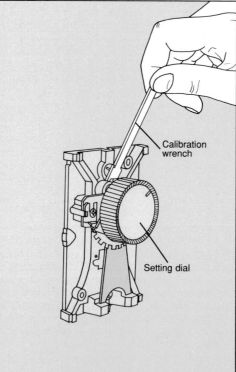

Recalibrating the thermostat. Turn up the setting dial *(far left)* just until you hear the thermostat click on. If the setting matches the temperature reading on the thermometer in the cover plate or on a room thermometer, the thermostat is calibrated properly. Otherwise, write down the two numbers, then turn off power to the heating system at the main service panel *(page 102)*. Rotate the setting dial to its highest setting and pull off the thermostat cover *(page 166)*. Fit a calibration wrench onto the calibration screw behind the setting dial *(near left)*. Refer to the numbers you recorded: If the setting was higher than the temperature reading, rotate the calibration nut one-eighth turn clockwise for each degree F of difference; if the temperature reading was higher, rotate the wrench one-eighth turn counterclockwise for each degree F of difference. Replace the thermostat cover and rotate the setting dial to normal room temperature. Allow the thermostat to stabilize for 10 minutes, then check the calibration again; it may require several adjustments. Once finished, apply a tiny drop of nail polish to secure the calibration screw.

AIR DISTRIBUTION

An air distribution system can provide the home with an ideal year-round climate. It circulates heated or cooled air through a gas, oil or electric furnace, or central air conditioning unit, via a network of ducts in the home. A blower, housed in the furnace and turned by a belt-drive or direct-drive motor, draws air from the return duct, through the filter, and into the furnace, where the air is heated or cooled. The air then goes out through the supply duct to branch ducts. On many systems, adjustable dampers in the ducts regulate the flow of air to different parts of the house; adjustable registers regulate air flow into a room. Gas and oil furnaces generally use a fan-and-limit control mounted on the furnace plenum to switch the blower on and off in response to plenum temperature. Electric furnaces *(page 201)* and central air conditioning *(page 216)* use separate blower relays or fan centers to switch the blower in direct response to the thermostat.

If properly maintained, an air distribution system will be relatively trouble-free. At least once a year, clean the blower blades, lubricate the blower motor and clean or replace the filter as necessary. Problems may be caused by another component in the system. Consult the Troubleshooting Guides of other chapters as well.

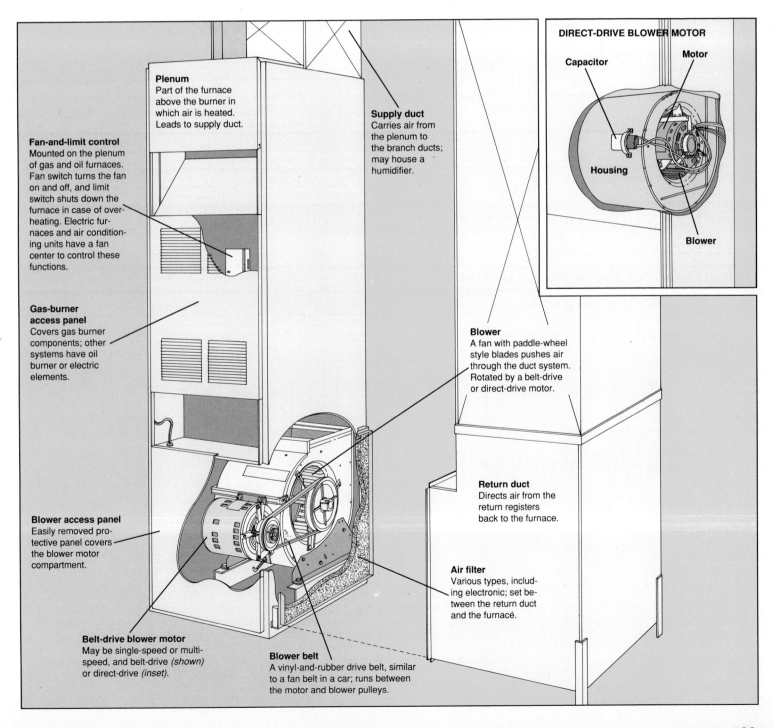

DIRECT-DRIVE BLOWER MOTOR

Capacitor

Motor

Housing

Blower

Plenum
Part of the furnace above the burner in which air is heated. Leads to supply duct.

Supply duct
Carries air from the plenum to the branch ducts; may house a humidifier.

Fan-and-limit control
Mounted on the plenum of gas and oil furnaces. Fan switch turns the fan on and off, and limit switch shuts down the furnace in case of overheating. Electric furnaces and air conditioning units have a fan center to control these functions.

Gas-burner access panel
Covers gas burner components; other systems have oil burner or electric elements.

Blower
A fan with paddle-wheel style blades pushes air through the duct system. Rotated by a belt-drive or direct-drive motor.

Blower access panel
Easily removed protective panel covers the blower motor compartment.

Return duct
Directs air from the return registers back to the furnace.

Air filter
Various types, including electronic; set between the return duct and the furnace.

Belt-drive blower motor
May be single-speed or multispeed, and belt-drive *(shown)* or direct-drive *(inset)*.

Blower belt
A vinyl-and-rubber drive belt, similar to a fan belt in a car; runs between the motor and blower pulleys.

TROUBLESHOOTING GUIDE

SYMPTOM	POSSIBLE CAUSE	PROCEDURE
Heating or central air conditioning does not run at all	No power to unit	Reset circuit breaker or replace fuse (p. 102) □○
System runs, but no hot or cold air flow	Blower belt broken or loose	Inspect and adjust belt tension (p. 172) □○ and pulley alignment (p. 173) □○; replace belt (p. 173) ◪○
	Fan-and-limit control faulty	Test fan-and-limit control (p. 174) ◪○▲; replace control (p. 175) ◪◗
	Blower relay faulty	Test blower relay (p. 176) ◪◗▲; replace if necessary
	Blower motor faulty	Inspect blower motor (p. 174) □○; call for service
Heating or cooling insufficient in part of the house	Register closed or blocked, or filter dirty	Open register and remove obstructions; replace dirty register filter
	Blower blades dirty	Clean blower blades (p. 174) □○
	Duct disconnected or damper closed	Reconnect duct or open damper
Heating or cooling insufficient throughout entire house	Air filter dirty	Clean or replace air filter (p. 171) □○
	Blower running poorly	Oil blower motor and bearings (p. 170) □○; adjust blower speed (p. 172) □○; adjust blower belt tension (p. 172) □○ and blower pulley alignment (p. 173) □○; clean blower blades (p. 174) □○
	Blower bearings dry or worn	Lubricate bearings (p. 170) □○; have bearings replaced
	Duct dampers adjusted improperly	Adjust dampers
Air flow noisy	Blower speed too high	Adjust blower speed (p. 172) □○
	Joints loose at duct corners	Tighten joints and adjust duct hangers; call for service
Blower noise excessive	Blower motor or bearings dry or worn	Lubricate motor and bearings (p. 170) □○; call for service
	Motor or blower mounting hardware loose	Tighten mounting hardware
Blower belt slips or squeals	Belt tension incorrect	Adjust belt tension (p. 172) □○; replace belt (p. 173) □○
	Pulley misaligned	Align blower pulleys (p. 173) ◪◗

DEGREE OF DIFFICULTY: □ Easy ◪ Moderate ■ Complex
ESTIMATED TIME: ○ Less than 1 hour ◗ 1 to 3 hours ● Over 3 hours

▲ Special tool required

LUBRICATING THE BLOWER AND MOTOR

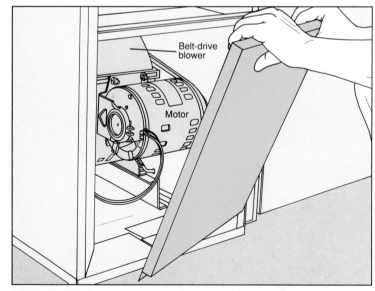

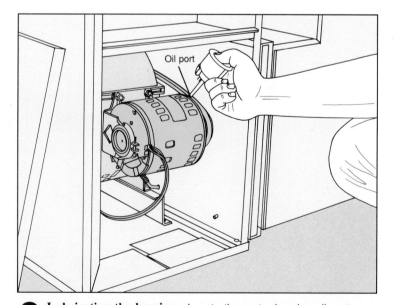

1 Accessing the blower. Turn off power to the furnace at the main service panel (page 102) and unit disconnect switch (page 22). The blower, usually located in the bottom of the unit, is covered by an access panel that should have a label with oiling instructions. Tug up and out to remove the panel (above). Most blowers with oil ports should be lubricated at least once a year. Often only the motor requires oiling; most belt-drive blowers turn on sealed bearings that should not be oiled at all. Direct-drive blowers turn on the motor's bearings.

2 Lubricating the bearings. Locate the motor-bearing oil ports, if any, at each end of the motor casing. If the ports are capped, use the blade of a flat-tipped screwdriver to pry up the caps. Squirt five drops of non-detergent SAE-30 motor oil into each port (above); do not over-oil. If there are oil ports at the bearings where the blower shaft is mounted, oil them also.

SERVICING FILTERS

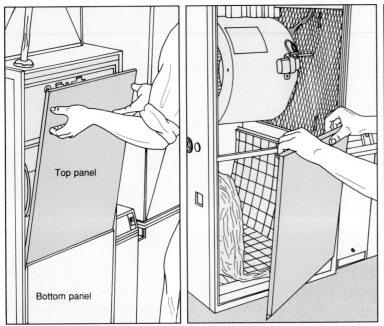

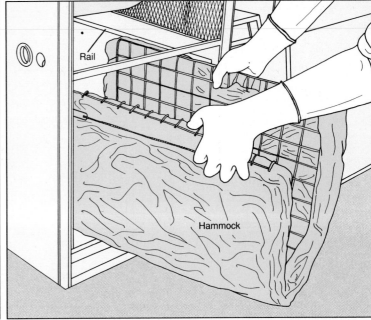

Replacing a hammock filter. Turn off power to the furnace at the main service panel *(page 102)* and unit disconnect switch *(page 22)*. Access the filter by removing the furnace cover panels *(above, left and center)*, releasing each with a sharp upward tug. Once a month during the heating and cooling seasons, inspect the filter by shining a light through it from behind. If the light is nearly or completely blocked, replace the filter. Wearing gloves, lift and release each side of the wire mesh hammock from the retaining rails, fold it inward, and pull the filter and hammock out of the furnace *(above, right)*. Hammock filters made of fiberglass batting are available in rolls from a heating and cooling supplies dealer. Use a utility knife to cut the batting to size, place it between the holders and slide the hammock onto the retaining rails. Reinstall the access panels and restore power to the furnace.

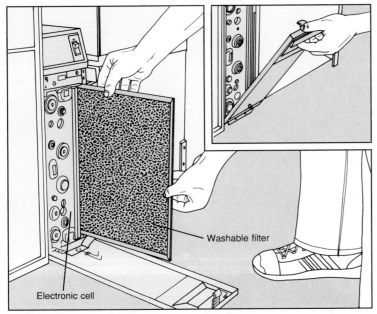

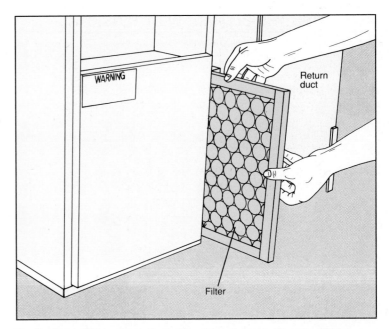

Cleaning an electronic filter. Turn off power to the furnace at the main service panel *(page 102)* and unit disconnect switch *(page 22)*. Pull open the filter door panel *(inset)*. Slide the filter out of its retainer sleeve *(above)*; push aside any spring tabs that secure the filter in place. Once a month during heating and cooling seasons, wash the filter with a detergent-and-water solution, rinse well, then allow it to drip dry before reinserting. If the filter is damaged, replace it with an identical one. Before each season, slide out the electronic cells and carefully wash them the same way. Close the door panel and turn on the power.

Replacing a filter element. Pull the filter element out of its slot between the return duct and the blower *(above)*. On some units, the filter is inside the furnace; turn off power to the furnace at the main service panel *(page 102)* and unit disconnect switch *(page 22)* and pull off any access panels. Remove the filter and inspect it for dirt by holding it up to a light bulb. If the light is nearly or completely blocked, replace a dirty cardboard-framed fiberglass filter with an exact replacement; wash a dirty metal or plastic element filter using a hose with a high-pressure nozzle, then let it drip dry. Reinstall the filter and turn on the power.

ADJUSTING THE BLOWER SPEED

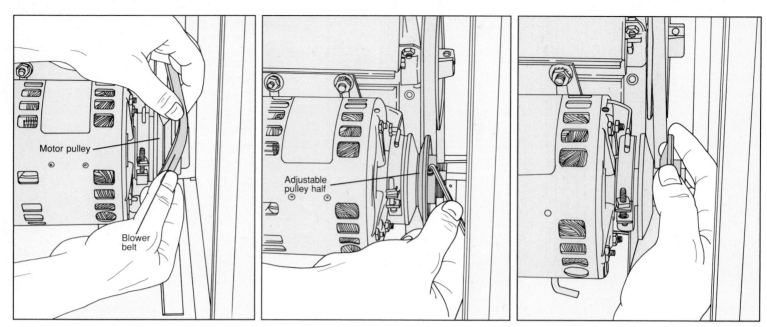

Adjusting the pulley width. The speed at which the adjustable motor pulley drives the blower belt is determined by the width set between the two halves of the pulley. Turn off power to the furnace at the main service panel *(page 102)* and unit disconnect switch *(page 22)*; access the blower *(page 170)*. Slip the blower belt over the outer lip of the motor pulley *(above, left)*; turn the pulley counterclockwise to help work the belt off. Use a hex wrench to loosen the pulley setscrew *(above, center)* until the adjustable pulley half can be turned on its threaded shaft. Turn the pulley one-half turn at a time: clockwise to increase blower speed and counterclockwise to decrease it *(above, right)*. Align the setscrew with the flat side of the motor shaft before retightening it. Slip the belt back on the pulley, and check its tension *(below)*.

ADJUSTING THE BLOWER BELT TENSION

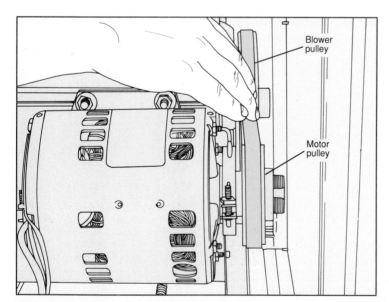

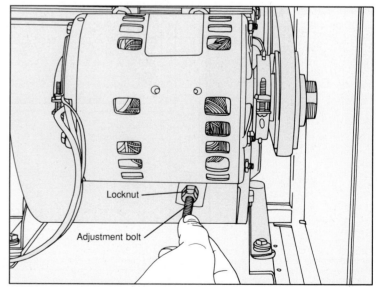

1 Checking the belt tension. Turn off power to the furnace at the main service panel *(page 102)* and unit disconnect switch *(page 22)*; remove the access panels *(page 170)*. Inspect the belt for cracks, brittleness or wear; replace it if damaged *(page 173)*. Test belt tension by pushing down on the belt midway between the pulleys until the belt is taut *(above)*; it should slacken about one inch. If it slackens more, it should be tightened or replaced, depending on your model; look for instructions on a label near the blower. If it slackens less than one inch, it is too tight; loosen it.

2 Adjusting the belt tension. With power to the furnace turned off, locate the locknut on the blower-belt adjustment bolt and loosen it with an open-end wrench. Next, turn the adjustment bolt by hand, clockwise to tighten the belt, or counterclockwise to loosen it *(above)*. Check the belt tension *(step 1)*, then retighten the locknut. Reinstall the access panel and turn on power to the furnace.

REPLACING THE BLOWER BELT

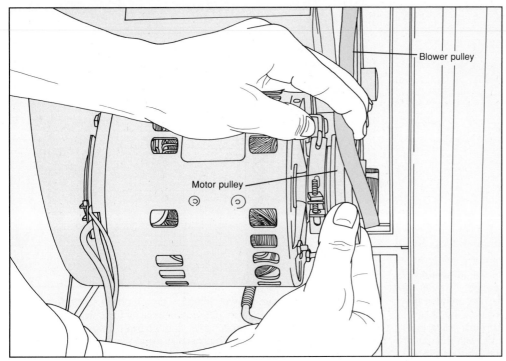

Blower pulley

Motor pulley

Installing a new blower belt. Turn off power to the furnace at the main service panel *(page 102)* and unit disconnect switch *(page 22)* and remove the access panels covering the blower *(page 170)*. Inspect the blower belt; if it is cracked, brittle, worn or stretched beyond adjustment limits, replace it. Remove the belt by pushing it over the top of the outer lip of the motor pulley with your thumb; if the belt is hard to remove, use your other hand to turn the pulley counterclockwise. Take the old belt with you to a heating supplies dealer and buy an exact replacement. Place the new belt over the blower pulley. Hold the belt in the top groove of the motor pulley with one hand and turn the pulley counterclockwise with the other hand *(left)*. Reassemble the unit and restore the power. Check belt tension and adjust if necessary *(page 172)*.

ALIGNING THE BLOWER AND MOTOR PULLEYS

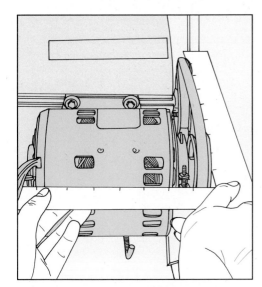

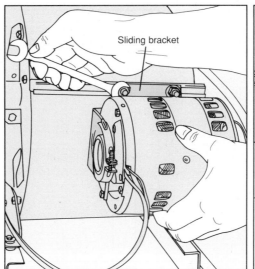

Sliding bracket

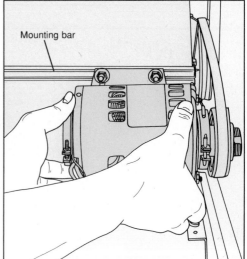

Mounting bar

1 Checking pulley alignment. Turn off power to the furnace at the service panel *(page 102)* and unit disconnect switch *(page 22)* and remove the access panels *(page 170)*. Hold a carpenter's square or straightedge across the faces of the motor and blower pulleys *(above)*. If the edge does not rest flush against both pulleys, shift the motor's position on its bracket until the pulleys align *(step 2)*.

2 Shifting the motor. Use an open-end wrench to loosen the nuts securing the sliding bracket to the mounting bar *(above, left)*. Grasp the motor in both hands and shift it slightly forward or backward, as needed *(above, right)*. Recheck the pulley alignment with the carpenter's square *(step 1)*; when the pulleys are aligned properly, retighten the mounting bolts. Check belt tension and adjust if necessary *(page 172)*. Restore power to the furnace and check that the belt runs smoothly and quietly.

CLEANING THE BLOWER BLADES

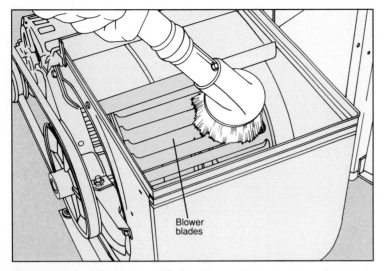

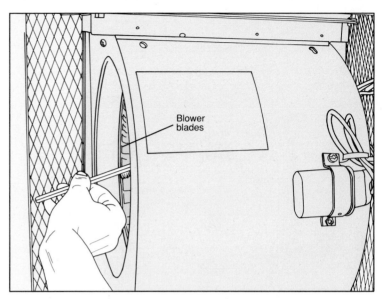

Cleaning belt-drive blower blades. Blower blades load up with dirt and become inefficient only if the filter has been neglected. Turn off power to the furnace at the main service panel *(page 102)* and unit disconnect switch *(page 22)*. Use a socket wrench to unscrew the bolts holding the blower's mounting brackets to the mounting rails; slide the blower assembly out of the furnace. Vacuum the blades with a brush attachment *(above)*. Tap the blower casing to dislodge the dirt. Replace the blower assembly, reassemble the unit and restore the power.

Cleaning direct-drive blower blades. Turn off power to the furnace at the main service panel *(page 102)* and unit disconnect switch *(page 22)* and remove the access panels covering the blower *(page 170)*. Reach into the blower cavity with a toothbrush to clean the inside and outside surfaces of each blade. If a vacuum nozzle will fit, use the vacuum to dislodge dirt. If the blades are inaccessible, use a socket wrench to unbolt and remove the direct-drive blower for cleaning. After cleaning the blades, reassemble the unit and restore the power.

TESTING THE FAN-AND-LIMIT CONTROL

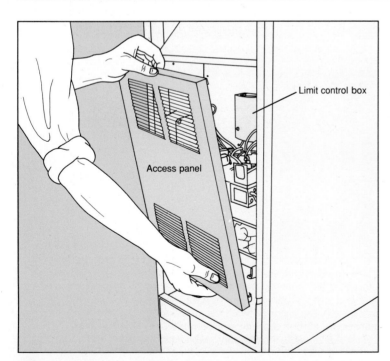

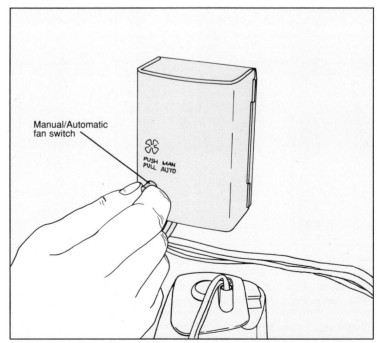

1 **Accessing the control box.** The fan-and-limit control used on gas and oil furnaces consists of a fan (blower) switch and a limit (shutoff) switch. On gas furnaces, the box is mounted near other controls: behind the access panel and against the plenum. Lift off the panel *(above)* and set it aside. An oil furnace fan-and-limit control is usually mounted directly on the plenum.

2 **Testing the blower motor.** Look on the limit control box for a rotating, push/pull or toggle switch marked MANUAL/AUTOMATIC or SUMMER/WINTER, or a switch mounted separately on an exterior panel. Set the button or toggle to MANUAL or SUMMER *(above)*. If the blower runs, the blower motor is OK. If the blower does not run, test the fan switch *(step 3)*.

TESTING THE FAN-AND-LIMIT CONTROL (continued)

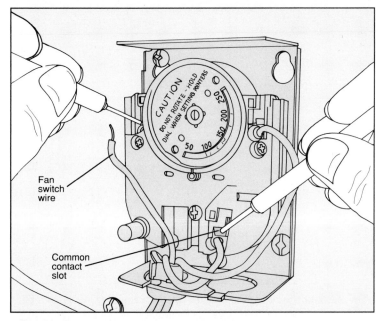

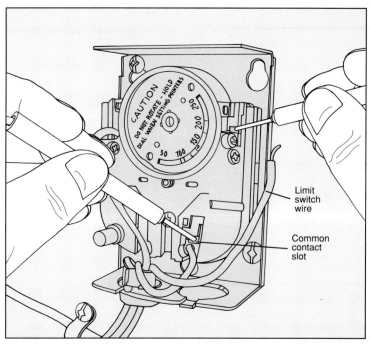

3 **Testing the fan switch.** Turn off power to the furnace at the main service panel *(page 102)* and unit disconnect switch *(page 22)*. Pull off the control cover. Disconnect the fan wire from its terminal. Set a multitester to test continuity *(page 417)*. With the switch on MANUAL or SUMMER, touch one probe to the fan contact slot and the other probe to the common contact slot *(above)*. If there is continuity, the fan switch is OK; go to step 2. If there is no continuity, replace the fan-and-limit control *(below)*.

4 **Testing the limit switch.** Set a multitester to the RX1K setting to test continuity. Disconnect the limit switch wire from its terminal. Touch one tester probe to the limit switch contact slot and the other probe to the common contact slot *(above)*. If there is no continuity, the limit control is faulty; replace it. Otherwise, reassemble the control.

REPLACING THE FAN-AND-LIMIT CONTROL BOX

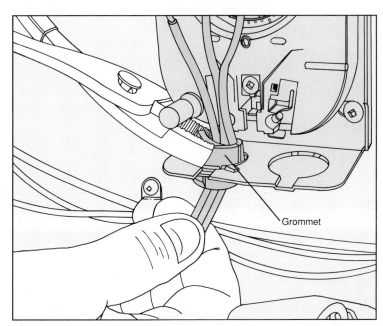

Grommet

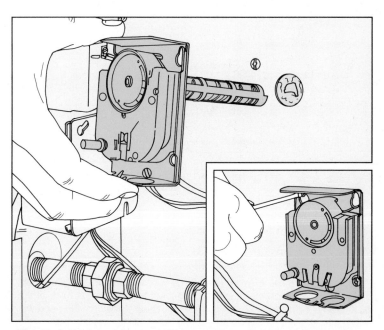

1 **Removing the wiring.** Turn off power to the furnace at the main service panel *(page 102)* and unit disconnect switch *(page 22)*. Pinch the inside rim of the wire grommet with pliers and push it out through the access hole in the bottom of the limit control box *(above)*.

2 **Unfastening a fan-and-limit control.** Label the wires and disconnect them. Use a screwdriver to remove the screws holding the limit control on the plenum *(inset)*. Pull the control out of the furnace *(above)*. Install an identical replacement, reversing these steps. Reassemble the furnace and restore power to the system.

TESTING AND REPLACING THE BLOWER RELAY

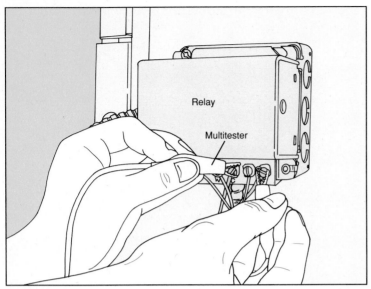

1 **Testing the thermostat circuit.** Turn off power to the heating and cooling system at the main service panel *(page 102)* and unit disconnect switch *(page 22)*. Set a multitester to the ACV setting, 50-volt range, to test voltage *(page 417)*. Attach one tester clip to the G terminal, and the other clip to the C or V terminal *(above)*. Without touching the clips or terminals, have someone turn on the power and turn up the thermostat. The tester should read about 24 volts and the blower should click on. If not, the thermostat circuit is faulty; see System Controls *(page 164)*. If the reading is 24 volts, turn off the power and go to step 2.

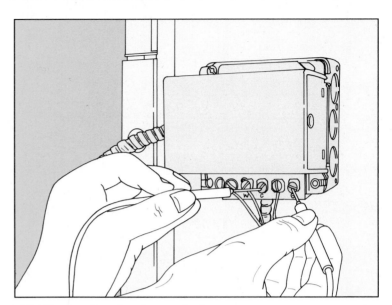

2 **Testing the relay for continuity.** With power to the system off, set a multitester to test continuity *(page 417)*. Touch one probe to the G terminal and the other to the C terminal *(above)*. There should be continuity. If there is no continuity, replace the relay *(step 3)*. If there is continuity through the relay, but the blower will not run, have the blower motor serviced.

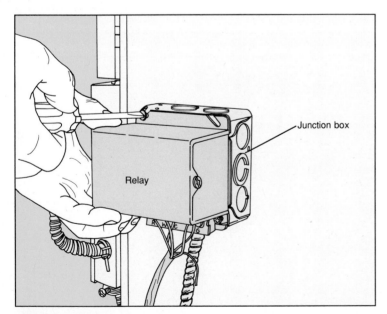

3 **Accessing the blower leads.** The wire leads from the blower enter the junction box and are connected to wires at the back of the relay. With power to the furnace off, remove the retaining screws with a screwdriver *(above)*, and pull the relay off the junction box. **Caution:** Check that power is off before disconnecting wires *(step 4)*.

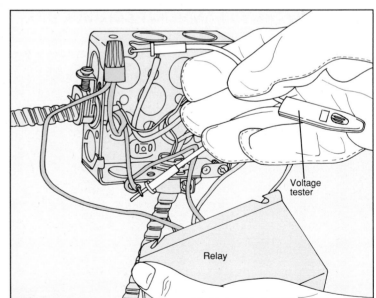

4 **Replacing the relay box.** Taking care not to touch any bare wires, uncap the black and white wires in the relay box. Holding a voltage tester in one hand, touch one probe to the black wire ends and the other to the grounded junction box *(above)*. Next, test between the white wires and the box. Finally, test between the black and white wires. The tester should not glow in any case; if it does, turn off the correct circuit and test again. Label all wires for correct reconnection and replace the relay with an identical new one. Reconnect the wires, reassemble the unit and turn on the power.

WATER DISTRIBUTION

Most water distribution systems found in homes today were installed before the 1950s. In fact, many boilers still in use are converted coal-burning units, like the one pictured below.

When the thermostat calls for heat, the burner turns on to heat the water inside the boiler. When the water reaches a preset temperature (usually 100°F to 120°F), the circulator pump turns on, and circulates the heated water throughout the house via a system of pipes to radiators or convectors. One or more aquastats monitor the water temperature. The burner aquastat acts as a safety device, turning off the burner if the water exceeds a safe temperature. When the thermostat is satisfied, the burner stops. The pump aquastat turns the circu-

lator pump on and off. Even with the burner off, the circulator pump continues to pump water through the system until the water cools to below the aquastat's preset temperature.

A pressure reducing valve lowers the incoming water pressure of around 70 to 75 psi (pounds per square inch) to the 15 psi minimum required by the boiler. Pressure within the boiler is registered on a pressure gauge. When the system is cold, the gauge should read about 15 psi, depending on the height of the radiators above the boiler. As the water heats, pressure increases to about 30 psi; a safety valve on or near the boiler protects it from bursting by releasing water through a discharge pipe at 30 psi and above.

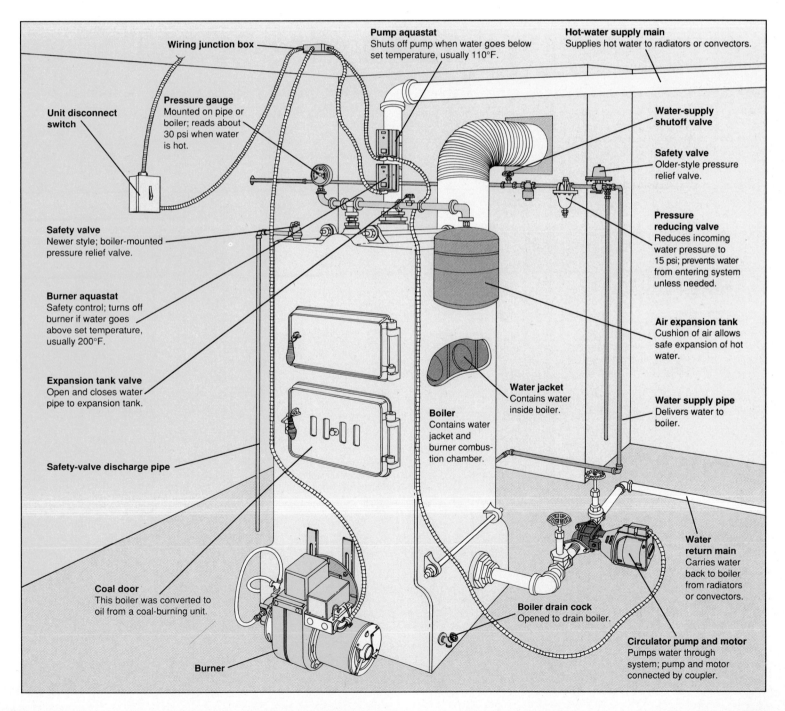

Wiring junction box

Pump aquastat
Shuts off pump when water goes below set temperature, usually 110°F.

Hot-water supply main
Supplies hot water to radiators or convectors.

Unit disconnect switch

Pressure gauge
Mounted on pipe or boiler; reads about 30 psi when water is hot.

Water-supply shutoff valve

Safety valve
Older-style pressure relief valve.

Safety valve
Newer style; boiler-mounted pressure relief valve.

Pressure reducing valve
Reduces incoming water pressure to 15 psi; prevents water from entering system unless needed.

Burner aquastat
Safety control; turns off burner if water goes above set temperature, usually 200°F.

Air expansion tank
Cushion of air allows safe expansion of hot water.

Expansion tank valve
Open and closes water pipe to expansion tank.

Water jacket
Contains water inside boiler.

Water supply pipe
Delivers water to boiler.

Boiler
Contains water jacket and burner combustion chamber.

Safety-valve discharge pipe

Coal door
This boiler was converted to oil from a coal-burning unit.

Boiler drain cock
Opened to drain boiler.

Water return main
Carries water back to boiler from radiators or convectors.

Burner

Circulator pump and motor
Pumps water through system; pump and motor connected by coupler.

Most systems use an air expansion tank, usually installed directly above or alongside the boiler; some large systems have two tanks. The expansion tank contains a pocket of air that is compressed when the hot water expands. If an old-style tank becomes completely full of water it must be drained and recharged *(page 183)*; the newer diaphragm-type tanks become waterlogged only when the diaphragm is worn out. In this case the tank must be replaced *(page 183)*.

Before each heating season, bleed all the radiators or convectors in your home and replace any faulty bleed valves *(page 180)*. Check the pressure reducing valve. Inspect the air expansion tank for leaks and recharge an old-style tank *(page 183)*. Test the aquastats *(page 184)* and oil the circulator pump and motor with non-detergent SAE-30 motor oil.

Before beginning most tests and repairs, turn off power to the boiler at the main service panel *(page 102)* and unit disconnect switch *(page 22)*. **Caution:** Working with wiring can be highly dangerous if the proper electrical circuit is not turned off; use a continuity tester to make sure the power is off *(page 417)*. Identify the components of your system in advance. If necessary, ask a plumber to point them out.

Heating problems may be caused by another system unit. Consult the Troubleshooting Guides in System Controls *(page 164)*, Oil Burners *(page 185)* and Gas Burners *(page 193)*.

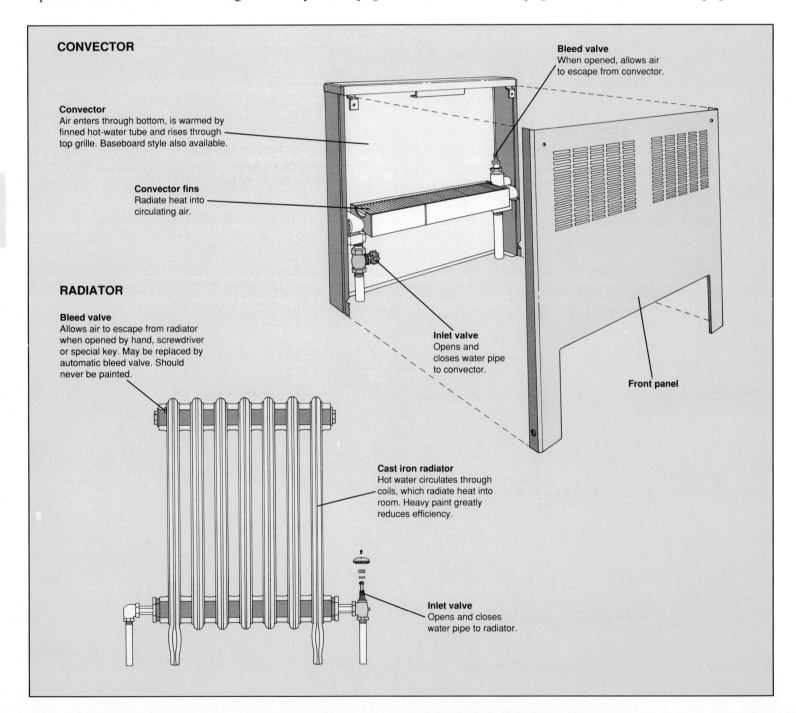

CONVECTOR

Bleed valve
When opened, allows air to escape from convector.

Convector
Air enters through bottom, is warmed by finned hot-water tube and rises through top grille. Baseboard style also available.

Convector fins
Radiate heat into circulating air.

RADIATOR

Bleed valve
Allows air to escape from radiator when opened by hand, screwdriver or special key. May be replaced by automatic bleed valve. Should never be painted.

Inlet valve
Opens and closes water pipe to convector.

Front panel

Cast iron radiator
Hot water circulates through coils, which radiate heat into room. Heavy paint greatly reduces efficiency.

Inlet valve
Opens and closes water pipe to radiator.

TROUBLESHOOTING GUIDE

SYMPTOM	POSSIBLE CAUSE	PROCEDURE
No heat	No power to system	Replace fuse or reset circuit breaker (p. 102) □○; restore power at unit disconnect switch (p. 22) □○
	Aquastat faulty	Test aquastats (p. 184) □○ and have replaced if necessary
	Air trapped in radiators or convectors	Bleed radiators or convectors (p. 180) □○; if frequent bleeding is required, install automatic bleed valves (p. 180) ▭●
	Coupler broken	Call for service to have coupler replaced
	Circulator pump faulty	Call for service
No heat, motor housing hot	Circulator motor burned out	Call for service
Gurgling sound in pipes or radiator	Air trapped in radiator	Bleed radiators (p. 180) □○; if frequent bleeding is required, install automatic bleed valves (p. 180) ▭◑
Burner does not turn off	Burner aquastat faulty	Test aquastat (p. 184) □○ and have replaced if necessary
Heat uneven throughout house	Air trapped in radiator or convector	Bleed radiators or convectors (p. 180) □○; if frequent bleeding is required, install automatic bleed valves (p. 180) ▭◑
	Coupler broken	Call for service to have coupler replaced
	Circulator pump faulty	Call for service
	Pressure reducing valve set too low	Call for service
Radiator is cold, hammering noise in pipes	Sagging floor makes radiator slope, trapping cold water or air pockets in radiator	Level sloping radiator with 1/4-inch wood shims, raising the leg below bleed valve
Not enough heat, convector is lukewarm	Convector fins dirty or bent	Vacuum convector fins, and straighten them with broad-billed pliers
	Air trapped in convector	Bleed convectors (p. 180) □○; if frequent bleeding is required, install automatic bleed valves (p. 180) ▭◑
	Circulator pump faulty	Call for service
Not enough heat, radiators are lukewarm (water pressure is too low)	Pressure gauge set too low	Call for service
	Pipes leaking	Tighten pipe joints with a wrench; call for service
	Pressure reducing valve faulty	Call for service
	Rust deposits in boiler or pipes	Drain and refill boiler system, adding rust inhibitor (p. 181) ▭●
	Circulator pump faulty	Call for service
Radiators are lukewarm (water pressure exceeds 30 psi soon after burner turns on, and safety valve discharges)	Old-style expansion tank waterlogged or leaking	Recharge expansion tank (p. 183) ▭●; if leaking, call for service
	Diaphragm-type expansion tank waterlogged or leaking	Replace expansion tank (p. 183) ▭◑
Radiators above boiler are lukewarm, others are cold	Pump aquastat faulty	Test aquastat (p. 184) □○ and have replaced if necessary
	Circulator pump or motor faulty	Call for service
Circulator motor noisy	Motor and pump not properly maintained	Pry open port caps and lubricate circulator pump and motor with 15 drops of non-detergent SAE-30 motor oil in each port
System sounds like chain being dragged through it	Coupler broken	Call for service to have coupler replaced
Water spills from safety-valve discharge pipe	Old-style expansion tank waterlogged or leaking	Recharge expansion tank (p. 183) ▭●; if leaking, call for service
	Diaphragm-type expansion tank waterlogged or leaking	Replace expansion tank (p. 183) ▭◑
Circulator pump leaks	Pump seal or impeller worn	Call for service
Inlet valve leaks	Valve packing deteriorated	Replace valve packing (p. 182) ▭◑
Bleed valve drips constantly or will not turn	Bleed valve faulty	Replace bleed valve (p. 180) ▭●

DEGREE OF DIFFICULTY: □ Easy ▭ Moderate ▣ Complex
ESTIMATED TIME: ○ Less than 1 hour ◑ 1 to 3 hours ● Over 3 hours ▲ Special tool required

BLEEDING THE SYSTEM

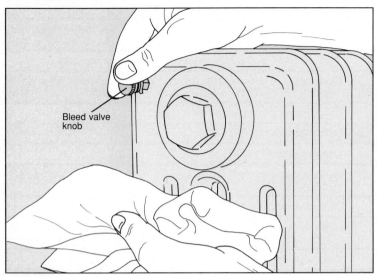
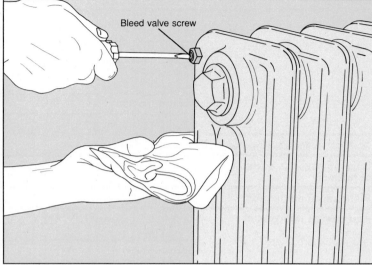

Bleeding a radiator or convector. At the beginning of each heating season, bleed the valve on each radiator or convector, starting on the top floor of your home. Have an absorbent rag handy; when the air is vented, water will escape from the valve. On models with a bleed-valve knob, turn the knob 180 degrees counterclockwise to purge the radiator or convector of air *(above, left)*. On models without a bleed-valve knob, use a screwdriver *(above, right)* or radiator venting key, as appropriate. Automatic bleed valves should bleed themselves, but water impurities can occasionally clog them. If a radiator with an automatic bleed valve is cool, bleed the valve: Take off the cap, turn it upside down and push it into the air valve, as for a car tire. On all bleed valves, as soon as water escapes in a steady stream the air has been bled; close the valve.

REPLACING A BLEED VALVE

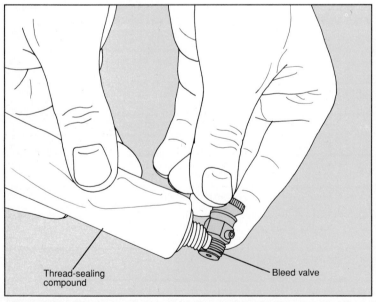
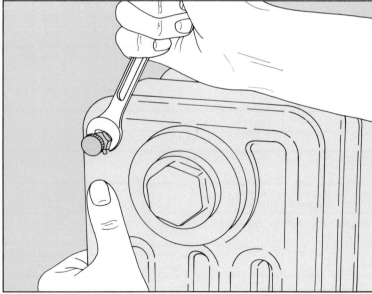

Removing and replacing the valve. If a bleed valve drips constantly or will not bleed at all, replace it. Buy a new bleed valve to fit your radiator, and coat its threads with thread-sealing compound *(above, left)* or wrap with pipe tape. If you are installing an automatic valve, buy the proper fittings for its upright, side-mounted or horizontal-mounted position. Turn off power to the boiler at the main service panel *(page 102)* and unit disconnect switch *(page 22)*; allow the boiler to cool. Drain the system *(page 181)* just until water stops leaking from the bleed valve. Use an open-end wrench to loosen the old bleed valve from its fitting *(above, right)*, and unscrew the valve. For an automatic valve, use a small pipe wrench to screw its fittings into the radiator. Then screw the new valve in place, taking care not to cross-thread the fitting. Refill the system *(page 181)*, then restore power. If the new valve leaks, try tightening the fitting.

DRAINING AND REFILLING THE SYSTEM

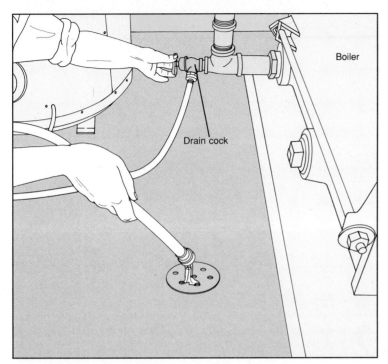

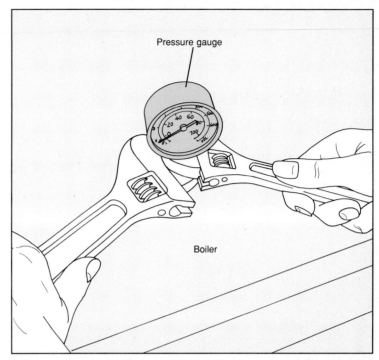

1 Draining the system. Turn off power to the boiler at the main service panel *(page 102)* and unit disconnect switch *(page 22)*. Turn off the water to the boiler, attach a hose to the drain cock and open a bleed valve on the top floor. Open the drain cock and let the system drain *(above)*; this can be a long process. An unpleasant odor is normal. When water no longer flows, open the pressure reducing valve and a ground-floor bleed valve to make sure there is no water in the system. Close the drain cock.

2 Accessing the boiler. With the boiler drained, remove the pressure gauge *(above)* or safety valve—whichever is boiler-mounted. Hold the boiler fitting with one wrench, and use another wrench to loosen the pressure gauge or safety valve from the fitting *(above)*. Then unscrew the gauge or valve by hand.

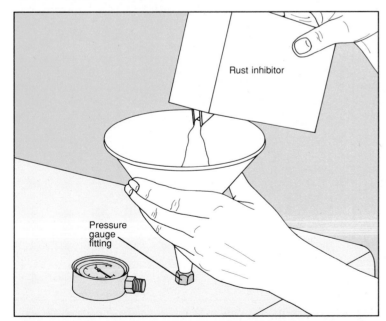

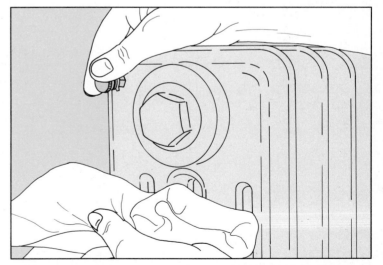

3 Adding rust inhibitor. Buy rust inhibitor, available from a heating supplies dealer. Insert a funnel into the pressure gauge or safety valve opening and, following the label instructions, pour the recommended amount of rust inhibitor for your system into the boiler *(above)*. Reinstall the pressure gauge or safety relief valve.

4 Refilling the system. Close the bleed valves that you opened in step 1, then close the pressure reducing valve. **Caution:** If any part of the system is still hot and cold water enters too quickly, the boiler could be damaged. Turn on the water supply to the boiler at the shutoff valve. When the boiler pressure reaches about 5 psi, bleed every radiator or convector in the house, starting on the ground floor. When boiler pressure stabilizes (on most systems, at 15 to 20 psi), restore power to the boiler. Allow the heated water to circulate for several hours, until the radiators or convectors are warm, to purge the water of dissolved air. Then bleed each radiator or convector again.

REPAIRING A LEAKY INLET VALVE

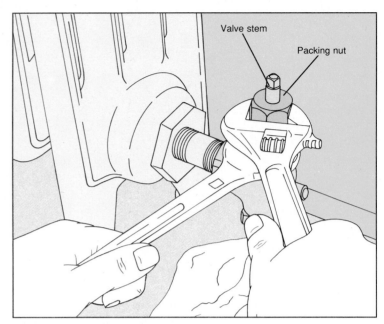

1 Unscrewing the handle. If a radiator or convector inlet valve leaks, try tightening the packing nut one-quarter turn. (Do not over-tighten—this will prevent the valve from turning.) If the valve still leaks, use a screwdriver to remove the handle screw, located in the middle of the valve stem *(above)*. Pull the handle straight off the stem.

2 Removing the packing nut. Wrap a few rags around the valve area; when you loosen the packing nut, the leaking may increase. Use two wrenches; one to hold the valve fitting steady, and the other to loosen the packing nut from the valve stem, turning counter-clockwise *(above)*. Unscrew the packing nut by hand and slip it off the valve stem. If excessive water leaks from the valve, reinstall the nut and drain the system *(page 181)*.

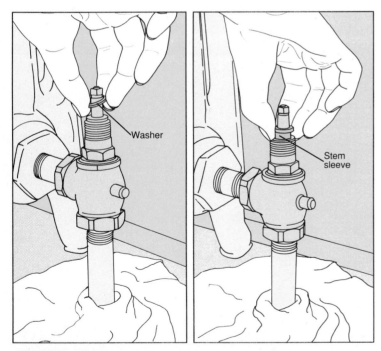

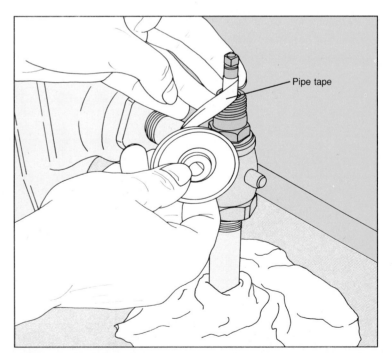

3 Dismantling the valve. With the packing nut removed, pull the washer, if any, off the stem *(above, left)*. Use the blade of a flat-tipped screwdriver to pry up the stem sleeve, if any. Once it is loosened, slip it off the stem by hand *(above, right)*.

4 Repacking the valve. Leaving the old packing in place, add pipe tape *(above)* or new packing string, available from a plumbing supplies dealer. Wrap the tape or string several times around the old packing, stretching it and pressing it down as you go. Replace the stem sleeve and washer, and reinstall the packing nut. Use a wrench to tighten the packing nut until it stops leaking. Screw on the valve handle.

REPLACING A DIAPHRAGM-TYPE EXPANSION TANK

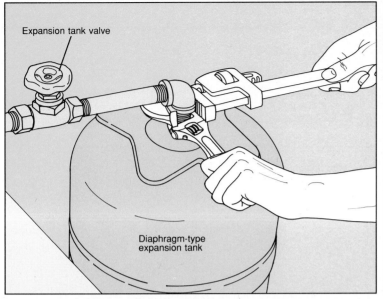

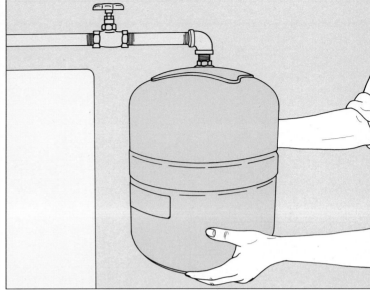

Freeing the expansion tank. Turn off power to the boiler at the main service panel *(page 102)* and unit disconnect switch *(page 22)*, and let the boiler cool. Close the expansion tank valve. Use a pipe wrench to grip the fitting connecting the expansion tank to the pipe *(above, left)*. Use another wrench to loosen the tank just until water starts to drip; wait until the water stops dripping. **Caution:** the tank is full of water, and will be heavy. Have a helper hold it for safety. Twist the tank off the pipe fitting by hand *(above, right)*. Purchase a new expansion tank from a heating supplies dealer. Wrap plumber's tape around the threads. Install the tank, reversing these instructions. Open the expansion tank valve slowly, then restore power to the boiler.

SERVICING AN OLD-STYLE EXPANSION TANK

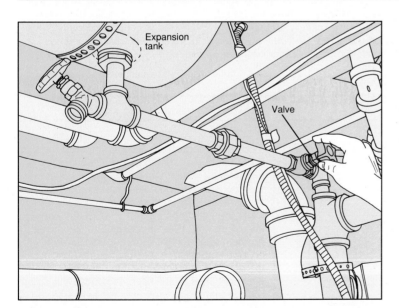

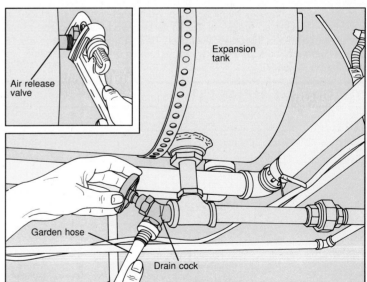

1 **Shutting off water to the tank.** If the pressure gauge reading rises to 30 psi or above and the safety valve spouts water, the expansion tank may be waterlogged and must be recharged. Turn off power to the boiler at the main service panel *(page 102)* and unit disconnect switch *(page 22)*, and allow the boiler to cool. Close the expansion tank valve *(above)*.

2 **Draining and refilling the tank.** Connect a garden hose to the drain cock on the bottom of the expansion tank. Open the drain cock; then use a pipe wrench to open the air release valve on the side of the tank *(inset)*. When the tank has drained completely, tighten the air release valve, close the drain cock and partially open the tank's shutoff valve. You will hear water slowly entering the tank; after the sound stops, open the valve completely. When the pressure gauge reads about 15 psi, restore power to the boiler. When the radiators or convectors are warm, bleed all of them *(page 180)*, beginning on the top floor.

183

AQUASTATS

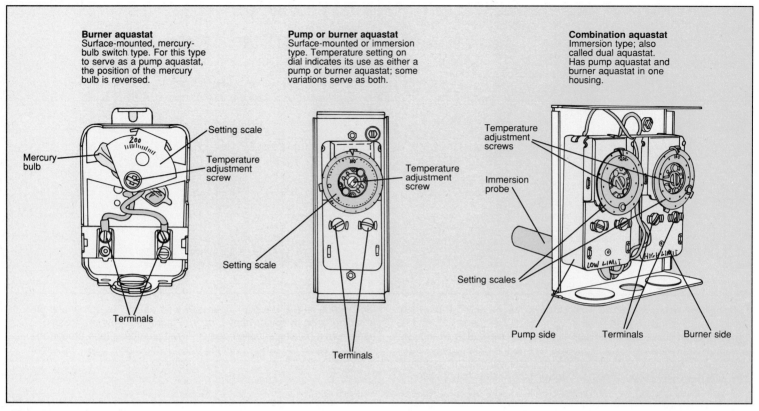

Burner aquastat
Surface-mounted, mercury-bulb switch type. For this type to serve as a pump aquastat, the position of the mercury bulb is reversed.

Mercury bulb

Setting scale

Temperature adjustment screw

Terminals

Pump or burner aquastat
Surface-mounted or immersion type. Temperature setting on dial indicates its use as either a pump or burner aquastat; some variations serve as both.

Temperature adjustment screw

Setting scale

Terminals

Combination aquastat
Immersion type; also called dual aquastat. Has pump aquastat and burner aquastat in one housing.

Temperature adjustment screws

Immersion probe

Setting scales

Pump side   Terminals   Burner side

Three types of aquastats. An aquastat is a device that senses the temperature of water in the system, and responds by turning the burner or circulator pump on or off, as appropriate. All systems have at least one aquastat; some have as many as three. An aquastat may be surface-mounted—located on a pipe; or the immersion type—with a probe inserted into a well in the boiler. All boilers have a burner aquastat *(above, left)* that acts as a safety switch, turning off the burner if the water temperature rises above a safe level, usually around 200°F. A second aquastat, the pump aquastat *(above, center)*, turns on the circulator pump when the temperature of the water is high enough to heat the house (usually around 110°F). When the water cools down, it turns off the pump. On some systems, a combination aquastat serves as both pump and burner aquastat *(above, right)*.

TESTING AN AQUASTAT

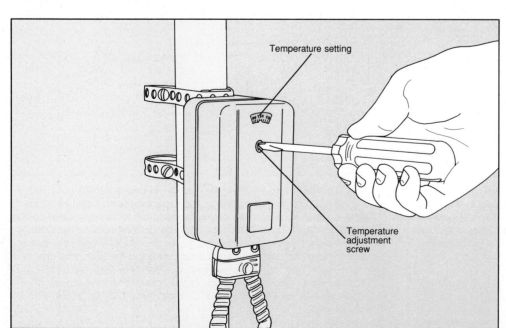

Temperature setting

Temperature adjustment screw

Testing the aquastat. Raise the thermostat to 80°F; the burner should go on. Then locate the temperature adjustment screw on the cover of the aquastat. On a burner aquastat, note the temperature setting, then use a screwdriver to lower the setting below 100°F *(left)*; the burner should turn off. Raise the setting to its original position; after a slight delay (up to 10 minutes on an oil burner with a stack-mounted relay), the burner should turn on. If the aquastat fails either test, it is faulty; have it replaced.

On a pump aquastat, note the temperature setting, then use a screwdriver to lower the setting below 100°F; the pump should turn on. Then raise the setting above 200°F; the pump should turn off. If the aquastat fails either test, it is faulty; have it replaced. Reset the thermostat.

OIL BURNERS

The oil burner is a team of small machines that produce and sustain a flame. The flame warms air or water, which circulates through the home to provide heat.

The pump supplies oil to the system, pressurizing it to about 100 pounds per square inch (psi). The oil is forced through a tiny opening in the nozzle, creating a finely-atomized mist that burns quickly and completely when mixed with air. In order to ignite this mixture, the ignition transformer raises household electrical current from roughly 120 volts to 10,000 volts. The stepped-up voltage runs to a pair of electrodes, creating a high-voltage spark that ignites the oil mist to start the system. The flame then continues burning on its own in the combustion chamber, fed by air supplied by the blower.

Periodic maintenance and efficiency tests can reduce the need for repairs, as well as lowering your fuel bill. In addition to cleaning the air intake gate and oiling the motor *(page 187)*, check the fuel tank gauge regularly to avoid running out of fuel. To conduct the tests in this chapter, you will need special tools available from a heating supplies dealer. These tools, and the proper way to use them, are presented in Tools & Techniques *(page 417)*.

If your oil-fired heating system is not working properly, the cause may be the oil burner, or it may be another unit in the heating system. Also consult the Troubleshooting Guides for System Controls *(page 164)*, and Water Distribution *(page 177)* or Air Distribution *(page 169)*.

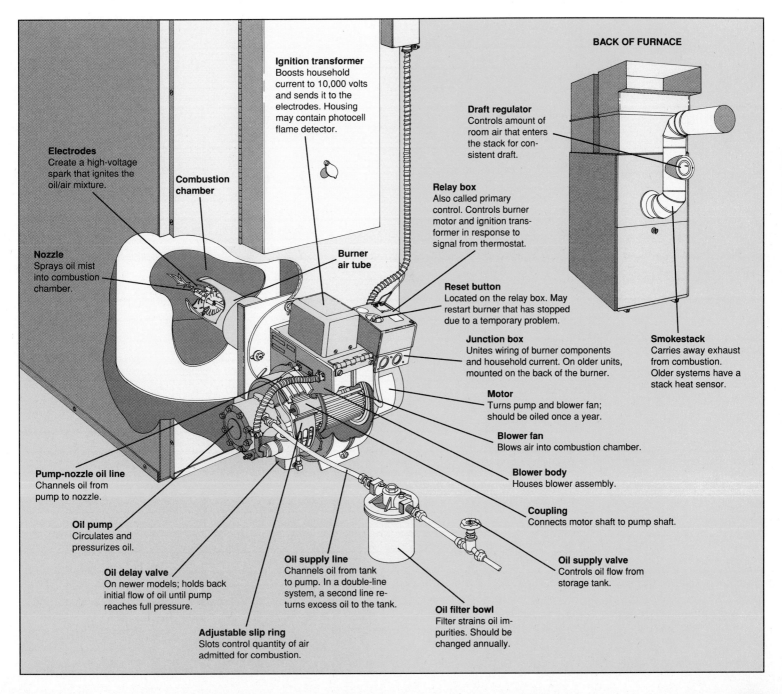

Ignition transformer
Boosts household current to 10,000 volts and sends it to the electrodes. Housing may contain photocell flame detector.

Electrodes
Create a high-voltage spark that ignites the oil/air mixture.

Combustion chamber

Nozzle
Sprays oil mist into combustion chamber.

Burner air tube

BACK OF FURNACE

Draft regulator
Controls amount of room air that enters the stack for consistent draft.

Relay box
Also called primary control. Controls burner motor and ignition transformer in response to signal from thermostat.

Reset button
Located on the relay box. May restart burner that has stopped due to a temporary problem.

Junction box
Unites wiring of burner components and household current. On older units, mounted on the back of the burner.

Smokestack
Carries away exhaust from combustion. Older systems have a stack heat sensor.

Motor
Turns pump and blower fan; should be oiled once a year.

Blower fan
Blows air into combustion chamber.

Blower body
Houses blower assembly.

Coupling
Connects motor shaft to pump shaft.

Pump-nozzle oil line
Channels oil from pump to nozzle.

Oil pump
Circulates and pressurizes oil.

Oil delay valve
On newer models; holds back initial flow of oil until pump reaches full pressure.

Oil supply line
Channels oil from tank to pump. In a double-line system, a second line returns excess oil to the tank.

Oil filter bowl
Filter strains oil impurities. Should be changed annually.

Oil supply valve
Controls oil flow from storage tank.

Adjustable slip ring
Slots control quantity of air admitted for combustion.

TROUBLESHOOTING GUIDE

SYMPTOM	POSSIBLE CAUSE	PROCEDURE
No heat or insufficient heat	No fuel	Check fuel tank gauge; have tank refilled if necessary
	No power to circuit	Replace fuse or reset circuit breaker *(p. 102)* □○
	Relay or stack heat sensor tripped	Press reset button no more than twice; if the system doesn't start, call for service
	Oil leaking at pump fittings	Tighten fittings; if no improvement, have pump replaced
	Electrodes faulty	Call for service
	Nozzle faulty	Replace nozzle *(p. 192)* ◪○
	Photocell dirty or faulty	Clean photocell *(p. 187)* □○; replace if necessary
	Stack heat sensor dirty	Clean soot buildup out of stack heat sensor *(p. 188)* □○
	Coupling broken	Call for service
	Pump seized	Test pump pressure *(p. 190)* □○▲; call for service
	Motor seized or overloaded	Press reset button; if motor is silent or hums but does not turn, call for service
	Pump pressure too low	Test pump pressure *(p. 190)* □○▲; call for service
	Oil filter dirty	Replace oil filter *(p. 189)* □○
	Oil strainer dirty	Clean strainer *(p. 190)* □○; replace if necessary
Intermittent heat	Fuel supply low	Check fuel tank gauge; have tank refilled if necessary
	Oil filter dirty	Replace oil filter *(p. 189)* □○
	Oil strainer dirty	Clean strainer *(p. 190)* □○; replace if necessary
	Pump pressure too high	Test pump pressure *(p. 190)* □○▲; call for service
	Motor overloaded	Press reset button; if motor is silent or hums but does not turn, call for service
	Pump seized	Test pump pressure *(p. 190)* □○▲; call for service
	Nozzle faulty	Replace nozzle *(p. 192)* ◪○
	Photocell dirty or faulty	Clean or replace photocell *(p. 187)* □○
	Stack heat sensor dirty	Clean soot buildup out of stack heat sensor *(p. 188)* □○
High fuel consumption	Nozzle faulty	Replace nozzle *(p. 192)* ◪○
	Pump pressure too low or too high	Test pump pressure *(p. 190)* □○▲; call for service
Burner system noisy	Motor bearings dry	Lubricate motor *(p. 187)* □○
	Coupling misaligned, loose or broken	Call for service
	Pump worn out	Test pump pressure *(p. 190)* □○▲; call for service
	Draft regulator misadjusted	Turn counterweight screw on draft regulator to allow more or less air flow
	Incorrect oil/air mix causing flame roar	Call for service
Diesel fuel odor from burner system	Draft regulator wide open	Adjust counterweight, screw on draft regulator
	Stack or heat exchanger blocked with soot	Call for service to have stack or heat exchanger cleaned
	Pump leaking	Call for service
	Nozzle faulty	Replace nozzle *(p. 192)* ◪○
	Electrodes faulty	Call for service
	Stack damaged	Call for service
Electrical insulation odor from burner system	Ignition transformer or motor overheating	Call for service

DEGREE OF DIFFICULTY: □ Easy ◪ Moderate ■ Complex
ESTIMATED TIME: ○ Less than 1 hour ◖ 1 to 3 hours ● Over 3 hours   ▲ Special tool required

CLEANING AND LUBRICATING THE BURNER

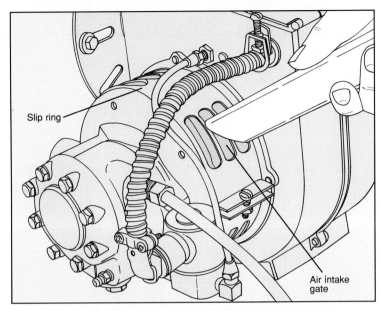

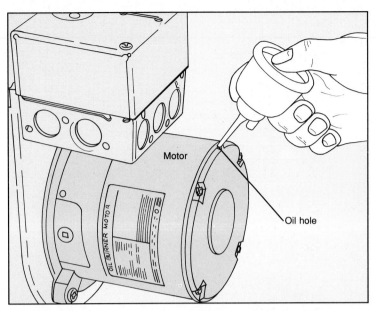

Vacuuming the air intake gate and blower. Turn off power to the burner at the main service panel *(page 102)* and unit disconnect switch *(page 22)*. Locate the air intake gate, usually at the left side of the burner assembly when you face the furnace or boiler; it is covered by a slotted slip ring. As air enters through the slots, dust, animal hair or dryer lint can accumulate. Using a crevice tool, vacuum the air intake gate *(above)*. If necessary, mark the slip ring position and detach it to remove heavy buildup. Reinstall the slip ring before turning on power to the burner.

Oiling the motor. Turn off power to the burner at the main service panel *(page 102)* and unit disconnect switch *(page 22)*. Locate the motor, usually at the right side of the burner assembly when you face the furnace or boiler. The motor has one or more oil holes at the top. Using an oil can, insert a drop of high-grade SAE 30 machine oil into each hole *(above)*. Oil sparingly, a total of four drops once per year; too much oil, or oiling too often, can damage the internal starting switch. Turn on power to the burner.

SERVICING THE PHOTOCELL FLAME DETECTOR

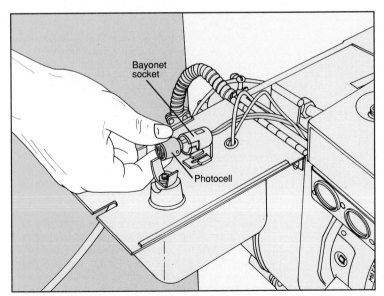

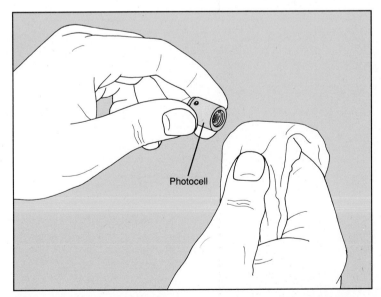

1 **Removing the photocell.** If your burner has no photocell, remove and clean the stack heat sensor *(below)*. On a unit with a photocell, turn off power to the burner at the main service panel *(page 102)* and unit disconnect switch *(page 22)*. Remove the screw from the transformer's hinged hatch and open the hatch. Remove a bayonet-style photocell by pushing it in, then twisting it out of its socket *(above)*; pull out a plug-in photocell.

2 **Cleaning the photocell.** Use a clean, moist cloth to wipe soot buildup off the photocell "eye" *(above)*. Reinstall the photocell in its socket, close the transformer hatch and reinstall the screw. Turn on power to the burner. If the photocell is still faulty, remove it again and replace it with an identical photocell.

SERVICING THE STACK HEAT SENSOR

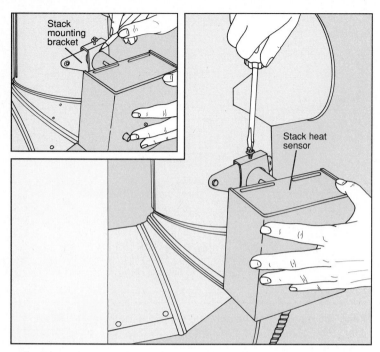

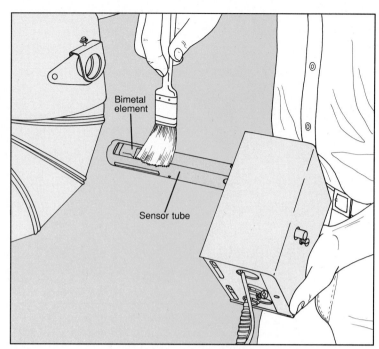

1 **Removing the stack heat sensor.** Turn off power to the burner at the main service panel *(page 102)* and unit disconnect switch *(page 22)*. Use a felt-tip pen to mark the tube of the heat sensor where it meets the stack mounting bracket *(inset)*. Loosen the lock screw on the mounting bracket *(above)* and pull the stack heat sensor out of the stack.

2 **Cleaning the sensor tube and bimetal element.** Use a soft paintbrush *(above)* to sweep away soot that has collected on the heat-sensor bimetal element and sensor tube. Replace the stack heat sensor to the depth indicated by the pen mark and tighten the mounting bracket screw. Turn on power to the burner.

PRIMING THE PUMP

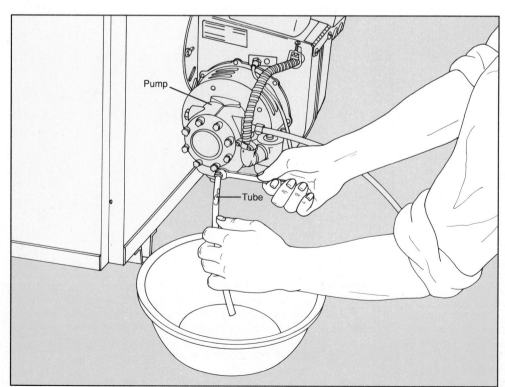

Loosening the bleeder nut. Set the thermostat 5°F above room temperature. If you have turned off power to the burner and closed the main oil-supply valve in order to work on the burner, restore the power and open the oil supply valve. If you suspect that the safety control system has shut off the burner, locate the reset button on the relay box and press it no more than twice to reset the relay. Once the burner is running, locate the bleeder nut, a small plug with a nipple in its center, on the pump. Slip a flexible clear-plastic tube over the bleeder nut nipple, and set out a container to catch dripping oil. Using an open-end wrench, slowly loosen the bleeder nut by turning it counterclockwise three-quarters of a turn *(left)*; you will see air bubbles in the oil flow. Bleed the pump until the oil runs smoothly, with no air bubbles. Tighten the bleeder nut and remove the tube. If the relay system shuts off the burner during bleeding, press the reset button once to reset the relay, then continue bleeding.

REPLACING THE OIL FILTER

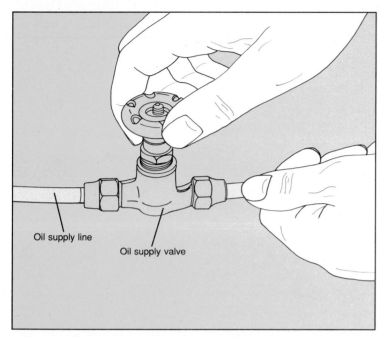

Oil supply line

Oil supply valve

1 Closing the oil supply valve. Turn off power to the burner at the main service panel *(page 102)* and unit disconnect switch *(page 22)*. Locate the oil supply valve on the oil supply line between the burner and the oil tank. Both the oil supply valve and the oil filter may be located at either end of the oil line: next to the oil tank or next to the burner assembly. Close the valve by turning its knob clockwise *(above)*.

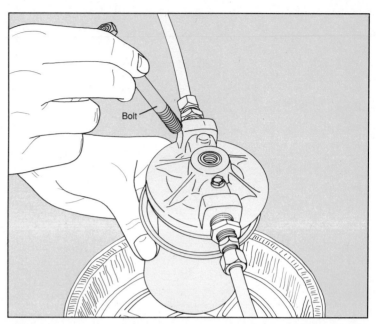

Bolt

2 Removing the filter bowl. Place a bucket or pan under the oil filter. Use an open-end wrench or screwdriver to unfasten the bolt or screw attaching the filter bowl to its lid *(above)*. If the bolt or screw is particularly stubborn, grip the lid firmly to avoid bending the oil line's copper tubing, and wear a glove to protect your other hand when the bolt jolts loose. As you loosen the bolt, hold the filter bowl to prevent it from spilling oil. Remove the bolt and washer, then pull the bowl down off the lid, taking care not to twist the oil line's copper tubing.

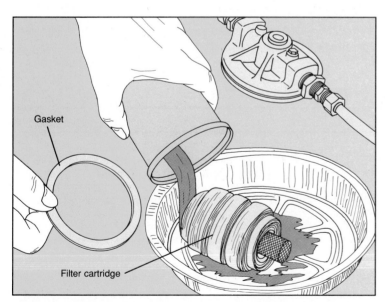

Gasket

Filter cartridge

3 Emptying the filter bowl. Turn the bowl upside down over the drain pan *(above)*. Oil and a filter cartridge should fall out of the bowl. The gasket around the top of the bowl will usually fall off; if it sticks to the bowl or the lid, pry it loose with a screwdriver. (Except in an emergency, don't worry about keeping the gasket intact; it should be replaced.) Using a clean rag, wipe oil and grit off the inside of the bowl and its lid, then wipe clean the outside of the filter bowl and the surrounding area. Buy exact replacements for the oil filter, cartridge and gasket, and rub fuel oil on both sides of the new gasket.

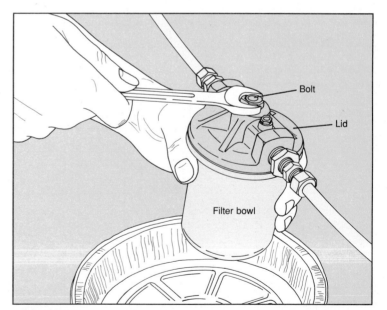

Bolt

Lid

Filter bowl

4 Replacing the filter cartridge. Push the new filter cartridge into the filter bowl. Fit the gasket onto the lip of the filter bowl, then press the bowl and gasket against the bowl lid. Tighten the lid bolt or screw. On a single-line system, prime the pump *(page 188)*. Locate the small nut blocking a hole in the lid of the filter bowl; this hole releases air as the filter bowl fills with oil. Use an open-end or adjustable wrench to remove the bleeder nut *(above)*. Open the oil supply valve *(step 1)*; in about 30 seconds the filter bowl should be full of oil. Screw in the bleeder nut and turn on power to the burner.

CLEANING THE PUMP STRAINER

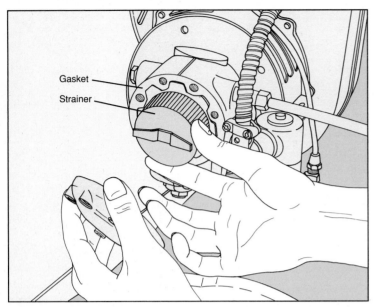

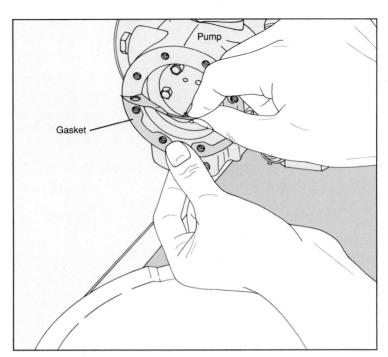

1 **Removing the pump cover and strainer.** Turn off power to the burner at the main service panel *(page 102)* and unit disconnect switch *(page 22)*, then close the oil supply valve *(page 189)*. Use an open-end or adjustable wrench to unbolt the pump cover and take it off. Locate the strainer, a small, squat cylinder of wire mesh, positioned horizontally inside the pump. (Some older models have a rotary filter, which is removed and cleaned the same way.) Pull the strainer or filter out of the pump *(above)*, and soak it in cleaning solvent for 15 minutes to loosen built-up sludge. Peel off the thin gasket sealing the rim of the pump; buy an identical replacement gasket.

2 **Replacing the gasket.** Examine the strainer closely for damage or pieces of grit. If the strainer is bent, or the wire mesh is torn, replace it with an identical strainer. Otherwise, use a toothbrush or fine-bristled nylon brush to dislodge all dirt and foreign particles from the mesh. Rinse the strainer with solvent, then reinsert it in the pump. Place the adhesive side of the gasket against the pump rim, pressing firmly to ensure a tight bond *(above)*. Replace the pump cover and screw in the bolts by hand. Tighten the bolts in a crisscross sequence: first, the bolt in the 12 o'clock position, then 6 o'clock, then 3 o'clock, then 9 o'clock, and so on. Open the oil supply valve and turn on power to the burner. For a single-line system, prime the pump *(page 188)*.

TESTING PUMP PRESSURE

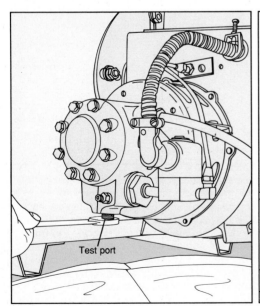

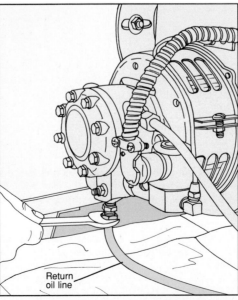

1 **Accessing the test port.** Turn off power to the burner at the main service panel *(page 102)* and unit disconnect switch *(page 22)*. Place newspaper or a drain pan under the pump to catch dripping oil. Using an open-end wrench, remove the bolt from the test port on the pump *(far left)*. On a two-line system *(near left)*, the test port is sometimes used as a return port for oil; in that case, disconnect the return oil line from the port.

TESTING PUMP PRESSURE (continued)

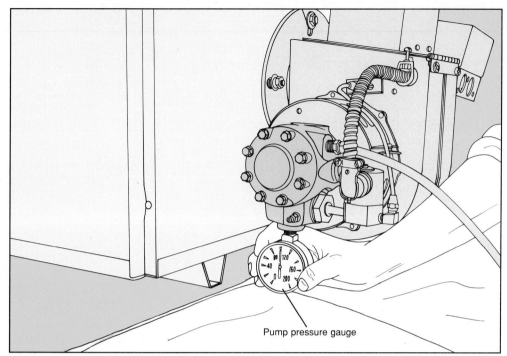

2 Reading the pump pressure. Screw a pump pressure gauge—available from a heating supplies dealer—into the threaded opening of the test port *(left)*. Turn on power to the burner. With the pump running, the gauge should show a reading of between 90 and 100 psi (pounds per square inch). If the reading is above or below these levels, turn off the power and remove the gauge. Call for service to have the pressure adjusted or replace the pump. If there is no pressure at all, bleed air from the filter bowl *(page 58)*, and test again. If the reading is OK, remove the gauge and reinstall the test port bolt in a single-line system, or the return oil line in a double-line system. If the problem persists, the pump may be seized; call for service.

Pump pressure gauge

SERVICING THE RELAY BOX

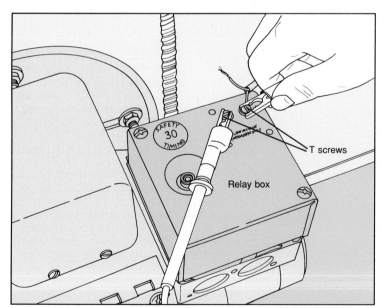

T screws

Relay box

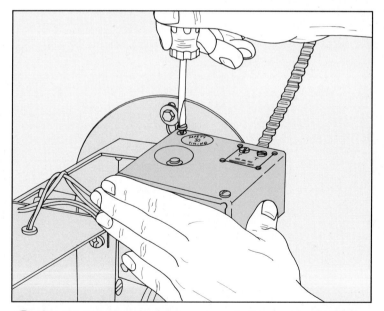

1 Testing for low voltage. Turn off power to the burner at the main service panel *(page 102)* and unit disconnect switch *(page 22)*. Disconnect a wire from one of the two thermostat screw connections (labeled "T") on the relay box. On a stack-mounted relay, unscrew the housing and open the box to find the T screws. Set a multitester to measure 24 volts AC *(page 417)*, then attach a probe with an alligator clip to each T screw. Without touching the relay box or multitester, turn on power to the burner. If the multitester shows a reading of about 24 volts, the relay is OK. Turn off power and reconnect the disconnected wire, then turn on the power. If there is no reading, remove the relay box from the junction box *(step 2)* and check the wiring.

2 Unscrewing the relay. With power to the burner turned off, locate the junction box. On newer units, it is located beneath the relay box, usually on top of the motor. On older units, the junction box is generally on the back of the burner; to find it, trace the electrical cable running to the burner. Remove the two screws securing the relay box to the junction box *(above)*. Make sure all connections inside the junction box are tight and that wire caps are correctly fastened. Reattach the junction box and test again *(step 1)*. If the test shows no voltage, turn off the power and replace the old relay box with an identical new one. Transfer the wires one by one from the old box to the new box, then screw the new box in place. Turn on power to the burner.

REPLACING THE NOZZLE

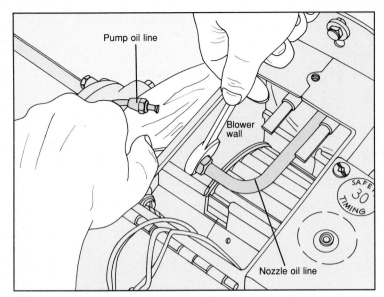

Pump oil line

Blower wall

Nozzle oil line

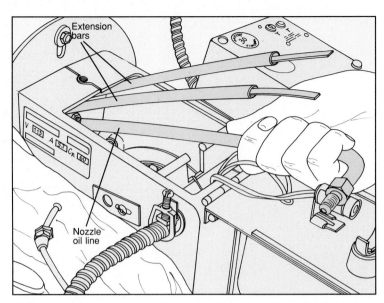

Extension bars

Nozzle oil line

1 **Accessing the firing assembly.** Turn off power to the burner at the main service panel *(page 102)* and unit disconnect switch *(page 22)*. Close the oil supply valve *(page 189)* and loosen the nuts attaching the two oil lines to the oil pump with a pair of open-end wrenches. Then disconnect the small oil line from the oil delay valve. Remove the screw from the ignition transformer and lift off the transformer, or tip it over if it has a hinge, as on the model shown. Locate the nozzle oil line inside the blower body, and the nut connecting it to the pump oil line on the blower walll. Place a rag underneath the pump oil line, and use an open-end wrench to loosen its nut. Then loosen the nut on the nozzle line and pull the pump line free *(above)*.

2 **Removing the firing assembly.** Detach the nozzle oil line from the blower wall. Gripping the oil line firmly, pull the entire firing assembly out of the air tube *(above)*. It may be necessary to turn or twist the assembly slightly as you pull it out. Avoid catching the electrode extension bars on the burner housing, or bumping the electrodes and nozzle. Replace the nozzle *(step 3)* and use a cloth dampened with cleaning solvent to wipe soot off the insulators, electrodes and extension bars.

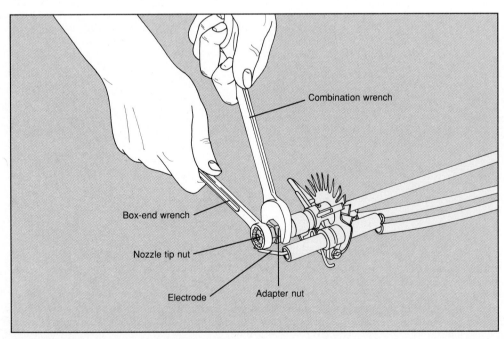

Combination wrench

Box-end wrench

Nozzle tip nut

Electrode

Adapter nut

3 **Removing and replacing the nozzle.** Locate the two nuts on the nozzle, one near the tip and one at the nozzle oil-line adapter. Taking care not to touch the electrodes or twist the oil line, loosen the nuts with a combination wrench and box-end wrench, and unscrew the nozzle *(left)*. When choosing a new nozzle, match the specifications stamped on the nozzle tip: firing rate in gallons of oil per hour (GPH); angle of spray in degrees; and spray pattern (identified by a letter of the alphabet). Screw on the new nozzle and reinstall the firing assembly by reversing the sequence above. Have a combustion test done by a professional as soon as possible.

GAS BURNERS

The gas burner is one of the simplest, most reliable elements in a home heating system. It burns cleaner than an oil burner, is easier to maintain, and promises a constant supply of fuel. Although a gas burner usually fires a forced-air furnace, as shown below, gas-fired boilers with circulating pumps are also in common use.

When the thermostat activates a valve in the combination control, gas flows from a supply line through a manifold, then to burner tubes that mix it with air. The mixture goes to ports where it is ignited by a pilot — or on some newer units, an electric spark igniter. A heat exchanger uses this flame to pro-duce warm air, hot water or steam for circulation through the house. Waste gases go up a vent. The thermocouple stops gas flow if the pilot light goes out or the electric igniter fails.

New technology has improved the efficiency of gas-fired systems. Electric ignition offers two gas-saving alternatives to the conventional pilot: A pilot is ignited electrically, or direct-ignition burners are ignited by a spark from an electrode. High efficiency, or condensing, furnaces operate on a "sealed combustion" principle, with no pilot light, burners or conventional vent; an automotive spark plug is used for ignition. Repairs to this type should be done by the gas company.

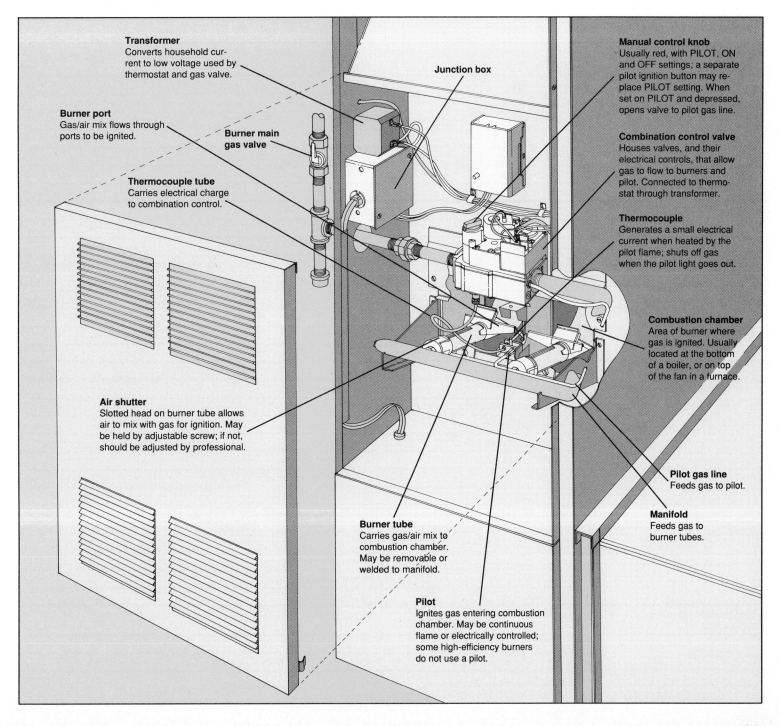

Transformer
Converts household current to low voltage used by thermostat and gas valve.

Junction box

Manual control knob
Usually red, with PILOT, ON and OFF settings; a separate pilot ignition button may replace PILOT setting. When set on PILOT and depressed, opens valve to pilot gas line.

Burner port
Gas/air mix flows through ports to be ignited.

Burner main gas valve

Combination control valve
Houses valves, and their electrical controls, that allow gas to flow to burners and pilot. Connected to thermostat through transformer.

Thermocouple tube
Carries electrical charge to combination control.

Thermocouple
Generates a small electrical current when heated by the pilot flame; shuts off gas when the pilot light goes out.

Combustion chamber
Area of burner where gas is ignited. Usually located at the bottom of a boiler, or on top of the fan in a furnace.

Air shutter
Slotted head on burner tube allows air to mix with gas for ignition. May be held by adjustable screw; if not, should be adjusted by professional.

Pilot gas line
Feeds gas to pilot.

Manifold
Feeds gas to burner tubes.

Burner tube
Carries gas/air mix to combustion chamber. May be removable or welded to manifold.

Pilot
Ignites gas entering combustion chamber. May be continuous flame or electrically controlled; some high-efficiency burners do not use a pilot.

Gas burner maintenance typically involves relighting the pilot *(page 195)*, or servicing the thermocouple *(page 196)* or transformer *(page 198)*. For safety reasons, the combination control and other components that carry gas under pressure should be adjusted or replaced only by a professional. Gas leaks are rare, but if you smell gas, follow the instructions in the Emergency Guide *(page 11)*.

Your gas burner should be cleaned periodically; how often depends on the burner's age and the type of system it fires. Newer burners require cleaning every few years, but more frequent cleaning is recommended for older models. Prevent rust-causing condensation inside the furnace by turning off the pilot at the end of each heating season.

Before beginning most repairs, turn off power to the burner at the main service panel *(page 102)* or unit disconnect switch *(page 22)*. **Caution:** Some repairs, such as replacing a thermocouple, require shutting off the burner gas valve *(page 197)*. If your gas-fired heating system is not working properly, the cause may be the gas burner itself, or another element of the heating system. Before attempting a repair, also consult the Troubleshooting Guides for System Controls *(page 164)*, and Air Distribution *(page 169)* or Water Distribution *(page 177)*.

TROUBLESHOOTING GUIDE

SYMPTOM	POSSIBLE CAUSE	PROCEDURE
No heat	No power to circuit	Replace fuse or reset circuit breaker *(p. 102)* □○
	Transformer faulty	Test transformer *(p. 198)* ◩●▲ ; replace if necessary
	Pilot light out	Relight pilot *(p. 195)* □○
	Combination control faulty	Call for service
Insufficient heat	Air shutter needs adjustment	Adjust burner air shutter *(p. 197)* □○
	Burner ports clogged	Clean burner ports *(p. 200)* □○
	Gas pressure too low	Call for service
Excessive fuel consumption	Pilot set too high	Adjust pilot *(p. 196)* □○
	Gas pressure too high	Call for service
Pilot does not light or does not stay lit	Pilot orifice dirty or clogged	Clean pilot *(p. 199)* □○
	Thermocouple loose or faulty	Test thermocouple *(p. 196)* □○▲ ; tighten or replace if necessary
	Electric pilot faulty	Call for service
	Combination control faulty	Call for service
Pilot lights, but burner does not ignite	Gas pressure too low	Call for service
	Combination control faulty	Call for service
	Transformer faulty	Test transformer *(p. 198)* ◩●▲ ; replace if necessary
Pilot flame flickers	Pilot set too low or too high	Adjust pilot *(p. 196)* □○
Exploding sound when burner ignites	Pilot set too low	Adjust pilot *(p. 196)* □○
	Pilot orifice dirty or clogged	Clean pilot *(p. 199)* □○
	Gas pressure too low or too high	Call for service
	Pilot light not positioned correctly	Call for service
	Burner ports clogged	Clean burner ports *(p. 200)* □○
Burner takes more than a few seconds to ignite	Burner ports clogged	Clean burner ports *(p. 200)* □○
	Pilot needs adjustment	Adjust pilot *(p. 196)* □○
Burner flame uneven	Burner ports clogged	Clean burner ports *(p. 200)* □○
Burner flame too yellow	Burner dirty	Clean burner *(p. 200)* □○
	Insufficient air for combustion	Provide air from outside by opening vents in furnace room; if problem persists, call for service
	Air shutter opening too small	Adjust air shutter *(p. 197)* □○
	Burners faulty	Call for service
Noisy furnace: rumbling when burners off	Pilot needs adjustment	Adjust pilot *(p. 196)* □○
Noisy furnace: rumbling when burners on	Burner ports clogged	Clean burner ports *(p. 200)* □○
	Air shutter needs adjustment	Adjust burner air shutter *(p. 197)* □○

DEGREE OF DIFFICULTY: □ Easy ◩ Moderate ■ Complex
ESTIMATED TIME: ○ Less than 1 hour ◖ 1 to 3 hours ● Over 3 hours   ▲ Special tool required

LIGHTING THE PILOT

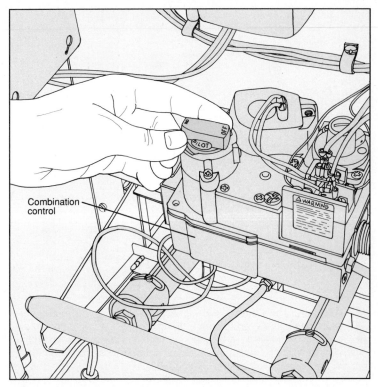

1 **Removing the front access panel.** Look for screws holding the panel in place, and remove them. Grasp the panel firmly and slide it up, then pull it off *(above)*. Loosen a panel that sticks by rapping it gently at the bottom.

2 **Turning off gas to the pilot.** Set the manual control knob, which is usually red, to the OFF position *(above)* and wait ten minutes for the gas to dissipate before lighting a flame. **Caution:** If the smell of gas persists, do not attempt to relight the pilot; call for service.

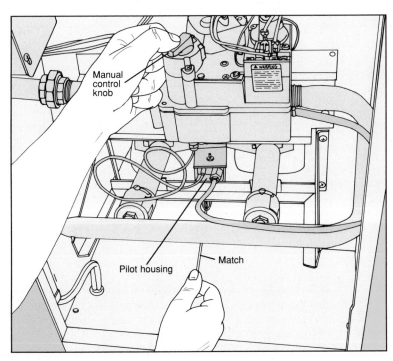

3 **Relighting the pilot.** Follow the manufacturer's instructions for relighting the pilot—usually labeled on, or near, the combination control. If there are no instructions, follow this general procedure: Turn on the gas to the pilot by setting the manual control knob to the PILOT position. While depressing the control knob or pilot ignition button, light the pilot with a long match *(left)* or a lit soda straw. Continue depressing the knob for 30 seconds. Release the control knob; if the pilot goes out, light it again, this time depressing the knob for one minute. If the pilot doesn't stay lit, the thermocouple may be faulty; service the thermocouple *(page 196)*. If the pilot stays lit, check to see that the pilot flame envelops the thermocouple properly; adjust the pilot if necessary *(page 196)*. Turn the manual control knob to the ON position. Replace the front access panel.

CHECKING AND ADJUSTING THE PILOT FLAME

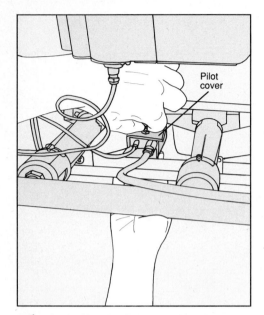

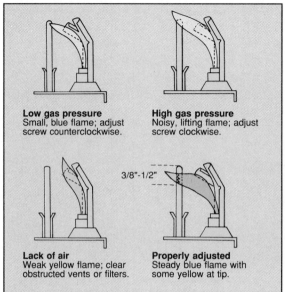

Low gas pressure
Small, blue flame; adjust screw counterclockwise.

High gas pressure
Noisy, lifting flame; adjust screw clockwise.

Lack of air
Weak yellow flame; clear obstructed vents or filters.

3/8"-1/2"

Properly adjusted
Steady blue flame with some yellow at tip.

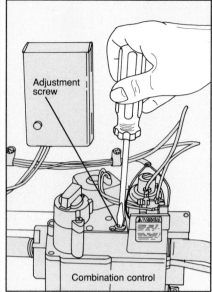

Adjustment screw

Combination control

1 Accessing the flame. If you can see the pilot flame clearly, go to step 2. If, however-er, view of the flame is blocked by a metal cover, first turn off the gas at the manual control knob on the combination control. Wait a few minutes for the cover to cool. Unscrew and re-move the cover *(above)*, then turn on the gas and relight the pilot *(page 195)*.

2 Adjusting the pilot screw. A properly adjusted flame is blue with some yellow at the tip, and contacts about 3/8 to 1/2 inch of the thermocouple. Compare the flame to the diagrams *(above, left)*, and use the guidelines given to make any necessary adjustments. The adjust-ment screw on the combination control regulates the amount of gas delivered to the pilot. On some models, the adjustment screw is recessed and covered by a cap screw that must first be removed; on others, the adjustment screw is on the surface of the combination control. Increase the height of the flame by turning the adjustment screw counterclockwise *(above, right)*; decrease it by turning clockwise. Adjust until the flame appears correct. If the flame cannot be correctly adjusted, clean the pilot *(below)*. If you removed a pilot cover in step 1, turn off the gas, replace the cover, then relight the pilot.

ADJUSTING AND REPLACING THE THERMOCOUPLE

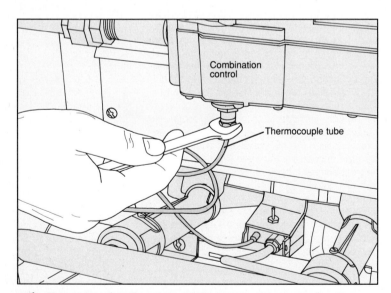

Combination control

Thermocouple tube

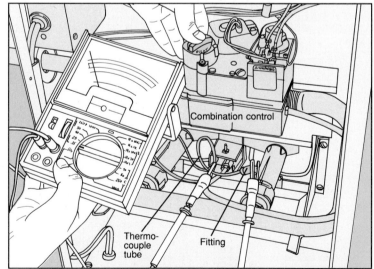

Combination control

Thermo-couple tube

Fitting

1 Removing the thermocouple tube. The thermocouple generates an electrical charge when it is heated by the pilot flame. To test it, the pilot must remain lit. Turn the manual control knob on the combination control to the PILOT setting and depress the knob or the pilot ignition button. Since it must remain depressed during removal and testing, this will be easier if someone helps you. Detach the thermocou-ple tube from the combination control by unscrewing the fitting with an open-end wrench *(above)*.

2 Testing the thermocouple. Set a multitester to the DCV scale, lowest volt range *(page 417)*. Keeping the manual control knob or button depressed, clip one multitester probe to the end of the thermocouple tube nearest the pilot and the other multitester probe to the fitting on the other end of the tube *(above)*. If the multitester shows a reading above or below zero, the thermocouple is generating sufficient voltage; put back the thermocouple tube. If there is no reading, release the manual control knob and go to step 3.

ADJUSTING AND REPLACING THE THERMOCOUPLE (continued)

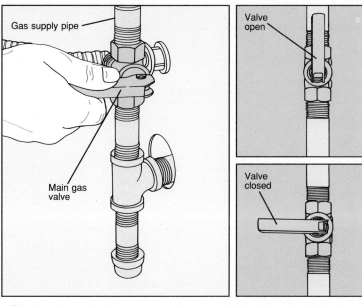

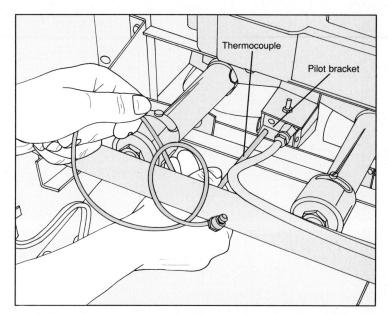

3 **Shutting off the burner main gas valve.** Before replacing the thermocouple, shut off the main gas valve *(above)*, located on the gas supply pipe that leads into the burner. When the handle is parallel to the pipe, the valve is open *(inset, top)*; when the handle is perpendicular to the pipe, the valve is closed *(inset, bottom)*. Turn off power to the burner at the main service panel *(page 102)* or unit disconnect switch *(page 22)*, and allow 30 minutes for metal parts to cool.

4 **Removing and replacing the thermocouple.** Slide the defective thermocouple out of the bracket that holds it in place next to the pilot *(above)*. Use a cloth to clean the fitting on the combination control and screw an identical replacement thermocouple tube into the fitting. After tightening it by hand, turn it a quarter turn with an open-end wrench. Insert the thermocouple into the pilot bracket, being careful not to crimp the tubing.

ADJUSTING THE BURNER FLAME

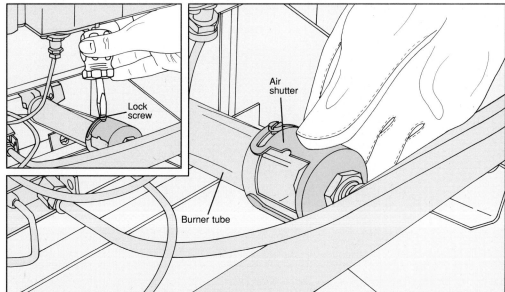

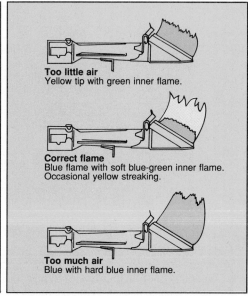

Too little air
Yellow tip with green inner flame.

Correct flame
Blue flame with soft blue-green inner flame. Occasional yellow streaking.

Too much air
Blue with hard blue inner flame.

Adjusting the air shutter. The burner may have an adjustable shutter, held in position by a lock screw on the end of the burner tube; or a fixed air shutter, which must be adjusted by a professional; or no air shutter at all. If your model has an adjustable shutter, turn the thermostat to its highest setting to start the burner and keep it running. Allow five minutes for the burners to ignite and heat up, then remove the burner access panel *(page 195)* and loosen the lock screw *(inset)*. Slowly rotate the shutter open *(above, left)* until the blue base of the flame appears to lift slightly from the burner port surface. Then close the shutter until the flame reseats itself on the surface, and looks correct *(above, right)*. Tighten the lock screw. Repeat this procedure to adjust the remaining burners, then replace the access panel and return the thermostat to its normal setting.

SERVICING THE TRANSFORMER

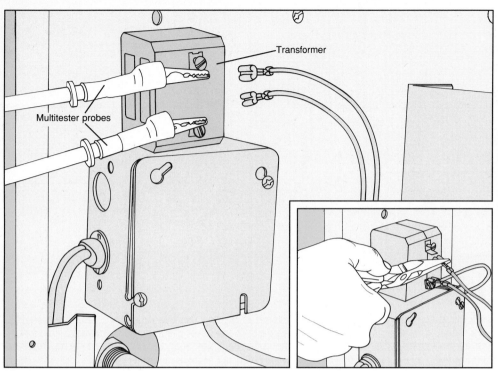

1 **Testing the transformer.** Turn off power to the burner at the main service panel *(page 102)* or unit disconnect switch *(page 22)*. Remove the access panel *(page 195)* and locate the two wires that connect the transformer to the combination control. Using long-nose pliers, gently wiggle these two wires off their terminals on the transformer *(inset)*. Also detach the ground wire. Set a multitester to the ACV scale, 50-volt range. Clip one multitester probe to each transformer terminal *(left)*. Without touching the probes or transformer, turn on power to the burner. If the multitester reads about 12 volts or 24 volts, the transformer is sending sufficient voltage; reattach the wires. If there is no reading, turn off power to the burner and go to step 2.

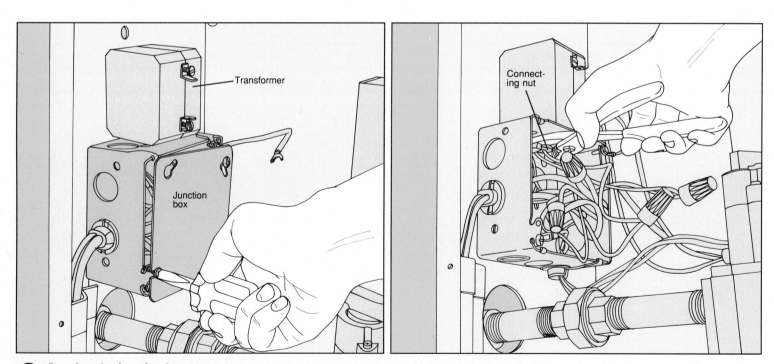

2 **Opening the junction box.** With power to the burner turned off, unscrew *(above, left)* and remove the junction box cover. Inside the junction box, locate the two wires leading to the transformer; inspect the wire cap connections that join them to other wires *(page 417)*. Reconnect the wires if they are loose and test again *(step 1)*. If the connections do not seem to be the problem, use pliers to unscrew the nut connecting the transformer to the junction box *(above, right)* and replace the transformer *(step 3)*.

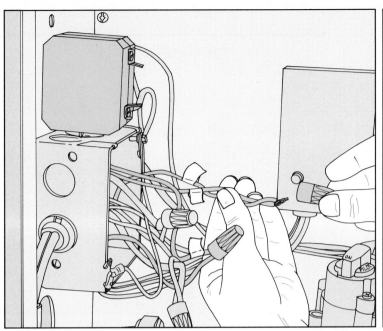

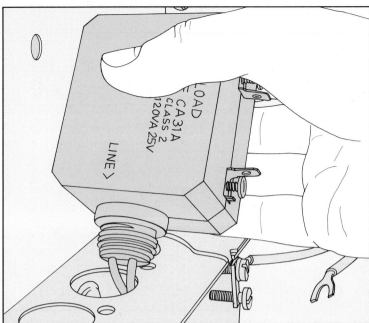

3 **Removing and replacing the transformer.** Remove the two wire caps securing the transformer wires *(above, left)*, first labeling all the wires as "bundle A" or "bundle B" for correct reconnection. Unwind and free the wires. Lift the transformer off the junction box *(above, right)*. Install an identical transformer. Tighten the nut and reconnect the transformer wires with their labeled counterparts. Screw on the junction box cover and turn on power to the burner.

CLEANING THE PILOT

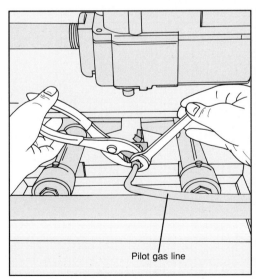

Pilot gas line

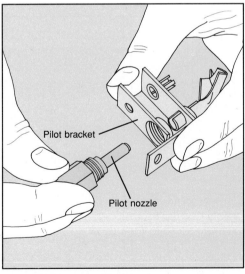

Pilot bracket

Pilot nozzle

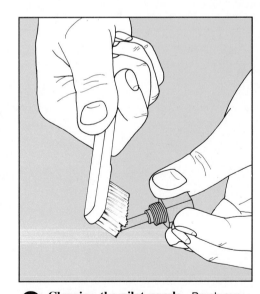

1 **Disassembling the pilot.** Shut off the gas to the burner by turning the main gas valve to the OFF position *(page 197)*. Turn off power to the burner at the main service panel *(page 102)* or unit disconnect switch *(page 22)*. If the burner has been running, wait 30 minutes to allow metal parts to cool. Disconnect and remove the thermocouple tube *(page 196)*. With a pair of pliers, steady the gas line connecting the pilot to the combination control; be careful not to bend or damage the line. With an open-end wrench in your other hand, loosen the nut attaching the pilot gas line *(above, left)*. Unscrew and remove the bracket holding the pilot/thermocouple assembly in place. Carefully unscrew the pilot nozzle from the bracket and pull the two apart *(above, right)*.

2 **Cleaning the pilot nozzle.** Brush surface dirt off the pilot nozzle with a toothbrush *(above)*. Use a soft wire to dislodge deposits from inside the pilot, being careful not to damage or chip it. Reassemble the pilot assembly and reinstall it in the burner. Turn on the gas and power to the burner and relight the pilot *(page 195)*.

CLEANING THE BURNERS AND SPUDS

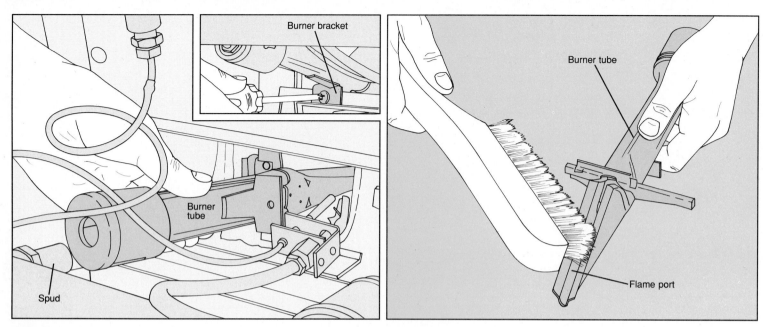

1 **Removing and cleaning the burner tubes.** Shut off the main gas valve *(page 197)* and turn off power to the burner at the main service panel *(page 102)* and unit disconnect switch *(page 22)*. If the burner tubes are housed in a metal drawer, pull out the drawer, then clean the ports gently with a brush. If the burner tubes are the removable type, such as the model shown, there will usually be a screw attaching each burner tube to the retaining bracket just underneath the tubes; remove these screws *(inset)*. On some models, the entire pilot assembly must be removed to gain access to the burner tubes. When the burner tube is free of the retaining bracket, gently twist it forward off the spud, then pull it out of the burner *(above, left)*. Rust and soot can accumulate on the exterior of the burner tubes; clean the tubes thoroughly with a stiff-bristled brush, paying special attention to the ports *(above, right)*. **Caution:** Clean gently to avoid enlarging or damaging the burner ports.

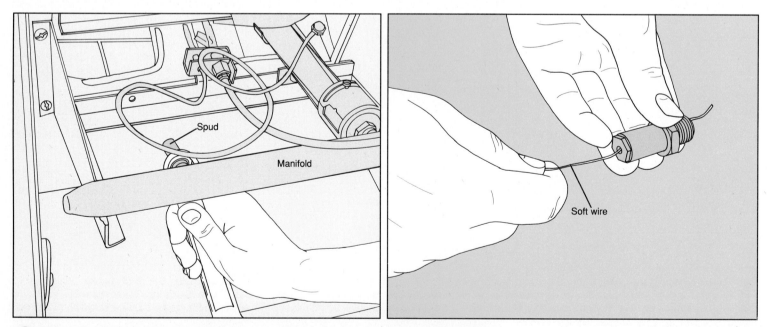

2 **Removing and cleaning the spuds.** Use a box-end wrench to unscrew the spud from the manifold *(above, left)*; remove the spud. Run a toothpick or soft wire through the spud opening to clear it, being careful not to chip or enlarge the opening *(above, right)*. Gently tighten the spud onto the manifold, then reinstall the burner assembly, reversing the procedure here.

ELECTRIC FURNACES

The heat produced by an electric furnace is cleaner than in oil- or gas-burning types, because no combustion takes place. In areas where electricity is still affordable, an electric furnace will heat efficiently, provided the house is well insulated. The electric furnace may be linked to a heat pump *(page 208)* or central air conditioning *(page 216)*, and is almost always used with a forced-air distribution system. The unit draws cool air from the return registers and blows it over three to six electric heating elements. A blower in the furnace housing *(Air Distribution, page 169)* sends the heated air through the plenum and into the rooms of the house via the ducts.

The home's 240-volt electrical current enters the unit from the main service panel and unit disconnect switch, then flows to the transformer and blower. The transformer steps down the line voltage to 24 volts, which flows to the control terminal block — the furnace's link to the thermostat. When the thermostat calls for heat, the control terminal block directs low voltage to the heat relay. The heat relay signals the first sequencer relay's contacts to close, allowing line voltage to flow to the first element. This sequencer then signals the next sequencer and the process continues, turning on as many elements as are needed to satisfy the thermostat. The blower also turns on, and sends heated air through the system. On some larger units, electrical current in the element circuit also flows through cartridge fuses to protect against overload.

Apart from filter, blower and humidifier maintenance or special maintenance required by central air conditioning, the electric furnace is virtually maintenance free. Once a year, access the control box and check inside connections; replace burned or damaged wires, and inspect the replacements periodically. If the damage recurs, call an electrician.

A unit disconnect switch is frequently required by the electrical code, and may be present with the furnace or with any electrically controlled system. The switch box is usually located indoors near the boiler or furnace, or outdoors, mounted on or near the heat pump or the central air conditioning unit. Outdoor boxes are protected with weatherproof covers. For safety instructions on turning off power to the disconnect switch, refer to the Emergency Guide *(page 22)*.

Troubleshooting an electric furnace may be as simple as testing and replacing a fuse *(page 204)* or as involved as replacing a heating element, which may require disconnecting a number of wires that are in the way. When disconnecting more than one wire, make sure to label the wires first, to ensure correct reconnection. The components in your electric furnace may vary from those pictured on page 202. If in doubt about how to proceed with a repair, call for professional service.

Follow all safety instructions in this chapter and in the Emergency Guide. Before beginning any repair or inspection, turn off power to the heating and cooling system at the main service panel and unit disconnect switch. Heating problems may also be caused by a component in the air distribution system, or by the thermostat. Consult the Troubleshooting Guides in System Controls *(page 164)* and Air Distribution *(page 169)*.

TROUBLESHOOTING FOR ELECTRICAL PROBLEMS

Inspect your furnace periodically for signs of overheating electrical circuits; burned wire insulation and scorched paint on the housing are common clues. You can usually solve the problem by tightening wire connections or replacing damaged wires.

If your house wiring is aluminum, however, the problem is more fundamental. Many homes built or enlarged between 1965 and 1973 may have branch circuits of old technology aluminum wiring. Over a 10-year period, some 500 fires were attributed to this type of wiring. Two factors make aluminum wiring potentially hazardous: Corrosion of the aluminum wire ends can cause high resistance to current at electrical terminals, generating a great deal of heat. In addition, since aluminum expands and contracts more than other metals when heated and cooled, aluminum wiring tends to wiggle loose from its terminals, adding to resistance and overheating. Especially in a vibrating furnace, which cycles on and off continually, it is almost impossible to maintain a good connection with aluminum wiring.

Check for aluminum wiring entering the furnace at the electrical-service terminal block; look for loose or corroded terminals, and burned insulation or paint. If the electric furnace in your home is wired with aluminum wiring, consider having an electrician replace or update the wiring.

Another tell-tale troubleshooting symptom is short cycling of the furnace. A furnace that turns on and off repeatedly may be linked to a thermostat that is not calibrated properly or that is simply the wrong thermostat for the system. Many of the electric furnaces in use today were installed as replacements for oil or gas furnaces, and the original thermostats were not adjusted or replaced accordingly. For efficient operation, an electric furnace requires a thermostat with a heat anticipator; if your thermostat does not have one, have it replaced with a model that does. If your thermostat does have a heat anticipator, it may not have been readjusted when the electric furnace was installed. Check the ampere rating of the furnace, and adjust the thermostat anticipator if necessary *(page 167)*.

Sequencer relays

With a heating filament and a bimetal switch, the sequencer relay uses one electrical circuit to turn on another circuit. When the thermostat calls for heat, 24-volt electrical current flows through the filament of the first relay. After several seconds, the heat created by the current flow causes the bimetal switch in the relay to expand, switching on 240-volt current to its heating element. At the same time, the relay allows 24-volt current to pass to the next sequencer relay in the series, which turns on the 240-volt current to its heating element. This process continues, turning on elements one at a time until the demands of the thermostat have been satisfied. To protect the household electrical supply against overload, each sequencer relay has a delayed reaction, switching on its element several seconds after the previous one. The wiring of sequencer relays varies according to the model they serve. To avoid any risk of disconnecting the wrong wires, call for service if your troubleshooting points to a faulty sequencer relay.

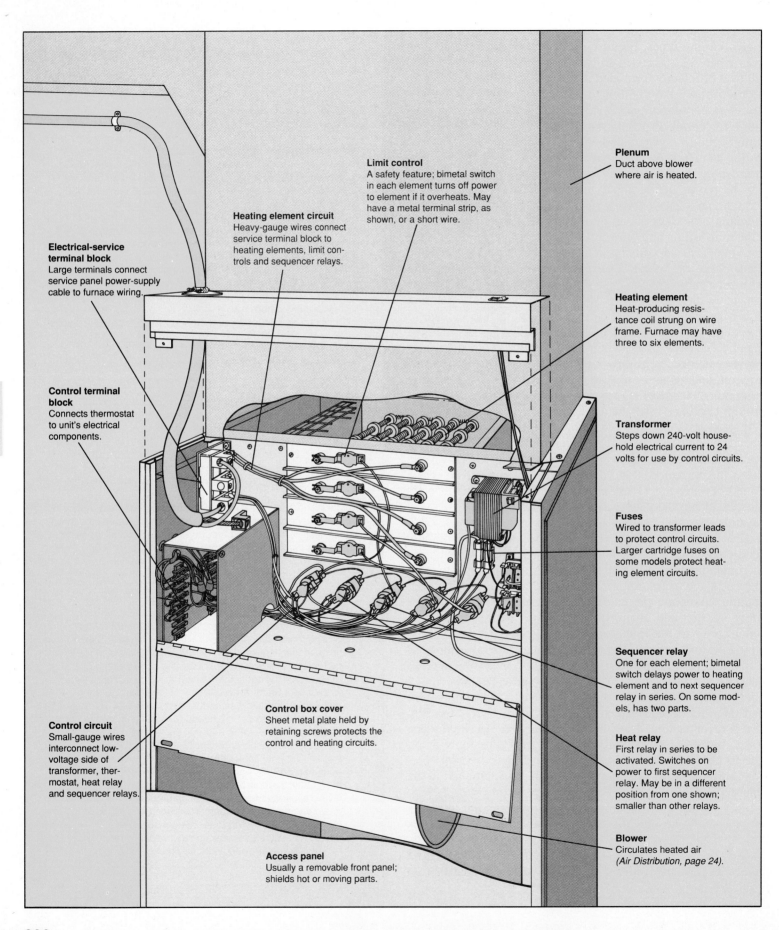

Limit control
A safety feature; bimetal switch in each element turns off power to element if it overheats. May have a metal terminal strip, as shown, or a short wire.

Heating element circuit
Heavy-gauge wires connect service terminal block to heating elements, limit controls and sequencer relays.

Electrical-service terminal block
Large terminals connect service panel power-supply cable to furnace wiring.

Control terminal block
Connects thermostat to unit's electrical components.

Plenum
Duct above blower where air is heated.

Heating element
Heat-producing resistance coil strung on wire frame. Furnace may have three to six elements.

Transformer
Steps down 240-volt household electrical current to 24 volts for use by control circuits.

Fuses
Wired to transformer leads to protect control circuits. Larger cartridge fuses on some models protect heating element circuits.

Sequencer relay
One for each element; bimetal switch delays power to heating element and to next sequencer relay in series. On some models, has two parts.

Heat relay
First relay in series to be activated. Switches on power to first sequencer relay. May be in a different position from one shown; smaller than other relays.

Control circuit
Small-gauge wires interconnect low-voltage side of transformer, thermostat, heat relay and sequencer relays.

Control box cover
Sheet metal plate held by retaining screws protects the control and heating circuits.

Access panel
Usually a removable front panel; shields hot or moving parts.

Blower
Circulates heated air (Air Distribution, page 24).

TROUBLESHOOTING GUIDE

SYMPTOM	POSSIBLE CAUSE	PROCEDURE
No heat	Circuit breaker tripped or fuse blown	Reset breaker or replace fuse *(p. 102)* □○; restore power at unit disconnect switch *(p. 22)* □○
	Wires broken or terminal connectors loose or faulty	Inspect furnace wiring. Replace wires or install new connectors *(p. 417)* ◨●; tighten wire connections *(p. 204)* □○
	Wires burned (may be accompanied by burned paint on furnace housing)	Inspect furnace wiring. Replace wires *(p. 417)* ◨●; if problem recurs, have electrician check for aluminum house wiring and replace it
	Control or heating circuit fuse faulty	Test fuse and replace *(p. 204)* □○▲ if necessary
	Transformer faulty	Test transformer and replace *(p. 205)* ◨●▲ if necessary
	Limit controls faulty	Identify faulty element circuit *(p. 206)* ◨○▲; test limit control and replace *(p. 206)* ◨●▲ if necessary
	Heating elements burned out, due to dirty air filter	Replace air filter *(Air Distribution, p. 169)* □○. Identify faulty element circuits *(p. 206)* ◨○▲; test heating elements and replace *(p. 207)* ◨●▲ if necessary
	Heating elements faulty	Identify faulty element circuit *(p. 206)* ◨○▲; test heating elements and replace *(p. 207)* ◨●▲ if necessary
	Heat relay faulty	Call for service
	Sequencer relay faulty	Call for service
Intermittent or insufficient heat	Wire connections loose	Inspect furnace wiring. Replace loose wire connectors *(p. 417)* □○; tighten wire connections *(p. 204)* □○
	Wires burned (may be accompanied by burned paint on furnace housing)	Inspect furnace wiring. Replace wires *(p. 417)* ◨●; if problem recurs, have electrician check for aluminum house wiring and replace it
	Thermostat anticipator not adjusted for electric furnace	Adjust thermostat anticipator *(System Controls, p. 164)* □○
	Old-style thermostat does not have anticipator	Have thermostat replaced with new style that has anticipator
	Limit control faulty	Identify faulty element circuit *(p. 206)* ◨○▲; test limit control and replace *(p. 206)* ◨●▲ if necessary
	Heating element faulty	Identify faulty element circuit *(p. 206)* ◨○▲; test heating element and replace *(p. 206)* ◨●▲ if necessary
	Sequencer relay faulty	Call for service

DEGREE OF DIFFICULTY: □ Easy ◨ Moderate ■ Complex
ESTIMATED TIME: ○ Less than 1 hour ◐ 1 to 3 hours ● Over 3 hours ▲ Special tool required

ACCESSING THE INTERNAL COMPONENTS

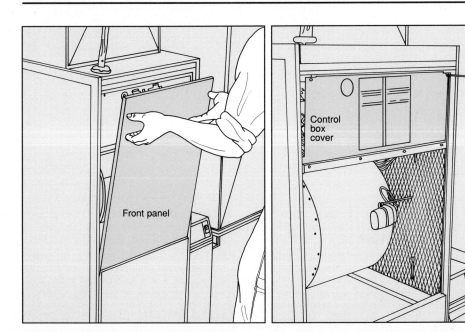

Front panel

Control box cover

Removing the access panels. Turn off power to the furnace at the main service panel *(page 102)* and unit disconnect switch *(page 22)*. Grasp the slotted handles on the front panel and pull the panel away with a sharp upward tug *(far left)*, exposing the control panel. Place the panel out of the way. Next, unscrew the retaining screws from the control box cover to gain access to the internal wiring and components.

SERVICING WIRE CONNECTIONS

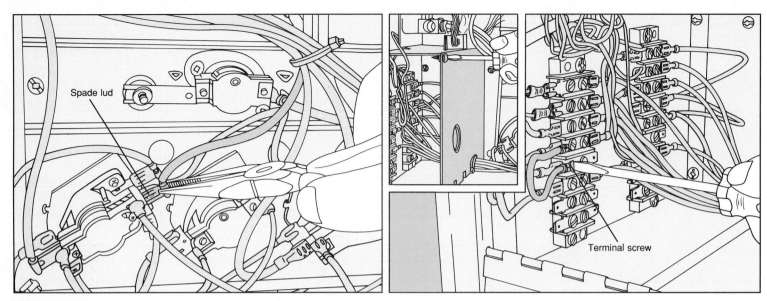

Inspecting wire connections. Turn off power to the furnace at the main service panel and unit disconnect switch, and access the control box *(page 203)*. Visually inspect the wiring in the control box for loose connectors, frayed wires, cracked insulation, and signs of overheating or burning. Repair any damaged wires *(page 417)*. Use long-nose pliers to tug gently on wires connecting individual components inside the control box *(above, left)*; tighten loose connections. Replace loose-fitting or damaged spade lug connectors. Remove the control terminal block cover *(inset)*, and use a screwdriver to tighten terminal screws that may have worked loose due to blower vibration *(above, right)*.

TESTING AND REPLACING FUSES

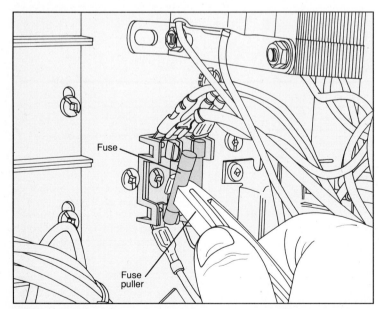

1 **Removing control circuit and heating circuit fuses.** Turn off power to the furnace at the main service panel *(page 102)* and unit disconnect switch *(page 22)*, and access the control box *(page 203)*. Locate the fuses, in a block wired to the transformer leads, such as the one shown, or larger cartridge fuses connected to a panel in the control box. (Some units have both types.) Use a fuse puller to hook the center of the fuse cartridge and, with a quick tug, free the fuse from its block *(above)*.

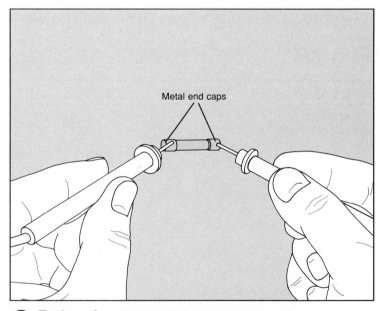

2 **Testing a fuse.** Set a multitester to the RX1 setting to test continuity. Touch one multitester probe to each end cap of the fuse *(above)*; test a larger cartridge fuse the same way. If the multitester shows continuity, the fuse is good; test all other fuses in the unit. If a fuse has no continuity, purchase an exact replacement—available at a hardware store—and install it in its block, or on its panel. Restore the power. If a replacement fuse blows, turn off power to the furnace and call for service.

SERVICING THE TRANSFORMER

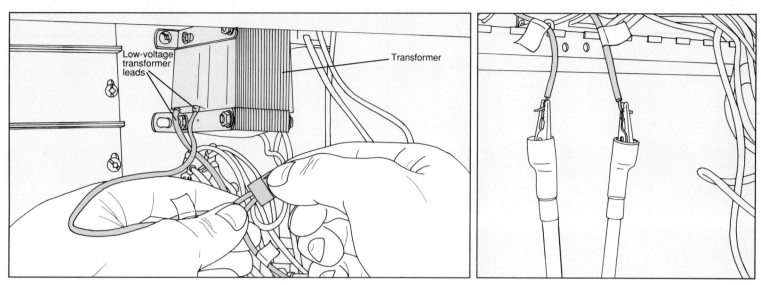

1 **Testing the transformer output.** Turn off power to the furnace at the main service panel *(page 102)* and unit disconnect switch *(page 22)*, and access the control box *(page 203)*. Locate the low-voltage wire leads running to the control terminal block from the transformer, and label them for correct reconnection. Disconnect the low-voltage wire leads by unscrewing their wire caps *(above, left)*. Set a multitester to the ACV setting and turn the dial to the 50-volt range to test voltage *(page 417)*. Using alligator clips, attach a multitester probe to each disconnected wire *(above, right)*. Being careful not to touch the furnace or any wire, turn on power to the furnace, note the multitester reading, then turn off the power. The tester should read about 24 volts. If not, test the transformer windings *(step 2)*.

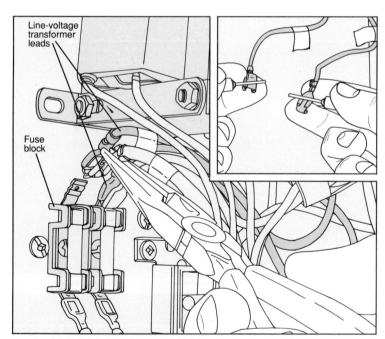

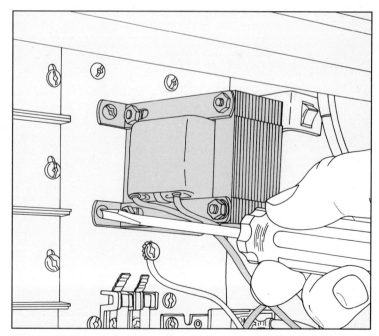

2 **Testing the transformer windings.** With power to the furnace turned off, trace the transformer's line-voltage wire leads to the control fuse block; label the wires for correct reconnection. Use long-nose pliers to detach their connectors from the terminals *(above)*. Set a multitester to the RX1K setting to test continuity. Touch a multitester probe to each wire lead *(inset)*. If the multitester shows continuity, test the other transformer leads *(step 1)* the same way. If either test shows no continuity, replace the transformer *(next step)*.

3 **Replacing the transformer.** With power to the furnace turned off, use a screwdriver to remove the retaining screws securing the transformer in the control box; support the transformer with one hand and lift it out of the furnace. Purchase an identical replacement transformer from an electrical supplies dealer or from the manufacturer, and screw it in place. Connect the wires to their terminals, and restore the power.

IDENTIFYING A FAULTY HEATING ELEMENT CIRCUIT

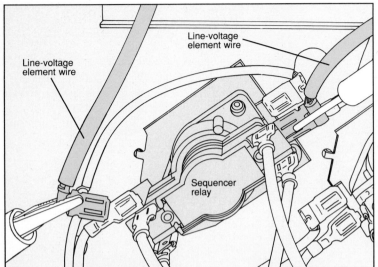

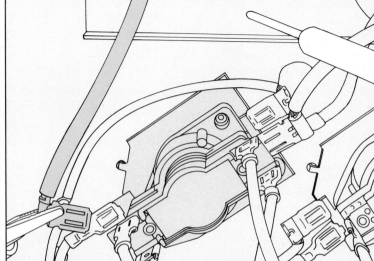

Testing the element circuits. Turn off power to the furnace at the main service panel *(page 102)* and unit disconnect switch *(page 22)*, and access the internal components *(page 203)*. Conduct two tests for each element. First, trace the line-voltage wire that leads from the element to the sequencer relay; then find the similar line-voltage wire connected to the other side of the relay. Use long-nose pliers to disconnect one of the wires. Set a multitester to the RX1K setting to test continuity. Attach one alligator clip to the disconnected wire end and touch one probe to the other wire's terminal on the sequencer *(above, left)*. The multitester should show continuity. Next, test for ground by touching one probe or clip to the detached wire and the other probe to bare metal inside the control box *(above, right)*; there should be no continuity. If the element fails either test, test the limit control for that circuit *(below)*. Otherwise, reconnect the wires and test the other element circuits. If all element circuits test OK, a sequencer relay may be faulty; call for service.

TESTING AND REPLACING THE LIMIT CONTROLS

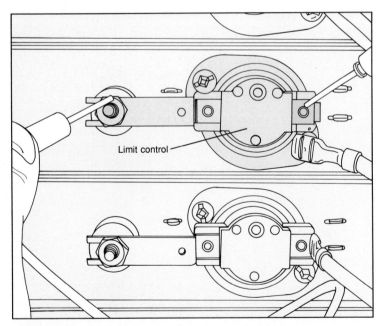

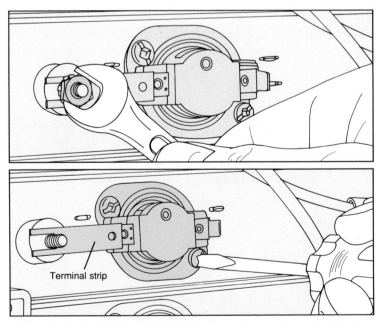

1 Testing a limit control. With power to the furnace turned off, test the limit control on the faulty element circuit *(step above)*. Use long-nose pliers to detach a wire from the limit control. Set a multitester to the RX1K setting to test continuity. Touch a multitester probe to the terminal on each side of the limit control *(above)*; the model shown above shares a terminal with the heating element. If the multitester does not show continuity for the limit control, replace it *(next step)*. If the limit control tests OK, test the element *(page 207)*.

2 Replacing the limit control. Label the limit control wires for correct reconnection. Using an open-end wrench, unscrew the nut securing the terminal strip to the element terminal *(above, top)*. On models with a short wire instead, pull off the connector. Remove the retaining screws holding the limit control bracket *(above, bottom)*, and pull out the limit control. Purchase an identical replacement from a heating and cooling supplies dealer. Install the new part, reversing these instructions. Reassemble the unit and restore the power.

SERVICING THE HEATING ELEMENT

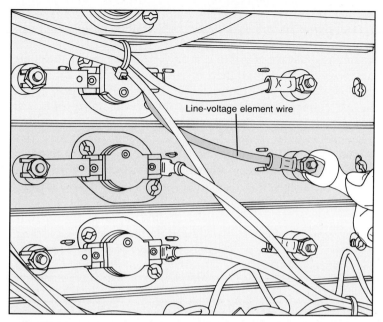

Line-voltage element wire

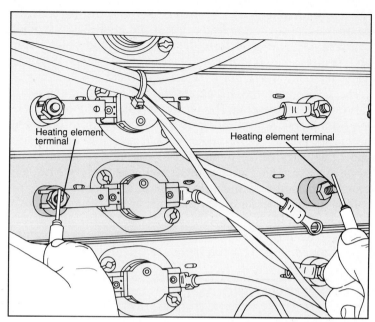

Heating element terminal

Heating element terminal

1 **Disconnecting the heating element from its circuit.** With power to the furnace turned off, detach one of the wires from the heating element in the faulty element circuit *(page 206)*: Using an open-end wrench, unscrew the nut securing the line-voltage element wire to the heating element terminal *(above)* and remove the wire.

2 **Testing the element.** With power to the unit off, set the multi-tester to the RX1K setting to test continuity. Touch a probe to each element terminal *(above)*. The multitester should show continuity; if not, replace the element *(step 3)*. If the element has continuity, and all other components in its circuit test OK *(page 206)*, a sequencer relay may be faulty; call for service.

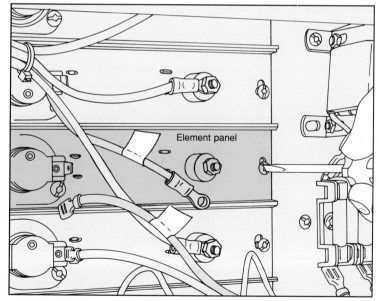

Element panel

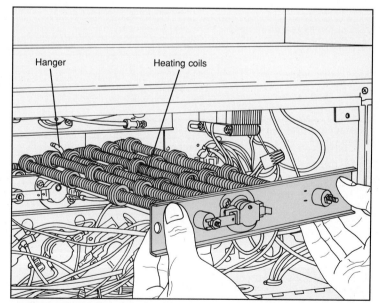

Hanger   Heating coils

3 **Removing the element.** With power to the unit off, label all wires connected to the faulty heating element. Detach any wire still connected to the element's terminals, then use a screwdriver to remove the retaining screws holding the element panel in place *(above)*.

4 **Replacing the element.** Grasp the element panel and pull it out *(above)*, working it back and forth gently to release it; avoid striking other elements. The hanger at the back of the element will drop out of its hole in the plenum. Purchase an identical replacement element from a heating and cooling supplies dealer or the manufacturer, and slide it into its slot. Insert the hanger into its hole in the plenum. Press the element panel in place, align it with the screw holes and replace the screws. Reattach all wires to the element, reassemble the unit and restore the power.

HEAT PUMPS

Instead of creating heat as conventional systems do, the heat pump uses refrigerant to transfer heat. Because the refrigerant can flow in either direction, the heat pump can be used for both heating and cooling the home. In cold weather, refrigerant in the outdoor coil, or heat exchanger, absorbs heat stored in the air. The compressor pumps the refrigerant, in hot vapor form, to the indoor coil. The blower circulates indoor air over the heated coil, warming the air for distribution through the home. As the hot vapor cools, it condenses into liquid form and flows back to the outdoor coil. During the summer, the cycle reverses; heat is absorbed from inside the home and transferred outdoors, much like central air conditioning.

Heat pumps operate most efficiently in temperatures above freezing. In mild climates, they can be used as the sole source of home heating. However, in areas where the temperature often drops below 32°F, an auxiliary heating system may be needed; electric heating is the system most commonly used.

Heat pump specialists claim that more than half of their service calls could be prevented if heat pumps were properly maintained. At the beginning of each heating season, clean the outdoor coils and straighten bent fins *(page 210)*. Check the level of the unit, and lubricate the motor and fan *(page 211)*. Before beginning most repairs or inspections, turn off power to the heat pump at the main service panel and outdoor-unit disconnect switch *(page 22)*. Leave the unit off at least five minutes before switching it back on, or excess pressure could overload the compressor. **Caution:** Before working inside the unit, make a capacitor discharger *(page 417)* and discharge all capacitors *(page 212)*.

Heating or cooling problems may be caused by another unit in the system. Also consult the Troubleshooting Guides in System Controls *(page 164)* and Air Distribution *(page 169)*.

TROUBLESHOOTING GUIDE

SYMPTOM	POSSIBLE CAUSE	PROCEDURE
Heat pump doesn't run at all	No power to unit	Replace fuse or reset circuit breaker *(p. 102)* □○; restore power at unit disconnect switch *(p. 22)* □○
	Compressor pump overloaded	Wait 30 minutes, then press reset button only once; if heat pump doesn't start, call for service
	Wiring loose or faulty	Check for loose or damaged wiring connections in the electrical control box *(p. 214)* □◗
	Compressor contactor faulty	Call for service
	Capacitor faulty	Discharge and test capacitors *(p. 212)* ◨◗▲; replace if necessary
Heat pump runs but doesn't heat or cool	Outdoor coils dirty	Clean coils *(p. 210)* □○
	Fan dirty or faulty	Lubricate fan motor *(p. 211)* □◗; have motor serviced
	Refrigerant leaking	Call for service
Heat pump cools but doesn't heat	Indoor thermostat set to COOL	Set thermostat to HEAT
	Reversing valve stuck or faulty	Set thermostat to COOL, wait 30 minutes, then reset to HEAT. If pump still doesn't heat, call for service
Heat pump heats but doesn't cool	Indoor thermostat set to HEAT	Set thermostat to COOL
	Refrigerant low	Call for service
	Reversing valve stuck or faulty	Set thermostat to COOL, wait 30 minutes, then reset to HEAT. If pump still doesn't heat, call for service
Heat pump fan doesn't run	Wiring loose or faulty	Check for loose or damaged wiring connections in the electrical control box *(p. 214)* □◗
	Fan motor burned out	Call for service
	Capacitor faulty	Discharge and test capacitors *(p. 212)* ◨◗▲; replace if necessary
	Obstruction in fan blades	Access blades *(p. 211)* □○; remove obstruction
Heat pump doesn't defrost automatically; ice buildup on coils	Indoor thermostat set to HEAT	Set thermostat to AUTOMATIC HEAT
	Air-flow sensor tube blocked	Clear air-flow sensor tube *(p. 211)* □◗
	Coil fins flattened	Clean and straighten coil fins *(p. 210)* □◗▲
	Reversing valve stuck or faulty, or defrost system faulty	Set thermostat to COOL, wait 30 minutes, then reset to HEAT. If ice not thawed, call for service
Auxiliary light on indoor thermostat lit constantly	Reversing valve stuck or faulty	Set thermostat to COOL, wait 30 minutes, then reset to HEAT. If pump still doesn't heat, call for service
	Outdoor temperature sensor faulty	Test sensor *(p. 214)* ◨◗▲; replace if necessary

DEGREE OF DIFFICULTY: □ Easy ◨ Moderate ■ Complex
ESTIMATED TIME: ○ Less than 1 hour ◗ 1 to 3 hours ● Over 3 hours   ▲ Special tool required

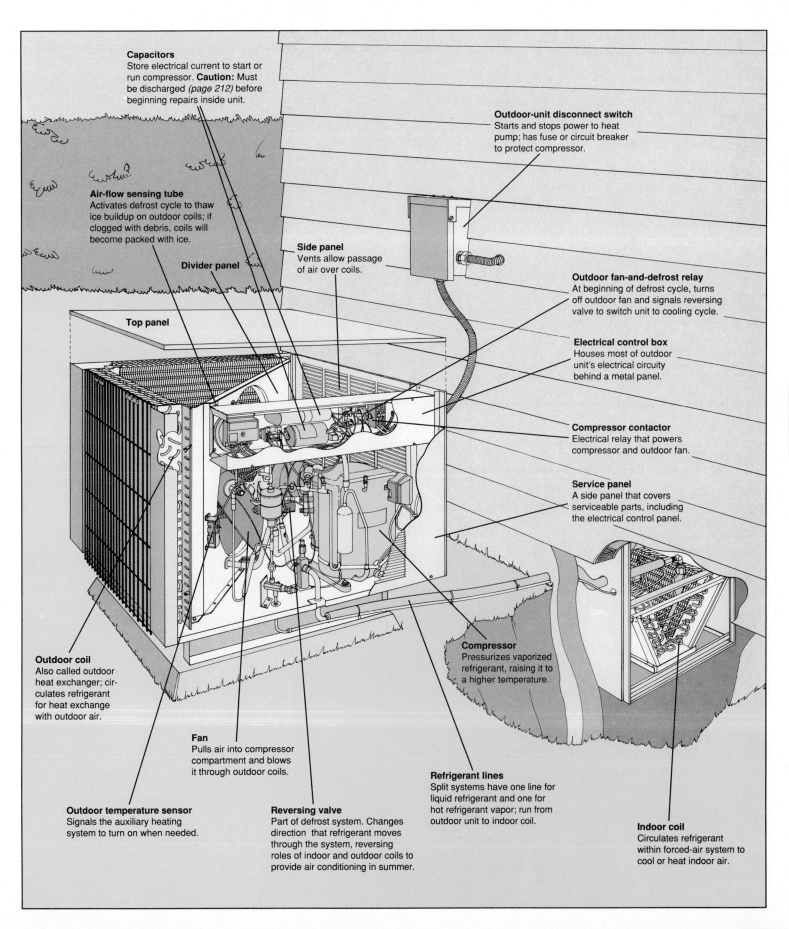

Capacitors
Store electrical current to start or run compressor. **Caution:** Must be discharged *(page 212)* before beginning repairs inside unit.

Air-flow sensing tube
Activates defrost cycle to thaw ice buildup on outdoor coils; if clogged with debris, coils will become packed with ice.

Divider panel

Top panel

Side panel
Vents allow passage of air over coils.

Outdoor-unit disconnect switch
Starts and stops power to heat pump; has fuse or circuit breaker to protect compressor.

Outdoor fan-and-defrost relay
At beginning of defrost cycle, turns off outdoor fan and signals reversing valve to switch unit to cooling cycle.

Electrical control box
Houses most of outdoor unit's electrical circuity behind a metal panel.

Compressor contactor
Electrical relay that powers compressor and outdoor fan.

Service panel
A side panel that covers serviceable parts, including the electrical control panel.

Outdoor coil
Also called outdoor heat exchanger; circulates refrigerant for heat exchange with outdoor air.

Fan
Pulls air into compressor compartment and blows it through outdoor coils.

Compressor
Pressurizes vaporized refrigerant, raising it to a higher temperature.

Outdoor temperature sensor
Signals the auxiliary heating system to turn on when needed.

Reversing valve
Part of defrost system. Changes direction that refrigerant moves through the system, reversing roles of indoor and outdoor coils to provide air conditioning in summer.

Refrigerant lines
Split systems have one line for liquid refrigerant and one for hot refrigerant vapor; run from outdoor unit to indoor coil.

Indoor coil
Circulates refrigerant within forced-air system to cool or heat indoor air.

209

ACCESS TO THE INTERNAL COMPONENTS

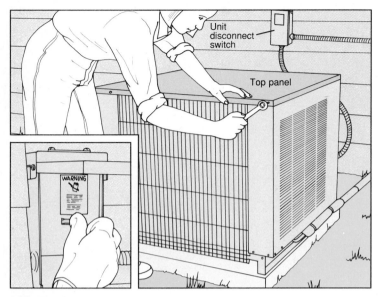

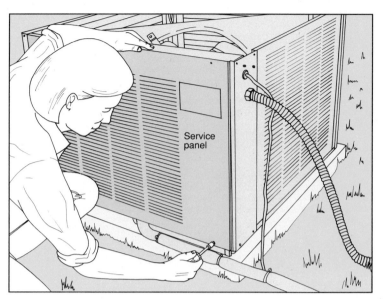

1 **Removing the top panel.** Turn off power to the heat pump at the main service panel *(page 102)* and at the outdoor-unit disconnect switch *(inset)*. Use a socket wrench or nut driver to remove the sheet metal screws securing the top panel around its edges *(above)*. If the screws are stubborn, loosen them with a few drops of penetrating oil. Wearing work gloves, lift off the panel; place it clear of the unit and refrigerant lines.

2 **Removing the side panels.** The service panel, usually identified by an information sticker, must be removed for access to the compressor and electrical control box. The other side panels must be removed for cleaning the evaporator coils. With power to the heat pump switched off *(step 1)*, use a nut driver to remove the sheet metal screws securing the side panels *(above)*. Wearing work gloves, pull the panels away from the unit and place them clear of the refrigerant lines.

MAINTAINING THE HEAT PUMP

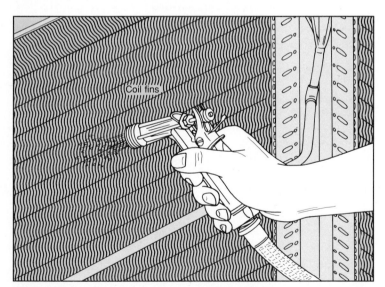

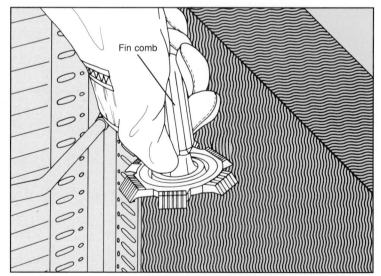

Cleaning the coils. With power to the heat pump turned off, remove the top and side panels *(steps above)* to access the coils. Use a soft brush and a portable cordless vacuum cleaner to clean the coil fins. To remove stubborn dirt buildup, spray water through the coil fins from inside, using a high-pressure nozzle on a garden hose *(above)*. **Caution:** Do not use a knife or screwdriver blade to dislodge dirt between fins; these tools can puncture the coils. Sweep debris accumulated on the bottom of the heat pump into a dustpan. Use a fin comb to straighten any bent coil fins *(right)*.

Straightening coil fins. With power to the heat pump turned off, remove the top and side panels *(steps above)* to access the coils. Wearing gloves, use a multi-head fin comb to straighten bent coil fins. Determine which head of the comb corresponds to the spacing of fins on the coils; the teeth on the head should fit easily between the fins. Gently fit the teeth of the fin comb between the coil fins in an undamaged section below the area to be straightened. Pull the fin comb up, sliding it through the damaged area *(above)*; at the same time, comb out any lodged debris. **Caution:** Do not use a knife or screwdriver blade to straighten fins; the coils could be damaged.

MAINTAINING THE HEAT PUMP (continued)

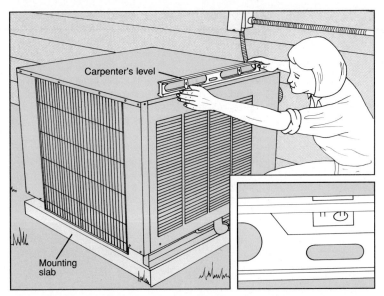

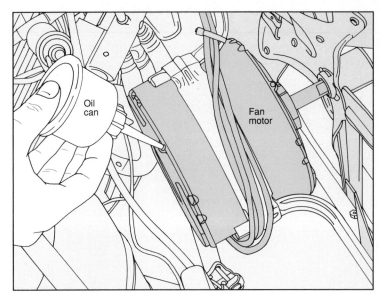

Checking the slope for proper drainage. If your heat pump is seated on a mounting slab, as shown above, check the slab's level each spring. Place a carpenter's level on top of the unit *(above)*. The level should read one-half to one bubble off center *(inset)*, sloping away from the house. Otherwise, the mounting slab has settled. Adjust the slab to its proper slope: Use a pry bar to lift the slab and slide a brick or other prop underneath, or call a professional to adjust it with concrete.

Lubricating the fan motor. Turn off power to the heat pump at the main service panel *(page 102)* and outdoor-unit disconnect switch. Remove the top panel *(page 210)*. Pry off the plastic or metal oil-port caps. Squirt a few drops of SAE-10 non-detergent oil into the oil ports *(above)*. If the fan motor is sealed and has no oil ports, squirt a little oil on the fan shaft where it meets the motor. Turn the fan blade back and forth a few times to work in the oil. Check for obstructions in the blade and remove them.

CLEARING THE AIR-FLOW SENSING TUBE

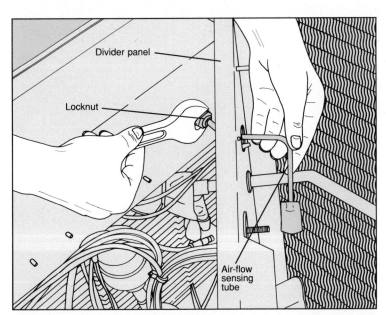

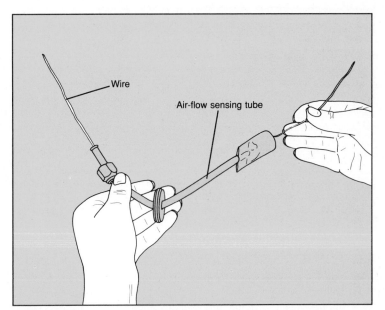

1 **Removing the air-flow sensing tube.** Turn off power to the heat pump at the service panel *(page 102)* and outdoor-unit disconnect switch. Remove the top panel *(page 210)*, and locate the air-flow sensing tube, a short, narrow pipe mounted on the divider panel. Use an open-end wrench to loosen the tube's locknut, and work the tube out of its opening in the divider panel *(above)*.

2 **Clearing the sensing tube.** To clear a debris-filled sensing tube, feed a flexible wire or pipe cleaner through the opening in the tube, sliding it in and out until the tube is cleaned *(above)*. Next, pull out the wire and test the tube by blowing air through it; the air should flow freely. Reinstall the tube, threading it back through its opening in the divider panel; tighten the locknut. Reassemble the heat pump and turn on the power.

DISCHARGING THE CAPACITORS

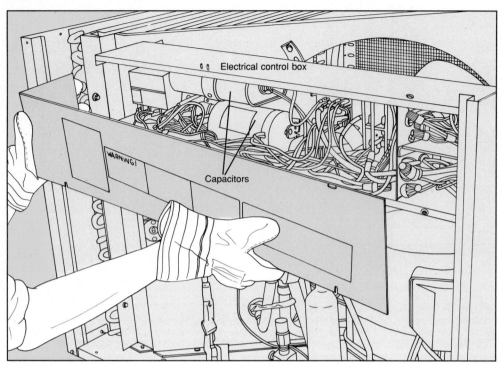

1 **Removing the electrical control-box panel. Caution:** Capacitors may store potentially dangerous voltage. Before servicing the control box components *(next step)*, make a capacitor discharging tool *(page 417)* and discharge the heat pump capacitors. Turn off power to the heat pump at the main service panel *(page 102)* and outdoor-unit disconnect switch *(page 22)*. Access the internal components *(page 210)*. Use a socket wrench or nut driver to remove the sheet metal screws holding the electrical control-box panel in place. Wearing work gloves to protect your hands, pull off the panel *(left)*.

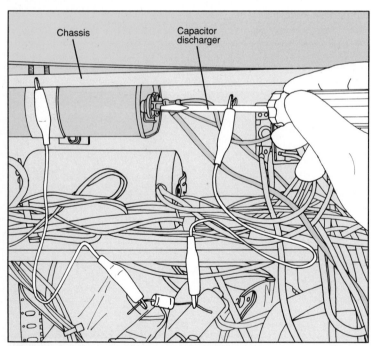

2 **Discharging an uncapped capacitor.** Make a capacitor discharger. With power to the heat pump turned off, clip one end of the capacitor discharger to the heat pump chassis. If a capacitor has more than two terminals and no bleed resistor, discharge it as shown in Tools & Techniques. If it has a bleed resistor, go to steps 3 and 4. If a capacitor has two terminals and no bleed resistor, as shown above, hold the insulated screwdriver handle of the capacitor discharger in one hand and touch each terminal, one at a time, with the tip of the screwdriver blade for one second *(above)*. Discharge all other capacitors in the unit.

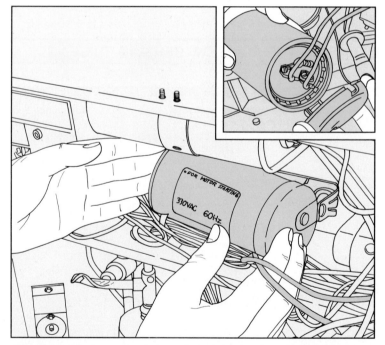

3 **Removing a capped capacitor.** With power to the heat pump turned off, place one hand at each end of the capacitor, holding the cap on, and pull the capacitor out of its mounting bracket in the electrical control box *(above)*. Lift off the cap to expose the capacitor wire terminals *(inset)*. **Caution:** Do not touch the terminals with your hands.

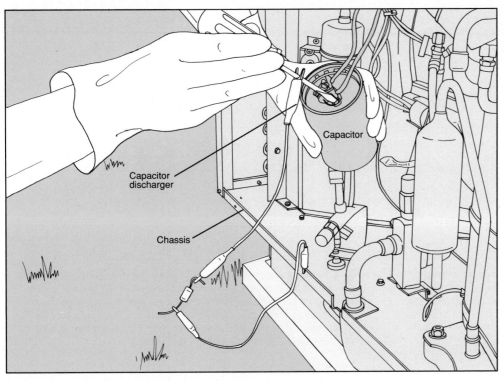

Capacitor

Capacitor discharger

Chassis

4 **Discharging a capped capacitor.** With power to the heat pump turned off, clip one end of the capacitor discharger to the heat pump chassis. If a capacitor has no bleed resistor and more than two terminals, discharge it as shown in Tools & Techniques *(page 417)*. If a capacitor has two terminals and a bleed resistor, as shown at left, hold the insulated screwdriver handle of the capacitor discharger in one hand. Touch each terminal, one at a time, with the tip of the screwdriver blade for one second. Discharge all other capacitors in the heat pump.

TESTING AND REPLACING THE CAPACITORS

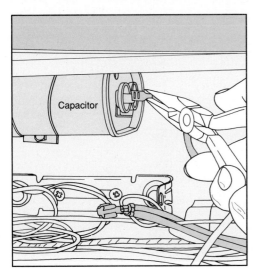

Capacitor

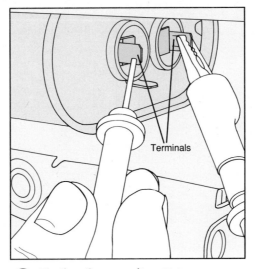

Terminals

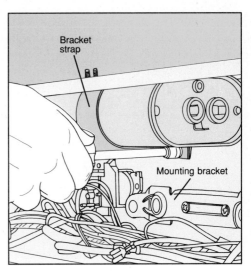

Bracket strap

Mounting bracket

1 **Inspecting the capacitor casing.** Turn off power to the heat pump at the main service panel *(page 102)* and outdoor-unit disconnect switch *(page 22)*. Discharge the capacitors *(page 212)*. Visually check each capacitor. If you see a bulging, broken or melted casing, replace the capacitor *(step 3)*. If the casing looks OK, use insulated long-nose pliers to slip the wire leads off the first capacitor you are testing *(above)*.

2 **Testing the capacitor.** Make sure power to the heat pump is off, and set a multitester to the RX1K scale. Test a three-terminal capacitor as shown in Tools & Techniques. Test a two-terminal capacitor by placing one multitester probe on each of the capacitor's terminals *(above)* while watching the tester needle. The needle should swing to zero resistance, then slowly move a third to halfway across the scale toward infinity. If the needle swings to zero resistance and stays there, or if there is no movement of the needle, replace the capacitor *(next step)*.

3 **Removing and replacing the capacitor.** A capped capacitor snaps out of a flexible mounting bracket. An uncapped capacitor is usually mounted with bracket straps to the back panel of the electrical control box; use a nut driver to remove the sheet metal screw holding the bracket in place *(above)*. **Caution:** Keep the capacitor out of the reach of children and do not incinerate. Replace it with one of identical rating.

CHECKING AND SERVICING WIRING CONNECTIONS

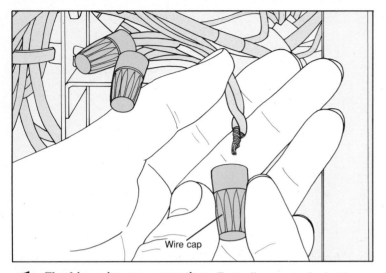

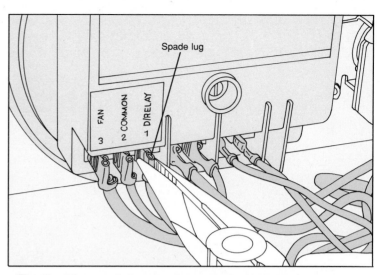

1 **Checking wire cap connections.** Turn off power to the heat pump at the main service panel *(page 102)* and outdoor-unit disconnect switch *(page 22)*. Access the electrical control box and discharge the capacitors *(page 212)*. Twist off each wire cap and check the wire leads. If the wires have separated, twist them together clockwise and screw on the wire cap *(above)*.

2 **Checking spade lug connectors and wires.** With power to the unit off and capacitors discharged, inspect the electrical wiring inside the electrical control box. Wires with frayed or charred insulation should be replaced; call a professional. Also inspect all wire connections: Using insulated long-nose pliers, push spade lug wire connectors securely onto their terminals *(above)*.

SERVICING THE OUTDOOR TEMPERATURE SENSOR

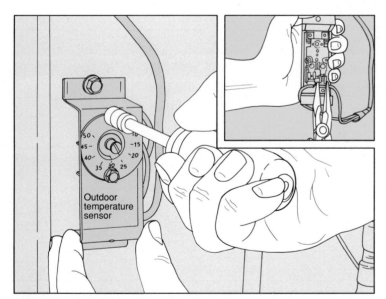

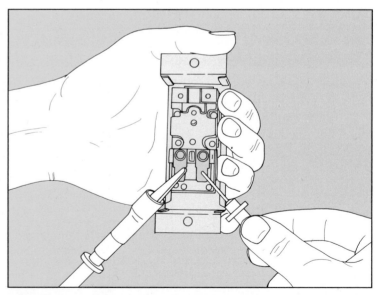

1 **Removing the temperature sensor.** If the auxiliary light on the indoor thermostat remains lit constantly, the outdoor temperature sensor—if your heat pump has one—may be faulty. Turn off power to the heat pump at the main service panel *(page 102)* and outdoor-unit disconnect switch *(page 22)*. Access the internal components *(page 210)*, and discharge all capacitors *(page 212)*. Locate the outdoor temperature sensor, usually mounted in the compressor compartment as shown above, but sometimes outside the heat pump in a mounting box. Use a nut driver to undo the screws that mount the sensor *(above)*. Label the wires, then use long-nose pliers to disconnect the sensor wire connectors from their terminals *(inset)*. Since the test shown in step 2 will work only at low temperatures, place the temperature sensor in the freezer for one-half hour.

2 **Testing the temperature sensor for continuity.** Remove the sensor from the freezer. Set a multitester to test continuity, then touch a probe to each sensor terminal *(above)*. If the multitester shows continuity, the temperature sensor is working; if there is no continuity, replace the sensor with an identical part, reassemble the heat pump and turn on the power.

TESTING THE COMPRESSOR

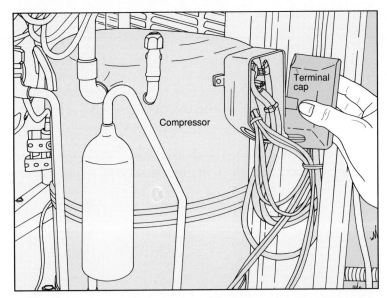

1 **Removing the compressor terminal cap.** Turn off power to the heat pump at the main service panel *(page 102)* and the outdoor-unit disconnect switch *(page 22)*. Access the electrical control box *(page 210)* and discharge the capacitors *(page 212)*. Locate the compressor terminal cap, a plastic cover that protects the compressor motor terminals, with an inlet hole for the motor leads. Grasp the cap and pull it straight off *(above)*.

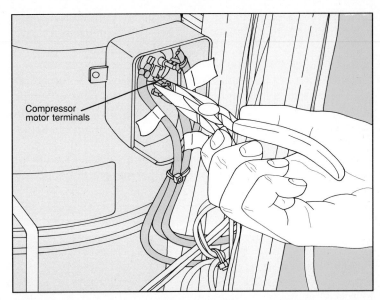

2 **Disconnecting the compressor leads.** Since each compressor manufacturer uses a different sequence of terminals (R for run winding, S for start winding, C for common), it is important to label each wire before removing it. If the terminals are not marked, draw a diagram of the wire lead positions on the compressor motor terminals. Use long-nose pliers to pull the wire connectors straight off their terminals *(above)*.

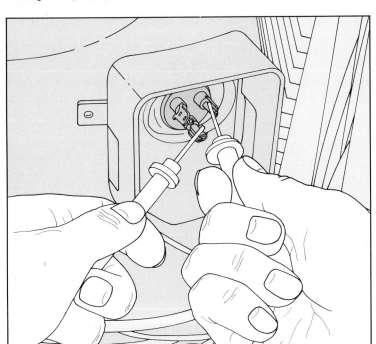

3 **Testing the compressor motor windings.** Set a multitester to test continuity. Touch one probe to one compressor motor terminal and touch the other probe to another terminal *(above)*. Repeat the test for all three possible combinations of terminals; there should be continuity each time. If there is continuity, the compressor motor windings are working; go to step 4. If there is no continuity in any one of the tests, the compressor must be replaced; call for service.

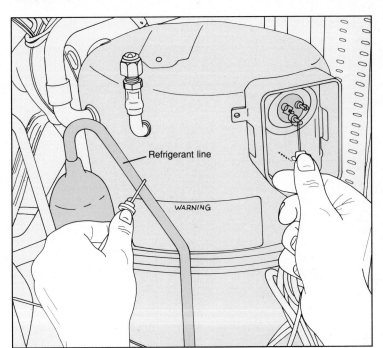

4 **Testing the compressor motor for ground.** To ensure a correct reading, allow the compressor motor to cool for three to four hours before conducting this test. Set a multitester to test continuity. Touch one probe to one of the compressor motor terminals, and touch the other probe to a clean, unpainted metal surface on the compressor dome or to one of the copper refrigerant lines leading from the compressor *(above)*. Repeat the test for the other two compressor terminals. If all tests show no continuity, the compressor motor windings are OK. If any test shows continuity, the windings are grounded, and the compressor must be replaced; call for service.

CENTRAL AIR CONDITIONING

In addition to cooling the air, central air conditioning also dehumidifies and circulates it. The system consists of two parts: the condenser unit, located outdoors, and the evaporator coil, mounted inside the furnace, usually in the plenum.

Central air conditioners are typically part of a forced-air heating system, allowing both heating and cooling to share the ducting and blower. In some cases, an integrated system located in either the attic or the basement contains both the condenser and evaporator coils, and has its own ducting.

When the thermostat calls for cooling, it switches on the air conditioner, which cools liquid refrigerant in the condenser coils. The compressor sends cooled refrigerant through one of two refrigerant lines to the evaporator coils inside the house. When the cooled refrigerant reaches the indoor evaporator coils, the furnace blower circulates warm air from the house over the cold coils. The evaporator coils absorb heat from the indoor air as the liquid refrigerant is transformed into a gaseous state. This gas is pumped outdoors through a second refrigerant line to the condenser coils. There the heat that was absorbed indoors is released.

At the beginning of each cooling season, clean outdoor condenser coils, and straighten the fins if necessary *(page 219)*.

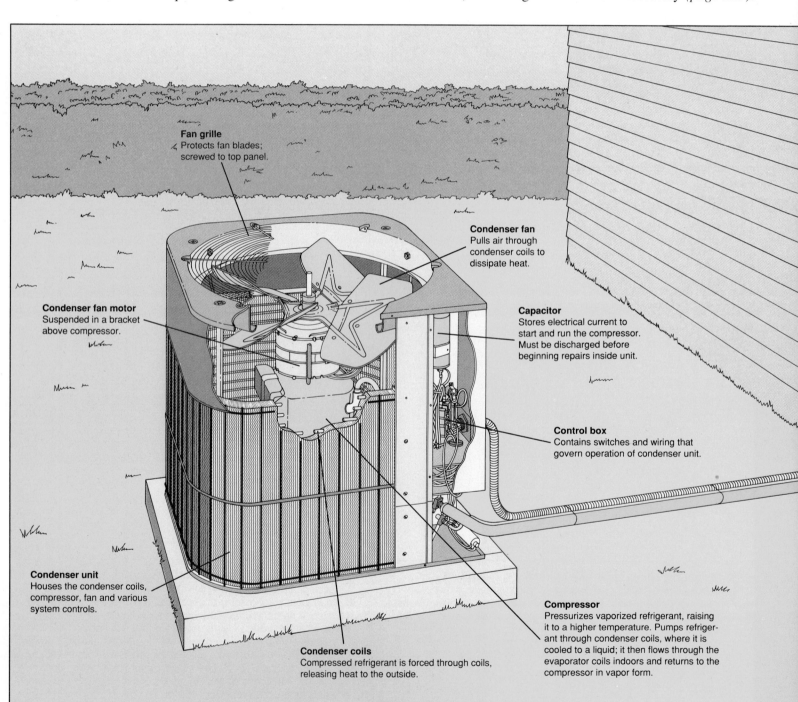

Fan grille
Protects fan blades; screwed to top panel.

Condenser fan
Pulls air through condenser coils to dissipate heat.

Condenser fan motor
Suspended in a bracket above compressor.

Capacitor
Stores electrical current to start and run the compressor. Must be discharged before beginning repairs inside unit.

Control box
Contains switches and wiring that govern operation of condenser unit.

Condenser unit
Houses the condenser coils, compressor, fan and various system controls.

Condenser coils
Compressed refrigerant is forced through coils, releasing heat to the outside.

Compressor
Pressurizes vaporized refrigerant, raising it to a higher temperature. Pumps refrigerant through condenser coils, where it is cooled to a liquid; it then flows through the evaporator coils indoors and returns to the compressor in vapor form.

Check the level of the outdoor condenser unit to ensure correct refrigerant flow between indoor and outdoor coils. Lubricate the motor *(page 220)* and make sure the air conditioner fan rotates properly.

Cold evaporator coils condense moisture out of the indoor air. This water drips into a drain pan beneath the coils. Clean the drain pan under a V-shaped evaporator coil, and clear the condensate drain pipe running from the drain pan under an A-shaped coil, to keep water from puddling inside the furnace and to prevent the growth of algae and bacteria. Before beginning a repair, turn off power to the air conditioner at the main service panel *(page 102)* and outdoor-unit disconnect switch *(page 22)*. Leave the unit off for at least five minutes before turning it back on to prevent excess refrigerant pressure from overloading the compressor. **Caution:** Discharge all capacitors *(page 221)* by making a capacitor discharger for repairs that advise it. Avoid handling fins, coils or refrigerant lines; these carry high-pressure refrigerant and should be serviced only by a professional.

Cooling problems may be caused by another unit in the system. Consult the Troubleshooting Guides in System Controls *(page 164)* and Air Distribution *(page 169)*.

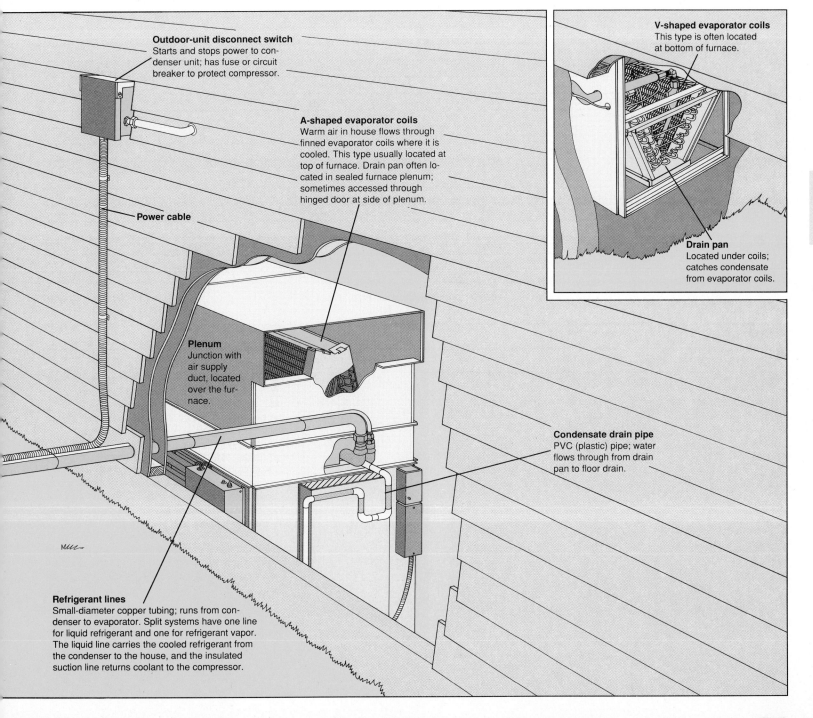

Outdoor-unit disconnect switch
Starts and stops power to condenser unit; has fuse or circuit breaker to protect compressor.

V-shaped evaporator coils
This type is often located at bottom of furnace.

A-shaped evaporator coils
Warm air in house flows through finned evaporator coils where it is cooled. This type usually located at top of furnace. Drain pan often located in sealed furnace plenum; sometimes accessed through hinged door at side of plenum.

Power cable

Drain pan
Located under coils; catches condensate from evaporator coils.

Plenum
Junction with air supply duct, located over the furnace.

Condensate drain pipe
PVC (plastic) pipe; water flows through from drain pan to floor drain.

Refrigerant lines
Small-diameter copper tubing; runs from condenser to evaporator. Split systems have one line for liquid refrigerant and one for refrigerant vapor. The liquid line carries the cooled refrigerant from the condenser to the house, and the insulated suction line returns coolant to the compressor.

TROUBLESHOOTING GUIDE

SYMPTOM	POSSIBLE CAUSE	PROCEDURE
Condenser unit does not turn on	No power to unit	Replace fuse or reset circuit breaker *(p. 102)* □○; restore power at outdoor-unit disconnect switch *(p. 22)* □○
	Thermostat set too high	Lower thermostat setting
	Outdoor temperature sensor faulty	Call for service
	High-pressure switch faulty	Call for service
	Capacitor faulty	Discharge capacitors *(p. 221)* □○▲; test and replace if necessary *(p. 222)* ◨●▲
	Compressor or fan motor faulty	Call for service
Condenser unit does not turn off	Contactor dirty or faulty	Clean contactor *(p. 222)* □○; test and replace if necessary *(p. 222)* ◨●▲
Condenser unit noisy	Fan blades hitting bracket or grille	Inspect fan blades; adjust or replace if necessary
	Fan motor faulty	Call for service
	Access panel screws loose	Tighten screws
	Fan motor bearings dry	Lubricate fan motor
Air conditioning does not cool	Thermostat set too high	Lower the thermostat setting
	Fan not cooling condenser coils	Call for service
	High-pressure switch faulty	Call for service
	Condenser coils blocked with dirt or grass	Clean coils and remove obstruction *(p. 220)* □○
	Condenser unit blocked; air cannot circulate	Clear debris from around unit; call for service to move unit
	Compressor faulty	Call for service
	Refrigerant level low	Call for service
Air conditioning short cycles (turns on and off repeatedly)	Evaporator coils frosted	Run blower in furnace with the air conditioning turned off for several hours
	Refrigerant level low	Call for service
Frost on evaporator coils	Blower in furnace turned off	Turn on blower *(Air Distribution, p. 169)*
	Blower motor faulty	Call for service
Water leaking inside furnace	Evaporator drain pan clogged	Clean drain pan *(p. 218)* □○
	Evaporator drain trap blocked	Call for service

DEGREE OF DIFFICULTY: □ Easy ◨ Moderate ■ Complex

ESTIMATED TIME: ○ Less than 1 hour ◖ 1 to 3 hours ● Over 3 hours

▲ Special tool required

MAINTAINING THE EVAPORATOR

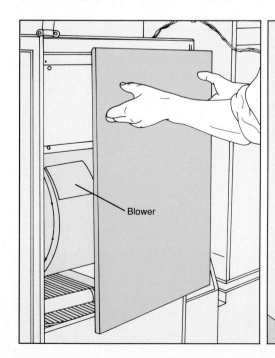

Blower

Evaporator coils

1 Accessing the evaporator coils. Turn off power to the air conditioner and the furnace at the main service panel *(page 102)* and outdoor-unit disconnect switch *(page 22)*. In most furnaces, the evaporator coils are top-mounted and often not accessible: The plenum that houses the coils may be a sealed unit, or ductwork and refrigerant lines may block access. A service technician may be able to install an access panel in a sealed plenum. In the air conditioner/electric furnace combination shown here, the evaporator coils are bottom-mounted and easily reached through access panels. First remove the blower panel *(far left)* by inserting your fingers in the slots and pulling it up and out. Then lift off the coil panel *(near left)*.

MAINTAINING THE EVAPORATOR (continued)

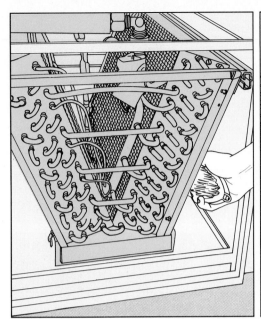
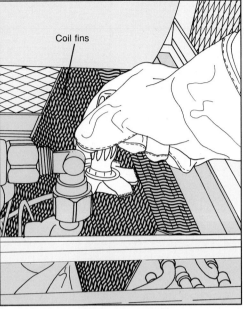
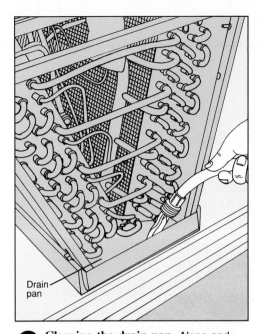

Coil fins

Drain pan

2 **Cleaning and straightening the coil fins.** Dirt that is not trapped by the air filter can lodge in the evaporator coil fins. With power to the unit off, clean the coils if necessary before each cooling season, or after running the air conditioner with a dirty filter. Using a very soft brush, gently stroke the coils up and down along the fins *(above, left)*. Brush all surfaces of the coils, paying special attention to the air-intake side (the side facing the air filter). Use a mild detergent-and-water solution for stubborn dirt; if the coils are top-mounted, do not let water drip on the heating elements or heat exchanger.

Check the coils for bent fins. Wearing work gloves, fit the teeth of a fin comb intö the fins near a damaged area, and gently pull the comb through the fins to unbend them *(above, right)*.

3 **Cleaning the drain pan.** Algae and sediment may collect in the drain pan. Wearing work gloves to protect your hands from the fins, wipe as much of the pan as you can reach, using a sponge. Flush out the pan and drain tube using a garden hose *(above)* or a pitcher of water. To prevent algae formation, add one-half cup bleach to the water in the drain pan—or use algaecide pills, following the manufacturer's instructions.

ACCESSING THE CONDENSER UNIT

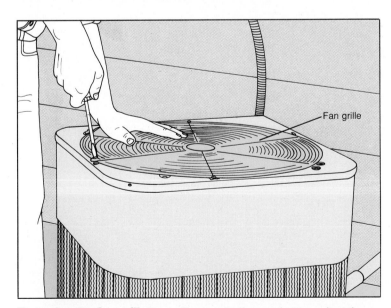

Fan grille

Removing the fan grille. Turn off power to the condenser unit at the main service panel *(page 102)* and outdoor-unit disconnect switch *(page 22)*. Using a screwdriver, remove the screws holding the fan grille to the top panel *(above)*, and lift it off. This grille provides access to the fan, fan motor and compressor.

Removing the control box cover. Turn off power to the condenser unit at the main service panel *(page 102)* and unit disconnect switch *(page 22)*. The control box is located near the entry point of the power cable and refrigerant lines. Using a screwdriver, remove the screws from the edges of the cover. For the control box shown here, pull the cover out, then down, to take it off *(above)*. The control box contains the capacitor, contactor, high-pressure switch and wiring connections. The condenser-unit wiring diagram is on the back of the control box cover.

MAINTAINING THE CONDENSER UNIT

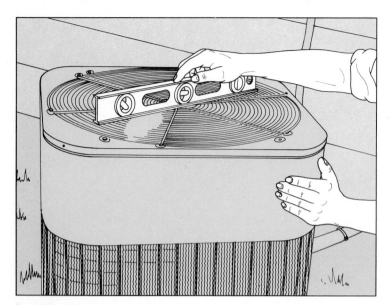

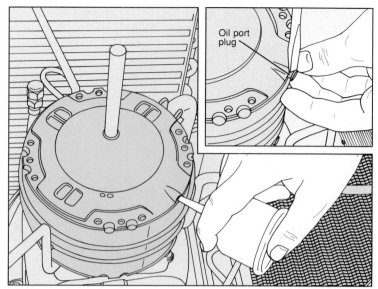

Leveling the condenser unit. For proper operation and longer life, the condenser unit should rest on a level slab. Each spring, check whether the unit has shifted: Rest a carpenter's level across the top of the unit *(above)*, first one direction, then the other. The bubble should be centered in the level each time; if not, the mounting slab has settled. With a helper, use a pry bar to lift the low edge of the slab and prop it with gravel or sand, or have a professional adjust it with concrete. Test its level again.

Oiling the fan motor. Oil the motor once before each cooling season. Turn off power to the condenser unit at the main service panel *(page 102)* and outdoor-unit disconnect switch *(page 22)*. Remove the top grille *(page 219)* and the fan blades: Loosen—but do not remove—the fan blade bolts and lift the blade assembly straight up off the motor shaft. Locate the oil ports, small holes in the motor housing. The ports may be sealed by small plastic plugs; pry out the plugs with a screwdriver *(inset)*. Insert two or three drops of non-detergent, light machine oil into each port *(above)*; do not over-oil. Replace the plugs.

MAINTAINING THE CONDENSER COILS

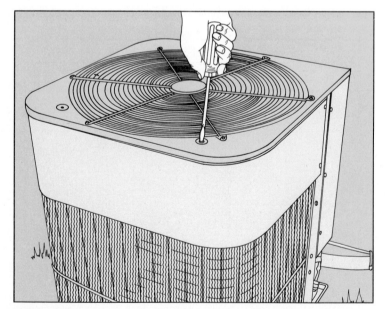

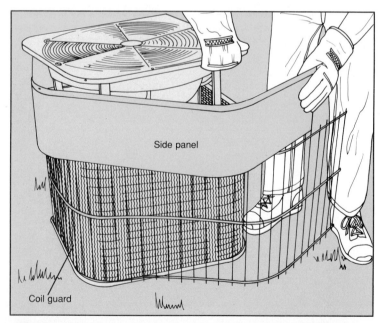

1 **Loosening the top panel.** For minor service to the condenser coils, such as picking off leaves or straightening a few fins, work without removing the coil guard. For heavier maintenance, you may need to unscrew the top panel to release the coil guard. Turn off power to the condenser unit at the main service panel *(page 102)* and outdoor-unit disconnect switch *(page 22)*. On the model shown, remove the screws on the top surface, near the corners *(above)*, to separate the top panel from the support rods inside.

2 **Removing the coil guard.** Take out the screws connecting the side panel to the top panel and to the condenser unit frame. Wearing work gloves, pull the top panel up slightly to disengage one end of the side panel and coil guard, and unwrap the panel and guard from the condenser unit frame. Your model may differ from the one shown; study the unit before disassembling it so that you do not remove more screws than necessary.

MAINTAINING THE CONDENSER COILS (continued)

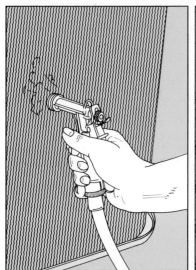

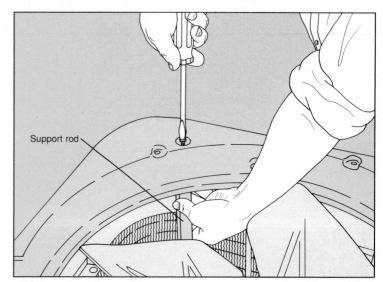

Support rod

3 **Cleaning and straightening the condenser coil fins.** The fan sucks in air—and debris—through the coils. Clean the coil fins before each cooling season; more often if they become clogged rapidly. Using a garden hose, spray water through the fins to dislodge dirt *(above, left)*; first spray from inside the unit outward, then spray the outside of the fins, as shown. Greasy or exceptionally dirty coils should be steam-cleaned professionally.

Check the coils for bent fins. Wearing work gloves, fit the teeth of a fin comb into the fins near a damaged area. Gently pull the comb through the fins to unbend them *(above, right)*.

4 **Reinstalling the panels.** Fasten the screws of the side panel at one end, wrap the panel and coil guard around the unit, and then fasten the screws at the other end. Settle the top panel onto the unit and unscrew the grille *(page 219)*. Reach into the unit and hold each support rod in position while screwing the top panel to it *(above)*. Reinstall the grille.

DISCHARGING THE CAPACITOR

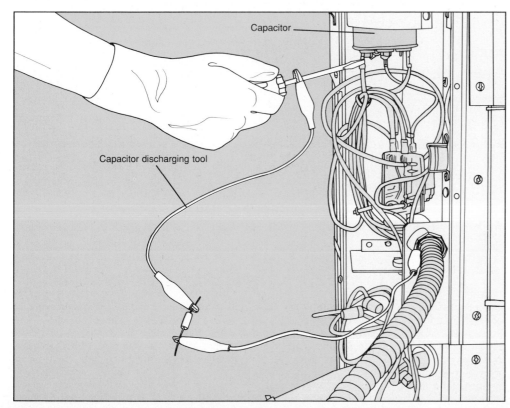

Capacitor

Capacitor discharging tool

Using a capacitor discharging tool. Caution: Capacitors may store potentially dangerous voltage. Before servicing control box components, the fan motor or the compressor, make a capacitor discharging tool *(page 417)* and discharge the capacitor. Turn off power to the condenser unit at the main service panel *(page 102)* and outdoor-unit disconnect switch *(page 22)*. Remove the control box cover *(page 219)* to access the capacitor. Clip the free end of the capacitor discharging tool to an unpainted metal part of the unit chassis. Hold the insulated screwdriver handle in one hand and touch the blade to each capacitor terminal, one at a time, for one second *(left)*. Look for other capacitors in the unit and discharge them the same way.

TESTING AND REPLACING A CAPACITOR

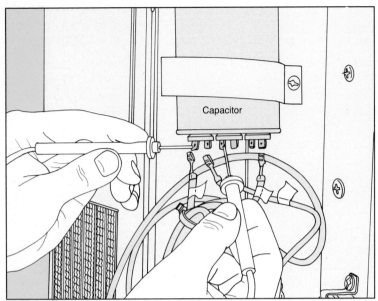

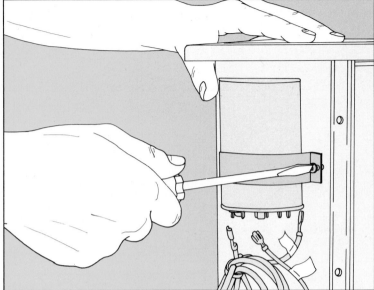

Testing and replacing the capacitor. Turn off power to the condenser unit at the main service panel *(page 102)* and outdoor-unit disconnect switch *(page 22)*. Remove the control box cover *(page 219)* and discharge the capacitor *(page 221)*. To test a three-terminal capacitor, as shown, label and disconnect its wires. Set a multitester to RX1K to measure resistance. Touch one probe to the common terminal, marked "C", and touch the other probe to one of the other terminals *(above, left)*. The multitester needle should swing toward zero resistance, then slowly move across the scale toward infinity. Test between "C" and the third terminal; if the needle responds the same way, the capacitor is good. If, for either test, the needle swings to zero and stays there, or it does not move at all, replace the capacitor. If the condenser unit has two, two-terminal capacitors, discharge them *(page 221)* and test each as on page 213. If a capacitor is faulty, unscrew the capacitor bracket *(above, right)* and slide out the capacitor. Purchase an identical replacement from a heating and cooling supplies dealer. Install the new capacitor in the bracket and screw the bracket in place. Reconnect the wires to the correct terminals.

SERVICING THE CONTACTOR

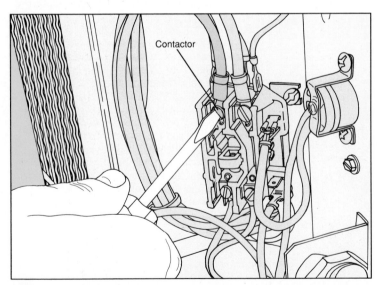

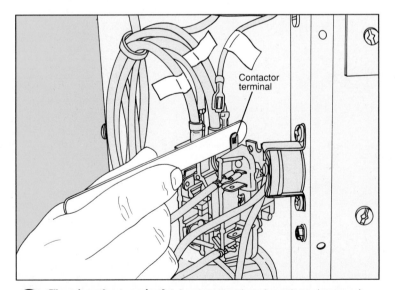

1 **Disconnecting the wires.** Turn off power to the condenser unit at the main service panel *(page 102)* and outdoor-unit disconnect switch *(page 22)*. Remove the control box cover *(page 219)* and discharge the capacitor *(page 221)*. Label the contactor wires. Disconnect the wires from the contactor, unscrewing screw terminals *(above)*, and pulling off spade lug connectors with long-nose pliers. For easier access, unscrew the contactor bracket and remove the contactor from the control box.

2 **Cleaning the terminals.** A contactor that doesn't work properly may simply be dirty. Inspect the contactor terminals for dirt or corrosion, and rub away any deposits with an ice cream stick *(above)*. Check the wire connectors you removed in step 1, and replace any that are loose-fitting or damaged *(page 417)*. Reconnect the wires.

SERVICING THE CONTACTOR (continued)

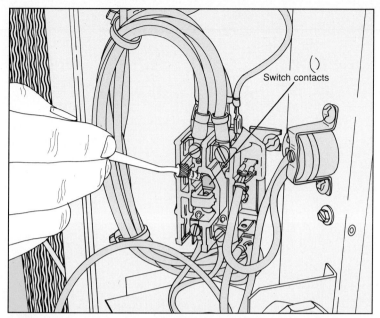

Switch contacts

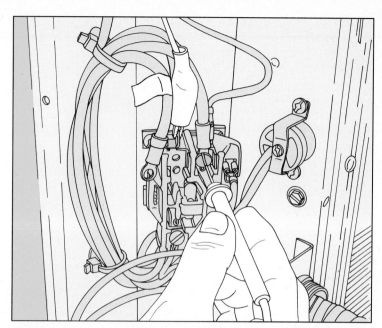

3 **Cleaning the switch contacts.** Inspect the reed-style switch contacts. If the contacts are stuck together or the spring is missing, replace the contactor *(step 6)*. Clean the contacts with contact cleaner solution, available at an electronics supply store. Use a small tool such as a dental brush *(above)* or a foam swab to reach the area where the contacts meet. Reconnect loose wires, reassemble the unit and turn on the power; if the contactor still doesn't work, test it *(step 4)*.

4 **Testing the contactor with the switch contacts open.** Turn off power to the unit and gain access to the contactor *(step 1)*. Disconnect the wires from one upper screw terminal. Set a multitester to test continuity *(page 417)*. Clip one probe to the disconnected terminal, and touch the other probe to the screw terminal next to it *(above)*. There should be no continuity. Test the lower pair of terminals the same way, first disconnecting the wires from one terminal. If either test shows continuity, the contactor is faulty; replace it *(step 6)*. If it is OK, test with the contacts closed *(step 5)*.

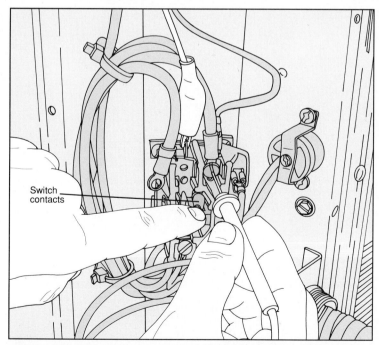

Switch contacts

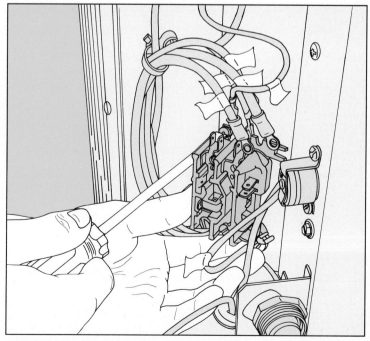

5 **Testing the contactor with the switch contacts closed.** With power to the unit still off, touch a multitester probe to each upper terminal as in step 4; but this time, depress the switch to close the contacts *(above)*. There should be continuity. Test the lower pair of terminals the same way. If either test does not show continuity, replace the contactor *(step 6)*. If the contactor is OK, reconnect the wires, reassemble the unit and turn on the power.

6 **Replacing the contactor.** Label and disconnect all contactor wires. Remove the mounting screws holding the contactor bracket to the control box wall *(above)* and take out the contactor. Purchase an identical replacement contactor from a heating and cooling supplies dealer or the manufacturer. Screw the new contactor in place and reconnect the wires. Reassemble the unit and turn on the power.

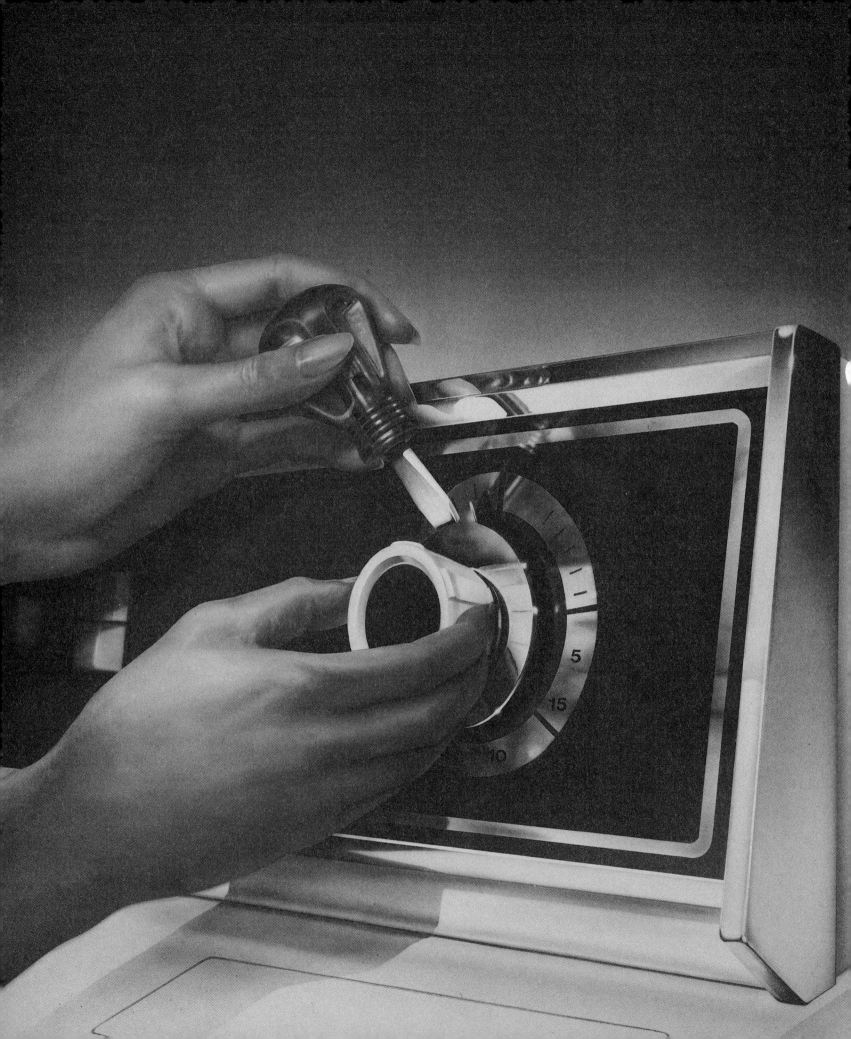

MAJOR APPLIANCES

REFRIGERATORS

An average lifespan of fifteen years puts refrigerators among the longest lasting and most trouble-free of all major appliances. All refrigerators work by means of a sealed cooling system. Refrigerant gas, liquefied by high pressure, passes through a narrow capillary tube and enters the evaporator coils inside the refrigerator. Under reduced pressure, it quickly boils into a gas, absorbing heat in the process. This gas flows to the compressor, which pumps it into the condenser coils on the outside of the refrigerator. Now under high pressure, the refrigerant gives off heat to the surrounding air as it returns to a liquid state. The refrigerant then passes back through the capillary tube into the evaporator coils as the cycle of heating

and cooling continues. When the desired temperature is reached, the thermostat control turns off the compressor.

The sealed cooling system limits the range of jobs that can be tackled by a do-it-yourselfer. Repairs to the compressor, evaporator or condenser require special skills and tools and must be handled by professionals. But many other problems can be diagnosed and repaired without any special tools.

Though they chill food the same way, refrigerators vary in style and features. When necessary, variations are described within each repair step. Shown below is a typical two-door, frost-free model with floor-level condenser coils. A frost-free refrigerator has a defrost heater that warms the evaporator

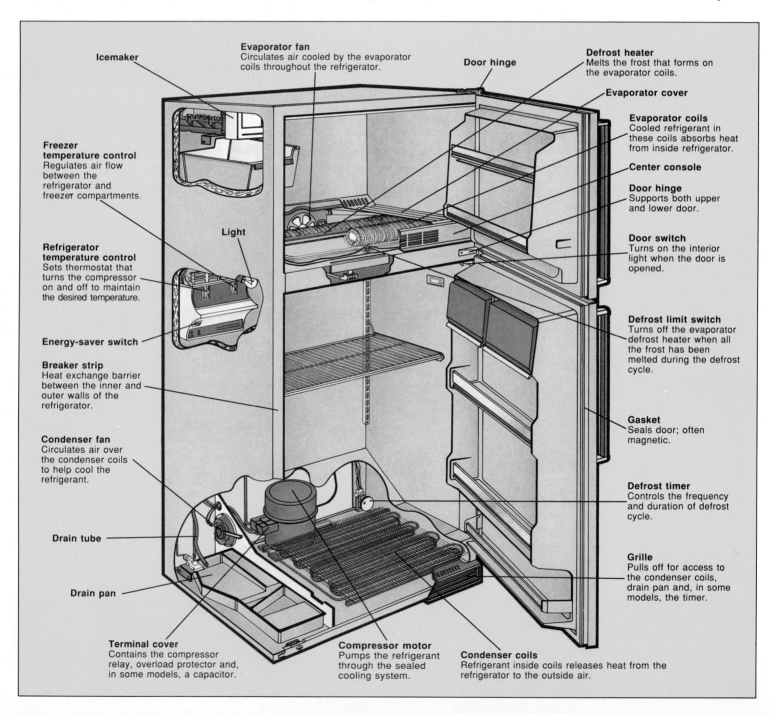

Icemaker

Evaporator fan
Circulates air cooled by the evaporator coils throughout the refrigerator.

Door hinge

Defrost heater
Melts the frost that forms on the evaporator coils.

Evaporator cover

Evaporator coils
Cooled refrigerant in these coils absorbs heat from inside refrigerator.

Center console

Door hinge
Supports both upper and lower door.

Door switch
Turns on the interior light when the door is opened.

Freezer temperature control
Regulates air flow between the refrigerator and freezer compartments.

Light

Refrigerator temperature control
Sets thermostat that turns the compressor on and off to maintain the desired temperature.

Energy-saver switch

Breaker strip
Heat exchange barrier between the inner and outer walls of the refrigerator.

Condenser fan
Circulates air over the condenser coils to help cool the refrigerant.

Defrost limit switch
Turns off the evaporator defrost heater when all the frost has been melted during the defrost cycle.

Gasket
Seals door; often magnetic.

Defrost timer
Controls the frequency and duration of defrost cycle.

Grille
Pulls off for access to the condenser coils, drain pan and, in some models, the timer.

Drain tube

Drain pan

Terminal cover
Contains the compressor relay, overload protector and, in some models, a capacitor.

Compressor motor
Pumps the refrigerant through the sealed cooling system.

Condenser coils
Refrigerant inside coils releases heat from the refrigerator to the outside air.

coils in both the refrigerator and freezer compartments. A semi-automatic refrigerator has a defrost heater that prevents frost in the refrigerator compartment only; the freezer compartment must be defrosted by hand. Turn off or unplug the machine and use a hair dryer on a low setting to melt a light layer of frost. For a heavy buildup, place a pan of hot water in each compartment and close the doors. Never hammer at ice buildup or try to pry it away with a sharp tool; this may puncture the evaporator.

Regular cleaning prolongs the life of a refrigerator and keeps energy costs down. Brush or vacuum the condenser coils regularly *(page 228)*, and keep the drain tubes and drain pan clean and unblocked *(page 229)*. Wash the compartments, trays, shelves and drain pan twice a year using a water and baking soda solution followed by a clear water rinse.

If the power goes out, food will keep in a closed refrigerator for 24 to 36 hours. If the power is out for a longer period, pack the food in dry ice (frozen carbon dioxide). Set the dry ice on heavy cardboard or layers of newspaper, not in direct contact with food. Keep the door closed as much as possible and handle dry ice with gloves; it causes frostbite.

Before starting any repair, always unplug the refrigerator. Before plugging it back in, wait an hour. This equalizes the pressure, lessening start-up strain on the compressor.

TROUBLESHOOTING GUIDE continued ►

SYMPTOM	POSSIBLE CAUSE	PROCEDURE
Refrigerator doesn't run and light doesn't work	No power to refrigerator	Check that refrigerator is plugged in; check for blown fuse or tripped circuit breaker *(p. 102)* □○
	Power cord loose or faulty	Test power cord *(p. 417)* ▣●
Refrigerator doesn't run, but light works	Temperature control turned off	Check temperature control
	Temperature control faulty	Test control *(dial type, p. 233; console type, p. 234)* ▣●
	Compressor overheated	Clean condenser coils *(p. 228)* □○
	Defrost timer faulty	Test defrost timer *(p. 239)* ▣●▲
	Condenser fan faulty	Call for service
	Overload protector faulty	Call for service
	Compressor or relay faulty	Call for service
Refrigerator starts and stops rapidly	Condenser coils dirty	Clean condenser coils *(p. 228)* □○
	Condenser fan faulty	Call for service
	Compressor faulty	Call for service
	Overload protector tripping repeatedly	Have an electrician check voltage at outlet
Refrigerator runs constantly	Frost buildup	Defrost refrigerator
	Door seal inadequate	Check door seal *(p. 229)* □○
	Door gasket damaged	Replace door gasket *(p. 231)* ▣●
	Condenser coils dirty	Clean condenser coils *(p. 228)* □○
	Evaporator plate or coils dirty (models with exposed evaporator)	Clean evaporator plate or coils with warm, soapy water
	Condenser fan faulty	Call for service
Refrigerator not cold enough	Temperature control set too high	Set temperature control to lower setting
	Temperature control faulty	Test control *(dial type, p. 233; console type, p. 234)* ▣●
	Condenser coils dirty	Clean condenser coils *(p. 228)* □○
	Door doesn't close automatically	Door should swing shut when left open halfway. If not, raise front leveling feet or rollers to tilt refrigerator backward slightly
	Door seal inadequate	Check door seal *(p. 229)* □○
	Door gasket damaged	Replace gasket *(p. 231)* ▣●
	Door switch faulty (some models)	Test door switch *(p. 232)* □○
	Evaporator fan faulty	Service evaporator fan *(p. 236)* ▣●
	Evaporator clogged by ice	Defrost refrigerator; test defrost heater *(p. 237)* ▣●▲ ; test defrost limit switch *(p. 238)* ▣●▲ ; test defrost timer *(p. 239)* ▣●▲
	Refrigerant leaking or contaminated	Call for service
Refrigerator too cold	Temperature control set too low	Set temperature control to higher setting
	Temperature control faulty	Test control *(dial type, p. 233; console type, p. 234)* ▣●

DEGREE OF DIFFICULTY: □ Easy ▣ Moderate ■ Complex
ESTIMATED TIME: ○ Less than 1 hour ● 1 to 3 hours ● Over 3 hours   ▲ Multitester required

TROUBLESHOOTING GUIDE (continued)

SYMPTOM	POSSIBLE CAUSE	PROCEDURE
Refrigerator doesn't defrost automatically	Defrost heater faulty	Test defrost heater (p. 237) ◩◖▲
	Defrost limit switch faulty	Test defrost limit switch (p. 238) ◩◖▲
	Defrost timer faulty	Test defrost timer (p. 239) ◩◖▲
Moisture around refrigerator door or frame	Breaker strips faulty	Inspect breaker strips (p. 235) ☐◖
	Energy saver switch on or faulty	Reset or test energy saver switch (p. 234) ◩◖
	Internal heater defective	Call for service
Ice in drain pan or water on bottom of refrigerator	Drain tube clogged	Clean drain tube (p. 229) ☐○
Water on floor around refrigerator	Drain pan damaged or misaligned	Check drain pan (p. 229) ☐○
	Drain tube clogged	Clean drain tube (p. 229) ☐○
	Icemaker water valve leaking	Call for service
Interior light doesn't work	Bulb loose or burned out	Check bulb (p. 232) ☐○
	Door switch faulty	Test door switch (p. 232) ☐○
Refrigerator smells bad	Contents spoiled	Remove spoiled food; wash interior of refrigerator with baking soda and warm water
	Drain pan dirty	Wash drain pan (p. 229) ☐○
	Insulation absorbing moisture through damaged breaker strips	Remove breaker strips and allow insulation to dry; replace strips if damaged (p. 235) ◩◖
Refrigerator noisy	Refrigerator not level	Adjust leveling feet
	Drain pan rattling	Reposition drain pan
	Evaporator fan damaged	Inspect evaporator fan (p. 236) ◩◖▲
	Compressor mountings loose or hardened	Call for service
	Condenser fan damaged	Call for service

DEGREE OF DIFFICULTY: ☐ Easy ◩ Moderate ■ Complex
ESTIMATED TIME: ○ Less than 1 hour ◖ 1 to 3 hours ● Over 3 hours   ▲ Multitester required

CLEANING THE CONDENSER COILS

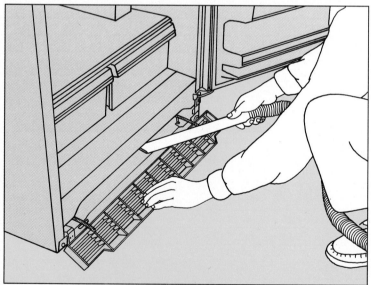

Cleaning two types of coils. An accumulation of dirt and dust prevents condenser coils from radiating heat, making the refrigerator cool poorly, run constantly, or even stop completely if the compressor overheats. Clean floor-level coils twice a year *(above, left)*; more often if you have pets. Unplug the refrigerator. Pull off the grille and use a vacuum cleaner with a wand attachment to remove dust and pet hair that accumulate behind the grille. Clean rear-mounted coils *(above, right)* yearly, using a stiff brush or a vacuum cleaner with a brush attachment. If the coils are greasy, wash them with warm, soapy water, taking care not to drip water on other parts of the refrigerator.

CLEANING THE DRAIN AND DRAIN PAN

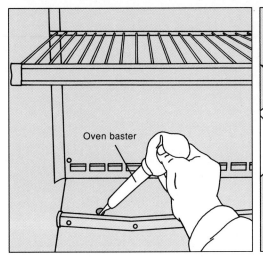

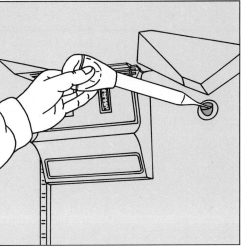

Cleaning the drain tube and drain pan. The drain opening may be in the floor of the refrigerator under the storage drawer *(far left)*, or at the top of the back wall, behind a pull-off drain trough *(near left)*. To clean the drain, use an oven baster to force a water solution (1/2 gallon hot water and 1 tablespoon baking soda or 1/2 cup household bleach) into the opening. To clear a stubborn clog, insert a length of 1/4-inch round plastic tubing into the drain and push it through to the drain pan below, then pull it out. The drain pan is located under the refrigerator, behind the front grille. Wash the pan regularly with a warm water and baking soda solution. If the pan rattles, it may be located too close to the compressor; reposition it.

CHECKING THE DOOR SEAL

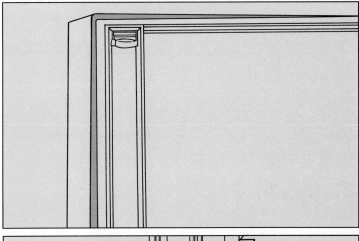

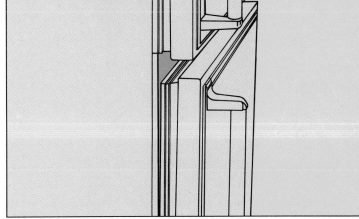

Checking the door seal. Open the door and examine all four sides of the door gasket for tears. Feel the gasket for brittleness or cracks. If the gasket shows damage, replace it *(page 231)*. If not, close the door and check the seal between gasket and cabinet for obvious gaps. Next open the door and shut it on a dollar bill, as shown. Slowly pull the dollar bill out of the door. If the gasket seals properly, you will feel tension as it grips the bill. Repeat this test all around the door.

For the door to close tightly and automatically, the refrigerator may have to tilt backward slightly. If the door seal isn't tight, have a helper push the refrigerator backward while you adjust the feet or rollers to raise the front of the refrigerator slightly. If the gasket still does not seal tightly, check the door for sagging or warping *(next step)*.

Checking the door for sagging or warping. If the refrigerator or freezer door sags on its hinges *(above, top)*, a poor seal will result. First adjust the hinges *(page 230)*. If the door gasket does not press flat against the cabinet, or the door appears warped *(above, bottom)*, the inner and outer door panels may be out of alignment. Try adjusting the hinges; if this doesn't work, reposition the door panels *(page 230)*.

CHECKING THE DOOR SEAL (continued)

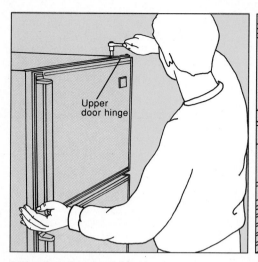

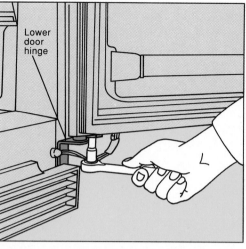

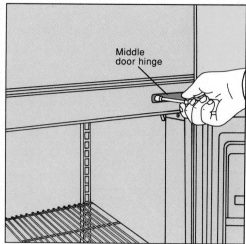

Adjusting the door hinges. Unplug the refrigerator. To correct a sag in an upper freezer door or in a full-length refrigerator door, use a socket wrench or hex wrench to loosen the bolts on the upper hinge *(above, left)*. Slight adjustments may also be made to a refrigerator door by loosening the bolts on the lower hinge *(above, center)*. Lift or push the door square with the refrigerator cabinet and retighten the hinge bolts. To correct a sag in a lower refrigerator door, open the door and loosen the screws on the middle hinge *(above, right)*. Shift the hinge slightly toward the outside of the cabinet and tighten the screws.

    To straighten a warped door, loosen the hinge bolts nearest the warped area, push the door tight to the cabinet and retighten the bolts. Check that the door rests flat against the cabinet all around the gasket. If not, the door panels must be realigned *(next step)*.

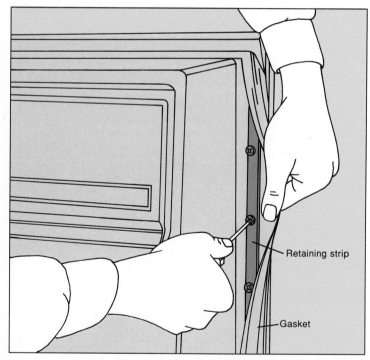

Loosening the retaining strip screws. Unplug the refrigerator. Open the door and pull back the door gasket to expose the metal or plastic retaining strips. Loosen, but do not remove, all the screws along the strip *(above)*.

Aligning the inner and outer door panels. Grasp the outer door panel at the top and side and twist it opposite to the warp, flattening the door. While you hold the door in this position, have a helper partially retighten the retaining screws *(above)*. Close the door and check that the warp has been corrected. If so, open the door and hold it while your helper tightens the screws securely. If the door is still warped, try adjusting it again. If the warp persists, the door may need to be replaced *(page 231)*.

REPLACING A DOOR GASKET

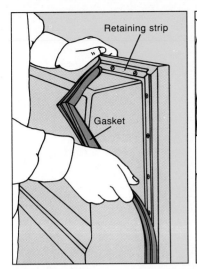

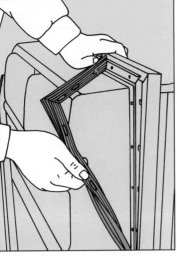

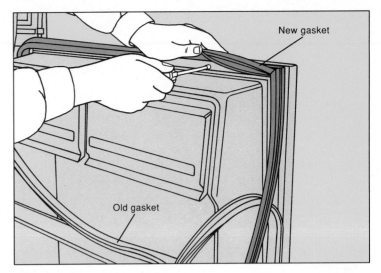

1 **Removing the gasket.** Before removing the old gasket, soak the new one in warm water to soften it and make installation easier. Unplug the refrigerator, pull back the gasket to expose the retaining strip and loosen the screws *(page 230)*. Try to pull out the gasket from behind the retaining strip. On newer models, it will come free *(above, left)*; on older models, the screws pass through holes in the gasket itself *(above, right)*. To free this type of gasket, remove the screws from the retaining strip along the top edge of the door and one-third of the way down each side. Pull the upper part of the gasket away from the retaining strip.

2 **Installing a new gasket.** On a newer model, start at an upper corner and simply insert the rear flange of the gasket behind the retaining strip, partially tightening the screws as you go. To keep the door from warping, have a helper hold it at the top and side as you tighten the screws *(page 230)*. When the gasket is installed all around the door, tighten the screws securely.

On an older model, push the flange of the new gasket behind the retaining strip. Install and partially tighten the screws *(above)*. Then remove the screws from the lower part of the retaining strip and pull out the rest of the old gasket. Push the rest of the new gasket into place. Starting at the bottom corners, reinstall and partially tighten the screws, then go back and tighten all the screws securely.

INSTALLING UPPER AND LOWER DOORS

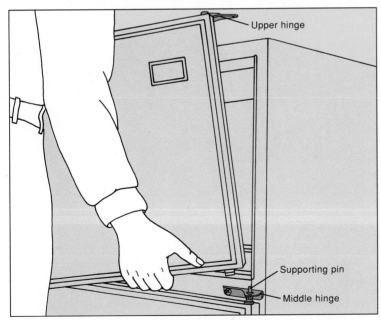

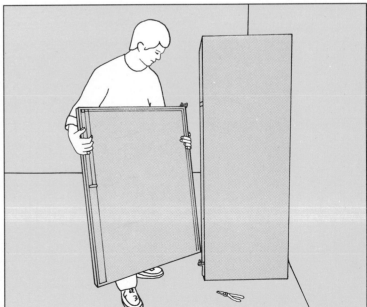

Removing and replacing the doors. Unplug the refrigerator. Use a socket wrench or hex wrench to remove the bolts holding the upper hinge to the refrigerator cabinet and lift the upper door off the supporting pin *(above, left)*; save any hinge washers. To install a new door, remove the upper hinge from the old door and insert it in the new door, replacing any washers. Rest the door on the lower supporting

pin and, aligning the door with the cabinet, install the upper hinge. To remove a lower door, you must first remove the upper door. Next, unscrew the middle hinge from the refrigerator cabinet and lift the door off the lower supporting pin *(above, right)*. Install a new door as described, replacing any hinge washers.

CHECKING THE LIGHT BULB AND DOOR SWITCH

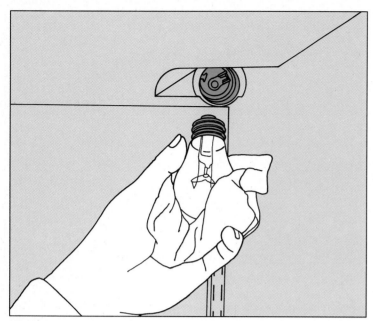

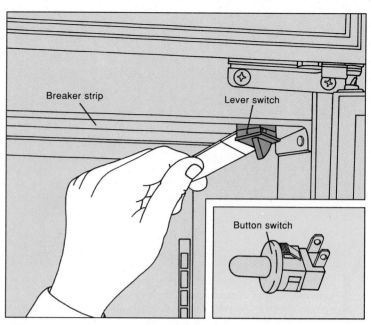

1 **Checking the light bulb.** In most refrigerators, a single door switch controls the interior light. In others, the same switch or a second door switch controls an evaporator fan as well. To test the evaporator fan switch only, go to step 2. If the interior light doesn't glow when you open the door, first check for a burned-out bulb. Protecting your hand with a rag or glove, unscrew the bulb *(above)*. Replace the bulb with a new one of the same wattage. If it does not light, the door switch may be faulty; remove and test it *(step 2)*. If you suspect that the light stays on when the refrigerator door is closed, warming the interior, press the door switch by hand. If the light stays on, remove and test the switch.

2 **Removing the door switch.** Unplug the refrigerator. Pry out a lever door switch *(above)* or a button switch *(inset)* using a putty knife, the blade padded with masking tape to prevent scratching the breaker strip. On some older refrigerators, the breaker strip must first be removed to free the switch from behind it *(page 235)*.

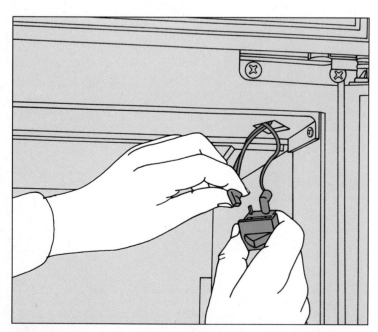

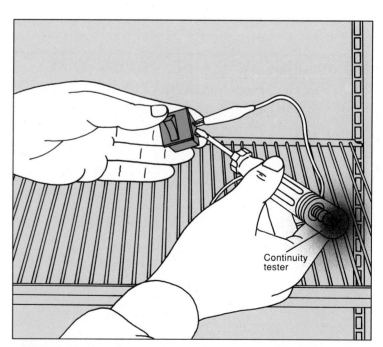

3 **Disconnecting the door switch.** Ease the switch housing from the breaker strip and pull it out to expose a few inches of wiring. The switch will have two or four terminals. Remove the push-on connectors *(above)*, labeling the wire positions for reassembly. If the wires are burned or corroded, repair them *(page 417)*.

4 **Testing the door switch.** Place a continuity tester probe on each terminal of a two-terminal switch. For a light switch, when the switch button is out the continuity tester should light *(above)*; when the button is depressed the continuity tester should not light. An evaporator fan switch will give the opposite result.

If the switch has four terminals, it is a combination evaporator fan and light switch. There should be continuity between one pair of terminals with the switch button out. Depress the switch button, and the other pair of terminals should show continuity. If the switch fails any test, replace it. Connect the new switch to the wire leads and snap the switch into the breaker strip.

TESTING AND REPLACING THE TEMPERATURE CONTROL (Dial type)

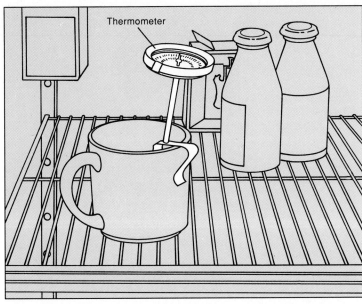

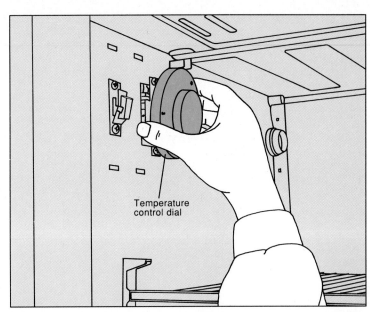

1 **Testing the refrigerator and freezer temperature.** The ideal temperature for the refrigerator is between 38°F and 40°F; for the freezer compartment, between 0°F and 8°F. (The freezer temperature may be about 10°F higher in a single-door refrigerator.) To test the temperature of the refrigerator, place a cup of water in it for 24 hours. (In a freezer, use cooking oil.) Place a cooking thermometer in the liquid for three minutes *(above)*. If the temperature is too cold or too warm, adjust the temperature control. If the problem persists, test the control *(dial type, step 2; console type, page 234)*.

2 **Removing the dial.** Unplug the refrigerator. Turn the dial to its coldest setting. If the dial has a screw in the center, unscrew it, then pull the dial straight off its shaft *(above)*.

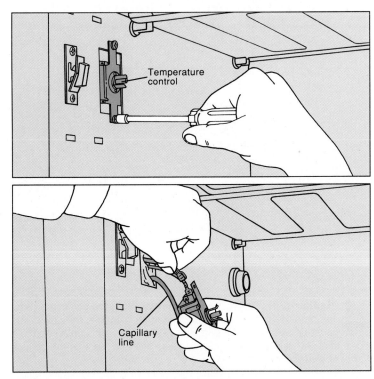

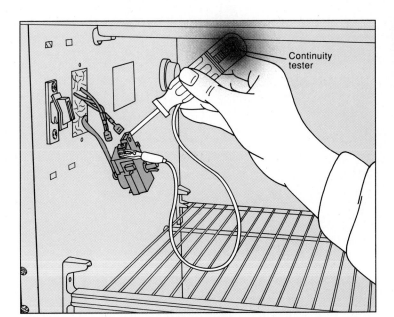

3 **Removing the temperature control.** Remove the screws securing the temperature control to the wall of the refrigerator *(above, top)*. Pull out the control to expose a few inches of electrical wiring, taking care not to bend or damage the metal capillary line. Pull off the wire connectors and the ground wire *(above, bottom)*.

4 **Testing and replacing the temperature control.** Touch a continuity tester probe to each terminal *(above)*. With the control at its coldest setting *(step 2)*, the tester should light, indicating a closed circuit. Turn off the control by twisting the shaft in the opposite direction until it stops, then retest; the tester should not light. To install a new temperature control, pull the capillary line of the old control out of its opening in the refrigerator wall. Set the new control to its coldest setting and carefully thread the capillary line into the opening without kinking it. Attach the wires to the terminals, screw the control in place on the wall, and reattach the dial.

TESTING AND REPLACING THE TEMPERATURE CONTROL (Console type)

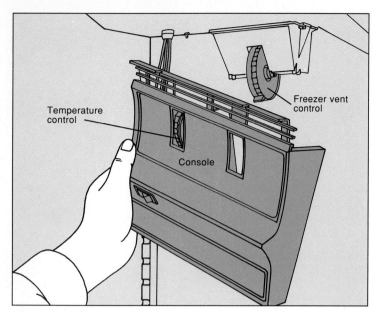

1 **Removing the temperature control console.** Test and adjust the temperature of the refrigerator or freezer *(page 233)*. If the temperature is not within the acceptable range, unplug the refrigerator. Unscrew the console and carefully remove it from the refrigerator wall *(above)*. The temperature control (and energy-saver switch, if any) is mounted on the console; let it dangle by its wiring. The freezer vent control will remain attached to the refrigerator wall.

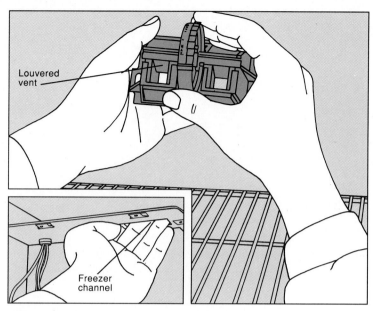

2 **Checking the freezer control.** Unscrew the freezer vent control from the refrigerator wall *(above)*. Use a hair dryer set on LOW to melt any ice blocking the louvered vent. Remove any food that might have fallen into the vent from the freezer. Finally, reach into the freezer channel in the refrigerator wall with your fingers *(inset)* and check for obstructions. Reinstall the freezer vent control.

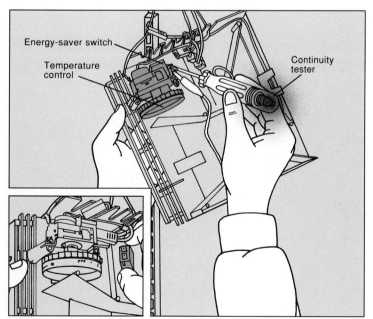

3 **Testing the energy-saver switch and temperature control.** If the console has an energy-saver switch, remove the push-on connectors *(inset)* and test the switch for continuity. With a probe on each terminal, the tester should light when the switch is on. If the switch is faulty, pull it off the console, snap on a new switch and reattach the push-on connectors. To test the temperature control, remove the push-on connectors and the ground wire from its terminals. Touch a tester probe to each terminal *(above)*. With the control turned to its coldest setting, the tester should light; with the control turned off, it should not light. Replace a faulty control.

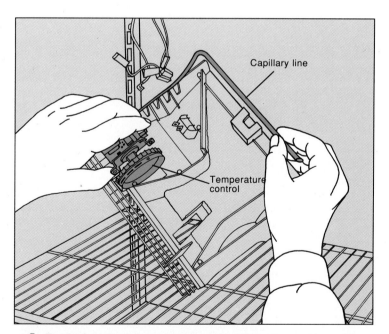

4 **Replacing the temperature control.** Note the position of the temperature control's capillary line in the console; the new one must be installed the same way. Pull out the old control and snap in a new one, threading the capillary line into place in the console *(above)*. Remount the console on the refrigerator wall.

REPLACING THE BREAKER STRIPS

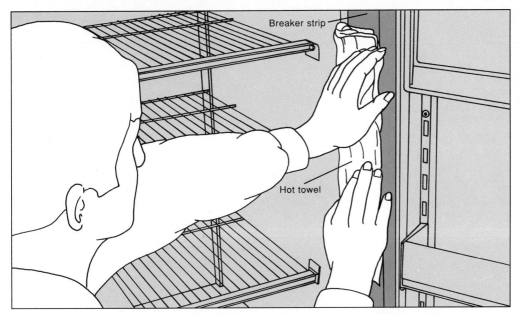

1 **Softening the breaker strip.** Damaged breaker strips allow moisture to enter the insulation between the inner and outer walls of the refrigerator or freezer, causing odor and reducing cooling efficiency. Inspect the breaker strips around the inner frame for warps or cracks. To replace a damaged breaker strip, first unplug the refrigerator. Because a breaker strip is brittle when cold, soften the strip before attempting removal by pressing a hot, wet towel against it along its entire length *(left)*.

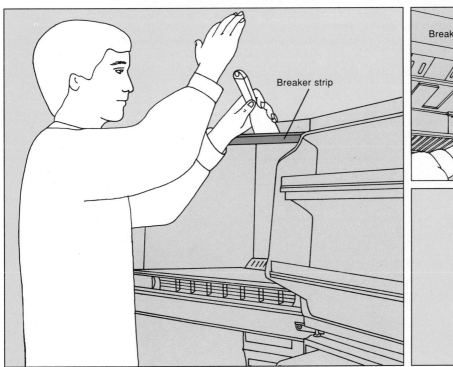

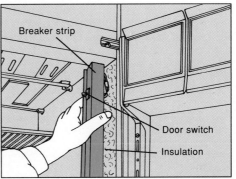

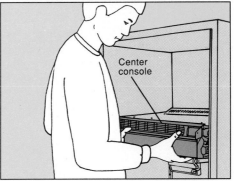

2 **Removing and replacing a breaker strip.** The way breaker strips are installed varies from model to model. Before beginning work, check to see how the strips are attached to each other and to the refrigerator cabinet. Most can be pried from the cabinet with a wide putty knife *(above, left)*. Be careful not to damage the foam insulation behind the breaker strip. If the insulation is damp or ice-clogged, or smells bad, leave it uncovered for a few hours or dry it with a hair dryer set on LOW. To replace the breaker strip, simply snap a new one in place.

Other kinds of breaker strips are more complicated to remove. On some models, you must first remove the unbroken strips to release the broken one. In other cases, the breaker strip may have a door switch mounted in it. Partially free the strip *(above, right, top)* and disconnect the wires from the back of the switch before removing the strip completely. Transfer the switch to the new breaker strip before installing it.

On some refrigerators, the top and bottom breaker strips are attached to the side strips with sealant. Cut through the sealant with a utility knife before removing the damaged breaker strip. After replacing the strip, reseal the corners with an arsenic-free sealant rated for use in food compartments.

The most difficult breakers to remove and replace are those that run from the bottom of the refrigerator to the top of the freezer and are held in place by the center console. To free these strips, first remove the screws that hold the console in place, then pull the console forward *(above, right, bottom)* and rest it in the freezer compartment without disconnecting the wires. Replace the breaker strip as described above and reinstall the console.

TESTING AND REPLACING THE EVAPORATOR FAN

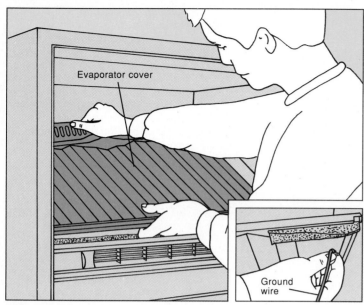

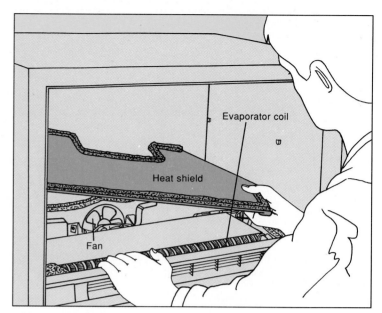

1 **Removing the evaporator cover.** The evaporator coils are part of the sealed refrigeration system and should only be serviced professionally. But the other components located under the evaporator cover are easily tested and replaced. On most models, the evaporator cover is also the freezer bottom. To remove it, first unplug the refrigerator. Remove the screws around the edges of the cover and lift it partway out. Unclip the ground wire from its underside *(inset)* and remove the cover from the freezer, as shown. If the freezer has an icemaker, remove it first by unscrewing the bottom bracket, then the top screws and clips. Lower out the icemaker and unplug it. On side-by-side models, the evaporator cover may be located at the top of the refrigerator compartment or at the back of the freezer.

2 **Removing the insulation and heat shield.** Carefully peel off the tape that holds the rigid sheet of foam insulation in place and remove it. Lift the metal heat shield from the evaporator coil compartment *(above)*. With a hair dryer set on LOW, melt any ice that has built up around the fan blades, taking care not to melt plastic components. Remove any objects that have fallen into the compartment through the air vent.

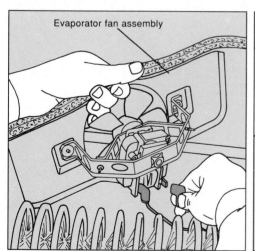

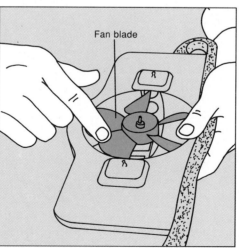

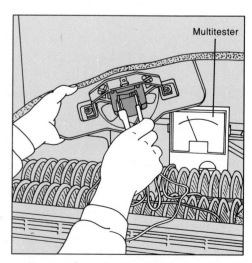

3 **Checking the evaporator fan.** If the fan housing is attached to the cabinet with screws, remove them. Lift the fan assembly a few inches and disconnect the push-on connectors and the ground wire *(above, left)*, using long-nose pliers if they do not pull off easily. If the fan blade is damaged, replace it. Unscrew the nut or setscrew at the center of the fan blade, pull the blade off the motor shaft and slide on a new blade, replacing any washers. Hold the fan horizontally and spin the blade to check for binding in the motor *(above, right)*. If the blade does not spin freely, replace the motor. Remove the fan blade, unscrew the smaller bracket at the front of the motor and remove the motor from the housing. Install the new motor and replace the bracket and the fan blade, taking care not to reverse the blade.

4 **Testing the evaporator fan motor.** Set a multitester to RX1 and touch a probe to each motor terminal. The meter should show some resistance. If not, install a new motor *(step 3)*, and reinstall the fan. Test the defrost heater *(page 237)* before replacing the evaporator cover.

TESTING AND REPLACING THE DEFROST HEATER

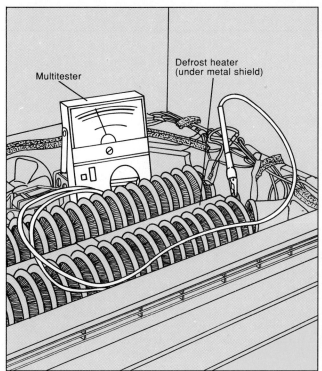

Multitester

Defrost heater
(under metal shield)

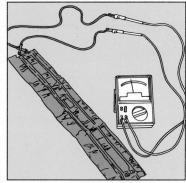

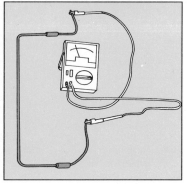

1 Testing the defrost heater. The defrost heater element may be enclosed within a glass tube and hidden beneath a metal reflector shield between the evaporator coils *(far left)*. Alternatively, it may be wrapped in aluminum foil *(near left, top)*, or it may be an exposed metal rod *(near left, bottom)*. All elements are tested the same way. Unplug the refrigerator and remove the evaporator cover, insulation, and heat shield *(page 236)*. Pull the wire connectors from the terminals at each end of the defrost heater. Set a multitester at RX1 and attach a probe to each terminal. The meter should show medium to high resistance. If not, replace the element. If the element is good, test the defrost limit switch *(page 238)*.

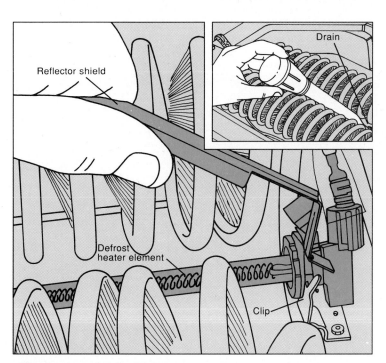

Reflector shield

Drain

Defrost heater element

Clip

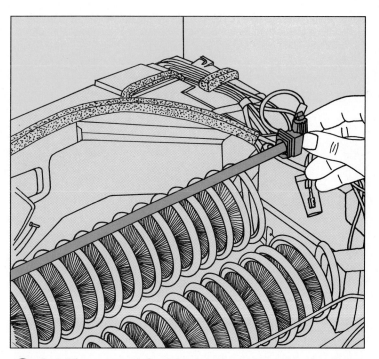

2 Removing the defrost heater. Unhook the element's reflector shield from the clips at each end *(above)*, and carefully lift the element out of its brackets. This will expose the opening to the drain tube. Before installing a new element, clean the drain tube by using an oven baster to force a solution of hot water and baking soda or bleach into the opening *(inset)*.

3 Installing a new defrost heater. Do not touch the glass surface of the new heater element; oils from your skin will cause hot spots. If you do touch the element, wipe it thoroughly with a paper towel. Plug the new element in the same position as the old one *(above)*, and replace all clips or fasteners. Next, reconnect the push-on connectors to the element terminals and snap in the reflector shield, if any. If you are not testing the defrost limit switch *(page 238)*, reinstall the evaporator cover, insulation and heat shield *(page 236)*. Take special care to reconnect the ground wire.

TESTING AND REPLACING THE DEFROST LIMIT SWITCH

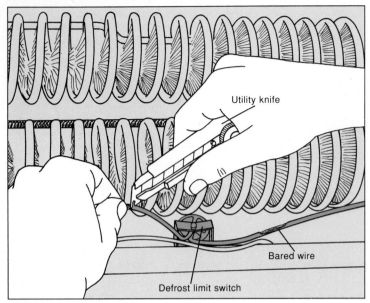

Utility knife

Bared wire

Defrost limit switch

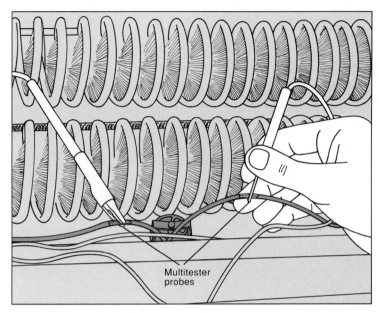

Multitester probes

1 **Baring the defrost limit switch wires.** The defrost limit switch, located next to the evaporator, turns off the defrost heater when all the frost has melted during the defrost cycle. To reach it, unplug the refrigerator and remove the evaporator cover, insulation, and heat shield *(page 236)*. If the defrost limit switch has push-on connectors, disconnect them. On most refrigerators, however, the switch is permanently wired. To test such a switch, you must bare the two switch wires. Taking care not to cut or fray the copper strands inside, use a sharp utility knife to remove a small patch of the plastic insulation around each wire *(above)*.

2 **Testing the defrost limit switch.** The switch should have complete continuity when it is cold, and no continuity when it is warm. To test the switch, place a plastic bag full of dry ice on it for 20 minutes. Remove the ice and touch a multitester probe to each of the two exposed wires *(above)*, or to each switch terminal. The tester should show continuity. Then warm the switch using a hair dryer set on LOW. The multitester needle should swing downscale to show resistance. If the switch fails either test, replace it. If the switch is good, tape the exposed wires *(step 3)*.

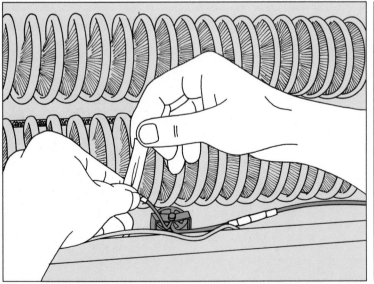

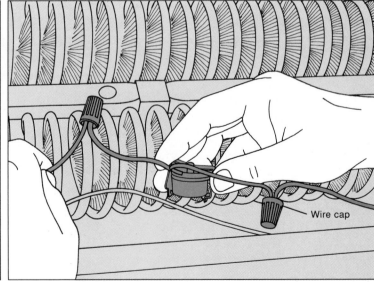

Wire cap

3 **Taping wires or replacing the defrost limit switch.** If the switch is good, reseal the bared wires with electrical tape, covering the cut patches and one inch on each side *(above, left)*. If the defrost limit switch has terminals, reconnect the push-on connectors. If the switch is faulty, cut the wires at the bared spots. Splice them to the wires of a new switch *(page 417)* using wire caps *(above, right)* or crimp connectors waterproofed with a dab of silicone sealant. Snap the new switch into place. Reinstall the evaporator cover *(page 236)*. Take special care to reconnect the ground wire.

TESTING AND REPLACING THE DEFROST TIMER

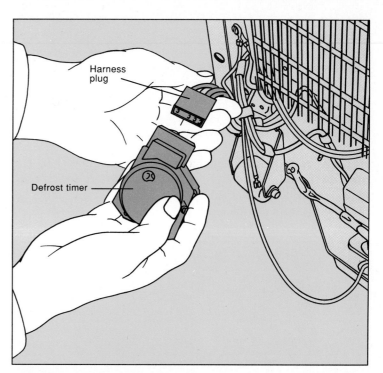

1 Removing the defrost timer. The defrost timer is usually located in the compressor compartment at the back of the refrigerator, as shown, but it may also be found behind the front grille, in the thermostat control console, or behind a cover plate inside the refrigerator *(inset)*. To remove the defrost timer, unplug the refrigerator and unscrew the timer from the cabinet *(above)*.

2 Disconnecting the wires. Disconnect the green ground wire from the timer. The timer is linked to the wiring by a harness plug *(above)*, which houses four connections. To help you reconnect it in the proper position, mark one side of both the plug and the defrost timer with masking tape before pulling apart the plug.

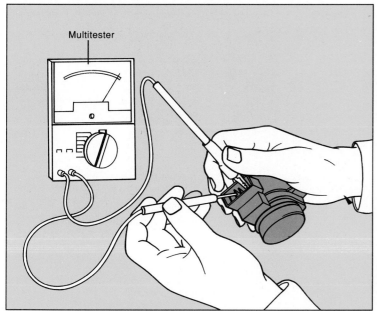

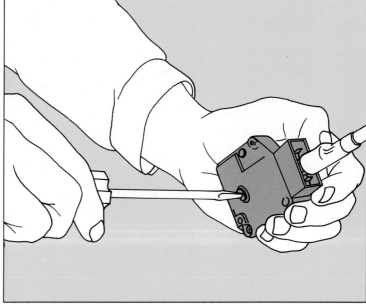

3 Testing the defrost timer. Find the common terminal of the timer, usually connected to the white wire of the harness plug (if the terminals are numbered, it is number 3). If you can't identify it this way, consult the wiring diagram. Attach one multitester probe to the common terminal and, with the meter set at RX100, touch the other probe to each of the other three terminals *(above, left)*. Two of these pairs should have full continuity while the third should have no continuity.

Then, using a screwdriver, turn the defrost timer switch manually *(above, right)* until you hear a click. Test the timer again the same way. Two of the three terminal pairs should show continuity, while the third—not the same one as before—should not. In either test, if all three pairs have continuity, or if only one does, the defrost timer is faulty. To install a new defrost timer or to reinstall the old one, reconnect the green ground wire and then reconnect the harness plug. Screw the defrost timer to the refrigerator cabinet and replace the back panel, if any.

ELECTRIC RANGES

Although the heart of an electric range seems a tangle of wires and switches, most repairs are based on simple deductive reasoning. An electric range operates on a 240/120-volt circuit—240 volts for the heating elements and 120 volts for the accessories (clock, lights and appliance receptacle). The range draws power though two separate fuses or breakers; if you suspect an electrical problem, check both fuses or breakers first.

The heating elements are controlled by electrical switches. A thermostat senses and regulates oven temperature. Self-cleaning ovens use extremely high temperatures—about 900°F—to burn food residue off the oven walls. A special door-lock mechanism prevents the oven door from being opened until the cleaning cycle is completed.

Electric ranges are made in a variety of styles—freestanding, slide-in, double-oven, cooktop or wall oven—but all operate in much the same way and use similar components. Once you understand the basic repair procedures, you can adapt them to your own range. The repairs in the following pages are shown with a freestanding range.

The Troubleshooting Guide at right lists the most common malfunctions in order from most to least likely. Before deciding that your range needs repair, check that the problem is not due to incorrect use. Follow the use and care recommendations in your owner's manual. Keeping your range clean is the most effective way to avoid breakdowns, but be careful not to get cleaning liquids inside the range where they can cause short

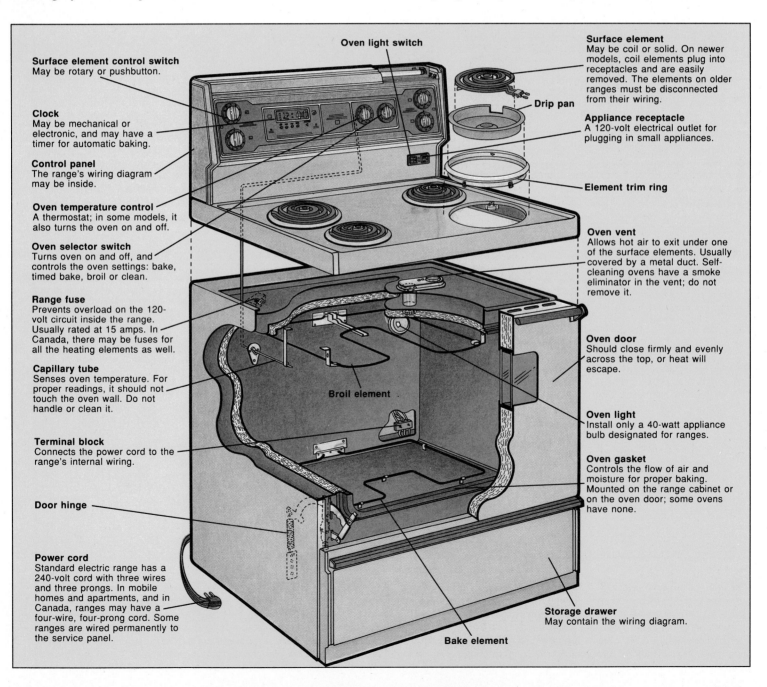

Surface element control switch
May be rotary or pushbutton.

Clock
May be mechanical or electronic, and may have a timer for automatic baking.

Control panel
The range's wiring diagram may be inside.

Oven temperature control
A thermostat; in some models, it also turns the oven on and off.

Oven selector switch
Turns oven on and off, and controls the oven settings: bake, timed bake, broil or clean.

Range fuse
Prevents overload on the 120-volt circuit inside the range. Usually rated at 15 amps. In Canada, there may be fuses for all the heating elements as well.

Capillary tube
Senses oven temperature. For proper readings, it should not touch the oven wall. Do not handle or clean it.

Terminal block
Connects the power cord to the range's internal wiring.

Door hinge

Power cord
Standard electric range has a 240-volt cord with three wires and three prongs. In mobile homes and apartments, and in Canada, ranges may have a four-wire, four-prong cord. Some ranges are wired permanently to the service panel.

Oven light switch

Surface element
May be coil or solid. On newer models, coil elements plug into receptacles and are easily removed. The elements on older ranges must be disconnected from their wiring.

Drip pan

Appliance receptacle
A 120-volt electrical outlet for plugging in small appliances.

Element trim ring

Oven vent
Allows hot air to exit under one of the surface elements. Usually covered by a metal duct. Self-cleaning ovens have a smoke eliminator in the vent; do not remove it.

Oven door
Should close firmly and evenly across the top, or heat will escape.

Broil element

Oven light
Install only a 40-watt appliance bulb designated for ranges.

Oven gasket
Controls the flow of air and moisture for proper baking. Mounted on the range cabinet or on the oven door; some ovens have none.

Storage drawer
May contain the wiring diagram.

Bake element

circuits. Don't use foil to line the drip pans under the burners—it can short the electrical connections of the element. Using burners without the drip pan can also harm the wiring. Never wash the gasket of a self-cleaning oven.

Most range repairs are electrical in nature, but they are not complex. Many malfunctions are caused by loose connections or burned wires; always check for these first. Clues to a loose connection are a metallic odor or a soft hissing or buzzing. A sharp odor of hot insulation indicates overheating in a switch or power cord. To repair wires or use a multitester, consult Tools & Techniques (page 417). If you must refer to your range's wiring diagram, look for it on the back panel, in the storage drawer, or inside the control panel.

Before starting repairs, turn off all the controls and then unplug the range, or turn off power at the main service panel (page 102). Check that you've disconnected the right fuses or breakers by turning on the heating elements—they should not warm up. While unplugging the range, don't touch the back panel; a loose wire inside could shock you. Before reconnecting the power, make sure that no uninsulated wires or terminals touch the cabinet, and that wiring is away from sharp edges and moving parts.

Many ranges are topped by a venting range hood. Range hood problems are usually caused by grease buildup in the aluminum mesh filter. Remove and wash the filter once a week with hot soapy water.

TROUBLESHOOTING GUIDE

SYMPTOM	POSSIBLE CAUSE:	PROCEDURE:
Nothing works	No power to range	Check that range is plugged in; check for blown fuse or tripped circuit breaker (p. 102) □○
	Power cord faulty	Test power cord (p. 417) ◨●
All elements do not heat, or heat only partially	Partial power to range	Check for blown fuse or tripped circuit breaker (p. 102) □○
	Power cord faulty or poor connection at terminal block	Test power cord and block connections (p. 417) ◨●
Surface element doesn't heat	Loose connection at element terminals	Reposition element (p. 243) □○
	Element shorted	Test element (plug-in elements, p. 243 □○; wired elements, p. 248) ◨●
	Receptacle faulty	Check receptacle (p. 243) ◨●▲
	Burner switch faulty	Test switch (p. 244) ◨●▲
Surface element provides only high heat	Burner switch faulty	Replace switch (p. 244) ◨●▲
Oven doesn't heat	Range fuse blown	Check range fuses under front element or control panel
	Clock timer incorrectly set	Reset clock timer
	Bake or broil element faulty	Test element (p. 245) ◨●▲
	Temperature control faulty	Test temperature control (p. 247) ◨●▲
	Oven selector switch faulty	Test switch (p. 248) ◨●▲
Oven doesn't hold set temperature	Capillary tube broken or touching oven wall	Check capillary tube (p. 246) ◨●
	Oven door not aligned	Adjust door (p. 251) □○
	Oven door gasket broken	Replace gasket (p. 250) ◨○
	Temperature control out of adjustment	Test oven temperature, recalibrate control (p. 246) ◨●
	Temperature control faulty	Test temperature control (p. 247) ◨●▲
Oven produces condensation	Oven vent clogged	Clean vent, wash duct (p. 246) □○
Self-cleaning oven doesn't clean	Oven door unlocked	Reclose and lock door
	Bake or broil element faulty	Test element (p. 245) ◨●▲
	Clock timer faulty	Check clock timer fuses; call for service
	Temperature control faulty	Test temperature control (p. 247) ◨●▲
	Oven selector switch faulty	Test switch (p. 248) ◨●▲
	Door lock faulty	Call for service
	Smoke eliminator faulty	Call for service
Oven light out	Bulb loose or burned out	Replace bulb (p. 249) □○
	Light switch broken	Test switch (p. 249) ◨●▲
	Socket faulty	Replace socket (p. 249) ◨○
Oven door doesn't close properly	Oven door not aligned	Adjust door (p. 251) □○
	Spring loose or broken	Adjust or replace springs (p. 251) □○
	Hinge broken	Call for service

DEGREE OF DIFFICULTY: □ Easy ◨ Moderate ■ Complex
ESTIMATED TIME: ○ Less than 1 hour ● 1 to 3 hours ● Over 3 hours   ▲ Multitester required

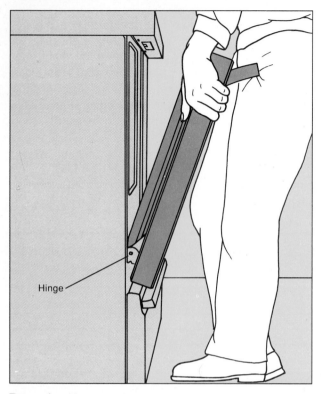

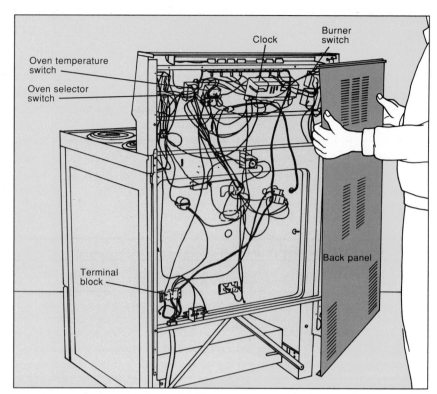

Removing the oven door. Many oven doors slide off their hinges, facilitating work inside the oven or on the door itself. (The door hinges of a self-cleaning range must be unscrewed). Open the door to its first stop, the broil position. Grip each side as shown, maintaining the door's angle, and pull the door straight off it hinges. Close the hinge arms against the oven for safety.

Removing the back of a freestanding range. The wiring and controls of a free-standing range are reached from the back. Unplug the range or turn off power at the service panel. Rock the range away from the wall. Supporting the back panel with a free hand or knee, remove the screws from around the panel's edges. Some ranges have a single panel *(above)*; others have a lower panel covering the terminal block where the power cord is attached, and one or more upper panels covering the wiring and controls.

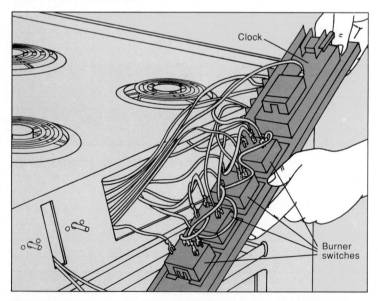

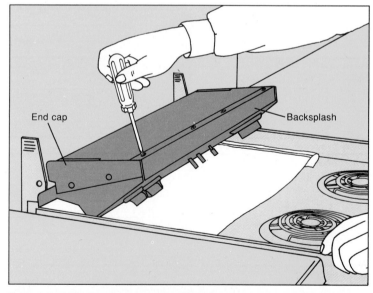

Reaching front-mounted controls. This type of control panel is attached with screws at each end. After disconnecting power to the range, remove them with a screwdriver. The panel may be held by a spring clip as well; pull up the panel to release it from the clip. Tilt the panel forward to expose the controls and wiring *(above)*; rest it on the top of the range or the edge of the door while working.

Removing the backsplash of a built-in range. Although similar in style to a freestanding range, the controls of a built-in range often can be serviced from the front, without moving the range from the wall. Disconnect power to the range and remove the screws from each end cap of the backsplash. Spread a towel on the cooktop to protect it. Pull the backsplash forward and rest it on the towel. To reach the range switches and controls, unscrew the rear panel of the backsplash *(above)* and set it aside.

REPAIRING PLUG-IN BURNER ELEMENTS

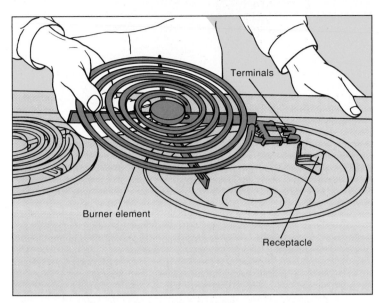

Terminals

Burner element

Receptacle

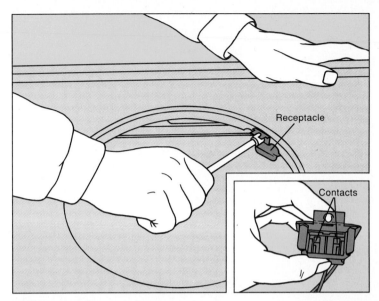

Receptacle

Contacts

1 **Checking a plug-in burner element.** Most modern ranges have sheathed coil elements with terminals that plug into an electrical receptacle within the burner opening. If a plug-in element doesn't heat, disconnect power to the range, grasp the element and reseat its terminals securely in the receptacle. If the problem persists, lift the element up about an inch and pull it out *(above)*. Inspect the element for damage; buff corroded terminals with fine steel wool and reinstall the element. If the element is burned or pitted, it must be replaced. If it shows no visible damage, test it by plugging it into the receptacle of a working element; if the element still does not heat, replace it. Otherwise, check its receptacle *(step 2)*.

2 **Examining an element receptacle.** Lift out the drip pan and its chrome ring. Unscrew the receptacle from the range *(above)*. Pull out the receptacle, taking care not to strain the wiring, and examine the metal contacts inside *(inset)*. If the contacts appear bent, burned or oxidized, replace the receptacle. Examine the terminals at the back of the receptacle where the wires are connected (you may first have to snap off two clips and remove a card-like insulator). If the wire terminals are burned, cut them off and install new terminal connectors *(page 417)*. On some ranges, you must lift and prop the cooktop to work on the receptacles. If screws secure the front edge of the cooktop, remove them before raising the top.

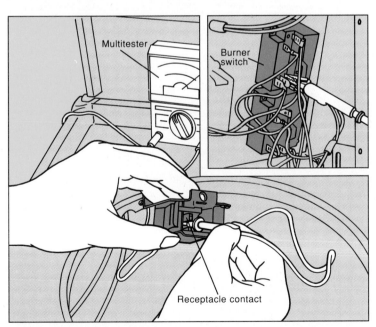

Multitester

Burner switch

Receptacle contact

3 **Testing the receptacle.** Since damage to a receptacle is not always visible, test it for continuity. With the power disconnected, gain access to the range switches and controls *(page 242)*. Trace the wires from the receptacle to the corresponding terminals on the burner switch (usually marked H1 and H2). Clip one probe of the multitester probe to a terminal *(inset)*, and touch the other to each of the receptacle contacts in turn *(above)*. Only one contact should show continuity. Repeat with a probe on the second switch terminal *(above)*. The other contact should show continuity.

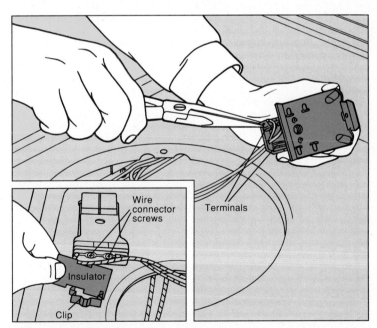

Wire connector screws

Terminals

Insulator

Clip

4 **Replacing the receptacle.** Use long-nose pliers to pull the wire connectors from the receptacle terminals *(above)*. To install a new receptacle, reattach a connector wire to each terminal and screw the receptacle firmly to the range. On some models, you must cut the wires leading to the receptacle and splice a new one in place with a wire connector *(page 417)*. If the receptacle's wiring connections are covered by a card-like insulator, snap off the clip with a screwdriver to remove the insulator, then unscrew the wires *(inset)*. Screw the wires to the new receptacle and clip on the insulator.

TESTING AND REPLACING BURNER ELEMENT SWITCHES

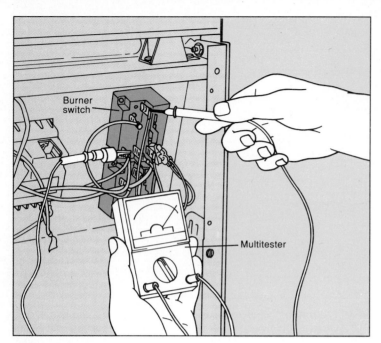

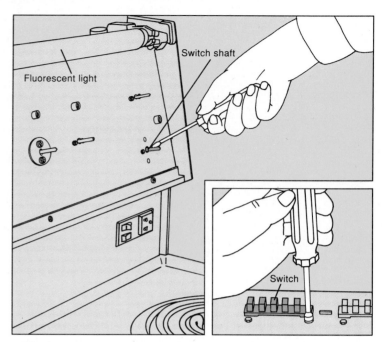

1 **Testing a burner switch.** Disconnect the power and gain access to the range controls and switches *(page 242)*. Replace any switch with a mechanical problem, such as a jammed button *(step 2)*. Check the switch wires for loose connections. If the switch terminals are damaged, replace the switch and any burned wire connectors *(page 417)*. If there is no visible damage, test the switch for continuity. The power supply wires are attached to terminals marked L1 and L2 (and a terminal marked N on some switches). Wires leading to the burner element are marked H1 and H2 (or just numbered). Turn on a working switch and test each power supply terminal, in turn, against each burner element terminal in the switch position that does not heat; disconnect one wire in each pair being tested. Then test the suspect switch *(above)*; if the results don't match, replace it.

2 **Removing the switch.** To remove a rotary switch, pull off the control knob and remove the two screws holding the switch to the control panel *(above)*. Pull the switch out through the back. If a glass panel covers the screws, first pull off all the control knobs and check for clips or trim pieces at the top or sides of the panel—you may have to raise the fluorescent light cover. Unclip the panel or unscrew the trim pieces, and lift out the panel. Pushbutton switches may be trimmed by a removable panel that covers the mounting screws; unfasten the clips holding the panel and pry it up by hand. Remove the switch screws *(inset)* and lift out the switch through the back .

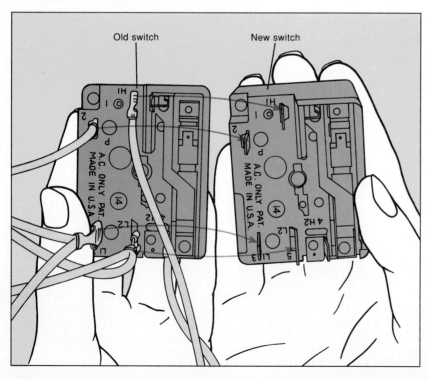

3 **Replacing the switch.** Leave the wires connected to the old switch while you buy a replacement part for the make and model of your appliance. (If you leave the control panel disassembled, leave a note taped to it warning other members of the household not to reconnect the power.) Replace the switch in one of two ways *(left)*: Transfer the wires from the old switch to the same terminals on the new switch one by one. Or, after labeling the position of each wire with masking tape, disconnect all the wires from the old switch, and connect them to the new switch. Screw the new switch to the control panel and replace the control panel cover, trim, and control knobs.

REPLACING OVEN ELEMENTS

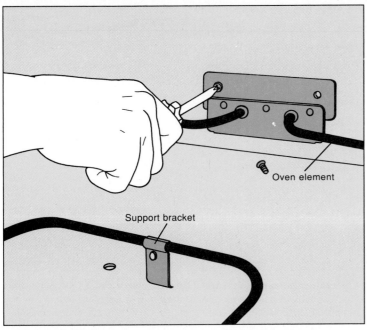

Oven element

Support bracket

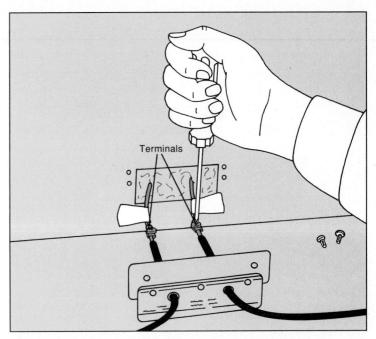

Terminals

1 **Dismounting the oven element.** Bake and broil elements are tested and replaced in the same way. Disconnect power to the range. For easy access to the oven, remove the door *(page 242)*. Remove the screws or nuts that fasten the element to the back of the oven *(above)*. The element may also have a front support bracket; unscrew it if necessary. Gently pull the element forward a few inches to expose its wiring. If the capillary tube is in the way of the broil element, unclip the tube from its support without bending it *(page 247)*. **Caution:** In self-cleaning ovens, the tube contains a caustic fluid—wear rubber gloves and use caution when handling it.

2 **Disconnecting the element.** Label the wire positions with masking tape and unscrew them from the element terminals *(above)*. Avoid bending the terminals. Do not allow the wires to fall back through the opening—otherwise, the range must be pulled out from the wall and opened to retrieve them. Check the wire connectors for burns; if damaged, cut them off and replace them *(page 417)*. Remove the element from the oven. Some older models have plug-in elements that can be pulled out rather than unscrewed.

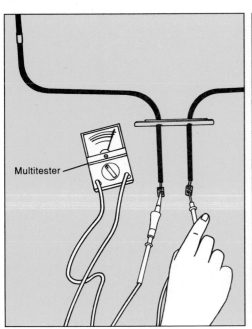

Multitester

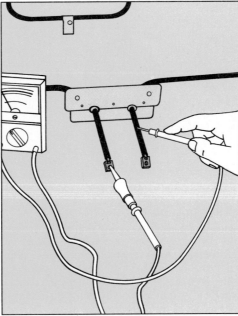

3 **Testing and replacing the oven element.** With a multitester set at RX1, touch a probe to each of the element terminals *(far left)*; there should be only partial resistance. If not, replace the element with a new one of the same wattage. Next, test for a ground with one probe on a terminal and the other on the metal sheath of the element *(near left)*; the multitester needle should not move. If the element fails either of these tests, replace it. To install a new element, reconnect the wires to the element terminals and screw the rear support bracket firmly in place for proper grounding. Reattach the support bracket if necessary and make sure the capillary tube is properly seated in its clips.

CHECKING AND ADJUSTING OVEN TEMPERATURE

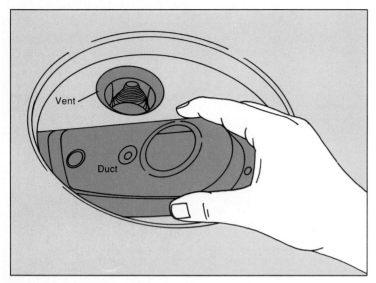

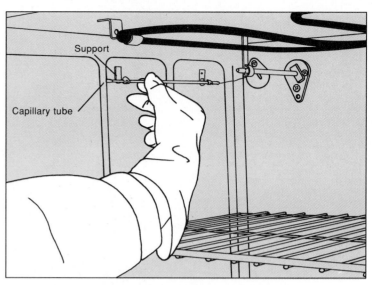

Checking and cleaning the oven vent. The vent helps control the circulation of air in the oven—and therefore the oven temperature—by conducting hot air through a duct under a burner, usually the right rear element. Disconnect power to the range. Pull out the burner, or raise it out of the way, and remove the drip pan. Lift out the vent duct *(above)* to expose the vent—you may need to unscrew the duct first. Clean the vent and wash the duct in hot, soapy water. When replacing the duct, be sure its opening will line up with the hole in the drip pan before screwing it in position. Replace the drip pan and burner.

Checking the capillary tube. Clipped to the inside of the oven, the capillary tube senses oven temperature and is adjusted by the oven temperature control. If the tube touches the oven wall, reposition it in its support clips *(above)*. If it is broken, both the tube and the temperature control switch must be replaced *(page 247)*. **Caution:** In self-cleaning ovens, the tube contains caustic chemicals. Wear rubber gloves and avoid bending the tube when handling it. If you should get the contents on your skin, wipe with a dry towel before washing with mild soap and water.

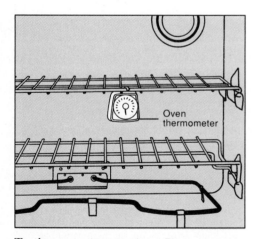

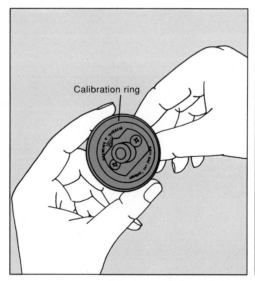

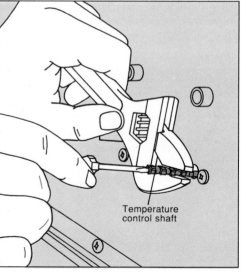

Testing oven temperature. Place an oven thermometer in the center of the oven *(above)* and set the temperature control switch at 350°F. Wait 20 minutes, then check the thermometer. Take three more readings, one every ten minutes. Add the readings and divide by four; the average should be 350°F. If your result is off by 25°F or less, the control is normal; by 25°F to 50°F, recalibrate it *(step, right)*. If it is off by more than 50°F, replace the control *(page 247)*.

Calibrating the temperature control. Pull the knob off the oven temperature control. If the back of the knob has a ring with marks indicating "Raise" and "Lower", turn the knob to move the ring *(above, left)*; you may first have to loosen two screws on the ring. If the calibration ring is mounted on the range under the knob, turn off the power *(page 102)*, then loosen the screws to adjust the ring. Give the shaft one-eighth turn *(above, right)* to the right to lower the temperature, or to the left to raise it. Check the temperature again after calibration. If calibration doesn't work, replace the temperature control *(page 247)*.

TESTING AND REPLACING THE OVEN TEMPERATURE CONTROL

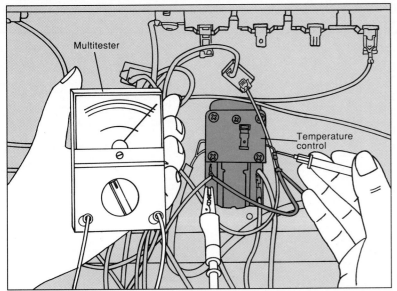

Multitester

Temperature control

1 Testing the temperature control. Turn off power to the range and open the control panel *(page 242)*. If any of the temperature control terminals are discolored or burned, replace the temperature control. Next, test the control for continuity. If it has more than two terminals, refer to the wiring diagram—on the rear panel, or inside the storage drawer or control panel—for the correct pairs of terminals to test. Disconnect one wire of the pair, clip a tester probe to one terminal, and turn the switch to 300°F. Then touch the tester probe to the other terminal *(left)*: If any of the circuits do not show continuity, replace the temperature control.

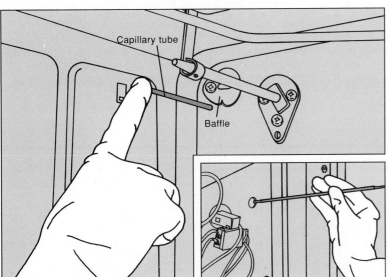

Capillary tube

Baffle

2 Removing the capillary tube. This tube leads from the temperature control into the oven. Gently unclip the tube from the supports in the oven and push it through the hole in the rear wall *(left)*; you may have to loosen a screw that secures a baffle over the hole and slide the baffle aside. From the back of the range, pull the tube completely out of the oven *(inset)*. **Caution:** In self-cleaning ovens, the tube is filled with caustic chemicals. Wear goggles and rubber gloves, and avoid bending the tube. If you should get the contents on your skin, wipe with a dry towel before washing with mild soap and water.

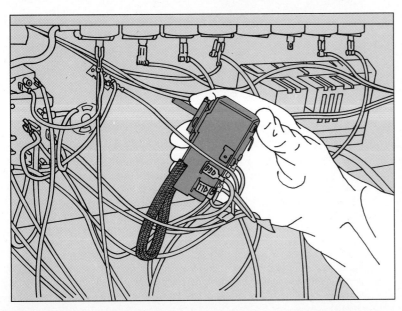

3 Removing and replacing the temperature control. Unscrew the two temperature control screws in front and remove the control from the back of the range *(left)*. Label the positions of the wires and disconnect them from the control. Replace any burned wire connectors *(page 417)*. To install a new temperature control, connect the wires to the terminals and screw the new switch to the control panel. Push the capillary tube gently into the oven through the the back, taking care not to bend or kink it, and clip it into its supports. Replace the rear panel, the front panel and the control knobs. Before replacing the knob, check that the calibration ring is centered. If not, reset it *(page 246)*.

TESTING AND REPLACING THE OVEN SELECTOR SWITCH

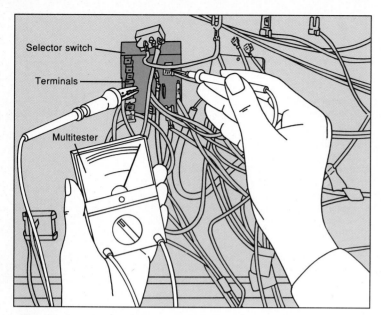

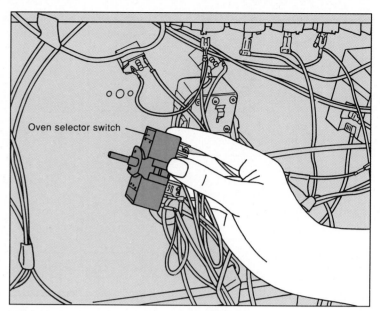

1 **Testing the oven selector switch.** Since it controls the bake, broil, timed bake, and clean functions, a broken selector switch can cause any of these cycles not to work. Disconnect power to the range and open the control panel *(page 242)*. Replace the switch if any terminals are burned. Test the switch for continuity; the correct pairs of terminals to test for each switch setting are indicated on the wiring diagram. Disconnect one wire from each pair of terminals being tested, and check for continuity at each position of the switch *(above)*. Replace the switch if it fails the test.

2 **Replacing the oven selector switch.** Remove the screws from the front of the control panel and pull the switch out from the back *(above)*. Label the wires and disconnect them. Replace any burned or corroded wire connectors *(page 417)*. To install a new switch, connect the wires to the terminals and screw the switch securely to the control panel to ensure proper grounding. Reassemble the control panel.

REPAIRING WIRED BURNER ELEMENTS

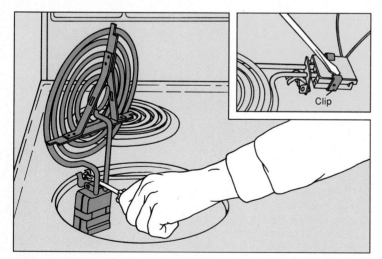

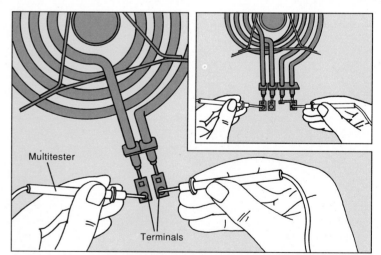

1 **Disconnecting a wired element.** The burners on some ranges are connected directly to the burner switch wires; this connection is protected by a glass or ceramic block. Lift the element and inspect its coils for burns or holes, and replace if damaged. To remove the element, turn off power to the range, remove the drip pan and unscrew the element and block from the range *(above)*. Use a screwdriver to pry off the clips joining the two halves of the block *(inset)*, and pull them apart to expose the screws that connect the wires. Tighten loose connections or repair burned wiring *(page 417)*. To test the element, unscrew the wires without bending the terminals. If there are more than two wires, label their positions with masking tape.

2 **Testing a wired element.** With a multitester set at RX1, touch one probe to each element terminal *(above)*; the meter should show only partial resistance. Next, test for a ground with one probe on a terminal and the other on the coil sheathing. The needle should not move. If the element has several terminals, half of them lead to a common terminal. Touch one probe to the common terminal and touch the other to each terminal in turn *(inset)*; the multitester should show partial resistance. Test for a ground by touching one probe to the coil sheathing and the other to each terminal in turn; there should be no continuity. To install a new element, screw the wires to the proper terminals, clip the insulating block in place and screw the element to the range.

SERVICING THE OVEN LIGHT, SWITCH AND SOCKET

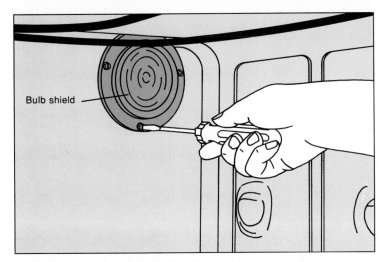

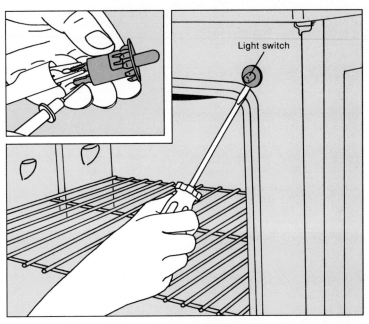

Replacing the oven light bulb. Disconnect power to the range *(page 102)*. In ovens with a wire protector or a glass shield covering the bulb, first pull down the wire protector, or unscrew the glass shield *(above)*. Unscrew the bulb, using a dry cloth to protect your hand. If the bulb breaks in the socket, be sure the power is disconnected before removing the remnants with long-nose pliers. Screw in a regular 40-watt bulb; if it works, the problem is simply a burned-out bulb. Replace it with an appliance bulb of the same size and wattage. If not, check the switch or the socket.

Testing and replacing a door-operated light switch. Disconnect power to the range and open the oven door. Pry out the switch, pushing in the spring clips with a screwdriver *(above)*. To test the switch, disconnect the wires and clip a continuity tester to each terminal *(inset)*. With the switch plunger in, there should be no continuity; when released, the plunger should show continuity. If it fails the test, replace the switch. Attach the wires to the new switch and snap it into place.

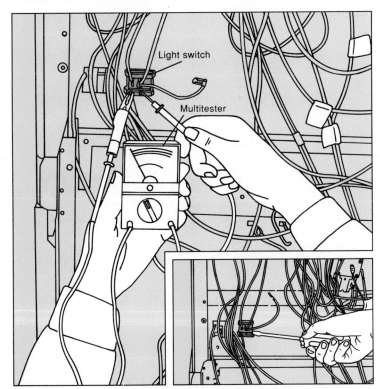

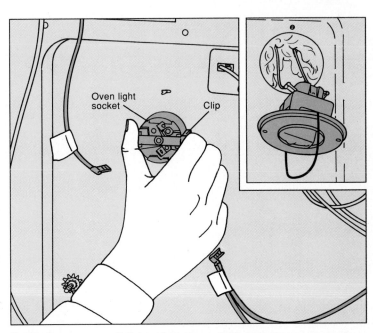

Testing and replacing a panel-mounted light switch. Disconnect power to the range *(page 102)* and open the control panel *(page 242)*. Remove one wire from the light switch and clip one multitester probe to each terminal *(above)*. With the switch off there should be no continuity. Flip the switch on; the tester should show continuity. To replace a faulty switch, press in the spring clips with a screwdriver *(inset)*. Push the switch out through the front of the range. Disconnect the wires; cut them if they are permanently attached. Connect or splice the wires to the new switch *(page 417)* and snap it into place.

Replacing an oven light socket. Some light sockets are removed through the back of the range. With the power disconnected, remove the rear panel *(page 242)*. The socket's ceramic base has spring clips; use a screwdriver to push in the clips, then pull out the socket *(above)*. On some models, you must first unscrew a socket assembly, and then push the socket out of the assembly. Disconnect the wires, insert a new socket and reconnect the wires. In other ranges, the light socket is accessible through the oven. Disconnect the power. Unscrew the socket assembly and pull it into the oven *(inset)*. Disconnect the wires and release the socket by squeezing the locking tabs on each side. Snap in a new socket, connect the wires and put back the assembly.

REPLACING THE OVEN GASKET

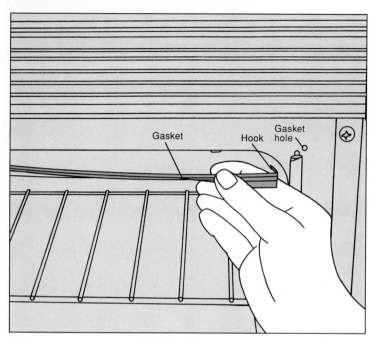

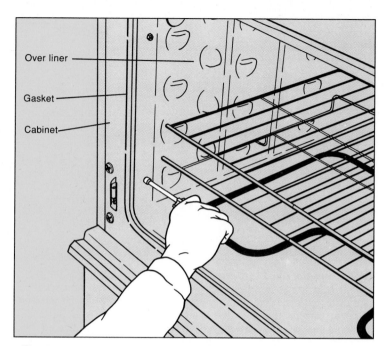

1 Checking the oven gasket. The gasket on many ovens is a simple rubber channel clipped onto the cabinet. To replace this gasket, disengage the damaged section by hand and hook a new one in place *(above)*. Other cabinet-mounted gaskets are clamped between the oven liner and the range cabinet *(step 2)*.

On self-cleaning ovens, the gasket is removed by disassembling the door; to ensure a secure seal, call for service.

2 Removing the oven retaining screws. To remove a gasket clamped between the oven liner and the range cabinet, you must free the oven liner and pull it forward. Disconnect power to the range *(page 102)* and remove the oven door to make the job easier. Check around the front edge of the oven for screws holding the oven liner in place; remove them *(above)* and go to step 4. If there are no screws, the oven liner is probably fastened at the back *(step 3)*.

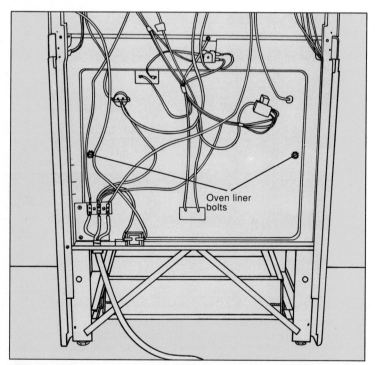

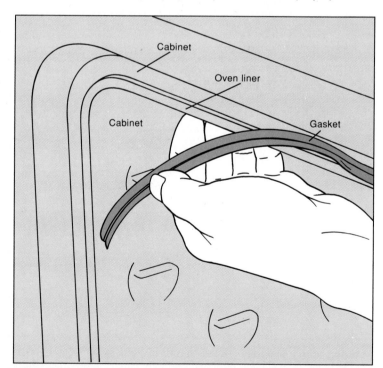

3 Loosening the oven liner bolts. With power to the range disconnected, pull it away from the wall. Unscrew the back panel *(page 242)*. Check for two bolts that protrude from the back of the range, one at each side *(above)*. If you can't find them, call a service technician to replace the gasket. Loosen the nuts on the bolts 1/4 inch.

4 Removing and replacing the gasket. Remove any retaining screws or clips at the front of the liner. Pull out the oven liner about 1/8 inch by rocking it back and forth. Disengage the gasket from between the liner and cabinet *(above)*. Position the lip of a new gasket behind the rim of the oven liner. Push the liner into place and replace the screws at the front or tighten the nuts at the back. Reinstall the oven door or rear panel and reconnect the power.

ADJUSTING THE OVEN DOOR

1 **Loosening the oven door panels.** The oven door can become warped over time, resulting in a poor seal. Discoloration or traces of soot around the door indicate that heat is escaping from the oven. Before adjusting a removable door, check that it is seated properly on its hinges. To adjust the door, first turn off power to the range *(page 102)*. Open the door and loosen—but don't remove—the screws that secure the inner door panel to the outer panel *(above)*. You may also have to loosen screws on the door handle and around the edge of the outer panel.

2 **Adjusting the door fit.** Holding the door at the top, twist it gently from side to side to straighten it *(above)*. On oven doors with a glass front or a window, be careful to shift the door only slightly. Partially tighten the door screws. Check the seal by pressing the top corners of the door against the oven. You may have to adjust the door several times for a good fit. Tighten the screws securely but do not overtighten—the porcelain could chip.

ADJUSTING THE OVEN DOOR SPRINGS

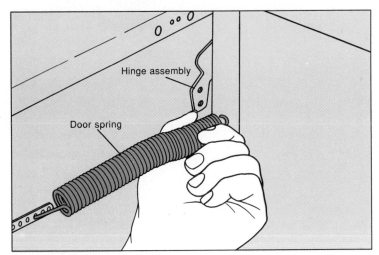

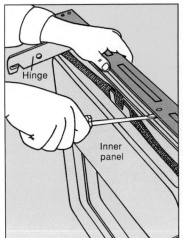

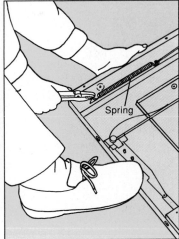

Adjusting cabinet-mounted springs. Turn off power to the range *(page 102)* and remove the oven door *(page 242)*. Hinge arms that protrude from the door indicate door-mounted springs, described at right. Otherwise, the springs are cabinet-mounted, as shown. Pull out the lower storage drawer. If you can't find the springs on each side of the cabinet, remove the side panels or call for service. (The springs on wall ovens and slide-in ranges are usually not accessible.) If one spring is broken, replace both. Wearing safety goggles, lift and unhook the hinge end *(above)*; if the spring is very stiff, grasp it with locking pliers. To increase the door tension, rehook the spring into a lower hole on the hinge assembly; to decrease tension hook it into a higher hole. Repeat with the other spring. Replace the door; if the tension is incorrect, readjust the springs.

Adjusting door-mounted springs. With the power off, remove the oven door *(page 242)*. Remove the screws on the inner door panel and along the edges of the outer panel. You may also have to remove the door handle. There may be tabs on one panel that fit into slots in the other; use a screwdriver to pry up the tabs *(above, left)*. Starting at the top, lift the inner panel free. Remove any insulation covering the springs. Lay the door on a table or the floor and inspect the springs; if one spring is worn or broken, replace both. Wearing safety goggles, unhook one end of the spring and insert it into the next hole in the hinge assembly. If the spring is stiff, brace the door with your hand or foot and use locking pliers to pry up one end of the spring and rehook it firmly in place *(above, right)*. Reassemble the door.

DISHWASHERS

The dishwasher combines water pressure, detergent and heat to clean dishes and kitchen utensils more thoroughly and efficiently than hand washing. Although a dishwasher is a complex machine, its most common problems are usually due to simple failures that are easy to fix.

During a typical 75-minute cycle, the dishwasher tub fills with hot water, which mixes with detergent released by the detergent dispenser. The detergent-and-water solution is then kept at about 150°F by the heating element and pumped through the spray tower and spray arm, which spins about 40 times a minute, hurling the mixture against the dishes and washing away even hardened food waste. After the dishes are rinsed and the dishwasher drained, the air inside the machine is warmed by the heating element, drying the dishes. (Some newer models have an energy-saver feature that turns off the heating element during the drying cycle, using a small blower to air dry the dishes.)

Built-in dishwashers are installed under a kitchen counter with permanent plumbing and wiring connections. Portable models have a plastic coupler so that they can be connected to the sink faucet and drain, casters that allow them to be rolled to and from the sink and a power cord that plugs into a grounded, 120-volt outlet.

The most common dishwasher problem is incomplete cleaning. Before repairing the appliance itself, check for other possible causes: improper loading, low water temperature, low water pressure, and ineffective detergent. Always scrape off dishes, pots and pans before loading. Large pieces of food can clog

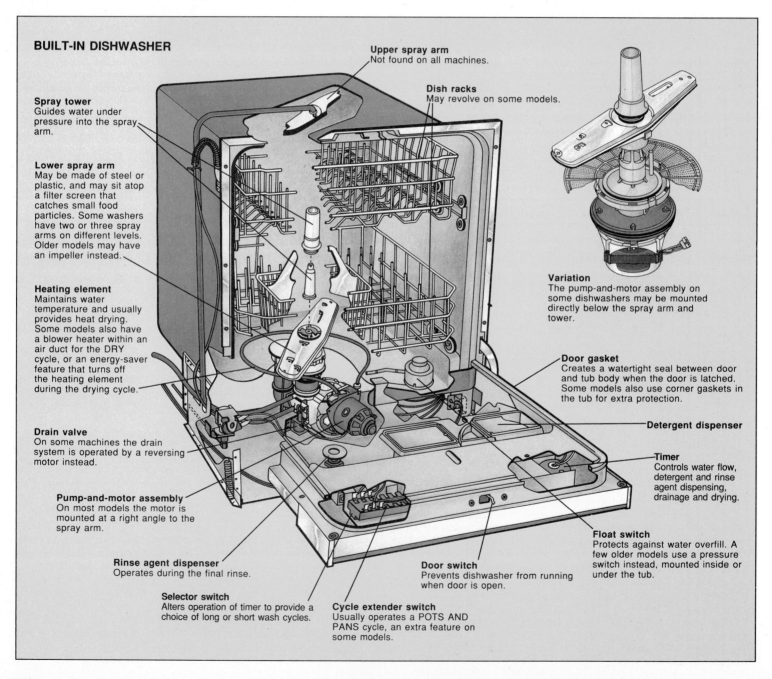

BUILT-IN DISHWASHER

Upper spray arm
Not found on all machines.

Dish racks
May revolve on some models.

Spray tower
Guides water under pressure into the spray arm.

Lower spray arm
May be made of steel or plastic, and may sit atop a filter screen that catches small food particles. Some washers have two or three spray arms on different levels. Older models may have an impeller instead.

Heating element
Maintains water temperature and usually provides heat drying. Some models also have a blower heater within an air duct for the DRY cycle, or an energy-saver feature that turns off the heating element during the drying cycle.

Drain valve
On some machines the drain system is operated by a reversing motor instead.

Pump-and-motor assembly
On most models the motor is mounted at a right angle to the spray arm.

Rinse agent dispenser
Operates during the final rinse.

Selector switch
Alters operation of timer to provide a choice of long or short wash cycles.

Cycle extender switch
Usually operates a POTS AND PANS cycle, an extra feature on some models.

Door switch
Prevents dishwasher from running when door is open.

Variation
The pump-and-motor assembly on some dishwashers may be mounted directly below the spray arm and tower.

Door gasket
Creates a watertight seal between door and tub body when the door is latched. Some models also use corner gaskets in the tub for extra protection.

Detergent dispenser

Timer
Controls water flow, detergent and rinse agent dispensing, drainage and drying.

Float switch
Protects against water overfill. A few older models use a pressure switch instead, mounted inside or under the tub.

filters and small, hard objects such as olive pits can stop up drainpipes. They can also block the air gap—a device required by many plumbing codes—which prevents water backing up into the dishwasher. (Portable models do not require one.)

Water temperature is critical. For clean dishes, the water must be between 140°F and 160°F; a lower temperature won't dissolve grease or detergent. The water pressure to the dishwasher must be adequate, too. If pressure is too low, run the dishwasher only when no water is being used elsewhere in the house.

Your use of detergent can also affect how well your dishes come clean. Avoid using old dishwashing detergent; it can become ineffective in as little as two weeks after the foil seal is broken. If the water in your area is hard—high in mineral content—you may need to use more detergent. Having a water softener installed (*page 94*) will help save on detergent. If your machine has a rinse agent dispenser; be sure it is filled. A rinse agent makes water flow off dishes faster than normal, reducing water spotting. Read the dishwasher's Use and Care manual for directions about arranging dishes in the machine.

The most difficult dishwasher repair involves servicing the pump and motor. An improperly installed pump seal, for example, can cause a leak into the motor, severely damaging the dishwasher. Therefore, if you suspect that the pump or motor is faulty, call for professional service.

When repairing a dishwasher, always turn off power at the main service panel or, for portable models, unplug the machine. For instructions on testing electrical components with a multitester, consult Tools & Techniques (*page 417*).

TROUBLESHOOTING GUIDE continued ►

SYMPTOM	POSSIBLE CAUSE	PROCEDURE
Dishes dirty or spotted after washing	Dishes loaded incorrectly	Rearrange dishes following manufacturer's loading instructions
	Water not hot enough	Test water temperature (*p. 263*) □○; if lower than 140°F, raise temperature at water heater
	Water pressure too low	Check water pressure (*p. 264*) □○; if low, avoid using house water supply while dishwasher is running
	Detergent ineffective	Make sure detergent is made for dishwashers; try different brands to find one effective for local water conditions
	Detergent dispenser faulty	Check for binding or broken parts (*p. 260*) □○
	Rinse agent dispenser empty	Refill dispenser
	Rinse agent leaking	Tighten loose fill cap; check rinse agent dispenser washers or gaskets; replace cracked dispenser (*p. 260*) □○
	Rinse agent dispenser faulty	Test bimetal terminals on rinse agent dispenser (*p. 260*) ▣●
	Spray arm stuck or clogged	Look for obstructions, such as measuring spoons, which fall under racks and block sprayer; check and clean spray arm (*p. 262*) □○
	Heating element faulty	Test heating element (*p. 263*) ▣●▲
	Selector switch or timer faulty	Test selector switch (*p. 257*) ▣●▲ and timer (*p. 258*) ▣●▲
	Pump clogged; impeller corroded, worn or chipped	Call for service
Dishwasher doesn't fill with water	Water supply line turned off	Open shutoff valve to dishwasher, faucet and main water supply
	Shutoff valve faulty	Replace dishwasher shutoff valve (*p. 417*) ▣●▲
	Water inlet valve fauty or valve screen clogged	Test water inlet valve solenoid ▣●▲ and inspect filter screen (*p. 261*) ▣●
	Float or float switch jammed or faulty	Inspect float; test float switch (*p. 264*) ▣●▲
	Door switch faulty	Adjust door catch; test door switch (*p. 259*) ▣●▲
	With a low buzzing sound: Filter under spray arm clogged (models with filter)	Remove filter and clean it under running water
	Faucet coupler clogged (portable models)	Clean or replace screen in coupler □○
Dishwasher drains during fill	Drain valve stuck open	Inspect drain valve; test-drain dishwasher with valve solenoid open and replace if necessary (*p. 265*) ▣●▲
Timer doesn't advance	Timer faulty	Test timer (*p. 258*) ▣●▲

DEGREE OF DIFFICULTY: □ Easy ▣ Moderate ▇ Complex
ESTIMATED TIME: ○ Less than 1 hour ◔ 1 to 3 hours ● Over 3 hours   ▲ Multitester required

TROUBLESHOOTING GUIDE (continued)

SYMPTOM	POSSIBLE CAUSE	PROCEDURE
Water doesn't shut off	Float or float switch jammed or faulty	Inspect float; test float switch (p. 264) ▭◕▲
	Water inlet valve solenoid faulty	Test water inlet valve solenoid; replace valve (p. 261) ▭◕▲
	Water inlet valve screen clogged	Remove water inlet valve; clean or replace screen (p. 261) ▭◕
	Timer faulty	Test timer (p. 258) ▭◕▲
Motor doesn't run	No power to dishwasher	Check for blown fuse or tripped circuit breaker (p. 102) □○
	Door switch faulty	Adjust door catch; test door switch (p. 259) ▭◕▲
	Timer faulty	Test timer (p. 258) ▭◕▲
	Motor faulty	Call for service
Motor hums, but doesn't run	Door switch faulty	Adjust door catch; test door switch (p. 259) ▭◕▲
	Timer faulty	Test timer (p. 258) ▭◕▲
	Motor faulty	Call for service
	Impeller jammed (older models)	Call for service
Poor water drainage	Air gap clogged	Clean air gap: remove cover, unscrew cap and use tweezers to remove obstruction in tube
	Spray arm or filter screen clogged	Clean spray arm (p. 262) □○; if model has filter screen underneath spray arm, inspect and clean
	Drain hose blocked	Inspect drain hose (p. 261) ▭◕
	Drain valve solenoid faulty	Test drain valve solenoid (p. 265) ▭◕▲
	Timer faulty	Test timer (p. 258) ▭◕▲
	Pump impeller clogged or broken	Call for service
	Reversing motor doesn't reverse	Check motor for number of wires (p. 265) □○; only motors with four wires are reversible. Call for service
Dishwasher leaks around door	Use of wrong detergent	Use detergent recommended for dishwashers; do not prewash dishes with liquid detergent
	Dishes deflecting water through door vent	Reposition dishes in racks
	Door not closing tightly on gasket	Adjust door catch (p. 259) □○
	Door gasket hardened or damaged	Replace door gasket (p. 260) □○
Dishwasher leaks from bottom	Tub cracked	Seal crack with silicone rubber sealant or waterproof epoxy glue
	Water inlet valve connection loose	Tighten water inlet connection (p. 261) □○
	Hose split; hose clamp loose	Inspect hoses; adjust or replace clamps (p. 261) ▭◕
	Spray arm broken	Check spray arm (p. 262) □○
	Pump seal faulty	Call for service
Dishwasher doesn't turn off	Timer faulty	Test timer (p. 258) ▭◕▲
	Cycle extender switch faulty	Test cycle extender switch (p. 257) ▭◕▲
Dishwasher noisy	Dishes loaded improperly	Reposition dishes according to manufacturer's recommendations
	Water pressure too low	Check water pressure; (p. 264) □○; if low, avoid using house water supply while dishwasher is running
	Water inlet valve screen clogged	Check water inlet valve screen (p. 261) ▭◕
	With a knocking sound during fill: Water inlet valve faulty	Test water inlet valve solenoid (p. 261) ▭◕▲
Door drops hard when opened	Door springs worn	Replace door springs (p. 259) □◕
Door is difficult to close	Door catch not closing properly	Adjust door catch (p. 259) □○
	Door catch bent or broken	Replace catch (p. 259) ▭◕

DEGREE OF DIFFICULTY: □ Easy ▭ Moderate ■ Complex
ESTIMATED TIME: ○ Less than 1 hour ◕ 1 to 3 hours ● Over 3 hours

▲ Multitester required

ACCESS THROUGH THE CONTROL PANEL

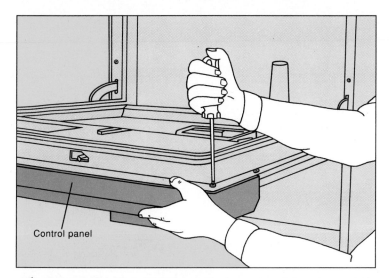

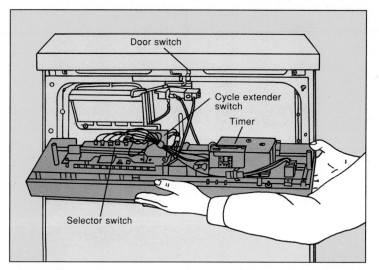

1 **Unscrewing the control panel.** Accessing dishwasher parts is often more than half the job. Turn off power to the dishwasher. Remove the control panel retaining screws located, in most cases, inside the dishwasher door. Hold the control panel to keep it from falling.

2 **Freeing the control panel.** Close the dishwasher door. Supporting the panel to avoid damaging wires, lower it away from the door *(above)*. (On some machines, you may first have to remove the door handle or door panel.) You now have access to the selector switch, cycle extender switch, door switch and timer.

ACCESS THROUGH THE DOOR PANEL

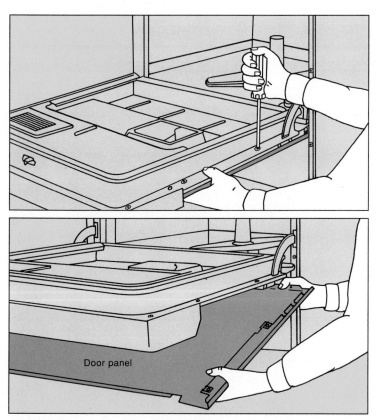

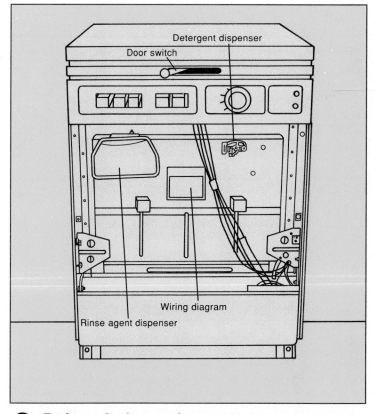

1 **Removing the door panel.** Turn off power to the dishwasher. Open the door and, keeping one hand underneath it to support the panel, remove the retaining screws *(above, top)* and lower the panel away *(above, bottom)*. On some dishwashers you must lift the metal strips to reach hidden screws.

2 **Getting to the door panel parts.** With the control panel and door panel removed, you now have access to the door switch, detergent and rinse agent dispensers, and the wiring diagram.

ACCESS THROUGH THE LOWER PANEL

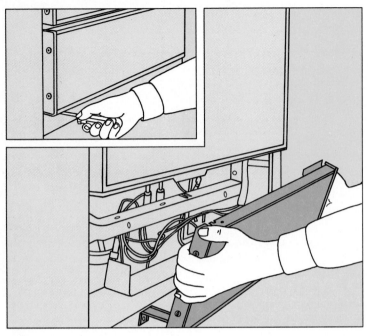

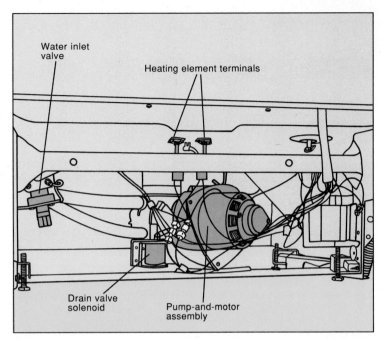

Water inlet valve

Heating element terminals

Drain valve solenoid

Pump-and-motor assembly

1 **Removing the lower panel.** Turn off power to the dishwasher. On some models, you must first remove retaining screws *(inset)* then, to free the panel, pull it down or lift it off hooks *(above)*.

2 **Gaining access to parts under the tub.** With the lower panel removed, you have access to the water inlet valve, heating element terminals, pump-and-motor assembly and drain valve solenoid. Some of these parts are hard to reach, so for complicated repairs on a built-in model, pull the machine free from the counter and tilt it on its back *(below)*.

FREEING AND TILTING THE MACHINE

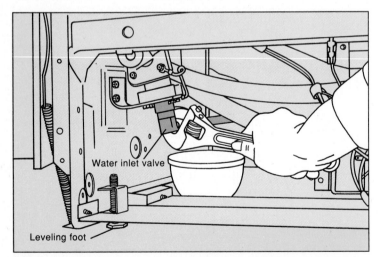

Water inlet valve

Leveling foot

1 **Disconnecting the power and water supply.** Turn off the water and power supply at their sources. Open the door and remove the screws that secure the top of the dishwasher to the kitchen counter. Remove the lower panel *(step 1, above),* then turn the threaded leveling feet to lower the dishwasher slightly. Keeping a shallow pan handy to catch dripping water, use a wrench to disconnect the water supply line from the water inlet valve *(above)*. Disconnect the drain hose from the sink drain or garbage disposer. Unscrew the cover of the power cord junction box, near floor level, and disconnect the power cord.

2 **Tilting the dishwasher.** Slide a blanket beneath the machine to protect the floor from scratches, then rock the appliance clear of the cabinet. Make sure you have a steady grip on the machine, and with your legs bent, gently lower it backward *(above)*.

SERVICING THE SELECTOR SWITCH

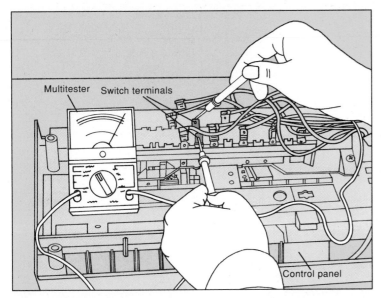

1 **Testing the selector switch.** After turning off the power or unplugging the power cord, remove the control panel *(page 255)* and inspect the selector switch. Repair any loose or broken wires *(page 417)*. Refer to the wiring diagram to test each pair of switch terminals for continuity, using a continuity tester or a multitester set at RX1 *(above)*. To make sure you reconnect the wires properly, disconnect only two at a time, reconnecting them before moving on to the next set. If any pair of terminals fails to show continuity with the appropriate switch button pressed, remove and replace that switch.

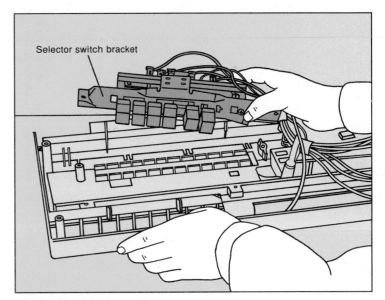

2 **Replacing the selector switch.** Detach the selector switch bracket from the control panel by removing the mounting screws and lifting the bracket from the control panel *(above)*. Pull the buttons off, keeping them in order for reinstallation. Unscrew the faulty switch from its bracket, leaving the wires attached. Install a new switch and replace the buttons. Finally, transfer the wires one by one from the old switch to the same terminals on the new switch. Replace the bracket in the control panel.

SERVICING THE CYCLE EXTENDER SWITCH

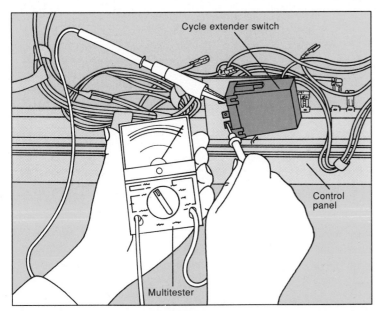

1 **Testing the cycle extender switch.** Turn off power to the dishwasher, remove the control panel *(page 255)* and inspect the switch. Repair any loose or broken wires *(page 417)*. Disconnect the wires from the switch terminals and label their positions. With a multitester set at RX1, test terminals H2 and L2 for continuity *(above)*. Then set the multitester at RX100 and test terminals H2 and H1; they should show resistance. If the switch is faulty, replace it.

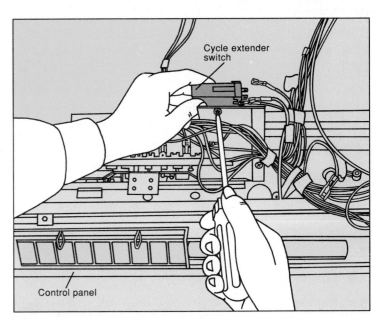

2 **Replacing the cycle extender switch.** Depending on your model, unscrew *(above)* or unclip the switch from the control panel. Install a new switch, reconnecting the wires one by one to the new terminals, and reinstall the control panel.

SERVICING THE TIMER

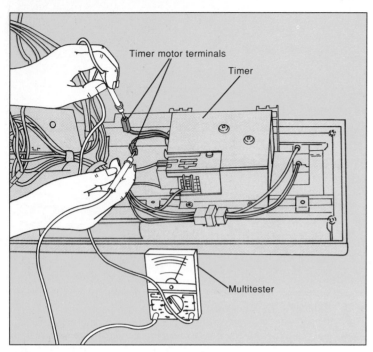

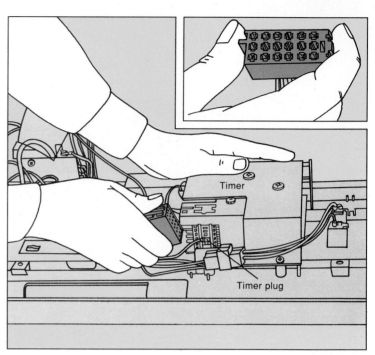

1 **Testing the timer motor.** After turning off power or unplugging the power cord, remove the control panel *(page 255)*. Disconnect the timer motor wires and, using a multitester set at RX100, test the timer motor terminals *(above)*; they should show partial resistance. If the motor is faulty, replace the entire timer *(step 4)*. If not, check the timer plug and terminals.

2 **Disconnecting the timer plug.** Keeping a solid grip on the timer plug, wiggle it away from the timer *(above)*. Once it is removed, inspect the plug *(inset)* for loose contacts. If any contacts protrude from the plug, push them back into place.

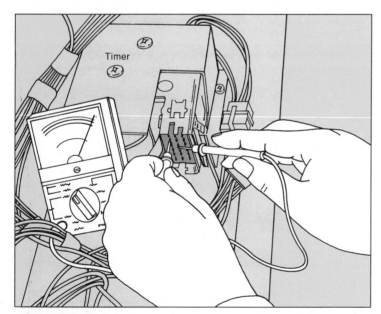

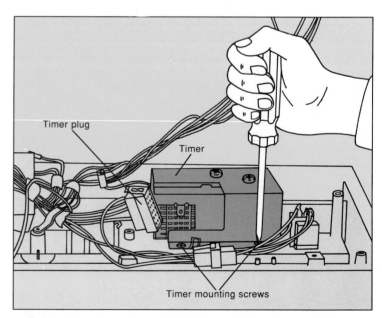

3 **Testing the timer terminals.** For this step, refer to the dishwasher's wiring diagram and timer chart, found inside the door panel or available from the manufacturer. Use the wiring diagram to identify the pairs of terminals that control the faulty cycle. Disconnect the wires from those terminals and test each pair for continuity with a multitester set at RX1 *(above)*. Turn the timer dial slowly through the full cycle. The timer chart will show at which points in the cycle there should be continuity. To make sure the wires are properly reconnected, replace each pair before disconnecting another pair. If any pair of terminals does not show continuity, replace the timer.

4 **Replacing the timer.** Pull off the timer dial by hand, then remove the timer mounting screws *(above)*. Disconnect all other wires, including the motor wires, and label them with masking tape for correct reassembly. Install a new timer, reconnect the wires and reinstall the timer plug. Replace the dial and the control panel.

SERVICING THE DOOR SWITCH

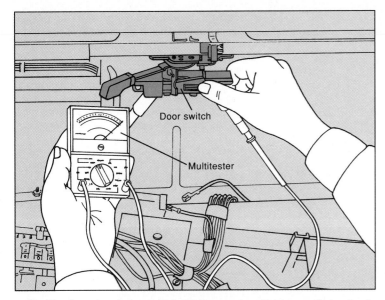

1 **Testing the door switch.** Before testing the door switch, check to see if the door catch closes securely. On many models, the catch can be tightened or repositioned by loosening the retaining screws, sliding the catch in or out, then retightening the screws. Otherwise shut off the power and remove the control panel *(page 255)*. With the door closed and locked, disconnect the wires from the door switch terminals and test for continuity using a multitester set at RX1 *(above)*. If there is no continuity, replace the switch.

2 **Replacing the door switch.** With the wires disconnected, remove the door switch retaining screws *(above)*, install a new switch and reconnect the wires.

REPLACING THE DOOR SPRINGS

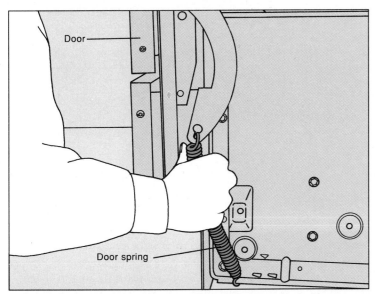

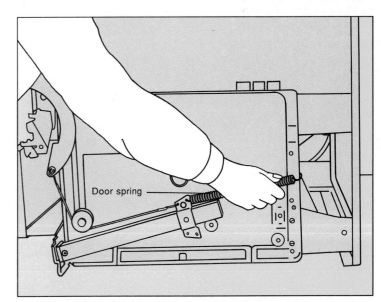

Replacing springs on built-in models. After turning off the power supply, locate the door springs. They are usually on the sides of the machine, under the front corners of the tub, so pull the dishwasher out from the counter *(page 256)*. If the springs are weak or broken, remove the ends from their holes by hand and replace them *(above)*. For proper tension, always replace door springs in pairs, even if only one is broken. If your dishwasher has a series of holes next to the pair on which the springs are hooked, you can adjust the tension by hooking each spring into a different hole.

Replacing springs on portable models. After unplugging the machine, remove the side panels by unscrewing the retaining screws that secure them to the frame. The springs are attached to an anti-tip mechanism that prevents the machine from falling forward when the door is opened and the racks pulled out. If the springs are weak or broken, replace them by hooking new springs into position *(above)*. For proper tension, always replace door springs in pairs, even if only one is broken.

REPLACING THE DOOR GASKET

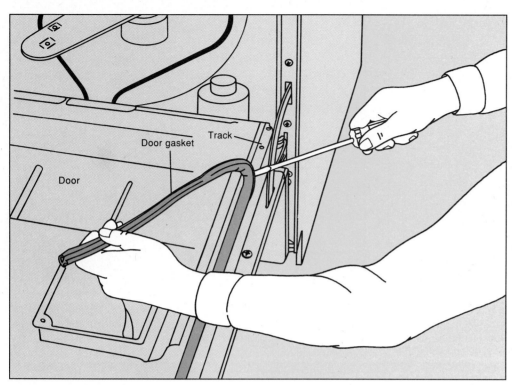

Inspecting and replacing the door gasket. Turn off power to the dishwasher. Open the dishwasher door, remove the dish racks and inspect the door gasket. If it is cracked or otherwise damaged, replace it with an identical gasket. Some may also have a tub gasket for extra protection; check this, too.

On some dishwashers, the gasket has clips or tabs that can be pried out with a screwdriver *(left)*. Other gaskets are secured with retaining screws. If the replacement gasket is kinked, soak it in warm water for a few minutes before installation. If the gasket slides into a track, lubricate the gasket with soapy water or silicone lubricant to make installation easier. (Do not use oil or grease.)

Press the center of the gasket into the top center of the door. Continue around the door, pressing into place several inches at a time. Secure the ends with the original clips or brackets.

If the gasket is good, check to see if the door catch closes securely. On many models, the catch can be tightened or repositioned by loosening the retaining screws, sliding the catch in or out, then retightening the screws.

CHECKING THE DETERGENT AND RINSE AGENT DISPENSERS

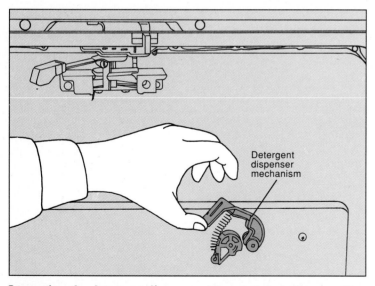

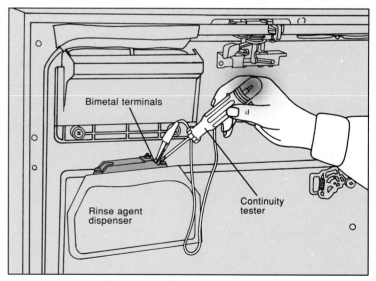

Inspecting the detergent dispenser. Although their design may differ, all detergent dispensers operate in much the same way. The dispenser is opened mechanically by the timer at a predetermined point during the cycle. Breakdowns, usually due to a damaged part, are infrequent. First turn off the power or unplug the dishwasher, then check the detergent cup inside the door for caked detergent; clean it if necessary. Also check the O-ring or gasket, if any, inside the cup's cover, and replace it if damaged. If your model has a movable cup, open and close it by hand to see if it is stuck or damaged. Next remove the door panel *(page 255)* and check the spring-and-lever mechanism for stuck or broken parts *(above)*. Replace any part that is damaged.

Inspecting the rinse agent dispenser. If your dishwasher has a rinse agent dispenser, the rinse agent is released either by an arm on the detergent dispenser or by the timer. First turn off power to the dishwasher and remove the door panel *(page 255)*. Make sure the fill cap is tight and inspect the rinse agent dispenser for signs of damage. If it is split or cracked, replace it. If your model resembles the one shown above, remove the wires to the bimetal terminals and test the terminals for continuity *(above)*. If there is no continuity, replace the bimetal assembly. If the dispenser leaks, check the washers or gaskets and replace them if cracked or brittle.

SERVICING THE WATER INLET VALVE

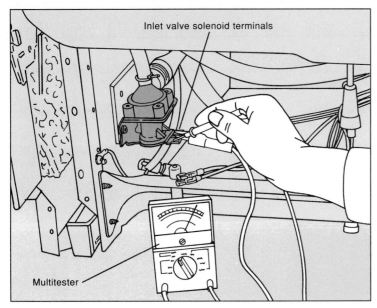

Inlet valve solenoid terminals

Multitester

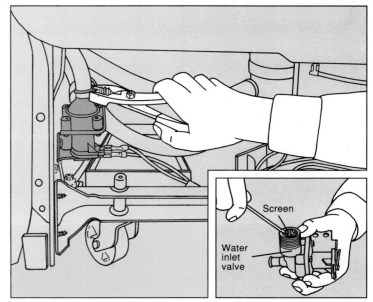

Screen

Water inlet valve

1 **Inspecting the water inlet valve solenoid.** Turn off the power and water supply to the dishwasher. Remove the lower panel *(page 256)*; you may also pull out the machine and tip it back for easier access. (On some portable models, remove the top of the machine to locate the water inlet valve.) If your machine leaks, make sure the incoming water line and the hose that connects the inlet valve to the tub are securely fastened. Tighten connections, if necessary, using an adjustable wrench or hose clamp pliers.

If you suspect the valve is faulty, remove the wires from the inlet valve solenoid terminals and test for continuity with a multitester set at RX1, as shown. If there is no continuity, remove and service the valve.

2 **Cleaning and replacing the water inlet valve.** With a shallow pan handy to catch dripping water, use hose clamp pliers to re-move the hose that connects the inlet valve to the tub *(above)*. Then use a wrench to disconnect the incoming water line. To free the water inlet valve, remove any screws that secure the valve bracket to the tub. If the valve is cracked or otherwise damaged, replace it.

Using a small screwdriver, pry out the water inlet valve screen *(inset)*. If it is a plastic screen, rinse it and clean it with an old tooth-brush, then replace it in the valve. If the screen is metal, it won't retain its shape; replace it with a new one. Reinstall the valve, water line and hose, tightening connections securely.

INSPECTING AND REPLACING THE DRAIN HOSE

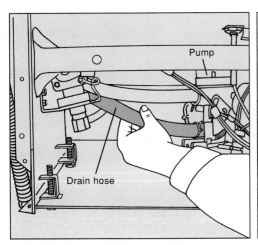

Pump

Drain hose

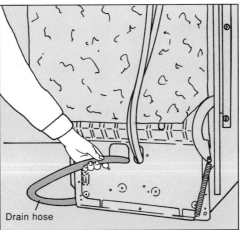

Drain hose

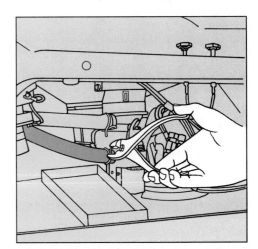

1 **Inspecting the drain hose.** Turn off the power and water supply to the dishwasher. Re-move the lower panel *(page 256)* and inspect the drain hose for kinks, cracks or splits. Begin at the pump, straightening kinks by hand *(above, left)*. If any kink remains, replace the hose. Also check that the hose clamp is secure; if not, reposition it with pliers.

If you don't find the problem under the dishwasher, follow the hose to the kitchen sink drain or garbage disposer (built-in model, *above, right*) or the faucet coupler (portable model). This means gaining access to the side of the dishwasher, so pull a built-in model away from the counter *(page 256)* or remove the side and top panels of a portable model *(page 259)*. If the hose is collapsed, kinked or cracked, replace it.

2 **Replacing the drain hose.** With a shallow pan handy to catch dripping water, disconnect the hose from the pump by squeezing the spring clamp with hose clamp pliers *(above)*. Then disconnect the hose under the kitchen sink drain (built-in models) or faucet coupler (portable models). Position the new hose and reconnect it at both ends with new clamps.

SERVICING THE SPRAY ARM

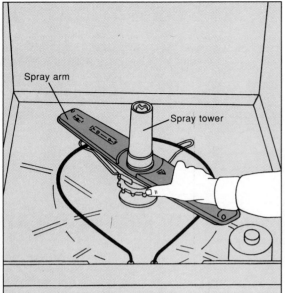

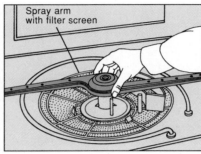

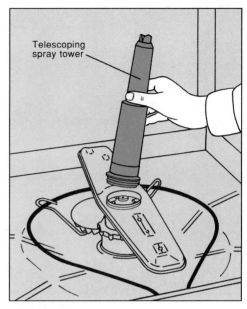

1 **Checking for obstructions.** Turn off power to the dishwasher and slide out the lower dish rack. Rotate the spray arm to see if it moves freely *(above)*; the ends of the arm should also move up and down slightly. If bent or damaged, replace the spray arm.

2 **Removing the spray tower.** If your model has a spray tower in addition to the spray arm, pull the telescoping parts to see if they move freely. Unscrew the tower by hand and remove it *(above)*. Check for clogs and clean if necessary.

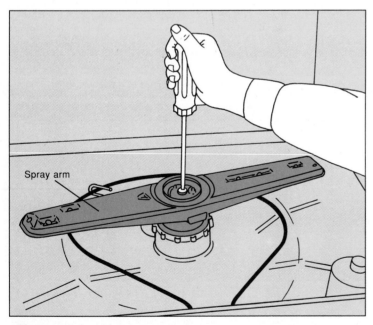

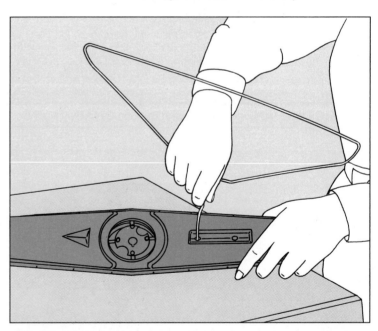

3 **Removing and replacing the spray arm.** Remove the spray arm by unscrewing it *(above)* or by removing a plastic cap. Keeping them in order, lift out the spray arm and its washers, gaskets or bearings. Clean or, if it is bent or damaged, replace the spray arm. If your model has a strainer below the spray arm, remove it and clean with an old toothbrush under running water.

4 **Cleaning the spray arm.** Check the spray arm for foreign objects. Using a stiff wire bent at a right angle at the tip, unclog the holes *(above)*. If your model has a second spray arm mounted above the first, clean it, too. Then rinse the spray arm, tower and strainer under running water and reassemble the parts.

MEASURING THE WATER TEMPERATURE

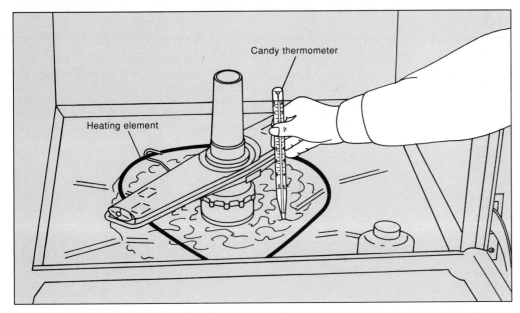

Candy thermometer

Heating element

Measuring the water temperature. Turn on the dishwasher, then interrupt it during the first wash cycle by opening the door. Steam will pour out, but the water will remain in the bottom of the tub. Place a candy or meat thermometer in the water *(left)*. It should read at least 140°F. If not, raise the temperature slightly at your water heater thermostat and make the test again after one hour.

If your water heater is already set to a higher temperature than is being delivered to the dishwasher, keep in mind that a loss of one degree per foot of pipe is normal. If the water temperature in the dishwasher continues to stay below 140°F, check the heating element *(below)*.

SERVICING THE HEATING ELEMENT

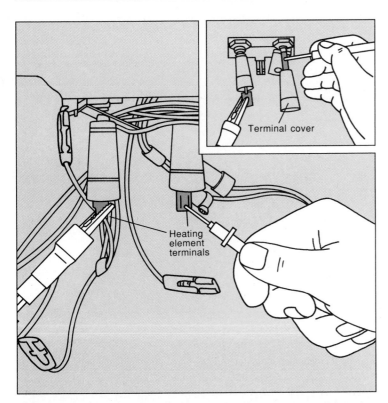

Terminal cover

Heating element terminals

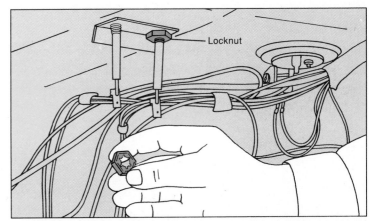

Locknut

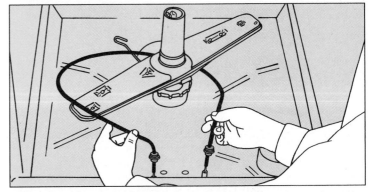

1 **Testing the heating element.** Turn off power to the dishwasher and remove the lower access panel *(page 256)*. Disconnect the heating element terminal wires, located under the tub, and test the terminals for continuity, using a multitester set at RX1 *(above)*. The tester should indicate partial resistance. If not, replace the element.

Also check the element for a ground. Pull one of the rubber covers to the end of the terminal. Touch one probe of the tester to the metal sheath and the other to a terminal *(inset)*. A continuity reading means the heating element is grounded and should be replaced.

2 **Replacing the heating element.** Slide off the rubber terminal covers and remove the locknuts that hold the element in place under the tub *(above, top)*. Then, from inside the tub, remove the element from its bracket *(above, bottom)*. Lift the element from the tub and install an exact replacement for your make and model. Reconnect the wires to the terminals, making sure the insulating covers completely hide the metal terminals.

CHECKING THE WATER PRESSURE

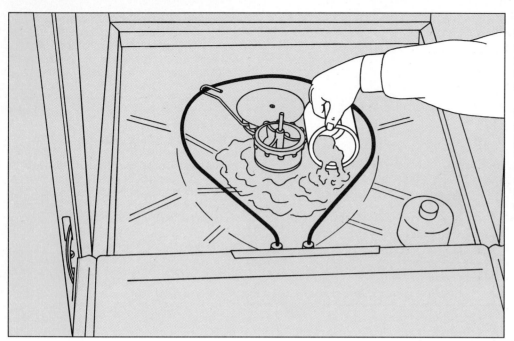

Checking the water pressure. Turn on the dishwasher and let it run until the dial reaches the first wash cycle. Then stop the machine by opening the door. Steam will pour out, but the water will remain in the bottom of the tub. Let the water cool, then bail it out *(left)* into a gallon container—emptying it into the sink as it becomes full. Remove the spray arm *(page 262)* if it is in your way. If there is less than 2 1/2 gallons (2 imperial gallons) of water in your dishwasher, the water pressure may be too low. First rule out all possible causes of insufficient water *(page 253)*. Otherwise, avoid using the house water supply while the dishwasher is in use.

SERVICING THE FLOAT SWITCH

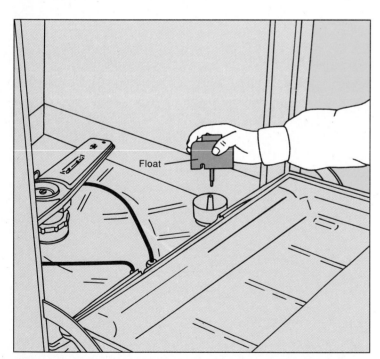

Float

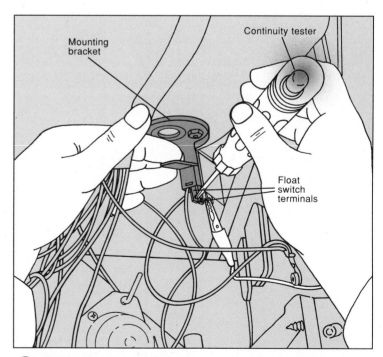

Mounting bracket

Continuity tester

Float switch terminals

1 **Inspecting the float.** Turn off power to the dishwasher. Open the dishwasher door, remove the lower dish rack and jiggle the float up and down to check that it moves freely. Then pull it out and look for obstructions *(above)*. On some models, the float is held in place by a clip under the tub. Remove the lower panel *(page 256)* and remove the clip. On other models, the float is hidden by a cover that first must be removed. Replace the float with a new one if it is damaged. If the float moves freely but the machine either doesn't fill or overflows, test the float switch.

2 **Testing the float switch.** Remove the lower panel *(page 256)* and detach the wires from the float switch terminals. Put the switch in the ON position by pulling down on the lever, and test the terminals for continuity. If there is no continuity, remove the switch by unscrewing it from its mounting bracket and replace it.

SERVICING THE DRAIN VALVE

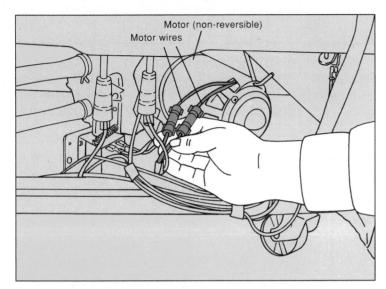

1 **Locating the drain valve.** Drain valves are used in dishwashers with non-reversible motors. Turn off power to the dishwasher and remove the lower panel *(page 256)*. Count the number of wires attached to the motor. A motor with two or three is non-reversible, as above; one with four wires is reversible.

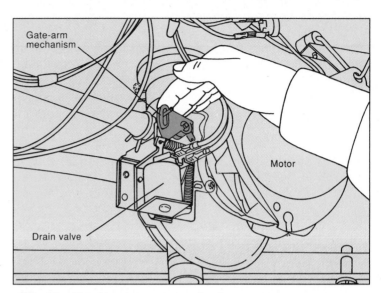

2 **Checking the gate arm mechanism.** Tilt the machine on its back *(page 256)* to make it easier to reach the drain valve. If your drain valve has a gate arm mechanism, move it by hand *(above)*; it should move freely up and down. There should be two springs; replace any that are broken or missing.

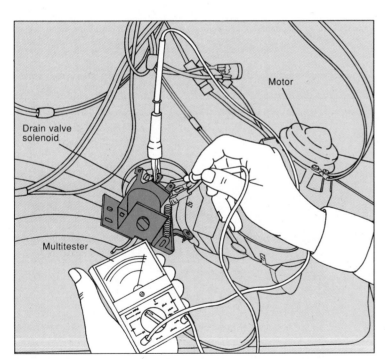

3 **Testing the drain valve solenoid.** Disconnect the wires from the drain valve solenoid terminals and, using a multitester set at RX1, test it for continuity *(above)*; the solenoid should show partial resistance. If there is no continuity, replace the solenoid.

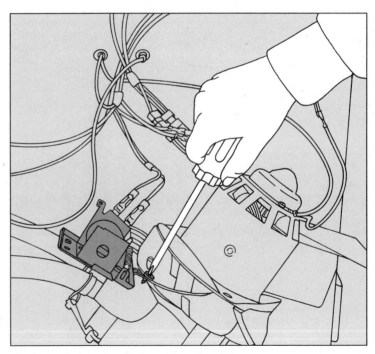

4 **Replacing the drain valve solenoid.** Noting carefully how they are attached, remove the mounting screws *(above)* and detach the solenoid springs and wires. Install a new solenoid and reattach the wires.

CLOTHES WASHERS

Its myriad cycles and settings make a clothes washer complex to fix. Indeed, some repairs are difficult, and require special tools designed specifically for the make and model of the machine. But if tackled logically and systematically, many washer repairs can be done by do-it-yourselfers.

To locate and fix a problem, service technicians divide the washer into three systems. The plumbing system brings in and circulates water through the pump and a network of hoses; the electrical system energizes the machine through the control switches, motor, timer, solenoids and their wiring; and the mechanical system—transmission, drive belt, agitator, basket and tub—powers the cleaning action.

To diagnose a problem, first determine where in the operating cycle the problem originated. Then consult the Troubleshooting Guide *(page 268);* its list of possible causes and repair procedures will help you pinpoint the problem and decide what to do. Even if you don't fix it yourself, this information will guide you when talking with the service technician and alert him to bring the proper replacement parts. Do not begin a repair without referring to the pages indicated in the chart. Disassembling your washer in the hope of finding the problem is usually a waste of time.

Though all automatic washers fill, agitate, pump out and spin dry in basically the same way, there are key differences in

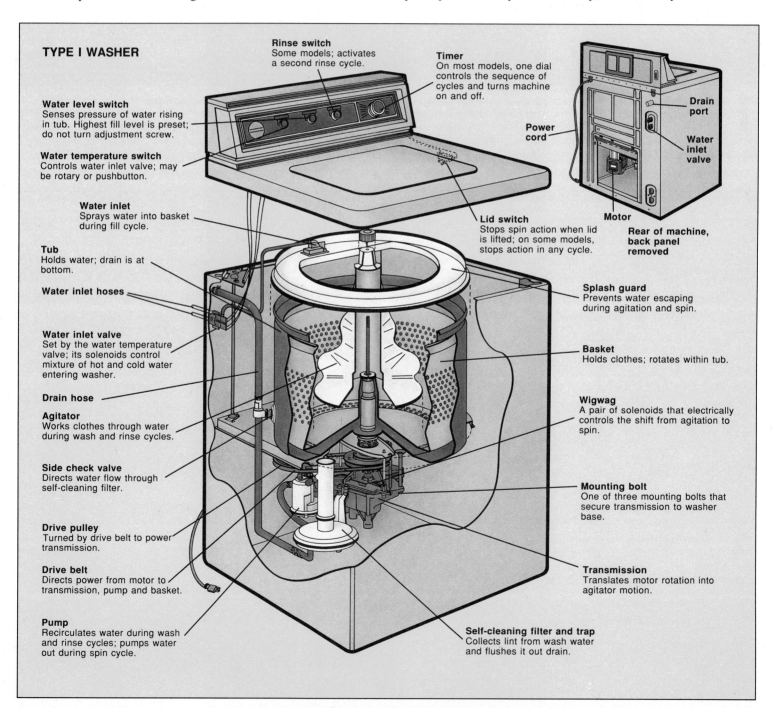

TYPE I WASHER

Rinse switch
Some models; activates a second rinse cycle.

Timer
On most models, one dial controls the sequence of cycles and turns machine on and off.

Water level switch
Senses pressure of water rising in tub. Highest fill level is preset; do not turn adjustment screw.

Water temperature switch
Controls water inlet valve; may be rotary or pushbutton.

Water inlet
Sprays water into basket during fill cycle.

Tub
Holds water; drain is at bottom.

Water inlet hoses

Water inlet valve
Set by the water temperature valve; its solenoids control mixture of hot and cold water entering washer.

Drain hose

Agitator
Works clothes through water during wash and rinse cycles.

Side check valve
Directs water flow through self-cleaning filter.

Drive pulley
Turned by drive belt to power transmission.

Drive belt
Directs power from motor to transmission, pump and basket.

Pump
Recirculates water during wash and rinse cycles; pumps water out during spin cycle.

Lid switch
Stops spin action when lid is lifted; on some models, stops action in any cycle.

Power cord

Drain port

Water inlet valve

Motor

Rear of machine, back panel removed

Splash guard
Prevents water escaping during agitation and spin.

Basket
Holds clothes; rotates within tub.

Wigwag
A pair of solenoids that electrically controls the shift from agitation to spin.

Mounting bolt
One of three mounting bolts that secure transmission to washer base.

Transmission
Translates motor rotation into agitator motion.

Self-cleaning filter and trap
Collects lint from wash water and flushes it out drain.

design and special features from model to model. The two washers pictured below—referred to as Type I and Type II throughout this chapter—illustrate most of the variations found in modern washers. Your machine will likely resemble one of these types. Front-loading tumbler washers, in spite of their lower energy costs, are not as popular as the top-loading agitator models shown here. Any differences will usually be in the location of parts, rather than in their function or testing procedure. The illustrations will help you recognize a part and understand its function, even if the position is not the same.

Always unplug your washer before attempting any repair. The washer repairs shown require only wrenches, screwdrivers and pliers. To service electrical parts, you will need a continuity tester or a multitester. For instructions on using these testers, consult Tools & Techniques *(page 417)*. Broken parts, including a faulty motor, are usually replaced rather than rebuilt, although the pump and several other plumbing components can be repaired. A faulty transmission, like its counterpart in the family car, can be professionally rebuilt.

A careful reading of your washer's Use and Care manual, available from the manufacturer, can help prevent problems caused by misuse. When repair is required, always turn off the water faucets to the machine, unplug the power cord, and have a container handy to catch water runoff.

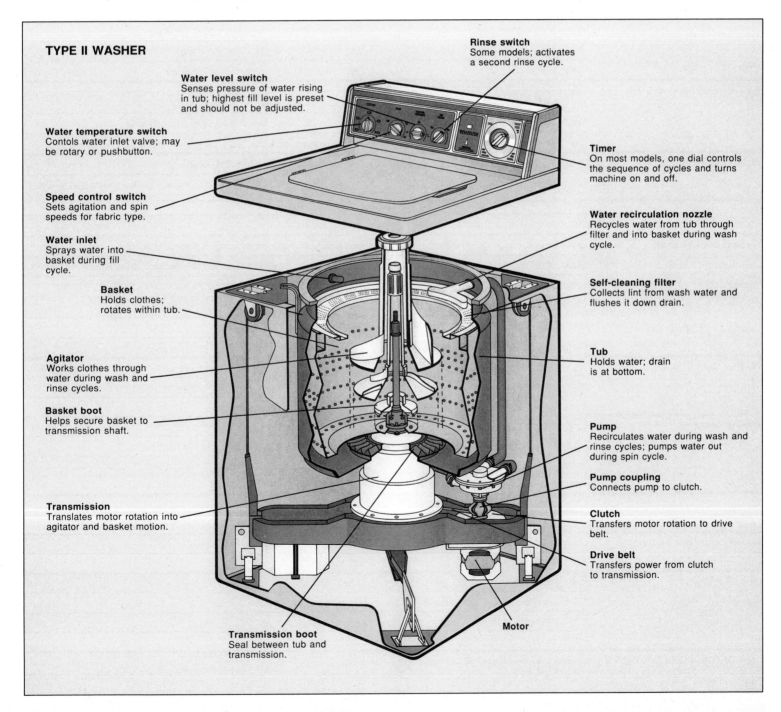

TYPE II WASHER

Water level switch
Senses pressure of water rising in tub; highest fill level is preset and should not be adjusted.

Water temperature switch
Contols water inlet valve; may be rotary or pushbutton.

Speed control switch
Sets agitation and spin speeds for fabric type.

Water inlet
Sprays water into basket during fill cycle.

Basket
Holds clothes; rotates within tub.

Agitator
Works clothes through water during wash and rinse cycles.

Basket boot
Helps secure basket to transmission shaft.

Transmission
Translates motor rotation into agitator and basket motion.

Transmission boot
Seal between tub and transmission.

Rinse switch
Some models; activates a second rinse cycle.

Timer
On most models, one dial controls the sequence of cycles and turns machine on and off.

Water recirculation nozzle
Recycles water from tub through filter and into basket during wash cycle.

Self-cleaning filter
Collects lint from wash water and flushes it down drain.

Tub
Holds water; drain is at bottom.

Pump
Recirculates water during wash and rinse cycles; pumps water out during spin cycle.

Pump coupling
Connects pump to clutch.

Clutch
Transfers motor rotation to drive belt.

Drive belt
Transfers power from clutch to transmission.

Motor

TROUBLESHOOTING GUIDE

SYMPTOM	POSSIBLE CAUSE	PROCEDURE
Washer doesn't run at all (in some cases, motor may hum)	No power to washer	Check that washer is plugged in; check for blown fuse or tripped circuit breaker (p. 102) □○; check for tripped GFCI (p. 105) □○
	Motor overheated	Turn off washer; allow motor to cool for one hour
	Lid switch or timer faulty	Test lid switch (p. 273) □○; test timer and its motor (p. 272) ■●▲
	Power cord loose or faulty	Test power cord (p. 417)
	Water level switch assembly faulty (Type I)	Service water level switch assembly (p. 271) ■●
	Motor or pump faulty	Call for service
Washer doesn't fill	No water or supply hoses kinked	Check faucets; disconnect and straighten or replace hoses
	Filter screens clogged	Clean or replace screens (p. 274) □○
	Water inlet valve faulty	Test water inlet valve (p. 274) ■●▲
	Water temperature switch faulty	Test water temperature switch (p. 273) ■●
	Water level switch, hose or dome faulty	Service water level switch assembly (p. 271) ■●
	Timer faulty	Test timer and timer motor (p. 272) ■●▲
Washer doesn't stop filling	Water inlet valve faulty	Unplug washer; if water continues to fill, inlet valve is faulty; repair or replace (p. 274) ●■▲
	Water level switch, hose or dome faulty	Service water level switch assembly (p. 271) ■●
	Timer faulty	Unplug washer; if water stops filling, test timer (p. 272) ■●▲
Washer doesn't agitate	Water level switch faulty	Test water level switch (p. 271) ■●
	Lid switch or timer faulty	Test lid switch (p. 273) □○; test timer and its motor (p. 272) ■●▲
	Drive belt or pulley loose	Call for service
	Motor or transmission faulty	Call for service
Washer doesn't drain	Drain hose too high or kinked	Reposition and straighten hose; replace if damaged
	Suds blocking drain	Turn off washer, bail out suds and hot water, and add cold water
	Self-cleaning filter or trap clogged (Type I)	Inspect filter and trap (p. 275) ■●
	Timer faulty	Test timer and timer motor (p. 272) ■●▲
	Tub drain blocked	Call for service
	Pump blocked or impeller jammed	Call for service
Washer doesn't spin	Lid switch or timer faulty	Test lid switch (p. 273) □○; test timer and its motor (p. 272) ■●▲
	Motor or transmission faulty	Call for service
	Pump blocked or impeller jammed	Call for service
Washer leaks	Filter clogged (models with manual filter)	Remove and clean filter
	Hose loose or cracked	Inspect and tighten or replace internal hoses
	Pump leaking	Call for service
	Transmission faulty	Call for service
Washer noisy or vibrates excessively	Load unbalanced or washer not level	Redistribute load; adjust leveling feet
	Transmission or pump faulty	Call for service
Washer damages clothing	Cleaning agents used improperly	Check Use and Care manual
	Agitator cracked	Call for service
Lint on clothing	Wrong mixture of fabrics in load	Check Use and Care manual
	Filter clogged (models with manual filter)	Remove and clean filter
	Self-cleaning filter or trap clogged (Type I)	Inspect filter or trap (p. 275) ■●
	Pump blocked or impeller jammed	Call for service

DEGREE OF DIFFICULTY: □ **Easy** ■ **Moderate** ■ **Complex**
ESTIMATED TIME: ○ **Less than 1 hour** ● **1 to 3 hours** ● **Over 3 hours**

▲ **Multitester required**

ACCESS THROUGH THE CONTROL CONSOLE

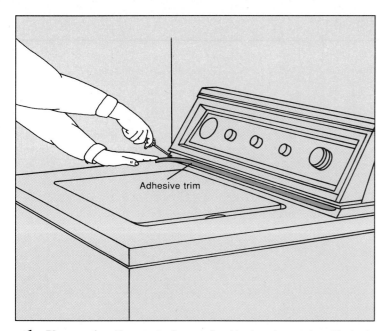

Adhesive trim

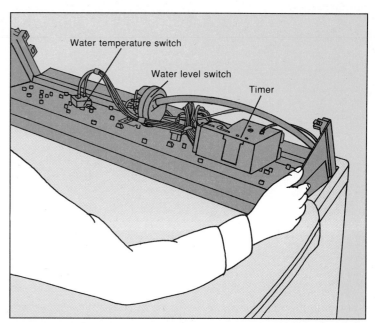

Water temperature switch

Water level switch

Timer

1 **Unscrewing the control console.** Unplug the washer. To free the control console of most washers, you must remove retaining screws from the bottom front corners of the console. The screws may be hidden by a strip of adhesive trim *(above)*. Other washers may have screws on the top or at the back of the console.

2 **Rolling the console panel foward.** Drape a towel over the top of the washer to protect its enamel finish. Tilt the control console forward and rest it on the washer top. If the console has a back panel, unscrew and remove it. You now have access to the timer and switches *(above)*. The wiring diagram for Type II washers is often located inside the console as well.

ACCESS THROUGH THE TOP

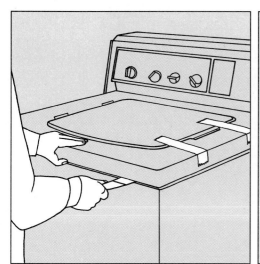

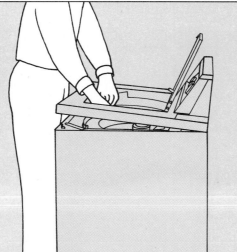

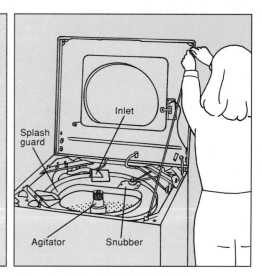

Inlet

Splash guard

Agitator   Snubber

Raising the washer top. Unplug the washer. Tape down the lid so that it will not swing open when the top is raised. On some Type II models, the recirculation nozzle under the lid must first be detached from the plastic cover shield. The washer top is held down by a spring clip near each corner. Slip a putty knife, the blade padded with masking tape, between the washer top and chassis near each corner, and push against the spring clips to release the top *(above, left)*. If the spring clips are too stiff to release easily with the putty knife, lift the lid and grasp the inner edge of the washer opening. Jerk the top forward and up to unlock the clips *(above, center)*. Lean the top against a wall, or support it with a length of heavy cord or a chain *(above, right)*. You now have access to the snubber, splash guard, inlet and agitator.

ACCESS THROUGH THE REAR PANEL

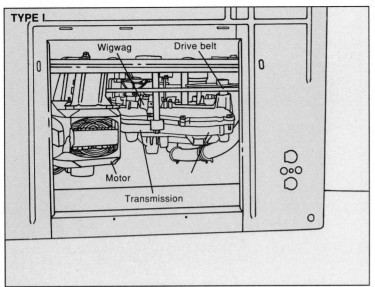

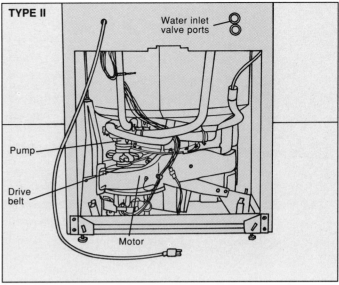

Removing the rear panel. Some washer components can be reached through an opening in the back of the chassis. Unplug the washer and pull it away from the wall. A Type II washer is very heavy; you may need help to move it. Unscrew the rear panel and set it aside. With the rear panel of a Type I washer removed *(above, left)*, you have access to the motor, drive belt, wigwag and back filter if your model has one. To top off the transmission lubricant from this position, use a syringe to inject non-detergent SAE-90 gear lubricant into the breather hole near the top center of the transmission. After removing the back panel of a Type II washer *(above, right)*, you have access to the water inlet valve, pump, drive belt, motor and motor start relay.

ACCESS THROUGH THE BOTTOM

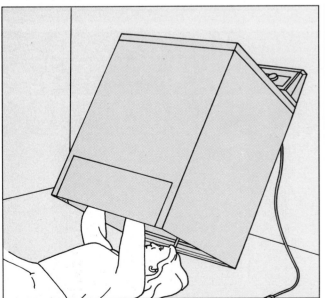

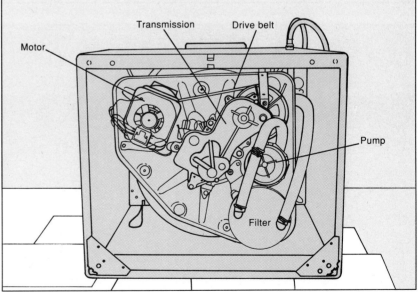

Inspecting parts through the bottom. Unplug the washer. Shut off the faucets and detach the water inlet hoses. Have a bucket handy to catch dripping water, and bail or siphon out any water in the tub. To perform a quick check, pull a Type I washer about 2 feet from the wall and tilt it back *(above, left)*. Be absolutely certain its position is secure, and the control console is firmly attached, before looking inside. For actual repairs, enlist a helper to lay a Type I washer front down on the floor *(above, right)*; most washers are very heavy. Protect the floor with newspaper; the transmission of a Type I washer will probably leak oil in this position—be sure to top it off *(step above)* once the machine is upright. With the bottom exposed, you have access to a Type I washer's trap and filter, pump, drive belt, transmission, motor and motor start switch. On a Type II washer, removing the drive motor is the only repair performed through the washer bottom. To check for a loose or worn belt, press it with your thumb; it should not deflect more than 1/2 inch. Ensure that hoses are not damaged or kinked and replace any broken hose clamps.

SERVICING THE WATER LEVEL SWITCH ASSEMBLY

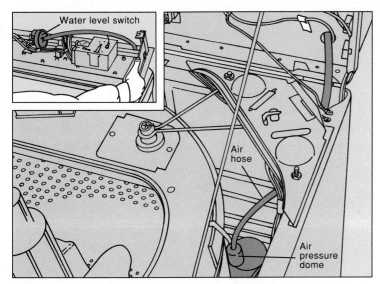

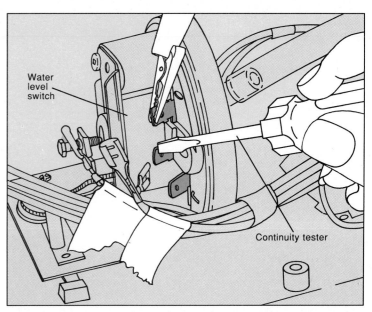

1 **Inspecting the air hose and air pressure dome.** Turn off and unplug the washer. Remove the control console *(page 269)*. Check the air hose *(inset)*; straighten any kinks and replace it if perforated. Remove the air hose from the water level switch and blow through it to clear any trapped water. Reconnect the air hose to the water level switch. Next, raise the top of the washer *(page 269)* and, on a Type I washer, follow the hose down the right side to the air pressure dome *(above)*. The connection should be completely airtight. If the dome is cracked, or if the seal between the dome and tub is broken, replace the dome. To remove it, pull off the hose, depress the dome and turn it counterclockwise one-quarter turn. Reverse the procedure to install a new dome.

2 **Testing a water level switch in the EMPTY position.** Inspect the wire connectors; if they are burned or loose, install new ones *(page 417)*. Label and remove the three wires from their terminals on the water level switch. Test each terminal against the other two with a continuity tester *(above)*. The tester should indicate continuity across one pair of terminals, and no continuity across the other two pairs. If not, the water level switch is broken and should be replaced *(step 4)*.

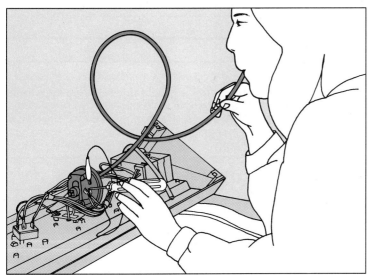

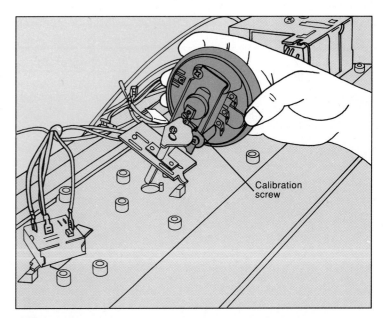

3 **Testing the water level switch in the FULL position.** After pulling the air hose off the switch's port, attach a shorter tube of the same diameter and blow very gently through it into the switch. You should hear a click when the switch trips to the FULL position. While blowing through the tube, test the terminals with a continuity tester as in step 2. This time a different pair of terminals should show continuity; the other two should not. If you do not hear a click, or you have trouble blowing gently and evenly into the tube, reconnect the air hose, fill the washer with water, unplug the machine and test the switch again. If the switch fails the test, replace it *(step 4)*.

4 **Replacing the water level switch.** Pull off the water level switch control knob, if any. Remove the tube from the switch's port and unscrew the water level switch bracket from inside the control console. Do not turn the calibration screw; the slightest adjustment could result in the tub overflowing. The mounting bracket of a Type I water level switch often has a tab that fits into a slot in the control panel. Screw the bracket of the new switch inside the console, reconnect the air hose and the terminal wires, push on the control knob and replace the console.

TESTING AND REPLACING THE TIMER

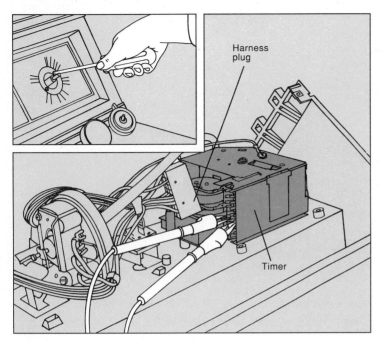

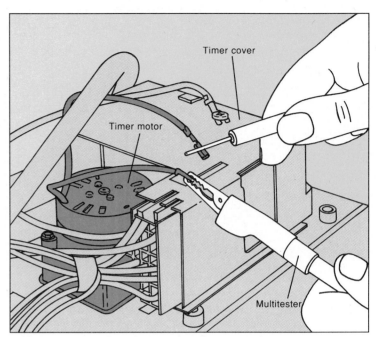

1 **Testing and replacing the timer.** Unplug the washer and remove the control panel *(page 269)*. Check the washer's wiring diagram for the terminals that control the affected cycle, and disconnect and label those wires. (Pull off the harness plug to expose the terminals.) Set the control knob to the affected cycle and touch the probe of a multitester set at RX1 to each terminal *(above)*. The tester should show continuity; if so, go to step 2. Otherwise, replace the timer. Remove the control knob and unscrew the timer from the front *(inset)* or from the back. Screw a new timer in place, plug in the wires and replace the control knob and the console.

2 **Testing the timer motor.** Label and remove both motor wires from their terminals. Set a multitester to RX100 and touch a probe to each terminal *(above)*; the motor should produce a reading of 2,000 to 3,000 ohms. Many timer motors can be replaced separately from the timer; simply remove the two screws that hold the motor on the timer. When installing a new timer motor, make sure that its gear fits back into the hole in the timer cover.

SERVICING A PLASTIC TIMER (Type II washers)

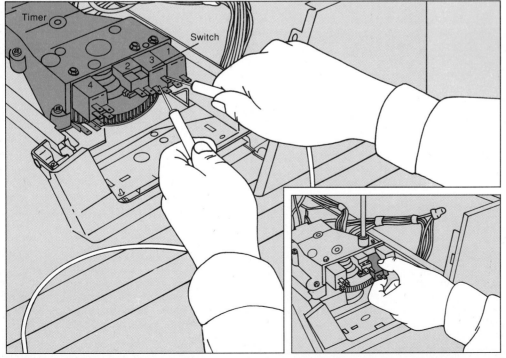

Testing a plastic timer. Unplug the washer and remove the control console *(page 269)*. If your Type II washer has a plastic timer, lift off the switch cover by releasing the plastic tab. Check the wiring diagram and timer chart to determine which switch controls the affected cycle. Label and disconnect the wires from those terminals. Testing with a continuity tester or a multitester set at RX1 *(left)* should show the following results:

CONTROL KNOB POSITION	SWITCH					
	1 Motor	2 Special Function	3 Main Power	3b Bypass	4 Wash	4b Spin
OFF	open	See timer chart	open	open	open	open
WASH	open		closed	open	closed	open
SPIN	open		closed	closed	open	closed

Replace a switch that fails any test. Switches 1 and 3 are easily replaced; remove the screw that secures the switch to the plastic casing and gently pull it free from the timer *(inset)*. The other switches can only be replaced by disassembling the timer; call for service.

TESTING AND REPLACING THE WATER TEMPERATURE SWITCH

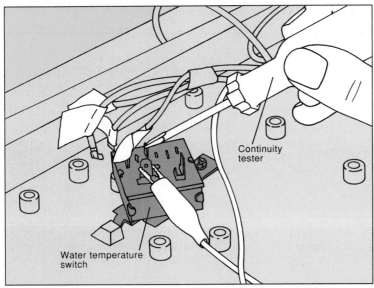

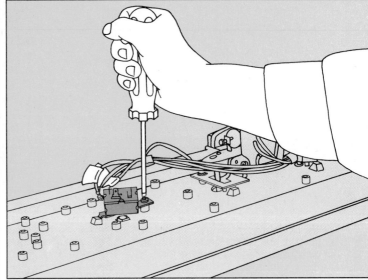

Testing the water temperature switch. Unplug the washer and remove the control console *(page 269)*. The water temperature switch may be rotary, as shown, or pushbutton; both are tested the same way. Check the wiring diagram for the markings used on the terminals that control the inoperative setting. Label and disconnect the wires from these terminals. Turn the knob to the inoperative setting or press the corresponding button. Touch one probe of a continuity tester to each terminal *(above, left)*. The tester should light; if not, replace the switch. Unscrew the old switch from the control console *(above, right)*, install the new switch and transfer the wires.

TESTING AND REPLACING THE LID SWITCH

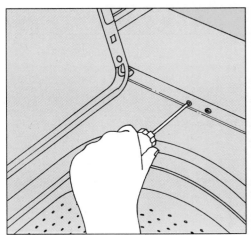

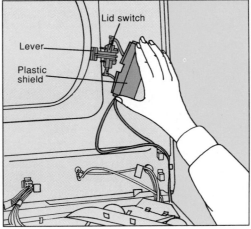

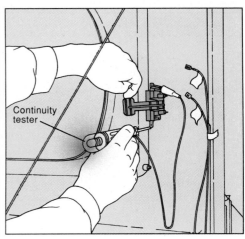

Inspecting the lid switch. Unplug the washer. To reach a Type I lid switch, loosen the two screws on the right side of the washer top *(above, left)*. Raise the top *(page 269)* and unsnap the plastic shield covering the switch *(above, center)*. Examine the switch; if both wires are secured to the terminals, the problem may be a damaged bracket or a broken switch. Lid switches vary in design. Some Type I washers have a mercury switch capsule in a bracket attached to the right lid hinge. Replace a damaged bracket by unscrewing it from the washer chassis. Type II shieldless lid switches have a metal lever; if bent, straighten it by hand. Make sure the lever covers the lid strike hole completely.

To test a switch, label and disconnect the wires. Clip a continuity tester probe to one of the terminals. Touch the second probe to the other terminal while lifting the lever with your finger *(above, right)*. The tester should light, indicating continuity. Release the lever; the continuity tester should not light. If the switch fails either test, replace it. Unscrew a Type I lid switch from inside the washer top and pull off the plastic lever. Fit the new switch in the lever and screw the switch on the washer just until the screws begin to grab. Then reconnect the wires, snap on the plastic shield, and tighten the screws completely. To replace a Type II lid switch, remove the two screws securing it to the inside edge of the washer top. Position the new switch over the lid strike hole.

SERVICING THE WATER INLET VALVE (Type I washers)

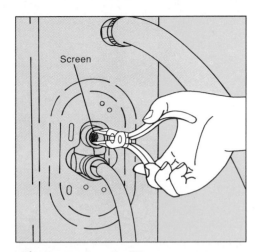

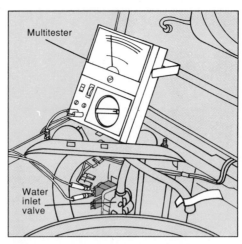

1 **Inspecting the filter screens.** Unplug the washer, turn off the faucets and disconnect the water inlet hoses at both ends. Check the screens regularly for blockage or rust. Using long-nose pliers, pry the screens out of the faucet couplers and the inlet valve ports *(above)*. Clean the screens with an old toothbrush under running water. Plastic screens can be replaced with metal ones but not vice versa.

2 **Testing the inlet valve solenoids.** Raise the top *(page 269)*. Unclip and remove the inlet hose. Remove the snubber, if present, then unhook the clips securing the splash guard and lift it up off the tub rim. The inlet valve is in the left rear corner behind the tub. Label and remove the wires from one solenoid. Set a multitester to RX100 and clip a probe to each terminal. You should get a reading of 500 to 2,000 ohms. Test the second solenoid, if any, the same way. If either solenoid is faulty, replace the entire valve assembly *(step 3)*.

3 **Replacing the inlet valve.** From inside the washer, unclamp the hose from the inlet valve port, then remove the screws that secure the valve to the back of the cabinet *(above)*. Hold on to the valve with your free hand and pull the valve out through the top. Hold the new valve in position and screw it to the cabinet. Reconnect the wires and hoses.

SERVICING THE WATER INLET VALVE (Type II washers)

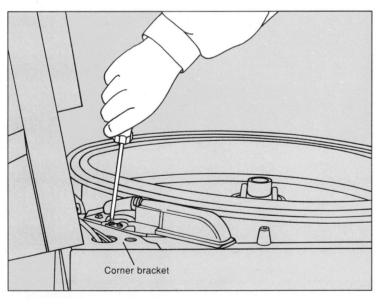

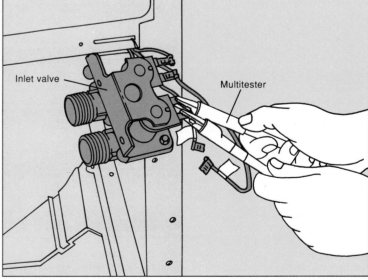

Servicing the inlet valve. Follow step 1 *(above)* to clean the filter screens. To service the valve, unplug the machine, lift the top *(page 269)* and remove the back panel *(page 270)*. Remove the screws holding the inlet valve to the corner bracket *(above, left)* and the washer cabinet. Then push the inlet valve down so that you can test it through the back of the machine *(above, right)*. Label and disconnect the wires. Set the multitester at RX100 and touch a probe to each terminal of one solenoid; the tester needle should sweep partially upscale, indicating resistance. Test the second solenoid the same way. If the inlet valve is faulty, remove it by unscrewing the clamp securing the hose to the inlet port. Install a new valve by reversing this procedure.

SERVICING THE SELF-CLEANING FILTER AND TRAP (Type I washers)

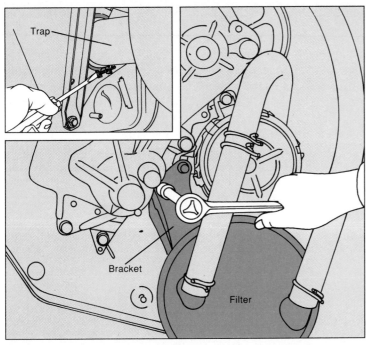

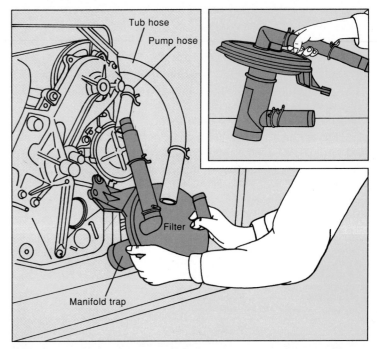

1 **Releasing the filter and trap.** Some Type I washers have self-cleaning filters connected to the tub outlet through a manifold trap. To remove a clogged filter and trap assembly, unplug the washer, turn off the water faucets and detach the hoses. Have a bucket handy to catch dripping water. Bail or siphon out any water remaining in the tub. Lay the washer flat on some newspapers *(page 269)*. Unscrew the clamp securing the pipe-like manifold trap to the tub outlet *(inset)*. Use a socket wrench *(above)* to remove the two bolts that hold the plastic filter bracket to the transmission.

2 **Removing and cleaning the trap.** The filter ports are clamped to a long hose leading to the tub, and a short hose leading to the pump. Disconnect the long hose from its port on the filter, and disconnect the short hose from its port on the pump. As you pull the filter and trap assembly free *(above)*, notice its proper position for reinstallation. Check the filter and manifold trap for cracks or for debris that may block the flow of water. Tap the end of the trap on the floor to knock out any objects caught inside *(inset)*; pins and buttons are common culprits. If the filter is clogged, replace it. To replace the filter and trap assembly, reverse this procedure.

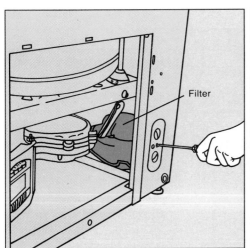

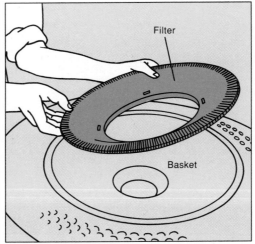

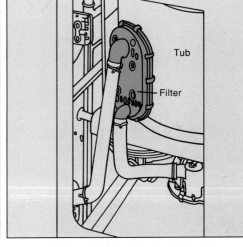

Alternate filters. Some older Type I washers have a self-cleaning filter in the lower right rear corner of the cabinet *(above, left)*. To replace it, remove the single screw that secures it to the cabinet and use pliers to unclamp the hoses. Other Type I models use a ring filter *(above, center)* that snaps on the bottom of the basket. To remove the basket, pull off the agitator, remove the basket boot and unscrew the bolts in the floor of the basket. Turn it over and use a screwdriver to pry off the clips securing the filter to the basket base. More recent models have a tub-mounted filter attached with a special locknut that also holds the side check valve in place *(above, right)*. The drain hose exits through the lower left rear corner of the cabinet. Replacement of this filter is difficult and rarely required. If it must be removed, call for service.

CLOTHES DRYERS

A dryer combines air, heat and motion to dry everything from soggy socks to damp dungarees. The motor turns a drive belt that revolves the drum. At the same time the blower, also powered by the motor, forces air past electric heater coils (or the flame from a gas burner) and into the drum. The air draws moisture and lint from the clothes through the lint screen and out the exhaust duct. Electric switches and the timer regulate the drying time and cycles, and thermostats control the temperature. Dryers have a long life expectancy—15 years or more—and fortunately, when things do go wrong, they are as simple as they are sturdy, making most repairs worth tackling yourself.

Most electric dryers in the U.S. and Canada resemble Type I *(below)*; another popular model is Type II *(page 277)*. A gas dryer substitutes a gas burner for the heater element or coils in either machine. Many common repairs, such as replacing the timer, are similar for all dryers. When repairs are significantly different—for example, replacing the heater element or coils—they are shown separately. Follow the instructions for the type of dryer that most resembles yours.

When a problem occurs, first check your home's main service panel for blown fuses or tripped circuit breakers *(page 102)*. Remember that an electric dryer runs on 240-volt

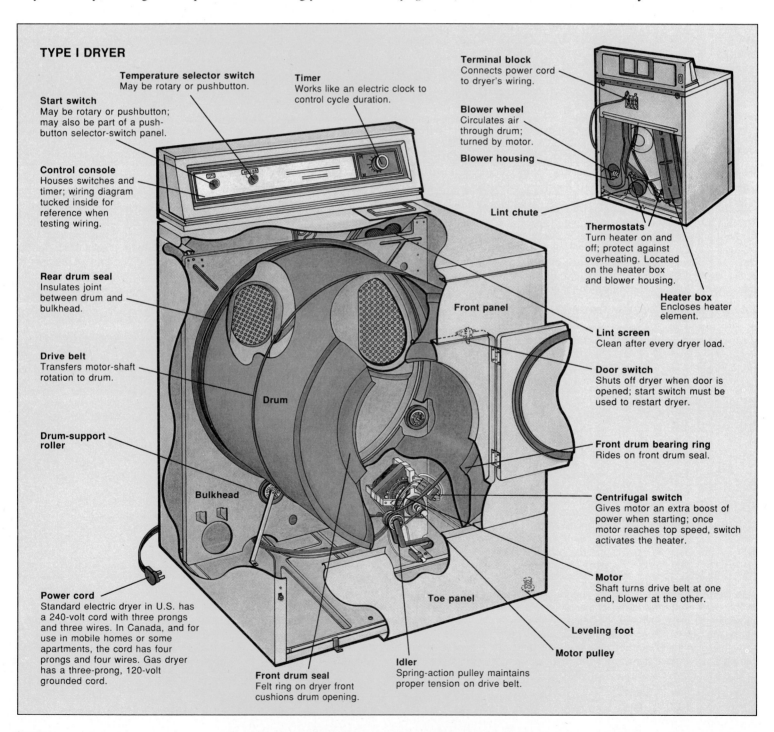

TYPE I DRYER

Start switch
May be rotary or pushbutton; may also be part of a push-button selector-switch panel.

Temperature selector switch
May be rotary or pushbutton.

Timer
Works like an electric clock to control cycle duration.

Terminal block
Connects power cord to dryer's wiring.

Blower wheel
Circulates air through drum; turned by motor.

Blower housing

Control console
Houses switches and timer; wiring diagram tucked inside for reference when testing wiring.

Lint chute

Thermostats
Turn heater on and off; protect against overheating. Located on the heater box and blower housing.

Rear drum seal
Insulates joint between drum and bulkhead.

Front panel

Heater box
Encloses heater element.

Lint screen
Clean after every dryer load.

Drive belt
Transfers motor-shaft rotation to drum.

Drum

Door switch
Shuts off dryer when door is opened; start switch must be used to restart dryer.

Drum-support roller

Front drum bearing ring
Rides on front drum seal.

Bulkhead

Centrifugal switch
Gives motor an extra boost of power when starting; once motor reaches top speed, switch activates the heater.

Motor
Shaft turns drive belt at one end, blower at the other.

Power cord
Standard electric dryer in U.S. has a 240-volt cord with three prongs and three wires. In Canada, and for use in mobile homes or some apartments, the cord has four prongs and four wires. Gas dryer has a three-prong, 120-volt grounded cord.

Toe panel

Leveling foot

Motor pulley

Front drum seal
Felt ring on dryer front cushions drum opening.

Idler
Spring-action pulley maintains proper tension on drive belt.

current and draws power through two separate fuses or breakers. As a result, if only one fuse has blown or breaker has tripped, the dryer motor may still run, although the dryer won't heat.

A dryer's greatest enemy is lint. Even if the lint filter is cleaned after every load, lint will still accumulate around the moving parts of a dryer as well as in the exhaust duct and vent, forcing the machine to work harder. At least once a year, turn off the power, remove the front and rear panels *(page 280)*, and vacuum or brush out lint from around the motor, idler and gas burner, if any. Disconnect the exhaust duct and remove lint from the internal exhaust pipe, the duct and the vent. Make sure

the duct has no kinks where lint and moisture can accumulate. The duct should be made of aluminum or of a plastic that won't soften and sag with heat. It must have no more than two bends of 90 degrees, spaced at least 4 feet apart.

Before working on the dryer, always unplug the power cord from the wall outlet. If the cord is wired directly into your home's electrical system, cut power to the machine at the main service panel. If you have a gas dryer, don't risk rupturing the gas line by moving the dryer or disconnecting the gas line yourself. Call the gas company or a service technician to disconnect and move it for you.

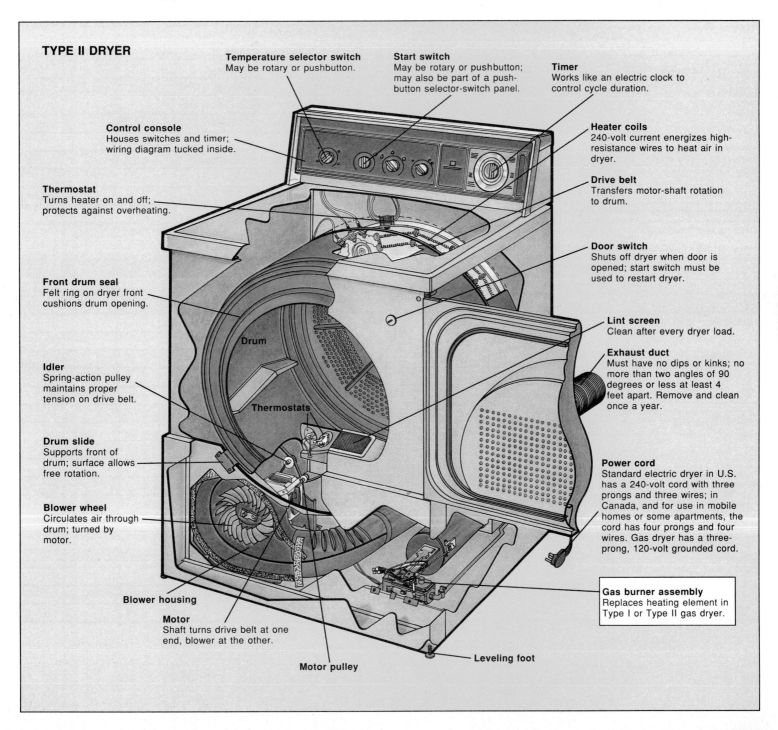

TYPE II DRYER

Temperature selector switch
May be rotary or pushbutton.

Start switch
May be rotary or pushbutton; may also be part of a pushbutton selector-switch panel.

Timer
Works like an electric clock to control cycle duration.

Control console
Houses switches and timer; wiring diagram tucked inside.

Heater coils
240-volt current energizes high-resistance wires to heat air in dryer.

Thermostat
Turns heater on and off; protects against overheating.

Drive belt
Transfers motor-shaft rotation to drum.

Front drum seal
Felt ring on dryer front cushions drum opening.

Door switch
Shuts off dryer when door is opened; start switch must be used to restart dryer.

Drum

Lint screen
Clean after every dryer load.

Idler
Spring-action pulley maintains proper tension on drive belt.

Exhaust duct
Must have no dips or kinks; no more than two angles of 90 degrees or less at least 4 feet apart. Remove and clean once a year.

Thermostats

Drum slide
Supports front of drum; surface allows free rotation.

Power cord
Standard electric dryer in U.S. has a 240-volt cord with three prongs and three wires; in Canada, and for use in mobile homes or some apartments, the cord has four prongs and four wires. Gas dryer has a three-prong, 120-volt grounded cord.

Blower wheel
Circulates air through drum; turned by motor.

Blower housing

Motor
Shaft turns drive belt at one end, blower at the other.

Gas burner assembly
Replaces heating element in Type I or Type II gas dryer.

Motor pulley

Leveling foot

TROUBLESHOOTING GUIDE

SYMPTOM	POSSIBLE CAUSE	PROCEDURE
Dryer doesn't run at all	No power to dryer	Check that dryer is plugged in; check for blown fuse or tripped circuit breaker *(p. 102)* □○
	Door switch faulty	Test door switch *(p. 282)* ⬓◒
	Start switch faulty	Test start switch *(p. 281)* ⬓◒
	Timer faulty	Test timer and timer motor *(p. 281)* ⬓◒▲
	Centrifugal switch faulty	Test centrifugal switch *(p. 281)* ⬓◒
	Thermostat faulty or thermal fuse blown (Type I)	Test thermostats and thermal fuse *(p. 282)* ⬓◒
	Power cord loose or faulty	Test power cord *(p. 417)* ⬓◒
	Motor faulty	Call for service
Motor runs, but dryer doesn't heat	Fuse blown or circuit breaker tripped	Check for blown fuse or tripped circuit breaker *(p. 102)* □○
	Temperature selector switch faulty	Test temperature selector switch *(p. 281)* ⬓◒
	Timer faulty	Test timer and timer motor *(p. 281)* ⬓◒▲
	Thermostats faulty	Test thermostats *(p. 282)* ⬓◒
	Centrifugal switch faulty	Test centrifugal switch *(p. 281)* ⬓◒
	Heater element faulty (Type I)	Test heater element *(p. 286)* ⬓◒▲
	Heater coils faulty (Type II)	Test heater coils *(p. 287)* ⬓●▲
	Gas burner faulty (gas dryers)	Call for service
Motor runs, but drum doesn't turn	Drive belt worn or broken	Check drive belt *(p. 283)* ⬓◒
	Idler faulty	Check idler *(p. 283)* ⬓◒
	Drum is binding	Service drum *(p. 284)* ⬓●
Dryer runs with door open	Door switch faulty	Test door switch *(p. 282)* ⬓◒
Dryer doesn't turn off	Room too cool	Raise room temperature to 50°F for dryer to work properly
	Timer faulty	Test timer and timer motor *(p. 281)* ⬓◒▲
	Thermostats faulty	Test thermostats *(p. 282)* ⬓◒
	Heater element faulty (Type I)	Test heater element *(p. 286)* ⬓◒
	Heater coils faulty (Type II)	Test heater coils *(p. 287)* ⬓●▲
Drying time too long	Lint screen full or exhaust duct blocked	Clean lint screen, exhaust duct and vent
	Thermostats faulty	Test thermostats *(p. 282)* ⬓◒
	Heater element faulty (Type I)	Test heater element *(p. 286)* ⬓◒▲
	Heater coils faulty (Type II)	Test heater coils *(p. 287)* ⬓●▲
	Gas burner faulty (gas dryers)	Call for service
Drying temperature too hot; clothes overheat	Exhaust duct or vent blocked	Clean or unkink exhaust duct; clean exhaust vent
	Thermostats faulty	Test thermostats *(p. 282)* ⬓◒
	Heater element grounded (Type I)	Test heater element *(p. 286)* ⬓◒▲
	Heater coils grounded (Type II)	Test heater coils *(p. 287)* ⬓●▲
Dryer noisy	Dryer not level	Adjust leveling feet
	Panel, trim or part loose	Tighten screws on loose part, panel or trim
	Drive belt worn	Check drive belt *(p. 283)* ⬓◒
	Idler worn or broken	Check idler *(p. 283)* ⬓◒
	Object in front or rear drum seal	Check drum seals *(Type I and II, p. 284; Type I, p. 285)* ⬓◒
	Support rollers worn (Type I)	Check drum support rollers *(p. 284)* ⬓◒
	Drum shaft bearing worn (Type II)	Check drum bearing *(p. 284)* ⬓◒
	Blower loose or obstructed	Call for service

DEGREE OF DIFFICULTY: □ Easy ⬓ Moderate ■ Complex
ESTIMATED TIME: ○ Less than 1 hour ◒ 1 to 3 hours ● Over 3 hours

▲ Multitester required

ACCESS THROUGH THE CONTROL CONSOLE

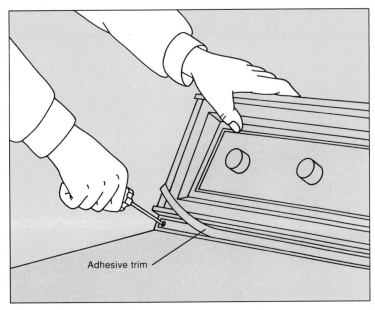

Adhesive trim

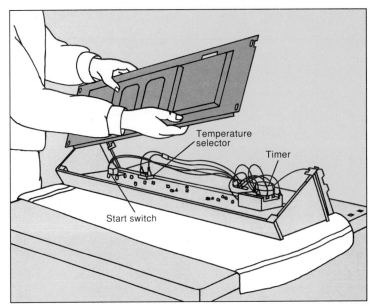

Temperature selector

Timer

Start switch

1 **Freeing the control console.** After unplugging the dryer, unscrew the control console at each end. On many machines, the screws are located at the bottom front of the console, and may be covered by adhesive trim *(above)*. On other machines, the screws are located at the top or sides of the console.

2 **Removing the console back panel.** Spread a towel on top of the dryer to protect its finish. Roll the console face down onto the towel; on some dryers, you must first slide the console forward to disengage tabs on the end panels from slots in the dryer top. If the console has a rear panel, unscrew it to expose the start switch, temperature selector, circuit diagram and timer.

ACCESS THROUGH THE TOP

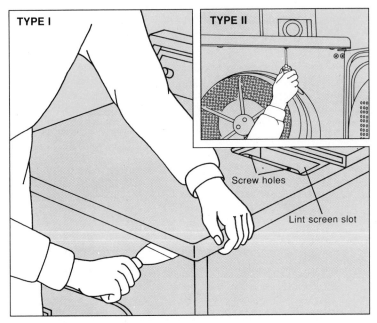

TYPE I

TYPE II

Screw holes

Lint screen slot

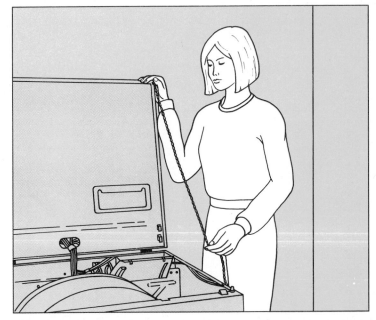

1 **Raising the dryer top.** For Type I dryers, which have a top-mounted lint screen, unplug the dryer, pull out the screen, and remove the two screws at the front edge of the screen slot. Then insert a putty knife wrapped in masking tape under the top *(above)* about two inches from each corner, and push in to disengage the hidden clips securing the top. For Type II dryers, unplug the dryer, open the door and remove the row of screws beneath the front edge of the dryer top *(inset)*.

2 **Securing the top.** The top of both models is hinged at the back; raise it and lean it against the wall behind the dryer. If the dryer is pulled out from the wall, attach a chain or cord to the top and cabinet *(above)* to keep it from falling backward and damaging wiring.

ACCESS THROUGH THE REAR PANEL AND TOE PANEL

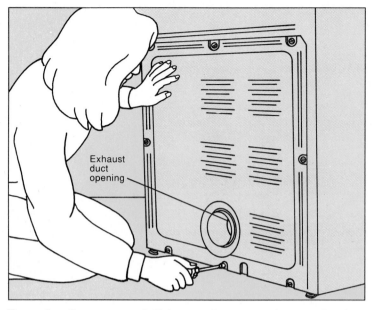

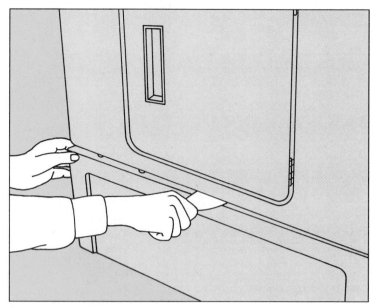

Removing the rear panel. Unless you have a gas dryer, unplug the machine, disconnect the exhaust duct and move the dryer out from the wall. **Caution:** If you have a gas dryer, do not move the dryer yourself—call the gas company or a service technician to move it for you. Most dryers have one large rear panel; remove the screws around its edges *(above)* and set it aside. Some models have two or three small panels; remove each as needed for a particular repair.

Removing the toe panel. Unplug the dryer, remove any retaining screws, and insert a putty knife near the center top of the toe panel *(above)*. Push down and in against the hidden clip while pulling the panel at one corner. Lift the panel off the two bottom brackets.

ACCESS THROUGH THE FRONT PANEL

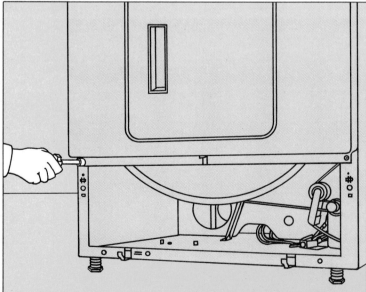

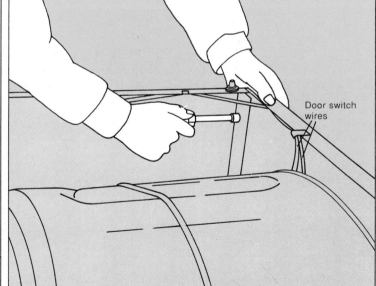

Removing the front panel. Unplug the dryer, raise the dryer top *(page 279)* and remove the toe panel, if any. (If, when you remove the toe panel, you see door hinge springs, tape the top of the door shut with masking tape to keep it from falling open. Then unhook the springs from the brackets at the bottom front of the dryer before removing the front panel.) For a Type I dryer, slip a length of scrap wood under the drum to keep it from falling when you remove the front panel.

Then, for both models, loosen but do not remove the screws, if any, at the bottom corners of the front panel *(above, left)*. Dryers without front panel screws have hidden brackets inside the machine. Move to the inside of the dryer and, taking care to label their positions, disconnect the wires leading to the door switch. Supporting the front panel with one hand, remove the screws at each inside corner *(above, right)*. Lift the panel off the lower screws or brackets.

TESTING AND REPLACING SWITCHES

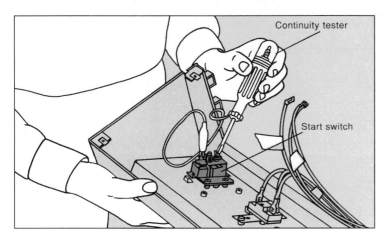

Continuity tester

Start switch

Testing the start switch. After unplugging the dryer, free the control console and tilt it forward *(page 279)*. Disconnect the wires from the start switch terminals and label their positions with masking tape. To test a two-terminal switch, place one probe of a continuity tester on terminal CO (or R2), and the other on NO (or R1) *(above)*. The tester should not light. Press the start button; the tester should now light, showing continuity. To test a three-terminal switch, place one probe on terminal NC (or CT1), and the other on CO (or R1); the tester should light. Press the start button; the tester should not light. If the switch fails this test, replace it. Pull off the control knob and unscrew the switch from the console. Remove and reuse the mounting bracket if the switch has one. Screw the new switch in place and reconnect the wires. If your dryer does not use these terminal configurations, consult the wiring diagram.

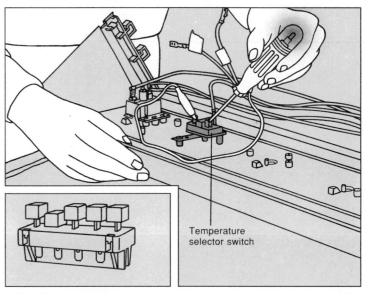

Temperature selector switch

Testing and replacing the temperature selector switch. The selector switch may be rotary or pushbutton *(inset)*; both are tested the same way. Unplug the dryer and free the control console *(page 279)*. Check the dryer's wiring diagram for the markings used on the terminals regulating the inoperative cycle. Disconnect the wires from these terminals and label them. Turn the knob to the inoperative cycle or press the corresponding button. Touch one probe of the continuity tester to each terminal *(above)*. The tester should light; if not, replace the switch. Unscrew the old switch from the control console, install the new switch and transfer the wires.

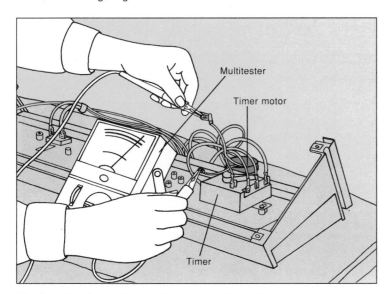

Multitester

Timer motor

Timer

Testing the timer. Unplug the dryer and free the control console *(page 279)*. To test the timer motor, disconnect its two black wires. Set a multitester to the RX1000 scale and connect a probe to each motor terminal *(above)*. The meter should show 2,000 to 3,000 ohms. If not, replace the motor by removing the two screws holding it to the timer and screwing a new motor in place. Reconnect the wires.

To test the timer itself, check the dryer's wiring diagram for the configuration of the affected cycle and disconnect the wires. Set the timer knob to the cycle. Touch one probe to each terminal; the needle should swing, indicating continuity. If the timer fails this test, replace it. Pull the control knob off the front (if the timer has a mounting bracket, reuse it). Install a new timer and transfer the wires from the old timer to the new one.

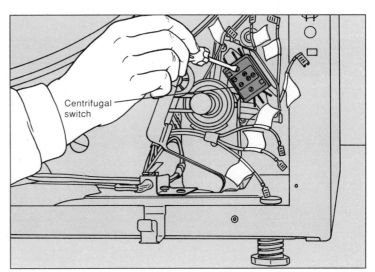

Centrifugal switch

Testing the centrifugal switch. Unplug the dryer. Mounted on the motor, the centrifugal switch is reached in most Type I dryers either by removing the toe panel *(page 280)* or by raising the top *(page 279)* and removing the front panel *(page 280)*. In Type II models, the centrifugal switch is reached through the rear panel *(page 280)*. Disconnect and label the wires, then unscrew the switch from the motor *(above)*. Place the probes of a continuity tester on terminals 1 and 2, then 5 and 6, then 5 and BK (or 3). Test with the switch button in, then out. Replace the switch if it does not show the following results:

TESTING AND REPLACING SWITCHES (continued)

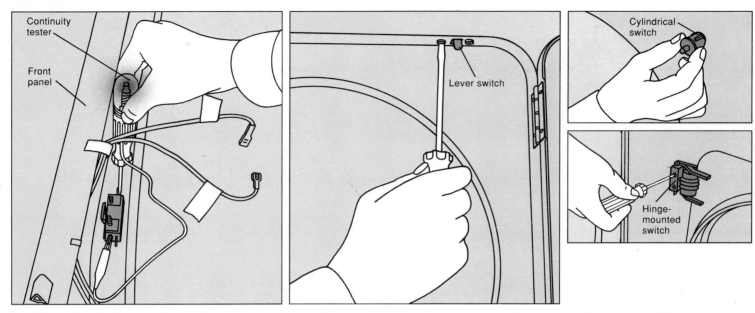

Testing and replacing the door switch. Unplug the dryer. Raise the top *(page 279)* to reach the switch, which is mounted near one of the upper corners of the dryer front. Disconnect the wires from the terminals. If the switch has two wires, touch a continuity tester probe to each terminal that was connected to a wire *(above, left)*; ignore any extra terminal. With the door closed, the tester should light, showing continuity; with the door open, it should not light.

In a dryer with a drum light, the door switch will have three wires and three terminals. Clip one probe to the common terminal (at one end of the switch or, on a cylindrical switch, the largest of the three) and touch the other probe to each of the other terminals in turn. With the door closed, the tester should light with one terminal and not light with the other; with the door open, the situation should reverse.

To replace a faulty lever-style switch *(above, center)*, remove the screws on either side of the lever. Lift out the switch from inside the dryer. To remove a cylindrical switch *(above, right, top)*, reach down inside the dryer, squeeze the retainer clips on the back of the switch and pull it out through the front. To remove a hinge-mounted switch *(above, right, bottom)*, take off the dryer front panel *(page 280)* and unscrew the switch from the door hinge.

TESTING AND REPLACING THERMOSTATS

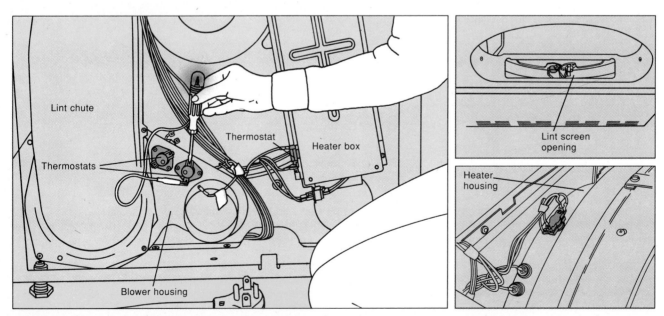

Testing and replacing thermostats or a thermal fuse. On Type I dryers, the thermostats and fuse are located on the blower housing and the heater box *(above)*. Type II dryers have thermostats under the lint screen *(above, right, top)*, on the heater housing *(above, right, bottom)*, or on the internal exhaust duct. All are tested the same way.

First, unplug the dryer. Disconnect the wires from the thermostat or fuse terminals and label their positions. Touch a continuity tester probe to each terminal, as shown; the tester should light. If either of the thermostats or the fuse fails this test, replace the faulty part. Reconnect the wires and replace the dryer panels.

SERVICING THE DRIVE BELT AND IDLER

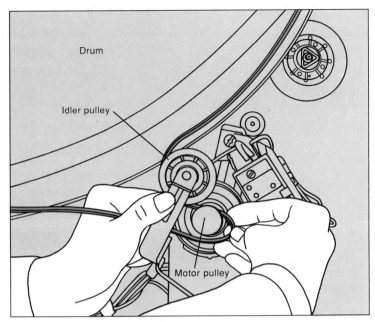

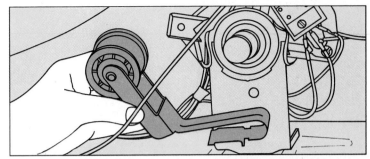

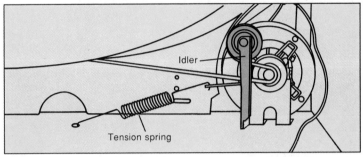

1 **Disengaging the drive belt.** Uplug the dryer. On a Type I dryer, remove the toe panel *(page 280)* or raise the top *(page 279)* and remove the front panel *(page 280)*. Prop the dryer drum on a piece of scrap wood. Push the idler pulley toward the motor pulley, releasing tension on the drive belt, and slip the belt off the motor pulley *(above)*. To access the drive belt in a Type II dryer, remove the rear panel *(page 280)*. Pull the idler pulley away from the motor pulley to release tension on the belt and slip it off the motor pulley.

2 **Removing the idler.** With the belt disengaged, inspect the idler bracket, pulley and spring. Idlers vary in style; many are one piece and are held in place in the dryer floor by belt tension *(above, top)*. Lift the idler out and check the pulley for uneven wear or wobbling. If it is damaged, install a new idler. Another type of idler has a tension spring *(above, bottom)*. Unhook the spring and replace it if worn or broken. This type of idler may also have a replaceable pulley; go to step 3 to inspect and replace it.

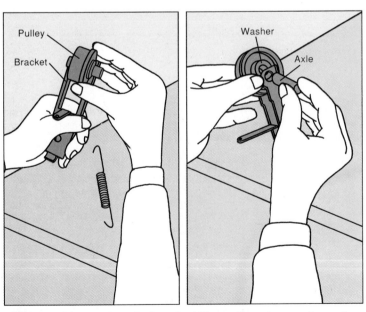

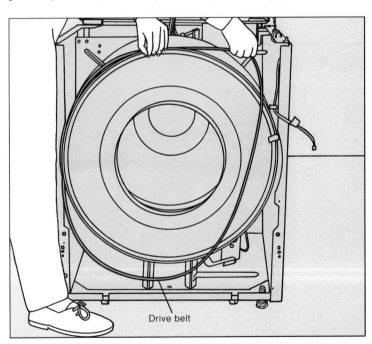

3 **Checking and replacing the idler pulley.** Inspect the surface of the pulley for uneven wear, and move it back and forth to check for wobbling *(above, left)*. To replace the pulley, use a nut driver to remove the screw at one end of the axle and slide the axle out of the pulley. Place a new pulley and washers in the bracket *(above, right)*, insert the axle, and replace the screw. Some idler pulleys have a retainer ring instead of a screw, and the axle is permanently connected to the bracket. Pry off the ring with long-nose pliers to remove and replace the pulley; snap the retainer ring back on the axle. When replacing the idler, engage the spring on the idler bracket before threading the drive belt around it.

4 **Removing and replacing the drive belt.** Raise the dryer top *(page 279)* and remove the front panel *(page 280)*. Lifting the drum slightly, slide the loose belt free. Align a new belt in the same position as the old one *(above)*, its grooved side against the drum. To rethread the belt in a Type I dryer, push a loop of the belt under the idler pulley and catch it on the motor pulley. Check that the rear drum seal rides properly on the bulkhead *(page 285)*. To rethread a Type II belt, loop it over the idler pulley and under the motor pulley. Turn the drum by hand to make sure the belt is properly positioned.

SERVICING THE DRUM

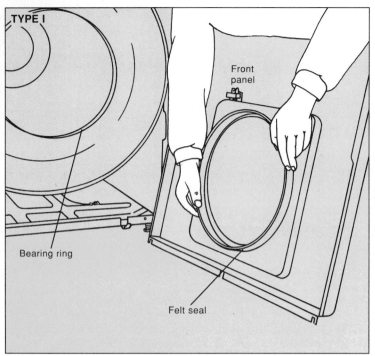

TYPE I

Front panel

Bearing ring

Felt seal

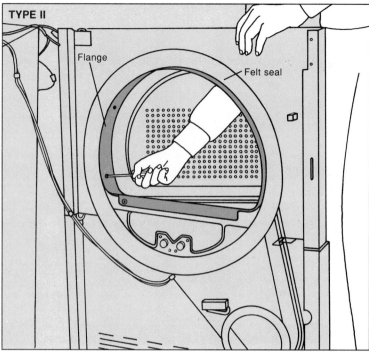

TYPE II

Flange

Felt seal

1 **Checking and replacing the front drum seal.** Unplug the dryer, lift the dryer top *(page 279)*, and remove the toe panel, if any, and the front panel *(page 280)*. Inspect the felt seal surrounding the door opening behind the front panel, and look for objects embedded in the felt. To replace the seal in a Type I dryer *(above, left)*, first peel off or unclip the old seal. Place a new seal with its folded

edge toward you and fit the holes in the seal over the clips on the rim of the door opening. Also check the plastic bearing ring within the drum opening; if it is rough or worn, snap it out and replace it. To replace a Type II seal *(above, right)*, unscrew the metal flange on which the felt is mounted, and screw on a new seal-and-flange assembly.

TYPE I

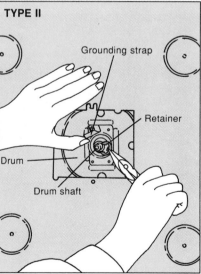

TYPE II

Grounding strap

Retainer

Drum

Drum shaft

2 **Removing the drum.** Disengage and remove the drive belt *(page 283)*. For a Type I dryer, lift the drum slightly and carefully slide it out through the front of the cabinet *(far left)*. For a Type II dryer, first unscrew the rear access panel *(page 280)* to expose the drum shaft. Loosen the grounding strap using a nut driver, then pry the retainer off the shaft with long-nose pliers *(near left)*. Carefully lift the drum out through the front of the cabinet.

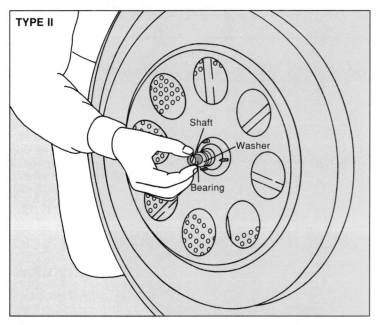

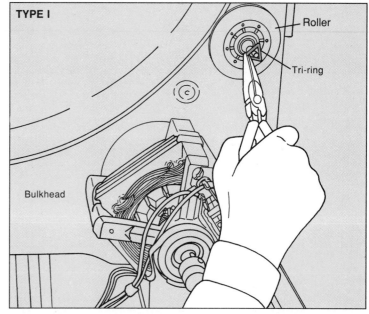

3 **Replacing the drum shaft bearing (Type II dryers).** A flexible, sleeve-like bearing cushions the drum shaft of a Type II dryer. Pull off the bearing *(above)*, and inspect it for wear. If it needs to be replaced, slide a new bearing onto the shaft, making sure the washers are in their proper positions. When reinstalling the drum *(step 6)*, be sure the bearing and washers do not slip off the shaft.

4 **Replacing drum support rollers (Type I dryers).** A pair of rubber rollers mounted on the bulkhead supports the drum in Type I dryers. With the drum removed, check each roller for wear and replace if damaged. To remove a roller, use long-nose pliers to pry off the tri-ring that secures it to the shaft *(above)*, and slide the roller off. (If the left roller has a support bracket, first unscrew it from the shaft.) Lightly lubricate the shaft with machine oil, slide on a new roller, and pop the tri-ring back onto the shaft. Screw the bracket back in place.

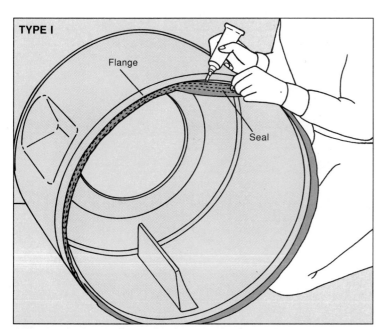

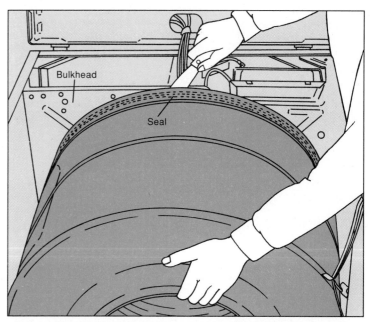

5 **Replacing the rear drum seal (Type I dryers).** With the drum removed, check the felt-and-plastic seal around its back edge; if the seal is damaged, scrape it off the drum with a putty knife. Clean any adhesive off the drum flange with a rag and paint thinner (do not use lacquer thinner). Slip a new seal around the drum flange, its stitched edge in. Lift the inner edge of the seal and apply a bead of adhesive around the drum flange *(above)*, pressing the seal down as you go. Let the adhesive set for one hour, then reinstall the drum.

6 **Reinstalling the drum.** For a Type I dryer, slide the drum in through the front of the dryer, and rest the rear drum flange on the support rollers. Rethread the drive belt *(page 283)*. Seat the rear seal against the bulkhead by inserting a putty knife between the seal and the bulkhead *(above)*; rotate the drum a full revolution to be sure the seal edge is not pinched. Replace the dryer panels.

On a Type II dryer, seat the front groove of the drum on the slides and, from the back, snap on the drum shaft retainer. Reinstall the grounding strap and the drive belt, and replace the dryer panels.

TESTING AND REPLACING THE HEATER ELEMENT (Type I dryers)

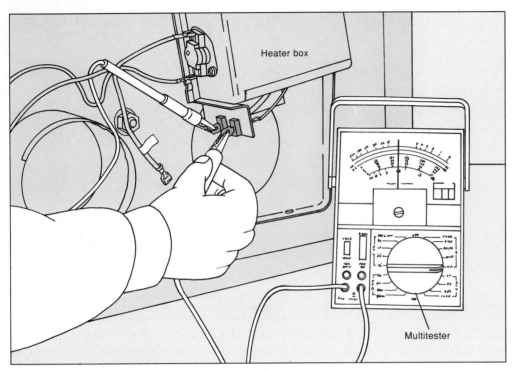

Heater box

Multitester

1 **Testing the heater element.** Unplug the dryer and remove the rear panel *(page 280)*. Disconnect the wires to the heater terminals and label their positions with masking tape. Set a multitester to the RX1 scale. If the heater has two terminals, touch one probe to each terminal *(left)*; the meter should show 5 to 50 ohms. Then touch one probe to the heater box and the other to each terminal in turn; the needle should not move from infinity. If the heater has three terminals, touch one probe to the middle terminal and the other probe to the outer terminals in turn; the meter should show 10 to 40 ohms. Then, to test for a ground, touch one probe to the heater box and the other to each terminal in turn; the meter should read infinity. If the element fails any of these tests, proceed to step 2 to remove and replace it.

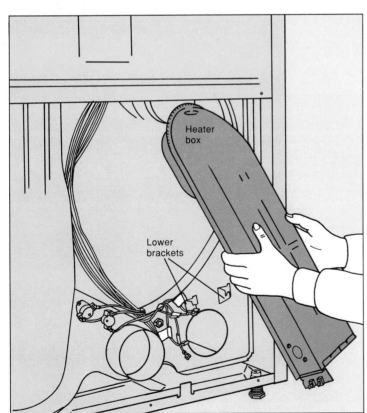

Heater box

Lower brackets

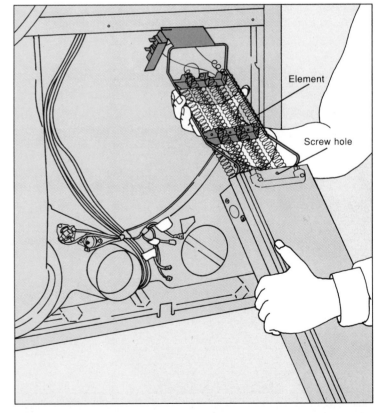

Element

Screw hole

2 **Removing the heater box.** Raise the dryer top *(page 279)* and unscrew the bracket holding the heater box to the bulkhead. Unscrew the thermostat from the side of the heater box. Lift the heater box slightly to free it from the lower brackets, and pull it down and out from the rear of the dryer *(above)*.

3 **Installing a new heater element.** Remove the screw holding the element in the heater box and carefully pull out the element *(above)*. Slide a new element into the box, same side up. Be sure the coils do not rub against the sides of the box. Insert and tighten the screw. Slide the heater box up into the rear of the dryer, hook the slots onto the lower brackets, and reattach the upper bracket. Screw the thermostat back on the heater box and replace the rear panel.

TESTING AND REPLACING THE HEATER COILS (Type II dryers)

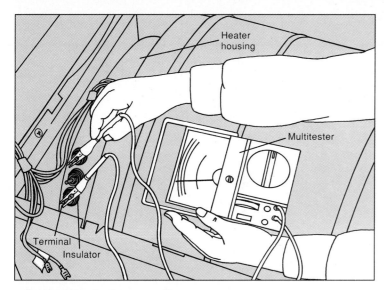

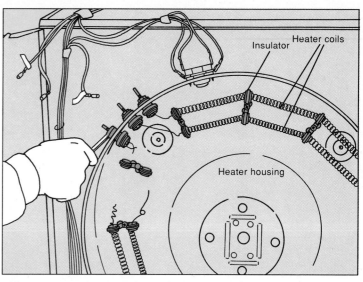

1 **Testing the heater coils.** Unplug the dryer and raise the dryer top *(page 279)*. Disconnect the wires from the insulator terminals on the heater housing and label their positions with masking tape. Set a multitester to the RX1 scale. Touch one probe to the left (common) terminal, and the other probe to each of the other terminals in turn *(above)*. In each case the multitester needle should move, showing continuity. Next, to test for a ground, touch one probe to the heater housing and the other probe to each terminal in turn. The needle should not move. If either coil fails any test, replace both coils.

2 **Removing the old heater coils.** Take out the drum *(page 284)*. Check the heater coils for breaks, burns or broken insulators. To remove the coils, use wire cutters to snip their ends near the terminals, and carefully unthread the coils through the insulators. Unscrew the nuts and washers holding the terminals to the heater housing *(above)*; discard the old terminals, but keep the ceramic insulators.

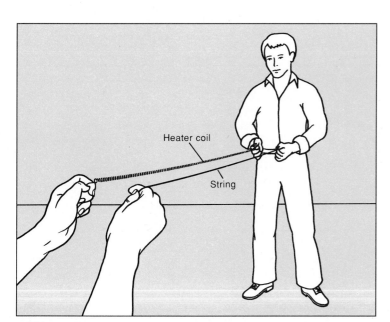

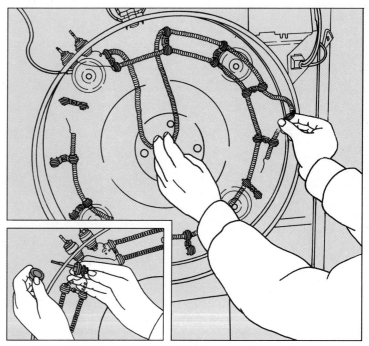

3 **Stretching a replacement coil.** New heater coils must be stretched to the required length before installation. The heater coil replacement kit indicates the length needed for your dryer model. Most often, the outer coil is stretched 63 inches to produce a relaxed length of 40 inches; the inner coil is stretched 56 inches, producing a 35-inch coil. To stretch a coil, cut a piece of string to the correct length, and hold one end of the coil and the string in each hand. With a helper, pull the coil slowly and evenly until the string is taut *(above)*. Do not stretch the coil in sections; the resulting unevenness causes hot spots. Cut and bend the ends of the outer coil to form 1-inch hooks, and the ends of the inner coil to form 1/2-inch hooks.

4 **Installing the heater coils and terminals.** Slip a nut and a washer on one end of a new terminal, hook the end of the heater coil around the terminal, and sandwich it tightly with another washer and nut. Place a ceramic insulator on the terminal and insert the terminal through a hole in the heater housing: The inner coil goes to the middle hole and the outer coil goes to the right-hand hole. Place a second insulator on each terminal from outside the housing and secure it with a nut. Gently thread each new coil clockwise through the insulators *(above)*. Wrap the two free ends around a single terminal, secure them with washers and nuts, and install the terminal with insulators in the remaining hole *(inset)*.

SMALL APPLIANCES

MICROWAVE OVENS

Unlike conventional ovens, which produce heat and transfer it to the food, microwave ovens enable food to create its own heat by bombarding it with electromagnetic waves. These microwaves set food molecules vibrating, causing friction that heats the food from within.

A typical countertop microwave oven is illustrated below. Although the wiring varies somewhat from model to model, the internal components are similar. The control center of a microwave oven is either an electronic circuit board or a mechanical timer assembly. Each regulates the cooking cycle by signaling the magnetron — a microwave generator — to turn on and off at set intervals. To produce microwaves, the magnetron requires a combination of low-voltage AC current and high-voltage DC current. The transformer takes incoming

household current of 120 volts AC and changes the voltage to higher and lower levels; a capacitor filters the high-voltage current and a diode converts it from AC to DC. The microwaves follow a wave guide from the magnetron to the oven cavity, and a stirrer, which is similar to a fan, distributes them evenly. With the door closed, microwaves cannot escape from the oven cavity; when it is opened, the door interlock switches turn off the oven. Several other safety switches and fuses protect both the oven and its user.

Most microwave oven problems are caused by inadequate cleaning or incorrect cooking techniques. Carefully follow the instructions for use in your owner's manual. Use a soft cloth and mild detergent to wash spattered food and grease off the oven cavity and door. If food cooks slowly or unevenly, stir or

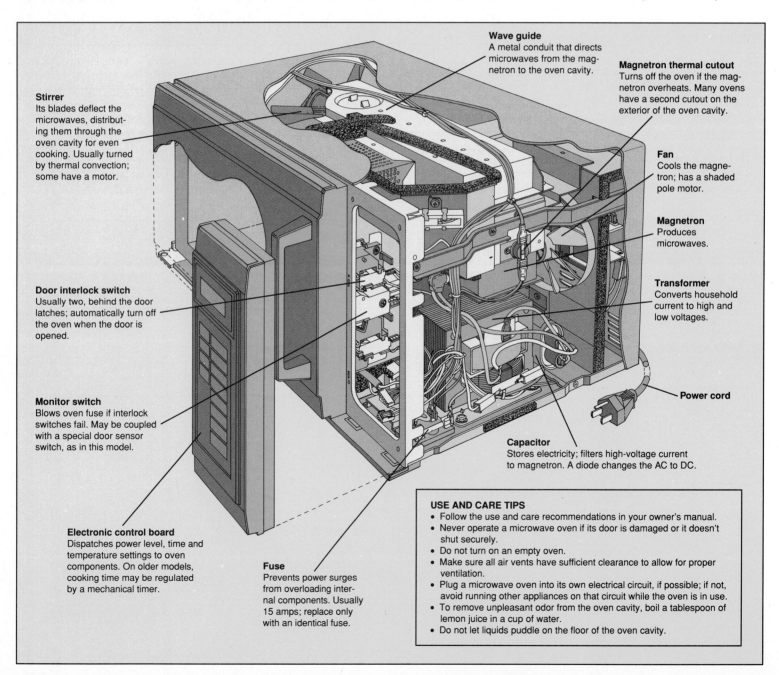

Wave guide
A metal conduit that directs microwaves from the magnetron to the oven cavity.

Magnetron thermal cutout
Turns off the oven if the magnetron overheats. Many ovens have a second cutout on the exterior of the oven cavity.

Stirrer
Its blades deflect the microwaves, distributing them through the oven cavity for even cooking. Usually turned by thermal convection; some have a motor.

Fan
Cools the magnetron; has a shaded pole motor.

Magnetron
Produces microwaves.

Door interlock switch
Usually two, behind the door latches; automatically turn off the oven when the door is opened.

Transformer
Converts household current to high and low voltages.

Monitor switch
Blows oven fuse if interlock switches fail. May be coupled with a special door sensor switch, as in this model.

Power cord

Capacitor
Stores electricity; filters high-voltage current to magnetron. A diode changes the AC to DC.

Electronic control board
Dispatches power level, time and temperature settings to oven components. On older models, cooking time may be regulated by a mechanical timer.

Fuse
Prevents power surges from overloading internal components. Usually 15 amps; replace only with an identical fuse.

USE AND CARE TIPS
- Follow the use and care recommendations in your owner's manual.
- Never operate a microwave oven if its door is damaged or it doesn't shut securely.
- Do not turn on an empty oven.
- Make sure all air vents have sufficient clearance to allow for proper ventilation.
- Plug a microwave oven into its own electrical circuit, if possible; if not, avoid running other appliances on that circuit while the oven is in use.
- To remove unpleasant odor from the oven cavity, boil a tablespoon of lemon juice in a cup of water.
- Do not let liquids puddle on the floor of the oven cavity.

turn the food halfway through the cooking cycle to balance its microwave exposure, and let it stand for a few minutes after cooking. Always put some food or drink in the oven before you turn it on; the microwaves must be absorbed or the magnetron will be damaged. Use only cookware recommended by the manufacturer, and avoid metallic containers, which can cause sparking and uneven cooking. To test whether a dish is microwave safe, place it in the oven alongside a cup of water and turn on the oven for one minute. Carefully touch the dish; if it is hot, do not use it.

In spite of its unconventional operation, a microwave oven is a sturdy, simple machine manufactured according to strict government regulations. If the oven doesn't work, first check your main service panel for a blown fuse or tripped circuit breaker. Make sure the oven is plugged into a grounded outlet; if possible, on a separate circuit from other kitchen appliances to avoid power overload.

Consult the Troubleshooting Guide below to help diagnose and fix problems, but if your oven is still under warranty, take it for professional service. Before working on any internal component, discharge the capacitor with a capacitor discharging tool. Many repairs call for a multitester; to learn how to use this and other tools correctly, read Tools and Techniques *(page 417)*. After any repair, test the oven fuse *(page 294)* and make sure that no bare wires are exposed or touching the chassis. After reassembling the oven but before plugging it in, do a cold check for leaking voltage, then take the oven for a microwave leakage test.

TROUBLESHOOTING GUIDE   continued ▶

SYMPTOM	POSSIBLE CAUSE	PROCEDURE
Microwave oven doesn't work at all	Oven unplugged or turned off, or door not closed properly	Plug in oven, close door securely and turn on oven
	No power to outlet or outlet faulty	Reset breaker or replace fuse *(p. 102)* □○; service outlet *(p. 148)*
	Power cord faulty	Test and replace power cord *(p. 417)* ◨○▲
	Oven fuse blown	Test and replace oven fuse *(p. 294)* ◨○
	Door interlock switch or monitor switch faulty	Check oven fuse *(p. 294)* ◨○; test and replace interlock switches *(p. 294)* □○ and monitor switch *(p. 295)* ◨○
	Thermal cutout faulty	Test and replace thermal cutouts *(p. 295)* ◨○
	Circuit board faulty	Take oven for professional service
Oven doesn't cook, but display lights are on	Door interlock switch or monitor switch faulty	Test and replace interlock switches *(p. 294)* □○ and monitor switch *(p. 295)* ◨○
	Thermal cutout faulty	Test and replace thermal cutouts *(p. 295)* ◨○
	Door, triac or circuit board faulty	Take oven for professional service
Oven doesn't cook, but emits humming sound	Transformer faulty	Test and replace transformer *(p. 296)* ■○▲
	Capacitor faulty	Test and replace capacitor *(p. 297)* ◨○▲
	Diode faulty	Test and replace diode *(p. 297)* ◨○▲
	Magnetron faulty	Take oven for professional service
Oven starts cooking, then stops	Other appliances on circuit draining power	Reset breaker or replace fuse *(p. 102)* □○ and plug oven into separate circuit
	Power cord faulty	Check oven fuse *(p. 294)* ◨○; test power cord *(p. 417)* ◨○▲
	Door interlock switch or monitor switch faulty	Check oven fuse *(p. 294)* ◨○; test and replace interlock switches *(p. 294)* □○ and monitor switch *(p. 295)* ◨○
	Thermal cutout faulty	Test thermal cutouts *(p. 295)* ◨○; check fuse *(p. 295)* ◨○
	Fan jammed or fan motor faulty	Service fan motor *(p. 298)* ◨◓▲; check oven fuse *(p. 294)* ◨○
	Transformer faulty	Test transformer *(p. 296)* ■○▲; check fuse *(p. 294)* ◨○
	Capacitor faulty	Test and replace capacitor *(p. 297)* ◨○▲; check fuse *(p. 294)* ◨○
	Diode faulty	Test and replace diode *(p. 297)* ◨○▲; check oven fuse *(p. 294)* ◨○
	Circuit board, triac or magnetron faulty	Take oven for professional service
Oven cooks slowly or intermittently	Power cord faulty	Test and replace power cord *(p. 417)* ◨○▲
	Voltage too low at wall outlet	Call an electrician for service
	Door interlock switch or monitor switch faulty	Check oven fuse *(p. 294)* ◨○; test and replace interlock switches *(p. 294)* □○ and monitor switch *(p. 295)* ◨○
	Fan jammed or fan motor faulty	Check whether blades turn freely; service fan motor *(p. 298)* ◨◓▲

DEGREE OF DIFFICULTY: □ Easy ◨ Moderate ■ Complex
ESTIMATED TIME: ○ Less than 1 hour ◓ 1 to 3 hours ● Over 3 hours   ▲ Multitester required

TROUBLESHOOTING GUIDE (continued)

SYMPTOM	POSSIBLE CAUSE	PROCEDURE
Oven cooks slowly or intermittently (continued)	Thermal cutout faulty	Test and replace thermal cutouts (p. 295) ▣○
	Mechanical timer assembly faulty	Test and replace mechanical timer assembly (p. 299) ▣○▲
	Transformer wire connections loose	Check wire connections; repair if necessary (p. 417) □○
	Circuit board, triac or magnetron faulty	Take oven for professional service
Oven burns or undercooks food regularly	Timer programmed incorrectly	Consult owner's manual and manufacturer's cookbook
	Mechanical timer assembly faulty	Test and replace mechanical timer assembly (p. 299) ▣○▲
	Stirrer, circuit board or triac faulty	Take oven for professional service
Oven cooks food unevenly	Cooking methods incorrect	Consult manufacturer's cookbook
	Dish not microwave safe	Consult owner's manual and use correct dish
	Microwave distribution uneven	Rearrange food halfway through cycle; install windup turntable
	Stirrer dirty or faulty, or oven cavity lining chipped or rusted	Take oven for professional service
Oven doesn't turn off	Mechanical timer assembly faulty	Test and replace mechanical timer assembly (p. 299) ▣○▲
	Circuit board or triac faulty	Take oven for professional service
Temperature probe doesn't work	Controls not set for probe, or probe faulty	Check setting for probe; test and replace probe (p. 292) ▣○▲
	Probe jack greasy or clogged	Unplug oven; clean jack with cotton swab dipped in soapy water
	Probe jack or circuit board faulty	Take oven for professional service
Door doesn't close properly	Door misaligned or gasket damaged	Take oven for professional service
Oven light doesn't work	Bulb burned out	Consult owner's manual and replace bulb
	Thermal cutout faulty	Test and replace thermal cutouts (p. 295) ▣○
Oven light doesn't turn off	Circuit board faulty	Take oven for professional service
Sparks in oven cavity while cooking	Dish, metal food wrap not microwave safe	Consult owner's manual and use correct dish or wrap
	Oven cavity lining chipped or rusted, or magnetron faulty	Take oven for professional service
Oven gives electrical shock	Components not properly grounded	Take oven for professional service

DEGREE OF DIFFICULTY: □ Easy ▣ Moderate ■ Complex
ESTIMATED TIME: ○ Less than 1 hour ◖ 1 to 3 hours ● Over 3 hours　　　　　▲ Multitiester required

SERVICING THE TEMPERATURE PROBE

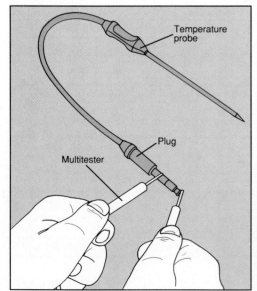

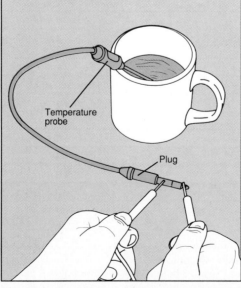

Testing the temperature probe. Set a multitester at RX10K to test resistance *(page 417)*. Touch one probe of the multitester to the tip of the plug and the second probe to the shaft of the plug, above the black ring *(far left)*. The multitester should register partial resistance. If the plug has infinite or zero resistance, replace the temperature probe. If it tests OK, perform a heat test: Heat a cup of water to boiling. Insert the thermometer end of the temperature probe into the water and repeat the resistance test *(near left)*. The multitester needle should swing to the middle of the scale, then gradually fall back toward infinite resistance as the water cools. If the temperature probe tests OK, suspect a faulty circuit board and take the microwave oven for professional service. If the probe fails any test, replace it with an exact duplicate from a microwave oven service center or from the manufacturer.

ACCESS TO OVEN COMPONENTS

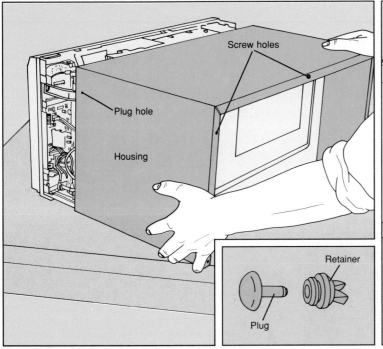

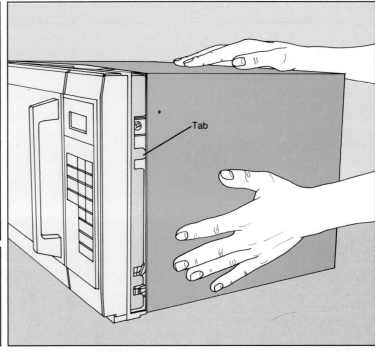

Removing and replacing the housing. Before working on a microwave oven, make a capacitor discharging tool *(page 417)*. If the oven is mounted under a cabinet or on the wall, consult the manufacturer's installation guide for the correct dismounting procedures. Unplug a countertop microwave oven and place it on a sturdy work table. The metal housing on the model shown above is secured to the oven chassis by screws in the back and by plastic plug fasteners *(inset)* through the sides. Use a screwdriver to remove all screws. Extract the plugs from their retainers using a narrow-tipped screwdriver padded with masking tape. Some oven housings

are secured by screws with splined washers; keep the washers for replacement later. When all screws and plugs have been removed, slide off the oven housing *(above, left)* to access the oven's internal components. Before servicing any of them, discharge the capacitor *(step below)*. After working on the microwave oven, reinstall the housing. Adjust its position so that the metal tabs on the front of the oven chassis fit into the slots on the housing *(above, right)*. Reinstall all screws and plastic plugs and cold check for leaking voltage *(page 417)* before plugging in the oven then take the oven for a microwave leakage test.

DISCHARGING THE CAPACITOR

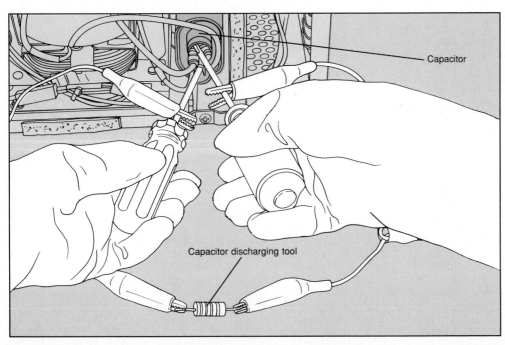

Discharging a capacitor. Unplug the oven and remove its housing *(step above)*. **Caution:** Capacitors store potentially dangerous voltage. Before working on any internal components, wait five minutes and then use a capacitor discharging tool *(page 417)* to drain the capacitor of stored charge. Locate the capacitor, an oblong metal canister with two terminals. Without touching any internal component, touch one screwdriver blade of the discharging tool to one capacitor terminal and the other blade to the other terminal at the same time, and hold for one second *(left)*. The capacitor may spark as it discharges.

TESTING AND REPLACING THE OVEN FUSE

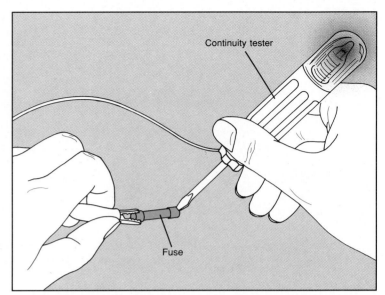

1 **Removing the fuse.** Unplug the oven, remove the housing and discharge the capacitor *(page 293)*. On the model shown here, the fuse is clearly visible on a junction board on the chassis floor. On some models, the fuse may be hidden by oven components; locate it by tracing the black wire and white wire from the power cord to their terminals on the power block next to the fuse. To remove the fuse for testing, use a fuse puller to gently pry it out of its retaining clips *(above)*.

2 **Testing the fuse.** To test the oven fuse for continuity, use a continuity tester. Touch a probe to each end of the fuse *(above)*. If the tester lights, reinstall the fuse. If it doesn't, replace the fuse with an exact duplicate purchased at an electronics parts supplier. Gently push the fuse into its retaining clips and reinstall the oven housing. Plug in the oven. If the fuse blows repeatedly, consult the Troubleshooting Guide for other possible causes for the problem.

SERVICING A DOOR INTERLOCK SWITCH

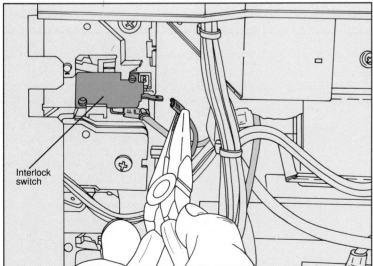

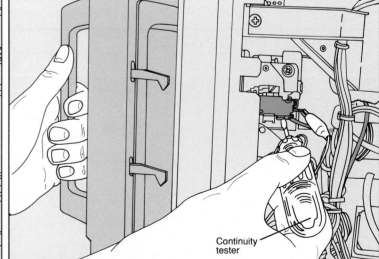

Testing an interlock switch. Unplug the oven, remove the housing and discharge the capacitor *(page 293)*. Locate the two door interlock switches behind the door latches. If a wire is loose or broken, repair the wire connection *(page 417)*. To test an interlock switch, use long-nose pliers to disconnect one wire from its terminal *(above, left)*. Attach the alligator clip of a continuity tester to this terminal and touch the probe to the second terminal *(above, right)*. With the oven door closed, the tester should light, and with the door open, the tester should not light. Test the second interlock switch the same way. If both switches test OK, return to the Troubleshooting Guide *(page 291)* to check for other possible

causes of oven malfunction before reinstalling the housing. If either switch fails this test, replace it: Label and disconnect the second wire. Unscrew or unclip the faulty switch from its mounting block and buy an exact replacement from a microwave oven service center or the manufacturer. Install the new switch, reversing the steps you took for removal. Reinstall the housing, cold check for leaking voltage *(page 417)* and take the oven to a microwave oven service center for a microwave leakage test. If you have trouble removing a switch, reinstall the housing and take the oven for professional service.

SERVICING THE MONITOR SWITCH

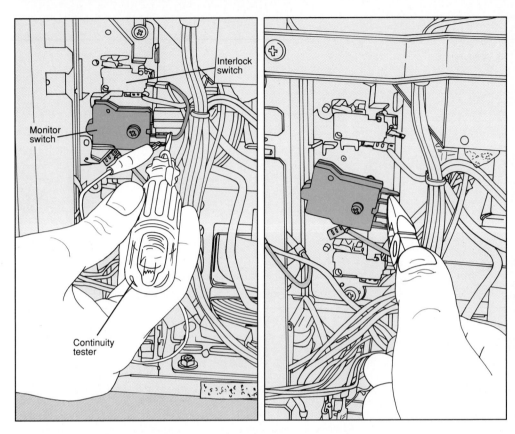

Interlock switch

Monitor switch

Continuity tester

Testing and replacing the monitor switch. Unplug the oven, remove the housing and discharge the capacitor *(page 293)*. Locate the monitor switch, between the door interlock switches behind the door latches. In the model shown here, it is coupled with a door sensor switch. Use long-nose pliers to disconnect the wire from the lowest terminal on the switch. Attach the alligator clip of a continuity tester to the free terminal and touch the probe to the terminal directly above it *(far left)*. With the door open, the tester should light, and with the door closed, it should not light. If the switch fails this test, replace it. If the switch tests OK, reconnect the wire and consult the Troubleshooting Guide for other possible causes of oven malfunction before reinstalling the housing. To replace a faulty switch, label and disconnect its second wire. Unscrew or unclip the switch and pull it off its mounting plate. Purchase an exact replacement switch from a microwave oven service center or the manufacturer. To install a new switch, use long-nose pliers to position the switch on the mounting plate *(near left),* then screw or clip it on. Reconnect the wires and reinstall the housing *(page 293)*.

TESTING AND REPLACING A THERMAL CUTOUT

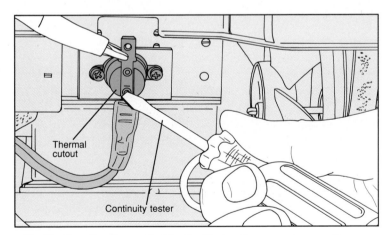

Thermal cutout

Continuity tester

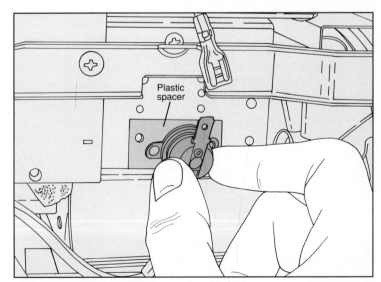

Plastic spacer

1 **Testing the thermal cutouts.** Unplug the oven, remove the housing and discharge the capacitor *(page 293)*. Locate the round, flat thermal cutout mounted on the magnetron. To test the cutout for continuity, disconnect one of its wires and attach the alligator clip of a continuity tester to the free terminal. Touch the probe to the second terminal *(above)*. The tester should light. If it doesn't, go to step 2 to replace the cutout. If it tests OK, reconnect the wire. Many microwave ovens have a second thermal cutout on the other side of the oven or on top. Test it the same way. If both thermal cutouts test OK, consult the Troubleshooting Guide *(page 291)* for other possible causes of oven malfunction before reinstalling the housing.

2 **Replacing a thermal cutout.** Label and disconnect the second wire. Use a screwdriver to remove the two screws holding the cutout in place and take it off, noting its exact position. If there is a plastic spacer on the magnetron's thermal cutout, keep it for reuse. Buy an identical thermal cutout from a microwave oven service center or the manufacturer. Mount the new cutout in the same spot, using the screws and spacer you removed. Reconnect the wires and reinstall the housing *(page 293)*.

SERVICING THE TRANSFORMER

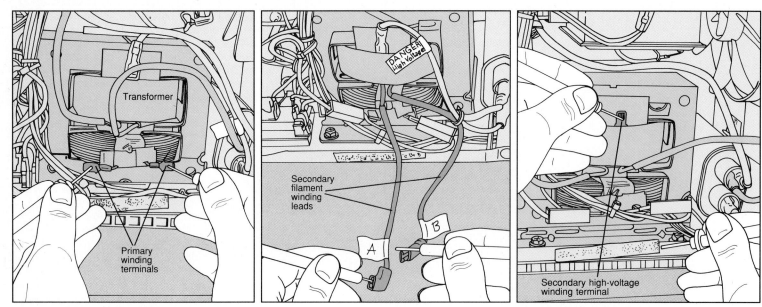

1 **Testing the transformer.** Unplug the oven, remove the housing and discharge the capacitor *(page 293)*. Locate the transformer, a large metal block with exposed windings. If the transformer smells or looks burned, take the oven for professional service. To test each of the three transformer windings for less obvious damage, set a multitester to RX1. First locate the primary winding, typically visible through an opening in the transformer. Label and disconnect the winding's two wires and touch a probe to each terminal *(above, left)*. The multitester should indicate very low resistance. If not, replace the transformer *(step 2)*. If the winding tests OK, reconnect the wires and test the secondary filament winding. Identify this winding by its two insulated wires that lead to terminals on the magnetron and the capacitor. Label and disonnect

the wires. Touch a probe to each wire *(above, center)*. The multitester should indicate very low resistance. If not, replace the transformer *(step 2)*. If it tests OK, reconnect the wires and go on to test the secondary high-voltage winding, which is generally hidden behind the manufacturer's label. If the transformer winding has only one terminal as shown above, disconnect the wire and test between the terminal and the chassis *(above, right)*. If the winding has two terminals, label and disconnect both wires and test between both terminals. The multitester should indicate some resistance. If not, replace the transformer *(step 2)*. If the windings test OK, suspect a faulty triac or control board and take the oven for professional service.

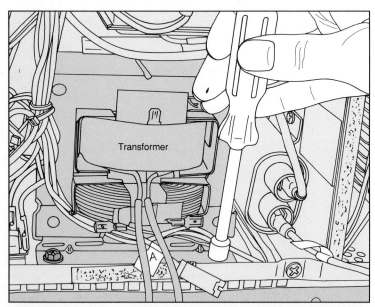

2 **Removing the transformer.** Label each transformer wire lead by its winding and position, and use long-nose pliers to disconnect it from its terminal. Locate the screws or bolts that secure the transformer to the oven chassis and unscrew them *(above)*. Pull the transformer out of the oven.

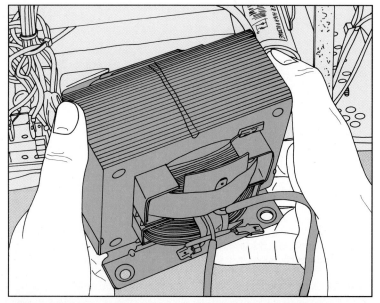

3 **Installing a new transformer.** Purchase an identical replacement transformer from a microwave oven service center or from the manufacturer. Position the new transformer *(above)*, securing it tightly to the chassis floor using the same screws or bolts you removed. Reconnect all wires to their correct terminals, and reinstall the oven housing *(page 293)*.

SERVICING THE CAPACITOR

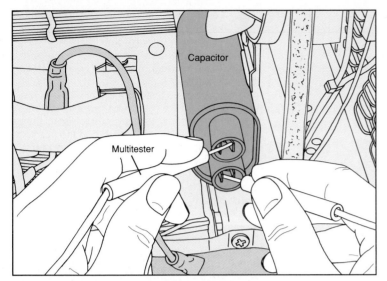

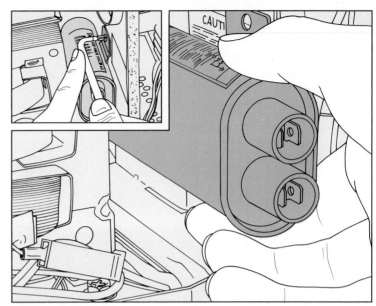

1 **Testing the capacitor.** Unplug the oven, remove the housing and discharge the capacitor *(page 293)*. Inspect the capacitor and replace one that is bulging or cracked *(step 2)*. To check for less evident damage, set a multitester to RX10K. Label the wires and disconnect them from the capacitor terminals. Touch a tester probe to each terminal *(above)*. The needle should rise, then fall immediately. If the capacitor tests OK, return to the Troubleshooting Guide and check for other possible causes of oven malfunction before reinstalling its housing. If the multitester needle swings to the right and stays, or if it doesn't move at all, replace the capacitor *(step 2)*.

2 **Replacing the capacitor.** Locate and remove the screws securing the capacitor to the oven chassis. On the model shown here, the capacitor mounting screw is difficult to reach; use an offset screwdriver to remove it *(inset)* and pull the capacitor free *(above)*. It may be necessary to remove the transformer *(page 296)* and/or the fan blade *(page 298)* before lifting out the capacitor. Purchase an exact replacement capacitor from a microwave oven service center or the manufacturer and screw it in place. Reconnect all wires and reinstall the housing *(page 293)*.

TESTING THE DIODE

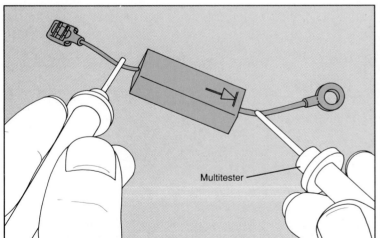

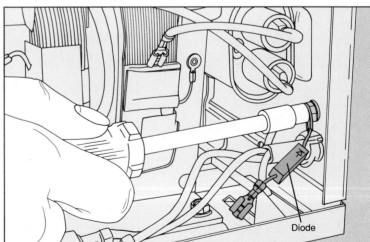

Testing the diode. Unplug the oven, remove the housing and discharge the capacitor *(page 293)*. Locate the diode, a small component connected to one of the capacitor terminals and to the chassis. If the diode isn't visible, it is encased within the capacitor housing and is difficult to test; take the oven for professional service. To test an externally-mounted diode, use a multitester set to its highest ohms setting to test resistance. Pull the diode connector off the capacitor terminal with long-nose pliers and unscrew the diode's ground wire from the chassis using a nut driver or screwdriver. Touch a multitester probe to each wire end

(above, left), then reverse the probe positions and repeat the test. In one test, the multitester needle should register partial resistance. In the other, it should register infinite resistance. If the diode tests faulty, buy an exact replacement from a microwave oven service center or the manufacturer. Position the diode so that its symbol points toward the chassis, and secure one wire to the chassis *(above, right)* and the other wire to the capacitor terminal. If the diode tests OK reinstall it, then return to the Troubleshooting Guide to check for other possible causes of oven malfunction before reinstalling the housing *(page 293)*.

INSPECTING AND REPLACING THE FAN MOTOR

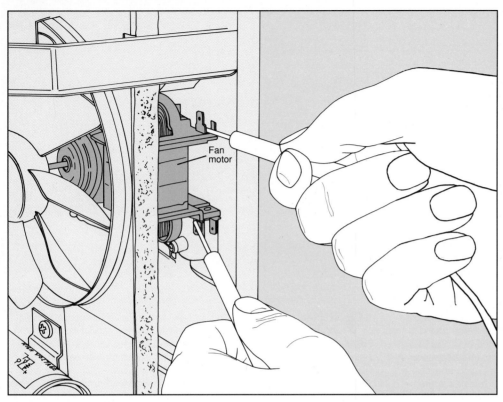

1 **Testing the fan motor.** To check whether the fan is operating, first remove the oven housing. **Caution:** Do not touch any internal components. Put a cup of water in the oven cavity, close the door, plug in the oven and turn it on for less than a minute. Do not touch the microwave oven. Observe the fan; if it does not revolve, unplug the oven, wait five minutes and discharge the capacitor *(page 293)*. Remove any obstructions that may be preventing the fan from rotating. Turn the blades by hand; if they don't move easily, disconnect the wires from the motor and take out the motor *(steps 2-5)* for professional service. If the fan blades move freely, check for a burning smell and examine the motor windings for discoloration. If a wire is loose or broken, repair the wire connection *(page 417)*. To test the motor for less visible damage, set a multitester to test resistance. Label and disconnect the wires. Touch a multitester probe to each motor terminal *(left)*. The motor should have low resistance. If not, replace it. If the motor tests OK, return to the Troubleshooting Guide and check for other causes of oven malfunction before reinstalling its housing.

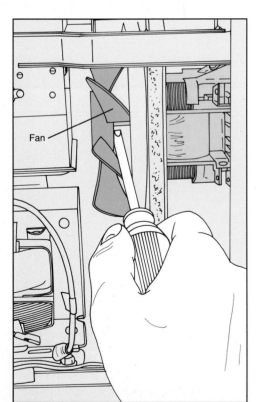

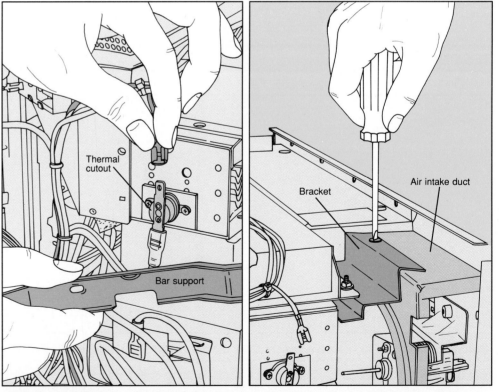

2 **Removing the fan.** Fan motors are mounted in various ways. On this model, remove several parts to access the motor: First, slip a screwdriver between the fan blades and the intake duct and pry the fan off the motor shaft *(above)*.

3 **Removing the bar support and bracket.** Unscrew the bar support from the front and back of the oven chassis and from the exterior of the magnetron. Pull the wire connector off the top terminal of the thermal cutout, and lift the bar support free *(above, left)*. Remove the screw securing the holding bracket to the air intake duct *(above, right)* and slide out the bracket.

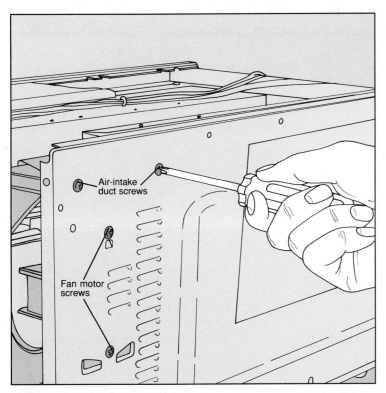

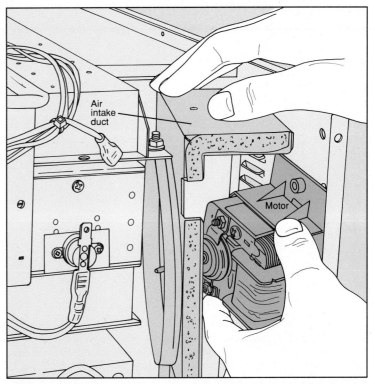

4 Freeing the fan motor. Remove the screws securing the air intake duct to the chassis *(above)*; on this model, two screws attach the duct to the back, while one screw attaches it to the floor. Then unscrew the motor from the back of the chassis. Do not remove more screws than necessary. Push the air intake duct toward the magnetron. If the duct is secured to the exterior of the oven cavity with a clip, lift the duct over the clip and then push the duct aside.

5 Replacing the fan motor. The motor is held in a casing that is in turn slotted into the chassis. Firmly grasp the motor and slide the casing out of the slots *(above)*. Then angle the motor shaft inward and pull the motor free. Have the motor serviced or purchase an exact replacement from a microwave oven service center or the manufacturer. To install the new motor, reverse the steps taken for removal, and reinstall the housing *(page 293)*.

SERVICING A MECHANICAL TIMER ASSEMBLY

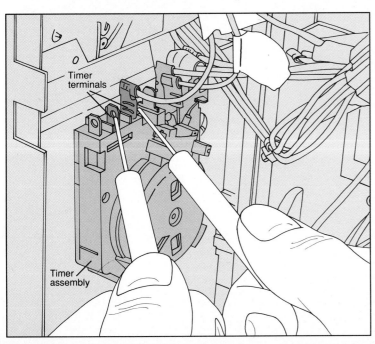

1 Testing the timer switch. Set the timer knob to 1 minute, place a cup of water in the oven cavity, and turn on the oven. Check the timer's accuracy with a wristwatch. If the timer keeps the correct time, suspect a faulty circuit board and take the oven for professional service. If the timer loses or gains time, replace the timer assembly *(step 3)*. If the timer knob doesn't move at all, turn on the oven again and press your fingers against the control panel next to the timer knob. If you do not feel a vibration, the timer motor may be faulty; test it *(step 2)*. If you feel a vibration, test the timer switch: Turn off the microwave, remove the housing and discharge the capacitor *(page 293)*. Locate the timer assembly behind the timer knob. If a wire connection is broken or loose, repair it *(page 417)*. Turn on the timer and set a multitester to test resistance, usually RX100. Some timer switches, like the one here, have three terminals. Label and disconnect two of the wires and test all three possible pairings of terminals *(left)*. The multitester should indicate some resistance at least once. If the timer switch has only two terminals, pull off one wire and test for continuity between the terminals. The multitester should indicate continuity. If the switch doesn't show resistance or continuity when it should, replace the timer assembly *(step 3)*. If it tests OK, test the timer motor *(step 2)*.

SERVICING A MECHANICAL TIMER ASSEMBLY (continued)

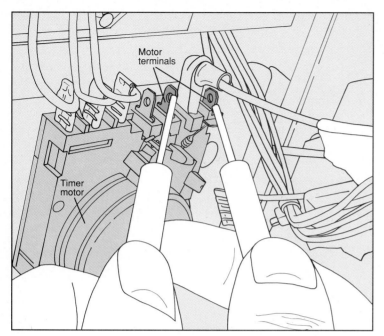

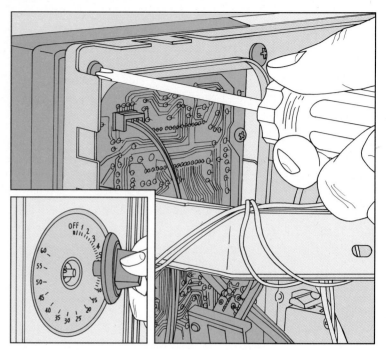

2 **Testing the timer motor.** Unplug the oven, remove the housing and discharge the capacitor *(page 293)*. The timer motor has two terminals, one wired to the fan motor and a thermal cutout, and a second wired to the circuit board. Label and disconnect a wire from each terminal. Set a multitester to RX100 and touch a probe to each terminal *(above)*. The multitester should indicate partial resistance. If the timer motor tests faulty, replace the timer assembly *(step 3)*. If it tests OK, suspect a faulty circuit board and take the oven for professional service.

3 **Removing the control panel frame.** With the housing removed and the capacitor discharged *(page 293)*, pull all knobs and buttons straight off the control panel *(inset)*. If a knob won't budge, slip a cloth behind it and pull the cloth to dislodge it. Label all wires on the back of the control panel, and disconnect them. Remove the screws attaching the control panel frame to the oven chassis *(above)*. Lift the panel frame off the front of the oven and set it face down on a padded work surface.

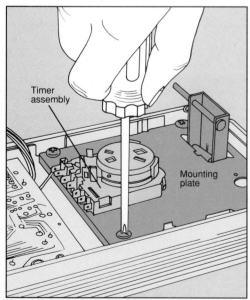

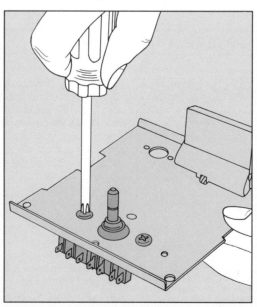

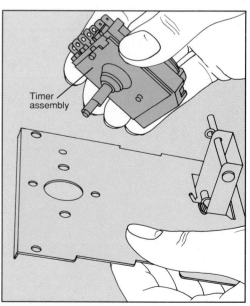

4 **Replacing the timer assembly.** Remove the screws attaching the timer-assembly mounting plate to the control panel frame *(above, left)*, then lift off the mounting plate. Turn the plate over, placing the timer assembly shaft up on the work surface. Unscrew the two screws securing the timer assembly to the mounting plate *(above, center)* and pull it off the plate *(above, right)*. Purchase an identical replacement timer assembly from a microwave oven service center or from the manufacturer. To install a new timer, reverse the steps taken for removal. Reattach the control panel frame to the oven chassis and reconnect all wires to the circuit board and the timer assembly. Reinstall the housing *(page 293)*.

TOASTERS AND TOASTER OVENS

The ubiquitous toaster and its versatile cousin, the toaster oven, are among the most frequently used of small kitchen appliances. Even so, with regular cleaning and proper care they will operate for years. Consult the Troubleshooting Guide below when a problem does arise. While cheaper models are uneconomical to repair, more expensive toasters and toaster ovens can be fixed at a fraction of their replacement price. Keep in mind, however, that some toaster parts are now riveted to the chassis, and most toaster-oven connections are spot welded. Replace rivets as described in this chapter *(page 304)*. Replace a welded connection with silver solder; consult Tools & Techniques *(page 417)*.

The deceptive ease with which a toaster browns bread belies a complicated interaction of mechanical and electrical events.

When the carriage lowers, it catches a latch that closes a main switch, completing a circuit to the heating elements. In some toasters a thermostat alone controls the heat, but in the model shown on page 302, the thermostat works with a solenoid switch and solenoid. When the thermostat's metal arm bends with the heat, it closes the switch, allowing current to magnetize the solenoid. The solenoid then pulls a metal latch release, freeing the latch so that the carriage can pop up.

The toaster oven works on virtually the same principles as a toaster, but since it also bakes and broils it has a radically different design. As illustrated on page 305, a typical toaster oven has two thermostats, one for toasting, the other for baking. In the unlikely event that either breaks, their repair is best left to an authorized repair center.

TROUBLESHOOTING GUIDE

SYMPTOM	POSSIBLE CAUSE	PROCEDURE
TOASTERS		
Carriage lowers and latches, but toaster doesn't turn on	No power to outlet or outlet faulty	Reset breaker or replace fuse *(p. 102)* □○; service outlet *(p. 148)*
	Power cord faulty	Test and replace power cord *(p. 417)* ■○▲
	Main switch contacts broken	Replace chassis *(p. 303)* ■○; replace toaster
Carriage lowers or latches stiffly or not at all	Slide rod or latches dirty or obstructed	Service carriage-and-latch assembly *(p. 304)* ■○
Toaster buzzes when latched and carriage pops up instantly	Toaster not cooling after toasting	Select darker color setting or wait longer between batches of toast
	Solenoid switch faulty	Test and replace solenoid switch *(p. 303)* ■○
Toaster stays on after carriage pops up	Main switch contacts fused	Access chassis and replace chassis if necessary *(p. 303)* ■○; or replace toaster
Carriage doesn't pop up and toast burns	Thermostat calibrated incorrectly	Recalibrate thermostat *(p. 302)* □○
	Solenoid switch or solenoid faulty	Test, replace solenoid switch *(p. 303)* ■○ or solenoid *(p. 304)* ■○▲
	Thermostat faulty	Replace toaster
Toast too dark or too light	Thermostat calibrated incorrectly	Recalibrate thermostat *(p. 302)* □○
Bread toasts on only one side	Element or elements faulty	Replace chassis *(p. 303)* ■○; or replace toaster
Toaster gives electrical shock	Internal component grounded to chassis	Take toaster for professional service
TOASTER OVENS		
Toaster oven doesn't work on toaster function and oven function	No power to outlet or outlet faulty	Reset breaker or replace fuse *(p. 102)* □○; service outlet *(p. 148)*
	Power cord faulty	Test and replace power cord *(p. 417)* ■○▲
	Main switch faulty	Service main switch *(p. 306)* ■○
	Thermal fuse or heating element faulty	Test and replace thermal fuse or heating element *(p. 308)* ■○
Toaster oven works on only one function	Oven control thermostat or toaster switch faulty	Take toaster oven for professional service
Toaster function doesn't turn off unless door is opened	Solenoid faulty	Test and replace solenoid *(p. 307)* ■○▲
	Toaster switch or toaster thermostat faulty	Take toaster oven for professional service
Toaster function buzzes and latch doesn't stay down	Toaster thermostat faulty	Take toaster oven for professional service
Toaster oven stays on when door is opened	Main switch faulty	Service main switch *(p. 306)* ■○
Upper or lower elements don't heat	Upper or lower element faulty	Test and replace element *(p. 308)* ■○▲
	Oven or toaster thermostat faulty	Take toaster oven for professional service
Oven gives electrical shock	Internal component grounded to chassis	Take toaster oven for professional service

DEGREE OF DIFFICULTY: □ Easy   ■ Moderate   ■ Complex
ESTIMATED TIME: ○ Less than 1 hour   ◖ 1 to 3 hours   ● Over 3 hours   ▲ Multitester required

TOASTERS

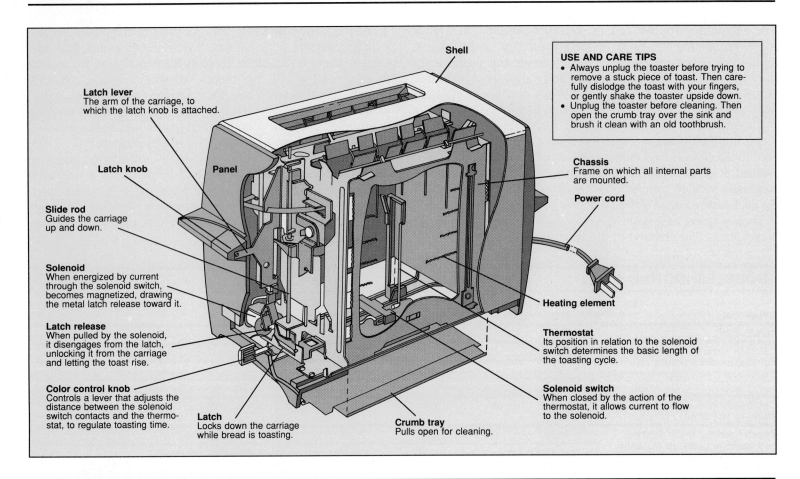

Shell

Latch lever
The arm of the carriage, to which the latch knob is attached.

Latch knob   **Panel**

Slide rod
Guides the carriage up and down.

Solenoid
When energized by current through the solenoid switch, becomes magnetized, drawing the metal latch release toward it.

Latch release
When pulled by the solenoid, it disengages from the latch, unlocking it from the carriage and letting the toast rise.

Color control knob
Controls a lever that adjusts the distance between the solenoid switch contacts and the thermostat, to regulate toasting time.

Latch
Locks down the carriage while bread is toasting.

Crumb tray
Pulls open for cleaning.

Chassis
Frame on which all internal parts are mounted.

Power cord

Heating element

Thermostat
Its position in relation to the solenoid switch determines the basic length of the toasting cycle.

Solenoid switch
When closed by the action of the thermostat, it allows current to flow to the solenoid.

USE AND CARE TIPS
- Always unplug the toaster before trying to remove a stuck piece of toast. Then carefully dislodge the toast with your fingers, or gently shake the toaster upside down.
- Unplug the toaster before cleaning. Then open the crumb tray over the sink and brush it clean with an old toothbrush.

RECALIBRATING THE THERMOSTAT

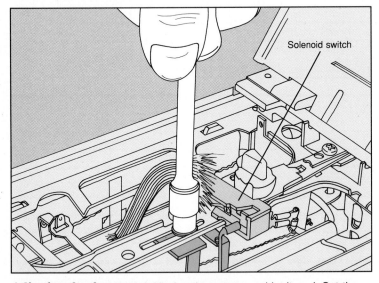

Solenoid switch

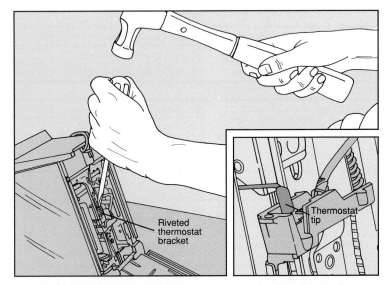

Riveted thermostat bracket

Thermostat tip

Adjusting the thermostat. Unplug the toaster and let it cool. Set the color control knob to its middle position. Turn over the toaster and open the crumb tray. Locate the thermostat bracket in a slot in the chassis. It may be screwed or riveted to the thermostat. Move the bracket toward the solenoid switch for a shorter toasting cycle and lighter-colored toast. Move the bracket away from the solenoid switch for a longer toasting cycle and darker-colored toast. To move a screwed bracket, loosen the screw *(above, left)* and slide the bracket with your fingers. Move a

riveted bracket by placing the blade of an old screwdriver at its edge and very gently tapping it with a hammer *(above, right)*. Never move the ceramic thermostat tip closer than 3/16 inch from the outer solenoid-switch contact *(inset)*. After moving a screwed bracket, retighten the screw. Close the crumb tray. Turn over and plug in the toaster and run a test cycle of toast. If the toast is still not the right color, repeat the adjustment until you get the desired result.

DISASSEMBLING AND INSPECTING A TOASTER

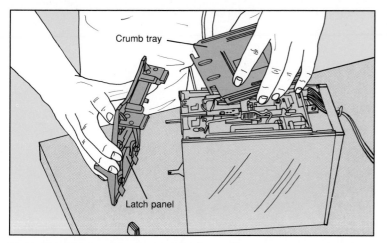

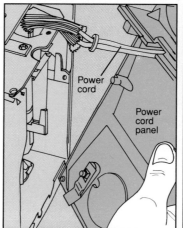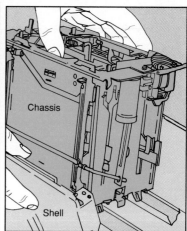

Removing the crumb tray and latch panel. Unplug the toaster and let it cool. Turn it over and open the crumb tray. Remove the color control knob; either unscrew the knob and pull it and its lever out of the side of the toaster, or just pull the knob off. Then remove the latch knob; slip the tips of a pair of long-nose pliers behind it on each side of its lever and pry it off, taking care not to lose the tiny clip that fits through a hole in the end of the lever to hold the knob in place. Unscrew the bottom of the latch panel from the chassis. Pull out on the bottom of the panel and lift off the crumb tray. Pull the latch panel up and out over the ends of the latch lever and color control lever, if it's still in place *(above)*. You can now service the latch assembly *(page 304)*.

Accessing and removing the chassis. To inspect the main switch contacts, remove the power cord panel: Unscrew the bottom of the panel and pull it away from the toaster. Then pull up on the panel and slide it along the power cord *(above, left)*. Check the main switch contacts; if they look fused or broken, replace the chassis or the toaster. To remove the chassis for replacement or to service the solenoid, pull off the crumb tray and latch panel *(left)*. Pull the chassis out of the shell by bending first one side of the shell and then the other, working its corner tabs free of the chassis *(above, right)*. If installing a new chassis, buy an exact replacement from an authorized service center and install it by reversing the steps you took to remove the old one. Cold check for leaking voltage *(page 417)* before plugging in the toaster.

SERVICING THE SOLENOID SWITCH

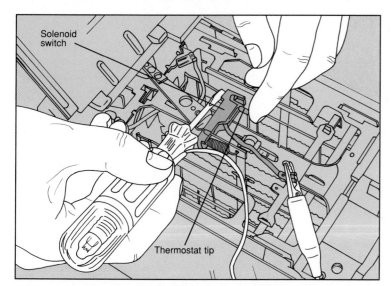

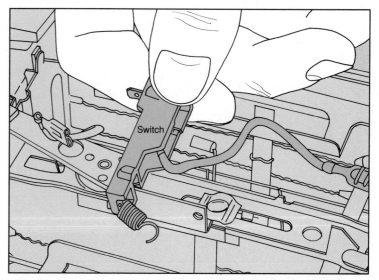

1 **Testing the solenoid switch.** Unplug the toaster and let it cool. Turn it over and open the crumb tray. The solenoid switch is attached to an element connecting rod and to a wire from the solenoid. Pull the switch wire connector off the rod and pull the solenoid wire connector off the switch. Clip a continuity tester to the switch wire connector and touch the tester probe to the switch terminal. The tester should not light. Press the ceramic thermostat tip firmly against the solenoid switch contacts *(above)*. The tester should light. If the solenoid switch fails either test, go to step 2 to replace the switch.

2 **Replacing the solenoid switch.** Use long-nose pliers to twist the solenoid switch spring out of its hole in the chassis, and take out the switch *(above)*. Unhook the spring from the switch and keep it for reuse. Buy an exact replacement switch from an authorized service center. Hook the spring onto the chassis, place the switch in position and use long-nose pliers to rehook the spring. Attach the switch wire connector to the element connecting-rod terminal and attach the solenoid wire connector to the switch terminal. Reassemble the toaster, reversing the steps taken to disassemble it, and cold check for leaking voltage *(page 417)*.

SERVICING THE CARRIAGE-AND-LATCH ASSEMBLY

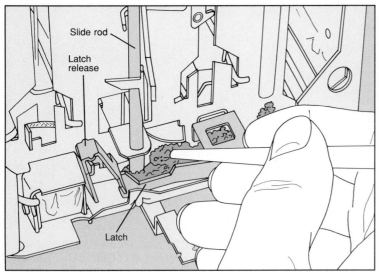
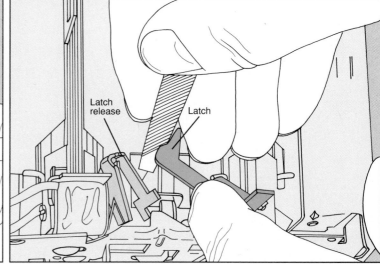

Inspecting and cleaning the carriage-and-latch assembly. Remove the crumb tray and latch panel *(page 303)*. Use a tool such as a wooden stick to clean away crumbs and deposits from the chassis floor *(above, left)*. Turn the toaster on its side and shake it to loosen hard-to-reach pieces of toast or foreign objects. Lower and raise the latch lever along the slide rod a few times; if the lever moves stiffly, lubricate the rod. Slip a piece of paper between the rod and the chassis and spray the rod lightly with a petroleum-based lubricant. Do not get lubricant on the chassis or carriage. Wait a few minutes, then wipe the rod clean with a soft cloth. Work the lever and spray again if necessary. Depress the lever completely and check whether the latch can hook the latch release. If the latch has worn too flat, use a small metal file to sharpen its hook so that it can catch the release *(above, right)*. Reassemble the toaster, reversing the steps taken to disassemble it.

SERVICING THE SOLENOID

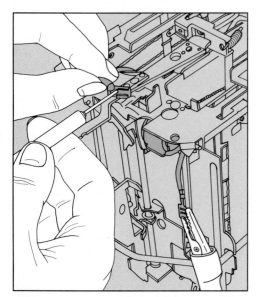
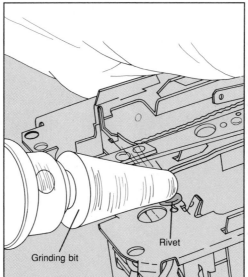
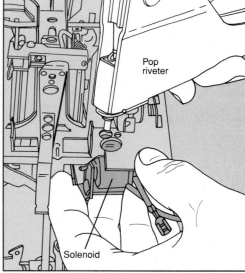

1 Testing the solenoid. Unplug the toaster. Remove the chassis *(page 303)*. Pull one solenoid wire connector off the solenoid switch and pull the other off the element connecting rod. Set a multitester to RX100. Clip a tester probe to the end of one wire and touch the other probe to the end of the other wire *(above)*. The multitester should register low resistance. If the solenoid tests faulty, go to step 2 to replace it.

2 Replacing the solenoid. To remove the solenoid, wear safety goggles and use a power drill fitted with a grinding bit to grind down the mounting rivet until it is flush with the chassis *(above, left)*. Do not grind the chassis. Pry off any remaining bits of rivet with a screwdriver. Buy an exact replacement solenoid from an authorized service center and position it in the chassis so that the hole in its bracket fits right over the old rivet hole in the chassis. Wearing safety goggles, use a pop riveter fitted with a short rivet the size of the bracket hole to secure the solenoid bracket to the chassis. Position the rivet head through the holes, press the riveter firmly against the chassis and squeeze its jaws closed to seat the rivet. Connect one solenoid wire to the solenoid switch terminal and the other to the element connecting-rod terminal. Reassemble the toaster, then cold check for leaking voltage *(page 417)*.

TOASTER OVENS

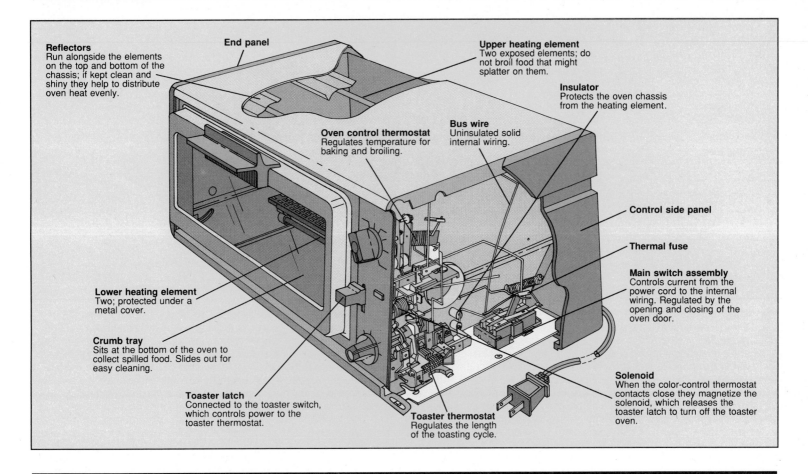

Reflectors
Run alongside the elements on the top and bottom of the chassis; if kept clean and shiny they help to distribute oven heat evenly.

End panel

Upper heating element
Two exposed elements; do not broil food that might splatter on them.

Insulator
Protects the oven chassis from the heating element.

Oven control thermostat
Regulates temperature for baking and broiling.

Bus wire
Uninsulated solid internal wiring.

Control side panel

Thermal fuse

Main switch assembly
Controls current from the power cord to the internal wiring. Regulated by the opening and closing of the oven door.

Lower heating element
Two; protected under a metal cover.

Crumb tray
Sits at the bottom of the oven to collect spilled food. Slides out for easy cleaning.

Toaster latch
Connected to the toaster switch, which controls power to the toaster thermostat.

Toaster thermostat
Regulates the length of the toasting cycle.

Solenoid
When the color-control thermostat contacts close they magnetize the solenoid, which releases the toaster latch to turn off the toaster oven.

ACCESSING THE INTERNAL COMPONENTS

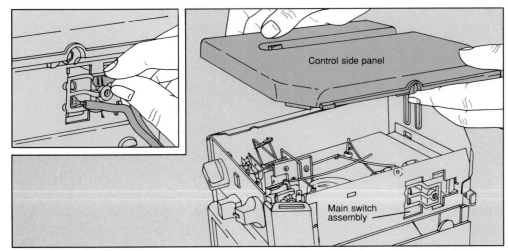

Control side panel

Main switch assembly

End panel

Bottom plate

1 **Removing the power cord and control side panel.** Turn off and unplug the toaster oven, and let it cool. Take the rack and broiler tray out of the oven. Trace the power cord to the main switch assembly on the bottom of the toaster oven. Turn the oven on end and remove the main switch assembly cover. Pull the power-cord wire connectors off the main switch terminals *(inset)*. You can now test the power cord *(page 417)*. To access the main switch, fuse, solenoid and heating-element terminal pins, locate and remove the screws from the control side panel. Slide the panel down to free it from the top edge tabs of the toaster oven, then lift it off the side of the oven *(above)*. To access the terminal pins on the other ends of the heating elements, go to step 2.

2 **Removing the end panel and bottom plate.** Stand the oven on its other end. Remove all screws that hold the bottom of the end panel to the bottom of the toaster oven. The model shown here has only one. Slide the panel down to free it from the top edge tabs of the toaster oven. Lift off the end panel and bottom plate *(above)*. You can now test the heating elements.

SERVICING THE MAIN SWITCH

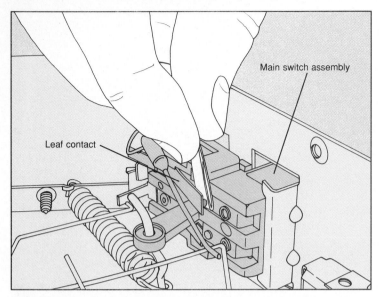

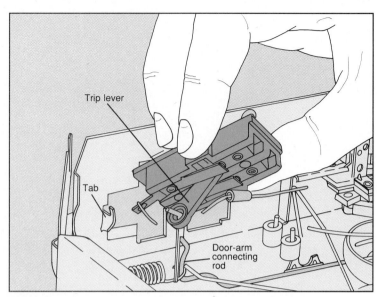

1 **Cleaning the main switch.** To access the main switch, unplug the unit and remove the power cord and the control side panel *(page 305)*. Open and close the toaster oven door and watch whether the switch leaf contacts open and close. If the contacts are broken, bent or fused, go to step 2 to replace the main switch. If the contacts look pitted or burned, lightly rub them until they are smooth and shiny with a piece of 600-grit emery paper folded in half *(above)*. After sanding, clean the contacts by drawing plain paper between them. Reassemble the toaster oven, reversing the steps taken to disassemble it.

2 **Removing the main switch.** Use diagonal-cutting pliers to cut the bus wires as close as possible to the switch terminals. To remove the switch assembly from the toaster oven shown here, use pliers to bend back the metal tab that holds the assembly to the oven chassis, then slide the switch off its support bracket. On some models, you can simply unscrew the assembly from the chassis. Lift the switch assembly and slide its trip lever off the door-arm connecting rod *(above)*. Buy an identical switch from an authorized service center.

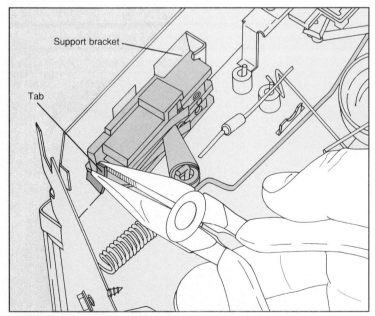

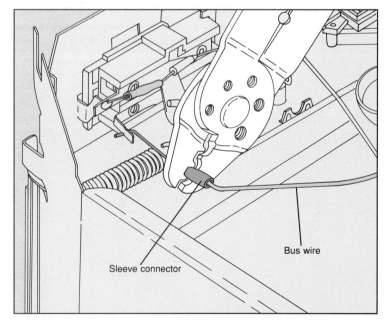

3 **Installing the main switch.** Replacement switches come with their own bus wire extensions. Slide the trip lever of the new switch assembly onto the door-arm connecting rod. Fit the assembly into its mounting hole in the toaster oven chassis and slide one end onto the support bracket. Secure the other end by bending the metal tab against it with long-nose pliers *(above)*.

4 **Connecting the main switch.** Use diagonal-cutting pliers to trim the bus wires you cut in step 2, so that they just overlap those of the new switch assembly. Install wire-to-wire uninsulated sleeve connectors on the bus wires and use a multipurpose tool to crimp their ends *(above)*. Before reassembling the toaster oven, check to make sure that no sleeve connectors or bus wires are bent or touching anywhere but at their proper connection points. Reassemble the toaster oven, reversing the steps taken to disassemble it, then cold check for leaking voltage *(page 417)*.

TESTING AND REPLACING THE SOLENOID

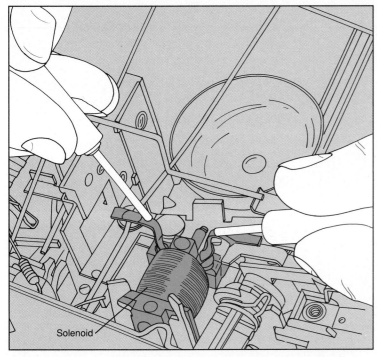

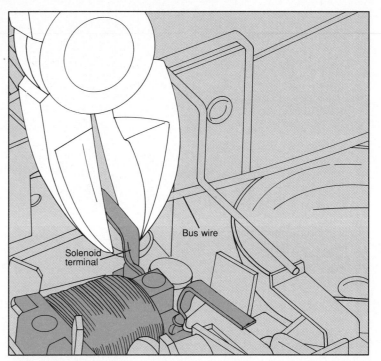

1 **Testing the solenoid.** To access the solenoid, unplug the unit and remove the control side panel *(page 305)*. Inspect the solenoid. If the coil looks burned or if the shaft through the center cannot be moved in and out easily, replace the solenoid *(step 2)*. To test for less visible damage, set a multitester to RX100. Touch a tester probe to each solenoid terminal *(above)*. The multitester should register low resistance. If the solenoid tests faulty, replace it.

2 **Replacing a faulty solenoid.** Use diagonal-cutting pliers to cut each solenoid terminal *(above)*. Use pliers to bend back the metal tabs that hold the solenoid and slide the solenoid out of its bracket on the toaster oven chassis. Purchase an exact replacement solenoid from the manufacturer or an authorized service center. A new solenoid comes with its own bus wire extension. Before you install it, cut the oven bus wire to remove the remaining bit of terminal.

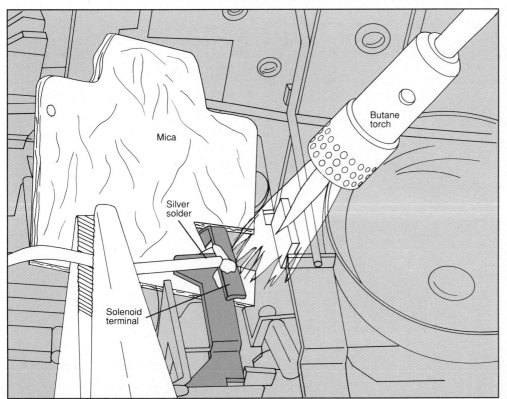

3 **Connecting the replacement solenoid.** Prepare to silver solder *(page 417)*. Slide the new solenoid into the mounting bracket on the oven chassis and bend the bracket tabs against the solenoid with pliers. Trim the bus wires of the new solenoid and the bus wires in the toaster oven so their ends just overlap. Clean the wires with emery paper to ensure a good solder. Protect the solenoid and adjacent components with a piece of mica or ceramic tile. Wearing safety glasses, use a miniature butane torch and a length of silver solder dipped in flux to solder the solenoid terminal to the toaster thermostat terminal *(left)* and its bus wires to the oven bus wires. Wipe off dried flux with a foam swab and hot water. Check the solidity of the connections by squeezing them with a pair of pliers. If a connection breaks, resolder it. Reassemble the toaster oven, reversing the steps taken to disassemble it, then cold check for leaking voltage *(page 417)*.

SERVICING THE THERMAL FUSE

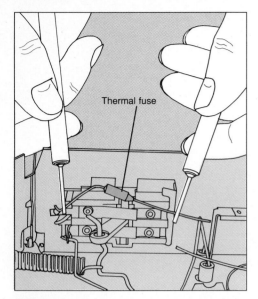

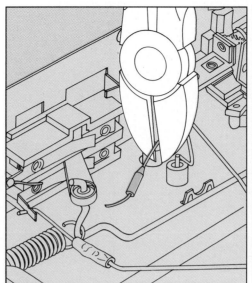

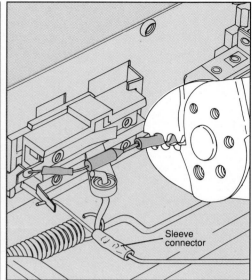

1 **Testing the thermal fuse.** Unplug the unit. Remove the control side panel *(page 305)*. On the model shown here, the fuse is located on a bus wire connected to the main switch. To test the fuse, use a continuity tester, or set a multitester to test continuity. Touch a tester probe to the bus wire at each end of the fuse *(above)*. The tester should show continuity. If the fuse tests OK, take the oven for service; if faulty, replace it *(step 2)*.

2 **Replacing the thermal fuse.** Use diagonal-cutting pliers to cut the bus wires as close to the fuse as possible *(above, left)*, being careful not to twist the wires as you cut. Remove the fuse, noting the position of its pointed end for replacement, and purchase an identical fuse from an authorized service center; it will come with its own bus wires. Trim the oven bus wires so that they just overlap the bus wires of the new fuse. Install wire-to-wire uninsulated sleeve connectors to join the fuse bus wires to the oven bus wires *(page 417)*, making sure the wires overlap inside the connector. Crimp each sleeve connector with a multipurpose tool *(above, right)*. Make sure that no connectors or bus wires touch other components. Reassemble the toaster oven, reversing the steps taken to disassemble it, then cold check for leaking voltage *(page 417)*. If a replacement thermal fuse blows, suspect a faulty control thermostat and take the toaster oven for professional service.

SERVICING THE HEATING ELEMENTS

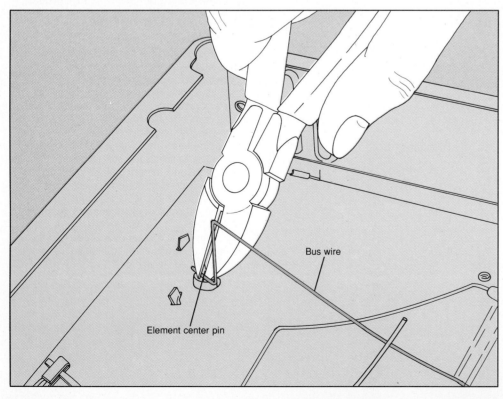

1 **Disconnecting a heating element.** Turn off and unplug the toaster oven, and let it cool. Remove the control side panel, the end panel and the bottom plate *(page 305)*. Inspect the heating elements; if an element is twisted, or burned in spots, replace it *(step 3)*. Check through both open ends of the toaster oven to inspect the connections between the center pins of the elements and their bus wires. If any connections are broken, resolder them *(step 5)*. If no damage is evident, determine which affected heating element requires replacement by removing them both from circuit for testing: Stand the oven on end with the control side facing up and use diagonal-cutting pliers to cut one bus wire of one affected element as close as possible to its center pin *(above)*. Go to step 2 to test the elements.

SERVICING THE HEATING ELEMENTS (continued)

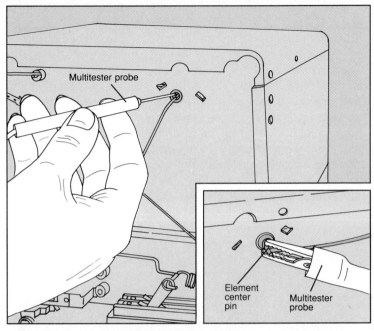

Multitester probe

Element center pin

Multitester probe

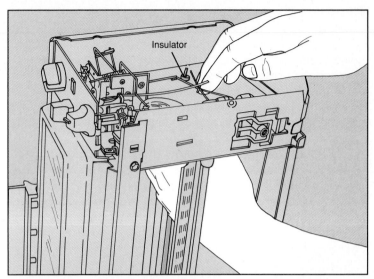

Insulator

2 **Testing a heating element.** Set a multitester to test resistance. Clip one tester probe to the center pin at one end of an affected element *(inset)* and touch the second probe to the other center pin of the element, at the opposite end of the toaster oven *(above)*. The multitester should show low resistance. Repeat the test for the other affected element. If both affected elements test OK, take the toaster oven for professional service. If either element or both elements test faulty, go to step 3.

3 **Removing a faulty heating element.** Use diagonal-cutting pliers to cut the bus wires connected to the ends of a faulty heating element, as close as possible to the element's center pins. Bend back the tabs that hold the upper element reflectors to the toaster oven frame with a pair of pliers. With one hand, reach through the oven bottom and push the side wall of the toaster oven up over the ends of the tabs *(above)*. With the other hand, push the element insulator down through the hole in the side wall. Then pull the element through the oven bottom toward you, working it free of the other side wall. If the element insulators are undamaged, remove them from the ends of the element and save them for installation on the replacement element.

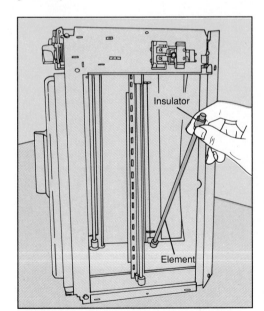

Insulator

Element

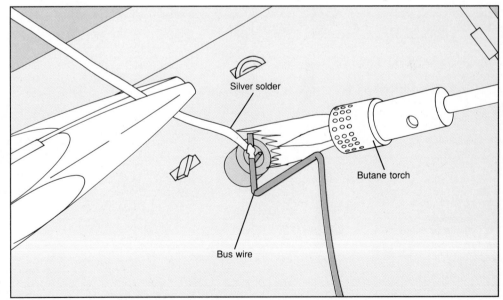

Silver solder

Butane torch

Bus wire

4 **Replacing a heating element.** Buy exact replacement elements, and insulators if necessary, from an authorized service center. Before installing a new element, clean its pins with a piece of emery paper and slip on the insulators. Install the new element *(above)* by reversing the steps taken to remove the faulty element, taking care not to bend it.

5 **Connecting a replacement heating element.** Prepare to silver solder *(page 417)* the oven bus wires to the heating-element center pins. Protect adjacent components with a piece of mica or ceramic tile. Clean the element center pin and bus wire tip with emery paper and push them together to make a good connection. To solder with silver solder, use a miniature butane torch and a length of silver solder dipped in flux. Use the torch to heat the connection, not the silver solder. Hold the torch and solder in position until the silver solder melts smoothly over the connection *(above)*. Turn off the torch. Repeat to connect the other end of the element. Check that all wire connections are securely soldered before reassembling the toaster oven, reversing the steps taken to disassemble it. Cold check for leaking voltage *(page 417)*.

STEAM IRONS

The steam iron produces water vapor that relaxes cloth fibers, enabling the soleplate to better smooth out wrinkles. When the steam button is popped up, a valve in the reservoir opens to release droplets of water into the steam chamber. The heating element, controlled by the thermostat, is encased in a waterproof housing in the soleplate. It turns the water to steam that escapes through the soleplate ports. To take out deep wrinkles, pushing the spray button makes the pump pull water from the reservoir and expel it through the nozzle.

The steam irons pictured below illustrate some differences between irons made prior to the late 1970s and more recent models. Although all steam irons work on the same principles, newer models are lighter and have fewer replaceable parts. Many also have a circuit board that provides automatic shut-off. Your iron's components may differ slightly; use the irons in this chapter as a general guide to repair.

Electronic components rarely break. More likely problems are a frayed power cord or a blockage in the water system due to inadequate cleaning. If the iron is self-cleaning, use this function once a month. If not, flush the iron *(page 312)* regularly to keep it free of mineral deposits that clog spray and steam apertures. To repair your iron, consult the Troubleshooting Guide at right, then contact an authorized service center or the manufacturer to make sure parts are available and that a repair is cost-efficient. In the case of an older iron, parts may sometimes be salvaged from used irons of the same make and model; check with a small-appliance repair shop. After repair, cold check for leaking voltage *(page 417)*.

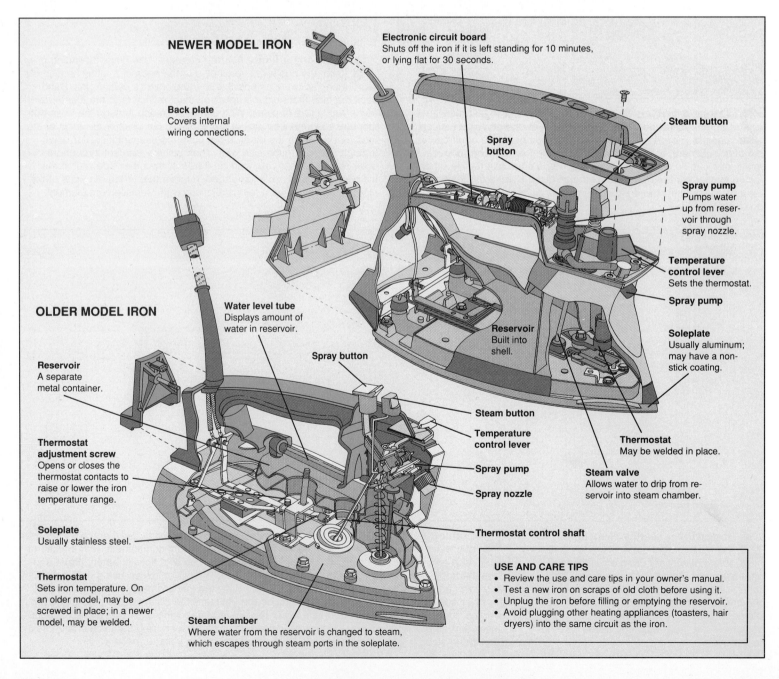

NEWER MODEL IRON

Electronic circuit board
Shuts off the iron if it is left standing for 10 minutes, or lying flat for 30 seconds.

Back plate
Covers internal wiring connections.

Spray button

Steam button

Spray pump
Pumps water up from reservoir through spray nozzle.

Temperature control lever
Sets the thermostat.

Spray pump

Soleplate
Usually aluminum; may have a non-stick coating.

Reservoir
Built into shell.

Thermostat
May be welded in place.

OLDER MODEL IRON

Water level tube
Displays amount of water in reservoir.

Spray button

Steam button

Temperature control lever

Thermostat

Steam valve
Allows water to drip from reservoir into steam chamber.

Reservoir
A separate metal container.

Thermostat adjustment screw
Opens or closes the thermostat contacts to raise or lower the iron temperature range.

Spray pump

Spray nozzle

Thermostat control shaft

Soleplate
Usually stainless steel.

Thermostat
Sets iron temperature. On an older model, may be screwed in place; in a newer model, may be welded.

Steam chamber
Where water from the reservoir is changed to steam, which escapes through steam ports in the soleplate.

USE AND CARE TIPS
- Review the use and care tips in your owner's manual.
- Test a new iron on scraps of old cloth before using it.
- Unplug the iron before filling or emptying the reservoir.
- Avoid plugging other heating appliances (toasters, hair dryers) into the same circuit as the iron.

TROUBLESHOOTING GUIDE

SYMPTOM	POSSIBLE CAUSE	PROCEDURE
Iron does not heat at all	Iron unplugged or turned off	Plug in and turn on iron
	No power to outlet or outlet faulty	Reset breaker or replace fuse (p. 102) □○; service outlet (p. 148)
	Power cord faulty	Test and replace power cord (p. 417) ▣○▲
	Thermostat and/or fuse faulty	Test heating element and thermostat (p. 313) ▣○▲; service thermostat (older model, p. 315 ▣◖; newer model, p. 318 ▣◖)
	Heating element faulty	Test heating element and thermostat (p. 313) ▣○▲; replace iron
	Circuit board faulty	Replace circuit board (p. 317) ▣○
Iron does not turn off, or becomes too hot	Thermostat calibrated incorrectly	Adjust thermostat (p. 312) ▣○▲
	Thermostat contacts stuck shut	Replace thermostat (older model, p. 315; newer model, p. 318) ▣◖
Iron does not become hot enough	Power cord loose or faulty	Test and replace power cord (p. 417) ▣○▲
	Thermostat calibrated incorrectly	Adjust thermostat (p. 312) ▣○▲
	Circuit board faulty	Replace circuit board (p. 317) ▣○
Little or no steam	Steam ports or steam chamber aperture clogged	Clean iron (p. 311) □○; service pump, reservoir and steam valve assembly (older model, p. 314; newer model, p. 317) ▣◖
Little or no spray	Spray nozzle clogged	Service spray nozzle (older model, p. 313; newer model, p. 317) □○
	Pump clogged or leaking	Service pump (older model, p. 314; newer model, p. 317) ▣◖
Iron leaves spots or stains on fabric	Water too hard	Use distilled water or add a demineralizing product
	Soleplate, steam ports or chamber dirty	Clean iron (p. 311) □○
Iron gives electrical shock	Ground fault in iron	Take iron for professional service
Iron leaks	Reservoir overfilled	Check owner's manual for correct filling instructions
	Spray nozzle assembly leaking	Service spray nozzle (older model, p. 313; newer model, p. 317) □○
	Pump gasket leaking, reservoir cracked, steam valve port clogged	Service pump, reservoir and steam valve assembly (older model, p. 314; newer model, p. 317) ▣◖
Water sputters from steam ports	Steam function used before iron warms up	Let iron heat for three to five minutes before using steam function
	Power cord loose or faulty	Test and replace power cord (p. 417) ▣○▲
Iron glides poorly or snags	Soleplate dirty or scratched	Clean soleplate (page 311) □○

DEGREE OF DIFFICULTY: □ Easy ▣ Moderate ■ Complex
ESTIMATED TIME: ○ Less than 1 hour ◖ 1 to 3 hours ● Over 3 hours   ▲ Special tool required

CLEANING THE IRON

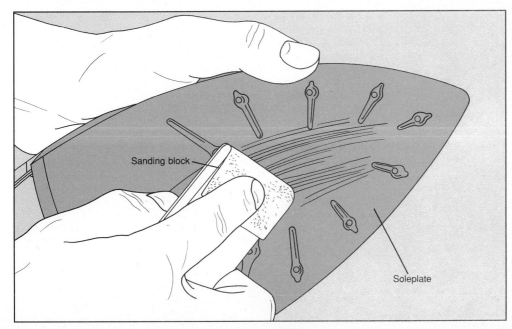

Sanding block

Soleplate

1 **Cleaning the soleplate.** Heat the iron, then turn it off and unplug it. Let it cool just enough to handle. Wipe a non-stick soleplate with a soft, damp cloth or sponge. To remove residue and scratches from aluminum and stainless steel soleplates, use a piece of 600-grit waterproof emery paper wrapped around a small block of wood. Sprinkle a bit of water on the soleplate and sand it with a steady back-and-forth motion, heel to tip, to produce an even, dull sheen (left). Wipe the sanded areas clean with a damp cloth. To finish off, buff the soleplate with 4/0 steel wool until it has a smooth satin finish. Wipe it again with a damp cloth to remove steel wool particles.

CLEANING THE IRON (continued)

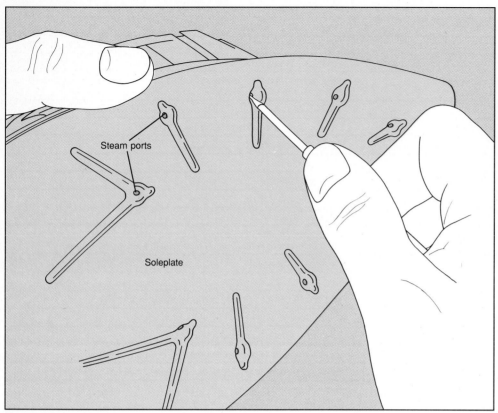

Steam ports

Soleplate

2 **Unclogging the steam ports and flushing the iron.** Heat the iron, then turn it off and unplug it. Let it cool just enough to handle. With the tip of a small screwdriver, scrape out mineral deposits encrusting the edges of the steam ports *(left)*. Take care not to scratch the soleplate, and hold the soleplate at an angle to prevent scrapings from falling into the steam chamber. Soften stubborn deposits by moistening them with a cotton swab dipped in vinegar and letting them soak for 15 minutes. After cleaning the steam ports, use the iron's self-cleaning function according to the directions in the owner's manual. If the iron is not self-cleaning, flush it clean: Mix a half-and-half solution of vinegar and water and fill the reservoir. Stand the iron upright in a sink. Set the steam button to OFF, in most cases by depressing it and locking it down. Plug in the iron, set the temperature at its highest setting and let the iron heat for five minutes. Turn off the iron and unplug it. Lay the iron flat in the sink, release the steam button and let the steam and water pour out until the iron is empty, usually 5 to 10 minutes. Repeat twice with clear water to flush the iron completely.

ADJUSTING THE THERMOSTAT

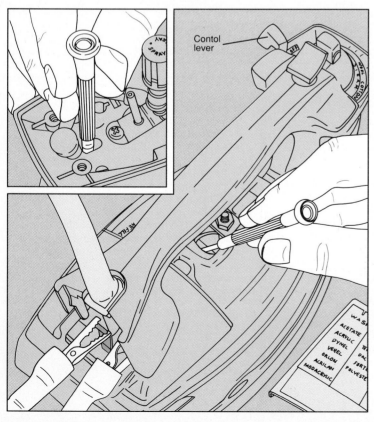

Control lever

Performing an ON/OFF calibration test. Turn off and unplug the iron. Let it cool to room temperature. Unscrew the back plate, and label and disconnect the wires from the main terminal posts. To check whether the thermostat is correctly calibrated in both the OFF and ON positions, set a multitester to test resistance and clip a multitester probe to each terminal. Set the control lever to OFF; the multitester should indicate infinite resistance. If not, adjust the thermostat contacts. To access the thermostat adjustment screw on many older irons, pry off the saddle plate *(page 314, step 3)*. On newer irons you may need to pull off the temperature button on the side of the shell or remove the handle plate *(page 317, step 1)* to reach the screw *(inset)*. Turn the screw clockwise *(left)*, one-quarter turn at a time, until the thermostat contacts open and the multitester measures infinite resistance. If the contacts are stuck shut, replace the thermostat *(older model, page 315; newer model, page 318)*. Once you have infinite resistance in the OFF position, check the thermostat in the ON position: Turn the control lever to the lowest possible ON setting. The contacts should close and the multitester should indicate about 12 ohms. If the multitester continues to show infinite resistance, turn the adjustment screw counterclockwise, one-quarter turn at a time, until the multitester shows about 12 ohms. Double-check to be sure that there is still infinite resistance in the OFF position. Test the iron on scraps of fabric before ironing clothes. If you had to turn the adjustment screw more than one full turn for either test, take the iron for professional service. If an iron with an automatic shutoff still doesn't heat up enough after the ON/OFF calibration test, suspect a faulty circuit board and replace it *(page 317)*.

TESTING THE HEATING ELEMENT AND THERMOSTAT

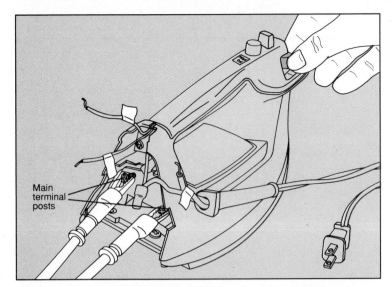

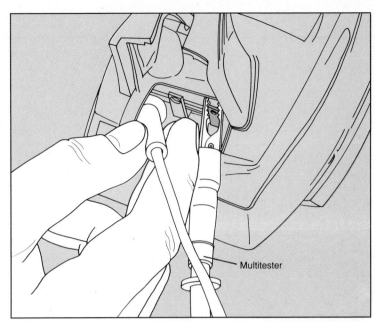

Main terminal posts

Multitester

1 **Testing the heating element and thermostat together.** Turn off and unplug the iron, and let it cool. Unscrew the back plate. If the iron does not have an automatic shutoff, go to step 2 to diagnose the electrical problem. On a model with automatic shutoff, locate the main terminal posts for the heating element and thermostat; one is connected to a power cord wire and the second to a circuit board wire. Label and disconnect the wires. Set a multitester to test resistance and clip a probe to each terminal post *(above)*. Turn on the iron. The multitester should register partial resistance. If not, go to step 2. If the iron tests OK, replace the circuit board *(page 317)*.

2 **Testing the heating element alone.** Locate the two heating element terminals on the far left and far right edges of the opening. Set a multitester to test resistance. Clip one probe to one terminal and touch the second probe to the other terminal *(above)*. The multitester should register partial resistance. If the heating element tests OK, suspect a faulty thermostat *(older model, page 315; newer model, page 318)*. If the heating element tests faulty, replace the iron.

SERVICING THE SPRAY NOZZLE AND FRONT PLATE ASSEMBLY (Older model)

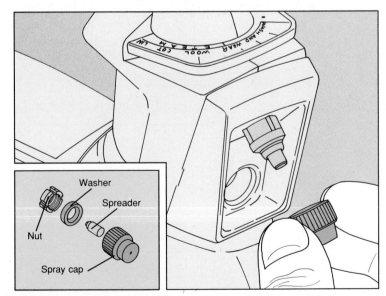

Washer
Spreader
Nut
Spray cap

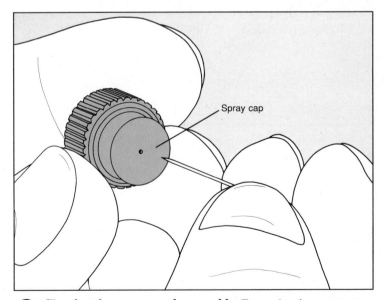

Spray cap

1 **Removing the spray nozzle assembly.** Turn off and unplug the iron. Let it cool to room temperature before removing the spray nozzle assembly. Unscrew and remove the spray cap *(above)*. Use long-nose pliers to loosen the cap if it is stuck. Pull off the spreader underneath, and the washer behind it. Then unscrew and remove the nut that holds the front plate in position. Note the position of the spray nozzle assembly parts for correct reassembly *(inset)*.

2 **Cleaning the spray nozzle assembly.** To service the spray nozzle assembly, inspect the center hole of the spray cap. If it is clogged, clear it with the tip of a fine needle *(above)*. Do not force the needle or you may enlarge the hole, damaging the spray action. Replace a dry or cracked washer or a damaged spray cap, spreader or nut with exact replacement parts. Reassemble the spray nozzle and flush the iron thoroughly *(page 312)*.

SERVICING THE PUMP, RESERVOIR AND STEAM VALVE ASSEMBLY (Older model)

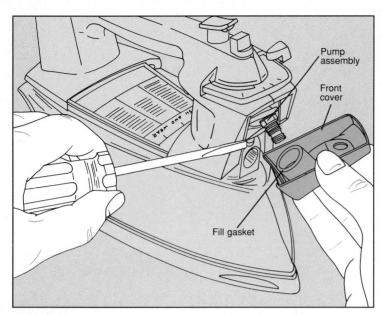

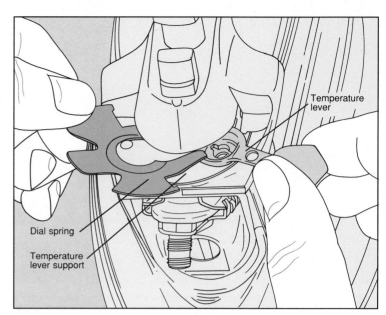

1 **Removing the front cover and replacing the fill gasket.** Turn off and unplug the iron, and let it cool. If you suspect a damaged pump, leaking reservoir or clogged steam-chamber aperture, disassemble the iron *(steps 1-4)*. First, remove the spray nozzle assembly *(page 313)*. Then remove the front cover by slipping a screwdriver blade into one of the notches on the side of the front cover and prying it loose *(above)*. Replace a dried or cracked fill gasket with an exact replacement from a small-appliance repair shop or the manufacturer. Reinstall the front cover and spray nozzle assembly, or go to step 2.

2 **Removing the temperature selector assembly.** Slip a screwdriver blade under the front edge of the handle in the center of the dial plate. Press down on the dial plate to release it. Slide the dial plate forward and out from under the edge of the handle. Pull the dial spring, the temperature lever and the temperature lever support out from beneath the handle *(above)*. Note the position of the temperature-selector assembly parts for correct reassembly *(page 316, step 4)*.

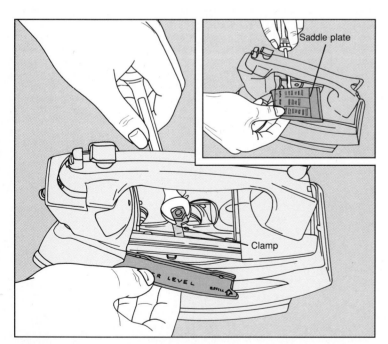

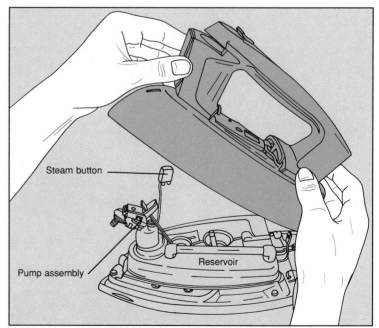

3 **Removing the saddle plate and water level plates.** Insert the screwdriver blade under the edge of the saddle plate and pry it off *(inset)*; the thermostat adjustment screw is now visible through the hole in the shell. To remove the water level plate, use a small open-end wrench to loosen the nut that holds the clamp over the edge of the water level plate. Slide the plate out from under the glass water-level tube *(above)*. Unscrew and remove the nut and clamp.

4 **Removing the handle and shell.** Unscrew the back plate and label and disconnect the power cord wires. Lift off the shell and handle *(above)* to reveal the pump assembly and reservoir. The steam button may remain attached to the reservoir or it may be pulled loose. Set the steam button and rod aside. Note the location of parts for correct reassembly. To clean or replace the pump, go to step 5. To replace the reservoir, clean the steam chamber aperture or service the thermostat, go to step 6.

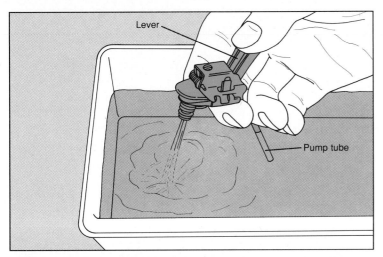

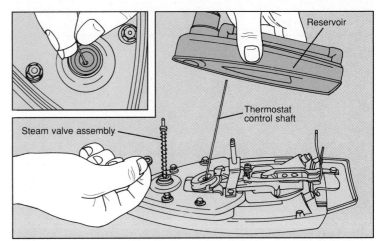

5 **Servicing the pump.** Pull the pump out of the reservoir. If you suspect the pump leaks, fill a container with water, insert the pump tube into the water and depress the lever a few times. If the pump is clogged and does not squirt water forcefully, clean it. Soak the pump in vinegar for 15 to 20 minutes to soften mineral buildup, then test it again. If the pump leaks or remains clogged after cleaning, purchase an exact replacement pump from a small-appliance repair shop or from the manufacturer. Install the pump in its hole in the reservoir and reassemble the iron *(page 316)*, or go to step 6.

6 **Replacing the reservoir and cleaning the steam chamber aperture.** Pull the small gasket off the top of the steam valve assembly. Unscrew the front clamp that holds the reservoir to the soleplate, and lift it off. Store the small gasket on the tip of the steam valve assembly *(above)*. Replace a reservoir that is cracked or corroded with a duplicate from a small-appliance repair shop or the manufacturer. Pull the steam valve assembly off the soleplate. Inspect the tiny aperture into the steam chamber; if clogged with mineral deposits, open it with a straight pin *(inset)*. Examine the thermostat *(step below)*. After completing repair, reassemble the iron *(page 316)*.

SERVICING THE THERMOSTAT (Older model)

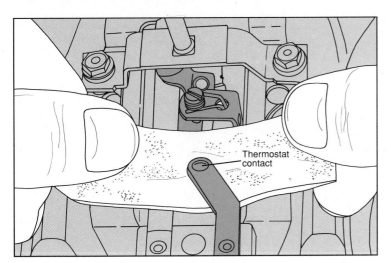

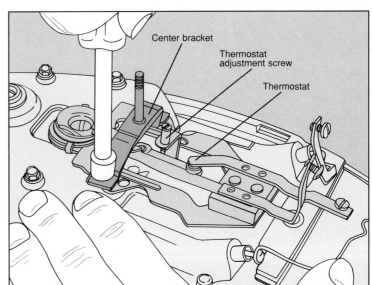

1 **Inspecting and cleaning the thermostat.** Turn off the iron, unplug it and allow it to cool. Unscrew the back plate, and label and disconnect the power cord wires. Remove the spray nozzle assembly *(page 313)* and the pump and reservoir *(page 314)*. Turn the thermostat control shaft back and forth and watch whether the contacts open and close. If they are stuck shut, replace the thermostat *(step 2)*. If the contacts look pitted or black, use a piece of 600-grit emery paper to smooth and polish them, then clean them with plain paper. Place the paper between the contacts, turn the control shaft to close them and pull the paper back and forth very gently *(above)*. After cleaning, check that the thermostat contacts open and close properly when the control shaft is turned. Reassemble the iron *(page 316)*. If the thermostat cannot be cleaned, replace the assembly *(step 2)*.

2 **Replacing the thermostat.** Buy an identical replacement assembly from a small-appliance repair shop or the manufacturer. Pull off the thermostat control shaft, noting its exact position. Disconnect the heating element from the thermostat. Unscrew the center bracket and thermostat from the soleplate *(above)*. Remove any washers and the center bracket. Unscrew the thermostat adjustment screw as far as you can without removing it. Slide the thermostat assembly toward the rear and lift it up over the adjustment screw bracket and off the soleplate. Position the new thermostat assembly on the soleplate and reassemble the iron *(page 316)*. Adjust the thermostat *(page 312)*.

REASSEMBLING THE IRON (Older model)

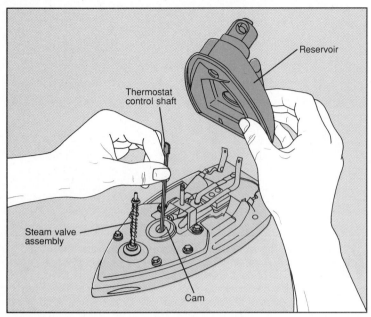

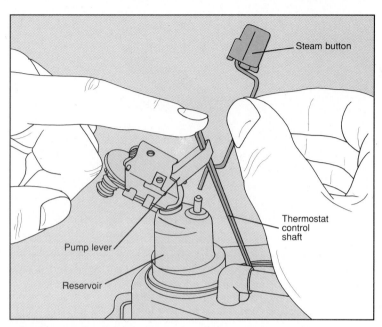

1 **Reinstalling the reservoir.** Fit the steam valve assembly into the steam valve seat, pressing the spring firmly in place so it stands upright. Take the small gasket off its tip. Reinstall the thermostat control shaft *(above)*, aligning the ridge on its side with the slot in the thermostat cam. Position the reservoir, feeding the steam valve assembly and thermostat control shaft through their holes in the front of the reservoir. Place the front clamp over the front edge of the reservoir and screw it to the soleplate below.

2 **Reinstalling the pump and steam knob.** Slip the small gasket onto the tip of the steam valve assembly. Reposition the pump in the reservoir, inserting the thermostat control shaft through its lever. Insert the steam button rod through the opening in the steam valve assembly *(above)*. Position the steam button so that you can read the lettering on the button from the back of the iron, and so that the bend in the rod fits behind the pump lever.

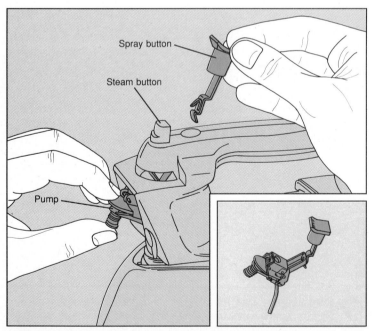

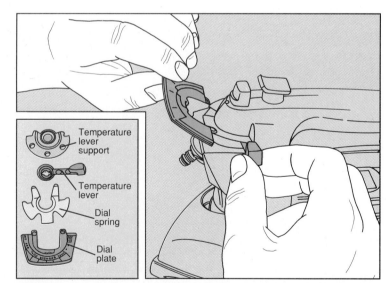

3 **Reinstalling the shell and spray button.** Working from the front of the iron, lower the shell over the iron with one hand. With the fingers of your other hand, guide the steam button up through its hole in the handle. If necessary, insert a screwdriver into the spray button hole to help push the steam button into place. Once the shell is in position, insert the spray button shaft into the handle *(above)*. Maneuver the button and the pump until the shaft clamps securely onto the pump lever inside *(inset)*.

4 **Reinstalling the temperature selector assembly.** Check the correct order of the temperature-selector assembly parts *(inset)*. Reinstall them one by one, beginning with the temperature lever support and finishing with the dial plate *(above)*. Fit the lever and control over the top of the temperature control shaft. Install the fill gasket and front cover. Check the proper order of the spray-nozzle assembly parts *(page 313, step 1)* and reinstall them. Resecure the water level plate with the clamp and nut. Before replacing the saddle plate, perform an ON/OFF calibration test *(page 312)*. Snap on the saddle plate, reconnect the power cord and screw on the back plate. Cold check for leaking voltage *(page 417)*. Clean and flush the iron thoroughly *(page 312)*.

SERVICING THE SPRAY NOZZLE AND PUMP ASSEMBLY (Newer model)

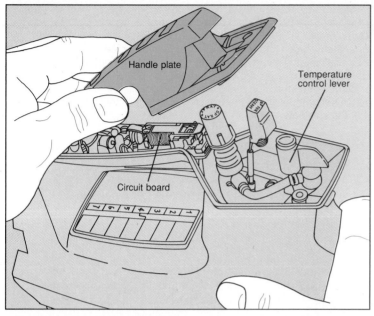

Handle plate

Temperature control lever

Circuit board

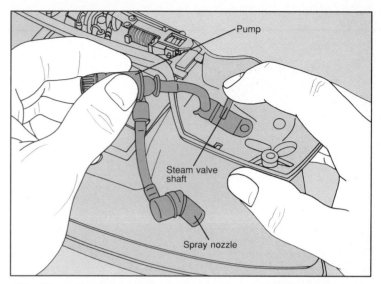

Pump

Steam valve shaft

Spray nozzle

1 **Removing the handle plate.** Turn off and unplug the iron, and let it cool. Turn the temperature lever to OFF. Push the dial plate back slightly with your fingers, then slip the blade of a screwdriver under its edge and pry it off. Unscrew and remove the two screws normally hidden under the dial plate. Turn the temperature control lever to the center position, aligning it with the slot in the center of the handle, and lift off the handle plate *(above).*

2 **Checking and replacing the spray nozzle and pump.** Pull the spray nozzle free and use the tip of a fine needle to clear its aperture of mineral deposits. (Do not force the needle or you may create a leak.) Pull out the temperature lever, the spray button, and the steam button and its rod. Remove the screw that holds the pump bracket in place. Steady the steam valve shaft with a finger while you slide the pump out from under the edge of the bracket with the other hand *(above).* Test the pump for leaks and clean it *(page 315, step 5).* Replace a damaged pump with an exact replacement purchased from a small-appliance repair shop or the manufacturer. Install the new pump and reassemble the iron, reversing these steps.

REPLACING THE ELECTRONIC CIRCUIT BOARD (Newer model)

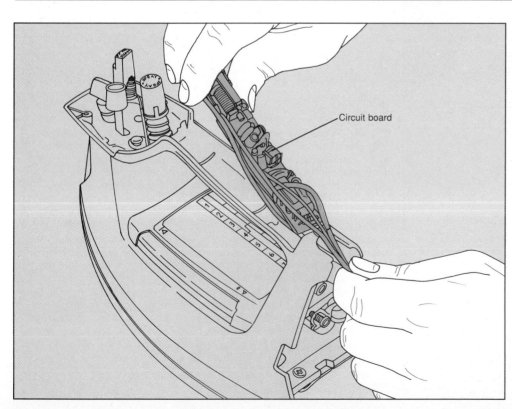

Circuit board

Taking out the circuit board. Unplug the iron and let it cool. Unscrew and remove the back plate. Label and disconnect the power cord wires and circuit board wires; unscrew screw-on connectors and use a pair of diagonal-cutting pliers to cut off any crimp connectors. If necessary, draw a diagram to help you remember where the wires go. Remove the handle plate *(step above).* Lift the circuit board out of its seat in the handle *(left)* and inspect it for cracks or evidence of water damage. Buy an exact replacement from an authorized service center or the manufacturer. Position the new circuit board in the handle. Reconnect the power cord wires and circuit board wires; if crimp connectors were used, crimp on new connectors. Reinstall the back plate, the handle plate and the dial plate, reversing the steps you took to remove them. Cold check for leaking voltage *(page 417).*

SERVICING THE THERMOSTAT (Newer model)

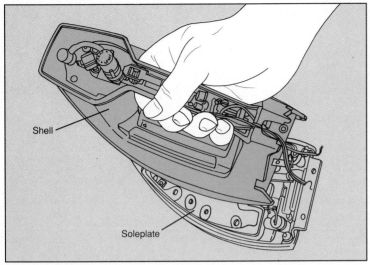

1 Removing the shell. Unplug the iron and let it cool. Unscrew and remove the back plate. If necessary, draw a diagram to help you remember where the wires go, then disconnect the power cord wires and any circuit board wires. Unscrew screw-on connectors and use a pair of diagonal-cutting pliers to cut off any crimp connectors. Remove the handle plate of the iron *(page 317)*. Pull out the temperature lever and the steam button and its rod. To separate the shell from the soleplate beneath, unscrew the two screws that hold the shell to the heel of the soleplate, and loosen (but do not remove) the two recessed screws that secure the shell to the tip of the soleplate. Lift the shell off the soleplate *(left)*.

Shell

Soleplate

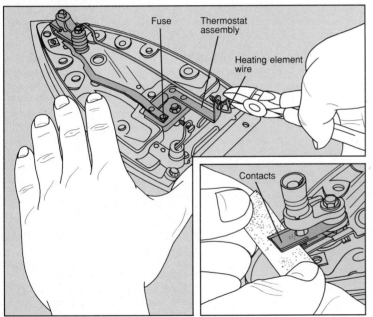

2 Removing the thermostat assembly. Inspect the thermostat contacts and clean them *(inset)* if necessary *(page 315, step 1)*. If the thermostat fuse has opened, or damage to the contacts is severe, replace the thermostat assembly. Most newer irons, such as the one shown, have a thermostat that is spot-welded to the heating element. When replaced, this type must be silver soldered *(page 417)*; have the right tools and materials on hand. Buy an exact replacement thermostat assembly from a small-appliance repair shop or the manufacturer. Lift the temperature control-arm seat off the front of the old thermostat assembly. Use diagonal-cutting pliers to sever the small piece of wire that connects the metal arm of the thermostat assembly to the heating element terminal *(left)*, cutting 1/8 inch from the terminal. Unscrew the thermostat from the soleplate. On the model shown, one screw is located at the back of the assembly on a small porcelain insulator, and the other is located in the front, on the thermostat. Lift off the old thermostat assembly.

Fuse   Thermostat assembly

Heating element wire

Contacts

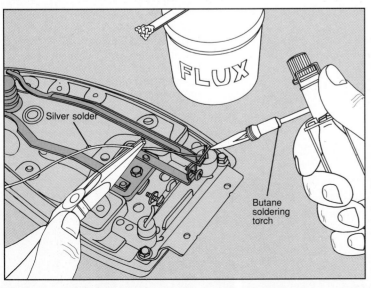

3 Soldering the new thermostat assembly. Lay the new thermostat assembly in position on the soleplate, and screw it in place. The metal arm of the new assembly should just touch the cut end of the wire connected to the heating element terminal. If the wire overlaps the arm of the thermostat assembly, cut it shorter with the diagonal-cutting pliers. Use a utility knife to make a vertical incision through the rubber insulator wrapped around the heating element terminal, and remove the insulator. Silver solder *(page 417)* the arm of the thermostat assembly to the heating element *(left)*. Wait five minutes for the area to cool. Slip the rubber insulator back around the heating element terminal. Reposition the temperature control-arm seat at the front of the thermostat assembly. To reassemble the iron, screw on the shell and reconnect the power cord wires and any circuit board wires. Perform an ON/OFF calibration test *(page 312)* and adjust the thermostat if necessary. Then replace the temperature control arm, steam button and rod, spray nozzle and pump. Screw on the back plate and reinstall the handle plate and the dial plate. Perform a cold check for leaking voltage *(page 417)*.

FLUX

Silver solder

Butane soldering torch

COFFEE MAKERS

The ritual of morning coffee rivals Mom and apple pie, and a kitchen without some sort of coffee machine hardly seems complete. The two most typical coffee makers are the automatic steam-pump drip brewer and the percolator. Automatic drip coffee makers *(page 320)* usually have one heating element controlled by a thermostat, which cycles it on and off until the unit is unplugged or it shuts off automatically. An electronic shutoff feature may be found with a digital timer that can be set to start the brewing cycle at a certain time. Percolators *(page 324)* have separate brewing and warming elements. Both elements go on the moment the unit is plugged in, but when the coffee gets hot enough, the thermostat cuts power to the brewing element. The warming element stays on as long as the unit is plugged in.

When your coffee maker malfunctions, use the Troubleshooting Guide below to diagnose the problem. On newer models, thermostat and element connections may be spot welded; be prepared to silver solder new connections by reading the instructions in Tools & Techniques *(page 417)*. If the coffee is too strong, too weak or bitter, don't immediately blame the coffee maker. Often such problems can be traced to the amount or type of coffee being used or inadequate cleaning. At least once a month, run an automatic drip coffee maker through a brewing cycle with a half-and-half solution of vinegar and water and then with cold water. Rinse a percolator's pump tube and basket with water after every use. To remove coffee stains from the basket, soak it in boiling water with two tablespoons of dishwasher powder, then rinse well.

TROUBLESHOOTING GUIDE

SYMPTOM	POSSIBLE CAUSE	PROCEDURE
AUTOMATIC DRIP COFFEE MAKERS		
Coffee maker doesn't work at all	No power to outlet or outlet faulty	Reset breaker or replace fuse *(p. 102)* □○; service outlet *(p. 148)*
	Power cord faulty	Test and replace power cord *(p. 417)* ▣○▲
	Fuse or thermostat faulty	Test and replace fuse and/or thermostat *(p. 321)* ▣○
	Heating element faulty	Test and replace heating element *(p. 322)* ▣○▲
	Wire connection loose or broken	Repair wire connection *(p. 417)* ▣○
	On/off switch faulty (non-electronic)	Test and replace on/off switch *(p. 323)* ▣○▲
	Circuit board faulty (electronic)	Replace circuit board *(p. 323)* ▣○
Coffee maker sputters and brews coffee slowly	Steam pump tubes clogged	Consult owner's manual to clean tubes
Coffee maker overflows	Reservoir overfilled	Consult owner's manual to fill reservoir correctly
	Filter basket clogged or overfilled	Consult owner's manual to clean and fill basket correctly
Coffee maker leaks	Reservoir or steam pump tubes cracked	Take coffee maker for professional service
Coffee maker blows circuit breaker or fuse	Wire connection loose or broken	Repair wire connection *(p. 417)* ▣○
	Power cord faulty	Test and replace power cord *(p. 417)* ▣○▲
PERCOLATORS		
Percolator doesn't work at all	No power to outlet or outlet faulty	Reset breaker or replace fuse *(p. 102)* □○; service outlet *(p. 148)*
	Power cord faulty	Test and replace power cord *(p. 417)* ▣○▲
	Power-cord receptacle terminal pins faulty	Service terminal pins *(p. 324)* ▣○
	Wire connection loose or broken	Repair wire connection *(p. 417)* ▣○
	Fuse or brewing element faulty	Take percolator for professional service
Percolator heats water but doesn't perk coffee	Steam tube or basket clogged	Consult owner's manual to clean tube and basket
	Thermostat faulty	Test and replace thermostat *(p. 325)* ▣○
Perked coffee boils and reperks	Thermostat faulty	Test and replace thermostat *(p. 325)* ▣○
	Warming element faulty	Test and replace warming element *(p. 325)* ▣○▲
Perked coffee doesn't stay hot	Warming element faulty	Test and replace warming element *(p. 325)* ▣○▲
Percolator blows circuit breaker or fuse	Power cord faulty	Test and replace power cord *(p. 417)* ▣○▲
Percolator gives electrical shock	Ground fault in percolator	Take percolator for professional service
Percolator leaks	Seals or gaskets worn	Take percolator for professional service

DEGREE OF DIFFICULTY: □ Easy ▣ Moderate ■ Complex
ESTIMATED TIME: ○ Less than 1 hour ◕ 1 to 3 hours ● Over 3 hours

▲ Multitester required

AUTOMATIC DRIP COFFEE MAKERS

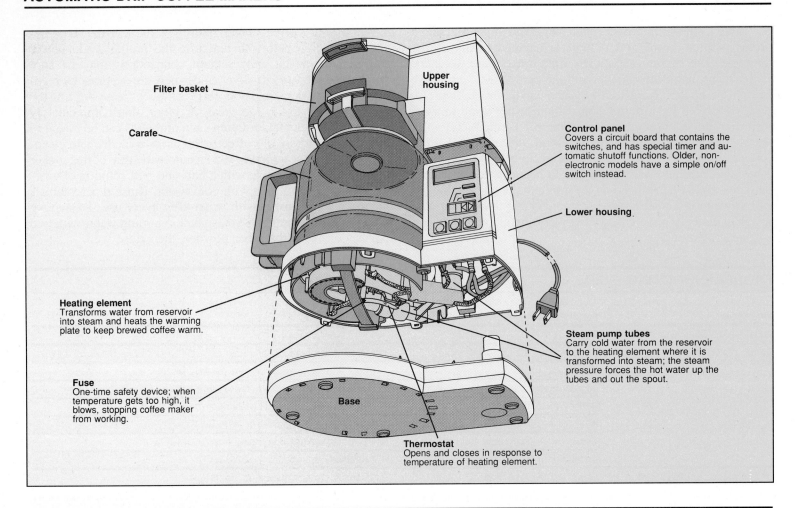

Filter basket

Carafe

Upper housing

Control panel
Covers a circuit board that contains the switches, and has special timer and automatic shutoff functions. Older, non-electronic models have a simple on/off switch instead.

Lower housing

Heating element
Transforms water from reservoir into steam and heats the warming plate to keep brewed coffee warm.

Steam pump tubes
Carry cold water from the reservoir to the heating element where it is transformed into steam; the steam pressure forces the hot water up the tubes and out the spout.

Fuse
One-time safety device; when temperature gets too high, it blows, stopping coffee maker from working.

Base

Thermostat
Opens and closes in response to temperature of heating element.

ACCESSING INTERNAL COMPONENTS

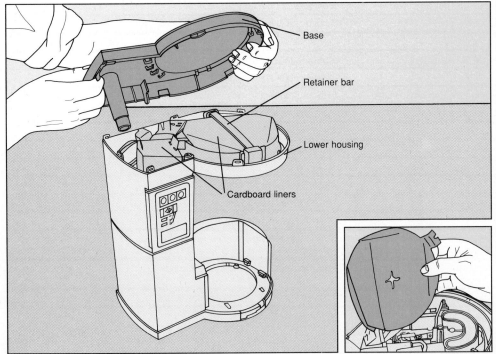

Base

Retainer bar

Lower housing

Cardboard liners

Removing the base. Turn off and unplug the coffee maker and let it cool. Remove the carafe and the filter basket and turn the unit upside down. Locate and remove the screws holding the base to the lower housing. On many models, you may then simply lift off the base. On the model shown here, gently work the base off the lower housing with the tip of a screwdriver and then lift it off *(left)*. If the internal components are covered by protective cardboard liners, remove them. On the model shown here, pull out the liner that protects the circuit board assembly, taking care not to tug on any wires. To remove the liner covering the heating element assembly, gently push down the retainer bar and rotate it clockwise to slip its ends out of the slots in the heating element housing. Remove it, then lift off the cardboard liner *(inset)*. You now have access to the heating element, thermostat, thermal fuse and circuit board.

TESTING AND REPLACING THE FUSE AND THERMOSTAT

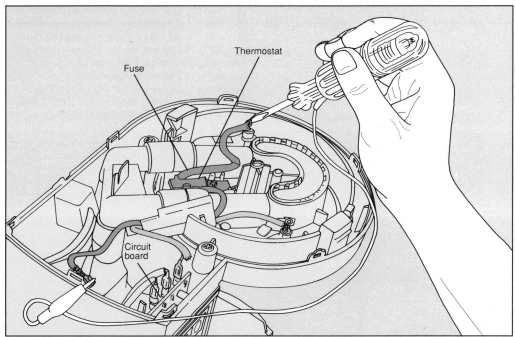

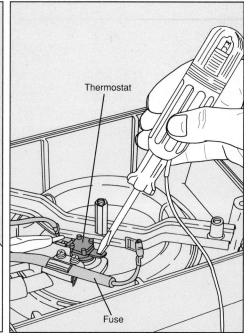

1 **Testing the fuse and thermostat.** To gain access to the thermostat and fuse, turn off and unplug the unit and remove the base *(page 320)*. Locate the small disc thermostat and the thick rubber- or plastic-covered fuse connected to one of its terminals. If you have a coffee maker in which the thermostat and fuse are spot welded together, disconnect the wire that connects the thermostat to the circuit board and test thermostat and fuse as a single assembly. Touch one continuity tester probe to the end of the free wire and touch the other to the end of the fuse wire where it is spot welded to a heating element terminal *(above, left)*. The tester should light. If the assembly tests faulty, replace it *(step 2)*. If the thermostat and fuse in your coffee maker are connected with wire terminal connectors, test them separately. To test a fuse, disconnect one of its wires and touch a continuity tester probe to each wire end. To test a thermostat, disconnect the wire from one of its terminals and touch a tester probe to each terminal *(above, right)*. In both cases, the tester should light. If either the fuse or the thermostat tests faulty, replace it *(step 2)*.

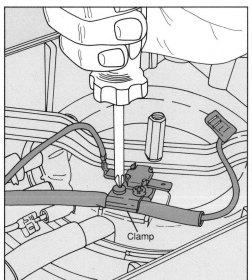

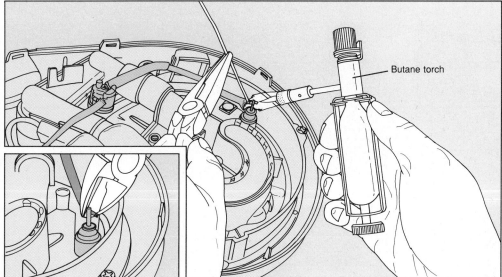

2 **Replacing a fuse and a thermostat.** To remove either a thermostat-and-fuse assembly or a separate thermostat or fuse, unscrew any clamps securing them to the element *(above, left)*. Disconnect their wires; if spot welded, use diagonal-cutting pliers to cut them loose near the terminal *(inset)*. Buy identical replacement parts from an authorized service center and install them, reversing the steps you took to remove the faulty ones. Silver solder *(page 417)* wires that were spot welded; wrap the wire around the terminal and use silver solder and a miniature butane torch *(above, right)*. Reassemble the coffee maker and cold check for leaking voltage *(page 417)*.

TESTING AND REPLACING THE HEATING ELEMENT

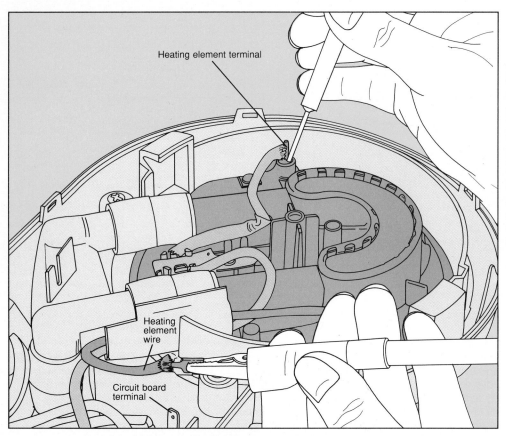

Heating element terminal

Heating element wire

Circuit board terminal

1 **Testing the heating element.** To gain access to the heating element, turn off and unplug the unit and remove the base *(page 320)*. Before testing the element, remove it from circuit: Either pull the wire off one of its terminals or, if the wire is spot welded as in the model shown here, pull it off the circuit board terminal. Set a multitester to RX1. Touch a tester probe to each heating element terminal or, as in the model shown here, touch one tester probe to the heating element terminal and the other to the end of the disconnected wire *(left)*. The multitester should show partial resistance. If the element tests OK, consult the Troubleshooting Guide for other possible causes of coffee maker malfunction before reassembling the unit. If the element tests faulty, go to step 2 to replace it.

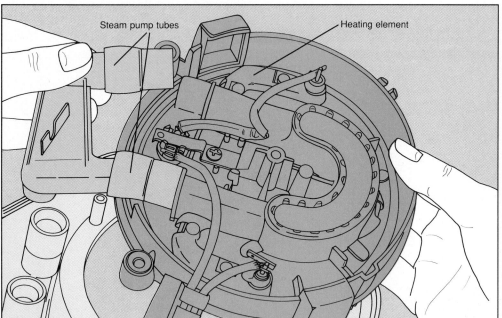

Steam pump tubes

Heating element

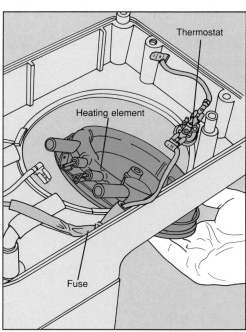

Thermostat

Heating element

Fuse

2 **Replacing the heating element.** Replacement heating elements for the model shown on page 320 come as an assembly with the fuse and thermostat. To remove the heating element, fuse and thermostat together, pull the thermostat wire off the circuit board terminal, then unscrew the heating element assembly from the lower housing. Lift the assembly off the lower housing with one hand while you pull the rubber steam-pump tubes off it with the other *(above, left)*. On many other coffee makers, the heating element may be replaced separately; label and disconnect the wires attached to the heating element terminals, and remove the thermostat and fuse from the element by unscrewing their mounting clamp. Then remove the center post that secures the element retainer bracket and lift off the bracket. Pull the steam pump hoses off the element and remove the element from the housing *(above, right)*. Buy exact replacement parts from an authorized service center, and reinstall them, reversing the steps taken to remove them. Reassemble the coffee maker and cold check for leaking voltage *(page 417)*.

REPLACING THE CIRCUIT BOARD

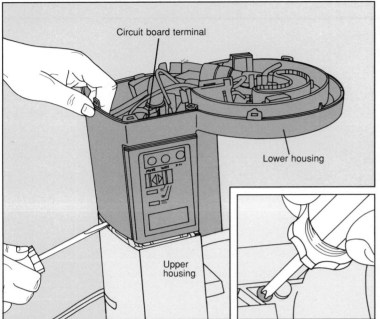

Circuit board terminal

Lower housing

Upper housing

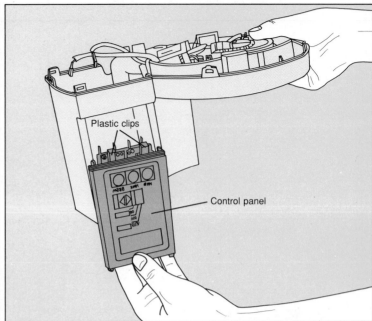

Plastic clips

Control panel

Replacing the circuit board. If the on/off function is faulty on an electronic coffee maker, replace the circuit board. To access the circuit board, turn off and unplug the unit and remove the base *(page 320)*. Label all wires and pull them off the circuit board terminals. Locate and remove any screws securing the circuit board to the housing. On the model shown here, reach behind the circuit board and remove the screw that holds the lower housing to the upper housing *(inset)*. Pull the ends of the steam pump tubes out of the rubber sleeves that hold them to the upper housing. Then separate the lower and upper housing

by working the tip of a screwdriver along the seam between the two sections *(above, left)*. Lift off the lower housing. Reach inside the housing with a screwdriver and pry back the plastic clips that secure the circuit board to the housing. Slide the circuit board (with the control panel attached) out of the lower housing *(above, right)*. Purchase a replacement circuit board from an authorized service center and install it by reversing the steps taken to remove the faulty one. Reassemble the coffee maker and cold check for leaking voltage *(page 417)*.

SERVICING THE ON/OFF SWITCH

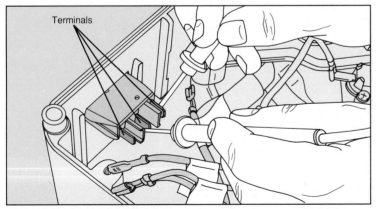

Terminals

1 **Testing the on/off switch.** Coffee makers without an electronic timer or automatic shutoff have a simple on/off switch. Turn off and unplug the unit, let it cool and remove its base *(page 320)*. Locate the switch, label its wires and pull them off the terminals. A typical on/off switch has a pilot light and three terminals. Set a multitester to RX1. Set the switch to OFF and touch the tester probes to each possible pairing of terminals *(above)*, in turn. The multitester should never indicate 0 ohms, although it may show low resistance between one pair of terminals. Set the switch to ON and repeat the test. The tester should register 0 ohms for only one pair of terminals. If the switch fails either test, go to step 2 to replace it.

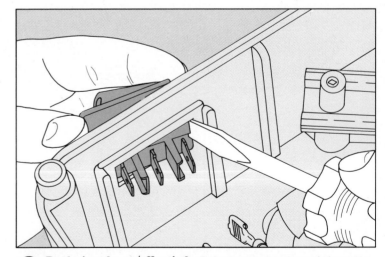

2 **Replacing the on/off switch.** Before removing the switch, note which side faces up so you can install the replacement the same way. To remove it, press in the retaining clips on one side with a screwdriver blade and angle it out through the housing; repeat on the other side until you can push the switch out completely *(above)*. Buy an identical switch from an authorized service center. Snap the new switch into the housing and reconnect the wires. Reassemble the coffee maker, reversing the steps taken to disassemble it, and cold check for leaking voltage *(page 417)*.

PERCOLATORS

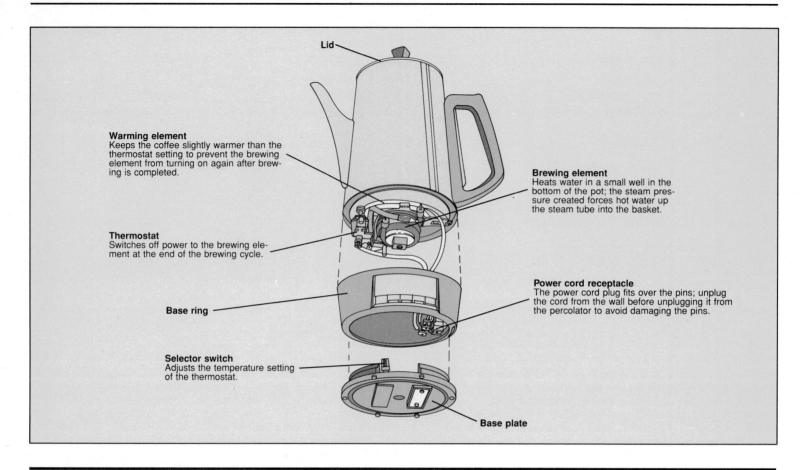

Warming element
Keeps the coffee slightly warmer than the thermostat setting to prevent the brewing element from turning on again after brewing is completed.

Thermostat
Switches off power to the brewing element at the end of the brewing cycle.

Base ring

Selector switch
Adjusts the temperature setting of the thermostat.

Lid

Brewing element
Heats water in a small well in the bottom of the pot; the steam pressure created forces hot water up the steam tube into the basket.

Power cord receptacle
The power cord plug fits over the pins; unplug the cord from the wall before unplugging it from the percolator to avoid damaging the pins.

Base plate

ACCESSING AND SERVICING THE PERCOLATOR COMPONENTS

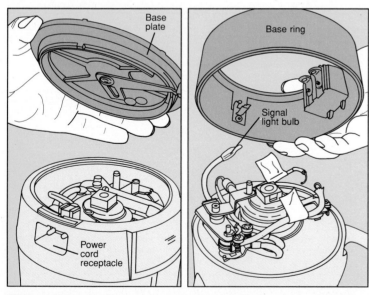

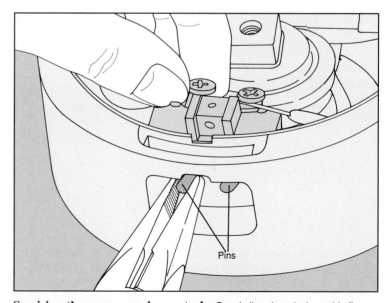

Disassembling the base. Turn off the percolator and unplug it from the wall outlet. Let it cool and empty it. Pull off the detachable power cord. Remove the lid, take out the basket and steam tube, and turn over the percolator. Remove the base-plate mounting screw and lift off the base plate *(above, left)*. Label and disconnect the wires to the power cord receptacle on the inside wall of the base ring. Gently pull the signal light bulb out of its clamp, then lift the ring off the bottom of the percolator *(above, right)*.

Servicing the power cord receptacle. Sand discolored pins with fine emery paper. If the pins are loose or damaged, disassemble the base *(left)*. To tighten loose pins, use long-nose pliers to turn their nuts clockwise while you hold the bracket terminals steady from behind *(above)*. To remove damaged pins and the flat washers beneath, turn the nuts counterclockwise. Buy identical replacements from an authorized service center. Install the pins and reassemble the percolator base. Cold check for leaking voltage *(page 417)*.

SERVICING THE PERCOLATOR

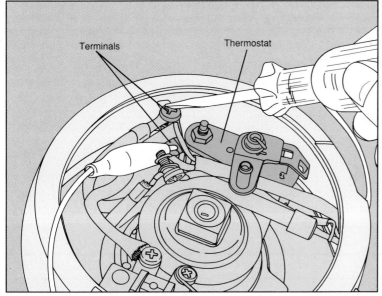

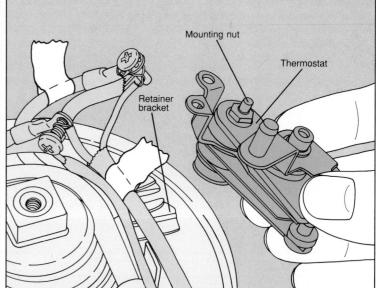

Servicing the thermostat. Unplug the unit. Wait until the percolator cools to room temperature, then disassemble the base *(page 324)*. Separate the thermostat contacts by hand and inspect them. If the contacts look pitted or black, slip a folded piece of fine emery paper between them and pull it back and forth gently, then follow with plain paper. If the thermostat leaves are bent or broken, or the contacts do not close or are fused shut, replace the thermostat. To check the thermostat for less visible damage, test it. Label and disconnect the wires from one thermostat terminal. Touch a continuity tester probe to each terminal

(above, left); the tester should light. To replace a faulty thermostat, label and disconnect the wires connected to the second thermostat terminal. Loosen the mounting nut on top of the thermostat assembly and slide the assembly sideways out of the retainer bracket *(above, right)*. Buy an identical replacement from an authorized service center. Install the new thermostat in the bracket and tighten the mounting nut. Reconnect the wires to the thermostat terminals. Reassemble the percolator by reinstalling the base ring and base plate, and cold check for leaking voltage *(page 417)*.

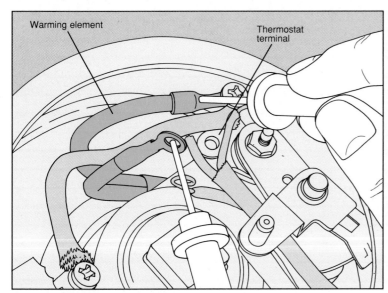

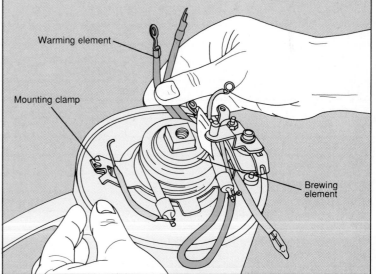

Testing and replacing the warming element. Unplug and turn off the percolator, and disassemble the base *(page 324)*. The warming element in the model shown here is an insulated wire coiled around the brewing element; label and disconnect one of its ends from a thermostat terminal. (You may also have to label and disconnect other wires from the same terminal in order to disconnect the warming element wire.) Set a multitester to test resistance. Touch one probe to the free end of the warming element and touch the other probe to the other end where it connects to the other thermostat terminal *(above, left)*. The tester should show partial

resistance. If the warming element tests faulty, replace it. Disconnect the other warming-element wire end. (Label and disconnect all other wires attached to the second thermostat terminal, if necessary.) To remove the warming element, gently bend up the mounting clamp with a screwdriver to release the looped end of the element, then slide the element out from around the brewing element *(above, right)*. Buy a replacement warming element from an authorized service center and install it reversing the steps taken to remove the faulty one. Reassemble the percolator base and cold check for leaking voltage *(page 417)*.

MIXERS

Using a variety of beaters and speed settings, an electric mixer can do everything from kneading bread dough to whipping egg whites. Most mixers have a universal motor that turns a worm gear, driving a pair of pinion gears in opposite directions from each other. When beaters are inserted into the spindles of the pinion gears, they create the opposing rotation that mixes food so efficiently.

A typical hand mixer is illustrated at right. If your mixer is a cordless rechargeable unit and it operates for shorter and shorter periods after charging, the nicad batteries may be at fault; have them replaced.

Most stand mixers look similar to the one pictured on page 328. This type uses a sensitive governor switch to control motor speed. When the control knob is rotated to the desired speed, it closes the switch contacts to start the motor. The rapid rotation of the motor armature activates a thrust rod, which repeatedly opens and closes the switch contacts to maintain precise speed control. Some newer stand mixers have an electronic circuit board instead of a governor switch. The electronic type is illustrated on page 331.

To avoid mixer problems caused by misuse, first review your owner's manual. When the mixer does not work properly, consult the categories that apply to your mixer in the Troubleshooting Guide below. For information on using a multitester, consult Tools & Techniques *(page 417)*.

If your mixer hums but doesn't work, or has a burning smell, turn it off at once to avoid damaging the motor or gears. If you suspect a faulty motor, have it serviced professionally. Keep in mind that many mixer motors are not easily serviced: replacing one can be more expensive than buying a new mixer.

TROUBLESHOOTING GUIDE

SYMPTOM	POSSIBLE CAUSE	PROCEDURE
ALL MIXERS		
Mixer doesn't run at all	No power to outlet or outlet faulty	Reset breaker or replace fuse *(p. 102)* □○; service outlet *(p. 148)*
	Power cord faulty	Test and replace power cord *(p. 417)* ▣○▲
	Internal wiring faulty	Inspect and repair wire connections *(p. 417)* ▣○
Motor hums; beaters don't turn	Motor bearing seized	Take mixer for professional service
Mixer overheats	Air intake vents clogged	Clean air intake vents with a toothbrush and vacuum cleaner
	Motor bearings worn or dry	Take mixer for professional service
Mixer vibrates noisily	Gears faulty	Service gears *(p. 333)* ▣○
	Motor faulty	Take mixer for professional service
Mixer gives electrical shock	Ground fault in mixer	Take mixer for professional service
Beaters hit one another, jam, grind, fall out, or won't turn	Gears faulty	Service gears *(p. 333)* ▣○
	Beater shafts worn or bent	Inspect and replace beaters
HAND MIXERS		
Mixer doesn't run at all	Speed control or power burst switch faulty	Test and replace main switch assembly *(p. 327)* ▣◐
	Motor faulty	Take mixer for professional service
GOVERNOR-TYPE STAND MIXERS		
Mixer doesn't run at all	Governor switch faulty	Service governor switch assembly *(p. 330)* ▣○
	Motor faulty	Take mixer for professional service
Mixer runs only on high speed, or doesn't turn off	Governor switch faulty	Service governor switch assembly *(p. 330)* ▣○
	Condenser faulty	Service condenser *(p. 330)* ▣○▲
Mixer runs sluggishly or erratically	Governor switch or resistor faulty	Service governor switch assembly *(p. 330)* ▣○
	Motor faulty	Take mixer for professional service
ELECTRONIC STAND MIXERS		
Mixer doesn't run at all	On/off switch faulty	Service on/off switch *(p. 332)* ▣○
	Fuse or motor faulty	Test fuse and motor circuit *(p. 332)* ▣○▲; service fuse *(p. 333)* ▣○ or have motor serviced
	Circuit board faulty	Replace circuit board *(p. 333)* ▣○
Mixer runs only on high speed	Circuit board faulty	Replace circuit board *(p. 333)* ▣○

DEGREE OF DIFFICULTY: □ Easy ▣ Moderate ■ Complex
ESTIMATED TIME: ○ Less than 1 hour ◐ 1 to 3 hours ● Over 3 hours

▲ Multitester required

HAND MIXERS

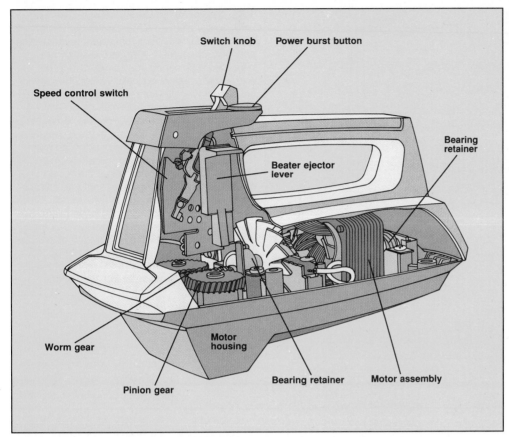

Switch knob   Power burst button

Speed control switch

Beater ejector lever

Bearing retainer

Worm gear

Motor housing

Pinion gear

Bearing retainer   Motor assembly

Accessing switches, motor and gears. Turn off and unplug the mixer. Remove the beaters and the detachable power cord, if it has one. Pry the switch knob off the lever. Turn over the mixer and remove the screws from the motor housing. Turn the mixer upright and work apart the housing, pulling the upper housing off over the beater ejector lever. You now have access to the motor and switch assembly. To access the gears, turn over the motor housing and pry off the small metal retaining rings and flat washers around the bottoms of the gear spindles, using a small screwdriver or long-nose pliers. Turn the motor housing upright. Unscrew the switch assembly from the top of the front bearing retainer and move the switch assembly to one side. You can now service the gears *(page 333)*.

SERVICING THE SWITCHES (Hand mixers)

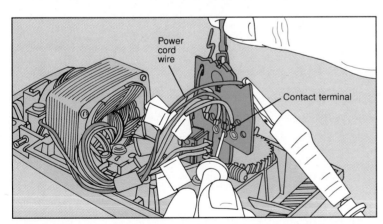

Power cord wire

Contact terminal

1 **Testing the speed control switch.** Turn off and unplug the mixer. Access the switches *(step above)*. Repair any loose or broken wire connections *(page 417)* and clean dirty switch contacts. To test a speed control switch like the one shown here, use a continuity tester, or set a multitester to test continuity. Identify the power cord wire connected to the switch and clip one tester probe to its terminal on the switch. Set the switch lever to the first contact terminal and touch the other probe to that terminal. The multitester should show continuity. Repeat the test at each switch lever setting, in turn *(above)*. If there is continuity at each setting, the switch is OK; go to step 2. If there is no continuity at a setting, replace the switch assembly *(step 3)*.

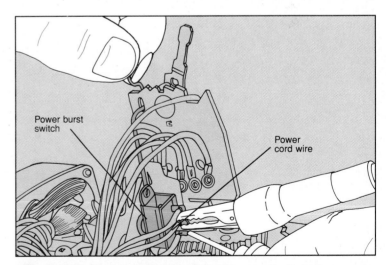

Power burst switch

Power cord wire

2 **Testing the power burst switch.** Use a continuity tester, or set a multitester to test continuity. Identify the power cord wire connected to the power burst switch, located on the main switch assembly. Clip one tester probe to the wire's terminal on the switch. Then touch the second probe to one of the other two terminals as you depress the shaft of the power burst switch *(above)*. The multitester should show continuity. Repeat the test for the other terminal. If there is continuity, the switch is OK. If there is no continuity in a test, go to step 3 to replace the switch assembly.

SERVICING THE SWITCHES (Hand mixers, continued)

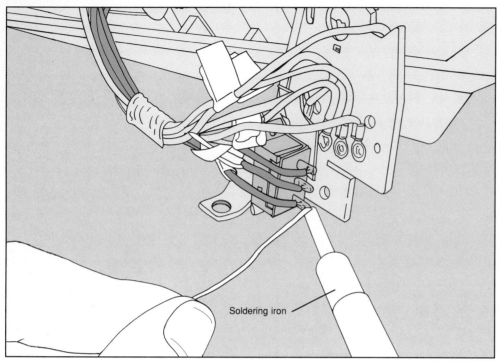

Soldering iron

3 **Replacing the main switch assembly.**
Label all main switch-assembly wires, noting their positions for correct reconnection, and disconnect them. On the model shown here, use a soldering iron *(page 417)* to desolder the power-burst switch wires. Use diagonal-cutting pliers to cut the speed-control switch wires as close to their terminals as possible. Unscrew the switch assembly from the top of the front bearing retainer. Buy an exact replacement from an authorized service center or the manufacturer. Use a wire stripper to strip a small piece of insulation off the tips of the speed control wires and slip each wire into its correct metal crimp connector on the new switch. Close each crimp connector with long-nose pliers. Solder each power-burst switch wire to its correct terminal *(left)*. Secure the new switch assembly to the front bearing retainer. Install the upper housing, reversing the steps taken to remove it. Cold check the mixer for leaking voltage *(page 417)*.

GOVERNOR-TYPE STAND MIXERS

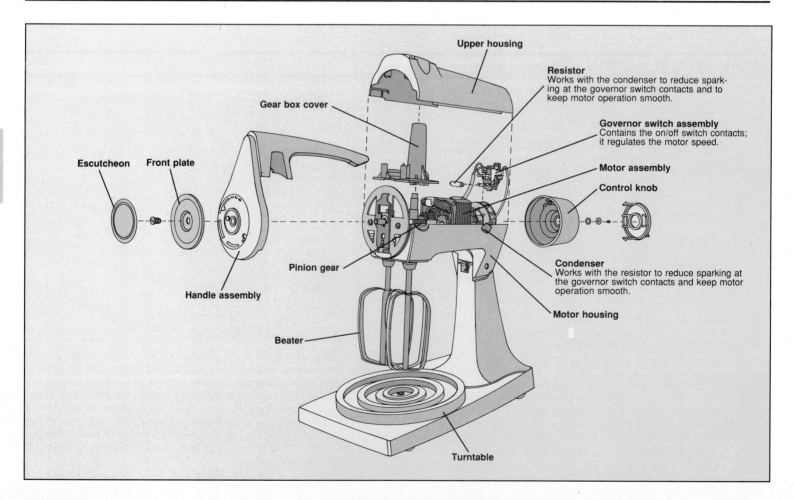

Upper housing

Resistor
Works with the condenser to reduce sparking at the governor switch contacts and to keep motor operation smooth.

Gear box cover

Governor switch assembly
Contains the on/off switch contacts; it regulates the motor speed.

Escutcheon   **Front plate**

Motor assembly

Control knob

Pinion gear

Handle assembly

Condenser
Works with the resistor to reduce sparking at the governor switch contacts and keep motor operation smooth.

Motor housing

Beater

Turntable

ACCESS TO INTERNAL PARTS (Governor-type stand mixers)

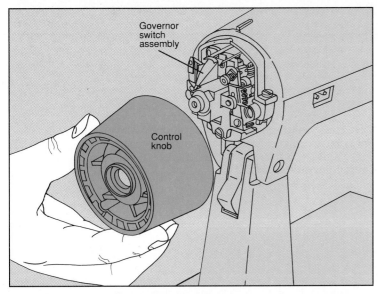

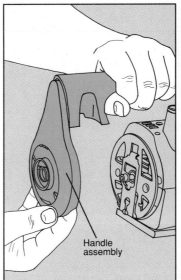

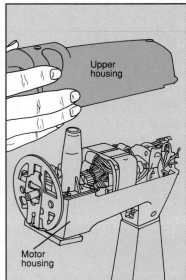

Removing and reinstalling the control knob. Turn off and unplug the mixer and remove the beaters. To remove the control knob on the model shown above, turn it to its highest setting, then use a screwdriver to pry the cap off its end. Note the order of the washers held by a screw to the center of the control knob. Remove the screw and catch the washers if they fall. Pull off the control knob *(above)*. Reverse this sequence to reinstall the knob, taking care that the washers are put back in the correct order.

Removing and reinstalling the handle and upper housing. Remove the control knob *(left)*. Then pry the escutcheon off the front of the mixer with the tip of a screwdriver. Unscrew the front plate and pull out the spring and washer beneath it. Grip the handle and rotate it counter-clockwise as far it goes, then pull to release the handle assembly from the mixer *(above, left)*. Unscrew the upper housing and lift it off the motor housing *(above, right)*. Reverse this sequence to reinstall the housing and handle.

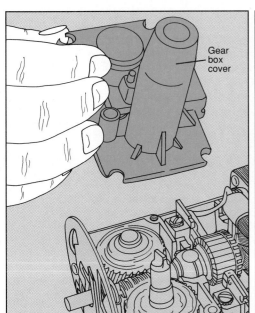

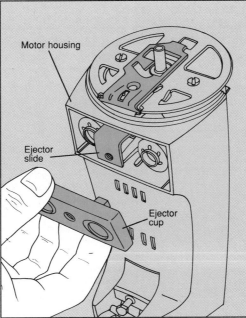

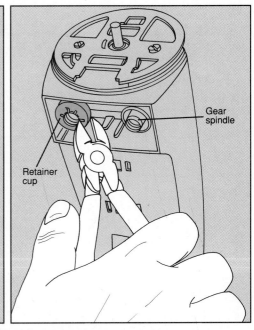

Accessing the gears. Remove the control knob *(step above, left)* and take off the handle and upper housing *(step above, right)*. Unscrew and lift off the gear box cover *(above, left)*. Tilt back the motor housing and unscrew and remove the ejector cup underneath it *(above, center)*, then pull out the ejector slide. Use diagonal-cutting pliers to cut the retainer cups off the bases of the gear spindles *(above, right)*. Then remove the two spindle seals beneath the retainer cups. You can now service the gears *(page 333)*. Before reassembling the mixer, purchase two identical retainer cups from the mixer manufacturer or an authorized service center to replace those you cut off. To put the mixer back together, reverse the sequence of steps taken to access the gears.

SERVICING THE GOVERNOR SWITCH ASSEMBLY AND CONDENSER (Governor-type stand mixers)

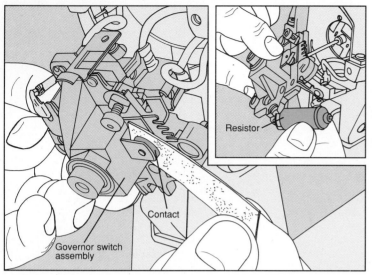

Resistor

Contact

Governor switch assembly

1 **Servicing the governor switch assembly.** Unplug the mixer. Remove the control knob *(page 329)*. Unscrew the governor switch from the back of the motor housing and pull it out of the mixer. Inspect the switch contacts. If the contacts can't close or are fused together, go to step 3 to replace the governor switch assembly. If the contacts are pitted or burned, clean them: Slip a small, folded piece of fine emery paper between them and gently rub their surfaces *(left)*. To remove the dust, pull a piece of plain paper between the contacts. After cleaning the contacts, inspect the resistor. If the resistor looks burned, flex one end of its bracket outward and pull it free *(inset)*. Replace it with an identical resistor purchased from an authorized service center.

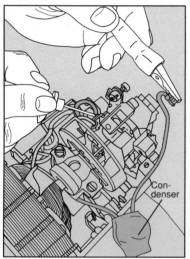
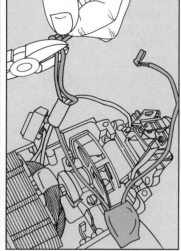

Con-denser

2 **Testing and replacing the condenser.** Remove the handle and upper housing *(page 329)*. Use a continuity tester, or set a multitester to test continuity. Locate the condenser and disconnect one of its wires. Touch a tester probe to each wire connector *(far left)*. The multitester should show resistance (although the needle may jump before it settles). If the condenser has continuity, replace it. Pull off the second wire connector and remove the condenser from the mixer. On the model shown here, a power cord wire is also attached to this wire connector. Use diagonal-cutting pliers to cut off the connector *(near left)*. Purchase an identical replacement condenser from an authorized service center or the mixer manufacturer. Install new wire connectors on the condenser wires, making sure to reconnect the power cord wire if it was disconnected earlier. Reconnect the condenser to the governor switch. Reinstall the upper housing, handle and control knob and cold check the mixer for leaking voltage *(page 417)*.

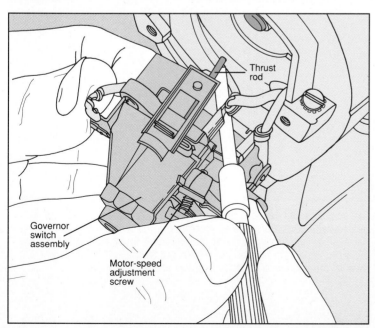

Thrust rod

Governor switch assembly

Motor-speed adjustment screw

3 **Replacing the governor switch assembly.** Label the wires and pull their connectors off the switch terminals with long-nose pliers. Buy an identical replacement switch from an authorized service center or the manufacturer. To install the new switch, first reconnect the wires. Then insert the flat end of the thrust rod into the slot in the back of the new switch. Use a magnetized screwdriver to guide the free end of the thrust rod into the armature hole as you push the switch assembly back into place *(left)*. Screw the assembly onto the motor housing and reinstall the control knob. After reassembling the mixer, cold check for leaking voltage *(page 417)*. Then plug in the mixer and slowly rotate the control knob. If the mixer turns on at a higher speed setting than normal, or if the mixer doesn't turn off at all or reaches its maximum speed below the highest speed setting, the switch contacts need adjusting. Turn off the mixer, unplug it and remove the control knob. Use a small hex wrench to turn the motor-speed adjustment screw one-quarter turn: clockwise if the mixer turns on too late, and counterclockwise if it reaches maximum speed too soon. Reinstall the control knob and operate the mixer again. Repeat the adjustment until the mixer turns on at the correct setting, turning the adjustment screw no more than one-quarter turn each time.

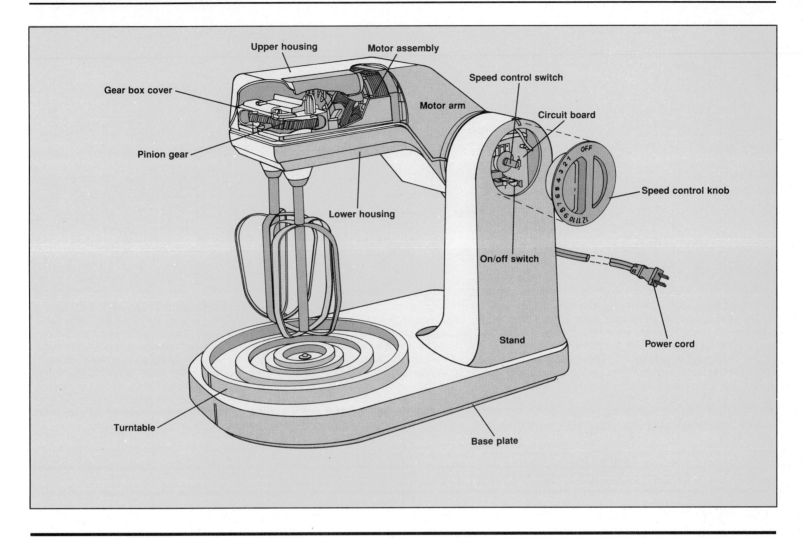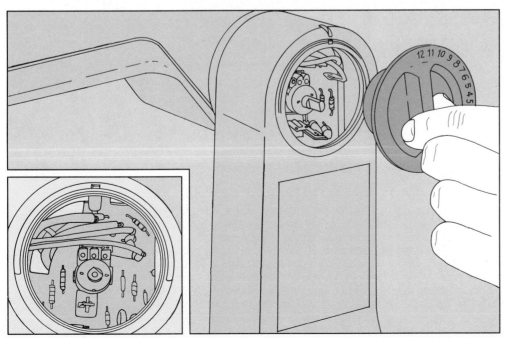

ACCESSING INTERNAL COMPONENTS (Electronic stand mixers, continued)

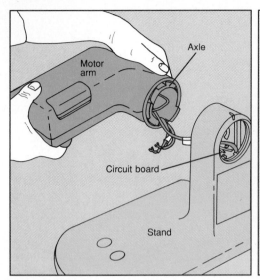

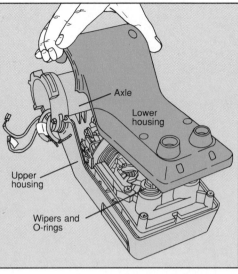

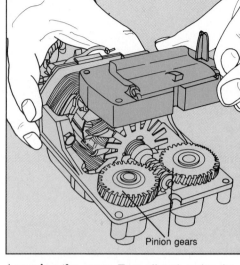

Disassembling and reassembling the motor arm. Turn off and unplug the mixer. Remove the control knob *(page 331)*. Label the wires and pull them off the circuit board. Reach through the speed-control knob hole and slide the circuit board down into the lower part of the stand until you can see the bracket that holds the motor arm axle to the stand. Unscrew the bracket and lift it out. Lift the motor arm up and back until the axle snaps free, then pull the arm off the stand *(above, left)*. Turn the motor arm upside down. Unscrew and lift off the lower housing *(above, right)*, and remove the motor-and-gear assembly from the upper housing. Keep track of the ejector spring that may fall off the bottom of the motor-and-gear assembly. Before reassembling the motor arm, roll the axle toward the back of the housing as far as it will go. Then reassemble the mixer, reversing the sequence of steps taken to disassemble it, and cold check for leaking voltage *(page 417)*.

Accessing the gears. Turn off and unplug the mixer. Disassemble the motor arm *(left)*. Remove the felt wipers and O-rings from the bottoms of the gear spindles and put them aside for reassembly. Remove the screws holding the gear box cover to the bottom of the motor-and-gear assembly. Then turn over the assembly and lift off the gear box cover *(above)*. After completing repair, reverse the sequence of steps taken to access the gears.

SERVICING THE ELECTRICAL COMPONENTS (Electronic stand mixers)

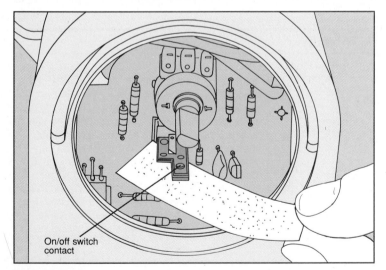

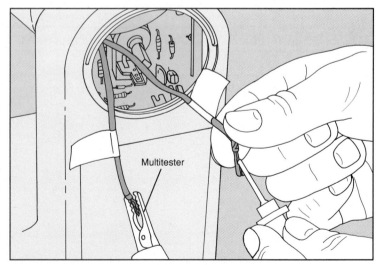

Servicing the on/off switch. Unplug the mixer and remove the speed control knob *(page 331)*. Inspect the contacts. If they are not touching, use long-nose pliers to bend them gently until they do. If the contacts are pitted, burned or dirty, clean them by slipping a small, folded piece of fine emery paper between the upper and lower contacts. Gently rub their surfaces *(above)*, then rub them with a piece of plain paper. After servicing the switch, reinstall the speed control knob and cold check the mixer for leaking voltage *(page 417)*. If the contacts can't be repaired or cleaned, replace the circuit board *(page 333)*.

Testing the fuse-and-motor circuit. Turn off and unplug the mixer. Remove the speed control knob *(page 331)*. Locate the fuse wire and motor wire on the circuit board; they are distinguished from the power cord wires by their smaller gauge. Label the wires and pull them off the circuit board. Set a multitester to RX10 and touch a tester probe to each wire end *(above)*. The multitester should show very low resistance. If it doesn't, suspect either a faulty fuse or a faulty motor. Test the fuse *(page 333)* to find out which one needs repair. If the fuse and motor test OK, repair any loose or broken wire connections *(page 417)*.

SERVICING THE ELECTRICAL COMPONENTS (Electronic stand mixers, continued)

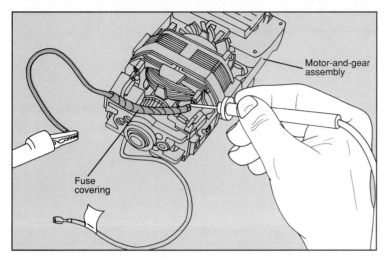

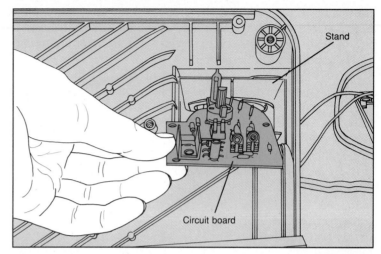

Testing and replacing the fuse. Turn off and unplug the mixer. Remove the speed control knob *(page 331)* and disassemble the motor arm *(page 332)*. Turn the motor-and-gear assembly over on its top. Locate the fuse; it may be hidden by a protective covering. Use a continuity tester, or set a multitester to test continuity. Touch a probe to the wire connector on the end of each fuse lead. The tester should show continuity. If the fuse tests OK, suspect a faulty motor and have it serviced. If the fuse tests faulty, remove it by pulling its wire off the motor terminal. Buy an exact replacement fuse from the mixer manufacturer or from an authorized service center. Connect the fuse to the motor and reassemble the mixer by reversing the steps taken to access the fuse. Cold check the mixer for leaking voltage *(page 417)*.

Replacing the circuit board. Turn off and unplug the mixer. Remove the speed control knob *(page 331)*. Label all wires to the circuit board, and disconnect them. Reach through the speed-control knob hole and slide the circuit board down into the lower part of the stand as far as you can. Lay the mixer on its side. Unscrew and remove the base plate; on the model shown here, peel off the rubber foot pads to access the base plate screws underneath. Remove the screws from the channel support and lift it off the bottom of the stand. Slide out the circuit board *(above)*. Buy a replacement circuit board from the mixer manufacturer or an authorized service center. Install the new board by reversing the sequence of steps taken to remove the old one. Cold check the mixer for leaking voltage *(page 417)*.

SERVICING THE GEARS (All mixers)

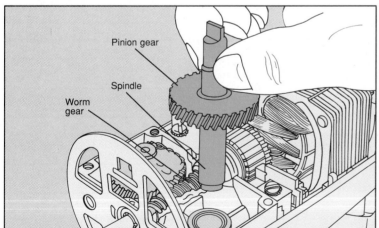

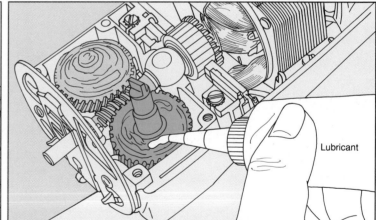

Cleaning and replacing the gears. Unplug the mixer. Access the mixer gears *(hand mixers, page 327; governor-type stand mixers, page 329; electronic stand mixers, page 332)*. Pull out the pinion gears *(above)* and inspect them for wear or cracks. Replace both gears if either is damaged. Buy identical replacement gears and the recommended gear lubricant from an authorized service center. Clean the gear box thoroughly with a soft cloth, and use a small brush to remove plastic shavings and old lubricant from the grooves of the worm gear. Seat the new gears in place. Then, while you hold them firmly in position with one hand, tip back the mixer housing and snap the beaters into the gear spindles underneath. If the beater blades intersect one another at a 45-degree angle, the gears are seated properly. If not, remove one of the beaters and lift out, rotate and reseat its gear. Snap the beater back in and check the beater positions again. Repeat until the beater blades intersect at a 45-degree angle. Once they do, secure the gears in place by reinstalling any washers, seals and clips. If the old gears were lubricated and housed in a separate box, apply a generous amount of the recommended lubricant around the teeth of the gears and on their tops *(above)*, or use a high-temperature, multipurpose, grease. Replace the gear box cover, if it has one, and reassemble the mixer, reversing the sequence of steps taken to access the gears. Cold check the mixer for leaking voltage *(page 417)*.

BLENDERS

The blades of a blender are driven by a small universal motor directly below the jar and blade assembly. A push-button switch regulates a variety of speeds, for functions ranging from chopping to liquefying.

The illustration below shows a typical blender with a removable blade assembly. The jar base, blades and seal ring can be taken apart for cleaning. When washing the blender, inspect the jar and blade assembly for cracks, bent blades or a dried-out seal ring; replace damaged parts. Wash the blade assembly immediately after each use to keep dried food from jamming its shaft. Inspect the blade socket that fits onto the drive stud, and replace the blade if it is stripped. Once a month, lubricate its moving metal parts with mineral oil; do not apply machine oil to parts that come in contact with food.

Blender problems are typically caused by overloading the jar. This slows the blades and puts a strain on the motor, causing it to overheat and burn out. Turn off the blender immediately if it begins to hum or has a burning odor—replacing the motor can cost as much as replacing the blender.

Testing a multi-speed switch is complicated. To determine whether the switch is at fault, consult the Troubleshooting Guide and rule out all other possible causes first. To service an on/off switch, see Food Processors *(page 339)*. After repair, perform a cold check for leaking voltage *(page 417)*.

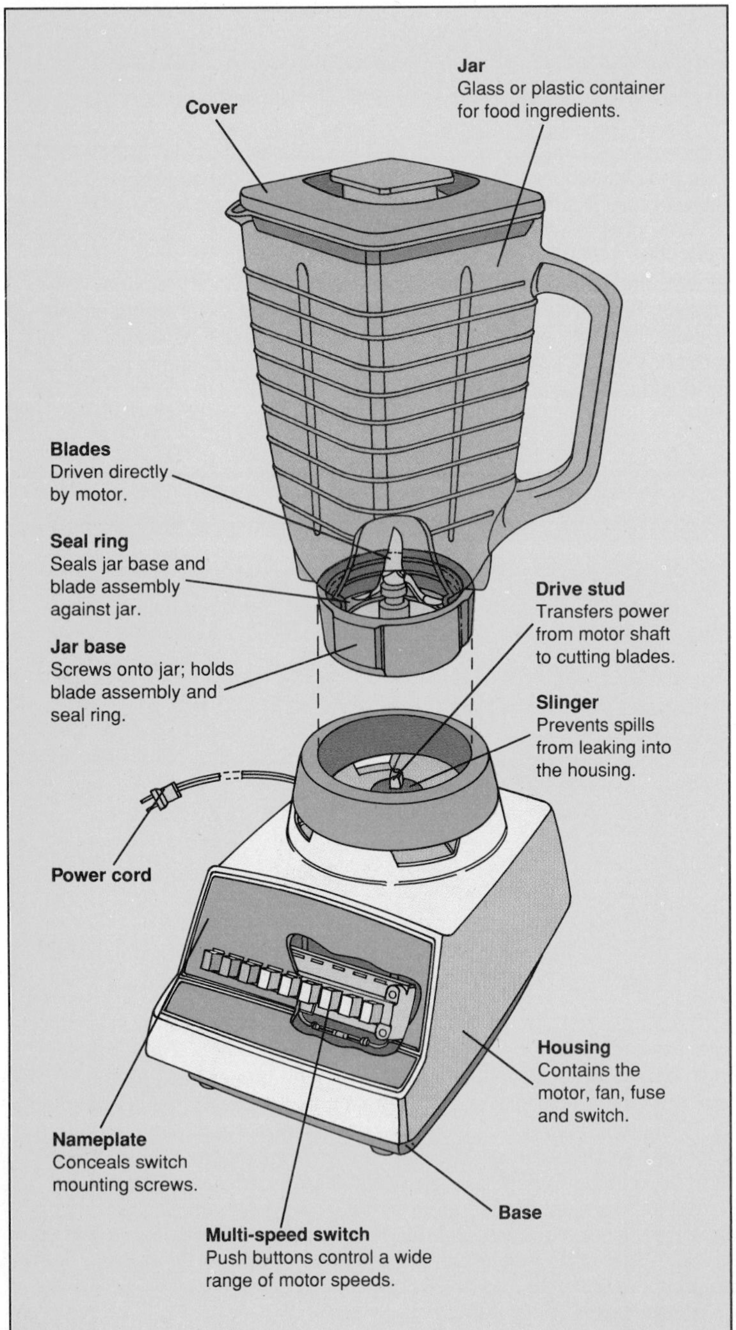

Cover

Jar
Glass or plastic container for food ingredients.

Blades
Driven directly by motor.

Seal ring
Seals jar base and blade assembly against jar.

Jar base
Screws onto jar; holds blade assembly and seal ring.

Drive stud
Transfers power from motor shaft to cutting blades.

Slinger
Prevents spills from leaking into the housing.

Power cord

Housing
Contains the motor, fan, fuse and switch.

Nameplate
Conceals switch mounting screws.

Base

Multi-speed switch
Push buttons control a wide range of motor speeds.

TROUBLESHOOTING GUIDE

SYMPTOM	PROCEDURE
Blender doesn't run at all	Reset breaker or replace fuse *(p. 102)* □○; service outlet *(p. 148)*
	Test power cord *(p. 417)* ▣○▲
	Clean or replace switch *(p. 335)* □◗
	Remove base *(p. 335)* □○; repair faulty wire connections *(p. 417)* ▣○
	Test and replace fuse *(p. 335)* □○▲
	Test motor *(p. 336)* ▣○▲
Blender runs intermittently	Test power cord *(p. 417)* ▣○▲
	Remove base *(p. 335)* □○; repair faulty wire connections *(p. 417)* ▣○
	Take blender for professional service
Blender doesn't run at some speeds	Remove base *(p. 335)* □○; repair faulty wire connections *(p. 417)* ▣○
	Test motor *(p. 336)* ▣○▲
	Clean or replace switch *(p. 335)* □◗
Motor hums but blades don't turn	Reduce load in jar
	Wash blade assembly and lubricate with mineral oil; or replace
	Inspect and replace blade assembly; replace drive stud *(p. 336)* □◗
	Test motor *(p. 336)* ▣○▲
Blender vibrates noisily	Inspect and replace blade assembly; replace drive stud *(p. 336)* □◗
	Tighten drive stud or fan locknut *(p. 336)* □○
	Test motor *(p. 336)* ▣○▲
Jar leaks	Tighten base onto jar
	Inspect and replace jar, seal ring or blade assembly
Blender overheats	Reduce load in jar
	Clean air screen in base
	Test motor *(p. 336)* ▣◗▲
Motor fuse blows repeatedly	Test motor *(p. 336)* ▣◗▲

DEGREE OF DIFFICULTY: □ **Easy** ▣ **Moderate** ■ **Complex**
ESTIMATED TIME: ○ **Less than 1 hour**
◗ **1 to 3 hours** ● **Over 3 hours**
▲ **Special tool required**

SERVICING THE MULTI-SPEED SWITCH

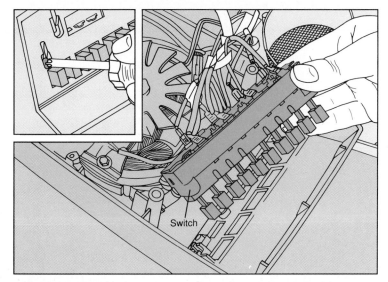

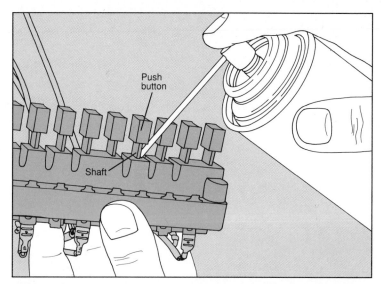

1 **Removing the base and accessing the switch.** Unplug the blender and remove the jar. Turn over the blender and remove the screws securing the base to the housing. Pull off the base to expose the switch, fan, motor and fuse. To service the switch, turn the blender upright and pry off the nameplate with a utility knife. Remove the mounting screws concealed beneath it *(inset)*, turn over the blender again and lift out the switch *(above)*.

2 **Cleaning or replacing the switch.** Scrape off hardened food deposits and wipe the push buttons with a damp cloth. Spray electrical contact cleaner into the button openings *(above)*, pressing each button two or three times. Clean the button shafts with a toothbrush and contact cleaner. If the buttons are jammed or the switch is faulty, label and disconnect the wires. Buy an exact replacement from an authorized service center and install it, making sure all wires are properly reconnected. Reassemble the blender and cold check for leaking voltage *(page 417)*.

TESTING AND REPLACING THE FUSE

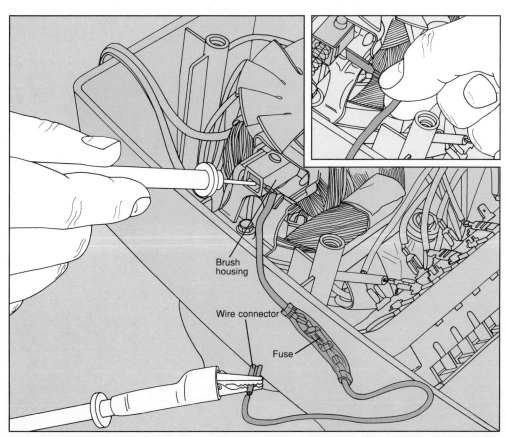

Testing and replacing the fuse. Unplug the blender and remove the jar. To access the fuse, remove the base *(step 1, above)*. Locate the fuse—usually encapsulated in clear plastic—and disconnect its wire from the switch. Set a multi-tester to RX1 and clip a probe to the wire connector. Touch the other probe to the fuse terminal at the brush housing *(left)*. The tester should show continuity. If it doesn't, replace the fuse. Use long-nose pliers to straighten the fuse terminal and pull it out of the brush housing *(inset)*. The brush spring will be released; immediately place your finger over the opening and remove the terminal slowly, so the spring and its motor brush stay in the housing.

Buy an exact replacement fuse from the manufacturer or an authorized service center. Use a small screwdriver to push the spring into the brush housing, then insert the the new fuse's terminal into the housing slot. Bend back the end of the terminal to secure it. Connect the other wire end to the switch. Reassemble the blender and cold check for leaking voltage *(page 417)*.

SERVICING THE MOTOR

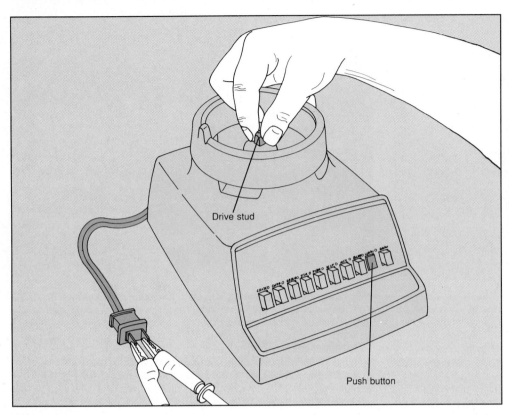

Drive stud

Push button

Testing the motor. Unplug the blender and remove the jar. Set a multitester to RX1 and clip a probe to each prong of the power cord plug. Press down one push button and read its resistance on the meter. With the button still depressed, rotate the drive stud one full turn *(left)*. If this causes the tester to register a change in resistance, have the motor serviced. Continue the test with each push button. Also note any deviation of more than about 15 ohms between buttons; this indicates a problem with the motor windings or the switch itself.

Remove the base *(page 335, step 1)* and inspect the motor assembly. If the motor smells burned or the windings are charred, take the unit for professional service. Otherwise, replace the switch *(page 335, step 2)*.

SERVICING THE DRIVE STUD AND SLINGER

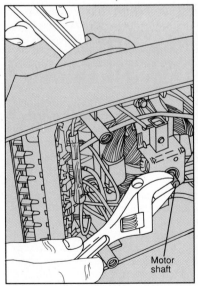

Motor shaft

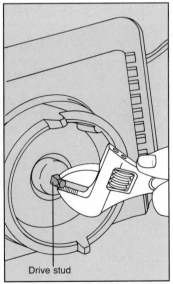

Drive stud

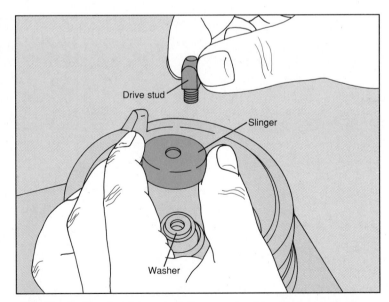

Drive stud

Slinger

Washer

1 **Freeing the drive stud.** Unplug the blender and remove the jar. Inspect the drive stud for worn edges; replace it if damaged. Remove the base *(page 335, step 1)* and lay the blender on its side. Locate the motor shaft. On the model shown, you must first remove the fan: Hold the fan with a rag, or wear a glove, and use an adjustable wrench to remove the fan locknut. Pull the fan and its washers off the shaft, taking care to lay the parts in correct order for reassembly. To free the drive stud, steady the motor shaft with the wrench *(above, left)*, while you use another wrench to unscrew the stud from the other side *(above, right)*.

2 **Replacing the drive stud.** Remove the drive stud and slinger, leaving the washer in place *(above)*. Use a toothbrush to clean the slinger of any hardened food deposits; replace it if rusted or worn. Buy exact replacement parts from the manufacturer or an authorized service center. Center the slinger and washer over the motor shaft, and insert the drive stud through them into the hole in the motor shaft. Tighten the stud with the two-handed technique you used to remove it, then reassemble the blender, reversing the steps you took to disassemble it. Cold check for leaking voltage *(page 417)*.

FOOD PROCESSORS

Food processors do what mixers and blenders do, only faster. Their powerful motors and razor-sharp blades can slice, shred or pulverize almost any food in a matter of seconds.

A belt-drive food processor *(page 338)* has a bowl capacity large enough to hold a shredded head of cabbage. The motor sits to one side of the bowl; a drive belt on a wheel-and-pulley assembly turns the blade. Switches control the speed and duration of the blade action. The direct-drive food processor is usually more compact. It houses the motor-and-gear assembly beneath the bowl; the blade is attached directly to the motor shaft or, as in the variation shown here *(page 340)*, the motor shaft drives a gear that turns the blade. Both types have a safety switch that activates the motor only when the cover is securely in position.

Most food processor malfunctions are caused by improper cleaning. Hardened food deposits in the drive shaft or spindle shaft cause noisy vibration, poor functioning and, eventually, permanent damage to the blade and the gear or drive assembly. Leaks and spills can short the switches and motor. The Troubleshooting Guide below will help you locate the most likely cause of your food processor's problem and direct you to its repair. Motor problems are often covered by the manufacturer's warranty.

For information on using electrical testers, consult Tools & Techniques *(page 417)*. Take safety precautions when working on a food processor. Always unplug the power cord before beginning a repair, and handle the sharp cutting discs and blades with care. When disassembling an older model, check carefully inside the housing for a capacitor—a battery-like component usually mounted beside the motor. The capacitor stores a potentially dangerous electrical charge; discharge it *(page 417)* before attempting a repair. If your food processor is much different from the models shown in this chapter, or if it is still under warranty, have it serviced professionally.

TROUBLESHOOTING GUIDE

SYMPTOM	POSSIBLE CAUSE	PROCEDURE
Food processor doesn't work at all	No power to outlet or outlet faulty	Reset breaker or replace fuse *(p. 102)* □○; service outlet *(p. 148)*
	Bowl and cover positioned incorrectly	Consult owner's manual for correct positioning
	Cam in edge of cover worn or broken	Inspect cover and replace if damaged
	Power cord faulty	Test and replace power cord *(p. 417)* ◨○▲
	Fuse blown (direct-drive type)	Test and replace food processor fuse *(p. 341)* ◨○▲
	Motor faulty	Take food processor for professional service
	Wire connections loose or faulty	Tighten or repair wire connections *(p. 417)* ◨○
	Switches faulty	Test and replace multi-control switches *(belt-drive type, p. 339)* ◨○▲; test and replace safety switch *(belt-drive type, p. 340)* ◨○▲; or take food processor for professional service *(direct-drive type)*
Food processor runs on only one speed setting (belt-drive type)	Speed control switch faulty	Test and replace speed control switch *(p. 339)* ◨○▲
	Wire connections loose or faulty	Tighten or repair wire connections *(p. 417)* ◨○
	Motor faulty	Take food processor for professional service
Motor runs but blades don't turn	Drive belt broken (belt-drive type)	Replace drive belt *(p. 338)* □○
	Drive belt tension incorrect (belt-drive type)	Adjust drive belt *(p. 338)* □○
	Spindle shaft broken (belt-drive type)	Replace spindle shaft *(p. 338)* □○
	Gear stripped or broken (direct-drive type)	Replace gear *(p. 341)* ◨◓
Blades slow down and speed up erratically (belt-drive type)	Drive belt worn	Replace drive belt *(p. 338)* □○
	Drive belt tension incorrect	Adjust drive belt *(p. 338)* □○
Food processor is noisy or vibrates excessively	Blades or blade shaft dirty, worn or broken	Clean or replace blade assembly
	Spindle shaft dirty or worn (belt-drive type)	Clean or replace spindle shaft *(p. 338)* □○
	Drive shaft dirty or worn (direct-drive type)	Clean or replace drive shaft *(p. 341)* □○
Food processor overheats	Bowl overloaded	Consult owner's manual for correct loading instructions
	Air intake screen clogged	Clean screen in lower housing with a toothbrush and vacuum cleaner
	Motor faulty	Take food processor for professional service
Food processor blows fuse or circuit breaker repeatedly	Household electrical circuit overloaded	Reduce number of appliances on circuit

DEGREE OF DIFFICULTY: □ Easy ◨ Moderate ■ Complex
ESTIMATED TIME: ○ Less than 1 hour ◓ 1 to 3 hours ● Over 3 hours   ▲ Multitester required

337

BELT-DRIVE FOOD PROCESSORS

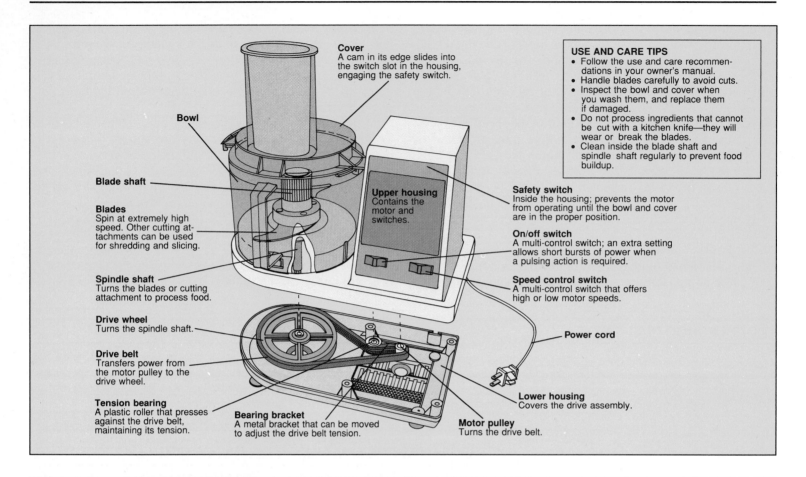

Cover
A cam in its edge slides into the switch slot in the housing, engaging the safety switch.

Bowl

Blade shaft

Blades
Spin at extremely high speed. Other cutting attachments can be used for shredding and slicing.

Spindle shaft
Turns the blades or cutting attachment to process food.

Drive wheel
Turns the spindle shaft.

Drive belt
Transfers power from the motor pulley to the drive wheel.

Tension bearing
A plastic roller that presses against the drive belt, maintaining its tension.

Bearing bracket
A metal bracket that can be moved to adjust the drive belt tension.

Upper housing
Contains the motor and switches.

Safety switch
Inside the housing; prevents the motor from operating until the bowl and cover are in the proper position.

On/off switch
A multi-control switch; an extra setting allows short bursts of power when a pulsing action is required.

Speed control switch
A multi-control switch that offers high or low motor speeds.

Power cord

Lower housing
Covers the drive assembly.

Motor pulley
Turns the drive belt.

USE AND CARE TIPS
- Follow the use and care recommendations in your owner's manual.
- Handle blades carefully to avoid cuts.
- Inspect the bowl and cover when you wash them, and replace them if damaged.
- Do not process ingredients that cannot be cut with a kitchen knife—they will wear or break the blades.
- Clean inside the blade shaft and spindle shaft regularly to prevent food buildup.

SERVICING THE DRIVE ASSEMBLY (Belt-drive food processors)

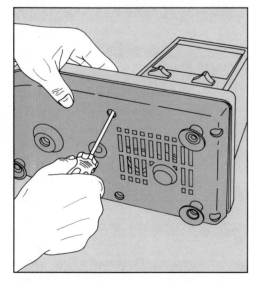

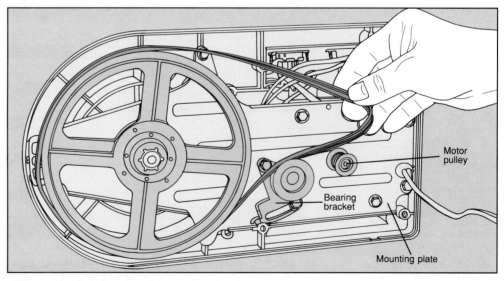

Motor pulley

Bearing bracket

Mounting plate

1 **Removing the lower housing.** Turn off and unplug the food processor. Take off the bowl and cover and lay the unit on its side. Remove the screws securing the lower housing *(above)* and lift it off to expose the drive assembly *(step 2)*. If you are simply adjusting the drive belt, go directly to step 4.

2 **Removing the drive belt.** Loosen, but do not remove, the screw securing the bearing bracket to the mounting plate. Shift the bracket to slacken the belt, then slip the belt up off the motor pulley and drive wheel *(above)*. Inspect the belt carefully; if it is cracked, worn, frayed or stretched, replace it. Purchase an identical replacement belt from the manufacturer or an authorized service center. If the blade assembly vibrates noisily when operating, go to step 3 to service the spindle shaft. Reinstall the belt by reversing the steps you took to remove it, and adjust its tension *(step 4)*.

SERVICING THE DRIVE ASSEMBLY (Belt-drive food processors, continued)

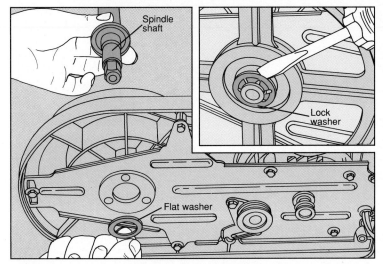

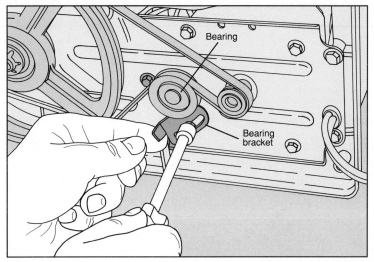

3 **Cleaning and replacing the spindle shaft.** Using a screwdriver, pry off the lock washer holding the spindle shaft to the center of the drive wheel *(inset)*. Remove the drive wheel and the flat washer beneath it, then pull the spindle shaft out through the top of the food processor *(above)*. Clean out food deposits inside the spindle shaft with a small bottle brush. If the shaft is broken, or the ridges inside are worn or damaged, replace the shaft with an identical part from the manufacturer or an authorized service center. Reinstall the flat washer, drive wheel and lock washer. Reinstall the drive belt and adjust its tension *(step 4)*.

4 **Adjusting the drive belt.** Rotate the drive belt by hand to check that it fits snugly and moves smoothly with the motor pulley and drive wheel. If the belt slips off while turning, or turns with difficulty, adjust the tension. Use a nut driver to loosen the screw securing the bearing bracket. Slide the bracket to tighten or loosen the belt *(above)*, then screw the bracket firmly in its new position. Reinstall the lower housing and try the food processor. Readjust the belt if necessary.

TESTING AND REPLACING MULTI-CONTROL SWITCHES (Belt-drive food processors)

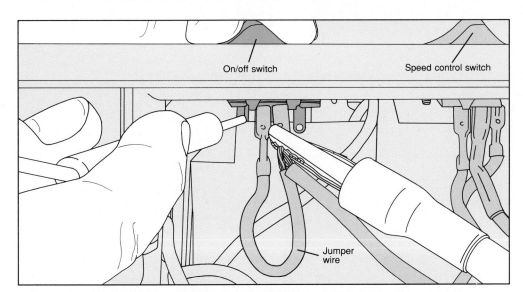

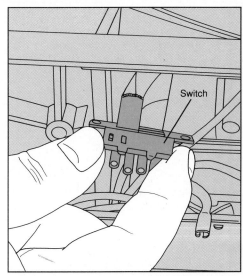

1 **Testing a multi-control switch.** The on/off and speed control switches are located in the upper housing. To gain access to them, unplug the food processor and remove the lower housing *(page 338)*. Test each switch separately. Push the switch to one of the ON positions. Use a continuity tester, or set a multitester to test continuity. Clip one probe to the switch's terminal connected to a power cord wire. (If this terminal is attached to a jumper wire, as shown, do not disconnect the jumper wire.) Label and disconnect the other wires. Touch the other tester probe to each of the other two terminals, in turn *(above)*. The tester should show continuity at one terminal only. Set the switch to its other ON position and repeat the test. The tester should show continuity at the other terminal only. If the switch fails either test, replace it *(step 2)*.

2 **Replacing a multi-control switch.** Label and disconnect the power cord wire. Pull off the switch cap and peel back the nameplate to expose the switch screws. Unscrew and pull out the faulty switch *(above)* and install an exact replacement purchased from an authorized service center. Reconnect the wires, reinstall the lower housing and cold check for leaking voltage *(page 417)*.

TESTING AND REPLACING THE SAFETY SWITCH (Belt-drive food processors)

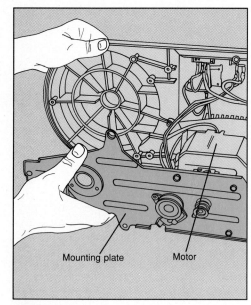
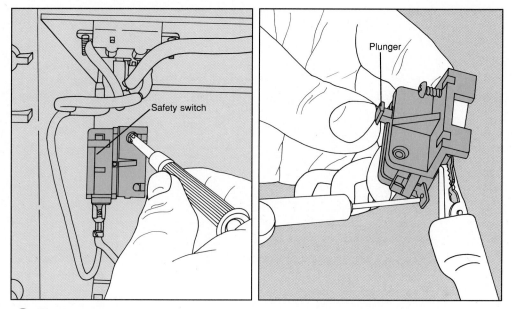

Mounting plate   Motor

Safety switch

Plunger

1 Removing the mounting plate. Unplug the food processor and take off the lower housing and drive assembly *(page 338)*. To gain access to the safety switch, remove the screws securing the mounting plate to the upper housing, then lift out the plate and motor *(above)* and slide it to one side, taking care not to damage or pull any wires.

2 Testing and replacing the safety switch. Locate the safety switch, deep inside the upper housing. Unscrew it from the housing wall *(above, left)* and lift it out. Label and disconnect the two wires. Use a continuity tester, or set a multitester to test continuity. Touch a probe to each terminal; the tester should show no continuity. Then depress the plunger on the side of the switch *(above, right)*; the tester should show continuity. If the switch fails either test, replace it with an exact replacement, purchased from an authorized service center. Reassemble the food processor, making sure all wires are properly reconnected, and cold check for leaking voltage *(page 417)*.

DIRECT-DRIVE FOOD PROCESSORS

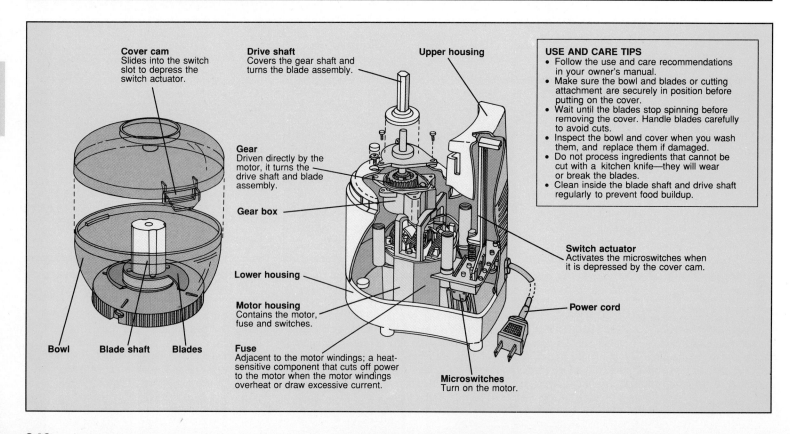

Cover cam
Slides into the switch slot to depress the switch actuator.

Drive shaft
Covers the gear shaft and turns the blade assembly.

Upper housing

Gear
Driven directly by the motor, it turns the drive shaft and blade assembly.

Gear box

Switch actuator
Activates the microswitches when it is depressed by the cover cam.

Power cord

Lower housing

Motor housing
Contains the motor, fuse and switches.

Bowl   **Blade shaft**   **Blades**

Fuse
Adjacent to the motor windings; a heat-sensitive component that cuts off power to the motor when the motor windings overheat or draw excessive current.

Microswitches
Turn on the motor.

USE AND CARE TIPS
- Follow the use and care recommendations in your owner's manual.
- Make sure the bowl and blades or cutting attachment are securely in position before putting on the cover.
- Wait until the blades stop spinning before removing the cover. Handle blades carefully to avoid cuts.
- Inspect the bowl and cover when you wash them, and replace them if damaged.
- Do not process ingredients that cannot be cut with a kitchen knife—they will wear or break the blades.
- Clean inside the blade shaft and drive shaft regularly to prevent food buildup.

SERVICING THE INTERNAL COMPONENTS (Direct-drive food processors)

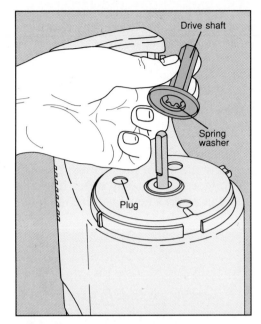

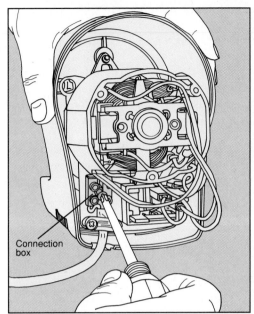

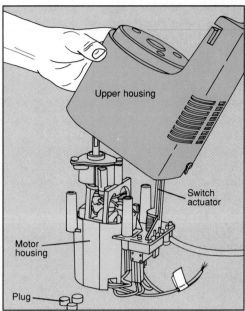

1 **Servicing the drive shaft.** Unplug the unit and remove the bowl and cover. If the drive shaft can be spun freely by hand or if its edges are worn, replace it with an exact duplicate from an authorized service center. Use a screwdriver to pry up the shaft and pull it off, with its spring washer attached *(above)*. Clean the drive shaft of any hardened food deposits.

2 **Inspecting the motor-and-gear assembly.** Unscrew the lower housing and pull it off. Remove the screw securing the connection box *(above, left)* and lift it up. Label and disconnect the wires attached to the box (one leads to the fuse), then remove the four screws recessed in the motor housing. Turn the unit upright and locate the plastic plugs in the top of the upper housing; they conceal the housing screws. Use a fine screwdriver to pry out the plugs, then unscrew and lift off the upper housing *(above, right)*. You now may service the gear assembly *(step 3)* or fuse *(step 4)*. If the motor smells burned or if the motor windings are charred, take the unit for professional service.

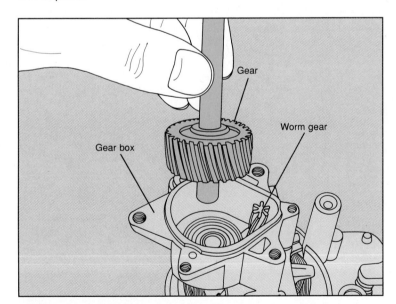

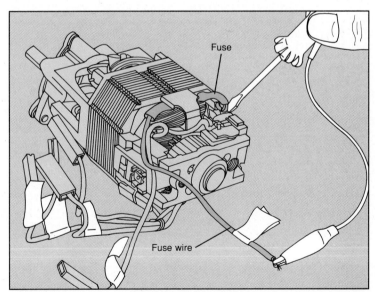

3 **Replacing the gear.** Unscrew and remove the gear box cover and lift out the gear *(above)*. If its teeth are worn or broken, buy an exact replacement gear from the manufacturer or an authorized service center. Before installing it, clean the worm gear with a small brush, and wipe old lubricant and debris from inside the gear box with a cloth. Lubricate the teeth of the new gear with a high-temperature multipurpose grease. Seat the gear, lubricate its top, and reinstall the cover. To test the fuse, go to step 4. Otherwise, reassemble the food processor, correctly reconnecting all wires, and cold check for leaking voltage *(page 417)*.

4 **Testing and replacing the fuse.** Lift out the switch actuator, then label and disconnect the wires to the switches. Slide the motor out of its housing. Follow the fuse wire to locate the fuse, near the motor windings, wrapped in a protective covering. Touch a continuity tester probe to each fuse-wire end *(above)*. The tester should show continuity. If the fuse tests OK, have the motor serviced. Otherwise, disconnect and replace the fuse. Buy an exact replacement fuse from an authorized service center and crimp on a new connector. Install the fuse and reassemble the food processor, making sure all wires are properly connected. Cold check for leaking voltage *(page 417)*.

VACUUM CLEANERS

The indispensable vacuum cleaner had its humble beginnings as an electric fan motor, mounted in a soap box, that collected dirt in a pillow case. Since then, it has been streamlined and modified into two basic styles: upright and canister. Two typical models are pictured below.

A vacuum cleaner sucks up dirt and air, filters out the dirt and allows the air to escape. All vacuum cleaners use a motor and fan to generate this suction; what distinguishes the two types is the route taken by the air flow. In an upright vacuum cleaner, dirt dislodged by the beater bar is pulled by the airstream into the dirt fan, which whirls it up into the dust bag. In a canister model, dirt is sucked through a hose and trapped in the dust bag as it enters the canister; only clean air passes the

fan. A major cause of vacuum cleaner malfunction is, of course, dirt. Change the dust bag often. Periodically check the filter in a canister vacuum cleaner, and wash or replace it as necessary. Keep spare dust bags and filters on hand.

Attentive maintenance will prevent many vacuum cleaner problems, but parts do wear out, most typically the drive belt and the beater bar brushes. If your vacuum cleaner does not operate quietly and efficiently, consult the Troubleshooting Guide at right. Vacuum cleaners are among the most easily serviced of household appliances. You can repair or replace most parts yourself, including the motor brushes and bearing. Canister types, especially older models, may differ from the ones shown here. Use this chapter as a general guide to repair.

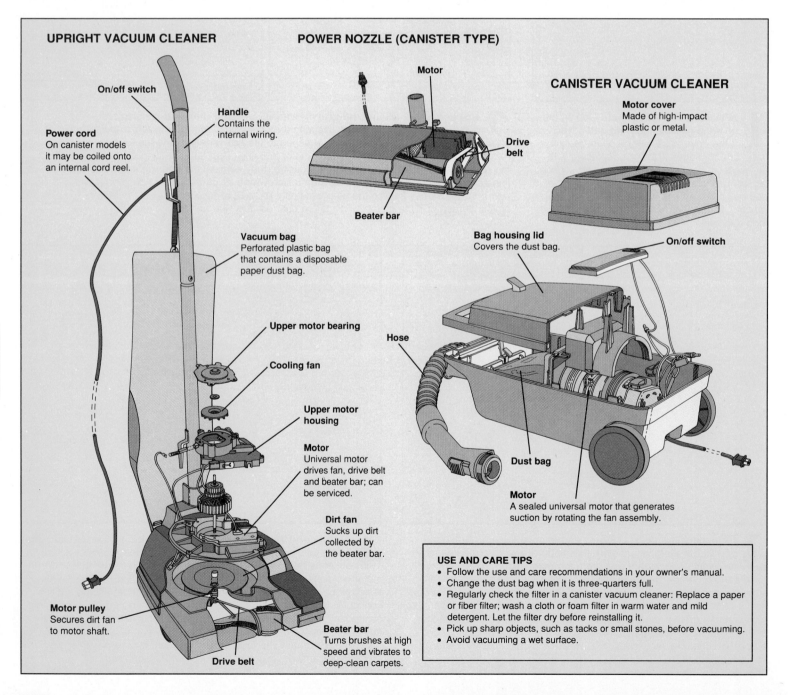

UPRIGHT VACUUM CLEANER

On/off switch

Power cord
On canister models it may be coiled onto an internal cord reel.

Handle
Contains the internal wiring.

Vacuum bag
Perforated plastic bag that contains a disposable paper dust bag.

Upper motor bearing

Cooling fan

Upper motor housing

Motor
Universal motor drives fan, drive belt and beater bar; can be serviced.

Dirt fan
Sucks up dirt collected by the beater bar.

Motor pulley
Secures dirt fan to motor shaft.

Drive belt

Beater bar
Turns brushes at high speed and vibrates to deep-clean carpets.

POWER NOZZLE (CANISTER TYPE)

Motor

Drive belt

Beater bar

CANISTER VACUUM CLEANER

Motor cover
Made of high-impact plastic or metal.

Bag housing lid
Covers the dust bag.

On/off switch

Hose

Dust bag

Motor
A sealed universal motor that generates suction by rotating the fan assembly.

USE AND CARE TIPS
- Follow the use and care recommendations in your owner's manual.
- Change the dust bag when it is three-quarters full.
- Regularly check the filter in a canister vacuum cleaner: Replace a paper or fiber filter; wash a cloth or foam filter in warm water and mild detergent. Let the filter dry before reinstalling it.
- Pick up sharp objects, such as tacks or small stones, before vacuuming.
- Avoid vacuuming a wet surface.

TROUBLESHOOTING GUIDE

SYMPTOM	POSSIBLE CAUSE	PROCEDURE
Vacuum cleaner doesn't turn on	Vacuum cleaner unplugged or turned off	Plug in and turn on vacuum cleaner
	No power to outlet or outlet faulty	Reset breaker or replace fuse (p. 102) □○; service outlet (p. 148)
	Power cord faulty	Test and replace power cord (p. 417) ◨○▲; have cord reel assembly serviced
	On/off switch faulty	Test and replace on/off switch (p. 346) ◨○▲
	Wire connections loose or broken	Inspect and test wiring (p. 349) ◨○
	Motor faulty	Service motor (p. 349) ◨◗▲
Vacuum cleaner turns on, then stops	Household electrical circuit overloaded	Reduce the number of appliances on circuit
	Motor overheated due to full dust bag or dirty filter	Turn off vacuum cleaner, replace dust bag and clean or replace filter; wait for motor to cool and thermal protector to reset itself before turning on vacuum cleaner
Vacuum cleaner runs intermittently	Power cord faulty	Test and replace power cord (p. 417) ◨○▲; have cord reel assembly serviced
	On/off switch faulty	Test and replace on/off switch (p. 346) ◨○▲
	Wire connections loose or broken	Inspect and test wiring (p. 349) ◨○
	Motor faulty	Service motor (p. 349) ◨◗▲
Vacuum cleaner hums, smokes or overheats	Fan jammed or dirty	Service fan (upright type, p. 347; canister type, p. 348) ◨○
	Motor brushes worn or field coil shorted	Service motor (p. 349) ◨◗▲
	Motor shaft bearing binding	Service motor (upright type, p. 349) ◨◗▲; take canister type for professional service
Vacuum cleaner doesn't clean any surface	Dust bag too full	Replace dust bag
	Filter dirty or blocked (canister type)	Clean or replace filter
	Hose clogged by dirt or foreign object (canister type)	Unblock hose with a broom handle
	Puncture in hose (canister type)	Tape or replace hose
Vacuum cleaner doesn't deep-clean carpets	Beater bar brushes clogged by debris (upright type and power nozzles)	Remove lint, hair and debris from beater bar (p. 345) □○
	Beater bar set too low or high (upright type)	Consult owner's manual and adjust wheel height
	Beater bar brushes worn (upright type and power nozzles)	Replace beater brushes (p. 345) ◨○
Beater bar rotates poorly or not at all (upright type and power nozzles)	Drive belt loose or broken	Replace drive belt (p. 345) □○
	Beater bar bearings jammed with dirt or lint	Clean and lubricate bearings (p. 345) □○
	Pressure clip holding beater bar broken	Replace broken clip (p. 345) □○
	Wire connection between vacuum cleaner and power nozzle loose or broken	Repair wire connection (p. 349) □○
Vacuum cleaners is noisy or vibrates excessively	Foreign object caught in fan; fan loose or damaged	Service fan (upright type, p. 347; canister type, p. 348) ◨○
	Drive belt worn or broken (upright type and power nozzles)	Replace drive belt (p. 345) □○
	Beater bar loose (upright type and power nozzles)	Replace beater-bar pressure clips (p. 345) □○
	Motor shaft bearing worn	Service motor (upright type, p. 349) ◨◗▲; take canister type for professional service
Vacuum cleaner gives electrical shock	Ground fault inside vacuum cleaner	Take vacuum cleaner for professional service

DEGREE OF DIFFICULTY: □ Easy ◨ Moderate ■ Complex

ESTIMATED TIME: ○ Less than 1 hour ◗ 1 to 3 hours ● Over 3 hours

▲ Multitester required

ACCESS TO INTERNAL PARTS (Upright type)

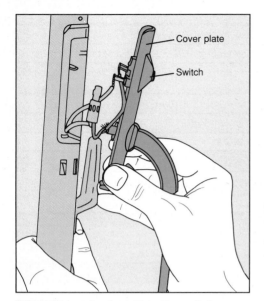

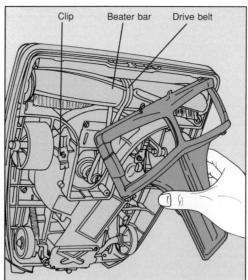

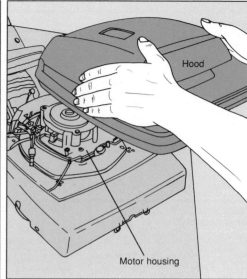

Removing and reinstalling the switch cover plate. Unplug the vacuum cleaner. Lock the handle in the upright position and unhook the vacuum cleaner bag. Unscrew the cover plate and slide it up off the handle *(above)*. After completing repair to the power cord or on/off switch, reinstall the cover plate and cold check for leaking voltage *(page 417)*.

Removing and reinstalling the bottom plate and the hood. Unplug the vacuum cleaner. Lock the handle in the upright position and lower it to the ground. Remove the bottom-plate mounting screws, or pivot the two retaining clips, then swing up the plate and pull it free *(above, left)*. You now have access to the drive belt and the beater bar. To repair the fan or motor, release the hood by unscrewing its mounting screws from the bottom. Then stand the vacuum cleaner back up and lower the handle to its lowest position. Lift off the hood *(above, right)*. After completing repairs, reinstall the hood and bottom plate and cold check for leaking voltage *(page 417)*.

ACCESS TO INTERNAL PARTS (Canister type)

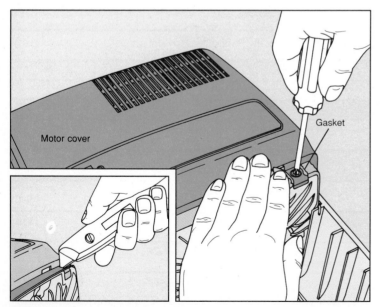

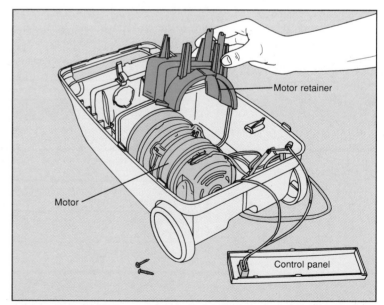

Removing and reinstalling the motor cover, control panel and motor retainer. Unplug the vacuum cleaner and protect the floor with old newspaper. Remove the bag housing lid and the dust bag. Locate the two screws that secure the motor cover to the filter support; rubber gaskets may conceal them. If so, use a utility knife to slit the gaskets *(inset)*, then peel away enough to reach the screw heads with a screwdriver. Remove the screws *(above, left)* and lift off the motor cover. The control panel on some canister models comes off with the motor

cover. On other models, such as the one shown above, it rests on the motor retainer and can be lifted off after the cover is removed. If the motor is shielded by a foam-and-cardboard muffler, remove it. Locate the screws that secure the motor retainer to the chassis, unscrew them and remove the retainer *(above, right)*. When repairs are complete, reinstall each part in order. Check that all wire connections are sound and cold check for leaking voltage *(page 417)*.

REPLACING THE DRIVE BELT (Upright type and power nozzles)

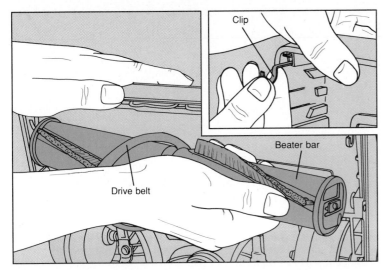

Clip

Beater bar

Drive belt

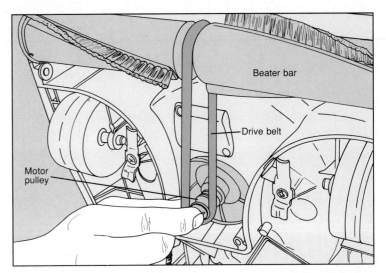

Beater bar

Drive belt

Motor
pulley

1 Removing the drive belt. Unplug the vacuum cleaner and re-move the bottom plate *(page 344)*. Inspect the drive belt; if the belt is broken, check the owner's manual for its correct position. If the belt is damaged, note how it is installed for reference. On an upright vacuum cleaner, unhook the belt from the motor pulley and pull the beater bar free of its clips *(above)*. On a power nozzle, lift off the retain-ing bracket, pull out the beater bar and then unhook the belt from the motor drive shaft. Sometimes the clips that hold the beater bar become loose. Use pliers to pull them out and buy exact replacements at a vac-uum cleaner service center. Fit a new clip back into its slot with your fingers *(inset)*.

2 Replacing the drive belt. Purchase an exact replacement belt at a vacuum cleaner service center. On the upright type, slide the belt onto its groove on the beater bar, snap the bar back into place and twist the belt around the motor pulley *(above)*. Make sure the high side of the belt aligns with the high-side mark. To reinstall a belt on a power nozzle, hook it around the drive shaft and then around its groove on the beater bar. Using both hands for added force, push the beater bar into its molded slots in the nozzle chassis, being careful not to pinch your fingers.

SERVICING THE BEATER BRUSH ASSEMBLY (Upright type and power nozzles)

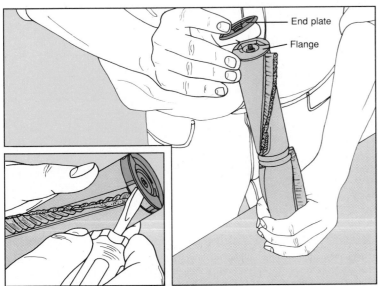

End plate

Flange

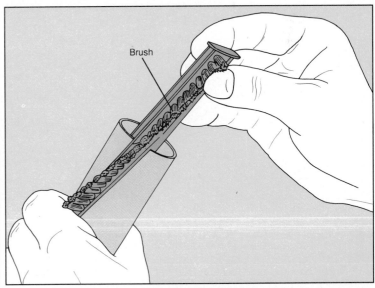

Brush

Disassembling the beater bar. Unplug the vacuum cleaner. Remove the bottom plate *(page 344)* and disengage the drive belt before pulling out the beater bar *(step above)*. Clean tangled hair, string and other debris from the bar and lubricate the beater bearings with graphite. To remove worn brushes, hold one end of the bar in each hand and turn them in opposite directions; one end plate will come off *(above, left)* revealing an inner metal flange and shaft. Pull off the other end plate; in some cases, you may have to tap the threaded end of the shaft with a hammer until the plate drops off the beater bar. Pry off the inner metal flange with a screwdriver *(inset)*. Replace both brushes if either is worn. To remove a brush, grasp one end and pull it out of the slot in the beater bar *(above, right)*. Buy exact replacement brushes from a vac-uum cleaner service center and slide them into their slots. Replace the inner flange, reinsert the threaded shaft and screw on the end plates tightly. Reinstall the drive belt and beater bar *(step above)* and the bottom plate.

SERVICING THE ON/OFF SWITCH (Upright type)

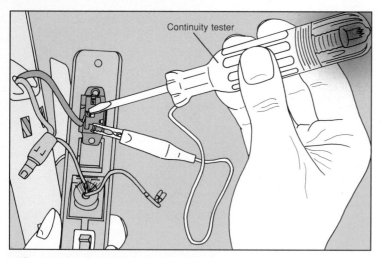

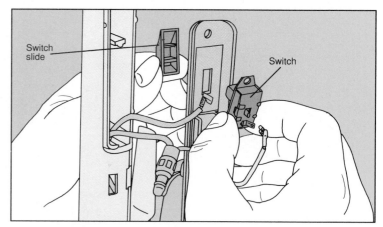

1 Testing the switch. Unplug the vacuum cleaner and remove the switch cover plate from the handle *(page 344)*. To test the single-speed switch, use a continuity tester. Disconnect one wire and attach the alligator clip of the tester to the free terminal. Touch the probe of the tester to the other terminal *(above)* and flip the switch to the ON position. If the tester lights only when ON, the switch is OK. Reconnect the wire, reinstall the cover plate and test the wiring *(page 349)*. If the tester fails to light, replace the switch *(step 2)*.

2 Replacing the switch. Use your fingers to pry off the switch slide. Buy an exact replacement switch from a vacuum cleaner service center or the manufacturer. Flick the new switch to OFF and turn it so that the lever points down. (If the on/off positions aren't marked, use a continuity tester to determine them; the tester will light with the switch in the ON position.) Fit the switch into the cover plate and snap on the switch slide *(above)*. Reconnect the wires to the switch terminals and reinstall the cover plate on the handle, tucking all wires into the plastic housing away from the screw hole and the metal handle. Screw on the cover plate and check for leaking voltage *(page 417)*.

SERVICING THE ON/OFF SWITCH (Canister type)

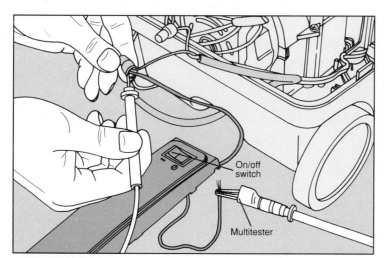

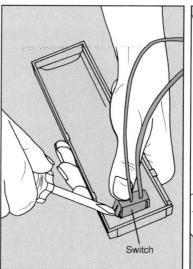

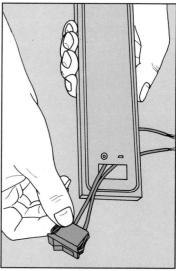

1 Testing the switch. Unplug the vacuum cleaner and remove the switch cover plate from the handle *(page 344)*. To test the single-speed switch, use a continuity tester. Disconnect one wire and attach the alligator clip of the tester to the free terminal. Touch the probe of the tester to the other terminal *(above)* and flip the switch to the ON position. If the tester lights only when ON, the switch is OK. Reconnect the wire, reinstall the cover plate and test the wiring *(page 349)*. If the tester fails to light, replace the switch *(step 2)*.

2 Replacing the switch. Use your fingers to pry off the switch slide. Buy an exact replacement switch from a vacuum cleaner service center or the manufacturer. Flick the new switch to OFF and turn it so that the lever points down. (If the on/off positions aren't marked, use a continuity tester to determine them; the tester will light with the switch in the ON position.) Fit the switch into the cover plate and snap on the switch slide *(above)*. Reconnect the wires to the switch terminals and reinstall the cover plate on the handle, tucking all wires into the plastic housing away from the screw hole and the metal handle. Screw on the cover plate and check for leaking voltage *(page 417)*.

SERVICING THE DIRT FAN (Upright type)

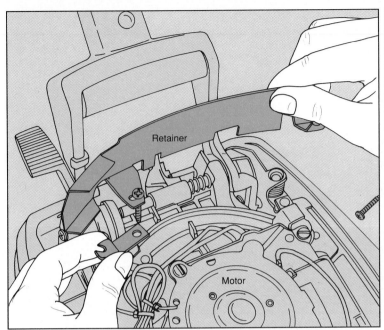

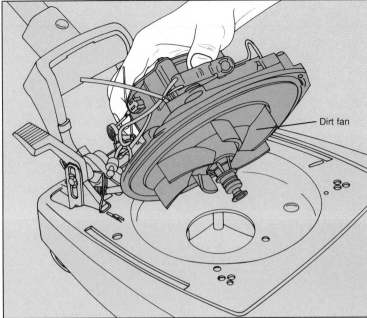

1 **Removing the fan and motor assembly.** Unplug the vacuum cleaner. Take off the bottom plate, unhook the drive belt from the motor pulley and remove the hood *(page 344)*. Use a screwdriver to unfasten the retainer and clip *(above, left)*. Locate the remaining motor mounting screws and unscrew them. Grasp the top of the motor housing and lift the fan-and-motor assembly out of the base *(above, right)*.

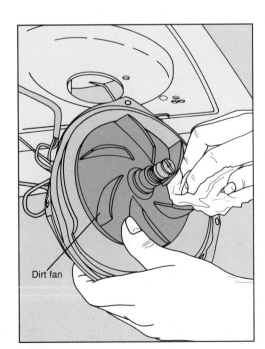

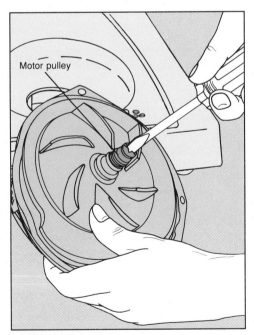

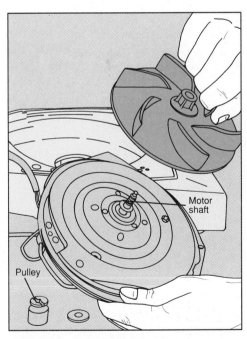

2 **Cleaning the dirt fan.** Use a soft, slightly damp cloth to wipe the fan blades *(above)* and the cavity in the vacuum cleaner base where the fan sits. Inspect a metal fan for bent blades, or a plastic fan for chipped or worn blades. Remove the fan if it is damaged *(step 3)* or to check for foreign objects caught beneath it.

3 **Removing the dirt fan.** Hold the dirt fan steady and unscrew the motor pulley *(above)*. Turn it counterclockwise; if it won't loosen, try turning it clockwise. Remove the motor pulley and its washer and set them aside. Pull the fan off the motor shaft. Note that another washer and a metal spacer are on the shaft itself; leave them in place.

4 **Replacing the dirt fan.** Purchase an exact replacement fan from a vacuum cleaner service center or the manufacturer. Slip the new fan onto the motor shaft *(above)*. Then reinstall the washer and motor pulley and screw on the pulley. Reinstall the fan-and-motor assembly, then the retainer. Put back the hood, reconnect the drive belt and reinstall the bottom plate. Check for leaking voltage *(page 417)*.

SERVICING THE FAN (Canister type)

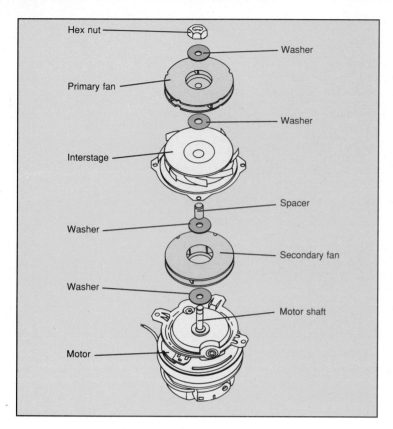

Hex nut
Washer
Primary fan
Washer
Interstage
Spacer
Washer
Secondary fan
Washer
Motor shaft
Motor

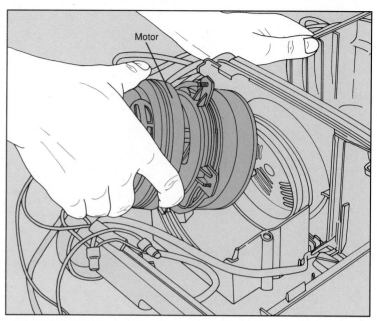

Motor

1 **Removing the canister motor.** Unplug the vacuum cleaner. Remove the bag housing lid and the dust bag. Next, remove the motor cover, the control panel, the muffler (if it has one) and the motor retainer *(page 344)*. Lift the motor out of the motor chamber *(above)* and lay it carefully on the table or workbench.

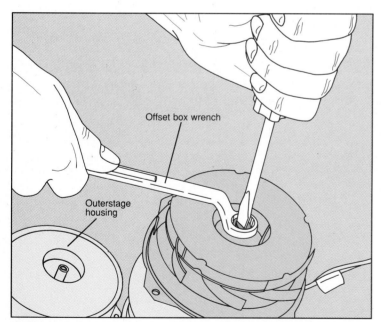

Offset box wrench

Outerstage housing

2 **Getting to the fans.** Remove the screws that hold the outerstage housing to the motor. Pull off the outerstage housing. Loosen the hex nut on the motor shaft by slipping an offset box wrench over the nut and fitting a large screwdriver into the slot of the motor shaft. (Some motors require a hex wrench rather than a screwdriver.) Hold the shaft stationary with the screwdriver and turn the wrench clockwise to loosen the nut *(above)*. If the nut won't budge, trying turning it counterclockwise. If it still sticks, squirt a few drops of penetrating oil on the shaft and let it soak for half an hour, then loosen the nut. Remove the nut and the washer.

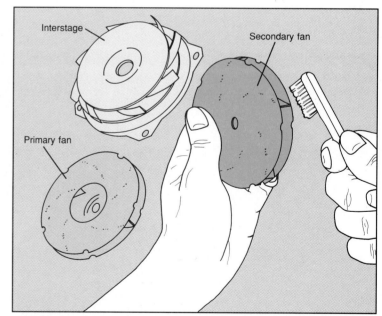

Interstage
Secondary fan
Primary fan

3 **Inspecting, cleaning and replacing the fans.** Take off the primary fan, the interstage and the secondary fan nested within the interstage. Keep track of where the spacers and washers fit between the fans. Use an old toothbrush *(above)* or a slightly damp cloth to clean the fans. Inspect them for dents or wear; the primary fan is more prone to damage since it is first in line. If a fan is damaged, take it to a vacuum cleaner service center and buy an exact replacement. Reassemble the fans using the anatomy picture *(top left)* as a guide. Reinstall the fan-and-motor assembly in the canister cavity, then reinstall the motor retainer, the muffler, the control panel and the motor cover.

SERVICING THE INTERNAL WIRING

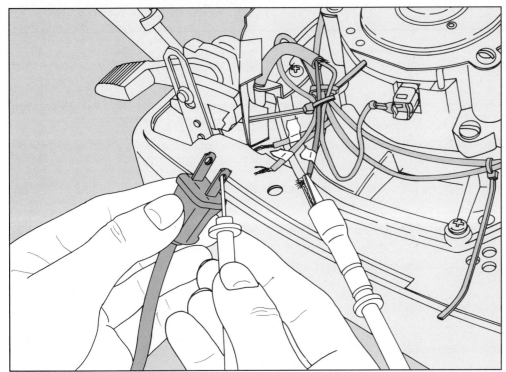

Testing the vacuum cleaner wiring. Unplug the vacuum cleaner. Access the vacuum cleaner motor by removing the bottom plate and the hood on an upright model, or the motor cover and control panel on a canister model *(page 344)*. Locate the power cord wires and disconnect one of them where it meets other wires in a crimp wire cap: Label the wires and cut off the cap with wire cutters. Flip the on/off switch to the ON position. Use a continuity tester, or set a multitester to test continuity. Attach the alligator clip of one probe to the disconnected power cord wire and touch the other probe to each plug prong, in turn *(left)*. The tester should register continuity once—and only once. If the wiring tests OK, repeat the test with the other power cord wire and each plug prong. If the wiring fails the tests, suspect a loose or broken wire connection and repair it if it is accessible *(page 417)*. If you cannot locate the problem in an upright vacuum cleaner, the damaged wiring may be in the handle; take the vacuum cleaner for professional service. If the wiring tests OK, recrimp the wires and check the motor brushes *(below)*.

SERVICING THE MOTOR

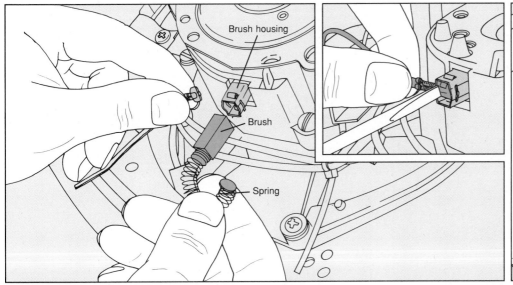

Brush housing

Brush

Spring

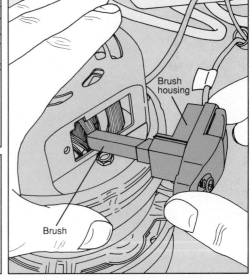

Brush housing

Brush

1 **Servicing the motor brushes.** Unplug the vacuum cleaner. Access the motor in your model *(page 344)*. If you suspect a binding or worn bearing on an upright model, go to step 3 to inspect the upper motor bearing. To remove a motor brush, disconnect its wire by depressing the terminal tab with a screwdriver *(inset)*. The brush will usually pop out in your hand *(above, left)*. Take out the second brush the same way. If the spring breaks off with the brush still in the housing, remove the upper motor bearing and cooling fan *(step 3)* and the upper motor housing *(step 6)*, then push out the brush from inside the housing with a small screwdriver. Some canister vacuum-cleaner motors have a brush housing that must be removed to check or change the brushes.

Unscrew the housing from the motor and pull it out *(above, right)*. Examine the brushes for pitting or wear; replace both if either is damaged. Purchase exact replacements from a vacuum cleaner service center. Fit each new brush into its housing and lock it in place with the wire terminal or by resecuring the brush housing to the motor housing. Reassemble the vacuum cleaner, reversing the steps you took to disassemble it. If the brushes are OK and the motor is a sealed unit (generally the case in canister vacuum-cleaner motors) take the vacuum cleaner for professional service. If the brushes are OK and the motor is a serviceable one, such as those found in upright vacuum cleaners, reinstall the brushes and go to step 2 to test the motor field coil.

SERVICING THE MOTOR (continued)

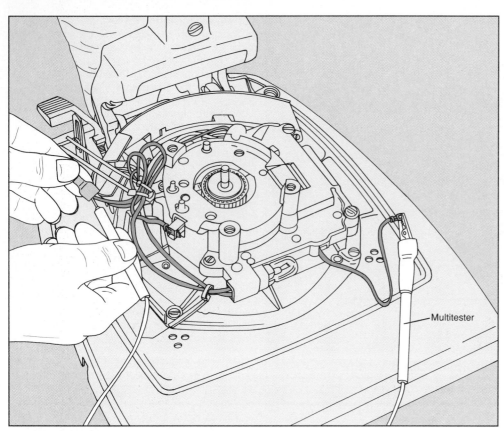

2 **Testing the motor field coil.** Have a multi-speed motor serviced professionally. To test the field coil of the more common single-speed vacuum cleaner motor, disconnect one of the motor's wire leads. If the wire is clipped to a motor brush, release it *(step 1)*. If the wire is connected to other wires in a crimp wire cap, label the wires and cut off the cap with wire cutters. Set a multitester to RX100 and attach the alligator clip of one probe to the end of the disconnected lead. Touch the other probe to the end of the second motor wire. If it is still connected to other wires in a crimp wire cap, try slipping the narrow tip of the probe into the cap, making sure it is in contact with the lead's copper filaments *(left)*. If there isn't enough space in the cap for the probe, label the wires, cut off the cap and touch the probe to the motor wire. The multitester should register partial resistance. If the field coil has continuity or infinite resistance, it is faulty; take the vacuum cleaner for professional service. If it tests OK, remove the upper motor bearing and fan *(step 3)* and test the commutator *(step 4)*.

Multitester

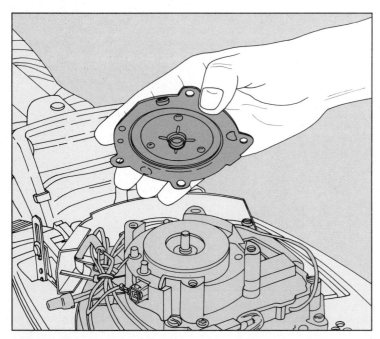

3 **Replacing the motor bearing.** The upper motor bearing consists of a sleeve inserted in a metal shield; to remove it from the upper motor casing, unscrew its mounting screws and lift it off *(above)*. Examine the bearing; if worn, install an exact replacement purchased at a vacuum cleaner service center. To reach the commutator for testing, remove the cooling fan: Hold the motor pulley underneath with one hand, while you turn the fan with the other. If it doesn't come off when turned counterclockwise, try turning it clockwise.

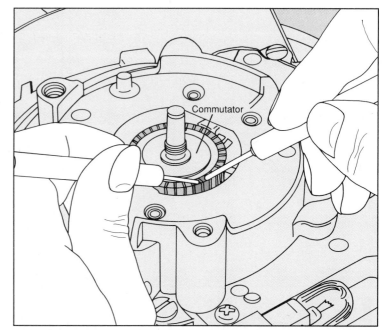

Commutator

4 **Performing a bar-to-bar commutator test.** To test whether there is a break in the armature wiring, set a multitester to RX1. Place the probes on adjacent commutator bars *(above)*; the multitester should indicate low resistance. Repeat this test between all adjacent bars on the commutator, and look for similar low resistance each time. If the commutator fails this test, remove the rotor *(step 6)* for service. If the commutator tests OK, go to step 5 to test for a ground fault in the motor.

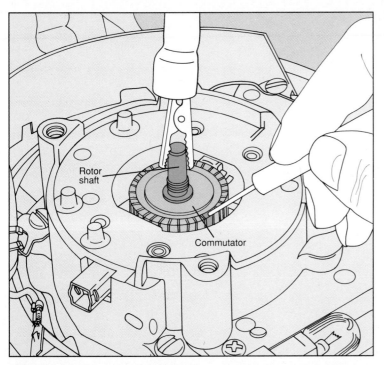 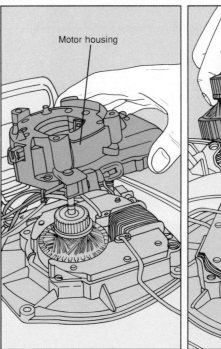 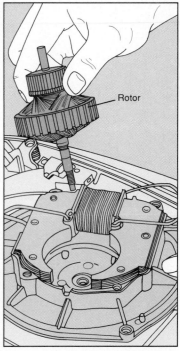

5 Testing for a ground fault. Set a multitester to test continuity. Attach a multitester probe with an alligator clip to the rotor shaft, and touch the second probe to each commutator bar, in turn *(above, right)*. The multitester should show no continuity. If the armature wiring fails this test, replace the rotor *(step 6)*. If it tests OK, remove the rotor and clean the commutator.

6 Removing the rotor. Remove the brushes *(step 2)*. Unscrew the upper motor housing from the lower housing, lift it off *(above, left)* and put it aside. Remove the dirt fan from underneath *(page 347)*. Take hold of the motor shaft, pull out the rotor *(above, right)*, and inspect it for service or replacement *(step 7)*.

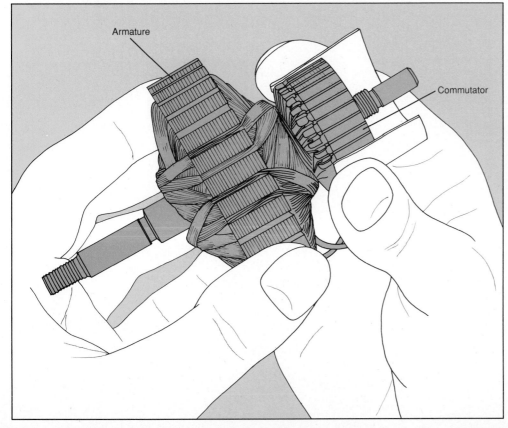

7 Cleaning the commutator. Check the commutator for pitting or carbon build-up. To remove roughness, smooth the surface with a piece of fine emery cloth. Use an old toothbrush to clean out grit and dirt between the bars. If the armature wiring is broken or shorted, or if the commutator bars are damaged, replace the rotor. Buy an exact replacement at a vacuum cleaner service center or from the manufacturer. Position it carefully inside the lower motor casing, resecure the dirt fan, and reinstall the fan-and-motor assembly *(page 347)*. Reinstall the upper motor housing and the motor brushes and put back the hood, drive belt and bottom cover. Cold check for leaking voltage *(page 417)* before plugging in the vacuum cleaner.

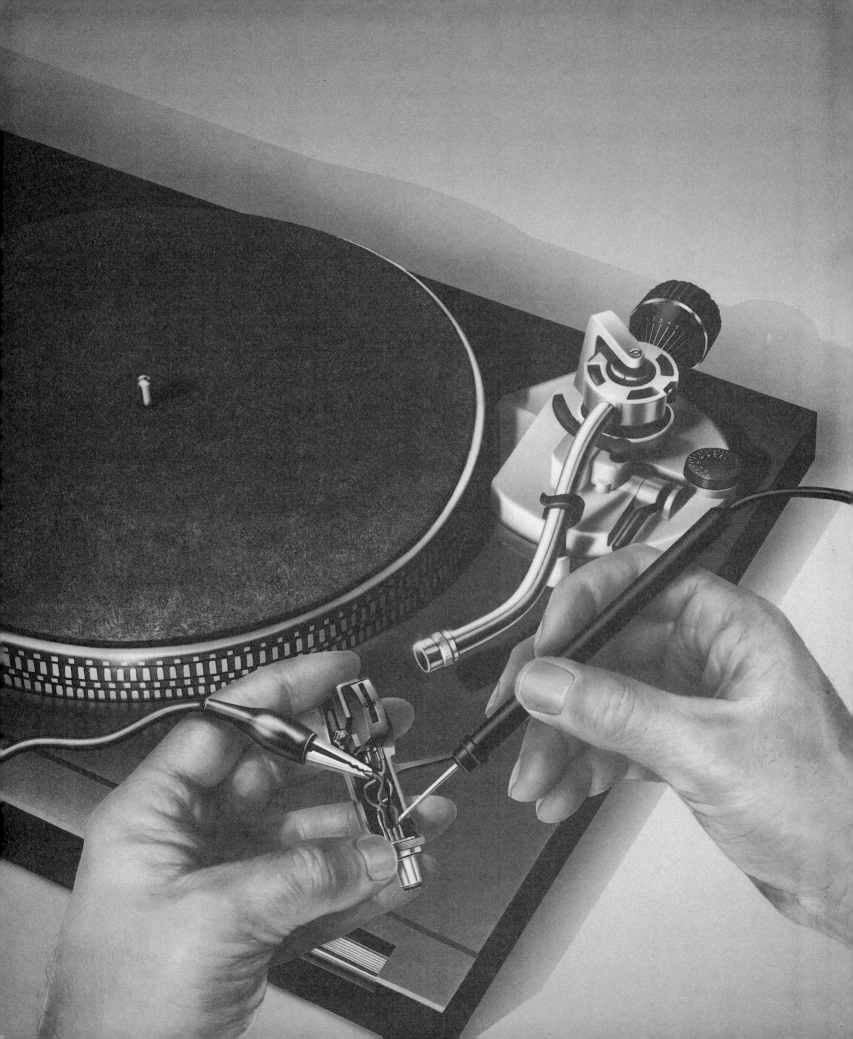

HOME ELECTRONICS

ENTERTAINMENT SYSTEMS

It may boast a top-of-the-line compact disc player and video-cassette recorder, or just a modest receiver, turntable and speakers, but a typical entertainment system *(below)* is an investment in leisure that can cost thousands of dollars. While each additional unit adds new entertainment options, it also complicates system hookups and problems diagnosis.

Thanks to solid-state circuitry, electronic problems are rare and can be logically deduced from their symptoms. Consult the Troubleshooting Guide in this chapter *(page 356)* first before referring to the chapter covering a specific audio or video entertainment unit.

To answer questions about the set-up or cable hookups for your entertainment system, check the owner's manual that came with each unit or consult the manufacturer. As a general rule, most units perform best if the cables between them are kept as short as possible, reducing electrical resistance and interference that weaken the audio or video signal; if the cable is coaxial, this is less of a worry. An exception is the turntable, which is highly sensitive to vibration and signal interference; position it at least 3 feet away from the speakers.

Many entertainment system problems can be resolved by adjusting cable hookups. Always turn off the units and unplug

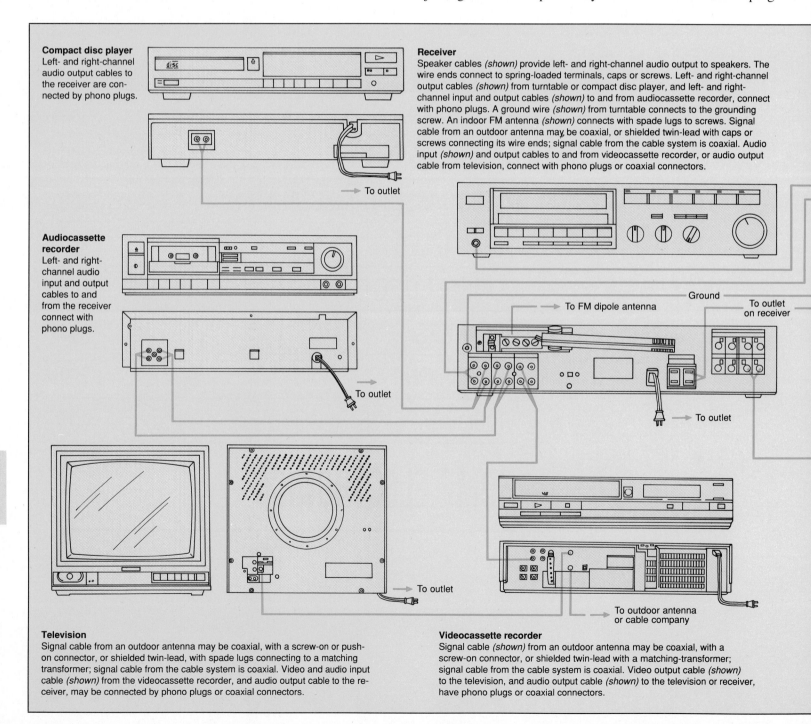

Compact disc player
Left- and right-channel audio output cables to the receiver are connected by phono plugs.

Audiocassette recorder
Left- and right-channel audio input and output cables to and from the receiver connect with phono plugs.

Receiver
Speaker cables *(shown)* provide left- and right-channel audio output to speakers. The wire ends connect to spring-loaded terminals, caps or screws. Left- and right-channel output cables *(shown)* from turntable or compact disc player, and left- and right-channel input and output cables *(shown)* to and from audiocassette recorder, connect with phono plugs. A ground wire *(shown)* from turntable connects to the grounding screw. An indoor FM antenna *(shown)* connects with spade lugs to screws. Signal cable from an outdoor antenna may be coaxial, or shielded twin-lead with caps or screws connecting its wire ends; signal cable from the cable system is coaxial. Audio input *(shown)* and output cables to and from videocassette recorder, or audio output cable from television, connect with phono plugs or coaxial connectors.

To outlet

To FM dipole antenna

Ground

To outlet on receiver

To outlet

To outlet

To outlet

To outdoor antenna or cable company

Television
Signal cable from an outdoor antenna may be coaxial, with a screw-on or push-on connector, or shielded twin-lead, with spade lugs connecting to a matching transformer; signal cable from the cable system is coaxial. Video and audio input cable *(shown)* from the videocassette recorder, and audio output cable to the receiver, may be connected by phono plugs or coaxial connectors.

Videocassette recorder
Signal cable *(shown)* from an outdoor antenna may be coaxial, with a screw-on connector, or shielded twin-lead with a matching-transformer; signal cable from the cable system is coaxial. Video output cable *(shown)* to the television, and audio output cable *(shown)* to the television or receiver, have phono plugs or coaxial connectors.

them before working with their cables. If you must disconnect a cable, tag it first, noting at each end the specific terminal to which it connects; if there is more than one wire or connector, tag each one. Cable connections at a splitter box, which routes a signal to more than one unit, should be labeled as carefully as those at the entertainment system units.

To tame the profusion of power cords in an entertainment system, install a grounded multiple-outlet plug in the wall outlet. Some are available with a voltage spike protector, which can shield sensitive electronic equipment from power surges. First check your fuse box or circuit breaker panel to make sure the circuit can handle the load, especially if other household appliances will be running at the same time. Do not use extension cords; reposition the units instead, if necessary. During an electrical storm, unplug the equipment.

Once you eliminate cable hookups as the source of a problem, service the unit itself. First locate labels on the electronic unit *(below)*, and read the valuable information they contain. Refer carefully to the Emergency Guide *(page 11)* and Tools and Techniques *(page 417)*. Then consult the unit's chapter; pay special attention to the introduction and familiarize yourself with the exploded diagram before beginning work.

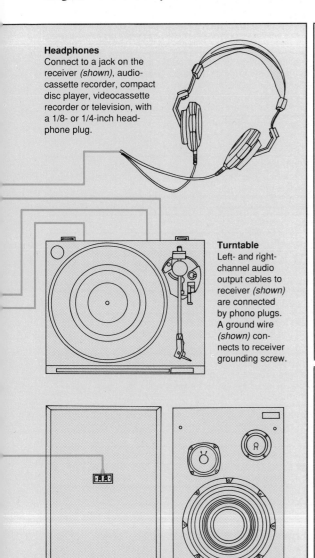

Headphones
Connect to a jack on the receiver *(shown)*, audio-cassette recorder, compact disc player, videocassette recorder or television, with a 1/8- or 1/4-inch head-phone plug.

Turntable
Left- and right-channel audio output cables to receiver *(shown)* are connected by phono plugs. A ground wire *(shown)* connects to receiver grounding screw.

Speaker
Positive and negative left-channel or right-channel audio output from the receiver is sent through speaker cable *(shown)*. The wire ends or spade lugs connect to spring-loaded terminals, caps or screws. Ensure that the wire connected to the positive terminal, indicated by the color red or a plus sign (+), is the same wire connected to the positive terminal at the receiver.

SAFETY SYMBOLS ON ELECTRONIC UNITS

Operation warning.
A triangle with an exclamation mark warns the user to consult the owner's manual *before* operating the unit.

Voltage warning.
A triangle with a lightning bolt warns of a potential electrical shock hazard. Usually, this symbol can be found on the back or bottom of the unit. If the symbol is posted on an internal component, do not touch the component; electrical current may be stored in it even though the unit is turned off and unplugged.

Laser warning.
A triangle or square with a sunburst symbol warns of possible danger from a laser. This symbol may be found on the back or bottom of a compact disc player. Never look directly at an operating laser; its intense light can cause permanent eye damage.

SERIAL NUMBER PLATE

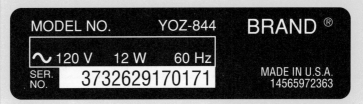

Reading make and model specifications. Locate the serial number plate—on some units this may be a sticker—on the back or bottom of your electronic unit. This label indicates the make *(above:* Brand), model *(above:* ZAB500) and serial number *(above:* 2580516630264) of your unit. Record this information immediately so that it is close at hand when ordering replacement parts, or to determine if repairs are covered under the manufacturer's warranty. For help ordering parts or talking to service technicians, consult the Emergency Guide *(page 31)*.

You will also find electrical specifications on this label. Voltage (V) rating—always 120 volts for home electronics—indicates the circuit power required. Wattage (W) rating, or volt-ampere (VA) rating, indicates the amount of electricity the unit will consume. Adding a unit to a full circuit will cause it to overload. To determine existing and maximum loads of the circuit refer to Tools & Techniques *(page 417)*.

TROUBLESHOOTING GUIDE

SYMPTOM	POSSIBLE CAUSE	PROCEDURE
AUDIO ENTERTAINMENT SYSTEMS		
No display lights, no sound	Receiver and/or other unit unplugged or turned off	Plug in and turn on receiver and/or audiocassette recorder, turntable or compact disc player
	Remote control dirty or faulty	Service remote control (p. 417) □○; replace batteries
	No power to outlet or outlet faulty	Reset breaker or replace fuse (p. 102) □○; service outlet (p. 148)
	Receiver, audiocassette recorder, turntable or compact disc player faulty	Service receiver (p. 360) or audiocassette recorder (p. 368) or turntable (p. 380) or compact disc player (p. 388)
Display lights, but no sound	Receiver and/or audiocassette recorder, turntable or compact disc player controls set incorrectly	Adjust receiver and/or audiocassette recorder, turntable or compact disc player controls; in particular, check receiver volume and tape-monitor controls
	Receiver, audiocassette recorder, turntable or compact disc player faulty	Adjust receiver selector control to other modes. If there is sound, service audiocassette recorder (p. 368), turntable (p. 380) or compact disc player (p. 388); if no sound, service receiver (p. 360)
Sound from only one speaker channel	Receiver controls set incorrectly	Adjust receiver controls; in particular, check balance control
	Cable hookup faulty between speaker and receiver or between receiver and audio-cassette recorder, turntable or compact disc player	Adjust receiver selector control to other modes. If there is sound from both speaker channels, check cable hookups between receiver and audiocassette recorder, turntable or compact disc player (p. 358) □○; if there is still sound from only one speaker channel, check cable hookups between speakers and receiver (p. 358) □○
	Audiocassette recorder, turntable or compact disc player faulty	Adjust receiver selector control to other modes. If there is sound from both speaker channels, service audiocassette recorder (p. 368), turntable (p. 380) or compact disc player (p. 388)
	Speaker or receiver faulty	Reverse receiver left- and right-channel cable connections. If no sound from same speaker, service speaker (p. 394); if no sound from other speaker, service receiver (p. 360)
Sound intermittent or distorted from the radio	Receiver tuner control set incorrectly	Adjust receiver tuner control
	Antenna positioned incorrectly	Adjust antenna
	Cable hookup faulty between speaker and receiver or between receiver and antenna or cable system	Adjust receiver selector control to other modes. If sound is OK, check cable hookups between receiver and antenna or cable system (p. 358) □○; if sound not OK, check cable hookups between speakers and receiver (p. 358) □○
	Antenna or cable system faulty	Adjust receiver selector control to other modes. If sound is OK, have antenna or cable system serviced
	Speaker or receiver faulty	Reverse receiver left- and right-channel cable connections. If sound not OK from same speaker, service speaker (p. 394); if sound not OK from other speaker, service receiver (p. 360)
Sound intermittent or distorted from the audiocassette recorder, turntable or compact disc player	Cable hookup faulty between speaker and receiver or between receiver and audio-cassette recorder, turntable, or compact disc player	Adjust receiver selector control to other modes. If sound is OK, check cable hookups between receiver and audiocassette recorder, turntable or compact disc player (p. 358) □○; if sound not OK, check cable hookups between speakers and receiver (p. 358) □○
	Audiocassette recorder, turntable or compact disc player faulty	Adjust receiver selector control to other modes. If sound is OK, service audiocassette recorder (p. 368), turntable (p. 380) or compact disc player (p. 388)
	Speaker or receiver faulty	Reverse receiver left- and right-channel cable connections. If sound not OK from same speaker, service speaker (p. 394); if sound not OK from other speaker, service receiver (p. 360)
Humming, buzzing or rumbling noise	Speaker vibrating or too close to turntable	Reposition speakers
	Cable hookup faulty between speaker and receiver, or between receiver and antenna or cable system, or between receiver and audiocassette recorder, turntable or compact disc player	Adjust receiver selector control to other modes. If sound is OK, check cable hookups between receiver and antenna or cable system (p. 358) □○ or between receiver and audiocassette recorder, turntable or compact disc player (p. 358) □○; if sound not OK, check cable hookups between speakers and receiver (p. 358) □○
	Ground wire hookup faulty	Check ground wire hookups (p. 359) □○
	Antenna or cable system (radio), or audio-cassette recorder, turntable or compact disc player faulty	Adjust receiver selector control to other modes. If sound is OK, service audiocassette recorder (p. 368), turntable (p. 380) or compact disc player (p. 388) or have antenna or cable system serviced
	Speaker or receiver faulty	Reverse receiver left- and right-channel cable connections. If sound not OK from same speaker, service speaker (p. 394); if sound not OK from other speaker, service receiver (p. 360)

DEGREE OF DIFFICULTY: □ Easy ▪ Moderate ■ Complex
ESTIMATED TIME: ○ Less than 1 hour ◖ 1 to 3 hours ● Over 3 hours

SYMPTOM	POSSIBLE CAUSE	PROCEDURE
VIDEO ENTERTAINMENT SYSTEMS		
No display lights, no picture and no sound	Television or videocassette recorder unplugged or turned off	Plug in and turn on television and videocassette recorder
	Cable converter unplugged	Plug in converter
	No power to outlet or outlet faulty	Reset breaker or replace fuse *(p. 102)* □○; service outlet *(p. 148)*
	Television or videocassette recorder faulty	Service television *(p. 399)* or videocassette recorder *(p. 407)*
Display lights, but no picture and no sound	Television or videocassette recorder controls set incorrectly	Adjust television and videocassette recorder controls; in particular, check channel selector controls
	Television or videocassette recorder faulty	Turn off videocassette recorder and tune in television. If still no picture and no sound, service television *(p. 399)*; if there are picture and sound, service videocassette recorder *(p. 407)*
Picture, but no sound	Television or receiver controls set incorrectly	Adjust television and receiver controls; in particular, check television and receiver volume controls and receiver tape-monitor control
	Audio cable hookup faulty between television and videocassette recorder, or between one of these units and receiver	Check audio cable hookups between television and videocassette recorder, and between receiver and television or videocassette recorder *(p. 358)* □○
	Receiver faulty	Adjust receiver selector control to other modes. If no sound, service receiver *(p. 360)*
	Television or videocassette recorder faulty	Turn off videocassette recorder and tune in television. If still no sound, service television *(p. 399)*; if there is sound, service videocassette recorder *(p. 407)*
Sound, but no picture	Television or videocassette recorder controls set incorrectly	Adjust television and videocassette recorder controls; in particular, check television brightness and contrast controls
	Video cable hookup faulty between television and videocassette recorder	Check video cable hookups between television and videocassette recorder *(p. 358)* □○
	Television or videocassette recorder faulty	Turn off videocassette recorder and tune in television. If still no picture, service television *(p. 399)*; if there is picture, service videocassette recorder *(p. 407)*
Sound from only one speaker channel	Television or receiver controls set incorrectly	Adjust television and receiver controls; in particular, balance controls
	Audio cable hookup faulty between television and videocassette recorder, or between receiver and television or videocassette recorder, or cable hookup faulty between receiver and speaker	Adjust receiver selector control to other modes. If there is sound from both speaker channels, check audio cable hookups between television and videocassette recorder and between receiver and television or videocassette recorder *(p. 358)* □○; if there is still sound from only one speaker channel, check cable hookups between receiver and speakers *(p. 358)* □○
	Television or videocassette recorder faulty	Turn off videocassette recorder and tune in television. If there is sound from both speaker channels, service videocassette recorder *(p. 407)*; if still sound from one speaker channel, service television *(p. 399)*
	Speaker or receiver faulty	See audio entertainment systems *(p. 356)*
Picture and sound intermittent or distorted	Antenna positioned incorrectly	Adjust antenna
	Cable hookup faulty between antenna or cable system and television or videocassette recorder	Check cable hookups between antenna or cable system and television or videocassette recorder *(p. 358)* □○
	Antenna or cable system, television or videocassette recorder faulty	Service videocassette recorder *(p. 407)*, television *(p. 399)* or have antenna or cable system serviced
Picture intermittent or distorted	Video cable hookup faulty between television and videocassette recorder	Check video cable hookups between television and videocassette recorder *(p. 358)* □○
	Television or videocassette recorder faulty	Turn off videocassette recorder and tune in television. If still no picture, service television *(p. 399)*; if there is picture, service videocassette recorder *(p. 407)*
Sound intermittent or distorted	Audio cable hookup faulty between television and videocassette recorder, or between receiver and television or videocassette recorder, or cable hookup faulty between receiver and speaker	Adjust receiver selector control to other modes. If sound is OK, check audio cable hookups between television and videocassette recorder, and between receiver and television or videocassette recorder *(p. 358)* □○; if sound not OK, check cable hookups between receiver and speakers *(p. 358)* □○
	Television or videocassette recorder faulty	Turn off videocassette recorder and tune in television. If still no sound, service television *(p. 399)*; if there is sound, service videocassette recorder *(p. 407)*
	Speaker or receiver faulty	See audio entertainment systems *(p. 356)*

DEGREE OF DIFFICULTY: □ **Easy** ◼ **Moderate** ■ **Complex**
ESTIMATED TIME: ○ **Less than 1 hour** ◖ **1 to 3 hours** ● **Over 3 hours**

SERVICING CABLE HOOKUPS

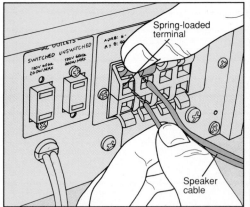

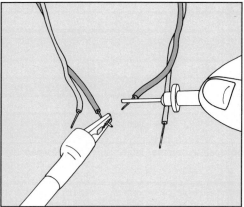

Checking speaker cable connections. Press the tabs *(far left)* or loosen the caps or screws and remove the cable wire ends or wire connections from the speaker and receiver terminals. If a wire end or connector is damaged, repair it *(page 417)*. Set a multitester to test continuity. Clip one probe to a wire and touch the other probe in turn to each wire at the other end *(near left)*; there should be continuity only once. Test the other wire the same way. If the cable tests faulty, replace it *(page 417)*. If the cable tests OK, reconnect it. Press the tabs and insert the wires; at cap or screw terminals, wrap the wires clockwise and tighten them.

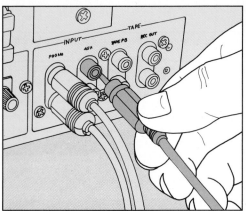

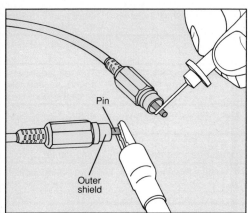

Checking phono cable connections. Pull the plugs out of the jacks on both units *(far left)*. If the center pin or outer shield is damaged, replace the plug *(page 417)*. Clean the plugs and jacks *(page 359)*. Set a multitester to test continuity. To test each plug, clip one probe to its center pin and touch the other probe to its outer shield; there should be no continuity. If either plug tests faulty, replace it. To test the cable, clip or touch a probe to each center pin *(near left)*, then to each shield; there should be continuity both times. If the cable tests faulty, replace it. Push back each plug firmly into its jack.

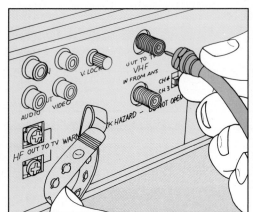

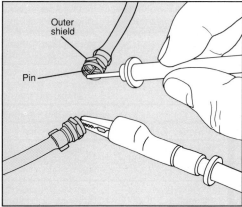

Checking coaxial cable connections. Unscrew or pull off the connectors at both ends *(far left)*. If the center pin or the outer shield is damaged, replace it *(page 417)*. Clean the connectors and terminals *(page 359)*. Set a multitester to test continuity. To test each connector, clip a probe to the center pin and touch the other probe to the outer shield; there should be no continuity. If a connector tests faulty, replace it *(page 417)*. To test the cable, clip or touch a probe to each center pin *(near left)*, then to each shield; there should be continuity both times. Replace a faulty cable. Screw or push each connector onto its terminal.

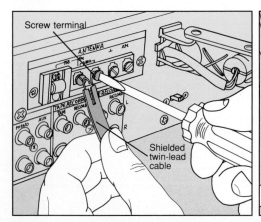

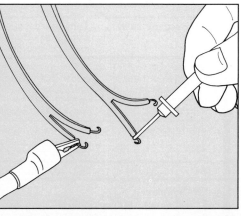

Checking shielded twin-lead cable connections. Loosen the caps or screws *(far left)* and remove the cable wire ends or wire connectors from the terminals on both units. If a wire end or connector is damaged, repair it *(page 417)*. Set a multitester to test continuity. Clip one probe to a wire at one end of the cable and touch the other probe in turn to each wire at the other end *(near left)*; there should be continuity once—and only once. Test again at the other wire. If the cable tests faulty, replace it. If the cable tests OK, reconnect it. Wrap the wires clockwise around the terminals and tighten the caps or screws.

CLEANING CONNECTIONS

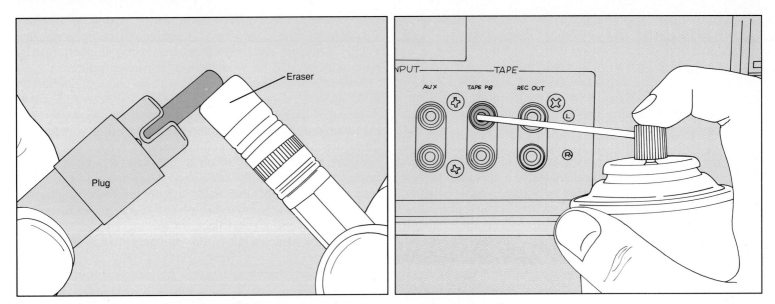

Cleaning cable connectors and unit terminals. To clean a plug connector, use the eraser end of a pencil. Rub thoroughly around the outer shield and along the center pin *(above, left)*; apply only moderate pressure to avoid bending the pin. Clear away particles by spraying electronic contact cleaner or compressed air into the connector, or use a foam swab moistened with denatured alcohol. Use the pencil eraser as well to clean any accessible contact points on the terminal. To clean inside the terminal, spray short bursts of electronic contact cleaner or compressed air through the opening *(above, right)*.

SERVICING GROUND WIRE CONNECTIONS

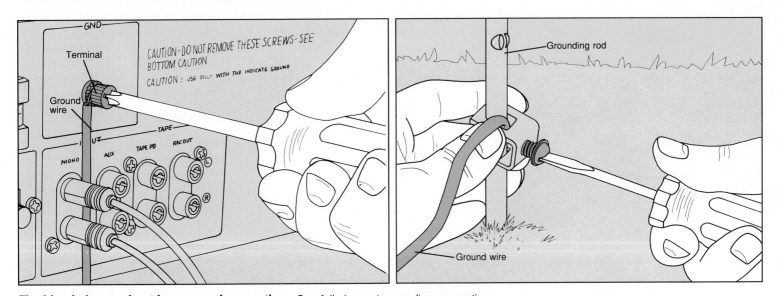

Checking indoor and outdoor ground connections. Carefully inspect grounding connections, both to troubleshoot problems and as a preventive measure. A loose or damaged ground wire can be an annoying source of humming noise. It can also be a hazard in the event a circuit is shorted or a cable is struck by lightning. Tighten a loose turntable ground wire at its terminal on the receiver *(above, left)*. Tighten the outdoor ground wire from the antenna system discharger or grounding block at the discharger or the grounding block, as well as at the grounding rod *(above, right)*: this may be a metal water pipe. Repair any damaged wire end or connector *(page 417)*. To test a ground wire, set a multitester to test continuity. Disconnect one end of the wire and touch a probe to each end of the wire. If the ground wire does not have continuity, replace it. Be sure to run an outdoor ground wire in the shortest and straightest possible path.

RECEIVERS

The cortex of most sophisticated audio systems is a receiver *(below)*, an integrated unit consisting of an analog or digital tuner, a preamplifier and a power amplifier. From the tuner, or from an auxiliary unit such as the turntable through cables hooked up to the receiver, the preamplifier accepts the incoming signal, amplifies it and routes it to the power amplifier. There, the signal is further strengthened and sent out through cables, usually to the speakers. Despite a jungle of cords and cables, receiver problems can be logically deduced from their symptoms. Consult the Troubleshooting Guide in Entertainment Systems *(page 356)* first, and then the one in this chapter.

Often, problems can be remedied by adjusting cable hookups or by cleaning switches and potentiometers—which play a key role in routing, reducing or stopping electrical current through circuits. Sometimes a wire may be loose or broken, or a compo-

nent may test defective. Make sure the air vent is not blocked. Cleaning materials, and most replacement components, are readily available from an electronics parts supplier. Special parts may have to be ordered from the manufacturer.

A set of small screwdrivers, a multitester and a soldering iron make up the basic tool kit for receiver repairs. Refer to Tools & Techniques *(page 417)* for tips on disassembly and reassembly, instructions for testing continuity, resistance and voltage, and directions for desoldering and soldering

Before attempting any repair to the receiver, turn it off and unplug it. Disconnect the cables and wires hooked up to it and set it on a clean work table. Store fasteners and other small parts in labeled containers and write down the sequence of disassembly steps. Perform a cold check for leaking voltage after reassembling the receiver but before plugging it back in.

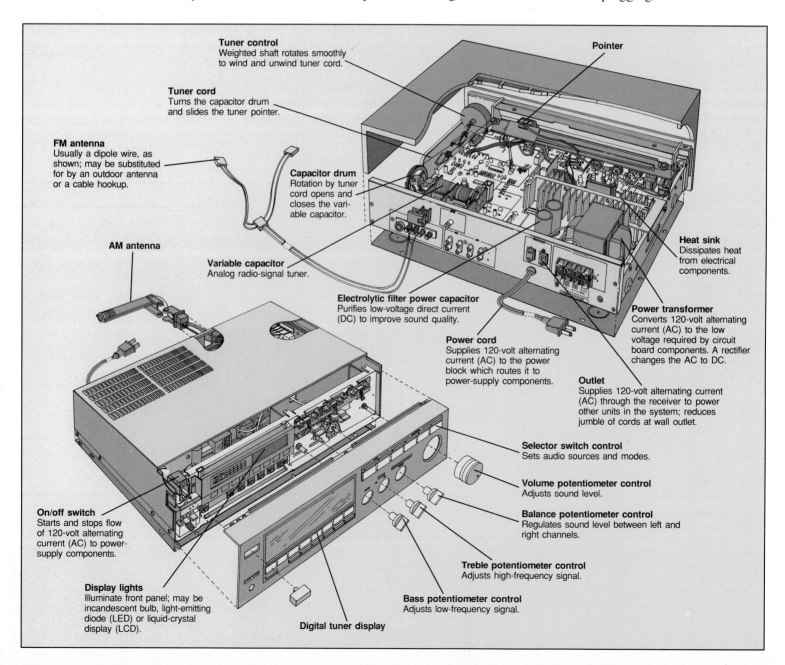

Tuner control
Weighted shaft rotates smoothly to wind and unwind tuner cord.

Pointer

Tuner cord
Turns the capacitor drum and slides the tuner pointer.

FM antenna
Usually a dipole wire, as shown; may be substituted for by an outdoor antenna or a cable hookup.

Capacitor drum
Rotation by tuner cord opens and closes the variable capacitor.

AM antenna

Variable capacitor
Analog radio-signal tuner.

Heat sink
Dissipates heat from electrical components.

Electrolytic filter power capacitor
Purifies low-voltage direct current (DC) to improve sound quality.

Power transformer
Converts 120-volt alternating current (AC) to the low voltage required by circuit board components. A rectifier changes the AC to DC.

Power cord
Supplies 120-volt alternating current (AC) to the power block which routes it to power-supply components.

Outlet
Supplies 120-volt alternating current (AC) through the receiver to power other units in the system; reduces jumble of cords at wall outlet.

Selector switch control
Sets audio sources and modes.

Volume potentiometer control
Adjusts sound level.

On/off switch
Starts and stops flow of 120-volt alternating current (AC) to power-supply components.

Balance potentiometer control
Regulates sound level between left and right channels.

Treble potentiometer control
Adjusts high-frequency signal.

Display lights
Illuminate front panel; may be incandescent bulb, light-emitting diode (LED) or liquid-crystal display (LCD).

Bass potentiometer control
Adjusts low-frequency signal.

Digital tuner display

TROUBLESHOOTING GUIDE

SYMPTOM	POSSIBLE CAUSE	PROCEDURE
No display lights, no sound	Receiver unplugged or turned off	Plug in and turn on receiver
	Remote control dirty or faulty	Service remote control (p. 417) □○; replace batteries
	No power to outlet or outlet faulty	Reset breaker or replace fuse (p. 102) □○; service outlet (p. 148)
	Power cord faulty	Test and replace power cord (p. 417) □○
	Power fuse blown	Test and replace power fuse (p. 417) □○
	On/off switch faulty	Test and replace on/off switch (p. 367) □○
	Power supply faulty	Take receiver for professional service
	Circuit board faulty	Take receiver for professional service
Display lights, no sound	Receiver controls set incorrectly	Adjust receiver controls
	Auxiliary unit faulty	Troubleshoot entertainment system (p. 356) □○
	Selector switch or circuit board faulty	Take receiver for professional service
Sound, no display lights	Display lights faulty	Take receiver for professional service
Sound from only one channel	Receiver controls set incorrectly	Adjust receiver controls
	Speaker or auxiliary unit faulty	Troubleshoot entertainment system (p. 356) □○
	Volume or balance control potentiometer dirty or faulty	Clean potentiometer (p. 366) □○; test and replace potentiometer (p. 366) ◨◕
	Circuit board faulty	Take receiver for professional service
Intermittent sound from an auxiliary unit	Speaker, cable or auxiliary unit faulty	Troubleshoot entertainment system (p. 356) □○
	Volume or balance control potentiometer dirty or faulty	Clean potentiometer (p. 366) □○; test and replace potentiometer (p. 366) ◨◕
	Circuit board faulty	Take receiver for professional service
Intermittent sound from the radio	Tuner control set incorrectly	Adjust tuner control
	Antenna positioned incorrectly	Adjust antenna
	Speaker or cable system faulty	Troubleshoot entertainment system (p. 356) □○
	Variable capacitor dirty	Clean variable capacitor (p. 364) □○
	Antenna loose or faulty	Check FM antenna wire connections; test and replace AM antenna (p. 365) □○
	Circuit board faulty	Take receiver for professional service
Humming noise	Auxiliary unit faulty	Troubleshoot entertainment system (p. 356) □○
	Electrolytic filter power capacitor faulty	Test and replace electrolytic filter power capacitor (p. 364) ◨○
Analog tuner control erratic or doesn't work	Tuner pulleys sticking or tuner cord slipping	Service tuner (p. 362) □○
	Tuner cord loose or broken	Restring tuner (p. 363) ◨◕
Scratching noise when analog tuner control is adjusted	Variable capacitor dirty	Clean variable capacitor (p. 364) □○
	Variable capacitor or circuit board faulty	Take receiver for professional service
Scratching noise when selector control is adjusted; background noise from another unit	Selector switch dirty	Clean selector switch (p. 365) □○
	Selector switch or circuit board faulty	Take receiver for professional service
Volume, balance or tone control abrupt, scratchy or doesn't work	Speaker faulty	Troubleshoot entertainment system (p. 356) □○
	Control potentiometer dirty or faulty	Clean potentiometer (p. 366) □○; test and replace potentiometer (p. 366) ◨◕
	Circuit board faulty	Take receiver for professional service
Burning odor	Air vents blocked or dirty	Reposition receiver or clean air vents
	Heat sink dirty	Clean heat sink
	Power fuse blown	Test and replace power fuse (p. 417) □○
	Power supply faulty	Take receiver for professional service
	Electrolytic filter power capacitor faulty	Test and replace electrolytic filter power capacitor (p. 364) ◨○
	Circuit board faulty	Take receiver for professional service

DEGREE OF DIFFICULTY: □ Easy ◨ Moderate ◼ Complex
ESTIMATED TIME: ○ Less than 1 hour ◕ 1 to 3 hours ● Over 3 hours

ACCESS TO THE COMPONENTS

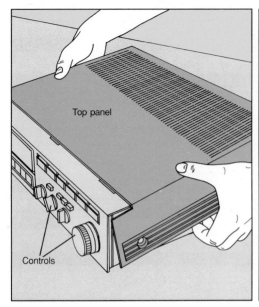

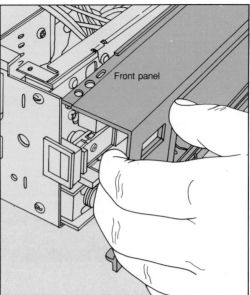

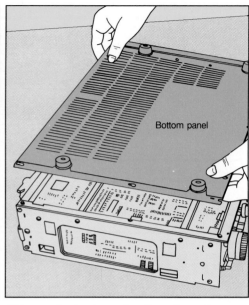

Removing and reinstalling top, front and bottom panels. Turn off the receiver, unplug it from the wall outlet and disconnect the cables and ground wire hooked up to it *(page 354)*. Top panel screws are usually located on the sides, and sometimes on the back or bottom. Unscrew the top panel, slide it out from under any lip on the front panel and lift it off the receiver frame *(above, left)*. Pull off or unscrew any controls too large to fit through the front panel. Front panel screws may be at the top, sides or bottom. Unscrew the front panel and gently pry it away from the frame *(above, center)*. Turn over the receiver. The bottom panel screws are on the edges and sometimes in the feet. Unscrew the bottom panel and lift it off the frame *(above, right)*. After working on the receiver, reverse this sequence to reinstall the panels, then cold check for leaking voltage *(page 417)*. Reconnect the cables *(page 358)* and ground wire *(page 359)*, plug in the receiver and turn it on.

SERVICING THE DIAL TUNER

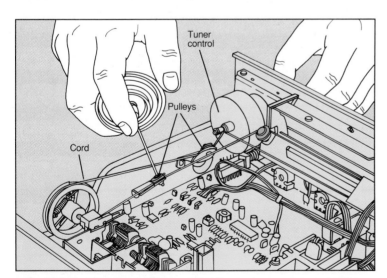

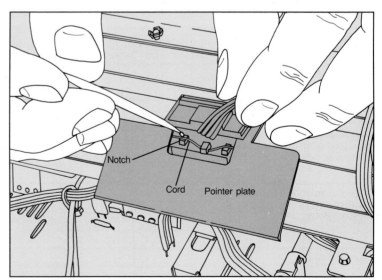

1 **Lubricating the pulleys and rail.** Unplug the receiver. Remove the top panel *(step above)*. Rotate the tuner control, checking the motion of the tuner cord and the tuner pointer inside the receiver. If the tuner cord is loose or broken, restring the tuner *(page 363)*. If the tuner cord does not travel easily, spray a tiny amount of silicone-based lubricant on the axles of the tuner pulleys, avoiding contact with the tuner cord. Work in the lubricant by rotating the tuner control *(above)*. Use a clean cloth to rub a little of the same lubricant on the pointer rail. If the tuner cord travels easily but the tuner pointer does not slide smoothly, reset the pointer *(step 2)*. When the tuner cord travels easily and the tuner pointer slides smoothly, reinstall the top panel *(step above)*.

2 **Resetting the pointer.** Unhook the tuner cord from the notches or clips on the pointer plate. Rotate the tuner control fully in one direction, then slide the pointer by hand fully in the same direction. Rethread the tuner cord snugly through the notches or clips on the pointer plate. Secure the tuner cord to the pointer plate by applying a small dab of nail polish to each notch *(above)* or by pressing down the clips with a small screwdriver. Reinstall the top panel *(step above)*.

RESTRINGING THE DIAL TUNER

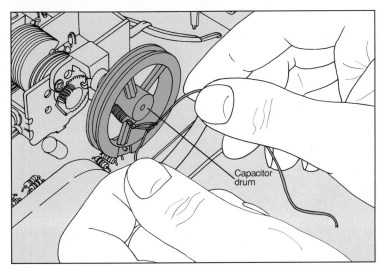

1 **Tying on cord at the capacitor drum.** Unplug the receiver. Remove the top panel *(page 362)* and check inside the receiver for a sketch of the tuner cord route. If there is no sketch, draw one; noting the sequence and the direction and number of turns the tuner cord makes around each component. If the tuner cord route cannot be determined, consult the manufacturer, or attempt to retrace the route using a replacement tuner cord of about the same length. Undo the knots securing the damaged tuner cord to the capacitor spring and remove the cord. Purchase the required length of tuner cord at an electronics parts supplier. Knot one end of the tuner cord to the capacitor spring *(above)*, then loop it around the capacitor drum. To keep the capacitor drum stationary, turn it fully in the direction of the loop.

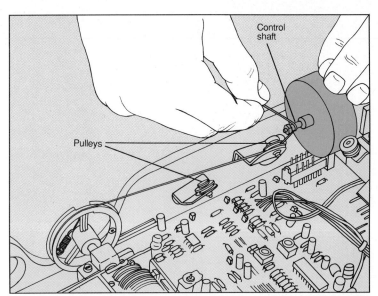

2 **Wrapping cord around the tuner control shaft.** Following the direction and number of turns noted in the sketch, wrap the tuner cord tautly around the tuner pulleys on the route to the tuner control shaft; if you are proceeding without a sketch, start by assuming once around each pulley in the same direction as the initial loop around the capacitor drum. Wrap the tuner cord around the tuner control shaft the direction and number of turns noted *(above)*. In most instances, at least two or three turns are required in the same direction as the initial loop around the capacitor drum, to allow the pointer to travel the full length of the tuner dial.

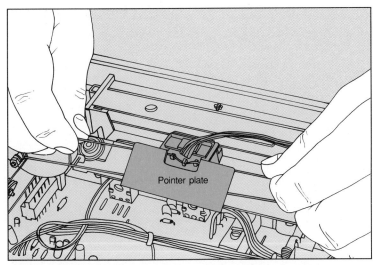

3 **Threading cord through the tuner pointer.** Pull the tuner cord across the back of the front panel, feeding it under the pointer plate. Still following the direction and number of turns noted in the sketch, wrap the tuner cord tautly around the tuner pulley at the end of the dial farthest from the tuner control shaft. Slide the pointer by hand as close as possible to the tuner control shaft. Pull the tuner cord to the pointer and thread it through the notches or clips on the pointer plate *(above)*. Finally, wrap the tuner cord around the tuner pulley at the end of the dial closest to the tuner control shaft and pull the cord back to the capacitor drum, wrapping it around any other pulleys indicated in the sketch.

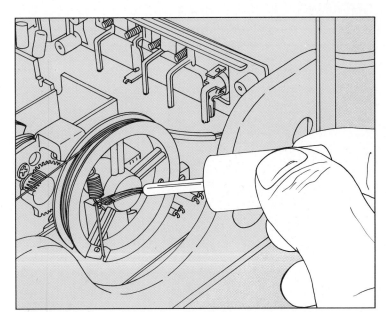

4 **Tying off cord at the capacitor drum.** Wrap the tuner cord once around the capacitor drum in the direction opposite to the initial loop. If the new tuner cord ends up much shorter or longer than the old tuner cord, retrace the route taken and look for errors. If the new tuner cord ends up about the same length as the old tuner cord, tie the cord to the capacitor spring, cut off any excess and apply a small dab of nail polish *(above)*. Rotate the tuner control to ensure that the capacitor blades can open and close fully and that the pointer can travel the full length of the tuner dial; if required, reset the pointer *(page 362)*. Reinstall the top panel.

SERVICING THE VARIABLE CAPACITOR

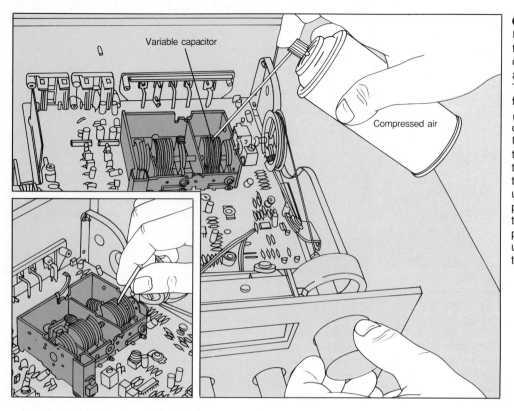

Variable capacitor

Compressed air

Cleaning a variable capacitor.
Unplug the receiver and remove the top panel *(page 362)*. Rotate the tuner control as shown, and inspect the variable capacitor blades for dirt or dust. To clean the blades, spray them carefully with short bursts of compressed air *(left)*, or apply a small amount of tuner cleaner or electronic contact cleaner. Use tuner cleaner and electronic contact cleaner sparingly, however; they tend to leave a slight sticky residue that traps dirt and dust. If necessary, gently use a toothpick or a folded sheet of paper to dislodge particles from between the blades *(inset)*. To dislodge particles that are difficult to reach, try using a vacuum cleaner. Reinstall the top panel.

SERVICING THE ELECTROLYTIC FILTER POWER CAPACITOR

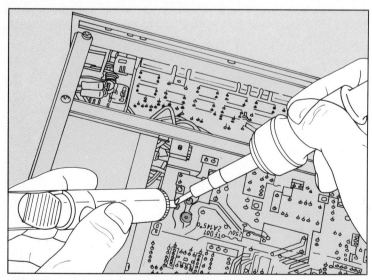

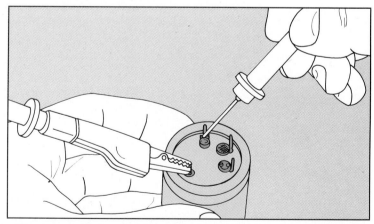

1 Removing the capacitor. Unplug the receiver and remove the top and bottom panels *(page 362)*. **Caution:** Wait 30 minutes for the capacitor to discharge completely any stored voltage. Find the capacitor near the power-supply components. Locate the capacitor contact pins on the circuit board, and carefully note their positions for reassembly. Desolder the pins *(page 417)* from the circuit board *(above)*, turn over the receiver and gently pull the capacitor off the circuit board.

2 Testing and replacing the capacitor. Set a multitester to test resistance. Clip the negative probe to the negative pin and touch the positive probe to each positive pin in turn *(above)*; if there are negative-and-positive pin pairs, test each pair. For each pair, the multitester should register low ohms and then a rise in ohms. If the capacitor tests OK, suspect a faulty circuit board and take the receiver for professional service. If the capacitor is faulty, purchase an exact replacement capacitor at an electronics parts supplier and solder it to the circuit board. Reinstall the bottom and top panels and cold check for leaking voltage *(page 417)*.

SERVICING THE AM ANTENNA

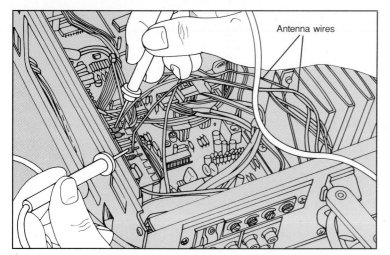

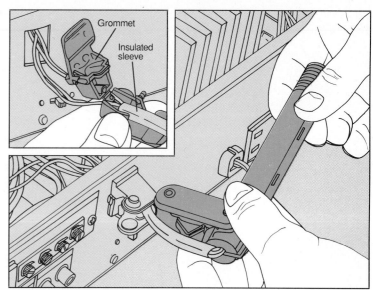

Antenna wires

Grommet

Insulated sleeve

1 **Testing the antenna.** Unplug the receiver. Remove the top panel *(page 362)* and locate the antenna wire terminals on the circuit board. If a wire is loose or broken, repair the wire connection *(page 417)*. Set a multitester to test continuity. Touch one probe to one antenna wire terminal on the circuit board and touch the other probe in turn to each of the other antenna wire terminals *(above)*. The multitester should register continuity at least once. Repeat this step to test each terminal against each other terminal. If the multitester does not register the correct results, replace the antenna *(step 2)*. If the multitester shows that the antenna is OK, reinstall the top panel.

2 **Replacing the antenna.** If the circuit board is not coded to the antenna wire colors, note the wire contact points. Desolder the wires from the circuit board *(page 417)* and pull the antenna off the grommet *(above)*. Pry the grommet off the back panel, open it and slip out the wires *(inset)*. Order a replacement antenna from the manufacturer. Slide the open grommet onto the wires, pressing it against the insulated sleeve. Close the grommet and thread the wires through the opening in the back panel. Fit the grommet into the back panel and push the antenna onto the grommet. Solder the wires to the circuit board. Reinstall the top panel and cold check for leaking voltage.

SERVICING THE SELECTOR SWITCH

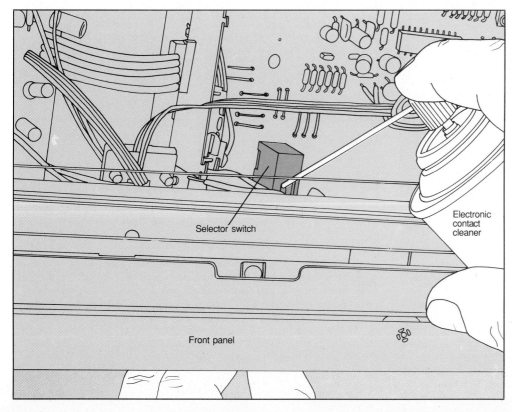

Selector switch

Electronic contact cleaner

Front panel

Cleaning the switch. Unplug the receiver. Remove the top panel *(page 362)* and locate the selector switch on the circuit board behind the selector control. Using electronic contact cleaner, direct the nozzle through the opening in the switch casing. Spray a short burst of cleaner into the switch and rotate the selector control fully clockwise and counterclockwise a number of times to work in the cleaner *(left)*. Reinstall the top panel. If the problem persists, suspect a faulty selector switch or circuit board and take the receiver for professional service.

SERVICING POTENTIOMETERS

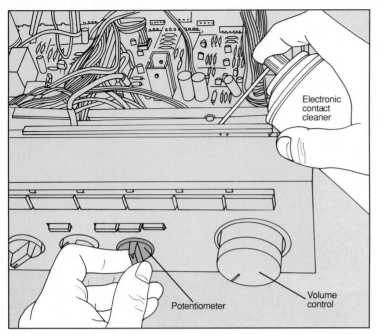

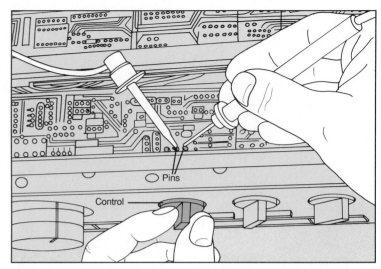

1 Cleaning a potentiometer. Unplug the receiver. Remove the top panel *(page 362)* and locate the potentiometer on the circuit board, behind its control. Spray electronic contact cleaner through the openings in the potentiometer casing and rotate the control back and forth to work in the cleaner *(above)*. Reinstall the top panel. If the problem persists, test the potentiometer *(step 2)*.

2 Testing a potentiometer. Remove the top and bottom panels *(page 362)*. Set the control fully left, and set a multitester to test resistance. If there is one row of pins, hook one probe to the middle pin in the row, and touch the other probe to one of the outer pins in the row. Rotate the control from left to right *(above)*: The multitester should register a variation in ohms as the control is rotated. Reset the control to its left and test the same way between the middle pin and the other outer pin in the row. If there are two rows of pins, test each row the same way. If you do not get a variation in ohms each time, replace the potentiometer. If the potentiometer is OK, reinstall the bottom and top panels and cold check for leaking voltage *(page 417)*.

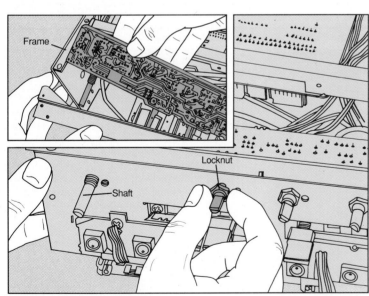

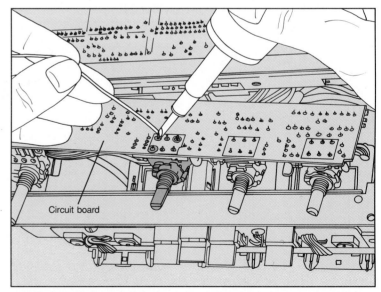

3 Removing a potentiometer. To take out the circuit board on which the potentiometer is located, remove the front panel *(page 362)* and unscrew the shaft locknut for each potentiometer on the circuit board *(above)*. Lift out the circuit board, pulling the shafts through the openings in the frame; if necessary, unscrew one end of the frame and pull it out slightly *(inset)*. Desolder the pins of the faulty potentiometer *(page 417)*, turn over the circuit board and gently pry off the potentiometer. Test its resistance again to confirm the potentiometer is faulty *(step 2)*. If the potentiometer tests faulty, replace it *(step 4)*; if it tests OK, suspect a faulty circuit board and take the receiver for service.

4 Replacing a potentiometer. Purchase an exact replacement potentiometer at an electronics parts supplier. Gently push the potentiometer pins into the circuit board openings, turn over the circuit board and solder the pins in place *(page 417)*. Slide the potentiometer shafts through the openings in the frame and reposition the circuit board; if required, pull out one end of the frame, then screw it back in place. Screw on the shaft locknuts for each potentiometer. Reinstall the bottom, front and top panels, then cold check for leaking voltage.

TESTING AND REPLACING THE ON/OFF SWITCH

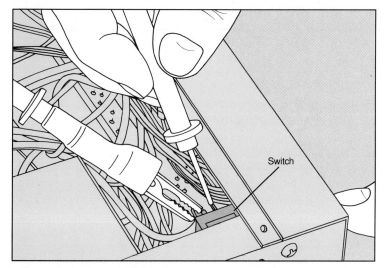

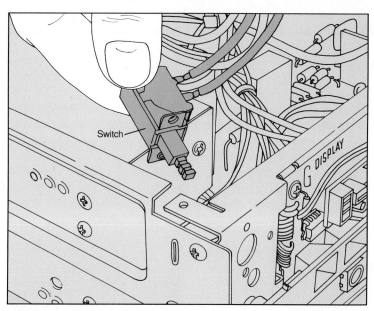

1 **Testing the switch**. Unplug the receiver. Remove the top panel *(page 362)* and locate the on/off switch terminals. If a wire is loose or broken, repair the wire connection *(page 417)*. Set a multitester to test continuity. Clip one probe to one switch terminal and touch the other probe to the other switch terminal. Set the switch to the ON position and then to the OFF position *(above)*. The switch should have continuity only in the ON position. If the switch is faulty, remove it *(step 2)*. If the switch tests OK, have the power supply serviced.

2 **Removing the switch.** Remove the front panel *(page 362)* and pull the control off the on/off switch shaft. Unscrew the switch, pull the shaft through the opening in the frame and lift the switch out of the receiver *(above)*. Desolder the wires from the switch terminals *(page 417)*. To confirm that the on/off switch is faulty, test for continuity again *(step 1)*. If the switch still tests defective, replace it *(step 3)*. If it now tests OK, resolder the wires, reinstall the on/off switch on the frame, put back the on/off control and have the power supply serviced.

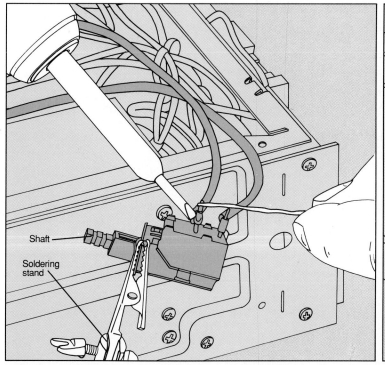

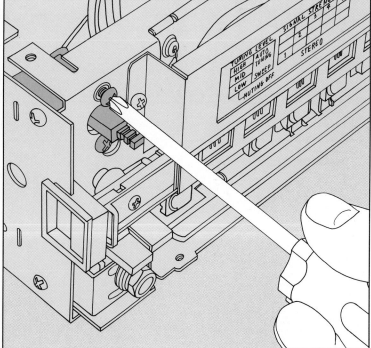

3 **Replacing the switch.** Purchase an exact replacement on/off switch at an electronics parts supplier. Solder the wires to the switch terminals, using a soldering stand if necessary to keep the switch stationary *(above, left)*. Release the switch from the soldering stand, slip the switch shaft through the opening in the frame and screw the switch in place *(above, right)*. Put back the on/off control and reinstall the front and top panels. Cold check for leaking voltage.

AUDIOCASSETTE RECORDERS

The audiocassette recorder routes sound in two directions—out of the unit in the play mode and into the unit in the record mode. During the play mode, invisible magnetic tracks on the audiocassette tape induce a varying electrical current in the head. The current is sent out of the recorder through cables, usually to the receiver and from there to the speakers. During the record mode, electrical current received from another audio unit is "written" by the head as magnetic tracks on the audiocassette tape for later play, when the head will route it back through the receiver and the speakers.

Many recorder problems can be remedied by adjusting cable hookups or by cleaning and demagnetizing the tape travel components. Consult the Troubleshooting Guide in Entertainment Systems (page 356) as well as in this chapter (page 369).

Cleaning supplies and most replacement components are available at an electronics parts supplier; some parts may have to be ordered from the manufacturer. Have the capstan motor and circuit board serviced professionally.

Refer to Tools & Techniques for the basic tool kit (page 417), as well as instructions for disassembly and reassembly, testing continuity and voltage, and desoldering and soldering.

Turn off and unplug the audiocassette recorder before attempting any repair. Disconnect the cables hooked up to it and set it on a clean work table. Store fasteners and other small parts in labeled containers and write down the sequence of disassembly steps. Perform a cold check for leaking voltage (page 417) after reassembling the audiocassette recorder but before you plug it back in.

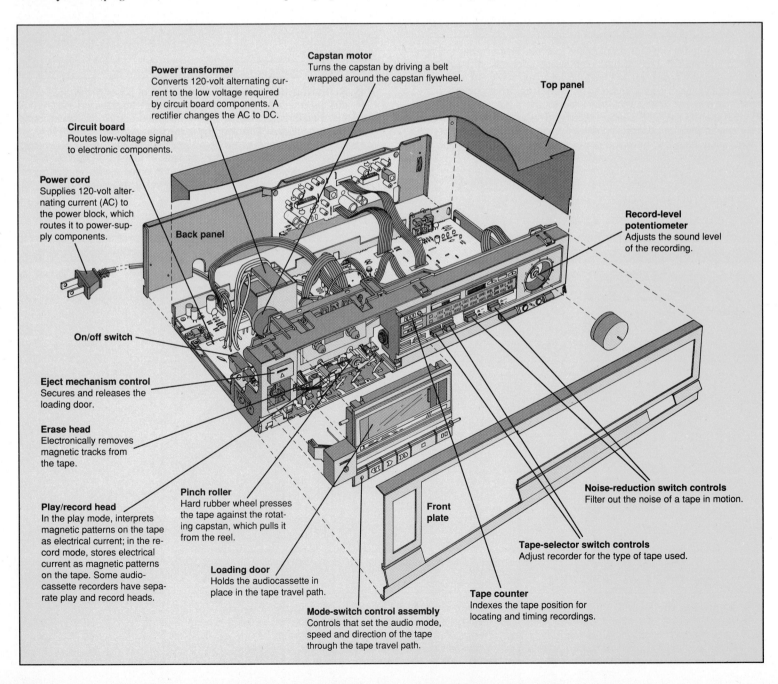

Capstan motor
Turns the capstan by driving a belt wrapped around the capstan flywheel.

Top panel

Power transformer
Converts 120-volt alternating current to the low voltage required by circuit board components. A rectifier changes the AC to DC.

Circuit board
Routes low-voltage signal to electronic components.

Power cord
Supplies 120-volt alternating current (AC) to the power block, which routes it to power-supply components.

Back panel

Record-level potentiometer
Adjusts the sound level of the recording.

On/off switch

Eject mechanism control
Secures and releases the loading door.

Erase head
Electronically removes magnetic tracks from the tape.

Play/record head
In the play mode, interprets magnetic patterns on the tape as electrical current; in the record mode, stores electrical current as magnetic patterns on the tape. Some audiocassette recorders have separate play and record heads.

Pinch roller
Hard rubber wheel presses the tape against the rotating capstan, which pulls it from the reel.

Loading door
Holds the audiocassette in place in the tape travel path.

Mode-switch control assembly
Controls that set the audio mode, speed and direction of the tape through the tape travel path.

Front plate

Tape counter
Indexes the tape position for locating and timing recordings.

Noise-reduction switch controls
Filter out the noise of a tape in motion.

Tape-selector switch controls
Adjust recorder for the type of tape used.

TROUBLESHOOTING GUIDE

SYMPTOM	POSSIBLE CAUSE	PROCEDURE
No display lights, no sound	Audiocassette recorder unplugged or off	Plug in and turn on audiocassette recorder
	No power to outlet or outlet faulty	Reset breaker or replace fuse (p. 102) □○; service outlet (p. 148)
	Power fuse blown	Test and replace power fuse (p. 417) □○
	Power cord faulty	Test and replace power cord (p. 417) □○
	On/off switch faulty	Test and replace on/off switch (p. 377) □○
	Power supply or circuit board faulty	Take audiocassette recorder for professional service
Display lights, no sound	Controls set incorrectly	Adjust audiocassette recorder controls
	Audiocassette tape torn or jammed	Splice tape (p. 370) □○; remove jammed tape (p. 372) □○
	Receiver faulty	Troubleshoot entertainment system (p. 356) □○
	Drive belt loose or broken	Service drive belts (p. 373) □○
	Play/record head faulty	Test and replace head (p. 375) □○
	Play/record switch dirty or faulty	Clean play/record switch (p. 378) □○; replace switch (p. 378) ■◐
	Capstan motor or circuit board faulty	Take audiocassette recorder for professional service
Sound, no display lights	Display lights faulty	Take audiocassette recorder for professional service
Sound from only one channel	Controls set incorrectly	Adjust audiocassette recorder controls
	Receiver or speaker faulty	Troubleshoot entertainment system (p. 356) □○
	Play/record head faulty	Test and replace play/record head (p. 375) □○
	Record level potentiometer dirty or faulty	Clean potentiometer (p. 379) □○; test and replace (p. 379) ◨○
	Circuit board faulty	Take audiocassette recorder for professional service
Sound intermittent or distorted	Receiver or speaker faulty	Troubleshoot entertainment system (p. 356) □○
	Audiocassette tape damaged	Splice audiocassette tape (p. 370) □○; replace audiocassette
	Tape travel path dirty	Clean and demagnetize tape travel path (p. 370) □○▲
	Play/record head misaligned	Adjust play/record head (p. 373) □○
	Drive belt dirty or loose	Service drive belts (p. 373) □○
	Capstan motor runs too fast or too slow	Adjust capstan motor speed (p. 374) □○
	Pinch roller faulty	Replace pinch roller (p. 374) □○
	Play/record head faulty	Test and replace play/record head (p. 375) □○
	Tape transport assembly dirty	Service tape transport assembly (p. 376) ◨○
	Record level potentiometer dirty or faulty	Clean potentiometer (p. 379) □○; test and replace (p. 379) ◨○
	Tape selector or noise reduction switch dirty or faulty	Clean switch (p. 379) □○; test and replace switch (p. 379) ■◐
	Capstan motor or circuit board faulty	Take audiocassette recorder for professional service
Record level control abrupt, scratchy, or doesn't work	Record level potentiometer dirty or faulty	Clean potentiometer (p. 379) □○; test and replace (p. 379) ◨○
	Circuit board faulty	Take audiocassette recorder for professional service
Mode control can't be set or releases prematurely	Play/record switch dirty or faulty	Clean play/record switch (p. 378) □○; replace switch (p. 378) ■◐
	Circuit board faulty	Take audiocassette recorder for professional service
Noise in fast forward, rewind, pause or stop mode	Mute switch faulty	Service mute switch (p. 377) □○
	Circuit board faulty	Take audiocassette recorder for professional service
Audiocassette tape can't be erased or recorded over	Audiocassette safety tab removed	Service audiocassette safety tab (p. 370) □○
	Play/record head misaligned	Adjust play/record head (p. 373) □○
	Erase head faulty	Test and replace erase head (p. 375) □○
	Play/record switch dirty or faulty	Clean play/record switch (p. 378) □○; replace switch (p. 378) ■◐
Loading door doesn't open	Eject mechanism faulty	Service eject mechanism (p. 372) □○
	Audiocassette tape jammed	Remove jammed audiocassette (p. 372) □○

DEGREE OF DIFFICULTY: □ Easy ◨ Moderate ■ Complex
ESTIMATED TIME: ○ Less than 1 hour ◐ 1 to 3 hours ● Over 3 hours ▲ Special tool required

369

SERVICING AUDIOCASSETTES

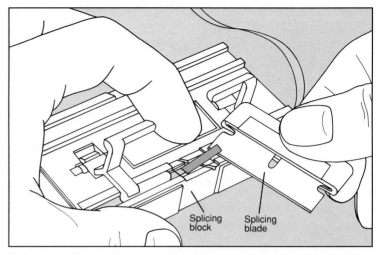

Removing and restoring the recording safety tabs. Locate the audio-cassette safety tabs on the top edge of the housing, usually indicated by arrows on the side edges. To prevent the audiocassette tape from being erased or recorded over, break off each safety tab using a small, flat screwdriver *(above)*; if the safety tab falls into the audiocassette, remove it using long-nose pliers. To erase or record over the audiocassette tape, cover each safety tab opening with a small piece of plastic tape.

Splicing audiocassette tape. Touching the undamaged audiocassette tape as little as possible, snip off a length of rumpled tape with scissors. Slip the tape ends, shiny side up, into a splicing block, overlapping them slightly at the cutting groove. Push down the levers, cutting through the tape ends with the splicing blade, and blow away the tape scraps. Use the blade to slice off 1/2 inch of splicing tape, taking care not to touch the sticky side. Pick up the splicing tape with the blade and center it, sticky side down, across the cut ends of the audiocassette tape *(above)*. Run a foam swab over the splicing tape to press it firmly onto the audio-cassette tape. Lift up the levers and remove the audiocassette tape from the splicing block. Turn the audiocassette takeup reel with a pencil to rewind the tape.

SERVICING THE TAPE TRAVEL PATH

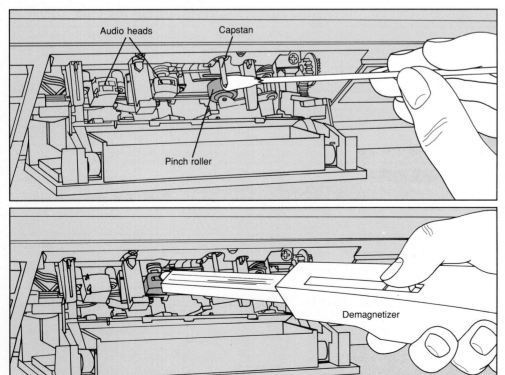

Cleaning and demagnetizing the tape travel path. Unload the audiocassette, if any. Turn off the audiocassette recorder and unplug it from the outlet. Using a foam swab dipped in dena-tured alcohol, wipe the audio heads, the capstan and the guides; for easier access to the heads, press the play or pause control. Use a cotton or foam swab dipped in rubber-cleaning compound to wipe the pinch roller *(left, top)*, turning it with a finger as you clean.

Purchase a demagnetizer at an electronics parts supplier. Plug the demagnetizer into a wall outlet and turn it on at least 2 feet away from the audiocassette recorder. Slowly bring the demag-netizer within 1/2 inch of an audio head *(left, bottom)*, draw it about 2 feet away and turn it off. Repeat this procedure for the other audio head as well as for the capstan, the guides and any other metal component that contacts an audio-cassette. Plug in the audiocassette recorder.

ACCESS TO THE INTERNAL COMPONENTS

Removing and reinstalling the top panel.
Unload the audiocassette, if any. Turn off and unplug the audiocassette recorder, and disconnect the cables hooked up to it *(page 354)*. Top panel screws may be located on the sides, back or bottom. Unscrew the top panel, slide it out from under any lip on the front panel and lift it off the frame *(above)*. To reinstall the top panel, slide it under the front panel lip and screw it to the frame. Cold check the audiocassette recorder for leaking voltage *(page 417)*. Reconnect the cables and plug in the audiocassette recorder.

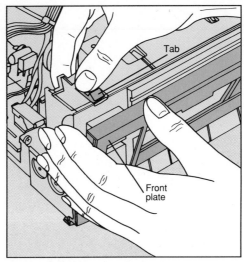

Removing and reinstalling the front plate or panel. Remove the top panel *(left)*. If there is a front plate, check for tabs and screws securing it to the frame. Unscrew the front plate, press in the tabs and pull off the front plate *(above)*. If there is no front plate, unscrew the front panel. Pull off or unscrew any controls too large to fit through their openings, and pull the front panel off the frame. To reinstall the front plate, snap it onto the frame and put back any screws. To reinstall the front panel, screw it onto the frame and put back any controls removed. Reinstall the top panel *(left)*.

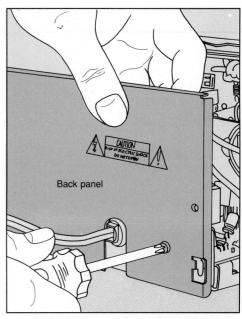

Removing and reinstalling the back panel. Remove the top panel *(far left)*. Unscrew the back panel, carefully pull it out from the frame *(above)* and turn it face down, exposing any interior wire connections, such as those leading to the power cord. To reinstall the back panel, set it against the frame and put back the screws. Reinstall the top panel *(far left)*.

ACCESS TO THE TAPE TRAVEL PATH COMPONENTS

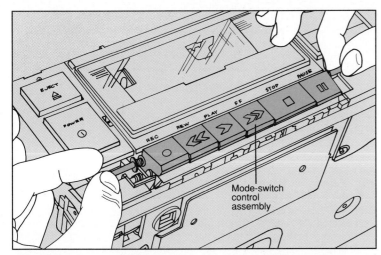

Removing and reinstalling the mode-switch control assembly.
Unplug the unit. Remove the top panel and the front plate or panel *(steps above)*. Press the tabs at each end of the mode-switch control assembly toward each other and pull the assembly off the frame; for easier access, upend the audiocassette recorder *(above)*. Tape the ends of the mode-switch control assembly to prevent losing the washers and springs. Reverse the sequence to reinstall the assembly.

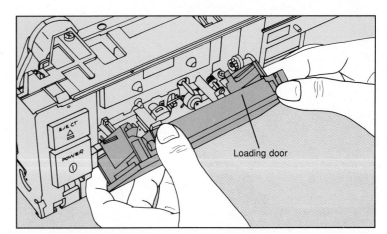

Removing and reinstalling the loading door. Push the eject mechanism control to open the loading door. Check for tabs securing a front plate on the loading door; press in the tabs and slide off the front plate. If there is no front plate, remove the mode-switch control assembly *(left)*. Press the tabs on each side of the loading door toward each other and pull off the loading door *(above)*. Reverse the sequence to reinstall the loading door.

SERVICING THE EJECT MECHANISM

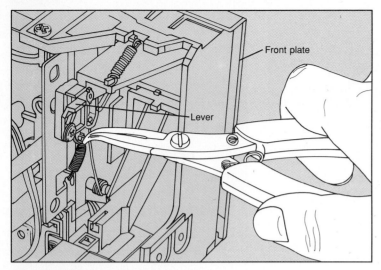

Front plate

Lever

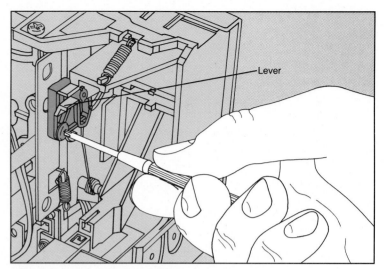

Lever

1 **Checking the mechanism.** Unplug the unit. Remove the top panel *(page 371)* and locate the eject mechanism components. If the lever is broken, replace it *(step 2)*. If the lever slides poorly, use a foam swab to apply a little white grease to it. If the lever has worked loose, tighten its mounting screw. Reconnect an unhooked spring using long-nose pliers *(above)* or tweezers; if a spring is damaged, replace it. Reinstall the top panel and check for leaking voltage.

2 **Replacing the mechanism.** Unhook any springs connected to the lever using long-nose pliers or tweezers. Remove the lever mounting screw *(above)* and pull the lever free of any retaining clips. Order an eject mechanism lever from the manufacturer or purchase a substitute at an electronics parts supplier. Press the lever into the retaining clips, put back the mounting screw and rehook the springs. Reinstall the top panel and cold check for leaking voltage.

REMOVING A JAMMED AUDIOCASSETTE

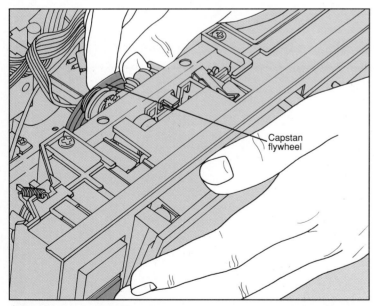

Capstan flywheel

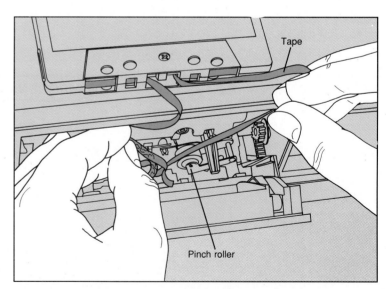

Tape

Pinch roller

1 **Releasing the audiocassette.** Turn off and unplug the audiocassette recorder. Press the eject control to open the loading door. If the loading door opens and the audiocassette can be lifted out easily, retrieve the jammed tape *(step 2)*. If the loading door does not open enough to reach the audiocassette, or if the audiocassette cannot be removed easily, take off the top panel *(page 371)* and the capstan plate *(page 376)*. Pull out the capstan flywheel to release the audiocassette from the capstan, then press the eject control *(above)*. Carefully lift out the audiocassette, push in the capstan flywheel and reinstall the capstan plate, reversing the sequence used to remove it.

2 **Retrieving jammed tape.** Resting the audiocassette on top of the audiocassette recorder, gently extract the tape from the tape travel path components *(above)*; avoid touching undamaged sections of tape with your fingers. If the tape is difficult to retrieve, cut it with scissors, making sure not to leave behind any stray pieces. Reinstall the top panel *(page 371)* if you removed it. If the tape has been cut or badly damaged, splice it *(page 370)*. If the tape is OK, turn the audiocassette takeup reel with a pencil to rewind the tape, being careful not to twist it.

ADJUSTING THE PLAY/RECORD HEAD

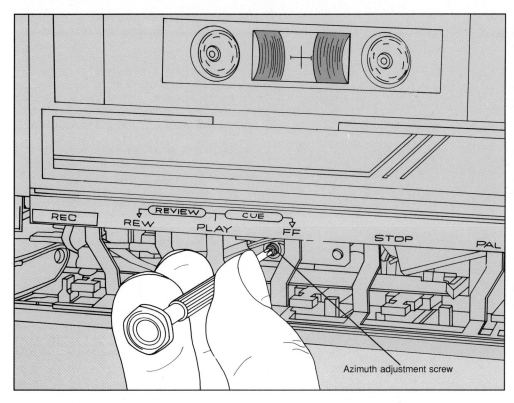

Azimuth adjustment screw

Resetting the azimuth adjustment screw.
Without disconnecting the cables hooked up to the audiocassette recorder, unplug it and remove the mode-switch control assembly *(page 371)*. Locate the green or red azimuth adjustment screw on the play/record head and twist it slightly with a screwdriver to break any bond. Plug in and turn on the audiocassette recorder. Load a prerecorded audiocassette, preferably one with considerable high frequency or treble sound. Fast/forward or rewind the audiocassette tape to midposition. Turn down the bass control, turn up the treble control and play the tape. While listening closely, slowly turn the azimuth adjustment screw clockwise and counterclockwise until the sound quality is optimum *(left)*. Lock the screw in position by applying a small dab of nail polish. Remove the audiocassette and turn off and unplug the audiocassette recorder. Reinstall the mode-switch control assembly.

SERVICING THE DRIVE BELTS

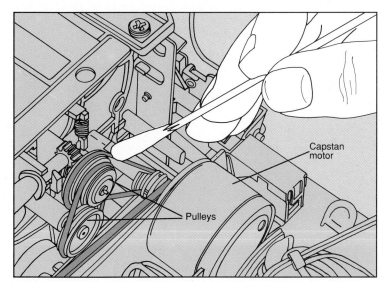

Capstan motor

Pulleys

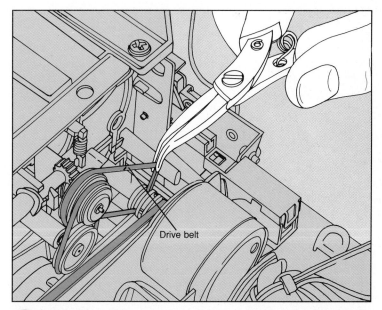

Drive belt

1 **Cleaning a belt.** Unplug the unit. Remove the top panel *(page 371)* and locate the drive belts on the tape transport assembly. If a belt is worn or broken, replace it *(step 2)*. If a belt is sticky or oily, clean it thoroughly on both sides using a cotton or foam swab dipped in rubber-cleaning compound *(above)*; never apply anything oily and avoid touching the belt with your fingers. Turn the belt pulleys or the capstan flywheel with a clean foam swab to reach the entire length of the belt. Reinstall the top panel.

2 **Replacing a belt.** Use long-nose pliers or tweezers to slip off the belt and any other belt in its way *(above)*. Note the belt positions on the pulleys or the capstan flywheel; be careful not to pinch a belt. To reach the capstan drive belt, remove the capstan plate *(page 376)*. Purchase an exact replacement belt at an electronics parts supplier. Holding the belt loosely, wrap it around its pulleys or the capstan flywheel. Reinstall any other belts you removed. Put back the capstan plate by reversing the sequence used to remove it. Reinstall the top panel, and cold check for leaking voltage *(page 417)*.

ADJUSTING THE CAPSTAN MOTOR SPEED

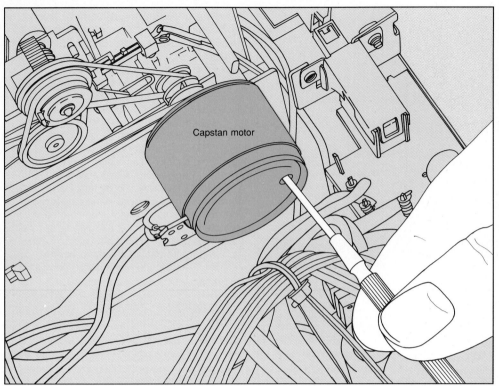

Capstan motor

Resetting the motor speed. Without disconnecting the cables hooked up to the audiocassette recorder, unplug it and remove the top panel *(page 371)*. Locate the motor-speed adjustment screw in the opening on the back of the motor. If there is no motor-speed adjustment screw, reinstall the top panel; to have the motor speed adjusted, take the audiocassette recorder for professional service. If there is a motor-speed adjustment screw, plug in the audiocassette recorder, turn it on and load a prerecorded audiocassette, preferably one with considerable mid-range frequency or voice passages. Play the audiocassette tape for about five minutes to warm up the motor, then fast/forward or rewind it to midposition. While listening closely to the tape, slowly turn the motor-speed adjustment screw clockwise and counterclockwise until the sound quality is optimum *(left)*. Remove the audiocassette, turn off the audiocassette recorder, unplug it and reinstall the top panel.

REPLACING THE PINCH ROLLER

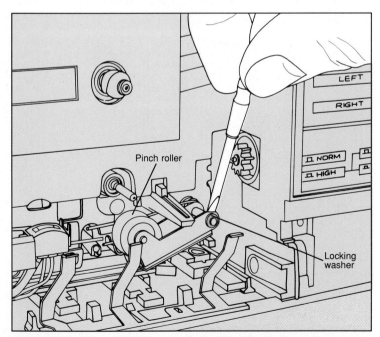

Pinch roller

Locking washer

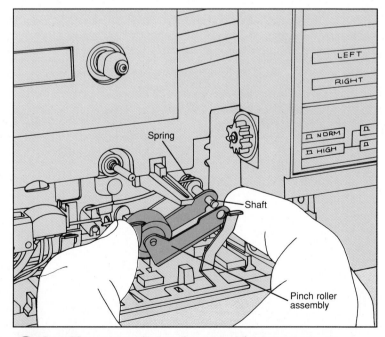

Spring

Shaft

Pinch roller assembly

1 Removing the pinch roller assembly. Unplug the unit. Remove the mode-switch control assembly and the loading door *(page 371)*. Locate the pinch roller assembly and note the pinch-roller spring position. Fit the tip of a small screwdriver under the locking washer and gently pry it off *(above)*; if required, use one hand to hold the pinch roller assembly stationary. Slide the pinch roller assembly off its shaft, noting its position.

2 Installing a new pinch roller assembly. If the pinch roller assembly spring is damaged, replace it; if the spring is OK, leave it in place. Purchase an exact replacement pinch roller assembly at an electronics parts supplier and slip it onto the shaft *(above)*. Pressing the pinch roller assembly against the spring, push the locking washer onto the shaft. Reinstall the loading door and the mode-switch control assembly.

TESTING AND REPLACING AN AUDIO HEAD

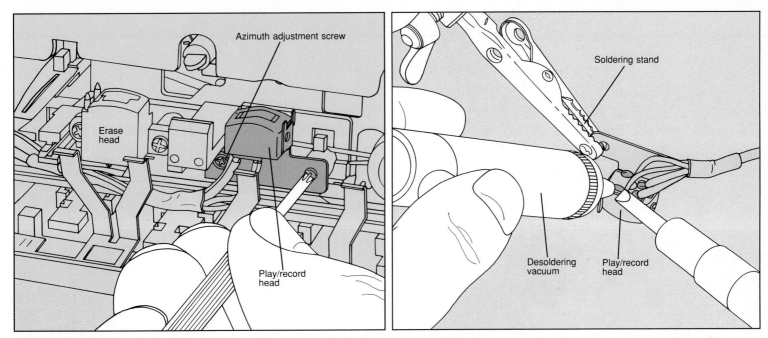

1 **Removing a head.** Unplug the unit. Remove the mode-switch control assembly and the loading door *(page 371)* and locate the play/record and erase heads; note the position of the green or red azimuth adjustment screw on the play/record head. Demagnetize a small screwdriver, unscrew the head being serviced *(above, left)* and gently lift it out of the audio-cassette recorder. If a wire connection is loose or broken, repair it *(page 417)*. Put back the head; for the play/record head, reset the azimuth adjustment screw *(page 373)*. Reinstall the loading door and the mode-switch control assembly. If the problem persists, test the head *(step 2)*. Access the head as above. Secure the head in a soldering stand and desolder *(page 417)* the wires *(above, right)*, noting their terminal positions.

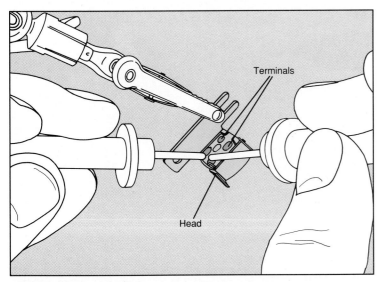

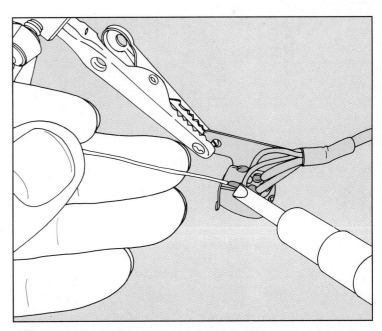

2 **Testing the head.** Set a multitester to test continuity. If the head has three wires, touch one probe to the ground terminal and the second probe to each other terminal, in turn. The multitester should register continuity. If the head has four wires, there are two ground wires; touch the probes to each ground/non-ground pair of terminals. The multitester should register continuity for each pair. If the head tests faulty, replace it *(step 3)*. If the head tests OK, solder the wires to the terminals and reinstall the head *(step 3)*.

3 **Replacing the head.** Order an exact replacement head from the manufacturer or purchase a substitute at an electronics parts supplier. Secure the head in the soldering stand, solder the wires to the head terminals *(above)* and screw in the head. If you serviced the play/record head, reset the azimuth adjustment screw *(page 373)*. Reinstall the loading door and the mode-switch control assembly and cold check the unit for leaking voltage *(page 417)*.

SERVICING THE TAPE TRANSPORT ASSEMBLY

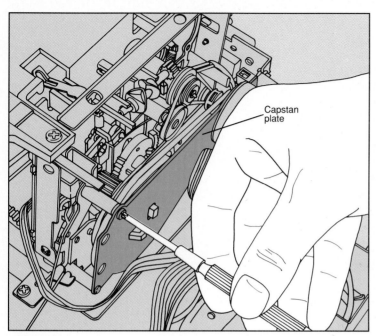

Capstan plate

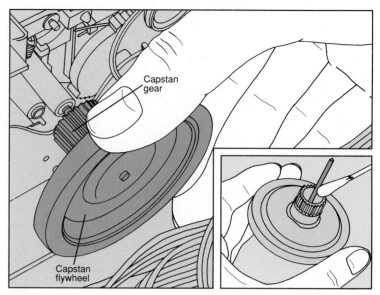

Capstan gear

Capstan flywheel

1 **Removing the capstan plate.** Unplug the unit. Remove the top panel *(page 371)* and unscrew the capstan plate *(above)*. Slip the drive belts off the motor pulley and the capstan flywheel using long-nose pliers or tweezers. Avoid touching or pinching any undamaged belt. Lift out the capstan plate and the motor along with the capstan drive belt, taking care not to damage the motor wires.

2 **Cleaning and lubricating the capstan.** Pull the capstan flywheel out of the tape transport assembly *(above)*, exposing the capstan. Clean the capstan flywheel and the capstan with a cotton or foam swab dipped in denatured alcohol *(inset)*. Use a toothpick to dislodge dirt from the capstan gear teeth. Lubricate the capstan base using a foam swab moistened with light machine oil, avoiding contact with the tip, which touches the audiocassette tape. Use a toothpick to apply a little white grease to the capstan gear teeth. Wipe off excess lubricant with a clean foam swab.

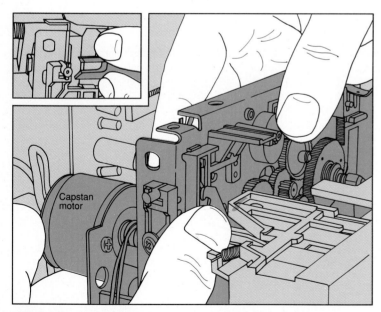

Capstan motor

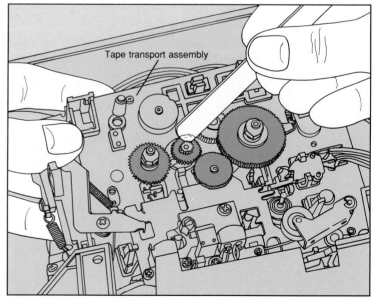

Tape transport assembly

3 **Removing the tape transport assembly.** Unscrew the tape transport assembly from the frame. Using long-nose pliers or tweezers, remove the play/record switch lever, any eject mechanism springs and the tape-counter drive belt, noting their positions for reassembly. Unclip the tape transport assembly from tabs securing it to the front panel *(inset)* and carefully lift it out of the audiocassette recorder *(above)*.

4 **Cleaning and lubricating the gears.** Clean the tape transport assembly gears using a foam swab dipped in denatured alcohol. Use a toothpick to dislodge any dirt from the gear teeth. Lubricate the gear teeth by applying white grease with a clean stick *(above)*; use a clean foam swab to wipe off excess lubricant. If a gear is damaged, remove any clip, washer or screw holding it in place and replace the gear. To reinstall the tape transport assembly, clip it under the tabs on the front panel, screw it to the frame, and insert the capstan flywheel. Put back the play/record switch lever, any eject mechanism springs and the tape-counter drive belt. Reinstall the capstan plate, reversing the sequence in step 1, then reinstall the top panel.

SERVICING THE MODE SWITCHES

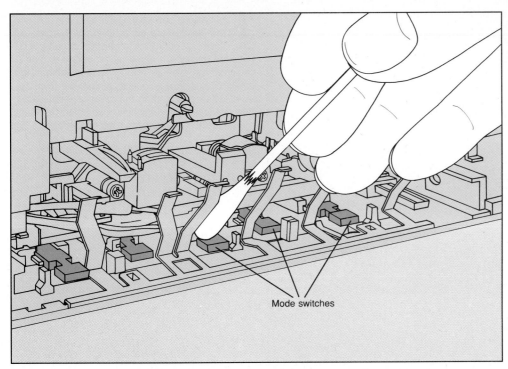

Mode switches

Cleaning and lubricating the switches.

Unplug the unit. Remove the mode-switch control assembly and the loading door *(page 371)*. Use a cotton or foam swab dipped in denatured alcohol to clean the entire surface of each switch *(left)*; for easier access, press in and release the switch lever so that it protrudes as far as possible. To lubricate the switch, use a toothpick to apply a little white grease where the switch lever enters the switch; press in and release the lever a number of times to work in the lubricant. Avoid applying lubricant to the control contact points. Wipe off excess lubricant with a clean foam swab. Reinstall the loading door and the mode-switch control assembly.

TESTING AND REPLACING THE ON/OFF SWITCH

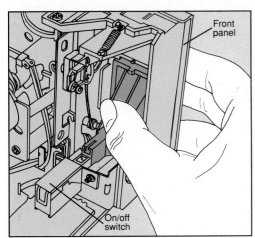

Front panel

On/off switch

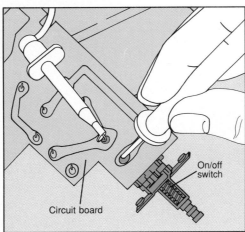

Circuit board

On/off switch

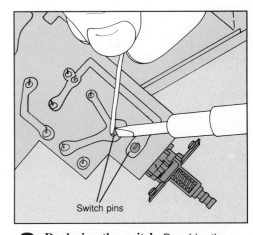

Switch pins

1 **Testing the switch.** Unplug the unit. Remove the top panel *(page 371)*. Disengage the control lever from the on/off switch *(above, left)*, unscrew the switch and the circuit board, and turn over the circuit board. Set a multitester to test continuity. Hook one probe to one switch pin and touch the other probe to the other switch pin *(above, right)*. Set the switch to the ON position, then to the OFF position. The multitester should register continuity only in the ON position. If the switch tests faulty, replace it *(step 2)*. If the switch tests OK, screw in the circuit board and the switch, reconnect the control lever, and take the unit for professional service.

2 **Replacing the switch.** Desolder the pins *(page 417)*, turn over the circuit board and pull off the switch. Purchase an exact replacement switch at an electronics parts supplier. Fit the pins into the circuit board and solder the pins *(above)*. Screw in the circuit board and the switch, put back the control lever, and reinstall the top panel. Cold check the unit for leaking voltage *(page 417)*.

SERVICING THE PLAY/RECORD SWITCH

Play/record switch

1 **Cleaning the switch.** Unplug the unit and remove the top panel *(page 371)*. Locate the play/record switch on the circuit board. To clean the switch, spray short bursts of electronic contact cleaner through the opening in the switch casing. Press in and release the switch several times to work in the cleaner *(left)*, taking care not to damage the hook-like switch lever connected to the tape transport assembly. Reinstall the top panel. If the problem persists, remove the top and back panels *(page 371)* and turn over the circuit board *(step 2)* to reach the play/record switch pins.

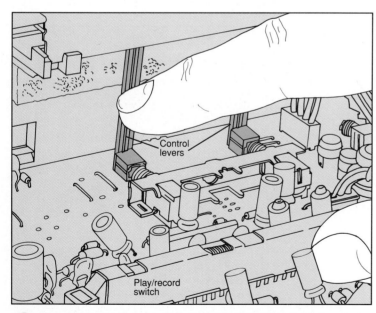

Control levers

Play/record switch

2 **Turning over the circuit board.** Carefully disengage the play/record switch lever connected to the tape transport assembly from the play/record switch; use long-nose pliers or tweezers, if required. Push the control levers off the tape selector and noise reduction switches *(above)*. To reach the switch pins, unscrew the circuit board, remove any components in the way and turn over the circuit board, avoiding damage to any wire connections.

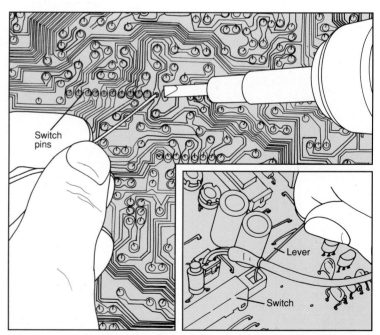

Switch pins

Lever

Switch

3 **Removing and replacing the switch.** Desolder the switch pins *(page 417)*. Turn over the circuit board and pull off the switch; wiggle it to help release the pins. Order an exact replacement play/record switch from the manufacturer or purchase a substitute at an electronics parts supplier. Fit the switch pins into the circuit board, turn over the circuit board and solder the pins *(above)*. Put back the circuit board, reversing the sequence used to remove it *(step 2)*. Carefully reconnect the switch lever to the play/record switch *(inset)*. Reinstall the back and top panels, and cold check for leaking voltage.

SERVICING THE RECORD LEVEL POTENTIOMETER

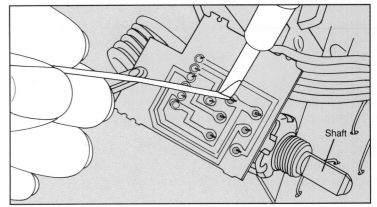

Potentiometer

1 **Cleaning and testing the potentiometer.** Unplug the unit. Remove the top panel *(page 371)* and locate the potentiometer on the circuit board behind its control. Spray electronic contact cleaner into the potentiometer casing *(inset)* and rotate the control back and forth to work it in. If the problem persists, test the potentiometer. Set a multitester to test resistance. Clip one probe to the center pin in one row on the circuit board and touch the other probe in turn to the other pins in the row *(above)*, turning the control back and forth. The multitester should register an ohms variation for each pin. Test the other row of pins the same way. If the potentiometer tests faulty, remove it *(step 2)*. Otherwise, suspect a faulty circuit board and take the audiocassette recorder for professional service.

Shaft

2 **Removing and replacing the potentiometer.** Pull the control knob off the potentiometer and unscrew the shaft locknut. Lift out the potentiometer and circuit board, pulling the shaft through the opening in the front panel. Desolder the potentiometer pins *(page 417)*, and pull off the potentiometer; wiggle it to help release the pins. Test resistance again to confirm the potentiometer is faulty *(step 1)*. Purchase an exact replacement potentiometer at an electronics parts supplier. Fit the potentiometer pins into the circuit board, turn it over and solder the pins *(above)*. Slide the shaft through the opening in the front panel, screw on the shaft locknut and put back the control. If the potentiometer now tests OK, but the problem persists, suspect a faulty circuit board and take the audiocassette recorder for professional service. Reinstall the top panel and cold check for leaking voltage *(page 417)*.

SERVICING THE FEATURE SWITCHES

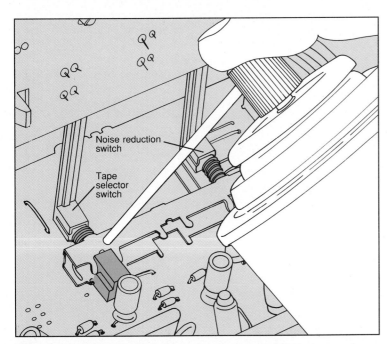

Noise reduction switch

Tape selector switch

1 **Cleaning the switch.** Unplug the unit. Remove the top panel *(page 371)* and locate the switch on the circuit board behind the control. Spray short bursts of electronic contact cleaner through the opening in the switch casing *(above)*; press in and release the control several times to work in the cleaner. Reinstall the top panel. If the problem persists, remove the top panel and turn over the circuit board *(page 378)* to reach the switch pins.

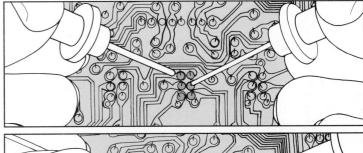

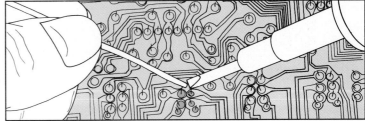

2 **Testing and replacing the switch.** Set a multitester to test continuity. Touch one probe to the center pin in one row and touch the other probe in turn to the other pins in the row *(above, top)*. For each switch setting, the multitester should register continuity with only one pair of pins. Test the other row of pins. If the switch tests faulty, desolder the pins *(page 417)* and pull off the switch. Purchase a replacement switch at an electronics parts supplier. Solder the pins into the circuit board *(above, bottom)*. If the switch tests OK, suspect a faulty circuit board and take the audiocassette recorder for professional service. Put back the circuit board, reversing the sequence used to remove it, and reinstall the panels. Cold check the unit for leaking voltage *(page 417)*.

TURNTABLES

The turntable *(below)*, whether belt-drive or direct-drive, automatic or manual, is the most mechanical unit of the audio system. The stylus tracks the grooves of a record turning on the platter. The cartridge transforms this motion into an electrical signal, sending it through wires in the tone arm to cables leading to the receiver. There, the signal is amplified and sent through cables to the speakers.

To diagnose the turntable as the source of audio problems, consult the Troubleshooting Guide in Entertainment Systems *(page 356)* and in this chapter *(page 381)*. Most problems can be remedied by securing cable hookups, rebalancing the tone arm, realigning the cartridge or servicing the power supply.

Make sure the turntable is level so that it can work properly. Replacement components are usually available at an electronics parts supplier; special parts, however, may have to be ordered from the turntable manufacturer.

A set of small screwdrivers, a multitester and a soldering iron make up the basic tool kit for turntable repairs. Refer to Tools & Techniques *(page 417)* for tips on disassembly and reassembly, electrical testing, and desoldering and soldering.

Turn off and unplug the turntable before attempting any repair. Disconnect its cables and set it on a clean work table. Perform a cold check for leaking voltage *(page 417)* after reassembling the turntable but before plugging it in.

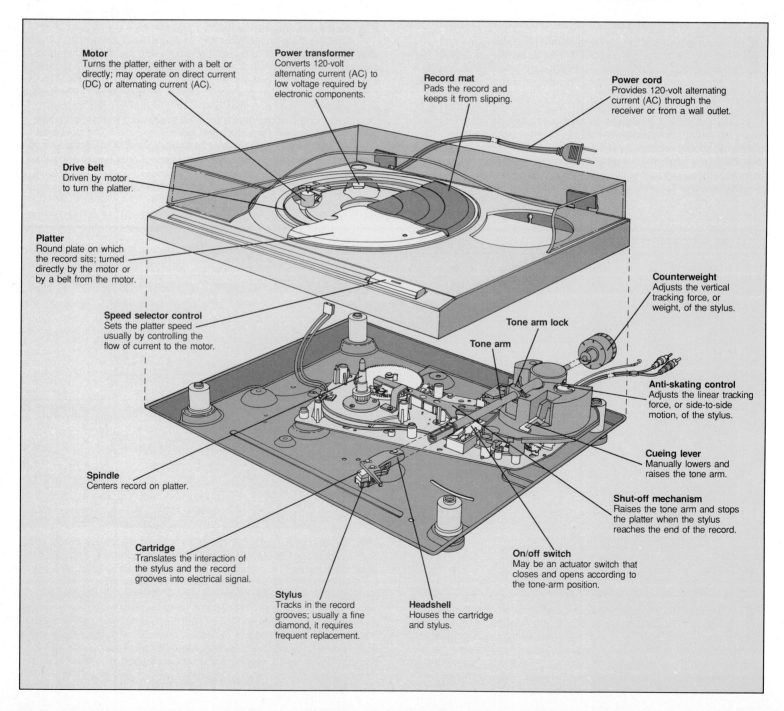

Motor
Turns the platter, either with a belt or directly; may operate on direct current (DC) or alternating current (AC).

Power transformer
Converts 120-volt alternating current (AC) to low voltage required by electronic components.

Record mat
Pads the record and keeps it from slipping.

Power cord
Provides 120-volt alternating current (AC) through the receiver or from a wall outlet.

Drive belt
Driven by motor to turn the platter.

Platter
Round plate on which the record sits; turned directly by the motor or by a belt from the motor.

Counterweight
Adjusts the vertical tracking force, or weight, of the stylus.

Speed selector control
Sets the platter speed usually by controlling the flow of current to the motor.

Tone arm lock

Tone arm

Anti-skating control
Adjusts the linear tracking force, or side-to-side motion, of the stylus.

Cueing lever
Manually lowers and raises the tone arm.

Spindle
Centers record on platter.

Shut-off mechanism
Raises the tone arm and stops the platter when the stylus reaches the end of the record.

Cartridge
Translates the interaction of the stylus and the record grooves into electrical signal.

On/off switch
May be an actuator switch that closes and opens according to the tone-arm position.

Stylus
Tracks in the record grooves; usually a fine diamond, it requires frequent replacement.

Headshell
Houses the cartridge and stylus.

TROUBLESHOOTING GUIDE

SYMPTOM	POSSIBLE CAUSE	PROCEDURE
Platter does not turn	Turntable unplugged or turned off	Plug in and turn on turntable
	No power to outlet or outlet faulty	Reset breaker or replace fuse *(p. 102)* □○; service outlet *(p. 148)*
	Receiver faulty	Troubleshoot entertainment system *(p. 356)* □○
	Power cord faulty	Test and replace power cord *(p. 417)* □○
	Drive belt loose or broken	Service drive belt *(p. 383)* □○
	Shutoff mechanism jammed	Clean shutoff gears and levers with foam swab and denatured alcohol; then lubricate with light machine oil
	On/off switch faulty	Test and replace on/off switch *(p. 387)* □○
	Power supply or motor faulty	Take turntable for professional service
	Circuit board faulty	Take turntable for professional service
Platter turns at wrong speed or at only one speed	Drive belt dirty or loose	Service drive belt *(p. 383)* □○
	Motor running too fast or too slow	Adjust motor speed *(p. 384)* □○
	Shutoff mechanism dirty	Clean shutoff gears and levers with foam swab and denatured alcohol; then lubricate with light machine oil
	Speed selector switch faulty	Test and replace speed selector switch *(p. 387)* □○
	Power supply or motor faulty	Take turntable for professional service
	Circuit board faulty	Take turntable for professional service
Platter does not stop turning or stops before end of record	Shutoff mechanism dirty or jammed	Clean shutoff gears and levers with foam swab and denatured alcohol; then lubricate with light machine oil
	Shutoff mechanism faulty	Take turntable for professional service
No sound	Receiver faulty	Troubleshoot entertainment system *(p. 356)* □○
	Cartridge faulty	Test and replace cartridge *(p. 385)* □○
	Tone arm wires loose or broken	Service tone arm *(p. 386)* □○
	Circuit board faulty	Take turntable for professional service
Sound from only one channel or intermittent sound	Record or stylus dusty	Clean record and stylus *(p. 382)* □○
	Receiver or speaker faulty	Troubleshoot entertainment system *(p. 356)* □○
	Tone arm unbalanced	Balance tone arm *(p. 382)* □○
	Cartridge misaligned	Adjust cartridge *(p. 383)* □○▲
	Stylus worn or broken	Replace stylus assembly *(p. 384)* □○
	Cartridge faulty	Test and replace cartridge *(p. 385)* □○
	Tone arm wire loose or broken	Service tone arm *(p. 386)* □○
	Circuit board faulty	Take turntable for professional service
Sound distorted; scratching or hissing noise	Record or stylus dusty	Clean record and stylus *(p. 382)* □○
	Receiver or speaker faulty	Troubleshoot entertainment system *(p. 356)* □○
	Tone arm unbalanced	Balance tone arm *(p. 382)* □○
	Cartridge misaligned	Adjust cartridge *(p. 383)* □○▲
	Stylus worn or broken	Replace stylus assembly *(p. 384)* □○
	Cartridge faulty	Test and replace cartridge *(p. 385)* □○
	Circuit board faulty	Take turntable for professional service
Humming, buzzing or rumbling noise	Ground wire loose	Check ground wire connection *(p. 359)* □○
	Receiver or speaker faulty	Troubleshoot entertainment system *(p. 356)* □○
	Cartridge faulty	Test and replace cartridge *(p. 385)* □○
	Circuit board faulty	Take turntable for professional service
Burning odor	Power supply or motor faulty	Take turntable for professional service
	Circuit board faulty	Take turntable for professional service

DEGREE OF DIFFICULTY: □ Easy ▨ Moderate ▪ Complex
ESTIMATED TIME: ○ Less than 1 hour ◖ 1 to 3 hours ● Over 3 hours ▲ Special tool required

CLEANING RECORDS AND THE STYLUS

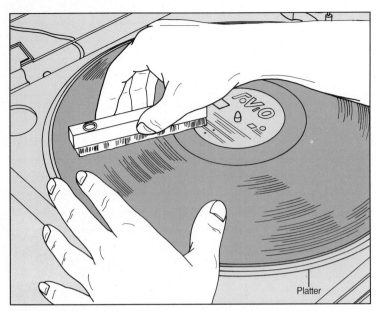

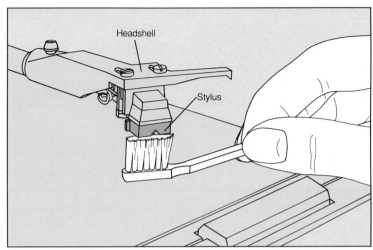

1 **Dusting records.** Turn off the turntable, leaving the record in place on the spindle. Position a nylon record brush across the record and lightly touch the bristles to the grooves. Applying steady, gentle pressure on the brush with one hand, slowly rotate the platter with the other hand *(above)*. Wipe off the brush on a clean, lint-free cloth. Turn over the record and repeat this step. Turn on the turntable. To prevent record damage, perform this procedure before each play. If the record sound quality is still poor, clean the stylus *(step 2)*.

2 **Brushing the stylus.** Turn off the turntable. With the tone arm at rest on its stand, position a nylon stylus brush behind the stylus, just below the headshell. Pull the brush slowly forward from under the headshell, lightly touching the bristles to the stylus *(above)*; avoid any side-to-side or front-to-back motion. Wipe off the brush on a clean, lint-free cloth. Turn on the turntable. To prevent damage to the stylus or records, perform this procedure before each record-playing session.

BALANCING THE TONE ARM

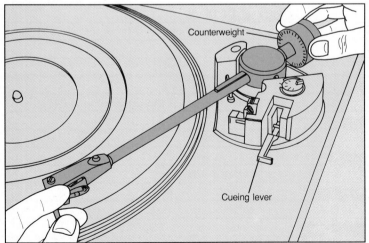

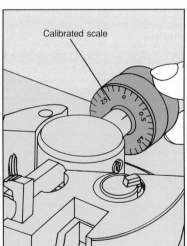

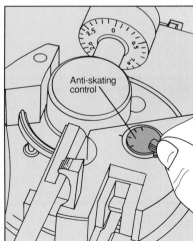

Adjusting the counterweight and the anti-skating control. Turn off the turntable and remove the record from the platter. With the tone arm at rest on its stand, flip down the stylus guard, if any, and set the anti-skating control to 0. With the cueing lever lowered, lift the tone arm and position it over the platter. Supporting the tone arm with one hand, rotate the counterweight with the other hand until the tone arm floats perpendicular above the platter; then turn the calibrated scale control until the 0 on the scale is aligned with the mark on the tone arm *(above, left)*. Place the tone arm back on its stand. Set the counterweight and calibrated scale to the midpoint of the range specified by the cartridge manufacturer *(above, center)*; adjust the anti-skating control to the identical setting *(above, right)*. Flip up the stylus guard, if any.

ADJUSTING THE CARTRIDGE

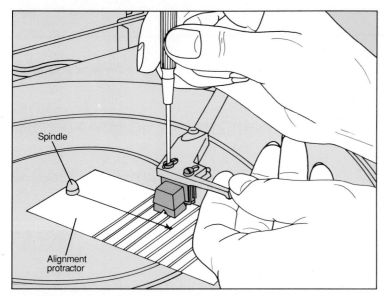

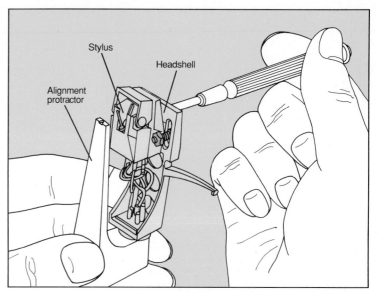

Realigning a straight tone-arm cartridge. Turn off the turntable and remove the record from the platter. If the tone arm starts and stops the platter, unplug the turntable from the receiver *(page 354)* or wall outlet. Use a straight tone-arm alignment protractor supplied by the turntable manufacturer or purchased at an electronics parts supplier. Position the protractor on the spindle and gently lower the tone arm to seat the stylus in the stylus opening on the protractor. Check the cartridge alignment by looking straight down from above the tone arm. If the cartridge is not exactly parallel to the grid lines, lift the tone arm and loosen the cartridge screws *(above)*. Lower the tone arm to reseat the stylus and adjust the cartridge so it is exactly parallel to the grid lines. Lift the tone arm and tighten the headshell screws. Place the tone arm back on its stand and remove the protractor.

Realigning a J- or S-shaped tone-arm cartridge. Turn off the turntable and remove the headshell *(page 385)*. Depending on the shape of the tone arm, use a J- or S-shaped tone-arm alignment protractor supplied by the turntable manufacturer or purchased at an electronics parts supplier. Position the headshell in the protractor and check the cartridge alignment by looking straight down at the cartridge from the front of the headshell. If the stylus is not exactly centered over the stylus mark on the protractor, loosen the cartridge screws *(above)*. Adjust the cartridge so the stylus is exactly centered over the stylus mark and tighten the headshell screws. Reinstall the headshell.

SERVICING THE DRIVE BELT

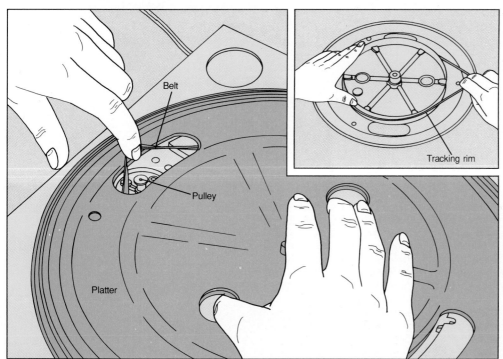

Cleaning and replacing the drive belt.
Unplug the turntable, remove the record from the platter and lock the tone arm. Lift off the record mat and locate the drive belt through the opening in the platter. Pull the belt away from the pulley *(left)*, lift off the platter and remove the belt. If the belt is worn or broken, order an exact replacement belt from the turntable manufacturer or purchase a substitute belt at an electronics parts supplier. If the belt is sticky or greasy, wipe it thoroughly using a clean, lint-free cloth sprinkled with rubber cleaning compound; never apply anything oily. To replace the belt, turn the platter face down and wrap the belt around the tracking rim *(inset)*, pulling it to the opening in the platter. Lift the platter enough to reach the belt through the opening from the other side and turn the platter upright without twisting the belt. Still holding the belt, reseat the platter and pull the belt around the pulley. Put back the record mat and unlock the tone arm. Adjust the motor speed *(page 384)* if necessary.

ADJUSTING THE MOTOR SPEED

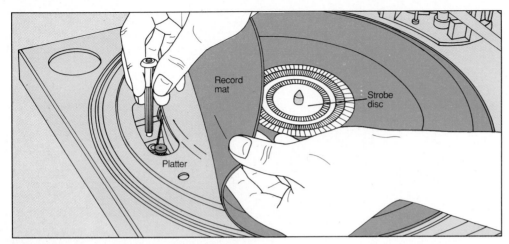

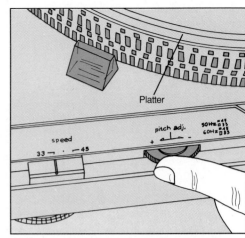

Fine-tuning the speed using a strobe disc. Turn off the turntable and remove the record from the platter. If the turntable is not equipped with a built-in stroboscope, use a strobe disc supplied by the turntable manufacturer or purchased at an electronics parts supplier. Locate the pitch adjustment screws, either on the top panel or reached through openings in the platter beneath the record mat, as shown. Position the strobe disc on the spindle and turn on the turntable. Shine a fluorescent light on the turntable and observe the strobe disc markings that correspond to the speed-selector switch setting. Adjust the screw corresponding to the switch setting to the exact point at which the markings appear as a solid, motionless band. If the screw is under the platter, you must turn off the turntable, lift up the record mat and adjust the screw *(above)*; then, put back the record mat, turn on the turntable and again observe the strobe disc markings. Repeat this procedure, if required, for each speed selector switch setting.

Fine-tuning the speed using a built-in stroboscope. Turn on the turntable and observe the stroboscope markings on the outer edge of the platter that correspond to the speed-selector switch setting. Adjust the pitch adjustment control dial on the front, top or side of the turntable to the exact point at which the markings appear as a solid, motionless band *(above)*. Repeat this procedure, if required, for each speed-selector switch setting.

REPLACING THE STYLUS ASSEMBLY

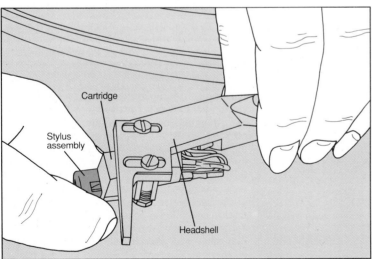

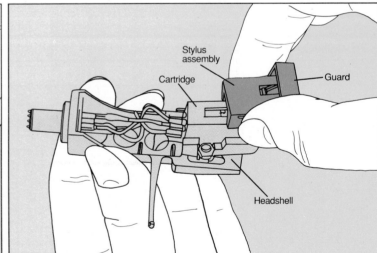

Installing a new stylus assembly. Turn off the turntable and flip down the stylus guard, if any. Lift up the tone arm to check how the stylus assembly fits into the cartridge; if you cannot determine how to take out the stylus assembly, remove the headshell *(page 385)* and take it to an electronics parts supplier. In many cases, the stylus assembly slides out from tracks under the cartridge. Grip the headshell in one hand and gently pull the stylus assembly straight out from under the cartridge using a thumb and forefinger *(above, left)*. In other cases, the stylus assembly is pulled straight off the cartridge. For better access to this type, remove the headshell *(page 385)* and turn it over. Grip the headshell in one hand and pull straight up on the stylus assembly with the other *(above, right)*. Purchase an identical replacement stylus assembly from an electronics parts supplier. Slide the stylus assembly along the tracks of the cartridge until it fits snugly, or press the stylus assembly into the cartridge and reinstall the headshell. Flip up the stylus guard, if any. If necessary, adjust the cartridge *(page 383)* and balance the tone arm *(page 382)*.

TESTING AND REPLACING THE CARTRIDGE

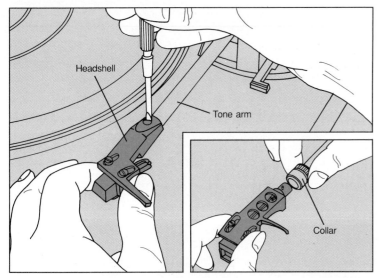

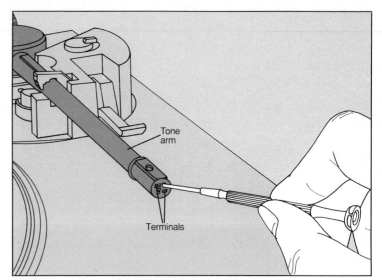

1 **Removing the headshell.** Turn off the turntable and lock the tone arm. Flip down the stylus guard, if any, or remove the stylus assembly if it slides out easily from under the cartridge *(page 384)*. Supporting the headshell with one hand, loosen the screw *(above)* or the collar *(inset)* securing it to the tone arm and gently slide it off. If the headshell cannot be detached, test the cartridge wires *(step 3)*. Turn over the headshell and check the cartridge wire connections. If the wire connections are secure, check for signal through the tone arm *(step 2)*. If a wire is loose, carefully reconnect it to its terminal using tweezers. Reinstall the headshell and, if required, put back the stylus assembly or flip up the stylus guard. Unlock the tone arm.

2 **Checking for signal through the tone arm.** To check the wire connections beyond the headshell, turn on the turntable and receiver, set the receiver selector control to PHONO and adjust the receiver volume control to slightly above its lowest setting. Using a small metal screwdriver or holding a larger screwdriver by its blade, lightly touch the screwdriver tip to each terminal at the end of the tone arm *(above)*. If there is an audible hum from the speakers at more or less than two tone-arm terminals, test the tone arm wires *(page 386)*. If there is an audible hum from the speakers at only two tone-arm terminals, turn off the turntable and test the cartridge wires *(step 3)*.

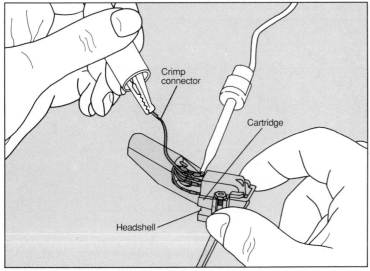

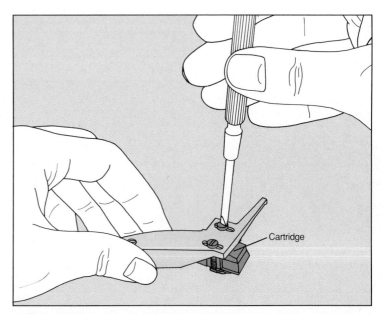

3 **Testing the cartridge wires.** Set a multitester to test continuity. Hook one probe to the crimp connector at the end of one wire and touch the other probe to the crimp connector at the other end of the wire; for easier access, pull the wire off its terminal *(above)*. Test each wire. If each wire registers continuity, install a new cartridge *(step 4)*. If each wire does not register continuity, purchase an identical replacement set of cartridge wires from an electronics parts supplier. If the cartridge wire terminals are not coded to the cartridge wire colors, note the terminal positions for the wires or remove and replace the wires one at a time. Reinstall the headshell *(step 1)*.

4 **Installing a new cartridge.** To remove the cartridge, disconnect the cartridge wires from the cartridge terminals and unscrew the cartridge from the headshell. If required, remove the stylus assembly *(page 384)*. Purchase a replacement cartridge at an electronics parts supplier. Reinstall the stylus assembly, screw the cartridge to the headshell *(above)* and connect the cartridge wires to the terminals using tweezers. If the cartridge terminals are not coded to the wire colors, connect the wires in the identical sequence as at the headshell terminals. Reinstall the headshell *(step 1)*. If necessary, adjust the cartridge *(page 383)* and balance the tone arm *(page 382)*.

ACCESS TO THE INTERNAL COMPONENTS

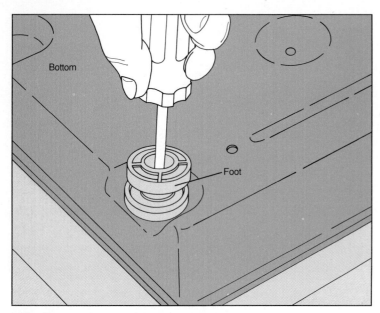

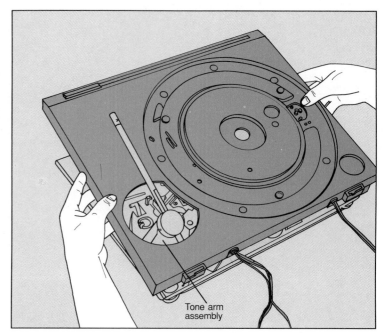

1 **Unscrewing the bottom panel.** Turn off the turntable and unplug it from the receiver or wall outlet. Remove any record from the platter and lock the tone arm. Disconnect the turntable cables and ground wire hooked up to the receiver *(page 354)*. Secure any transit screws, remove the record mat and lift off the platter; if required, first remove the drive belt *(page 383)*. Turn over the turntable and unscrew the bottom panel, checking for hidden screws in the turntable feet *(above)*. Lift off the bottom panel if the tone arm assembly is mounted on the top panel. If the tone arm assembly is mounted through an opening in the top panel, remove the top panel *(step 2)*.

2 **Lifting off the top panel.** Carefully turn the turntable upright, pull off the dust cover, and remove the headshell *(page 385)*. Screw off the counterweight, remove the counterweight shaft and unlock the tone arm. Lift up the top panel, slide the tone arm through the opening for the tone arm assembly *(above)* and relock the tone arm. Gently turn the top panel face down beside the bottom panel. Reinstall the top and bottom panel, and reconnect the cables *(page 358)* and ground wire *(page 359)*. Rebalance the tone arm *(page 382)*.

SERVICING THE TONE ARM

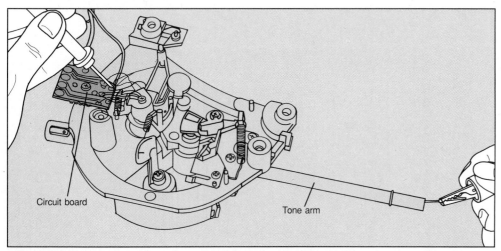

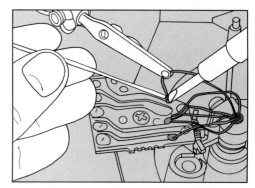

1 **Testing the tone arm wires.** Unplug the unit. Remove the top or bottom panel *(step above)*. If the tone arm assembly is mounted on the bottom panel, unscrew it and carefully turn it over, as shown, to reach the tone-arm wire contact points on the circuit board. If a wire is loose or broken, repair it *(page 417)*. Set a multitester to test continuity. Touch one probe to a wire terminal on the tone arm and touch the other probe in turn to each wire contact point on the circuit board *(above)*. The multitester should register continuity once—and only once. Test each wire; if one is faulty, replace the tone arm *(step 2)*. If each wire tests OK, screw the tone arm assembly in place, if required, and reinstall the top or bottom panel *(step above)*. If the problem persists, suspect a faulty circuit board and take the turntable for professional service.

2 **Replacing the tone arm.** Note the wire positions and desolder the wires *(page 417)*. Remove the headshell *(page 385)*, unlock the tone arm and unscrew it from the tone arm assembly. Order an exact replacement from the manufacturer or purchase a substitute at an electronics parts supplier. Thread the tone arm wires through the opening in the tone arm assembly, screw in the tone arm and lock it. Solder the wires to the circuit board, turning over the turntable, if required. Reinstall the top or bottom panel *(step above)* and the headshell, then cold check for leaking voltage *(page 417)*.

SERVICING THE ON/OFF SWITCH

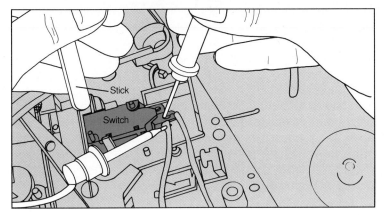

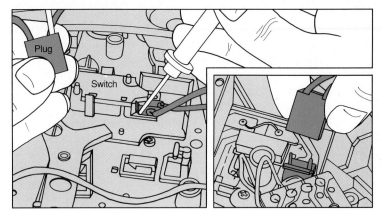

1 **Testing the switch.** Unplug the unit. Remove the top or bottom panel *(page 386)* and locate the on/off switch terminals. Set a multitester to test continuity. Hook one probe to one switch terminal and touch the other probe to the other switch terminal. Set the switch to the ON position and then to the OFF position; for an actuator switch, use a small stick to press in and release the side button *(above)*. The switch should have continuity only in the ON position. If the switch tests OK, test the switch wires *(step 2)*. If the switch tests faulty, desolder the wires *(page 417)* from the switch terminals and install a replacement switch. Solder the wires and reinstall the top or bottom panel.

2 **Testing the wires.** Locate the contact points on the circuit board for the wires connected to the switch terminals; if the wires are connected to contact pins in a plug, remove the plug from the circuit board *(inset)*. Touch one probe to a wire terminal on the switch and touch the other probe to the wire's contact point in the plug *(above)* or on the circuit board. Repeat this procedure for the other switch wire. If a wire does not have continuity, replace it *(page 417)*. If each wire has continuity, service the power supply *(below)*.

SERVICING THE SPEED SELECTOR SWITCH

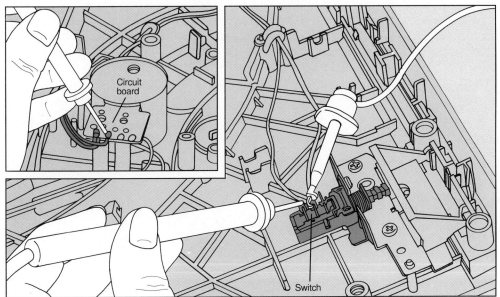

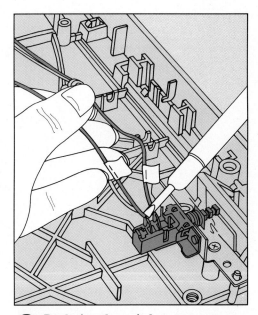

1 **Testing the switch.** Unplug the unit. Remove the top or bottom panel *(page 386)* and locate the speed-selector switch terminals. Set a multitester to test continuity. If the switch has two wires, hook one probe to one switch wire terminal and touch the other probe to the other switch wire terminal *(above)*. Set the switch to one position, then the other. The multitester should register continuity in only one position. If the switch has three wires, hook one probe to the center terminal and touch the other probe, in turn, to each of the other two terminals. In each switch position, the multitester should register continuity between only one pair of wires. If the switch tests faulty, replace it *(step 2)*. If the switch tests OK, locate the contact points for the switch wires on the circuit board. Hook one probe to a wire terminal at the switch and touch the other probe to the wire's contact point on the circuit board *(inset)*. Repeat this test for the other switch wire. If a wire does not have continuity, replace it. If each wire has continuity, have the motor tested.

2 **Replacing the switch.** Label each switch wire, noting its terminal, and desolder the wires. Unscrew the switch from its mounting. Buy an exact replacement switch at an electronics parts supplier. Screw in the switch and solder the wires to the terminals *(above)*. Reinstall the top or bottom panel and cold check for leaking voltage *(page 417)*. If the problem persists, have the motor tested.

COMPACT DISC PLAYERS

The compact disc player is the most intricate unit of the audio system, performing complex optical functions. The objective lens focuses the laser onto digitally-encoded tracks stamped in the rotating compact disc. The optical pickup assembly transforms the patterns of reflected light into an electrical signal. After further electronic modification, this signal is sent out by cables to the receiver, which amplifies it.

To diagnose problems, consult the Troubleshooting Guide in Entertainment Systems *(page 356)* and in this chapter *(page 389)*. Many problems can be remedied by adjusting cable hookups, cleaning the compact disc or the objective lens, or servicing a drive belt or a wire. Cleaning supplies and replace-ment components are available at an electronics parts supplier; specific parts may have to be ordered from the manufacturer.

A set of small screwdrivers, a multitester and a soldering iron compose the basic tool kit for compact-disc player re-pairs. Refer to Tools & Techniques *(page 417)* for instructions on disassembly and reassembly, testing continuity and volt-age, and desoldering and soldering. While working, store fas-teners and other small parts in labeled containers and write down the sequence of disassembly steps. Never look directly at the laser with the power on. Cold check for leaking voltage *(page 417)* after reassembling the compact disc player, but before plugging it in.

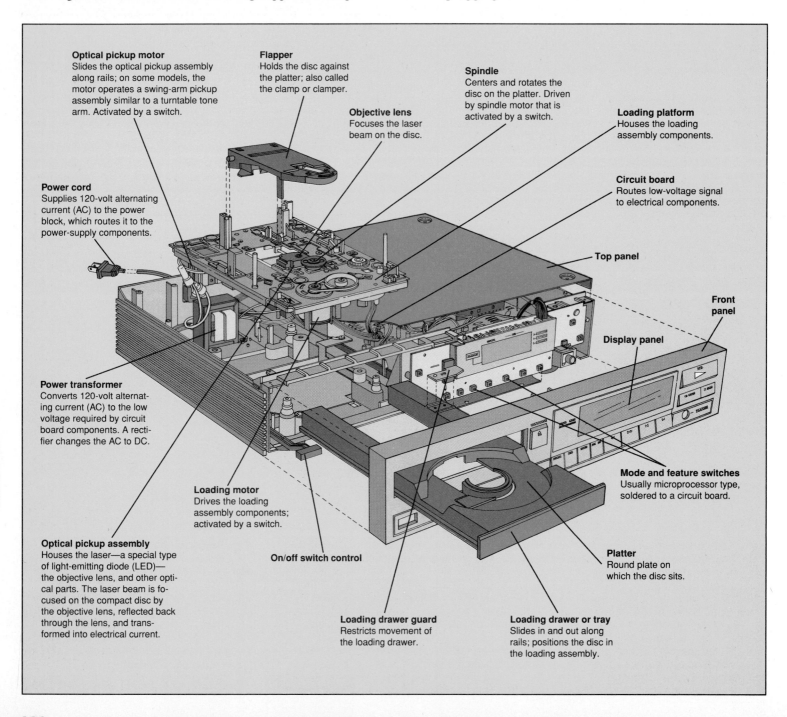

Optical pickup motor
Slides the optical pickup assembly along rails; on some models, the motor operates a swing-arm pickup assembly similar to a turntable tone arm. Activated by a switch.

Flapper
Holds the disc against the platter; also called the clamp or clamper.

Spindle
Centers and rotates the disc on the platter. Driven by spindle motor that is activated by a switch.

Objective lens
Focuses the laser beam on the disc.

Loading platform
Houses the loading assembly components.

Power cord
Supplies 120-volt alternating current (AC) to the power block, which routes it to the power-supply components.

Circuit board
Routes low-voltage signal to electrical components.

Top panel

Front panel

Power transformer
Converts 120-volt alternat-ing current (AC) to the low voltage required by circuit board components. A recti-fier changes the AC to DC.

Display panel

Loading motor
Drives the loading assembly components; activated by a switch.

Mode and feature switches
Usually microprocessor type, soldered to a circuit board.

Optical pickup assembly
Houses the laser—a special type of light-emitting diode (LED)— the objective lens, and other opti-cal parts. The laser beam is fo-cused on the compact disc by the objective lens, reflected back through the lens, and trans-formed into electrical current.

On/off switch control

Platter
Round plate on which the disc sits.

Loading drawer guard
Restricts movement of the loading drawer.

Loading drawer or tray
Slides in and out along rails; positions the disc in the loading assembly.

TROUBLESHOOTING GUIDE

SYMPTOM	POSSIBLE CAUSE	PROCEDURE
No display lights, no sound	Compact disc player unplugged or off	Plug in and turn on compact disc player
	Remote control faulty	Service remote control *(p. 417)* □○; replace batteries
	No power to outlet or outlet faulty	Reset breaker or replace fuse *(p. 102)* □○; service outlet *(p. 148)*
	Power cord faulty	Test and replace power cord *(p. 417)* □○
	Power fuse faulty	Test and replace power fuse *(p. 417)* □○
	On/off switch faulty	Test and replace on/off switch *(p. 393)* ■◐
	Power supply faulty	Take compact disc player for professional service
	Laser or circuit board faulty	Take compact disc player for professional service
Display lights, no sound	Controls set incorrectly	Adjust compact disc player controls
	Transit screws secured	Loosen transit screws on bottom of unit
	Receiver faulty	Troubleshoot entertainment system *(p. 356)* □○
	Objective lens dirty	Clean objective lens *(p. 391)* □○
	Drive belt loose or broken	Service drive belts *(p. 392)* □○
	Optical pickup/spindle motor switch faulty	Clean, test and replace motor switch *(p. 392)* □○
	Mode or feature switch dirty or faulty	Clean switch *(p. 393)* □○; test and replace switch *(p. 393)* ◨○
	Optical pickup motor faulty	Take compact disc player for professional service
	Spindle motor faulty	Take compact disc player for professional service
	Laser or circuit board faulty	Take compact disc player for professional service
Sound, no display lights	Display lights faulty	Take compact disc player for professional service
Sound from only one channel	Controls set incorrectly	Adjust compact disc player controls
	Receiver or speaker faulty	Troubleshoot entertainment system *(p. 356)* □○
	Circuit board faulty	Take compact disc player for professional service
Sound intermittent or distorted	Receiver or speaker faulty	Troubleshoot entertainment system *(p. 356)* □○
	Compact disc dirty or faulty	Clean compact disc *(p. 390)* □○; replace compact disc
	Objective lens dirty	Clean objective lens *(p. 391)* □○
	Drive belt dirty or loose	Service drive belts *(p. 392)* □○
	Optical pickup/spindle motor switch faulty	Clean, test and replace motor switch *(p. 392)* □○
	Mode or feature switch dirty or faulty	Clean switch *(p. 393)* □○; test and replace switch *(p. 393)* ◨○
	Optical pickup motor faulty	Take compact disc player for professional service
	Spindle motor faulty	Take compact disc player for professional service
	Circuit board faulty	Take compact disc player for professional service
Mode or feature control doesn't work	Mode or feature switch dirty or faulty	Clean switch *(p. 393)* □○; test and replace switch *(p. 393)* ◨○
	Laser or circuit board faulty	Take compact disc player for professional service
Compact disc loads, plays, then stops prematurely	Transit screws secured	Loosen transit screws on bottom of unit
	Compact disc dirty or faulty	Clean compact disc *(p. 390)* □○; replace compact disc
	Objective lens dirty	Clean objective lens *(p. 391)* □○
	Drive belt loose or broken	Service drive belts *(p. 392)* □○
	Optical pickup/spindle motor switch faulty	Clean, test and replace motor switch *(p. 392)* □○
	Optical pickup motor faulty	Take compact disc player for professional service
	Spindle motor faulty	Take compact disc player for professional service
	Laser or circuit board faulty	Take compact disc player for professional service
Loading drawer doesn't open or doesn't close	Drive belt loose or broken	Service drive belts *(p. 392)* □○
	Loading motor switch faulty	Clean, test and replace loading motor switch *(p. 392)* □○
	On/off switch faulty	Test and replace on/off switch *(p. 393)* ■◐
	Loading motor faulty	Take compact disc player for professional service

DEGREE OF DIFFICULTY: □ Easy ◨ Moderate ■ Complex
ESTIMATED TIME: ○ Less than 1 hour ◐ 1 to 3 hours ● Over 3 hours

SERVICING COMPACT DISCS

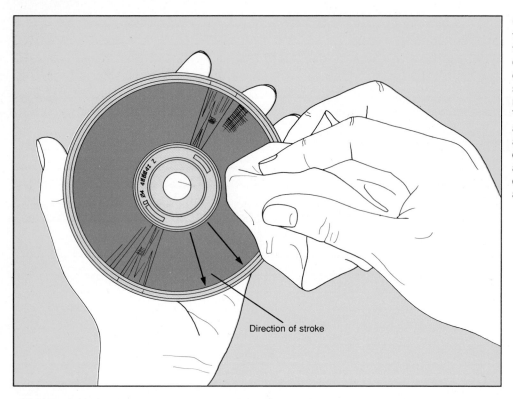

Direction of stroke

Cleaning a disc. Unload the compact disc from the compact disc player. Using a clean, dry, lint-free cloth, wipe dust off the disc. Holding the disc by its outside edge, gently wipe from the center toward the edge in smooth, straight strokes *(left)*; avoid any circular motion and never wipe around the disc circumference. To clean sticky fingerprints or dirt from the disc, apply a commercial compact-disc cleaner, available at an electronics parts supplier. Or, use a clean, lint-free cloth moistened with denatured alcohol. A disc may be washed with a solution of mild detergent and warm water; rinse well and dry with a lint-free cloth.

ACCESS TO THE INTERNAL COMPONENTS

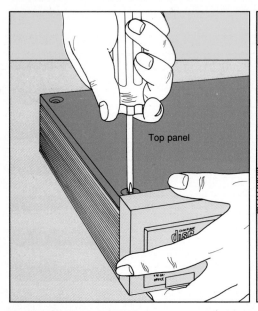

Top panel

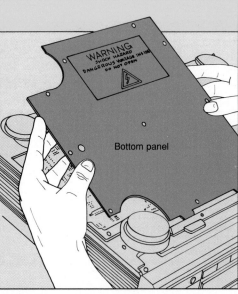

WARNING
SHOCK HAZARD
DANGEROUS VOLTAGE INSIDE
DO NOT OPEN

Bottom panel

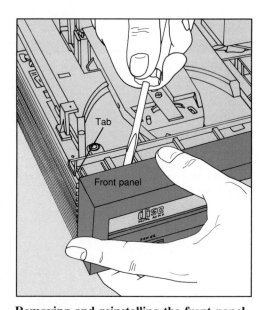

Tab

Front panel

Removing and reinstalling the top and bottom panels. To reach components beneath the loading assembly, first open the loading door *(page 391)*. Unload any compact disc, turn off and unplug the compact disc player, and disconnect the cables hooked up to it *(page 354)*. Secure any transit screws. To remove the top panel, check for screws on the top, sides, back or bottom. Unscrew the top panel *(above, left)*, slide it out from under any lip on the front panel, and lift it off the frame. To remove the bottom panel, check for hidden screws in the feet; unscrew the panel and lift it off the frame *(above, right)*. Reverse this sequence to reinstall the panels. Cold check the compact disc player for leaking voltage *(page 417)*. Reconnect the cables *(page 358)* and plug in the compact disc player.

Removing and reinstalling the front panel or plate. Remove the top panel *(left)*. Check the top, sides and bottom for tabs and screws securing the front panel or plate to the frame. Unscrew the front panel or plate, press in the tabs *(above)* and pull it off. To reinstall the front panel or plate, push it onto the frame to lock the tabs and put back the screws. Reinstall the top panel *(left)*, and cold check for leaking voltage *(page 417)*.

ACCESS TO THE INTERNAL COMPONENTS (continued)

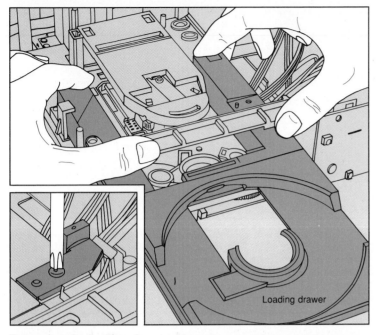

Loading drawer

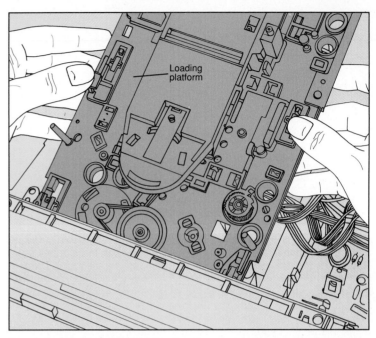

Loading platform

Removing the loading drawer. Press the open/close control to open the loading drawer, then remove the top panel *(page 390)*. Unscrew the loading drawer guard *(inset)* and set it aside. Gently slide out the loading drawer through the front panel *(above)*. To reach components beneath the loading assembly, remove the loading platform *(right)*. To reinstall the loading drawer, slide it in through the front panel and screw on the guard. Reinstall the top panel and press the open/close control to close the loading drawer.

Removing the loading platform. Press the open/close control to open the loading drawer. Remove the top panel *(page 390)* and the loading drawer *(left)*. Unscrew the loading platform and disconnect any ground wire connected to it. Lift out the loading platform, sliding it toward the back panel *(above)*. Turn it face down inside the compact disc player, taking care not to damage wire connections. Reverse this sequence to reinstall the loading platform. Reinstall the loading drawer *(left)* and the top panel.

SERVICING THE OBJECTIVE LENS

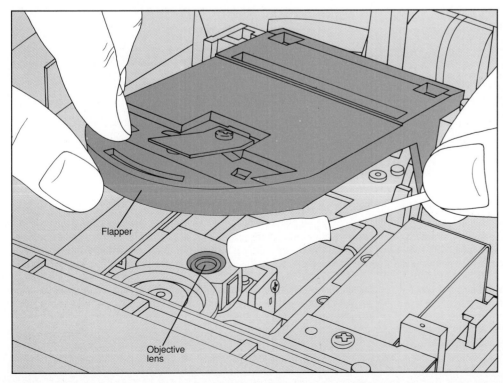

Flapper

Objective lens

Cleaning the objective lens. Press the open/close control to open the loading drawer, and then remove the top panel *(page 390)*. Carefully lift up the flapper and blow dust off the lens with short bursts of compressed air. To clean the lens, use a foam swab moistened with photographic lens cleaner, available at a photographic supplier. Gently wipe the swab across the lens *(left)*; use a fresh, dry swab to wipe off excess cleaner. Reposition the flapper over the lens and reinstall the top panel.

SERVICING THE DRIVE BELTS

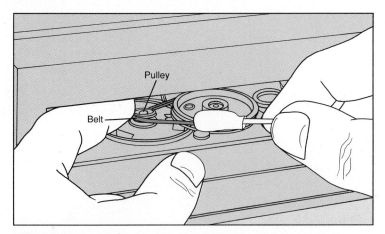

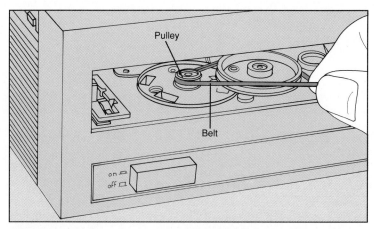

1 **Cleaning a belt.** Unplug the unit. Remove the top panel *(page 390)* and then the loading drawer *(page 391)*; to reach a belt on the bottom of the loading platform, also remove the loading platform *(page 391)*. If a belt is loose or broken, replace it *(step 2)*. If a belt is sticky or greasy, clean it using a foam swab dipped in rubber-cleaning compound *(above)*; never apply anything oily and avoid touching the belt with your fingers. Turn the belt pulleys to reach the entire length of the belt. Put back the loading platform if you removed it. Reinstall the loading drawer and the top panel.

2 **Replacing a belt.** Slip the damaged belt off the pulleys *(above)*, noting its position. First use long-nose pliers or tweezers to remove any other belt in the way; be careful not to pinch a belt. Purchase an exact replacement at an electronics parts supplier. Holding the belt loosely with long-nose pliers or tweezers, wrap it around the pulleys; then reinstall any other belt removed. Put back the loading platform, the loading drawer, and reinstall the top panel.

SERVICING THE MOTOR SWITCHES

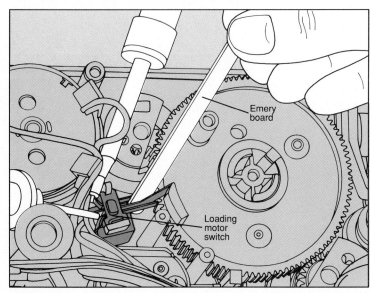

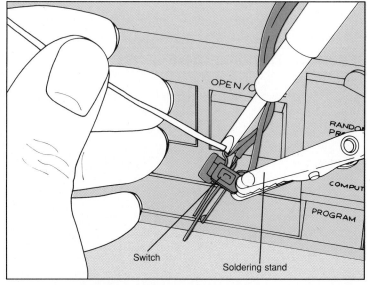

1 **Cleaning and testing a switch.** Remove the top panel *(page 390)* and the loading platform *(page 391)*. The loading motor switch is near the loading gears and lever, as shown; the optical pickup/spindle motor switch is next to the optical pickup assembly rail. If a switch leaf is damaged, replace the switch *(step 2)*. If a switch wire is loose or broken, repair it *(page 417)*. Set a multitester to test continuity. Touch one probe to a wire terminal on the switch and touch the other probe in turn to each switch-wire terminal on the circuit board. The multitester should register continuity once—and only once. Test each switch wire. If a wire tests faulty, replace it. If each wire tests OK, gently run an emery board over each leaf to clean the contacts *(above)*. Reinstall the loading platform and the top panel.

2 **Removing and replacing a switch.** Unclip or unscrew the switch from the loading platform. Tag the switch wires, noting their terminals, and desolder *(page 417)* the wires from the switch terminals. Order an exact replacement switch from the manufacturer or purchase one at an electronics parts supplier. Set the switch in a soldering stand and solder the wires to the switch terminals *(above)*. Clip or screw the switch to the loading platform. Reinstall the loading platform and the top panel, and cold check the unit for leaking voltage *(page 417)* before plugging it in.

SERVICING THE MODE AND FEATURE SWITCHES

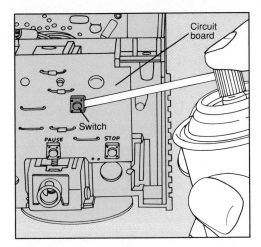

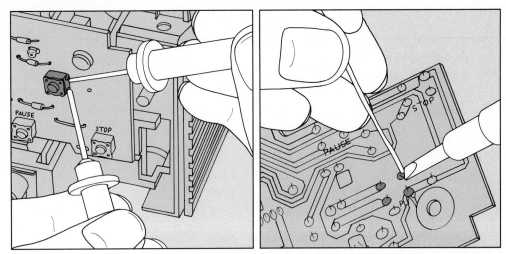

1 **Cleaning a switch.** Unplug the unit. Remove the top panel and the front panel or plate *(page 390)*. Locate the switch on the circuit board, behind its control. Clean the switch with electronic contact cleaner, directing a short burst into the switch opening *(above)*. Press the switch several times to work in the cleaner. Reinstall the front panel or plate and the top panel. If the problem persists, remove the panels again to test the switch *(step 2)*.

2 **Testing and replacing a switch.** Set a multitester to test continuity. Set the switch to one position and touch a probe to each pin on one side of the switch *(above, left)*; repeat this step with the switch set in the other position. The switch should register continuity in only one position. Repeat the procedure at the pins on the other side of the switch. If the switch tests faulty, unscrew and turn over the circuit board. Desolder the switch pins *(page 417)* and wiggle off the switch. Test continuity again to confirm the switch is faulty. Order an exact replacement switch from the manufacturer or purchase one at an electronics parts supplier. Fit the switch pins onto the circuit board and solder the pins *(above)*. If the switch tests OK, suspect a faulty circuit board and take the compact disc player for professional service. Put back the circuit board and reinstall the panels. Cold check for leaking voltage *(page 417)*.

SERVICING THE ON/OFF SWITCH

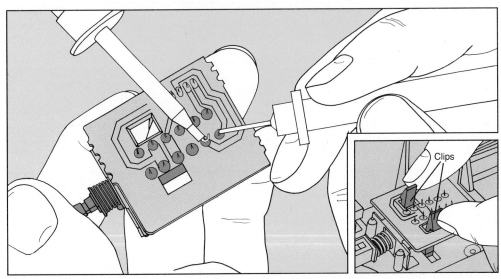

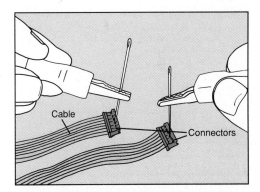

1 **Testing and replacing the switch.** Unplug the unit. Remove the top panel, the front panel or plate *(page 390)* and the loading platform *(page 391)*. Push off the switch control lever, unclip the switch circuit board *(inset)* and lift it out. Unplug or desolder *(page 417)* the wires from the switch. Set a multitester to test continuity. Hook one probe to a switch contact point and touch the other probe in turn to the other switch contact points, pressing in and releasing the switch for each test *(above)*. Test each contact point with each other contact point, checking for a continuity pattern. If there is a pattern, test the switch wires *(step 2)*. If not, desolder the switch pins and pull off the switch. Order an exact replacement switch from the manufacturer or purchase one at an electronics parts supplier. Solder the switch pins onto the circuit board. Put back the switch circuit board, and reinstall the loading platform and the panels.

2 **Testing and replacing the switch wires.** If the wires are housed in a cable with connectors at the ends, unplug it. Set a multitester to test continuity. Clip a needle to each probe. Touch one needle to a contact point at one end of a wire and touch the other needle to each contact point at the other end of the cable *(above)*. The multitester should register continuity once—and only once. Repeat the procedure for each wire. If a wire tests faulty, replace it. If each wire tests OK, plug in the cable or solder the wires to the switch circuit board. Put back the circuit board, reversing the sequence used to remove it *(step 1)*. Reinstall the loading platform and the panels. Cold check for leaking voltage *(page 417)*.

SPEAKERS

The final step in sound transmission by an audio system is performed by your speakers *(below)*. Incoming electrical signals are routed to the crossover network, where they are divided into frequency ranges and directed to the drivers, which reproduce the signals as various sound frequencies.

Many audio problems are experienced through the speakers; often these units are not the cause, but can be a valuable tool in troubleshooting other units in the audio system. Consult the Troubleshooting Guide in Entertainment Systems *(page 356)* and in this chapter.

Often, problems can be remedied by adjusting cable hook-ups. A wire may be loose or broken, or a component may test faulty. Replacement components are usually available from an electronics parts supplier. A special driver or crossover network may have to be ordered from the manufacturer.

Refer to Tools & Techniques *(page 417)* for instructions on testing continuity and resistance and for directions on de-soldering and soldering. When disconnecting a speaker cable, label the positive wire to maintain the polarity *(page 105)* of the electrical connection.

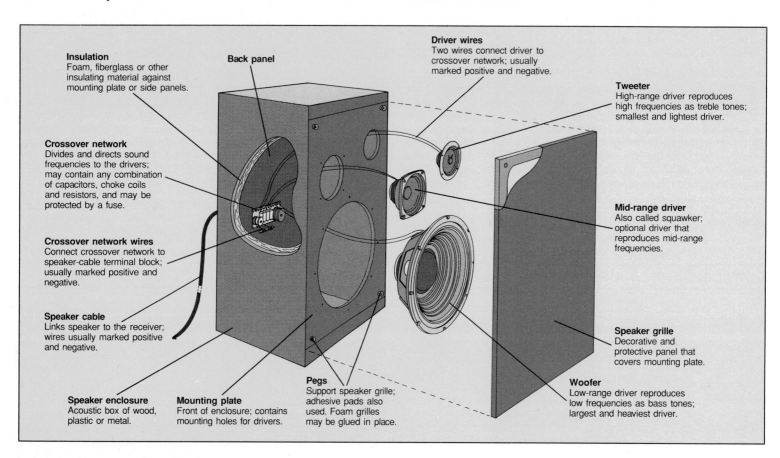

Insulation
Foam, fiberglass or other insulating material against mounting plate or side panels.

Back panel

Driver wires
Two wires connect driver to crossover network; usually marked positive and negative.

Tweeter
High-range driver reproduces high frequencies as treble tones; smallest and lightest driver.

Crossover network
Divides and directs sound frequencies to the drivers; may contain any combination of capacitors, choke coils and resistors, and may be protected by a fuse.

Mid-range driver
Also called squawker; optional driver that reproduces mid-range frequencies.

Crossover network wires
Connect crossover network to speaker-cable terminal block; usually marked positive and negative.

Speaker cable
Links speaker to the receiver; wires usually marked positive and negative.

Speaker grille
Decorative and protective panel that covers mounting plate.

Speaker enclosure
Acoustic box of wood, plastic or metal.

Mounting plate
Front of enclosure; contains mounting holes for drivers.

Pegs
Support speaker grille; adhesive pads also used. Foam grilles may be glued in place.

Woofer
Low-range driver reproduces low frequencies as bass tones; largest and heaviest driver.

TROUBLESHOOTING GUIDE

SYMPTOM	POSSIBLE CAUSE	PROCEDURE
No sound at all	Receiver, cable or auxiliary unit faulty	Troubleshoot entertainment system *(p. 356)* □○
	Speaker fuses blown	Test and replace fuses *(p. 417)* □○
Sound from only one speaker	Receiver, cable or auxiliary unit faulty	Troubleshoot entertainment system *(p. 356)* □○
	Speaker fuse blown	Test and replace fuses *(p. 417)* □○
	Crossover network faulty	Service crossover network *(p. 397)* □○
Intermittent sound from speaker	Receiver, cable or auxiliary unit faulty	Troubleshoot entertainment system *(p. 356)* □○
	Driver faulty	Test and replace drivers *(p. 396)* □○
	Crossover network faulty	Service crossover network *(p. 397)* □○
Speaker grille damaged	Wear and tear	Replace speaker grille *(p. 395)* □○

DEGREE OF DIFFICULTY: □ Easy ◨ Moderate ■ Complex
ESTIMATED TIME: ○ Less than 1 hour ◖ 1 to 3 hours ● Over 3 hours

TROUBLESHOOTING GUIDE (continued)

SYMPTOM	POSSIBLE CAUSE	PROCEDURE
Distorted sound from speaker	Receiver or auxiliary unit faulty	Troubleshoot entertainment system *(p. 356)* □○
	Cone loose or punctured	Repair speaker cone *(p. 396)* □○
	Driver faulty	Test and replace drivers *(p. 396)* □○
	Crossover network faulty	Service crossover network *(p. 397)* □○
Humming, buzzing or rumbling noise from speaker	Receiver, cable or auxiliary unit faulty	Troubleshoot entertainment system *(p. 356)* □○
	Speaker vibrating or too close to turntable	Reposition speakers
	Cone or driver faulty	Repair speaker cone or drivers *(p. 396)* □○
	Insulation loose	Apply rubber cement to corners of insulation
	Crossover network faulty	Service crossover network *(p. 397)* □○
No low-range (bass) sound from speaker	Receiver or auxiliary unit faulty	Troubleshoot entertainment system *(p. 356)* □○
	Woofer faulty	Test and replace drivers *(p. 396)* □○
	Crossover network faulty	Service crossover network *(p. 397)* □○
No high-range (treble) sound from speaker	Receiver or auxiliary unit faulty	Troubleshoot entertainment system *(p. 356)* □○
	Tweeter faulty	Test and replace drivers *(p. 396)* □○
	Crossover network faulty	Service crossover network *(p. 397)* □○
No mid-range (voice) sound from speaker	Receiver or auxiliary unit faulty	Troubleshoot entertainment system *(p. 356)* □○
	Mid-range driver faulty	Test and replace drivers *(p. 396)* □○
	Crossover network faulty	Service crossover network *(p. 397)* □○

DEGREE OF DIFFICULTY: □ Easy ◩ Moderate ■ Complex
ESTIMATED TIME: ○ Less than 1 hour ◑ 1 to 3 hours ● Over 3 hours

ACCESS TO THE COMPONENTS

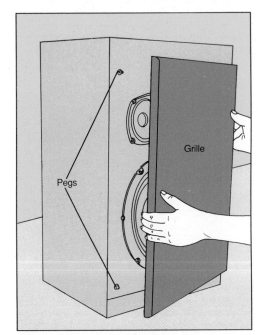

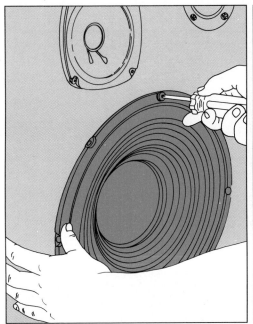

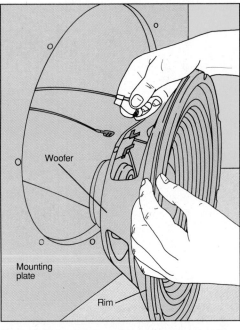

1 **Removing the speaker grille.** Remove any screws securing the front grille and gently pull it off the pegs or adhesive tabs *(above)*. If necessary, run a small putty knife under each corner to break any glue bond. To reach internal components, remove the woofer *(step 2)*. To reinstall the speaker grille, apply a small dab of cement to the corners if required.

2 **Removing and reinstalling the woofer.** Turn off the receiver and any other input unit and disconnect the cable from the speaker terminals *(page 354)*, labeling the positive terminal wire. Unscrew the woofer from the mounting plate *(above, left)*. Hold the woofer securely by the rim and gently pull it free of the mounting plate. Supporting the woofer on its rim or turning it face down, label the positive wire and disconnect or desolder *(page 417)* the wires from the woofer terminals *(above, right)*. Carefully set the woofer aside. If required, repeat this procedure to remove the tweeter or the mid-range driver. To reinstall a driver, reconnect or solder the wires to the driver terminals, screw the driver to the mounting plate, and put back the grille *(step 1)*. Reconnect the cable to the speaker terminals *(page 358)*.

REPAIRING DRIVER CONES

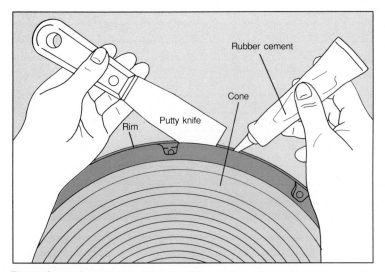

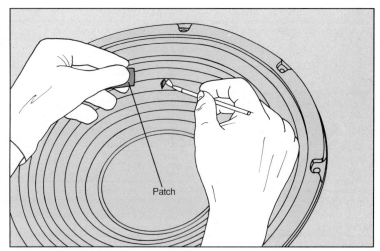

Reseating a loose cone. Remove the speaker grille *(page 395, step 1)*. If the woofer, tweeter or mid-range driver cone is damaged, remove the driver *(page 395, step 2)*. If the driver cone is badly torn or separated from the spider, or frame, replace the driver *(page 397)*. If there is a small hole in the driver cone, seal the puncture *(right)*. If a small section of the driver cone is separated from the rim, gently raise the cone away from the rim with a small putty knife and spread a small amount of rubber cement along the edges of the cone and rim *(above)*. Allow the cement to dry, then lightly press the cone against the rim until the rubber cement adheres. Reinstall the driver and the speaker grille.

Sealing a punctured cone. Remove the speaker grille *(page 395, step 1)*. If the woofer, tweeter or mid-range driver cone is damaged, remove the driver *(page 395, step 2)*. If the driver cone is badly torn or separated from the spider, or frame, replace the driver *(page 397)*. If a small section of the driver cone is separated from the rim, reseat the cone *(left)*. If there is a small hole in the driver cone, cut a patch slightly larger than the puncture from paper about the same thickness as the cone. Wearing a rubber glove, saturate the patch with rubber cement and use a small brush to apply a light coat of rubber cement around the cone puncture *(above)*. Allow the cement to dry, then set the patch over the puncture and gently press it until the cement adheres. Reinstall the driver and the speaker grille.

SERVICING THE DRIVERS

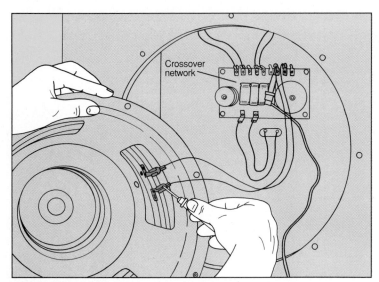

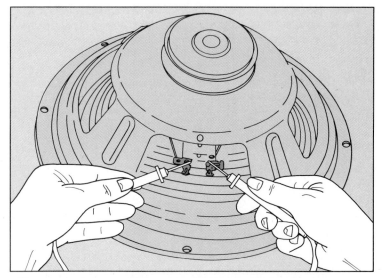

1 **Testing between the driver and the crossover network.** Remove the speaker grille and the woofer *(page 395, step 1)*. To test from the woofer, the tweeter or the mid-range driver, remove the driver *(page 395, step 2)* but leave the wires connected to the terminals. If a wire connecting to the crossover network is loose or broken, tighten or replace it *(page 417)*. Set a multitester to test continuity. Hook one probe to a wire terminal on the crossover network and touch the other probe to that wire's terminal on the driver *(above)*. Repeat this step for the other wire. If a wire does not have continuity, replace it. If each wire has continuity, test the driver *(step 2)*.

2 **Testing the driver.** Label the positive terminal wire and disconnect or desolder *(page 417)* the wires from the driver terminals. Place the driver face down on a work table and set a multitester to test resistance. Touch the positive probe to the positive driver terminal and touch the negative probe to the negative driver terminal *(above)*. The multitester should register close to the ohms rating indicated on the driver or specified by the speaker manufacturer. If the driver does not register what it should, replace it *(step 3)*. If the driver registers what it should, service the crossover network *(page 397)*.

SERVICING THE DRIVERS (continued)

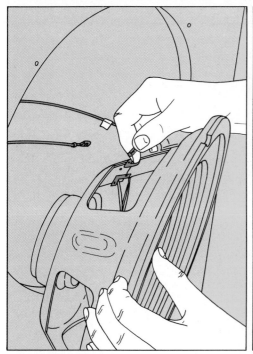
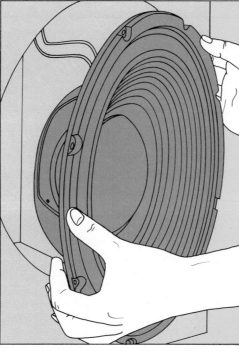

3 **Replacing the driver.** Purchase an exact replacement driver at an electronics parts supplier. Connect or solder *(page 417)* the labeled positive wire to the positive driver terminal *(far left)* and connect or solder the other wire to the negative driver terminal. Supporting the driver by its rim, set it into the opening in the mounting plate *(near left)* and screw it securely in place. Reinstall the woofer, if required, and the speaker grille.

SERVICING THE CROSSOVER NETWORK

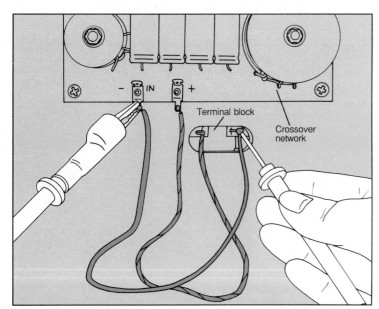
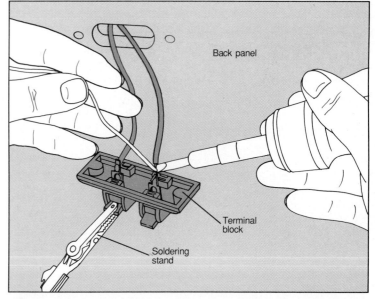

1 **Testing between the crossover and the terminal block.** Remove the speaker grille and the woofer *(page 395)*. Locate the two wires connecting the crossover network to the terminal block. If a wire is loose or broken, tighten or replace it. If required, remove the terminal block *(step 2)*. Set a multitester to test continuity. Clip one probe to a wire terminal on the crossover network and touch the other probe to that wire's terminal on the terminal block. Repeat this step for the other wire. If a wire does not have continuity, replace it *(step 2)*. If each wire has continuity, test the crossover network *(step 3)*.

2 **Repairing the wire connections.** Disconnect or desolder *(page 417)* the wire from the crossover network terminal. To gain access to the wire terminal on the terminal block, remove the exterior terminal block screws and pull the terminal block off the back panel. Secure the terminal block in a soldering stand and desolder the wire. Purchase a length of replacement wire the identical gauge at an electronics parts supplier; if required, also purchase a set of crimp connectors. Cut the wire to length and crimp on a connector at one end. Connect the end with the crimp connector to the terminal on the crossover network and solder the other wire end to the terminal on the terminal block *(above)*. Screw in the terminal block and reinstall the woofer and the speaker grille.

SERVICING THE CROSSOVER NETWORK (continued)

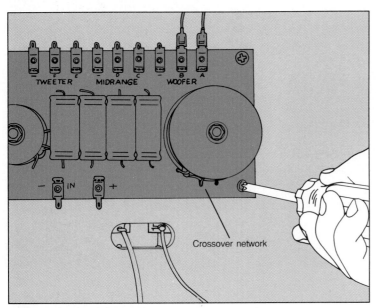

3 **Removing the crossover network.** Label the wires connecting the crossover network to the tweeter, any mid-range driver and the terminal block, noting the terminal positions. Disconnect or desolder the wires from the crossover network, leaving the woofer wires connected. Unscrew the crossover network from the back panel *(above)* and lift it out. Test the crossover network capacitors *(step 4)* and choke coils *(step 5)*; or, Label and disconnect the wires to the woofer, noting the terminal positions, and install an exact replacement crossover network purchased at an electronics parts supplier *(step 6)*.

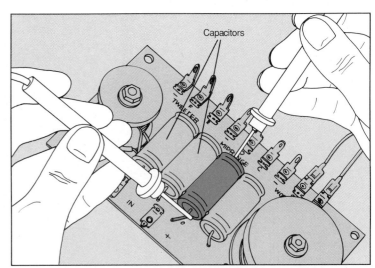

4 **Testing and replacing the capacitors.** Desolder one capacitor wire and pull it off the circuit board with long-nose pliers. Set a multitester to test resistance and touch the positive probe to the positive wire and the negative probe to the negative wire *(above)*. The multitester should register a sharp drop and then a rise in ohms. Repeat this procedure for each capacitor. If each capacitor registers what it should, resolder the capacitor wires and test the choke coils *(step 5)*. If a capacitor does not register what it should, desolder its other wire and remove the capacitor. Purchase an exact replacement capacitor at an electronics parts supplier. Position the capacitor on the circuit board, thread the wires through the openings and solder them. Reinstall the crossover network *(step 6)*.

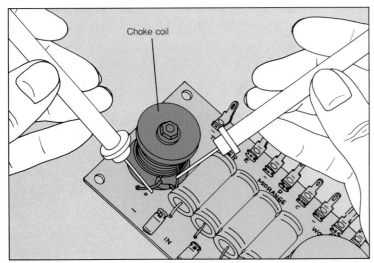

5 **Testing and replacing the choke coils.** Desolder one choke coil wire and pull it off the circuit board with long-nose pliers. Set a multitester to test resistance. Touch one probe to the middle choke coil wire and touch the other probe in turn to each other choke coil wire *(above)*. The multitester should register low, steady ohms for both tests. Repeat this test for the other choke coil. If each choke coil registers what it should, resolder the choke coil wires and reinstall the crossover network *(step 6)*. If a choke coil does not register what it should, desolder the other choke coil wires, noting their positions, and remove the choke coil. Purchase an exact replacement at an electronics parts supplier. Position it on the circuit board, thread the wires through the openings and solder them. Reinstall the crossover network *(step 6)*.

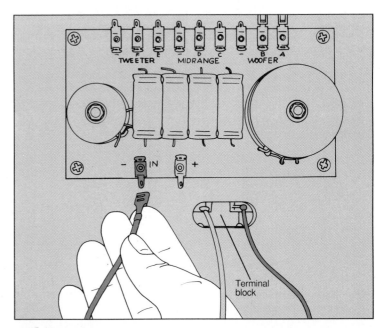

6 **Reinstalling the crossover network.** Position the crossover network against the back panel and screw it securely in place. Reconnect or solder the wires for the terminal block *(above)*, any mid-range driver and the tweeter to the crossover network terminals; if required, also reconnect the wires for the woofer. Reinstall the woofer and the speaker grille. If the problem persists, take the speaker for professional service.

TELEVISIONS

Through cables from the antenna or cable system, the television tuner receives a broadcast signal and changes it into electrical video and audio signals. The video signal is sent to the picture tube. A cathode ray tube, it projects visual images by beaming electrons through a vacuum against the phosphorescent inside face of the screen. The audio signal is routed to one or more drivers inside the television, or possibly through cables to the receiver and then to the speakers.

Thanks to its solid-state circuitry, little goes wrong with a modern television *(below)*. To diagnose problems, consult the Troubleshooting Guide in Entertainment Systems *(page 356)* and in this chapter *(page 400)*. Often, problems can be reme-

died by adjusting cable hookups; on an older television, the mechanical tuner may need cleaning. On older models, clean and demagnetize the screen to remove static electricity. Cleaning supplies and most replacement components are available at an electronics parts supplier.

Refer to Tools & Techniques *(page 417)* for instructions on disassembly and reassembly, testing continuity and resistance, and desoldering and soldering. Turn off and unplug the television before any repair. Perform a cold check for leaking voltage both before disassembling and after reassembling the television. Stay away from the picture tube when working; there may be high voltage stored in it, even after 24 hours.

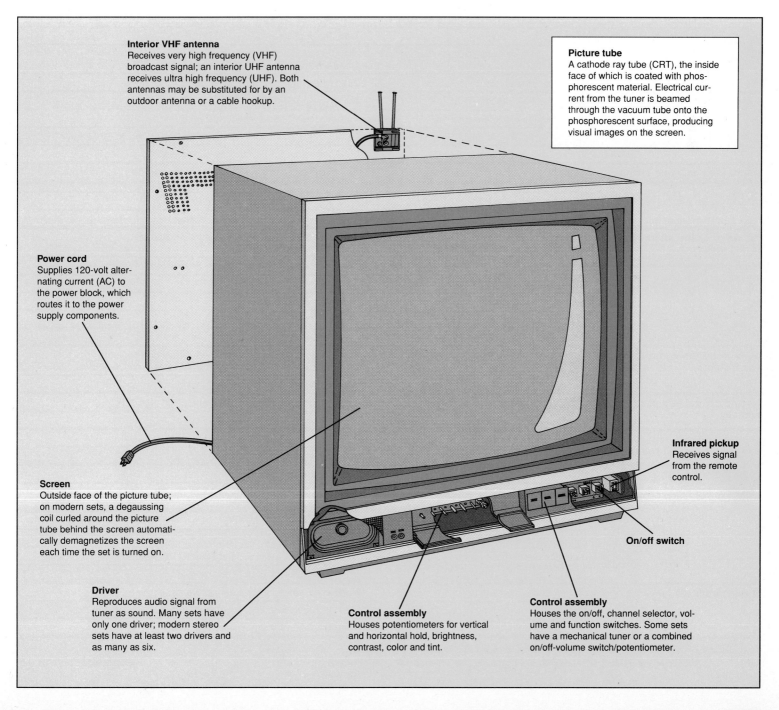

Interior VHF antenna
Receives very high frequency (VHF) broadcast signal; an interior UHF antenna receives ultra high frequency (UHF). Both antennas may be substituted for by an outdoor antenna or a cable hookup.

Picture tube
A cathode ray tube (CRT), the inside face of which is coated with phosphorescent material. Electrical current from the tuner is beamed through the vacuum tube onto the phosphorescent surface, producing visual images on the screen.

Power cord
Supplies 120-volt alternating current (AC) to the power block, which routes it to the power supply components.

Screen
Outside face of the picture tube; on modern sets, a degaussing coil curled around the picture tube behind the screen automatically demagnetizes the screen each time the set is turned on.

Infrared pickup
Receives signal from the remote control.

On/off switch

Driver
Reproduces audio signal from tuner as sound. Many sets have only one driver; modern stereo sets have at least two drivers and as many as six.

Control assembly
Houses potentiometers for vertical and horizontal hold, brightness, contrast, color and tint.

Control assembly
Houses the on/off, channel selector, volume and function switches. Some sets have a mechanical tuner or a combined on/off-volume switch/potentiometer.

TROUBLESHOOTING GUIDE

SYMPTOM	POSSIBLE CAUSE	PROCEDURE
No display lights, no picture and no sound	Television unplugged or turned off	Plug in and turn on television
	Remote control dirty or faulty	Service remote control *(p. 417)* □○; replace batteries
	No power to outlet or outlet faulty	Reset breaker or replace fuse *(p. 102)* □○; service outlet *(p. 148)*
	Power cord faulty	Test and replace power cord *(p. 417)* □○
	Power fuse blown	Test and replace power fuse *(p. 403)* □○
	On/off switch faulty	Test and replace combined switch/potentiometer *(p. 404)* □○ or test and replace mode switch *(p. 405)* □○
	Power supply or circuit board faulty	Take television for professional service
Display lights, but no picture and no sound	Videocassette recorder faulty	Troubleshoot entertainment system *(p. 356)* □○
	Circuit board faulty	Take television for professional service
Picture, but no sound	Controls set incorrectly	Adjust television controls
	Videocassette recorder or receiver faulty	Troubleshoot entertainment system *(p. 356)* □○
	Driver faulty	Test and replace driver *(p. 403)* □○
	Volume switch or potentiometer dirty or faulty	Clean, test and replace combined switch/potentiometer *(p. 404)* □○, or switch *(p. 405)* □○ or potentiometer *(p. 406)* □○
	Circuit board faulty	Take television for professional service
Sound, but no picture	Controls set incorrectly	Adjust television controls
	Videocassette recorder faulty	Troubleshoot entertainment system *(p. 356)* □○
	Potentiometer dirty or faulty	Clean, test and replace potentiometer *(p. 406)* □○
	Picture tube or circuit board faulty	Take television for professional service
Sound from only one channel	Videocassette recorder, receiver or speaker faulty	Troubleshoot entertainment system *(p. 356)* □○
	Driver faulty	Test and replace driver *(p. 403)* □○
	Circuit board faulty	Take television for professional service
Picture or sound intermittent or distorted	Antenna or cable system, videocassette recorder, receiver or speaker faulty	Troubleshoot entertainment system *(p. 356)* □○
	Screen static	Service screen *(p. 401)* □○▲
	Interior antenna broken	Replace antenna *(p. 402)* □○
	Mechanical tuner dirty	Service mechanical tuner *(p. 402)* □○
	Driver faulty	Test and replace driver *(p. 403)* □○
	Circuit board faulty	Take television for professional service
Mode or feature control doesn't work	Mode or feature switch or potentiometer dirty or faulty	Clean, test and replace combined switch/potentiometer *(p. 404)* □○, or mode or feature switch *(p. 405)* □○ or potentiometer *(p. 406)* □○
	Circuit board faulty	Take television for professional service
Feature control abrupt or scratchy	Feature potentiometer dirty or faulty	Clean, test and replace potentiometer *(p. 406)* □○
	Circuit board faulty	Take television for professional service
Mechanical tuner abrupt, scratchy or doesn't work	Mechanical tuner dirty	Service mechanical tuner *(p. 402)* □○
	Mechanical tuner or circuit board faulty	Take television for professional service
Color tones wrong	Controls set incorrectly	Adjust television controls
	Antenna or cable system or videocassette recorder faulty	Troubleshoot entertainment system *(p. 356)* □○
	Screen static	Service screen *(p. 401)* □○
	Interior antenna broken	Replace antenna *(p. 402)* □○
	Potentiometer dirty or faulty	Clean, test and replace potentiometer *(p. 406)* □○
	Tuner or circuit board faulty	Take television for professional service
Burning odor	Air vents blocked or dirty	Reposition television or clean air vents
	Power fuse blown	Test and replace power fuse *(p. 403)* □○
	Internal component faulty	Take television for professional service

DEGREE OF DIFFICULTY: □ Easy ◨ Moderate ■ Complex
ESTIMATED TIME: ○ Less than 1 hour ◖ 1 to 3 hours ● Over 3 hours

▲ Special tool required

SERVICING THE SCREEN

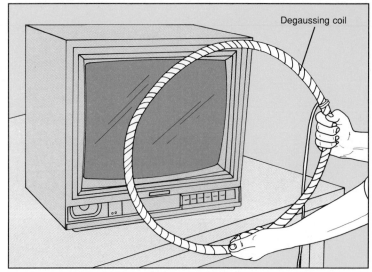

Degaussing coil

1 Cleaning the screen. Turn off the television. Wipe dust and finger-prints off the television screen using a clean, lint-free cloth moistened with window cleaner or a solution of mild detergent and warm water *(above)*. Rinse detergent off the screen, then dry it using a fresh cloth. Wash the screen at least once a month. If your television has a built-in degaussing coil, the screen is demagnetized automatically. If your television has no degaussing coil, or if the coil no longer functions, demagnetize the screen *(step 2)*.

2 Demagnetizing the screen. Purchase a degaussing coil at an electronics parts supplier. Unplug the television from the wall outlet and plug in the degaussing coil. Turn on the degaussing coil about 6 feet away from the television and bring it within an inch of the screen. Slowly circle the coil several times around the front of the screen without touching it *(above)*. Gradually draw the coil 6 feet away and turn it off. Unplug the degaussing coil and plug in and turn on the television. Demagnetize after each cleaning.

ACCESS TO THE INTERNAL COMPONENTS

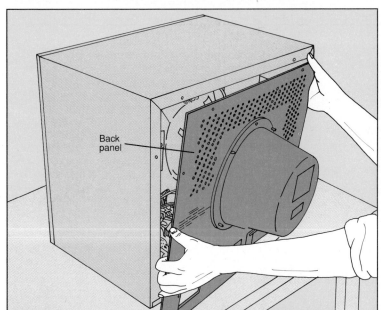

Back panel

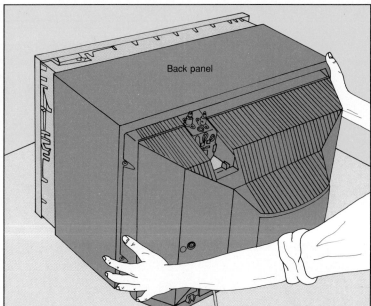

Back panel

Removing and reinstalling the back panel. Turn off the television, unplug it from the wall outlet and disconnect the cables hooked up to it *(page 354)*. Wait at least 24 hours for the picture tube to discharge stored voltage. Cold check the television for leaking voltage *(page 417)*. If there is an interior antenna mounted on the back panel, unscrew and remove the mounting plate; if the wires interfere with removing the back panel, note their terminal positions and disconnect them. On some models, the back panel is flat *(above, left)*; on other models, the back panel is a molded casing with a top, sides and bottom *(above, right)*. Check the back panel for screws or clips. Unscrew or unclip the back panel and slide it out from under any lip on the top panel. Slide the power cord and any interior antenna through their openings and pull the back panel off the frame. On some models, the power cord may unplug from terminals inside the television and come off with the back panel. Reverse the sequence to reinstall the back panel, then cold check the television again for leaking voltage.

REPLACING THE ANTENNA

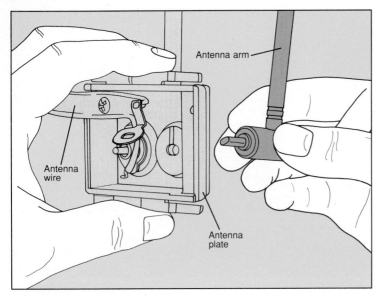

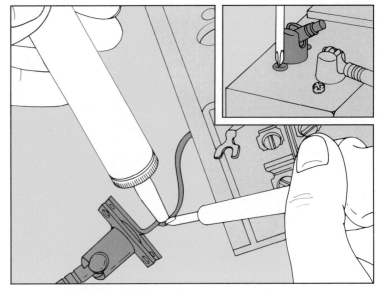

Reinstalling an externally mounted interior antenna. Turn off and unplug the television. Unscrew the antenna plate from the back panel. Remove the locknut securing the antenna arm to the back of the antenna plate, disconnect the antenna wire and pull out the antenna arm. Order an exact replacement antenna arm from the manufacturer or purchase a substitute at an electronics parts supplier. Fit the antenna arm into the antenna plate *(above)*, connect the antenna wire and install the locknut. Screw the antenna plate to the back panel. Plug in the television.

Reinstalling an internally-mounted interior antenna. Unplug the set and remove the back panel *(page 401)*. Disconnect the antenna wire from the antenna housing terminal. Unscrew the antenna arm *(inset)* and slip it down through the opening in the antenna housing. Desolder *(page 417)* the antenna wire from the antenna arm *(above)*. Order an exact replacement antenna arm from the manufacturer or purchase a substitute at an electronics parts supplier. Slide the antenna arm through the opening in the antenna housing and solder the antenna wire to it. Screw in the antenna arm and reconnect the wire to the antenna housing terminal. Reinstall the back panel.

SERVICING A MECHANICAL TUNER

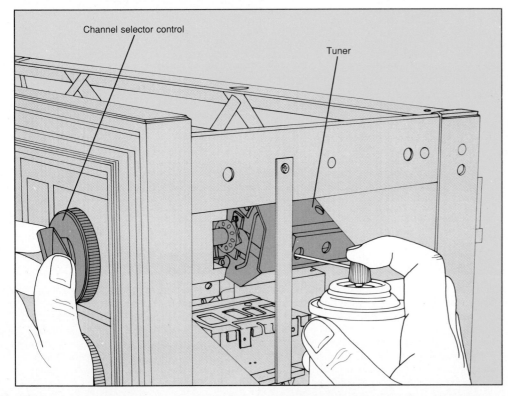

Cleaning a mechanical tuner. Unplug the set. Remove the back panel *(page 401)* and locate the tuner behind the channel selector control on the front panel. Using tuner cleaner, direct the nozzle through an opening in the tuner casing and spray short bursts of cleaner; gently rotate the channel selector control back and forth several times to work in the cleaner *(left)*. Repeat this procedure at each opening in the tuner casing. Reinstall the back panel and cold check for leaking voltage *(page 417)*. If the problem persists, suspect a faulty tuner and take the television for professional service.

SERVICING THE DRIVERS

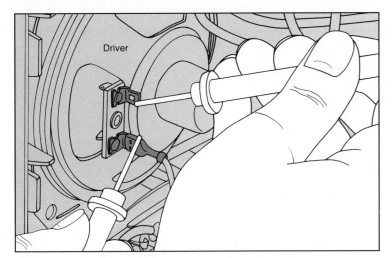

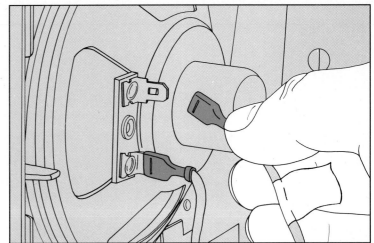

1 **Testing a driver.** Unplug the set. Remove the back panel *(page 401)* and locate the driver wire terminals. If a wire connection is loose or broken, repair it *(page 417)*. Reinstall the back panel; remove it again if the problem persists. Tag the positive wire and disconnect or desolder it from the terminal. Set a multitester to test resistance. Touch one probe to the positive terminal and touch the other probe to the negative terminal *(above)*. The multitester should register close to the ohms rating indicated on the driver or specified by the manufacturer. If the driver tests faulty, replace it *(step 2)*. If it tests OK, suspect a faulty circuit board; reinstall the back panel and take the television for professional service.

2 **Replacing a driver.** Disconnect or desolder *(page 417)* the negative wire. Unscrew the driver from the frame and remove it from the television. Order an exact replacement driver from the manufacturer or purchase a substitute at an electronics parts supplier. Position the driver in the television and screw it to the frame. Connect or solder the tagged wire to the positive driver terminal *(above)* and the other wire to the negative driver terminal. Reinstall the back panel *(page 401)*. If the problem persists, suspect a faulty circuit board and take the television for professional service.

REPLACING THE POWER FUSE

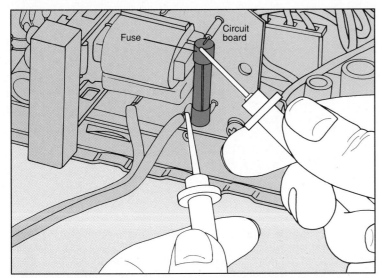

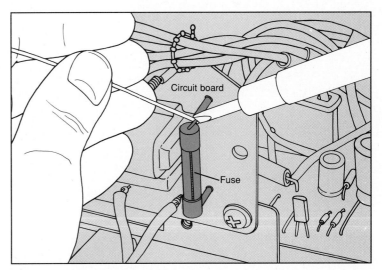

1 **Testing the fuse.** Remove the back panel *(page 401)* and locate the power fuse on the power-supply circuit board. If the fuse is held by retaining clips, use a fuse puller to remove it. If the fuse is soldered to posts, leave it in place. Set a multitester to test continuity. Touch a probe to the cap at each end of the fuse *(above)*. If a soldered fuse does not register continuity, desolder it *(page 417)* and test again. If the fuse does not register continuity out of circuit, replace it *(step 2)*. If the fuse registers continuity out of circuit, put it back and reinstall the back panel. If the problem persists, suspect a faulty circuit board and take the television for professional service.

2 **Installing a new fuse.** Purchase an exact replacement fuse at an electronics parts supplier. Gently push the fuse into the retaining clips on the circuit board; if the old fuse was soldered to posts on the circuit board, carefully solder the new fuse in place *(above)*. Reinstall the back panel *(page 401)*. If the fuse blows repeatedly, suspect a faulty power supply and take the television for professional service.

SERVICING A COMBINED SWITCH/POTENTIOMETER

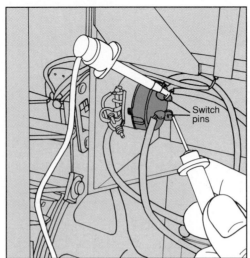

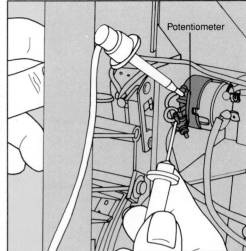

1 **Cleaning the potentiometer.** Unplug the set. Remove the back panel *(page 401)* and locate the switch/potentiometer behind its control on the front panel; the switch has two pins and the potentiometer has three pins. To clean the potentiometer, spray electronic contact cleaner into the openings in the casing and rotate the control back and forth to work in the cleaner *(above)*. Never apply cleaner to the on/off switch. Reinstall the back panel. If the problem persists, test the switch/potentiometer *(step 2)*.

2 **Testing the switch/potentiometer.** Remove the back panel *(page 401)*. To test the switch, set a multitester to test continuity. Hook one probe to one switch pin and touch the other probe to the other switch pin *(above, left)*. Set the switch to the ON position, then to the OFF position. The switch should register continuity only in the ON position. If the switch tests faulty, remove the switch/potentiometer *(step 3)*. If the switch tests OK, test the potentiometer. Set the multitester to test resistance. Hook one probe to the center potentiometer pin and touch the other probe in turn to the outer potentiometer pins, rotating the control back and forth *(above, right)*. The multitester should register a variation in ohms. If there is no variation, remove the switch/potentiometer *(step 3)*. If there is an ohms variation, suspect a faulty circuit board; reinstall the back panel and take the television for professional service.

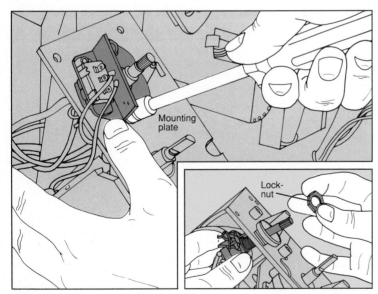

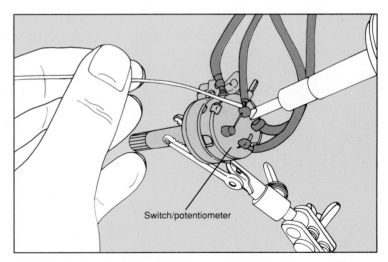

3 **Removing the switch/potentiometer.** Unscrew and lift out the switch/potentiometer mounting plate and unscrew the switch/potentiometer from it *(above)*. Remove the locknut from the potentiometer shaft and slide the shaft through the opening in the mounting plate *(inset)*. Label the switch/potentiometer wires, noting their terminal positions, and desolder them *(page 417)*. To confirm the switch/potentiometer is faulty, test it again *(step 2)*. If the switch/potentiometer once more tests faulty, replace it *(step 4)*. If it now tests OK, suspect a faulty circuit board; put back the switch/potentiometer, reinstall the back panel and take the television for professional service.

4 **Replacing the switch/potentiometer.** Purchase an exact replacement switch/potentiometer at an electronics parts supplier. Solder the wires to the switch/potentiometer terminals *(above)*. Slide the potentiometer shaft through the opening in the mounting plate and twist on the locknut. Screw the switch/potentiometer to the mounting plate and screw the plate to the frame. Reinstall the back panel and cold check for leaking voltage *(page 417)*. If the problem persists, suspect a faulty circuit board and take the television for professional service.

SERVICING MODE AND FEATURE SWITCHES

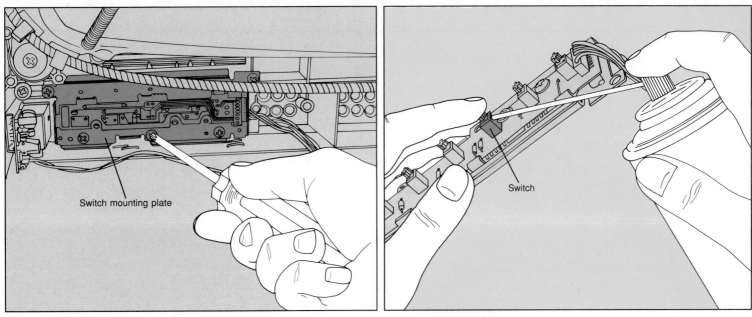

Switch mounting plate

Switch

1 **Cleaning a mode or feature switch.** Unplug the set. Remove the back panel *(page 401)* and locate the switch mounting plate behind its control on the front panel. Unscrew the mounting plate from the frame *(above, left)* and carefully pull it out of the television. To clean a switch other than the on/off control, use electronic contact cleaner; never apply cleaner to an on/off switch. Spray short bursts of cleaner through the opening in the switch casing; press and release the switch several times to work in the cleaner *(above, right)*. Screw in the mounting plate and reinstall the back panel. Cold check for leaking voltage *(page 417)*. If the problem persists, test the switch *(step 2)*.

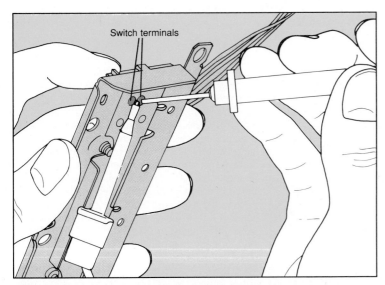

Switch terminals

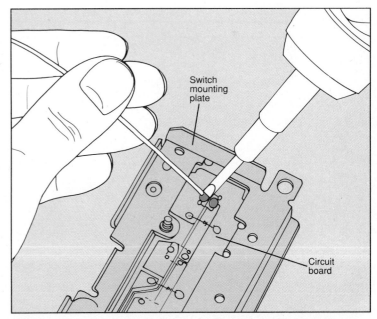

Switch mounting plate

Circuit board

2 **Testing a mode or feature switch.** Remove the back panel *(page 401)*. Unscrew and lift out the switch mounting plate. Set a multitester to test continuity. Hook one probe to one switch terminal and touch the other probe to the other switch terminal. Set the switch in the ON position, then in the OFF position *(above)*. The switch should register continuity only in the ON position. If the switch tests faulty, replace it *(step 3)*. If the switch tests OK, suspect a faulty circuit board; put back the mounting plate, reinstall the back panel and take the television for professional service.

3 **Replacing a mode or feature switch.** Desolder the switch pins *(page 417)* and pull the switch off the circuit board; wiggle the switch to help release the pins. To confirm the switch is faulty, test it again *(step 2)*. If the switch once more tests faulty, purchase an exact replacement switch at an electronics parts supplier. Fit the switch into the circuit board and solder the pins *(above)*. Test the new switch. If the switch now tests OK, suspect a faulty circuit board and take the television for professional service. Put back the mounting plate and reinstall the back panel. Cold check for leaking voltage *(page 417)*.

SERVICING POTENTIOMETERS

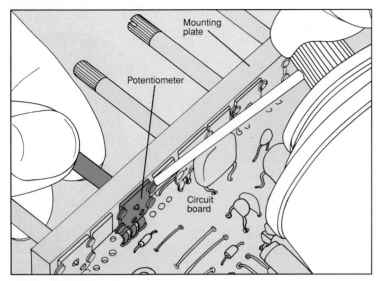

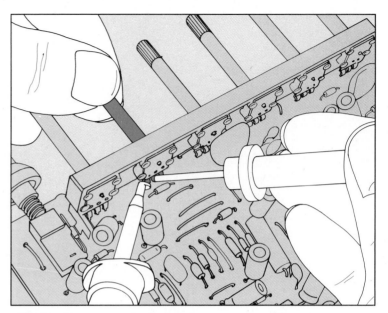

1 **Cleaning a potentiometer.** Unplug the set. Remove the back panel *(page 401)* and locate the potentiometer on the circuit board behind its control. Unscrew the potentiometer mounting plate from the frame and carefully pull it out of the television; remove any obstructing controls or locknuts. Spray short bursts of electronic contact cleaner into the opening in the potentiometer casing; rotate the potentiometer shaft back and forth several times to work in the cleaner *(above)*. Screw in the mounting plate, put back any locknuts or controls and reinstall the back panel. Cold check for leaking voltage *(page 417)*. If the problem persists, test the potentiometer *(step 2)*.

2 **Testing a potentiometer.** Remove the back panel *(page 401)* and access the potentiometer as in step 1. Set a multitester to test resistance. Hook one probe to the center potentiometer pin and touch the other probe in turn to the outer potentiometer pins, rotating the control back and forth for each position *(above)*. The multitester should register a variation in ohms. If there is no ohms variation, remove the potentiometer *(step 3)*. If there is an ohms variation, the problem may be a faulty circuit board; put back the mounting plate and any controls or locknuts removed, reinstall the back panel and take the television for professional service.

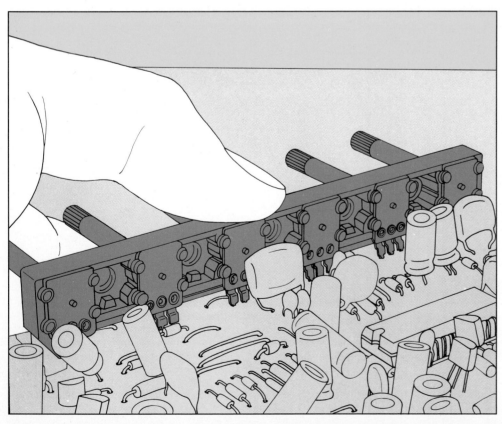

3 **Replacing a potentiometer.** To replace one potentiometer or the entire mounting plate/potentiometer assembly, you must desolder *(page 417)* all the potentiometer pins from the circuit board. Pull the mounting plate off the circuit board; wiggle it to help release the pins. Order an exact replacement mounting plate/potentiometer assembly from the manufacturer, if necessary. Otherwise, remove and replace only the faulty potentiometer: Drill out or snap off the rivets securing its backing and slide the potentiometer out of the mounting plate. Slide in the new potentiometer and secure the backing with screws or glue. Fit the mounting plate onto the circuit board *(left)* and solder the pins for each potentiometer. Screw the mounting plate to the frame, put back any locknuts or controls removed, and reinstall the back panel. Cold check for leaking voltage *(page 417)*. If the problem persists, suspect a faulty circuit board and take the television for professional service.

VIDEOCASSETTE RECORDERS

A videocassette recorder, or VCR, can tune in a television program and show it on the television, or record it on tape, or do both at the same time. It can also play back a prerecorded tape on the television. Because the VCR and the television have separate tuners, you can watch one program while recording another, or record a program with the television off. The audio and video heads in the VCR read and store magnetic tracks on tape, much like an audiocassette recorder.

VCRs are made in two styles, called formats: Beta and VHS. They differ mainly in how they thread the tape internally. The machine shown in this chapter is VHS; Beta components and repairs are similar. Most VCRs are programmable, meaning that their clock/timers can be preset to turn on the record function automatically.

With all these functions, the most common reason for VCR problems is simply programming errors. Check the owner's manual before consulting the Troubleshooting Guide in Entertainment Systems *(page 356)* and in this chapter *(page 408)*. Many problems can be solved by adjusting cable hookups or by cleaning and demagnetizing the tape travel components.

Cleaning supplies and most replacement parts are available at an electronics parts supplier; however, special parts have to be ordered from the manufacturer. Refer to Tools & Techniques *(page 417)* before beginning any repair.

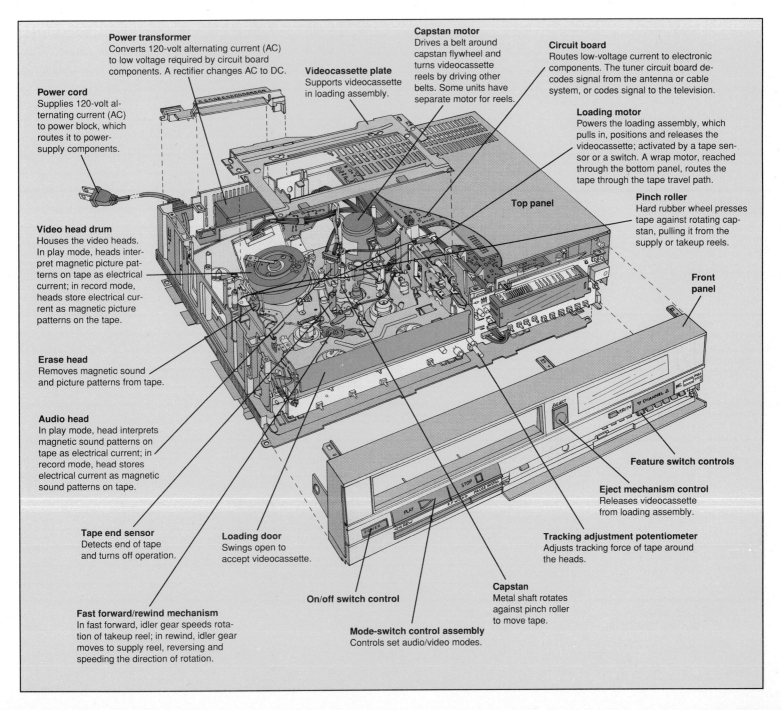

Power transformer
Converts 120-volt alternating current (AC) to low voltage required by circuit board components. A rectifier changes AC to DC.

Capstan motor
Drives a belt around capstan flywheel and turns videocassette reels by driving other belts. Some units have separate motor for reels.

Circuit board
Routes low-voltage current to electronic components. The tuner circuit board decodes signal from the antenna or cable system, or codes signal to the television.

Videocassette plate
Supports videocassette in loading assembly.

Power cord
Supplies 120-volt alternating current (AC) to power block, which routes it to power-supply components.

Loading motor
Powers the loading assembly, which pulls in, positions and releases the videocassette; activated by a tape sensor or a switch. A wrap motor, reached through the bottom panel, routes the tape through the tape travel path.

Top panel

Pinch roller
Hard rubber wheel presses tape against rotating capstan, pulling it from the supply or takeup reels.

Video head drum
Houses the video heads. In play mode, heads interpret magnetic picture patterns on tape as electrical current; in record mode, heads store electrical current as magnetic picture patterns on the tape.

Front panel

Erase head
Removes magnetic sound and picture patterns from tape.

Audio head
In play mode, head interprets magnetic sound patterns on tape as electrical current; in record mode, head stores electrical current as magnetic sound patterns on tape.

Feature switch controls

Eject mechanism control
Releases videocassette from loading assembly.

Tape end sensor
Detects end of tape and turns off operation.

Loading door
Swings open to accept videocassette.

Tracking adjustment potentiometer
Adjusts tracking force of tape around the heads.

On/off switch control

Capstan
Metal shaft rotates against pinch roller to move tape.

Fast forward/rewind mechanism
In fast forward, idler gear speeds rotation of takeup reel; in rewind, idler gear moves to supply reel, reversing and speeding the direction of rotation.

Mode-switch control assembly
Controls set audio/video modes.

TROUBLESHOOTING GUIDE

SYMPTOM	POSSIBLE CAUSE	PROCEDURE
No display lights, no picture and no sound	Videocassette recorder unplugged or off	Plug in and turn on videocassette recorder
	Remote control dirty or faulty	Service remote control (p. 417) □○; replace batteries
	No power to outlet or outlet faulty	Reset breaker or replace fuse (p. 102) □○; service outlet (p. 148)
	Power cord faulty	Test and replace power cord (p. 417) □○
	Power fuse blown	Test and replace power fuse (p. 414) □○
	On/off switch faulty	Test and replace on/off switch (p. 415) ◪○
	Power supply faulty	Take videocassette recorder for professional service
	Circuit board faulty	Take videocassette recorder for professional service
Display lights, but no picture and no sound	Videocassette tape torn or jammed	Replace tape or have it serviced; remove jammed tape (p. 412) □○
	Television or cables faulty	Troubleshoot entertainment system (p. 356) □○
	Drive belt loose or broken	Service drive belts (p. 413) □○
	Pinch roller faulty	Replace pinch roller (p. 414) □○
	On/off switch faulty	Test and replace on/off switch (p. 415) ◪○
	Motor faulty	Take videocassette recorder for professional service
	Circuit board faulty	Take videocassette recorder for professional service
Picture and sound, but no display lights	Display lights faulty	Take videocassette recorder for professional service
Picture, but no sound; or sound, but no picture	Receiver or television or cables faulty	Troubleshoot entertainment system (p. 356) □○
	Video or audio head or circuit board faulty	Take videocassette recorder for professional service
Sound from only one channel	Receiver, speaker or cables faulty	Troubleshoot entertainment system (p. 356) □○
	Audio head or circuit board faulty	Take videocassette recorder for professional service
Picture and/or sound intermittent or distorted	Videocassette tape tracking poorly	Adjust tracking force control
	Television, receiver or other unit faulty	Troubleshoot entertainment system (p. 356) □○
	Tape travel path dirty	Clean and demagnetize tape travel path (p. 410) □○▲
	Drive belt dirty or loose	Service drive belts (p. 413) □○
	Pinch roller faulty	Replace pinch roller (p. 414) □○
	Capstan/reel motor faulty	Take videocassette recorder for professional service
	Circuit board faulty	Take videocassette recorder for professional service
Mode or feature control doesn't work	Mode or feature switch dirty or faulty	Clean, test and replace mode or feature switch (p. 415) ◪○
	Circuit board faulty	Take videocassette recorder for professional service
Videocassette tape doesn't fast forward or doesn't rewind	Fast forward/rewind mechanism dirty	Service fast forward/rewind mechanism (p. 413) □○
	Fast/forward or rewind switch dirty or faulty	Clean, test and replace switch (p. 415) ◪○
	Circuit board faulty	Take videocassette recorder for professional service
Videocassette tape can't be erased or recorded over	Videocassette safety tab removed	Restore videocassette safety tab (p. 409) □○
	Erase head or circuit board faulty	Take videocassette recorder for professional service
Videocassette tape jams or tears repeatedly	Tape travel path dirty	Clean and demagnetize tape travel path (p. 410) □○▲
	Loading assembly dirty	Clean and lubricate loading assembly (p. 412) □○
	Fast forward/rewind mechanism dirty	Service fast forward/rewind mechanism (p. 413) □○
	Pinch roller faulty	Replace pinch roller (p. 414) □○
	Wrap motor faulty	Take videocassette recorder for professional service
	Capstan/reel motor faulty	Take videocassette recorder for professional service
Videocassette doesn't load or doesn't unload	Loading assembly dirty	Clean and lubricate loading assembly (p. 412) □○
	Videocassette tape jammed	Remove jammed tape (p. 412) □○
	Loading motor faulty	Take videocassette recorder for professional service

DEGREE OF DIFFICULTY: □ Easy ◪ Moderate ◼ Complex
ESTIMATED TIME: ○ Less than 1 hour ◑ 1 to 3 hours ● Over 3 hours   ▲ Special tool required

SERVICING VIDEOCASSETTES

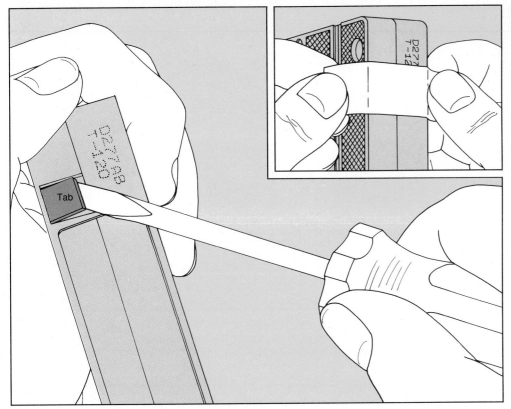

Removing and restoring the videocassette safety tab. Locate the videocassette safety tab on the top edge of the housing. To prevent the videocassette tape from being erased or recorded over, break off the safety tab using a small, flat screwdriver *(left)*; if the safety tab falls into the videocassette tape housing, remove it using long-nose pliers. To restore the ability to erase or record over the videocassette tape, cover the safety tab opening with a small piece of plastic tape *(inset)*. Avoid touching the videocassette tape with your fingers; replace the videocassette or have it serviced if the tape is damaged.

ACCESS TO THE INTERNAL COMPONENTS

Removing and reinstalling the top or bottom panel. Unload the videocassette, turn off and unplug the videocassette recorder, and disconnect the cables hooked up to it *(page 354)*. To remove the top panel, check for screws on the sides, back or bottom. Unscrew the top panel *(inset)*, slide it out from under any lip on the front panel and lift it off the frame. To remove the bottom panel, turn over the videocassette recorder, unscrew the bottom panel and lift it off *(left)*. To reinstall the top panel, slide it under any lip on the front panel and screw it to the frame. To reinstall the bottom panel, set it on the frame, put back the screws and turn the videocassette recorder upright. Cold check the videocassette recorder for leaking voltage *(page 417)* any time it has been opened. Reconnect the cables *(page 358)* and plug in the videocassette recorder.

ACCESS TO THE INTERNAL COMPONENTS (continued)

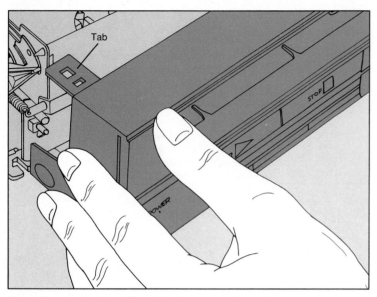

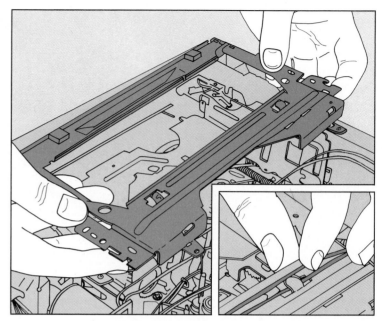

Removing and reinstalling the front panel or plate. If the machine has a front plate, remove it for access; otherwise, take off the front panel itself. Remove the top panel *(page 409)*. Check the top, sides and bottom for tabs and screws securing the front panel or plate. Pull off or unscrew any controls too large to fit through their openings. Unscrew the front panel or plate, press in the tabs at the corners and pull off the front panel or plate *(above)*. To reinstall the front panel or plate, snap it onto the frame, put back any screws, and push on or screw on the controls. Reinstall the top panel *(page 409)*.

Removing and reinstalling the videocassette plate. Remove the top panel *(page 409)* and locate the videocassette plate covering the tape travel path. Note the positions of any springs securing the videocassette plate and disconnect them from the plate using long-nose pliers or tweezers. Unhook any wires from tabs on the plate *(inset)*. Unscrew and lift out the plate *(above)*. To reinstall the videocassette plate, screw it in, hook the wires under their tabs and put back the springs. Reinstall the top panel *(page 409)*.

SERVICING THE TAPE TRAVEL PATH

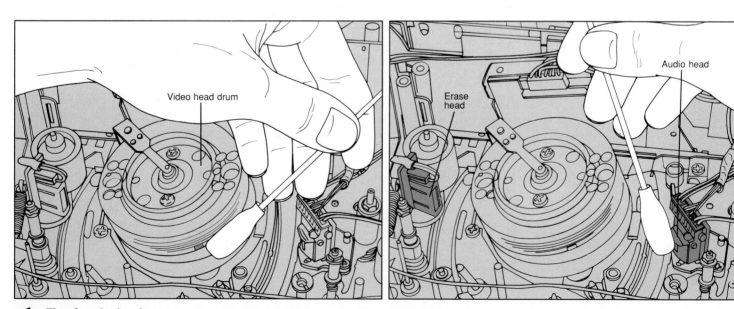

1 **Cleaning the heads.** Unplug the VCR. Remove the top panel *(page 409)* and the videocassette plate *(step above)*. To clean the video heads, the audio head and the erase head, use a foam swab dipped in denatured alcohol. For VHS video heads, gently hold the swab against the upper half of the video head drum and slowly rotate the drum counterclockwise several times *(above, left)*. For Beta video heads, wipe evenly across each head. Apply extremely light pressure and wipe only horizontally; up-and-down rubbing with the swab can damage a video head. Next, use a fresh foam swab dipped in denatured alcohol to wipe in turn the entire surface of both the audio head and the erase head *(above, right)*.

SERVICING THE TAPE TRAVEL PATH (continued)

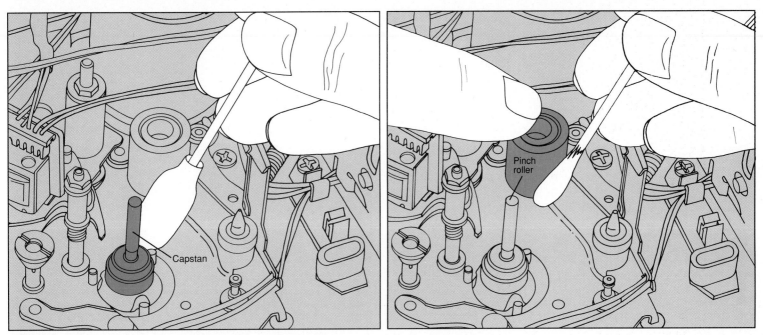

2 **Cleaning the capstan, the guides and the pinch roller.** Use a foam swab dipped in denatured alcohol to clean the entire surface of the capstan, the guides and any other metal or plastic component that contacts the videocassette tape *(above, left)*; apply only moderate pressure and change often to a fresh foam swab. To clean the pinch roller, use a fresh foam swab dipped in rubber-cleaning compound; slowly turn the pinch roller with a finger as you wipe, to reach the entire surface *(above, right)*. Check the condition of the pinch roller; if it is worn or damaged, replace it *(page 414)*.

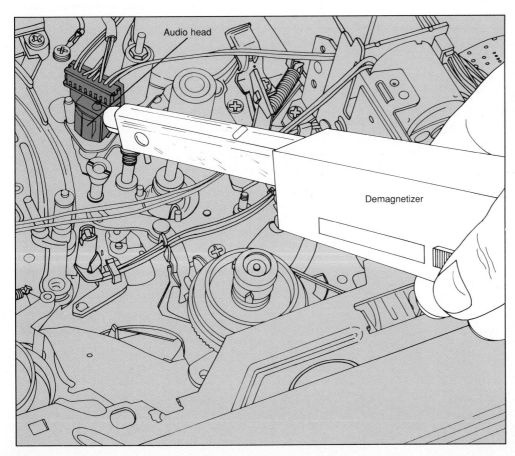

3 **Demagnetizing the tape travel path.** Purchase a demagnetizer at an electronics parts supplier. Plug the demagnetizer into a wall outlet and turn it on at least 2 feet away from the videocassette recorder. Slowly bring the demagnetizer within 1/2 inch of the video head drum, draw it about 2 feet away and turn it off; be especially careful not to touch a video head with the demagnetizer. Repeat this procedure for the audio head *(left)* and the erase head, as well as for the capstan, the guides and any other metal component that contacts a videocassette. Reinstall the videocassette plate and the top panel, and cold check for leaking voltage *(page 417)*.

SERVICING THE LOADING ASSEMBLY

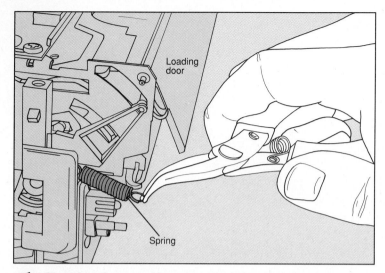

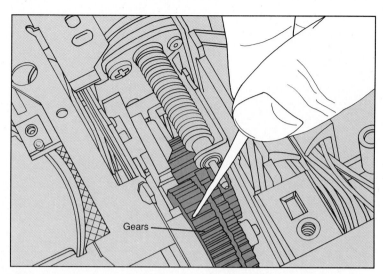

1 **Checking the assembly.** Unplug the VCR. Remove the top panel *(page 409)* and the front panel or plate *(page 410)*. Check the loading assembly and take out any obstructions. If the gears are dirty, clean and lubricate them *(step 2)*. Reconnect any unhooked spring using long-nose pliers *(above)* or tweezers; if a spring is damaged, replace it. If the supply-reel drive belt is dirty, clean it with a foam swab dipped in rubber-cleaning compound; if the drive belt is worn or broken, replace it *(page 413)*.

2 **Cleaning and lubricating the gears.** Clean the loading assembly gears using a foam swab dipped in denatured alcohol. Use a toothpick to dislodge particles from the gear teeth *(above)*. Spray gears that are difficult to reach with short bursts of compressed air. If it is necessary to turn the gears, slide in a videocassette and hold it in place. To lubricate the gears, use a toothpick to apply a little white grease. Wipe off the excess with a clean foam swab. Reinstall the front panel or plate and the top panel, and cold check for leaking voltage *(page 417)*.

REMOVING A JAMMED VIDEOCASSETTE

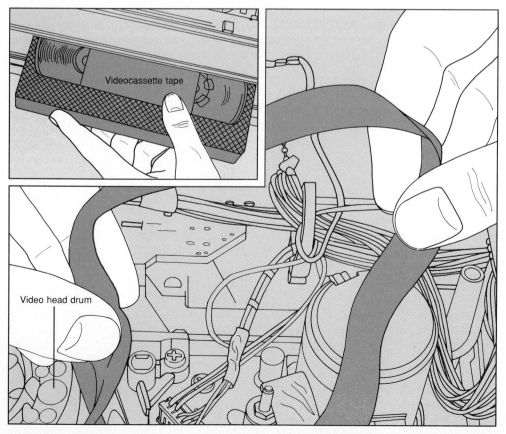

Retrieving jammed tape. Unplug the VCR. Remove the top panel *(page 409)* and gently try to extract the videocassette tape from the tape travel path components by hand *(left)*; avoid touching the undamaged tape with your fingers or applying pressure to any components. If the tape is difficult to retrieve, cut it with scissors, making sure not to leave behind any stray scraps. Once the tape is disentangled, pull out the videocassette through the loading door *(inset)*. If the videocassette cannot be removed easily, take off its plate *(page 410)*, lift out the videocassette and put back the plate. Then reinstall the top panel. If the tape has been cut or is badly damaged, replace the videocassette or have it serviced. If the tape is OK, press the button on the side of the videocassette to open the flap, and turn the takeup reel with a flat-bladed tool to rewind the tape, being careful not to twist it. Close the videocassette flap. Avoid replaying a videocassette tape that has jammed except to make a copy.

SERVICING THE FAST FORWARD/REWIND MECHANISM

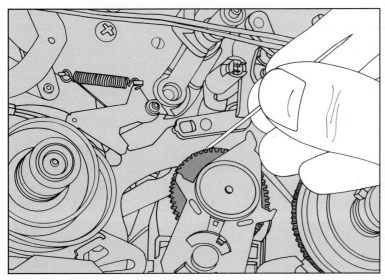
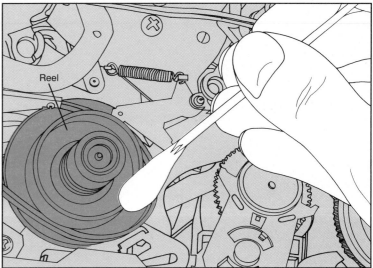

Cleaning the idler gears and the supply and takeup reels. Unplug the VCR. Remove the top panel *(page 409)* and locate the idler gears and the supply and takeup reels. Clean the gears using a foam swab dipped in denatured alcohol. Use a toothpick to dislodge particles from the gear teeth *(above, left)*. Lubricate the gears by applying a little white grease with a small stick or toothpick, and wipe off any excess using a clean foam swab. To clean the reels, use a clean foam swab *(above, right)*, applying denatured alcohol if they are plastic or rubber-cleaning compound if they are rubber. Clean drive belts with rubber-cleaning compound, using a foam swab. Reinstall the top panel and cold check for leaking voltage *(page 417)*.

SERVICING DRIVE BELTS

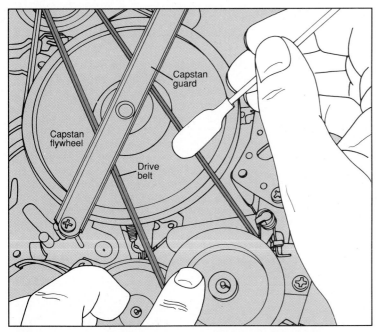
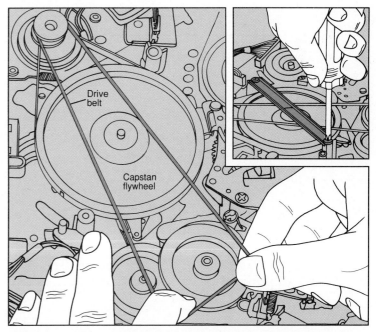

1 Cleaning a belt. Unplug the VCR. Remove the bottom panel *(page 409)* and locate the drive belts on the tape transport assembly. If a belt is worn or broken, replace it *(step 2)*. If a belt is sticky or greasy, clean the belt thoroughly using a foam swab dipped in rubber-cleaning compound *(above)*. Never apply anything oily, and avoid touching the belt with your fingers. Turn the belt pulleys or the capstan flywheel with a clean foam swab to reach the entire length of the belt. Reinstall the bottom panel and check for leaking voltage.

2 Removing and replacing a belt. Unscrew and remove the capstan guard *(inset)* and slip off the belt *(above)*, noting its position on the pulleys or the capstan flywheel. If necessary, use long-nose pliers or tweezers to remove any other belt in the way. Purchase an exact replacement belt at an electronics parts supplier. Holding the belt loosely with long-nose pliers or tweezers, wrap it around the pulleys or the capstan flywheel. Screw in the capstan guard and reinstall the bottom panel. Cold check for leaking voltage *(page 417)*.

REPLACING THE PINCH ROLLER

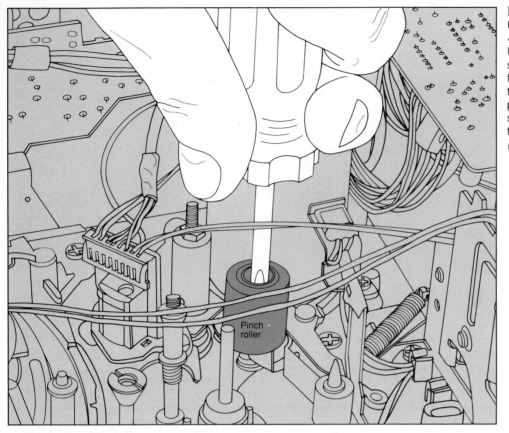

Pinch roller

Removing and reinstalling the pinch roller. Unplug the VCR. Remove the top panel *(page 409)* and the videocassette plate *(page 410)*. Unscrew the pinch roller *(left)* and lift it off the shaft. Order an exact replacement pinch roller from the manufacturer, or purchase a substitute at an electronics parts supplier. Slide the pinch roller onto the shaft and screw it into position. Reinstall the videocassette plate and the top panel. Cold check for leaking voltage *(page 417)*.

REPLACING THE POWER FUSE

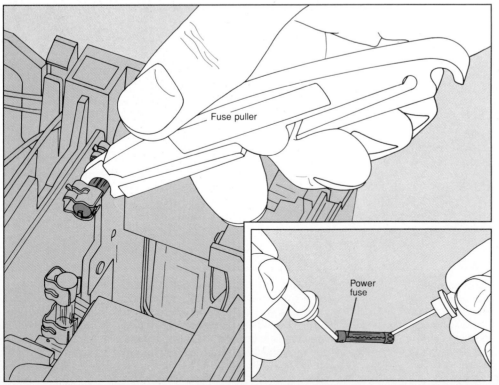

Fuse puller

Power fuse

Removing and testing the fuse. Unplug the VCR. Remove the top panel *(page 409)* and locate the fuse on the circuit board nearest the power supply components. Grasp the fuse with a fuse puller and gently pry it out of the retaining clips *(left)*. To test the fuse, set a multitester to test continuity. Touch one probe to the cap at one end of the fuse and touch the other probe to the cap at the other end of the fuse *(inset)*. If the multitester does not register continuity, purchase an exact replacement fuse at an electronics parts supplier. If the multitester registers continuity, reinstall the fuse. Gently push the fuse into the retaining clips and reinstall the top panel. Cold check for leaking voltage *(page 417)*. If the fuse blows repeatedly, have the power supply serviced.

SERVICING THE ON/OFF, MODE AND FEATURE SWITCHES

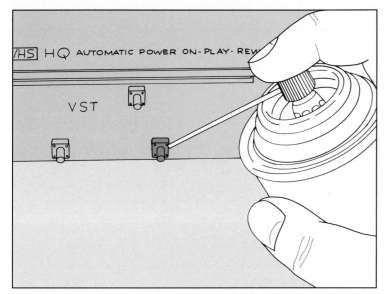

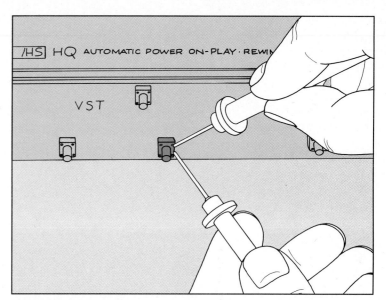

1 **Cleaning a mode or feature switch.** Unplug the VCR. Remove the top panel *(page 409)* and the front panel or plate *(page 410)*. Find the on/off, mode and feature switches on the circuit board. If you suspect the on/off switch is faulty, test it *(step 2)*; never apply cleaner to an on/off switch. To clean a mode or feature switch, spray a small amount of electronic contact cleaner into the opening between the switch and the circuit board *(above)*. Press in and release the switch several times to work in the cleaner. Reinstall the front panel or plate and the top panel. Cold check for leaking voltage *(page 417)*. If the problem persists, test the switch *(step 2)*.

2 **Testing a switch.** Unplug the VCR and access the switch *(step 1)*. Set a multitester to test continuity. Set the switch to one position and touch a probe to each pin on one side of the switch; repeat this step with the switch set in the other position. The switch should register continuity in only one position. Repeat this procedure with the pins on the other side of the switch. If the switch tests faulty, remove it *(step 3)*. If the switch tests OK, suspect a faulty circuit board and take the videocassette recorder for professional service; reinstall the front panel or plate and the top panel.

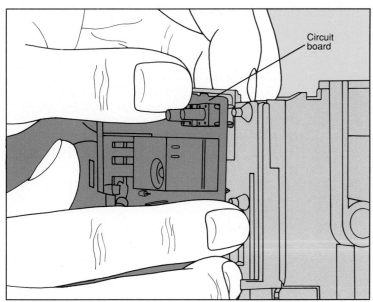

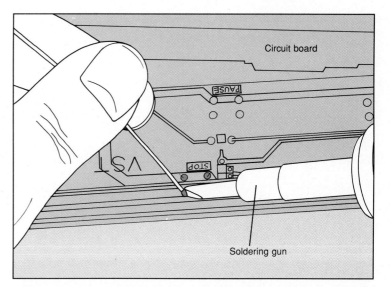

3 **Removing a switch.** Unscrew the circuit board for the switch, press in any tabs securing it to the frame *(above)*, and carefully turn it over. Desolder the switch pins *(page 417)* and pull off the switch; wiggle it to help release the pins from the circuit board. Test continuity again to confirm the switch is faulty *(step 2)*. If the switch still tests faulty, replace it *(step 4)*. If the switch now tests OK, suspect a faulty circuit board and take the videocassette recorder for professional service; put back the circuit board and reinstall the front panel or plate and the top panel. Cold check for leaking voltage *(page 417)*.

4 **Replacing a switch.** Order an exact replacement switch from the manufacturer or purchase a substitute at an electronics parts supplier. Fit the switch pins into the circuit board, turn over the circuit board and solder the pins *(above)*. Screw the circuit board in place. Reinstall the front panel or plate and the top panel. Cold check for leaking voltage *(page 417)*. If a problem persists with the on/off switch, have the power supply serviced. If a problem persists with a mode or feature switch, suspect a faulty circuit board and take the videocassette recorder for professional service.

TOOLS & TECHNIQUES

417

TOOLS & TECHNIQUES

This section introduces basic tests and procedures that help you perform the repairs shown in this book, from using electrical testers to soldering wires and electrical components. The repairs are common to the appliances, fixtures and units covered in the various chapters. A malfunction in an appliance, for example, may be traced to a faulty power cord, or to a loose or disconnected wire in the outlet. Water under the sink or clothes washer may be due to a leaking shutoff valve.

You can handle most repairs with the tools and supplies shown on pages 418–421. Specialized tools can sometimes be rented or borrowed from the suppliers that carry replacement parts. For the best results, buy the highest quality tools you can afford and use the right tool for the job. Take the time to care for and store your tools properly. Clean metal tools—but never their handles—using a cloth moistenend with light machine oil. Remove rust by rubbing the metal with fine steel wool. Protect tools in a sturdy plastic or metal toolbox, with a secure lock if stored around children.

Review the owner's manual for the unit or appliance before undertaking any repair; even a quick and simple job, such as replacing the power cord, may void the warranty. When an appliance stops working, determine whether the problem originates outside the unit before you take the appliance apart. If a fuse blows repeatedly, calculate the electrical load on the circuit *(page 443)* and move several appliances to another circuit if necessary.

Getting inside a small appliance or electronic unit to make a repair is often the most difficult part of the job. Check for hidden screws and tabs *(pages 441–442)* rather than forcing panels or casings apart. Magnetize screwdrivers to avoid time-

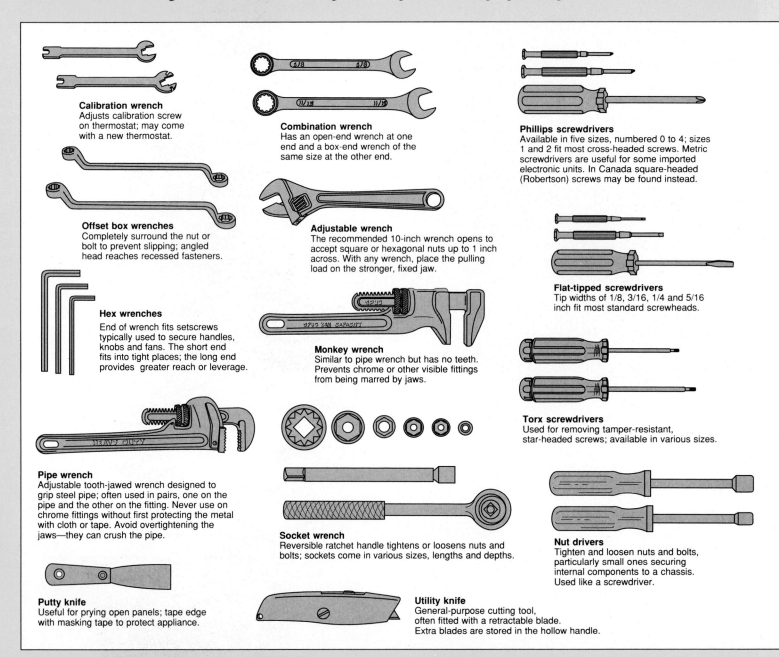

Calibration wrench
Adjusts calibration screw on thermostat; may come with a new thermostat.

Offset box wrenches
Completely surround the nut or bolt to prevent slipping; angled head reaches recessed fasteners.

Hex wrenches
End of wrench fits setscrews typically used to secure handles, knobs and fans. The short end fits into tight places; the long end provides greater reach or leverage.

Pipe wrench
Adjustable tooth-jawed wrench designed to grip steel pipe; often used in pairs, one on the pipe and the other on the fitting. Never use on chrome fittings without first protecting the metal with cloth or tape. Avoid overtightening the jaws—they can crush the pipe.

Putty knife
Useful for prying open panels; tape edge with masking tape to protect appliance.

Combination wrench
Has an open-end wrench at one end and a box-end wrench of the same size at the other end.

Adjustable wrench
The recommended 10-inch wrench opens to accept square or hexagonal nuts up to 1 inch across. With any wrench, place the pulling load on the stronger, fixed jaw.

Monkey wrench
Similar to pipe wrench but has no teeth. Prevents chrome or other visible fittings from being marred by jaws.

Socket wrench
Reversible ratchet handle tightens or loosens nuts and bolts; sockets come in various sizes, lengths and depths.

Utility knife
General-purpose cutting tool, often fitted with a retractable blade. Extra blades are stored in the hollow handle.

Phillips screwdrivers
Available in five sizes, numbered 0 to 4; sizes 1 and 2 fit most cross-headed screws. Metric screwdrivers are useful for some imported electronic units. In Canada square-headed (Robertson) screws may be found instead.

Flat-tipped screwdrivers
Tip widths of 1/8, 3/16, 1/4 and 5/16 inch fit most standard screwheads.

Torx screwdrivers
Used for removing tamper-resistant, star-headed screws; available in various sizes.

Nut drivers
Tighten and loosen nuts and bolts, particularly small ones securing internal components to a chassis. Used like a screwdriver.

consuming hunts for a screw dropped inside the unit. To avoid stripping screw heads, choose a screwdriver that fits and don't use excessive force. Always substitute a faulty component with an identical replacement. To free a rusted or corroded fitting, first try tightening it before loosening it. Or apply penetrating oil and let it sit for 15 to 30 minutes, or even overnight, to allow the oil to work its way between parts. Work patiently and methodically; never take short cuts. Keep in mind that even seemingly complicated tasks are seldom more than a sequence of easy steps.

Throughout this book, the use of a multitester *(page 425)*, also known as a volt-ohmmeter, is called for to test continuity, resistance and voltage. Be aware that although you may be performing the same test using the same procedure, the purpose of the test may vary from one instance to another. For example, in one situation continuity may mean a component is OK; in another, it may mean a component is faulty. Perform a cold check for leaking voltage before plugging a unit back in *(page 427)*, to ensure that no wires are crossed or disconnected and that there is no ground fault in the appliance.

Repairs can be done safely if you observe basic precautions. Keep the work area well-lit, clean and free of clutter. Don't wear loose clothing or jewelry, and tie back long hair to keep it out of the way. Use safety equipment such as insulated gloves or safety goggles wherever recommended. Don't smoke or cause a spark around gas appliances or oil burners. Always unplug an appliance or unit before working on it, and discharge the capacitors of a heat pump or microwave oven when recommended. After turning off power at the service panel, confirm that the power is off *(page 424)*.

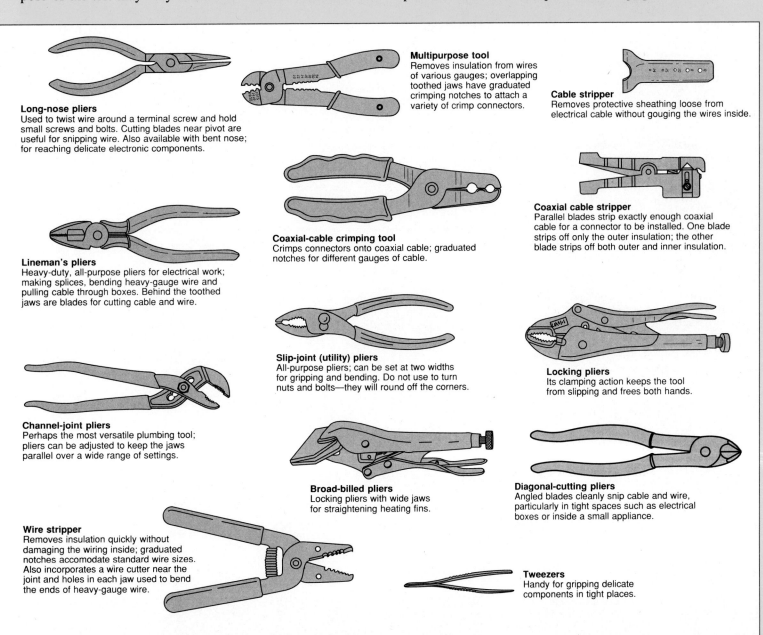

Long-nose pliers
Used to twist wire around a terminal screw and hold small screws and bolts. Cutting blades near pivot are useful for snipping wire. Also available with bent nose; for reaching delicate electronic components.

Lineman's pliers
Heavy-duty, all-purpose pliers for electrical work; making splices, bending heavy-gauge wire and pulling cable through boxes. Behind the toothed jaws are blades for cutting cable and wire.

Channel-joint pliers
Perhaps the most versatile plumbing tool; pliers can be adjusted to keep the jaws parallel over a wide range of settings.

Wire stripper
Removes insulation quickly without damaging the wiring inside; graduated notches accomodate standard wire sizes. Also incorporates a wire cutter near the joint and holes in each jaw used to bend the ends of heavy-gauge wire.

Multipurpose tool
Removes insulation from wires of various gauges; overlapping toothed jaws have graduated crimping notches to attach a variety of crimp connectors.

Coaxial-cable crimping tool
Crimps connectors onto coaxial cable; graduated notches for different gauges of cable.

Slip-joint (utility) pliers
All-purpose pliers; can be set at two widths for gripping and bending. Do not use to turn nuts and bolts—they will round off the corners.

Broad-billed pliers
Locking pliers with wide jaws for straightening heating fins.

Cable stripper
Removes protective sheathing loose from electrical cable without gouging the wires inside.

Coaxial cable stripper
Parallel blades strip exactly enough coaxial cable for a connector to be installed. One blade strips off only the outer insulation; the other blade strips off both outer and inner insulation.

Locking pliers
Its clamping action keeps the tool from slipping and frees both hands.

Diagonal-cutting pliers
Angled blades cleanly snip cable and wire, particularly in tight spaces such as electrical boxes or inside a small appliance.

Tweezers
Handy for gripping delicate components in tight places.

BASIC AND SPECIALIZED TOOLS

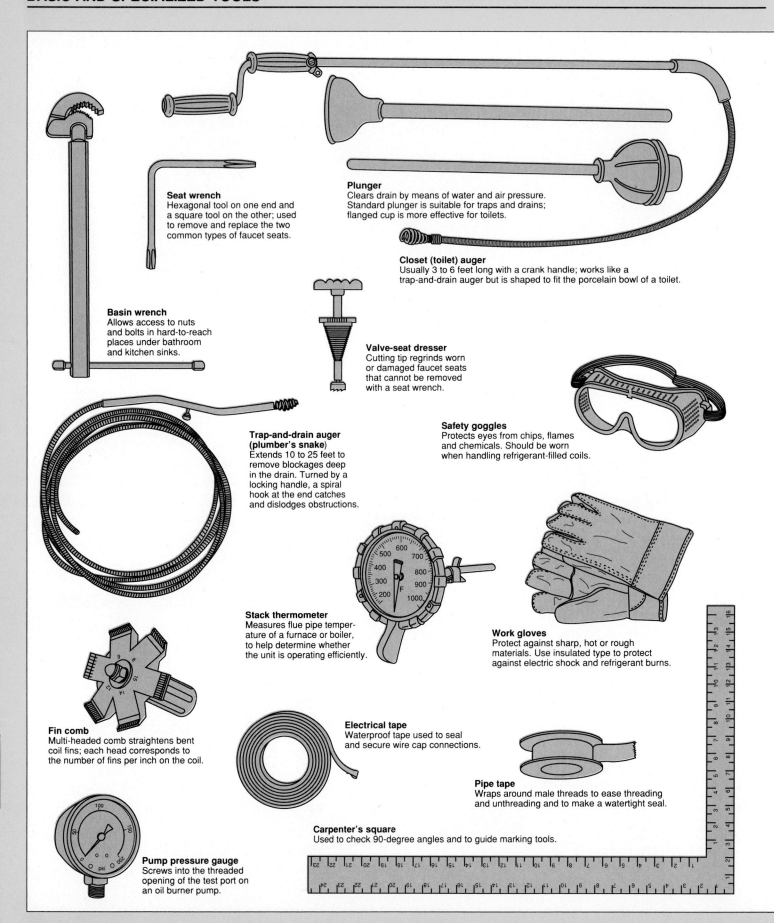

Seat wrench
Hexagonal tool on one end and a square tool on the other; used to remove and replace the two common types of faucet seats.

Plunger
Clears drain by means of water and air pressure. Standard plunger is suitable for traps and drains; flanged cup is more effective for toilets.

Closet (toilet) auger
Usually 3 to 6 feet long with a crank handle; works like a trap-and-drain auger but is shaped to fit the porcelain bowl of a toilet.

Basin wrench
Allows access to nuts and bolts in hard-to-reach places under bathroom and kitchen sinks.

Valve-seat dresser
Cutting tip regrinds worn or damaged faucet seats that cannot be removed with a seat wrench.

Safety goggles
Protects eyes from chips, flames and chemicals. Should be worn when handling refrigerant-filled coils.

Trap-and-drain auger (plumber's snake)
Extends 10 to 25 feet to remove blockages deep in the drain. Turned by a locking handle, a spiral hook at the end catches and dislodges obstructions.

Stack thermometer
Measures flue pipe temperature of a furnace or boiler, to help determine whether the unit is operating efficiently.

Work gloves
Protect against sharp, hot or rough materials. Use insulated type to protect against electric shock and refrigerant burns.

Fin comb
Multi-headed comb straightens bent coil fins; each head corresponds to the number of fins per inch on the coil.

Electrical tape
Waterproof tape used to seal and secure wire cap connections.

Pipe tape
Wraps around male threads to ease threading and unthreading and to make a watertight seal.

Carpenter's square
Used to check 90-degree angles and to guide marking tools.

Pump pressure gauge
Screws into the threaded opening of the test port on an oil burner pump.

BASIC AND SPECIALIZED TOOLS (continued)

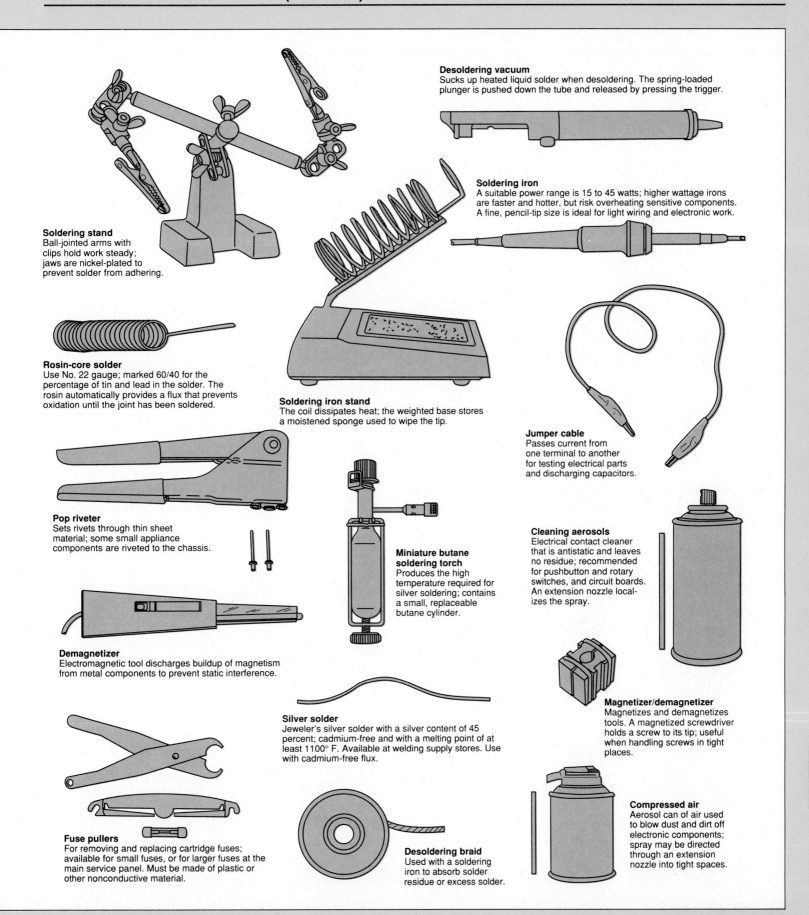

Desoldering vacuum
Sucks up heated liquid solder when desoldering. The spring-loaded plunger is pushed down the tube and released by pressing the trigger.

Soldering iron
A suitable power range is 15 to 45 watts; higher wattage irons are faster and hotter, but risk overheating sensitive components. A fine, pencil-tip size is ideal for light wiring and electronic work.

Soldering stand
Ball-jointed arms with clips hold work steady; jaws are nickel-plated to prevent solder from adhering.

Rosin-core solder
Use No. 22 gauge; marked 60/40 for the percentage of tin and lead in the solder. The rosin automatically provides a flux that prevents oxidation until the joint has been soldered.

Soldering iron stand
The coil dissipates heat; the weighted base stores a moistened sponge used to wipe the tip.

Jumper cable
Passes current from one terminal to another for testing electrical parts and discharging capacitors.

Pop riveter
Sets rivets through thin sheet material; some small appliance components are riveted to the chassis.

Miniature butane soldering torch
Produces the high temperature required for silver soldering; contains a small, replaceable butane cylinder.

Cleaning aerosols
Electrical contact cleaner that is antistatic and leaves no residue; recommended for pushbutton and rotary switches, and circuit boards. An extension nozzle localizes the spray.

Demagnetizer
Electromagnetic tool discharges buildup of magnetism from metal components to prevent static interference.

Magnetizer/demagnetizer
Magnetizes and demagnetizes tools. A magnetized screwdriver holds a screw to its tip; useful when handling screws in tight places.

Silver solder
Jeweler's silver solder with a silver content of 45 percent; cadmium-free and with a melting point of at least 1100° F. Available at welding supply stores. Use with cadmium-free flux.

Fuse pullers
For removing and replacing cartridge fuses; available for small fuses, or for larger fuses at the main service panel. Must be made of plastic or other nonconductive material.

Desoldering braid
Used with a soldering iron to absorb solder residue or excess solder.

Compressed air
Aerosol can of air used to blow dust and dirt off electronic components; spray may be directed through an extension nozzle into tight spaces.

SHUTOFF VALVES

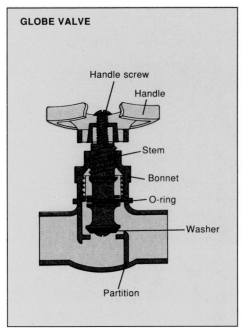

GLOBE VALVE

Handle screw
Handle
Stem
Bonnet
O-ring
Washer
Partition

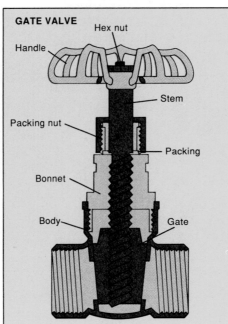

GATE VALVE

Hex nut
Handle
Stem
Packing nut
Packing
Bonnet
Body
Gate

Globe valves *(far left)* are installed on branch lines and fixtures, which may be opened and closed frequently. A partition within the valve body slows the flow of incoming water and therefore reduces water pressure in a supply line. When the handle is turned clockwise to close the valve, a rubber washer or disc presses against a matching seat to block the flow of water. Globe valves must be installed in the proper direction of flow; an arrow is usually stamped on the valve body.

Gate valves *(near left)* are located on the main water supply line. When the handle is turned clockwise to close the valve, a gate lowers to block the flow of water. Since a gate valve does not divert the flow of water from one direction to another, the pressure of the water is the same at both ends of the valve. On a horizontal run, installing the valve in an upright position prevents sediment from collecting in the closing mechanism.

Servicing valves. Close the main shutoff valve and open a faucet farther along the run to drain the supply line. If the main shutoff is faulty, call your local water department to close the curb valve outside the house *(page 18)*. Grip the valve body with a pipe wrench, and with the other hand, use an adjustable wrench to loosen the bonnet. Apply penetrating oil and wait, if necessary.

Remove the bonnet and valve stem. To clean out mineral deposits and sediment, bend the shaft of a wire brush for copper fittings, and scrub as far inside the valve body as possible. To cure leaks around the stem and handle, replace the washer, O-ring or packing, and reassemble the valve. Restore the water supply. If the valve continues to leak, or doesn't close, have it replaced.

SHUTOFF VALVES: ADDING A FIXTURE VALVE

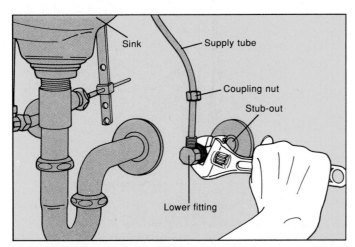

Sink
Supply tube
Coupling nut
Stub-out
Lower fitting

1 **Removing the lower fitting.** Close the main shutoff valve and drain the supply lines. With an adjustable wrench, unscrew the coupling nut on the lower fitting, then the nut on the stub-out *(above)*. Pull the fitting off the stub-out and supply tube. Cut off the stub-out's compression ring with a hacksaw.

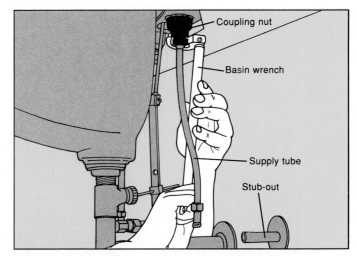

Coupling nut
Basin wrench
Supply tube
Stub-out

2 **Removing the supply tube.** Use a basin wrench to unscrew the coupling nut securing the supply tube to the faucet. Rotate the handle of the wrench counterclockwise *(above)* to loosen the nut, then unscrew it by hand.

SHUTOFF VALVES: ADDING A FIXTURE VALVE (continued)

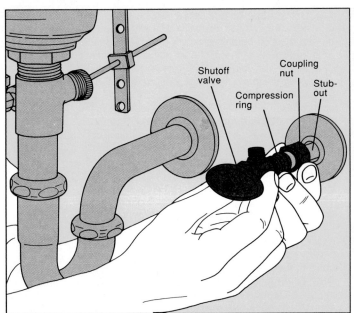

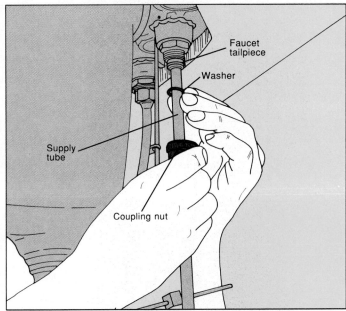

3 **Adding the shutoff valve and flexible supply tube.** Slip a new coupling nut and compression ring onto the stub-out, then fit the valve by hand *(above, left)* so that its outlet points up. Grip the valve with an adjustable wrench and tighten the coupling nut with a second wrench. (For a steel pipe, you will need a threaded union. For a copper pipe, you may need to have the valve soldered onto the stub-out). Insert one end of a new supply tube into the faucet tailpiece. Slip the washer, if any, and plastic coupling nut up the tube *(above, right)* and tighten the connection by hand.

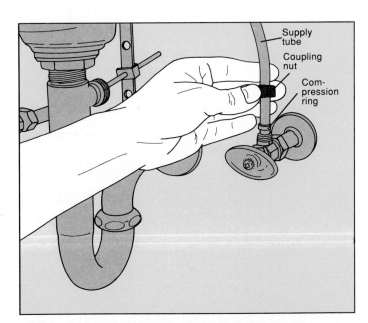

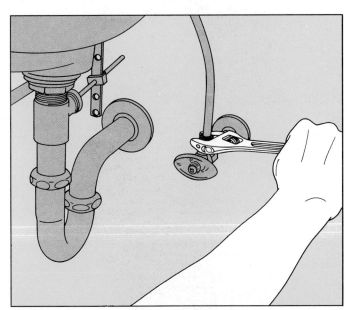

4 **Connecting the valve.** Slip the coupling nut and the compression ring onto the free end of the supply tube. Push the tube into the valve outlet as far as it will go. Slide the compression ring into the joint, making sure that is squarely aligned, then slide the coupling nut over the fitting and screw it down by hand *(above)*.

5 **Testing the repair.** Tighten the coupling nut by hand. If a joint leaks, tighten the coupling nut one-half turn *(above)* with a wrench and test again. Otherwise, you must disassemble the fitting and start again. If the faucet has an aerator, remove it and open the faucet to allow the running water to clear debris loosened by the repair.

DIAGNOSING ELECTRICAL PROBLEMS

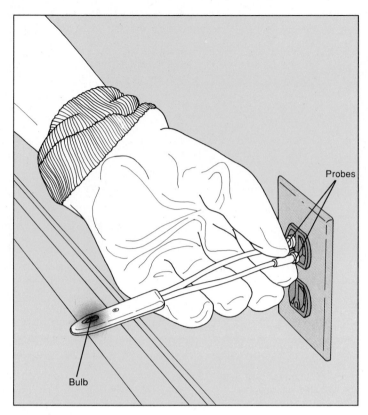

Using a voltage tester. Use a voltage tester *(left)* to make sure that the electricity to a circuit has been turned off before you work on it. (To test the amount of voltage in the circuit, use a multitester: page 426). The voltage tester has no power source of its own; it lights when its probes are touched to terminals or wires, or inserted in slots that are charged with electricity. The voltage tester is primarily a safeguard against shock, used to make sure that there is no current in the circuit you are working on.

In some cases the voltage tester is used with the power on to locate a hot (current-carrying) wire or to test the grounding at an outlet. Work with care when performing a live voltage test. Hold the tester probes by the insulated handles and use one hand only, as shown. (For additional protection against shock, wear an insulated glove.)

Buy a voltage tester rated for 240-volt household current. Always hold the two probes by their insulation—never touch the bare metal ends. Before using the voltage tester, check to make sure it works. Insert the probes of the voltage tester into the slots of a working outlet. If the bulb glows without flickering, the tester is good. Follow the specific directions in each chapter to turn off power to a circuit, then confirm that it is off using the voltage tester.

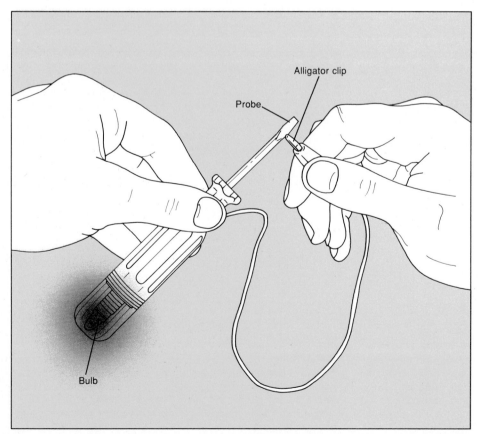

Using a continuity tester. The continuity tester sends a small current through a circuit to determine if its electrical path is intact. (A multitester can also be used for this: page 425). Because it is battery-powered, the tester must be used only when power to a circuit has been turned off. First check the battery by touching the alligator clip to the probe *(left)*; the bulb should light. To test for continuity, attach the alligator clip to one end of the circuit (a plug prong, for example) and touch the probe to the other end (the bare cord wire). If the circuit is complete, the bulb will glow. If it fails to light, there is a break in the circuit. When the tester is not in use, attach the alligator clip to its plastic insulation to prevent it from accidentally contacting the probe and wearing out the battery.

USING A MULTITESTER

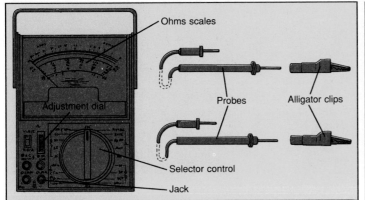

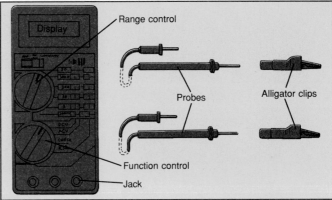

Troubleshooting with a multitester. A multitester, or volt-ohm-meter, is used to send a low-voltage electrical current from its batteries through the part being tested. It displays, in ohms, the precise amount of resistance the part has to electrical current. Zero ohms—total lack of resistance—indicates a completed circuit, or continuity. A multitester is also used to test voltage, measuring the precise amount of electrical current flowing in a completed circuit. A multitester may be analog *(above, left)*, with a needle that sweeps across a scale, or digital *(above, right)*, with a numerical display. On either type, connect the black cable to the negative, or common, jack and the red cable to the positive jack. To use an analog multitester, first "zero" the meter: With the multitester set at RX1, touch the probes together, or clip the alligator clips together. The needle should sweep from left or right toward ZERO; turn the adjustment dial until the needle lies directly over the zero on the scale. (If the multitester won't "zero" the batteries are low.) A digital multitester can be easier to use and read; consult the instructions that come with it. When testing, the alligator clips or probes should contact bare metal, terminals or wire ends; not insulated, painted or dirty ones.

USING A MULTITESTER: TESTING CONTINUITY

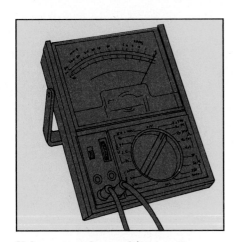

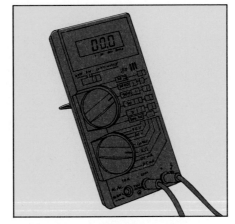

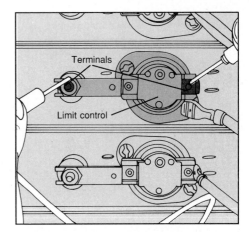

Using an analog multitester. Prepare the multitester as described above. Set the selector control to the RX1 setting *(above)*, or other setting specified for the repair. Touch each probe—or attach each clip—to a terminal of the component you are testing, as shown far right. If the needle swings to zero ohms, there is continuity. If the needle does not move from infinite ohms, there is no continuity.

Using a digital multitester. Prepare the multitester as described above. With the multitester turned on, turn the range control to its lowest setting and set the function control to OHMS *(above)*. Touch each probe—or attach each clip—to a terminal of the component you are testing, as shown at right. If the reading is 0.00, or if you hear a beep, there is continuity.

Testing continuity. A limit control in an electric furnace is being tested for continuity *(above)*. When each probe contacts a switch terminal the multitester tries to send low-voltage electrical current from its batteries through one probe. If the current passes through the control to the other probe, there is a complete circuit and continuity. If the current does not pass through to the other probe, there is no complete circuit and no continuity.

USING A MULTITESTER: TESTING VOLTAGE

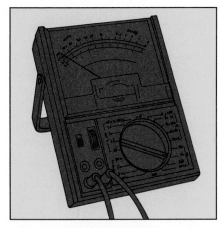

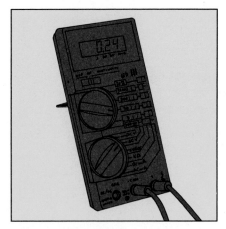

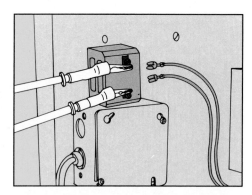

Using an analog multitester. Prepare the multitester as described on page 425. Set the selector control to 50 ACV for a transformer or a motor not connected to a circuit board; use DCV for a thermocouple or a motor connected to a circuit board. Turn off power to the system *(page 102)*. Attach each clip to a terminal, as shown at far right. Turn on the power: the multitester needle will show the amount of voltage in the circuit.

Using a digital multitester. Prepare the multitester as described on page 425, and turn it on. Set the range control to 30. If testing a transformer, set the function control to ACV. Turn off power to the system *(page 102)*. Attach each alligator clip to a terminal of the component, as shown at right. Turn on the power: the multitester display will show the amount of voltage in the circuit.

Testing voltage. Caution: Make sure power is off when attaching multitester clips to the component you are testing: do not touch the clips or the unit while power is on. In the example above, the power from a gas furnace transformer is tested. With each clip contacting a transformer terminal *(above)*, a low-voltage electrical current is sent through the multitester by turning on power to the furnace. The amount of electrical current flowing through the component is shown by the multitester's needle or display.

USING A MULTITESTER: TESTING RESISTANCE

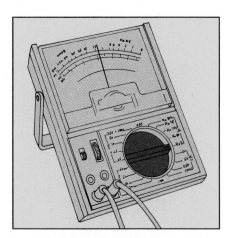

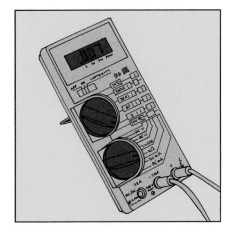

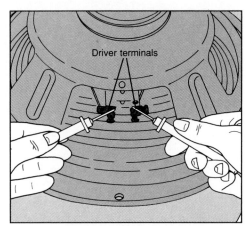

Driver terminals

Using an analog multitester. Prepare the multitester as described on page 425. Set the selector control to RX1; or RX1K when testing large capacitors. Touch each probe—or attach each clip—to a terminal of the component you are testing, as shown at far right. The needle position on the scale indicates the resistance level.

Using a digital multitester. Prepare the multitester as described on page 425. With the multitester turned on, set the range control to its lowest setting and set the function control to OHMS. Touch each probe—or attach each clip—to a terminal of the component you are testing, as shown at right.

Testing resistance. When each probe contacts a terminal *(above)*, the multitester tries to send low-voltage electrical current from its batteries through one probe. The amount of electrical current that passes through the component to the other probe is limited by the driver circuitry; this is displayed, in ohms, as resistance to the electrical current.

COLD CHECK FOR LEAKING VOLTAGE

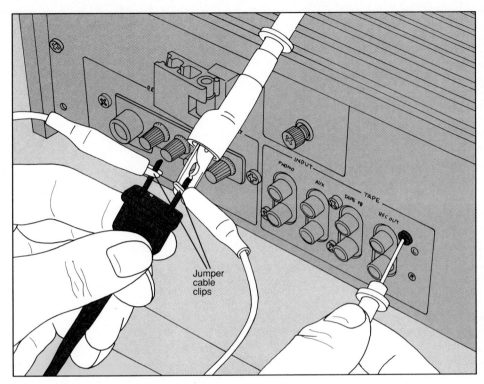

Jumper
cable
clips

Testing for a potential electrical hazard.
Before plugging in a unit that has undergone
an internal repair, perform a simple test to
confirm that no internal electrical circuits have
been damaged or shorted and that current
cannot leak to the chassis. Clip a jumper cable to the prongs on the power cord plug and
set the on/off control to the ON position. Set
a multitester to test continuity *(page 425)*.

Clip one multitester probe to a plug prong
and touch the other probe in turn to at least
two or three unpainted metal surfaces on the
unit *(left)*; screws through the panels into the
frame and cable terminals make ideal test
points. In each test, there should be no continuity. Unclip the jumper cable and touch a
probe to each prong on the power cord plug;
in this test, there should be continuity. If the
unit tests faulty in any test, do not plug it into
an outlet until you have located the problem
and remedied it: check for wires touching the
chassis. If you cannot determine the cause
of the problem, take the unit for professional
service. If the unit tests OK in each test, set
the on/off control to the OFF position and
plug the unit into an outlet.

DISCHARGING CAPACITORS

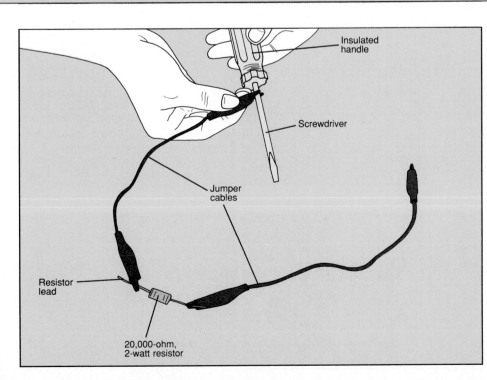

Insulated
handle

Screwdriver

Jumper
cables

Resistor
lead

20,000-ohm,
2-watt resistor

Making a capacitor discharging tool.
This simple tool discharges capacitors
without damage to them or injury to you.
Assemble two jumper cables with alligator
clips; a 20,000-ohm, 2-watt resistor, available from an electronics supplies store;
and a screwdriver with an insulated handle. Clip one end of a jumper cable to one
resistor lead and clip the other end to the
blade of the screwdriver. Clip one end of
the other jumper cable to the remaining
resistor lead *(left)*.

DISCHARGING CAPACITORS (continued)

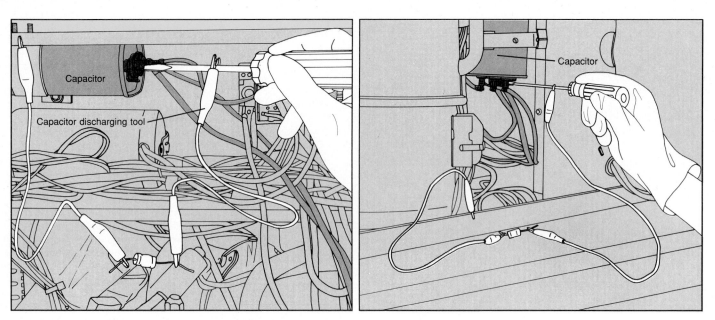

Discharging a capacitor with exposed terminals. Turn off power to the heating or cooling unit *(page 102)*. Using a capacitor discharging tool *(page 427)*, attach the free alligator clip to a clean, unpainted metal part of the unit's chassis. Hold the insulated handle of the screwdriver with one hand and touch the screwdriver blade to each of the capacitor's two *(above, left)* or three *(above, right)* terminals, in turn, for one second. Discharge all capacitors in the unit.

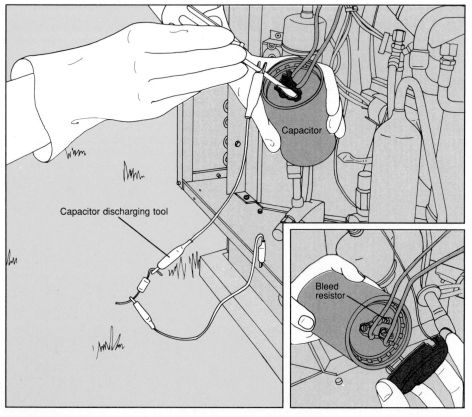

Discharging a capped capacitor. Turn off power to the unit *(page 102)*. Attach the free alligator clip of a capacitor discharging tool *(page 427)* to a clean, unpainted metal part of the unit's chassis. Release the capacitor from its clips and carefully remove the cap covering the capacitor terminals *(inset)*. **Caution:** Do not touch the capacitor terminals. Hold the capacitor in one hand and, holding the insulated handle of the screwdriver with the other hand, touch the screwdriver blade to each terminal on the capacitor, in turn, for one second *(left)*. Discharge all capacitors in the unit.

SERVICING 120-VOLT POWER CORDS

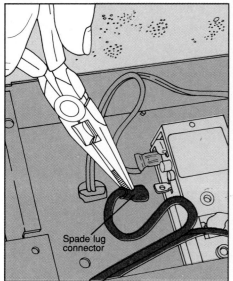

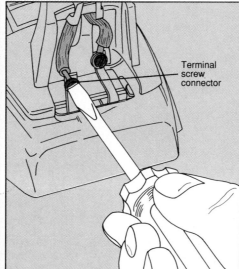

Terminal
screw
connector

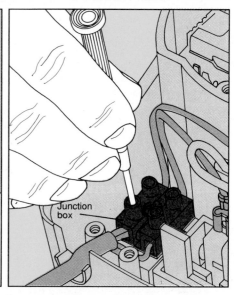

Junction
box

Spade lug
connector

1 **Disconnecting a power cord wire.** Unplug the appliance. Consult the appliance's chapter and the tips on disassembly *(pages 441–442)* to access the power cord terminals. Disconnect one of the power cord wires by pulling the spade lug connector off its terminal *(above, left)*; unscrewing one connector *(above, center)*; or removing the screw that clamps it inside a junction box *(above, right)*. If the wires are connected to other wires by a crimp wire cap, label the wires and cut off the cap; if they are soldered, desolder one wire *(page 439)*. In a major appliance, pull apart the small plastic plug.

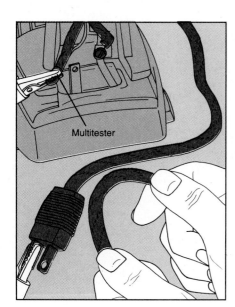

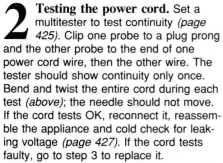

Multitester

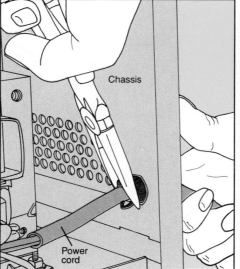

Chassis

Power
cord

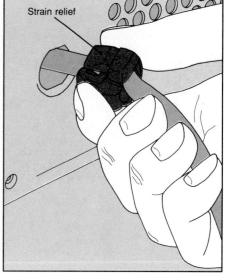

Strain relief

2 **Testing the power cord.** Set a multitester to test continuity *(page 425)*. Clip one probe to a plug prong and the other probe to the end of one power cord wire, then the other wire. The tester should show continuity only once. Bend and twist the entire cord during each test *(above)*; the needle should not move. If the cord tests OK, reconnect it, reassemble the appliance and cold check for leaking voltage *(page 427)*. If the cord tests faulty, go to step 3 to replace it.

3 **Replacing the power cord.** Disconnect the remaining power cord wire and remove the cord. If the power cord is held to the chassis with a strain relief grommet, squeeze the grommet with pliers and push it through its hole *(above, left)*. Then pull the power cord free and remove the grommet, keeping it for the new power cord. Buy an exact replacement power cord of the correct gauge insulation and number of wires *(page 432)* from an electrical parts supplier. Cut off a short length of the outer insulation at the end of the cord with a utility knife, then strip back the inner insulation from each wire end *(page 434)*. If the old power cord had terminal connectors, install identical connectors. Thread the power cord through the chassis, install the strain relief grommet on the cord *(above, right)* and push the grommet back into its hole. Clip, screw or solder the wires to their terminals, or install new crimp wire caps *(page 436)*. Reassemble the appliance, reversing the steps taken to disassemble it, and cold check for leaking voltage *(page 427)*.

SERVICING 240-VOLT POWER CORDS

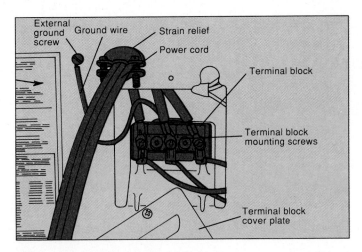

1 **Access to the terminal block.** The power cords of 240-volt appliances are connected to the machine's internal wiring via a terminal block. (Some 120-volt refrigerators also have terminal blocks.) If the appliance fails, or if a heating element doesn't heat, both the power cord and terminal block should be checked for damage. Unplug the appliance and remove the cover plate where the cord enters the back of the machine *(above)*. Inspect the terminal block for loose, burned, broken or corroded wires. At any visible sign of damage, have the block replaced.

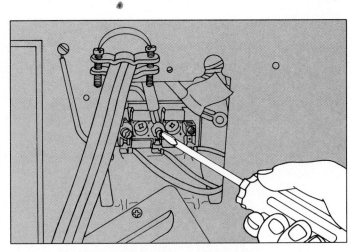

2 **Disconnecting the power cord.** To test the power cord for internal damage, first disconnect it from the terminal block. Label the wires for reassembly and, depending on your machine, either pull off the wire connectors or remove the screws or hex nuts holding the wires in place *(above)*.

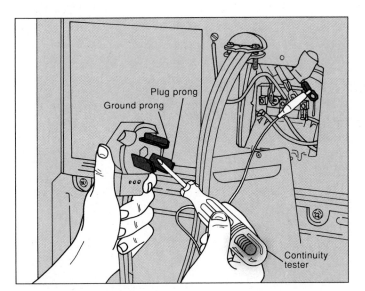

3 **Testing the power cord.** Touch the probe of a continuity tester to one of the flat prongs on the power cord plug. Touch the other tester probe to the terminals of the three wires in turn. The tester should glow against only one of the terminals. Repeat this test with the other flat prong *(above)*; the tester should glow against a different terminal. Replace the cord if faulty.
  Next, touch the tester probe to the ground prong, and the other probe to the teminal of the middle wire; the tester should light. If you have a four-prong, four-wire power cord, test the top middle ground prong against the grounding wire. Test the bottom middle prong against the middle wire to the terminal block. The tester bulb should glow; if not, replace the cord.

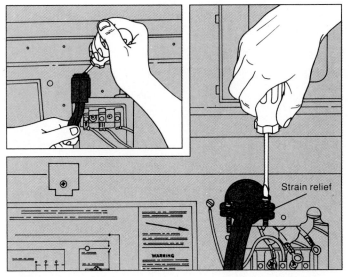

4 **Replacing the power cord.** To replace a power cord with a four-prong plug, first remove the screw securing the grounding wire to the cabinet. If the cord is protected by a metal strain relief, loosen it *(above)*, and pull the cord through the back of the cabinet. Newer appliances may have a plastic strain relief that is molded to the cord; pry the cord free with a flat-tipped screwdriver *(inset)*. Feed the new power cord through the back of the cabinet, wire it to the terminal block, and replace the cover plate.

SERVICING ELECTRICAL BOXES

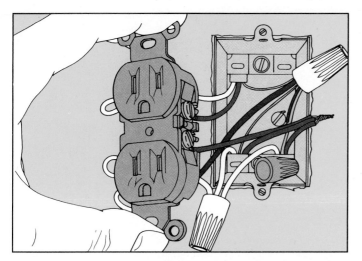

Reconnecting a loose wire. When a wire works loose from a wire cap *(above)* or terminal screw, and its bare metal end contacts the box or another bare wire, a short circuit results, blowing the fuse or tripping the circuit breaker. When a wire works loose from a connection but does not touch the box or another wire end, the current will not flow beyond that point. Turn off power to the outlet *(page 102)* and confirm that it is off. To reinstall a wire cap connection, make sure that the wire ends are firmly twisted together, then screw on a wire cap of the correct size. Reconnect a detached wire by hooking the end clockwise around its terminal and tightening the screw. Gently fold the wires back into the box.

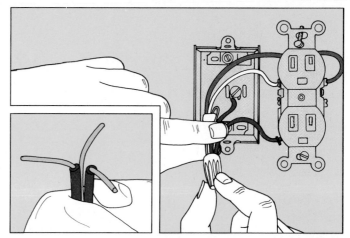

Joining jumper wires in a pigtail connection. To join more than one wire to the same terminal, use a jumper wire to make the connection. A jumper is usually 6 inches long and must match the gauge of the wires it joins. When grounding an outlet wih one cable in the box, for example, you will need two jumpers. With the power off, cut the first wire, strip back both ends *(page 434)*, then form one end into a hook and attach it to the ground screw at the back of the box. Prepare the second jumper and attach it to the grounding terminal on the outlet. Join the jumpers and the bare copper grounding wire using a pigtail connection. Hold the wire ends together and bend each at a right angle *(inset)*. With lineman's pliers, grip the wire ends and twist them together in a clockwise direction so that turns are tight and uniform along the length of the bare wires. Clip 1/4 inch off the end of the twisted wires, then screw a wire cap onto the connection *(above)*.

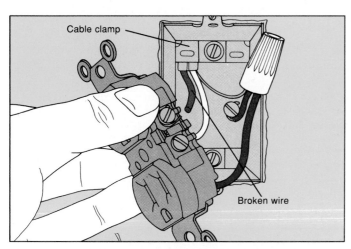

Repairing a broken wire. A broken wire that is touching the metal box or another wire end can cause a short circuit. With the power off, loosen the terminal screw holding the broken wire and unhook the wire from the outlet switch. Clip back the wire to remove the damage, then strip back the insulation, taking care not to nick or gouge the wire *(page 434)*. If the clipped wire is too short to reach the terminal, loosen the cable clamp in the box and pull in some cable, or attach a jumper wire to extend it *(step above)*. Use long-nose pliers to curl the wire end, hook it clockwise around the terminal and tighten securely.

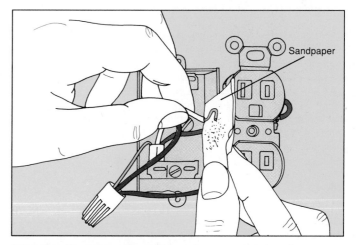

Cleaning the connections. Dirty or loose connections in an electrical box can produce sparks or shocks. Once you have confirmed that the power is off, remove the device from the box and examine the wire connections. If they appear dirty or corroded, disconnect them, then use fine sandpaper to burnish them *(above)*. If they are discolored, cleaning won't help. Blackened wire should be clipped back and restripped; a switch or outlet with blackened terminals should be replaced. If your house has aluminum wiring, it should be inspected by an electrician.

WIRES AND CABLES

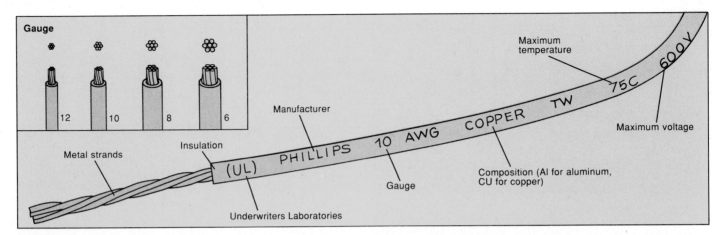

Reading a wire. The internal wiring of an appliance *(above)* is made of many thin copper or aluminum strands wrapped together and sheathed in plastic, rubber or heat-resistant insulation. Solid uninsulated wires, called bus wires, are sometimes used in small appliances. The diameter, or thickness, of the wire is indicated by a gauge number *(inset)*, usually printed on the insulation beside AWG (American Wire Gauge).

Electrical parts suppliers stock a wide assortment of wires and cables. When in doubt about the type of wire required *(page 433)*, snip off a length of old wire and take it with you. Make sure that wire for a heating appliance has heat-resistant insulation (TW). If a wire is burned, broken, corroded or shows resistance when checked with a continuity tester or multitester, it should be repaired or replaced *(page 434)*.

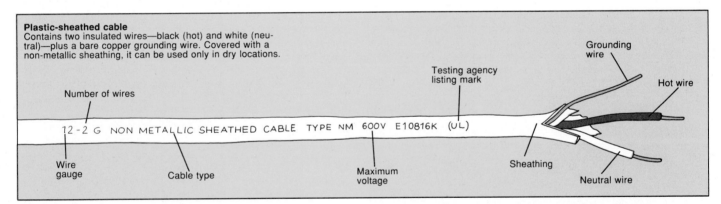

Reading a cable. When more than one insulated wire is enclosed in a covering, it is generally referred to as a cable. Plastic-sheathed cable *(above)* is the type most often used to carry electricity throughout the home. It contains insulated black and white wires, along with a grounding wire (G). Three-wire cable has a third (hot) wire, which is coded red. It is used to connect three- and four-way switches and split-circuit outlets.

Type NM or NMB cable—non-metallic sheathed cable—is widely used in home wiring where it will not be exposed to dampness. The solid plastic sheathing of type NMC cable keeps out moisture, and is used in basements or laundry rooms. Wiring protected by flexible steel armor is commonly called BX cable. The chart *(below)* provides information on wire gauge and ampere rating requirements.

WIRE GAUGE AND AMPERE RATING

Wire Gauge (AWG)	NO.6	NO.8	NO.10	NO.12	NO.14	NO.16	NO.18	NO.20
Amperes	55	40	30	20	15	10	7	5

Matching wire gauge and ampere rating. The diameter, or thickness of a wire—or of each of the wires in a cable—is indicated by a gauge number, usually printed on the insulation. The smaller the number, the thicker the wire and the more current it can carry *(above)*. The smallest wires, No. 20, No. 18 and No. 16, are used in low-voltage systems. (Wires narrower than 18 are usually unmarked.) No. 14 or No. 12 wire is installed on most 120-volt circuits. No. 10 wire is used for dishwashers and clothes dryers. A 240-volt appliance takes heavy-duty No. 8 or No. 6 wire.

Be sure to match the ampere rating of the appliance with that of the wiring. To determine an appliance's ampere rating, divide its wattage by 120 volts, or 240 volts, according to its circuit. The number of watts used by the appliance will be marked next to the model number on the unit's base or side *(page 443)*. Never install wire or cable of a smaller gauge; if necessary use a larger gauge. Overloaded wiring can pose a fire hazard. When in doubt about the gauge of wire required, snip off a length of old wire and take it with you to the supplier.

WIRES AND CABLES(continued)

Choosing the right wire, cord or cable. Most electrical parts suppliers stock a wide assortment of wires and cables. The wire and cable chart *(below)* describes the types most commonly used. Read the markings on the old wire *(page 432)* to determine the gauge and ampere rating required. To buy coaxial cable, refer to its ohms rating. When purchasing power cord cable, keep in mind that three-prong plugs require 3-conductor (grounding) cable. Many small appliances, however, use 2-prong plugs and must be replaced only by 2-conductor cable. Make sure that wire for a heating appliance has heat-resistant insulation. When in doubt about the gauge or type of wire required, snip off a length of the wire and take it with you to the supplier. Repair damaged wiring as shown on page 434, install connectors as shown on page 436.

Low-voltage wire
Solid or stranded inner conductor covered with plastic insulation.

Low-voltage multi-conductor cable
Three to five insulated wires; may have outer insulation. Use the color-code or mark to connect the wires without reversing polarity.

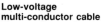

Speaker cable
Two-conductor cable covered with plastic insulation. Use the color-code or mark to connect the wires without reversing polarity.

Shielded one-conductor cable
Spiral or braided shield acts as a ground and protects the insulated wire from interference; commonly referred to as patch cord.

Shielded two-conductor cable
Spiral or braided shield acts as a ground and protects the two insulated wires from interference.

Low-voltage or bell wire
Single-strand No. 16 or No. 18 wire is used for doorbells and patio lights. Wire ends can be joined by twisting them together and screwing on a wire cap of the appropriate size or by securing them in a crimp wire connector.

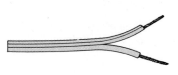

Zip cord
Nos. 16 and 18 wire are made of fine metal strands covered with rubber or plastic insulation, and are used for lamps and small appliances. Polarized cord is used where the hot and neutral wires must be aligned throughout a circuit. One of the two wires is keyed as neutral—usually with a molded ridge on its insulation.

insulated small-gauge wire
Copper or aluminum strands wrapped together and sheathed in plastic, rubber or heat-resistant insulation.

Two-conductor power cord cable
Insulated stranded wire used to replace power cords with two-prong (non-grounding) plugs. Commonly used with steam irons, coffee makers and toasters.

Coaxial cable
Stranded or solid center conductor protected by foam insulation. Spiral or braided outer conductor acts as a ground. Outer insulation protects the cable from weather.

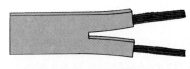

Shielded twin-lead cable
Two inner conductors protected by foam insulation; may contain an inner foil sheathing to protect the inner conductors from interference. Outer insulation protects the cable from weather.

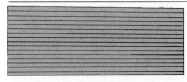

Ribbon cable
Multi-conductor; low-voltage wires within plastic insulation. Ribbon cable connectors pierce the insulation to contact the wires.

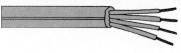

Telephone cable
Four insulated wires; use the color code to connect the wires without reversing polarity.

Grounding wire
Solid 10-gauge wire; often uninsulated, or coded green.

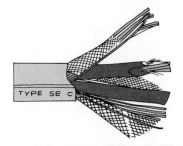

Service cable
No. 1/0 to 4/0 cable carries electricity from the utility company`s power lines into the house`s main service panel. Only the power company or an electrician should work on this wiring.

TYPE SE C

Armored cable (Type AC)
Often found in older homes, armored cable contains two wires and a metal bonding strip or grounding wire wrapped in paper and sheathed in a flexible steel housing. When no grounding wire is present, the housing and bonding strip act as ground.

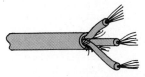

Three-conductor power cord cable
Insulated stranded wire for use with three-prong (grounding) plugs.

STRIPPING ELECTRICAL WIRES

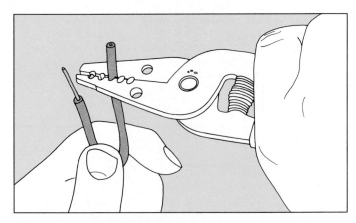

Using wire strippers. A stripping tool with a series of holes to fit various wire gauges snips through insulation without damaging the metal wire. Insert the wire into a matching slot on a pair of wire strippers *(above)* or multipurpose tool. (The gauges of the wire and slot must be the same.) Close the tool and twist it back and forth until the insulation is severed and can be pulled off the wire. Strip back 3/4 inch of insulation from the new wire to make most connections.

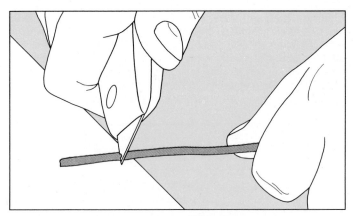

Using a knife. A sharp knife requires more care than wire strippers, but can also be used to strip the insulation from a wire. Place the wire on a firm surface and carefully cut into the insulation, paring it away at an angle *(above)*. Take care not to gouge the wire or wire strands inside. Always cut away from you in case the knife slips. Turn the wire over and make a second cut, then pull off the insulation. If you have nicked the wire, use diagonal-cutting pliers to snip off the wire end, then start again.

REPAIRING DAMAGED WIRING

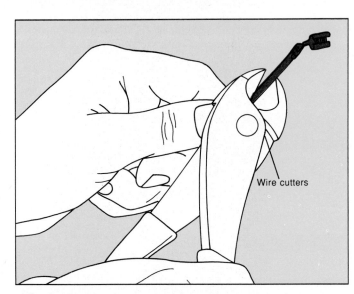

Wire cutters

1 **Removing damaged wiring.** Most damage, particularly burned or oxidized terminals, is visible. But if you suspect a wire has hidden damage, run your fingers along it from terminal to terminal while gently bending and twisting it. If you locate a bump or sudden limpness, that section should be replaced. Snip off the damaged length with wire cutters *(above)*. Then strip back 1/4 inch of insulation from each wire end. Replace the wire connector, or rejoin the same wire with a sleeve connector *(page 436)*. To splice a lower gauge (thick) wire, go to step 2.

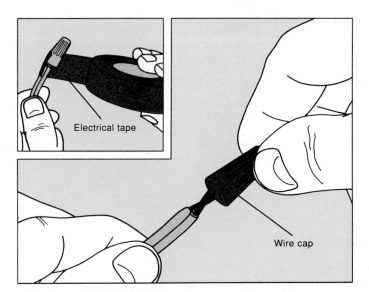

Electrical tape

Wire cap

2 **Securing the splice.** Hold the wires side by side with one hand, grip the bare ends with pliers and twist the wires together clockwise into a pigtail. Slip a wire cap over the connection *(above)* and screw the cap clockwise until it is tight and no bare wire remains exposed. Test the connection with a slight tug. To make sure the wires will not jar loose, secure the connection with electrical tape *(inset)*. Wrap the tape around the base of the cap, then once or twice around the wires, and finally around the base of the cap again.

WIRE CONNECTIONS: MAKING TERMINAL CONNECTIONS

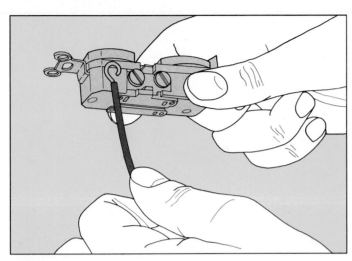

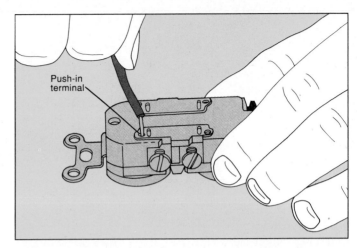

Making a hook connection. Strip back the insulation from the wire end, then bend it at a 45-degree angle with long-nose pliers. Starting near the insulation, make progressive bends to the right, moving the pliers toward the wire end until an open hook is formed. Loosen the terminal screw, but do not force it out of its threads. Attach the wire end to the terminal so that its hook will close in the same clockwise direction as the screw *(above)*. Make sure that the hook loops at least three-quarters of the way around the screw. Tighten the screw so that it grips the wire end securely (it should flatten the wire slightly). If part of the bare wire end is exposed, take apart the connection and start again.

Making a push-in connection. Some switches and outlets are fitted with push-in terminals that automatically grip the wire ends. This feature eliminates the need to bend the wire ends into a hook, but does not provide as secure a connection as screw terminals. To attach a wire to a push-in terminal, strip back the insulation according to the strip gauge marked on the device—usually 1/2 inch—and push the bare wire end into the hole up to its insulation. Make sure that no uninsulated wire is exposed. Note that stranded or aluminum wire should never be used with push-in terminals. To free the wire from a push-in terminal, insert a small screwdriver or stiff wire into the release slot next to the terminal hole, then pull on the wire. If the wire end breaks off in the terminal, replace the switch or outlet.

WIRE CONNECTIONS: TINNING STRANDED WIRE

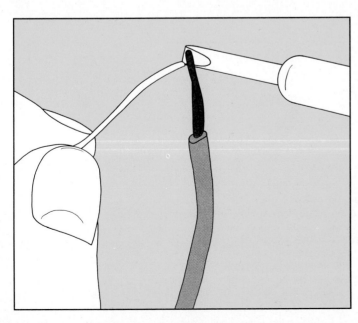

Tinning a wire lead. When making connections with thin stranded wire, solder the wire strands to prevent them from breaking and causing an electrical short. Strip back 1/4 inch of the wire's insulation *(page 434)*; for a cable, cut off the outer insulation with a utility knife, then strip back the insulation from each wire. Prepare a soldering iron *(page 439)*. Support the wire in a soldering stand and twist the strands together clockwise between your thumb and forefinger. Hold the soldering iron tip against the wire; after a few seconds, touch the solder to the wire *(left)*. Apply just enough solder to coat the wire strands evenly. Snip off any protruding untinned wire strands using wire cutters. After tinning the lead, solder the wire *(page 440)* or install a wire connector *(page 436)*.

WIRE CONNECTIONS: INSTALLING WIRE CONNECTORS

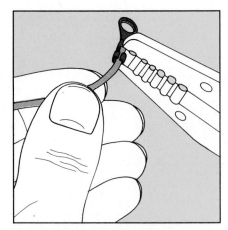

Crimping a connector. Purchase crimp or solderless connectors at an electronics parts supplier; be sure they are appropriate to the use, the terminals and the wire gauge. To install a crimp connector, strip back the wire *(page 434)*, fit it into the connector sleeve and crimp it using the crimping notches on a wire stripper *(above)*. Gently tug the wire to ensure it is held securely.

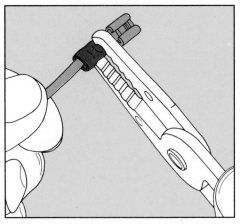

Soldering and crimping a spade lug. Purchase spade lugs to fit the terminals and the wire at an electronics parts supplier. To install a spade lug, strip 1/2 inch of insulation from the wire *(page 434)*. If you are working with thinly stranded wire, first tin the wire leads *(page 435)*. Fit the wire into the spade lug sleeve. then crimp it with a wire stripper *(above)* or multipurpose tool.

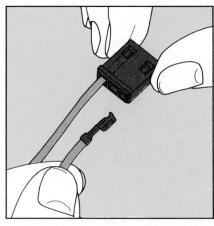

Crimping for a plug. Purchase a plug and crimp connectors to fit its terminals and the wires at an electronics parts supplier. Strip back each wire *(page 434)* and install a crimp connector *(far left)*. Snap each crimp connector into the plug *(above)*. Gently tug each wire to ensure it is held securely. If you install a plug at the other end of the wires, take care not to cross the wires.

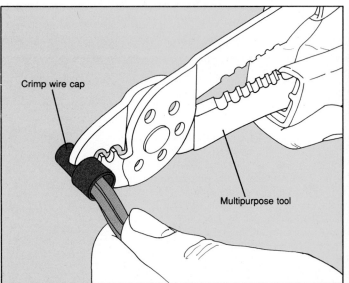
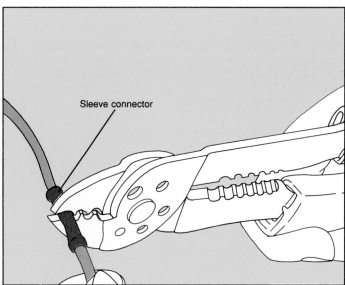

Installing wire-to-wire connectors. Sometimes two or more wires in an appliance are joined in a crimp wire cap. When a wire connection works loose, or after testing or replacing one of the wires, you must install a new wire cap. Strip the insulation off the wire ends *(page 434)* and twist them together. Slide the wire cap over the wire ends until no wire is exposed. Fit the jaws of the multipurpose tool around the wire cap just above the collar and squeeze the handles together *(above, left)*. Test the connection with a slight tug. When joining two wires with a sleeve connector, strip 1/2 inch of insulation from each wire and slip them into opposite ends of the connector. To secure the connection, use the crimping jaws of a multipurpose tool to squeeze each end of the connector *(above, right)*. Test the connection with a slight tug.

AUDIO AND VIDEO CABLE CONNECTORS

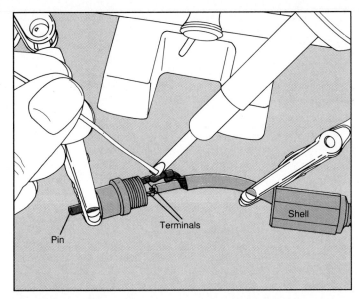

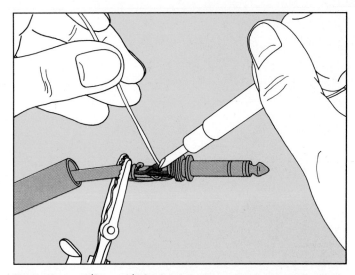

Replacing a phono plug. Snip off the old plug using wire cutters or a utility knife. Purchase an exact replacement plug at an electronics parts supplier. Unscrew the shell and slide it onto the cable. If the plug pin is solid, cut off 1/2 inch of outer insulation, strip back 1/4 inch of wire insulation *(page 434)* and solder *(page 440)* the insulated wire to the terminal closest to the plug tip. If the plug pin has a hole, cut off 1 1/2 inches of outer insulation and strip back 3/4 inch of wire insulation. Insert the insulated wire into the pin and solder the wire to the pin tip. Solder the uninsulated wire to the remaining terminal *(above)* or to a plug clip. Using pliers, squeeze the plug clips together to secure the cable. Screw the shell onto the plug.

Replacing a 1/8- or 1/4-inch plug. Snip off the old plug using wire cutters or a utility knife. Purchase an exact replacement plug at an electronics parts supplier. Unscrew the shell and slide it and any insulating sleeve onto the cable. Cut 1 1/2 inches of outer insulation off the cable and strip back 1/2 inch of insulation from the wires *(page 434)*. Solder *(page 440)* the uninsulated wire to the terminal farthest from the plug tip, and solder the insulated wires to the other plug terminals *(above)*. Using pliers, squeeze the plug clips together to secure the cable. Slide any insulating sleeve and the shell over the plug and screw on the shell.

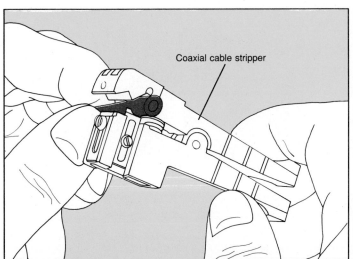

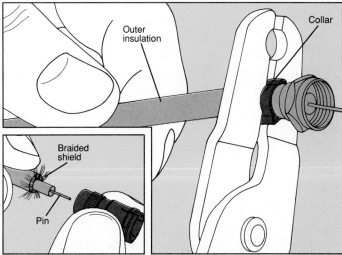

Replacing a coaxial connector. Cut off the old connector using wire cutters or a utility knife. Purchase an exact replacement connector at an electronics parts supplier. Slide the collar onto the cable, then fit the cable into a coaxial cable stripper, with the longer blade 1/2 inch from the end. Squeeze the handles and turn the stripper around the cable *(above, left)*, cutting it in two places.

Pull the outer insulation off the second cut, exposing the braided shield, and pull the braided shield off the first cut, exposing the pin. Unravel the braided shield and fold it back over the outer insulation. Push the connector onto the cable *(inset)* and slide the collar over the connector. Crimp the collar securely using a coaxial-cable crimping tool *(above, right)*.

REPLACING A POWER FUSE

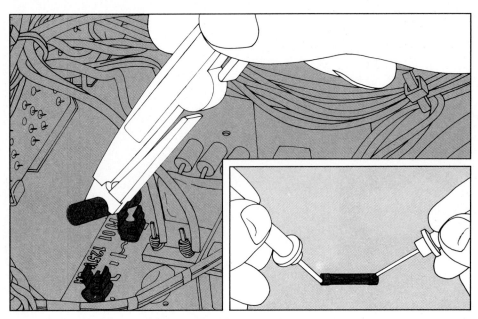

Removing and replacing a fuse. Consult the chapter on the unit to remove any panels. If the fuse is externally mounted in the back panel, turn the fuse cap counterclockwise and pull the fuse out of its casing. If the fuse is internally mounted and its caps are held in retaining clips, grip the fuse with a fuse puller and gently pry it out *(left)*. If the fuse is internally mounted and its caps are soldered to posts, leave it in place. Set a multitester to test continuity *(page 425)*. Touch a probe to each fuse cap *(inset)*. If a fuse does not register continuity out of circuit, purchase an exact replacement at an electronics parts supplier and install it. If you remove any panels, reinstall them, then cold check for leaking voltage *(page 427)*. If a fuse blows repeatedly, take the unit for professional service.

SERVICING A REMOTE CONTROL

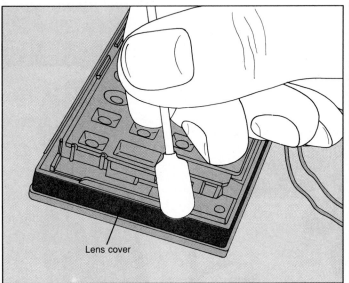

Lens cover

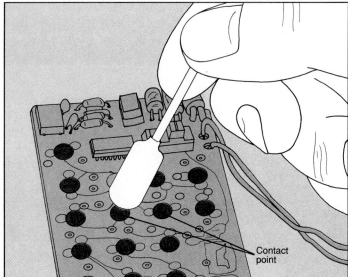

Contact point

Cleaning a remote control. To clean the outside of the lens cover, wipe with a damp, lint-free cloth. Check the battery terminals each time you change the batteries; if the terminals are dirty, rub them gently using a pencil eraser or spray them with short bursts of electronic contact cleaner. To clean inside the remote control, remove the screws holding the top and bottom casings together; check for hidden screws inside the battery compartment or under the manufacturer's label. If the casings do not separate easily, gently pry them apart using a small putty knife. Unscrew and lift out the circuit board. Use a foam swab moistened with denatured alcohol to clean the inside of the lens cover *(above, left)*. To reach the key assembly, remove the key pad from the circuit board. Clean the key assembly contact points by gently rubbing them with a pencil eraser and then wiping them using a clean foam swab moistened with denatured alcohol *(above, right)*. Reinstall the circuit board and the pad, snap the casings back together and reinstall the screws.

PREPARING A SOLDERING IRON

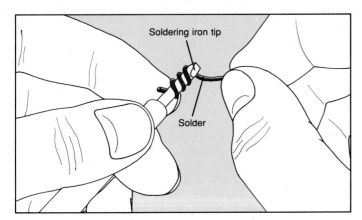

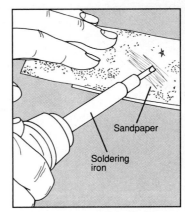

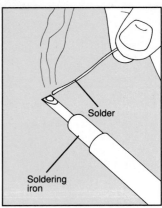

Tinning a new soldering iron. To ensure precise and tarnish-free soldering, the tip of a new soldering iron must be tinned, that is, coated with solder. Set up a soldering iron stand and place a dampened sponge on its base. Wrap a short spiral of rosin-core solder around the soldering iron tip *(above)*; use just enough to cover the entire tip evenly. Plug in the soldering iron and let it melt the solder: turn the iron's handle to help spread the solder evenly. Lightly wipe the tip across the sponge to distribute the solder over the entire tip and to remove excess. Keep the soldering iron in its stand when not in use and unplug it when you take a break.

Preparing a used soldering iron tip. If the soldering iron tip is pitted or blackened from use, rub it back and forth on a piece of medium-grade sandpaper *(above, left)* until the copper shows through. Set up a soldering iron stand and place a dampened sponge on its base. Plug in the iron and allow it to heat. Hold rosin-core solder against the sanded area *(above, right)* until it melts. Turn the iron's handle to help spread the solder evenly, then lightly wipe the tip across the damp sponge. Keep the soldering iron in its stand until you are ready to use it and unplug it when you take a break.

DESOLDERING

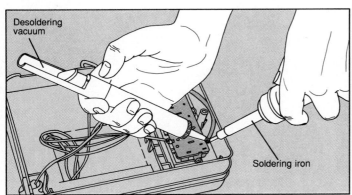

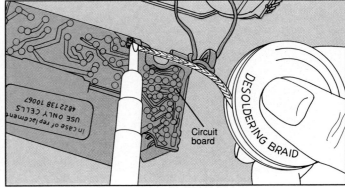

Removing old solder. Prepare the soldering iron *(steps above)*. Lightly press the tip of the iron directly on the old solder for a few seconds, until it begins to melt: if the iron is held any longer, the heat generated may damage nearby components. To remove large deposits of solder, use a desoldering vacuum. Push down the plunger, position its nozzle directly over the molten solder and use your thumb to press the trigger *(above, left)*, sucking up the melted solder. Repeat the procedure until all the solder has been removed from the terminal and the wire connection is loosened. Use long-nose pliers to remove a wire wrapped around a terminal. Remove solder from a circuit board or clean up stubborn traces of solder

with desoldering braid. Place the braid over the old solder, gently touch the tip of the iron to the braid for a few seconds *(above, right)* and pull up the braid. Repeat the procedure until all the old solder is absorbed, cutting away used braid when necessary. Clean up accidental solder drops by desoldering them the same way. After desoldering, wipe the tip of the soldering iron on the sponge, and unplug it from the wall outlet. To clean off flux residue left by old solder, rub it gently using a foam swab moistened with denatured alcohol or with flux-cleaning solvent, available from an electronics parts supplier.

SOLDERING

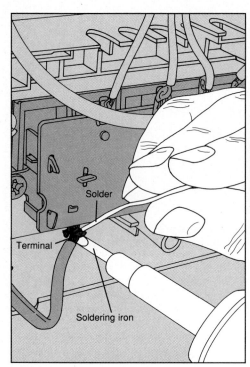

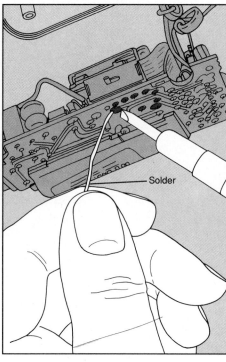

Connecting parts with solder. If you have never used a soldering iron, practice soldering lengths of scrap wire or discarded components. Prepare a soldering iron and remove old solder *(page 439)*. If soldering a wire, strip back the insulation *(page 434)* and tin the wire lead *(page 435)*. To solder a wire to a terminal, support the wire against the terminal or wrap it around the terminal. Touch the iron's tip to the wire for a few seconds and touch the solder to the heated wire *(far left)*; do not let the iron and solder touch each other directly. Keep the iron in position until enough solder has melted to secure the joint; the soldered joint should look smooth and rounded. While soldering, wipe the iron's tip on the sponge frequently. If soldering on a circuit board *(near left)*, keep in mind that less solder is needed than for a typical electrical connection, and take special care to avoid touching nearby components. After soldering, wipe the tip of the soldering iron on the sponge, and unplug it.

SILVER SOLDERING

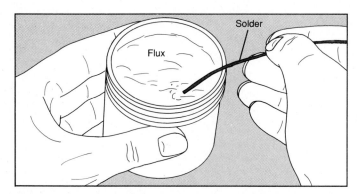

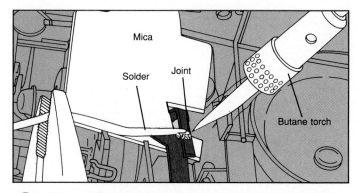

1 **Preparing to silver solder.** To replace a spot-welded electrical connection, use silver solder and a miniature butane torch. If you have never soldered before, practice first with rosin-core solder and a soldering iron *(step above)*, and then with silver solder and a butane torch. Purchase silver solder and flux paste from a welding supply store, and a miniature butane torch from an electronics parts supplier. Prepare to work in a well-ventilated area. Position the joint as securely as possible and mask adjacent components with a piece of ceramic tile or mica. Wearing safety goggles, dip the solder into the flux *(above)*, taking care not to let the flux touch your skin. Spread flux on the joint with a foam swab.

2 **Silver soldering.** Set the solder aside while you light the butane torch. Adjust it according to the manufacturer's instructions until the flame is cone-like with a bright blue center. Pick up the solder with long-nose pliers and position it near the joint, while you heat the joint with the blue part of the flame *(above)*. As soon as a small puddle of solder spreads over the joint, withdraw the solder and the flame. Turn off the torch. To check that the connection is solid, squeeze it with the jaws of the pliers. Wipe away flux residue using a foam swab moistened with hot water. After storing the flux, solder and torch, wash your hands thoroughly.

TIPS ON DISASSEMBLY AND REASSEMBLY: HOME ELECTRONICS

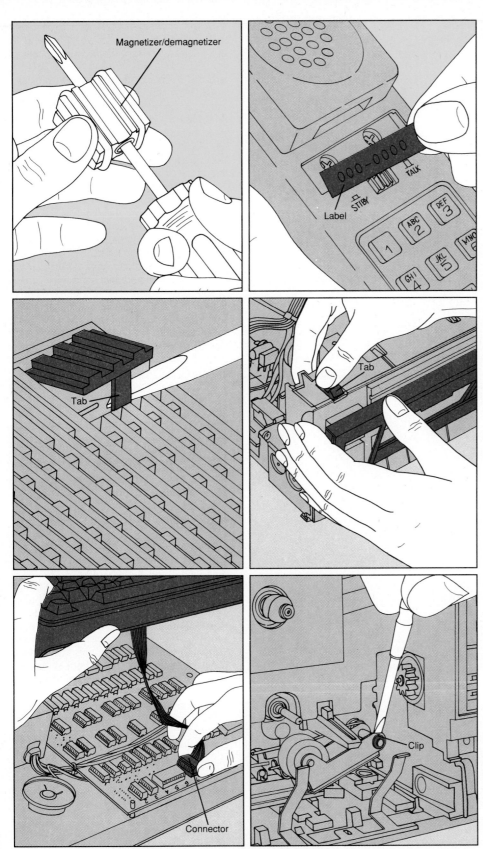

Magnetizer/demagnetizer

Label

Tab

Tab

Connector

Clip

Working methodically and safely.

Adhering to a few simple disassembly and reassembly guidelines ensures that your experiences in home electronics repair are rewarding and accident-free. Keep in mind the warnings you are likely to find on the back and bottom panels of a unit *(page 354)*. Before undertaking a major repair, review the owner's manual and check whether the unit is still under warranty.

Set up for repairs on a clean, well-lit work table; a wooden surface is ideal. Protect the unit from scratches by covering the table with a clean, insulating pad; an old blanket will do.

Magnetize screwdrivers before you start to work by passing their heads through a magnetizer/demagnetizer *(top, left)*. Keep screws and other small parts in labeled trays, jars or film containers.

Discharge any static buildup from yourself by touching an exposed, unpainted metal surface on the unit, such as a screw; hold the frame to ground yourself before handling circuit boards.

Study the unit panels before beginning, to determine the sequence in which they were installed. Check for hidden screws under labels *(top, right)* and recessed screws covered by a tab *(center, left)*. To release a stubborn screw, press the screwdriver firmly into the screwhead and snap any glue seal with a sharp counterclockwise twist. Pull or slide off panels gently; never force them. If a panel resists being removed, check the edges for tabs securing it to another panel or to the frame *(center, right)*.

Disassemble only what is needed to reach parts being repaired. Refer to the unit service manual, if it is available from the manufacturer or an electronic parts supplier. Write down your sequence of disassembly steps for reference in reassembly.

As you remove a panel, check behind it for wires connecting it to internal components. Before unplugging a connector *(bottom, left)*, note its terminal positions: soldered connections rarely need to be removed.

Unscrew circuit boards using as little pressure as possible; they are very easily damaged. Carefully pry any small clip off a component *(bottom, right)*; keep one hand ready to catch it.

Before reinstalling panels, check that no tools are left inside and that all components are back in place. After reassembly, but before plugging in the unit, perform a cold check for leaking voltage *(page 427)*.

TIPS ON DISASSEMBLY AND REASSEMBLY: SMALL APPLIANCES

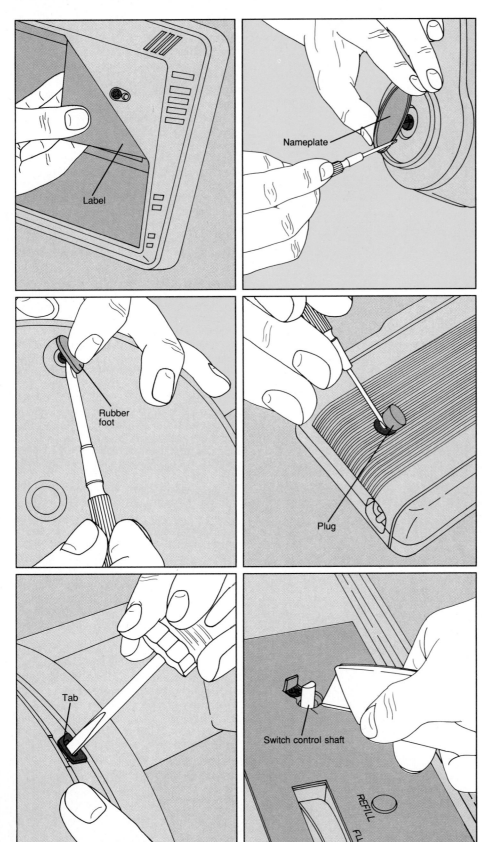

Label

Nameplate

Rubber foot

Plug

Tab

Switch control shaft

REFILL

Finding concealed fasteners. Before trying to disassemble an appliance, review the owner's manual. Check whether the appliance is still under warranty. If it is, take the unit for service. If not, set up for repair on a clean, well-lit work table. Magnetize screwdrivers before you start to work by passing their heads through a magnetizer/demagnetizer *(page 441)*. Label small jars or film canisters for storing screws and small parts, or use an egg carton, placing parts in the cups in the sequence of removal.

First study the appliance to determine how the housing is put together. On many appliances, the fasteners are recessed or completely hidden from view. Check for screws under labels and nameplates: run your fingers over the label to feel for screw heads and gently peel back a corner of the label *(top, left)*. Undo the nameplate's mounting screws or slip a screwdriver blade under a glued plate to pry it off *(top, right)*. Lift off rubber, felt or plastic feet with your fingers or the tip of a screwdriver to find screws *(center, left)*. Sometimes the only sign of a hidden screw is a small circular seam in the housing, indicating a plug set flush with the surface. Work the tip of a small screwdriver gently along the seam to pry out the plug *(center, right)*. To release a stubborn screw, press the screwdriver firmly into the screw head and snap any glue seal with a sharp counterclockwise twist.

If you cannot find any assembly screws, the housing may be held together with tabs. Slip a screwdriver blade into the seam of the housing and gently work the housing apart. Then press the tab with the blade tip to release it from its notch *(bottom, left)*.

Disassemble only what is needed to reach the parts being repaired. As you work, write down the sequence of disassembly steps for reference in reassembly. Once a part's mounting screws have been removed, carefully lift the part out of the unit without pulling wires or dislodging other parts. If the part's mounting fasteners are not visible, do the same detective work as for housing screws. The part may be secured from the exterior: Look beneath labels and control knobs, and as a last resort, cut away part of the control panel with a sharp utility knife to expose the screw heads *(bottom, right)*.

Before reinstalling the housing, make sure all parts are in place and that wires are secure. After reassembly but before plugging in the appliance, perform a cold check for leaking voltage *(page 427)*.

CALCULATING ELECTRICAL LOAD

Determining a circuit overload. If you suspect that a circuit is overloaded, calculate the existing load, then compare it to the capacity of the circuit. The maximum load is indicated by the ampere rating of the fuse or circuit breaker. For example, a general lighting circuit might have a maximum load of 15 amperes.

To calculate the load on a circuit, list all the fixtures and appliances on the circuit and the volt-ampere—also known as wattage—rating for each device. Find this information on a sticker near the socket of a lamp or lighting fixture, or on a small plate on the back or bottom of an appliance *(right)*. Typical ratings are listed in the chart below. Add the volt-ampere ratings for all appliances and fixtures on the circuit, then divide by 120 volts to convert to amperes. If the total is higher than the capacity of the circuit, the circuit is overloaded. Move a high-power using appliance, such as a toaster, to another circuit or have an electrician run a new circuit from the service panel. Do this calculation when adding a new appliance to the circuit.

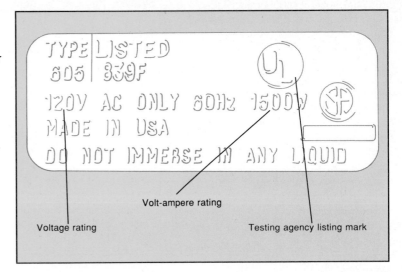

Voltage rating

Volt-ampere rating

Testing agency listing mark

TYPICAL APPLIANCE LOADS

APPLIANCE	APPROXIMATE VOLT-AMPERE RATING
Household appliances and equipment	
Ceiling fan	50
Clock	5
Computer	150 - 600
Dehumidifier	575
Humidifier	50 - 150
Iron	1200
Lamp or fixture	25 - 150
Portable heater	1500
Projector	350 - 500
Radio	10 - 100
Sewing machine	100
Stereo system	200 - 500
Television	150 - 450
Typewriter	45
Vacuum cleaner	300 - 600
Videocassette recorder	50

APPLIANCE	APPROXIMATE VOLT-AMPERE RATING
Bedroom and bathroom appliances	
Electric blanket	150 - 500
Hair dryer	400 - 1500
Heating pad	60
Shaver	15
240-volt appliances	
Air conditioner	5000
Clothes dryer	5000
Range (per burner)	5000
(oven)	4500
Water heater	2500 - 5000
Large 120-volt appliances	
Dishwasher	1200 - 1500
Freezer	300 - 600
Garbage disposer	300 - 900
Microwave oven	500 - 800
Refrigerator	150 - 300

APPLIANCE	APPROXIMATE VOLT-AMPERE RATING
Kitchen appliances	
Blender	200 - 400
Can opener	150
Coffee grinder	150
Coffee maker	600 - 750
Food processor	500 - 1500
Frying pan	1000 - 1200
Kettle	1200 - 1400
Mixer	100 - 225
Toaster	800 - 1200
Toaster oven	1500
Trash compactor	500 - 1000
Power tools	
Drill	360
Sander	540
Saw	600 - 1500
Soldering iron	150

Page references in *italics* indicate an illustration of the subject mentioned. Page refereces in **bold** indicate a Troubleshooting Guide for the subject mentioned.